SMALL UNMANNED AIRCRAFT SYSTEMS GUIDE

SMALL UNMANNED AIRCRAFT SYSTEMS GUIDE

Exploring Designs, Operations, Regulations, and Economics

Brent Terwilliger, Ph.D.
David Ison, Ph.D.
John Robbins, Ph.D.
Dennis Vincenzi, Ph.D.

AVIATION SUPPLIES & ACADEMICS
NEWCASTLE, WASHINGTON

Small Unmanned Aircraft Systems Guide: Exploring Designs, Operations, Regulations, and Economics
by Brent Terwilliger, David Ison, John Robbins, and Dennis Vincenzi

Aviation Supplies & Academics, Inc.
7005 132nd Place SE
Newcastle, Washington 98059-3153
asa@asa2fly.com | www.asa2fly.com

See the ASA website at **www.asa2fly.com/reader/SUAS** for the "Reader Resources" page containing additional information and updates relating to this book.

ASA-UAS-SUAS
ISBN 978-1-61954-394-2

Printed in the United States of America
2022   2021   2020   2019   9   8   7   6   5   4   3   2

Cover photo: istock.com/seregalsv
Credits for many of the images used in this book are listed in the Figure Credits on page 247.

Library of Congress Cataloging-in-Publication Data
Names: Terwilliger, Brent, author. | Ison, David C., author. | Robbins, John, author. | Vincenzi, Dennis A., author.
Title: Small unmanned aircraft systems guide : exploring designs, operations, regulations, and economics / Brent Terwilliger, Ph.D., David Ison, Ph.D., John Robbins, Ph.D., Dennis Vincenzi, Ph.D.
Description: Newcastle, Washington : Aviation Supplies & Academics, Inc., [2017] | Includes bibliographical references and index.
Identifiers: LCCN 2016037988| ISBN 9781619543942 (trade paper : alk. paper) | ISBN 161954394X (trade paper : alk. paper)
Subjects: LCSH: Drone aircraft. | Drone aircraft—History.
Classification: LCC TL685.35 .T47 2016 | DDC 629.133/39—dc23
LC record available at https://lccn.loc.gov/2016037988

CONTENTS

Chapter 5   203
Business of Unmanned Aviation: From Agencies to Startups

Chapter 6   233
Preparing for the Future: Accurate Information Makes All the Difference

ILLUSTRATIONS

NOTE: Credits for images used in this book are listed in the Figure Credits starting on page 247.

TABLES

FOREWORD

There aren't many "firsts" remaining in aviation. Aviation has become commonplace, over-shadowed by advancements in technology that make the miracle of flight seem mundane and archaic to the current generation. The passion for careers and advances in aviation and aeronautics so prevalent through the 1960s and 1970s has been surpassed by the readily available ability to live in a virtual world, inundated with low-cost, intuitive gismos and gadgets that connect us all at the touch of a button. The glamour and excitement associated with traditional aviation endeavors that drove so many of us to dedicate our lives to the science seemed to have waned. All of this was true until the advent of unmanned aviation!

It's quite remarkable to realize that emerging unmanned aviation has such crossover appeal to so many. The technological developments that could have doomed the aviation industry are actually enhancing it through the advent of unmanned aircraft. The skills and interest of a non-traditional pool of engineers and entrepreneurs have driven this new and unanticipated "first" in aviation in directions no one expected even a few years ago. The same technologies we take for granted today have enabled unique and unexpected opportunities to advance an entirely new and exciting path for aviation. The proliferation of "drones" for civil applications and the challenges to integrate them into routine use has birthed a new industry that seems to have no limits. The opportunity to be an active contributor to the possible last significant "first" in aviation should not be taken lightly.

While it may seem that the emergence and acceptance of unmanned aviation would be logical and relatively obvious, it is clear to those of us involved in advancing the industry that significant challenges remain. Global routine use of UAS won't occur until the current aviation "system" evolves, ultimately allowing the safe and full integration of UAS. The current airspace construct and operation, while extremely safe, was never designed to accommodate non-segregated access of unmanned aircraft.

While the technical challenges are significant, the emergence of UAS into everyday life has sparked a debate on a number of social issues associated with their use. Concerns about privacy, security, and the potential for harm caused by inadvertent misuse or hardware failures has prompted a proliferation of state-sponsored rules and restrictions that clearly hinder growth of the UAS industry. While the concerns may very well be legitimate, it is clear that viable solutions exist and that with the concerted effort of the professional UAS community, we will achieve our goals. Education is key. Armed with an understanding and appreciation of the rules and regulations associated with operation of aircraft, the new generation of "pilots" flying unmanned aircraft *will* safely become a reality.

You are taking the first significant step in that direction. This textbook will provide you with a solid, fundamental understanding of the history, technology, and challenges facing unmanned aviation. Elegant solutions to many of the challenges are yet to be discovered. The opportunity lies ahead. You are a pioneer in your own right and have a chance to shape what may be the most significant chapter in aviation history. Seize the moment!

Paul E. McDuffee
Vice President of Commercial Business Development
Insitu, Inc.

ACKNOWLEDGMENTS

We wish to express our gratitude to all those who made this book possible, especially our families and colleagues who provided essential support and encouragement throughout the writing process. We would also like to highlight the contributions of and support from our fellow faculty members at Embry-Riddle, including Dr. Kenneth Witcher, Dr. Ian McAndrew, Dr. Robert "Buck" Joslin, Dr. Joseph Cerreta, Dr. Brian Sanders, Dr. Robert Deters, Dr. Timothy Holt, Dr. James Marion, Dr. Sarah Nilsson (Esq.), Stefan Kleinke, David Thirtyacre, Scott Burgess, Felix Brito, Teena Deering, Michael Millard, and Brad Opp, as well as the input from the operational community provided by Fred Judson, Andrew Wentworth, Brad Hayden, Robert Lamond, Dr. Richard Baker, Stephen Luxion, Christopher Broyhill, John Kelley, Jonathan Rupprecht (Esq.), and David Peller. These individuals provided critical and in-depth technical review and suggestions. A special thank you is also due to Jackie Spanitz, Laura Fisher, Greg Robbins, and the rest of the team at our publisher, Aviation Supplies & Academics, Inc., for initiating and supporting this project; their guidance and assistance made this effort possible. Finally, we extend our gratitude to all UAS stakeholders actively collaborating to grow public awareness, pursue and fund research, and ensure UAS continue to be applied in an appropriate and responsible manner. Only by continuing to push the boundaries of what is known, endeavoring against complacency, and dreaming of new possibilities, will we realize truly amazing achievements.

> A single lifetime, even though entirely devoted to the sky, would not be enough for the study of so vast a subject. A time will come when our descendants will be amazed that we did not know things that are so plain to them.
> —Seneca, Book 7, first century CE

ABOUT THE AUTHORS

Dr. Brent Terwilliger is an Assistant Professor of Aeronautics and the Program Chair for the M.S. in Unmanned Systems degree at the Embry-Riddle Aeronautical University (ERAU), Worldwide Campus, College of Aeronautics, in Daytona Beach, Florida. He holds a Ph.D. in Business Administration from Northcentral University, a Master's in Aeronautical Science (MAS) degree and B.S. in Aerospace Studies from ERAU, and more than a decade of experience in defense contracting.

Dr. David Ison is an Assistant Professor of Aeronautics and the Research Chair of ERAU, Worldwide Campus, College of Aeronautics. He holds a Ph.D. in Educational Studies/ Higher Education Leadership/Aviation Higher Education from the University of Nebraska–Lincoln, a Master's in Aeronautical Science (MAS) degree from ERAU, and a B.S. in Aviation Management from Auburn University.

Dr. John Robbins is an Assistant Professor and the Program Coordinator for the B.S in Unmanned Aircraft System Science degree at the ERAU Daytona Beach campus. He holds a Ph.D. in Agricultural and Biological Engineering from the University of Florida (UF), a Master's in Aeronautical Science (MAS) degree from ERAU, and a B.A. in Geology from UF.

Dr. Dennis Vincenzi is an Assistant Professor of Aeronautics and the Department Chair of the ERAU, Worldwide Campus, College of Aeronautics, Department of Aeronautics, Undergraduate Studies. He received his Ph.D. in Human Factors Psychology in 1998 from the University of Central Florida, Orlando, Florida.

INTRODUCTION

The utility and benefits of unmanned aircraft systems (UAS), as valuable capabilities modifiers, are now emerging and being recognized across multiple industries. While this technology is not new, the ability to support domestic operation is becoming better understood, opening up new uses to government organizations and commercial enterprise. Analysis of the unmanned aviation market indicates that small UAS (sUAS) will become the most prevalent and affordable form of unmanned aircraft available, featuring technology developed by contributors ranging from the "do-it-yourself" (DIY) and model aircraft communities to defense contractors. This book contains descriptions of typical sUAS architecture, related technology, common uses, and suggested safety practices, while also providing a narrative to help you determine the most appropriate path forward through complex legal, business, operational, and support considerations. Understanding how these pieces fit together, from the technical and legal perspectives, will shape your own strategy for the safe, efficient, and effective use of this (r)evolutionary technology.

▋ INTENT

There has been an observable swell in public desire to access and domestically operate sUAS. However, there is also a significant learning curve to properly understand the multitude of designs, equipment, operational cases, capabilities, limitations, regulations, and strategies supporting safe and appropriate use. Our intent is to help readers better understand sUAS technology to achieve such use, in accordance with published advisory circulars, guidelines, and regulations. We developed this book to share critical background, concepts, guidance, and lessons learned from our collective experience as researchers, operators, and academic instructors to dispel common myths and provide a starting point to explore how sUAS can be applied to solve challenges and support economic pursuits.

The presentation of information has been structured to help readers better understand how sUAS can be used to realize cost and efficiency gains, while considering how to incorporate potential benefits and address limits and challenges. The following represents the topics and material presented:

- *History of UAS*—history and current path of UAS development, operations, and regulations
- *Application of sUAS*—current, developmental, and perceived uses of sUAS platforms and technology
- *Variety of Design*—types and configurations of platforms, detailed descriptions of elements and their purpose, and an overview of design-specific considerations
- *Legal, Environmental, and Operational Considerations*—major factors affecting use of sUAS, including a detailed overview of the current U.S. regulatory framework, operational requirements and prohibitions, unique considerations of various operational environments, and recommended application processes

- *Business of Unmanned Aviation*—types of organizational structures, purchase and usage considerations, and anticipated economic growth areas
- *Preparing for the Future*—reference sources to stay connected to the rapidly changing landscape

This book was written to support ease of comprehension by the general public, even without a background in aviation. It simplifies and explains existing and impending regulation to address the segment of the public expected to adopt and use this technology for organizational, business, and recreational pursuits. However, it contains sufficient detail to be featured as a suggested text in many UAS-related academic and training programs, ranging from high-school to graduate-level readers.

Upon completion of this book, readers can expect to:

1. Understand what an sUAS is, including common types, configurations, and components, to make well-informed decisions regarding purchase and use.

2. Evaluate how sUAS and their various configuration options can be used to address or support evolving business needs.

3. Formulate a plan to acquire necessary certification approvals and system components to operate sUAS in a safe, efficient, and effective manner.

▮ NOTE TO THE READER

Thank you for taking this first step to learn about and explore the world of unmanned aviation. As sUAS and larger UAS platform technologies are integrated into our society, it will be imperative for users to understand the complexity, benefits, and options, as well as the limitations and major considerations, that affect their responsible application. A broad range of material is covered in this book, from the history of UAS to recommendations for supporting your operation of sUAS.

Information has been presented to help make informed decisions as you consider potential sUAS selection and application options. Many critical aeronautical concepts are introduced and briefly discussed, but may not be described in detail. Rest assured that such material is presented in a manner supporting basic understanding, within the related context, to support further investigation on your own. I strongly encourage you to examine and explore such concepts, in depth and independently, using the resources and references provided throughout the book as well as those found on U.S. government websites, such as the Federal Aviation Administration's (FAA) Unmanned Aircraft Systems webpage (www.faa.gov/uas). The ASA "Reader Resources" webpage for this book (www.asa2fly.com/reader/SUAS) contains additional information and resources relating to sUAS, and will be updated to serve as a valuable reference as the industry continues to grow. Conducting personal research is an essential component of staying informed about the many changes occurring in this rapidly evolving field. We hope you find this book as enjoyable to read and reference as it was for us to write.

Brent A. Terwilliger, Ph.D.

ABBREVIATIONS

2-DOF	two degrees of freedom
3-DOF	three degrees of freedom
AC	advisory circular
ADC	analog-to-digital converter
ADM	aeronautical decision making
ADS-B	Automatic Dependent Surveillance–Broadcast
AGL	above ground level
AMA	Academy of Model Aeronautics
AME	Aviation Medical Examiner
API	application programming interface
APKWS	Advanced Precision Kill Weapon Systems
ARC	Aviation Rulemaking Committee
ARF	almost ready-to-fly
ARP	airport reference point
ASSURE	Alliance for System Safety of UAS through Research Excellence
ATC	air traffic control
AUVSI	Association for Unmanned Vehicle Systems International
BEC	battery elimination circuitry
BIOS	basic input/output system
BLOS	beyond line-of-sight
BNF	bind-and-fly
BTT	Basic Target Training
BVLOS	beyond visual line-of-sight
C3	command, control, and communication
CBO	community-based organization
CCD	charged coupled device
CCPM	cyclic/collective pitch mixing
CFIT	controlled flight into terrain
CFR	Code of Federal Regulations
CG	center of gravity
CMOS	complementary metal oxide semiconductor
COA	certificate of waiver or authorization
COE	Center of Excellence
COTS	commercial off-the-shelf
CRM	crew resource management
CTAF	common traffic advisory frequency
DAC	digital-to-analog converter
DC	direct current
DIY	do it yourself
DOD	Department of Defense
DOT	Department of Transportation
DSA	detect, sense, and avoidance
EAR	Export Administration Regulations
EMI	electrical magnetic interference
EO	electro-optical
ESC	electronic speed control
EVLOS	extended visual line-of-sight
FAA	Federal Aviation Administration
FARs	Federal Aviation Regulations
FL	flight level
FMRA	FAA Modernization and Reform Act
FPV	first-person view
FSDO	Flight Standards District Office
FSTD	flight simulation training device
GCS	ground control station
GHz	gigahertz
GIS	geographic information system
GNC	guidance, navigation, and control
GPIO	general purpose input/output

GPS	global positioning system
GUI	graphical user interface
HALE	high-altitude long-endurance
HMD	helmet-mounted/ head-mounted display
HMI	human-machine interface
HTOL	horizontal takeoff and landing
I2C	inter-integrated circuit
IDE	integrated development environment
IFR	instrument flight rules
IMC	instrument meteorological conditions
IMINT	imagery intelligence
IMU	inertial measurement unit
I/O	input/output
IR	infrared
ISM	industrial, scientific, and medical
ISR	intelligence, surveillance, and reconnaissance
ITAR	International Traffic in Arms Regulations
KSAs	knowledge, skills, and abilities
kts	knots
LBA	lifting body airship
LiDAR	light detection and ranging
Li-ion	lithium-ion
LiPo	lithium-polymer
LOA	letter of agreement
LOS	line-of-sight
LRE	launch and recovery element
mAh	milliampere hour

MALE	medium-altitude, long-endurance
MARS	mid-air retrieval system
MAV	micro air vehicle
MCE	mission control element
MHz	megahertz
mph	miles per hour
MSL	mean sea level
MSRP	manufacturer's suggested retail price
MTI	moving target identification
MTOW	maximum takeoff weight
MTS	multi-spectral targeting system
NAS	National Airspace System
NBC	nuclear, biological, and chemical
NDVI	normalized difference vegetation index
NiCd	nickel-cadmium
NiMH	nickel-metal hydride
NM	nautical mile
nm	nanometer
NOTAM	Notice to Airmen
NPRM	notice of proposed rulemaking
OEM	original equipment manufacturer
OPA	optionally piloted aircraft
OpsCon	Operational Concept
OS	operating system
OSD	on-screen display
PC	personal computer
PIC	pilot-in-command
PWM	pulse width modulation
RADAR	radio detection and ranging
RC	remote control

RC	radio controlled	UTM	unmanned traffic management
R&D	research and development	UV	ultraviolet
RPA	remotely piloted aircraft	VFR	visual flight rules
RPM	revolutions per minute	VLOS	visual line-of-sight
RPV	remotely piloted vehicle	VMC	visual meteorological conditions
RSSI	received signal strength indication	VO	visual observer
RTF	ready-to-fly	VTOL	vertical takeoff and landing
RX	receiver	Wh	watt hours
SAC	special airworthiness certificate		
SAC-EC	special airworthiness certificate —experimental category		
SAC-RC	special airworthiness certificate —restricted category		
SAR	synthetic aperture radar		
SDK	software development kit		
SIGINT	signals intelligence		
SM	statute mile		
SME	subject matter expert		
SPDT	single pole double throw		
SPST	single pole single throw		
STOL	short takeoff and landing		
sUAS	small unmanned aircraft system		
SUAV	small unmanned aerial vehicle		
TFR	temporary flight restriction		
TSA	Transportation Security Administration		
TX	transmitter		
UA	unmanned aircraft		
UAS	unmanned aircraft system		
UAS	unmanned aerial system		
UAV	unmanned aerial vehicle		
USB	universal serial bus		

CHAPTER 1

HISTORY OF UAS: WHERE DID THEY COME FROM AND WHERE ARE THEY HEADED?

INTRODUCTION

Although unmanned aircraft may seem like a relatively recent development, these systems have been in use for quite some time, dating back to as early as the late nineteenth century. Many of the technologies and principles required for operation of modern systems were first envisioned, uncovered, and developed by various scientists and inventors in these early eras. This chapter contains an examination and discussion of crucial pioneers of technology and aeronautics, periods of technological development and operational expansion, the changing role in the modern era, and the technological and regulatory landscape influencing application of unmanned aviation.

EARLY PREDECESSORS

Early aeronautics pioneers and their precursor models and technologies eventually led to the development of early unmanned aircraft, which were used for a range of functions, such as aerial research platforms, weapons, and targets. While the list of contributors to the success of unmanned aircraft provided here is not exhaustive, it does highlight some of the significant research and experimentation that has led to the technologies necessary to successfully operate such unmanned systems.

■ SIR GEORGE CAYLEY

Born in 1773, Sir George Cayley was an early pioneer of aeronautical vehicle design and aerodynamics research. In 1804, he designed a monoplane glider that appears sophisticated even by today's standards. Cayley is credited with discovering that curved surfaces generate lift more effectively than flat ones. Also, he found that some modifications to wings, such as canting them upwards (commonly referred to as dihedral), added stability to his aircraft. In 1849, he created a glider with space for a pilot, which he successfully flew with a young boy as the occupant. Several years later, Cayley built a larger glider, which also successfully flew (see Figure 1-1). Cayley's discoveries provided essential foundations for aircraft design and aerodynamics theory.

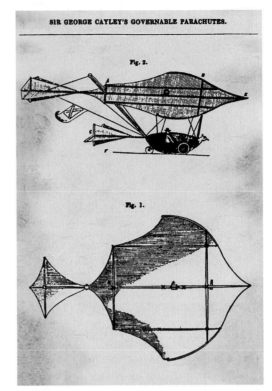

■ JOHN STRINGFELLOW

John Stringfellow, born in 1799, was fascinated with machinery, in particular with carriages and steam engines. Stringfellow experimented with light steam engines in an effort to propel aircraft designs developed by fellow aviation enthusiasts of the time. By 1848, he had worked to create an aircraft with counter-rotating "propellers" driven by a lightweight steam engine. After several failed attempts, he was able to properly balance the aircraft, resulting in a successful short-distance flight with the ship being guided by wires. Stringfellow's work demonstrated the importance and utility of adding reliable propulsion to aircraft (see Figure 1-2). His foundational work would inspire those who followed his efforts.

■ ALPHONSE PÉNAUD

By age 21, Alphonse Pénaud had established himself as an accomplished aviation inventor, demonstrating one of his early flying inventions in Paris in 1871. Credited with harnessing the power of rubber bands to power aircraft propellers and rotors, Pénaud's designs reliably and successfully flew with ease (see Figure 1-3). Pénaud's work is credited with inspiring the Wright brothers early in their lives. In 1876, he developed a sophisticated amphibious aircraft including seemingly modern flight controls

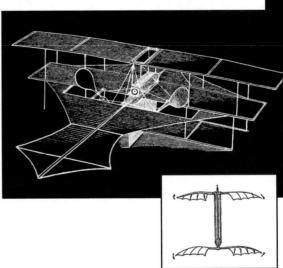

FIGURE 1-1. Cayley glider design (*top*).

FIGURE 1-2. Stringfellow's steam engine aircraft (*middle*).

FIGURE 1-3. Pénaud's rubber band-powered helicopter (*bottom*).

and instrumentation with the help of other aviation enthusiasts, but this design never moved forward. The works of Pénaud certainly were influential to future aircraft experimenters.

■ OTTO LILIENTHAL

Born in Prussia in 1848, Otto Lilienthal went on to study engineering, leading him to the design of numerous successful gliding aircraft. First experimenting with kites, Lilienthal began to work with different shapes of wings to determine which was the most utilitarian for flight. Most notably, in 1890, Lilienthal began working diligently on flying machines that allowed for the carriage of a pilot. The initial iteration of Lilienthal's glider was flown in 1891 and achieved a flight of approximately 80 feet. By the next year, the distance capability of his revised glider was doubled, and Lilienthal began work on a derivative that used a motor to flap its wings. Lilienthal worked diligently to better understand flight through repeated tests of his works. He was able to successfully fly his numerous models in more than 1,500 total flights, eventually reaching distances of nearly a quarter of a mile (see Figure 1-4). By the time of his death in 1896, he had published numerous articles about flight and his endeavors, which were noted by the Wright brothers years later as inspirational to their work.

FIGURE 1-4. Test flight of a Lilienthal glider in 1895.

■ NIKOLA TESLA

Nikola Tesla fulfilled a peripheral, yet critical, contribution to the advent of modern unmanned aircraft. While not directly associated with the development of aircraft as were Lilienthal, Cayley, and Stringfellow, Tesla developed electrical components essential to the creation of the modern radio. Born in 1856 in Smiljan (modern day Croatia), Tesla went on to study math and philosophy in Graz (Austria) and Prague (Czech Republic), respectively. At age 26, Tesla devised the concept of a brushless alternating current (AC) motor. Tesla then moved to New York and began to work with Thomas Edison, making improvements to Edison's direct current (DC) designs. Within a few years, Tesla began his own company, which eventually led to the adoption of an AC power grid in Massachusetts. This began a competition of sorts between Tesla and Edison as to the future power supply, pitting Tesla's AC power against Edison's DC. In the 1890s, Tesla created a variety of electrical component inventions and improvements including his namesake transformer, the Tesla Coil. He was also able to demonstrate radio communications years before Marconi. In fact, some of Marconi's patents would later be cancelled as a nod to the true originator of the concepts. Tesla used this type of communication to control a model boat in a demonstration in New York City. This last feat truly laid the foundation for future remote control on which current unmanned systems rely. Also, Tesla's legacy of AC power transmission is still the source of choice for the developed world.

■ GUGLIELMO MARCONI

Guglielmo Marconi was born in Italy in 1874. By age 20, he was already interested in the works of Heinrich Hertz, in particular the use of radio waves. Marconi soon developed a means of transmitting messages

FIGURE 1-5. Marconi operating his wireless radio system.

through the use of such waves from up to a mile away. In 1896, he moved to England and within a year developed a wireless station used to communicate with ships over 10 miles away. By 1899, Marconi was able to send transmissions across the English Channel. Soon thereafter, with a bit of ingenuity (including flying an antenna on a kite), he successfully sent Morse Code across the Atlantic Ocean (see Figure 1-5). The radio capabilities realized by Marconi, coupled with the work of Tesla, paved the way for modern radio and the transmission capabilities used to remotely control a range of systems, including unmanned aircraft.

■ OCTAVE CHANUTE

Chanute, born in 1832, did not get involved in aviation until later in life. He began to experiment with various different aircraft designs including a glider (see Figure 1-6) that used numerous adjustable wings for self-compensating stability. He also successfully experimented with automatic flight control utilizing movable control surfaces with several of his designs successfully and reliably taking individuals aloft. He published an influential book, Progress in Flying Machines, in 1894, which helped to interest the Wright brothers. Beginning in 1899, Chanute worked with the famous brothers, acting as a mentor to the inventors.

■ SAMUEL P. LANGLEY

Langley is often credited with coming very close to beating the Wright brothers to manned, powered flight. He began experimenting with rubber powered aircraft, as he called them "aerodromes," in 1887 with some success. In 1891 he began to work with steam engines on his model Aerodrome 0, which did not live up to expectations, failing to work as planned. He then continued with a series of Aerodromes, eventually building a houseboat from which to launch his inventions (see Figure 1-7), which would float on the Potomac River. By the time he reached iterations 5 and 6, the design was sound enough to allow the craft to climb several thousand feet above the launching point. Langley desired for his craft to be able to hoist a person aloft. By 1901, a radial engine was housed on Aerodrome A, which did not provide much success toward manned flight, crashing during the test flight. Langley would rebuild the craft for 1903 launch. Sadly, this also ended badly, crashing immediately on launch. This failure was followed by harsh and negative press. Aerodrome A would live on another day, modified and rebuilt by pioneer Glenn Curtiss, it would take flight in 1914.

FIGURE 1-6. Replica of Chanute 1896 glider (*left*).

FIGURE 1-7. Langley Aerodrome (*center*).

FIGURE 1-8. Wright brothers' famous first controlled, powered flight, December 17, 1903 (*right*).

▌ARCHIBALD LOW

Labeled the "Father of Radio Guided Systems," Archibald Low began working with the British government to develop a variety of theoretical and actual radio-controlled systems and weapons. In 1917 he began work on an unmanned aircraft, which included the use of a gyroscope to maintain stability. Soon thereafter, Low began work on an electrically guided missile, which the Germans viewed as so threatening that they made attempts to assassinate Low. In an odd twist of fate, the Germans would take Low's findings and improve upon them to develop and implement one of the first regularly used unmanned flying weapon systems, the V-1 rocket.

▌WRIGHT BROTHERS

While the Wright brothers, Orville and Wilbur, are credited with inventing the modern-day aircraft, much of the foundation work to develop such craft (including that described earlier in this chapter) had already been accomplished prior to their experimentations with flight. The brothers experimented with lift calculations outlined by their mentors, such as Lilienthal and Chanute, and even developed a test bay wind tunnel. What was especially problematic about flying machines when the Wrights became interested in aviation was the general lack of reliable control of the vehicles. The Wrights began to tackle this issue in 1901 using gliders with a wing-warping technique that caused an imbalance in lift on one side of the aircraft versus the other, causing the craft to tilt in one direction and resulting in a change in direction. Other flight controls for pitch and yaw were also developed by 1902. By 1903, the Wrights were finalizing the design of a lightweight gasoline engine to help keep their designs aloft. They designed the predecessor of today's modern propeller and even designed a primitive flight data recorder, which would accompany them on their first flight. Of course, the brothers were successful in flying their Wright Flyer on December 17, 1903 (*see Figure 1-8*), but the craft was far from practical. It was not until 1905 that their updated Flyer showed promise of a practical flying machine with utility beyond demonstration and exhibition. The Wrights continued to make improvements to their designs through 1910, including the ability to carry a passenger. But by 1911, Wright aircraft were increasingly becoming outdated. Wilbur died soon thereafter in 1912, and Orville exited the business four years later. Clearly, the Wrights' inventions and innovations had direct impacts on the practicality of aircraft and, in turn, made modern unmanned aircraft a distinct possibility.

▌ ELMER SPERRY

Elmer Sperry started a career in engineering, but soon became bored and turned instead to research and development. In 1907, while working with a range of electrical components, he became interested in the use of gyroscopes to stabilize vehicles. Sperry originally aimed to help stabilize ships in rough seas using the principle of precession (the reaction of a rotating gyro when a force is applied to it whereby that force is transposed 90 degrees in the direction of the motion of the gyro). By 1910, Sperry had established a business specializing in gyroscopes, which would become essential components in aircraft navigation systems as well as autopilot applications. Although many modern aircraft, both manned and unmanned, use more sophisticated accelerometers and stabilizers rather than gyros, the principles developed by Sperry allowed for reliable, all-weather, and automated flight operations. Gyroscopes were eventually integrated into aircraft for all-weather navigation and guidance. They have also been used to direct autopilot systems, critical to both manned and unmanned flight. Although many aircraft today use updated, solid state accelerometers and sensors for flight instruments and autopilots, the principles developed by Sperry laid the foundations for automated flight control systems in all types of aircraft.

▌ ADVENT OF AEROMODELING

Many of today's civilian unmanned aircraft have more in common with remote-control model aircraft than larger and more sophisticated military platforms. Interestingly, model aircraft of varying sorts have been in use throughout history. One of the first model flying devices, as well as possibly the first rudimentary robot, was created between 400 and 350 BC by a Greek mathematician named Archytas. The device, a steam-powered "pigeon," was constructed of wood and used steam to power its wings. It is purported that Archytas's pigeon could fly up to 600 feet. Most early flying models were based on observable capabilities of birds (biomimicry) or employed basic aeronautical concepts (e.g., kites, parachutes, rotor-wings, and balloons) (see Figure 1-9).

Hydrogen airships from the late nineteenth century were used for entertainment purposes in theaters or auditoriums and represent one of the earliest forms of controllable aircraft models. These airships were manipulated by a rudimentary radio signal generated using spark gap transmitters. Once manned aircraft began to become more commonplace, interest in aviation grew as did the market for replications in the form of user-assembled models. Initially, such models were limited to A-frame pusher-propeller designs, but these models were continuously updated to replicate contemporary aircraft configurations and capabilities (see Figure 1-10).

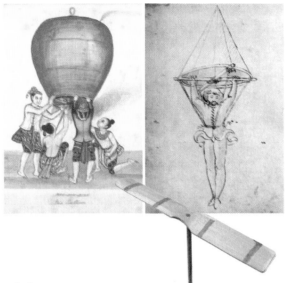

FIGURE 1-9. Depictions of various early aeromodeling designs.

Several European countries founded clubs aimed to increase interest and the study of aviation, as well as to foster aeronautic competitions. Examples included Aero-Club de France (1898), Belgium's Aero Club Royal de Belgique (1901), and the U.K.'s Royal Aero Club (1901). In response to the growing interest in aviation, in particular competitions and record-breaking activities, in addition to efforts by the aforementioned clubs and their counterparts, the Fédération Aéronautique Internationale (FAI) was founded in 1905. Within the FAI is the Commission Internationale d'Aero-Modelisme, which acts as a governing body for international aeromodeling activities and entities.

Aeromodeling continued to grow, truly taking off with the rapid adoption of air travel and power in the 1930s and 1940s. Miniature gas engines and lightweight, inexpensive materials, which enabled the construction of more realistic and capable models, escalated the interest in aeromodeling. In reaction to the growing interest, further clubs and associations were established. In the United States, one of the foremost and currently active organizations supporting development and use of modeling, the Academy of Model Aeronautics (AMA), was founded

FIGURE 1-10. Examples of modern operational model aircraft.

in 1936. Since its inception, the AMA has sanctioned competitions and fly-ins, developed procedures and guidelines (national community-based programs[1]), provided education and training, advocated on behalf of membership, and provided insurance to recreational pilots (members). The AMA has been instrumental in working with its membership and the federal government to coordinate the use of recreational models (e.g., access to radio frequencies, airspace access, maintaining safety) throughout its history. Other countries have aeromodeling clubs with similar histories and functions. For example, the British Model Flying Association stems back to 1922 and provides for encouragement of model flying in the U.K. and coordinates with applicable government agencies to protect and promote such activities. Other examples include the Aero Modelers Association (associate of the Aero Club of India), the Model Aeronautical Association of Australia, the Club Aeromodelistas Newbery (Argentina), Choshi Aeromodellers (Japan), RC Pattaya Flying Club (Thailand), and the Dubai RC Flying Club (United Arab Emirates). These clubs have proliferated interest in remote-controlled model aircraft and are key organizations during the rapid escalation of recreational unmanned aircraft use across the globe.

UNMANNED AIRCRAFT DEVELOPMENT

To grasp the level of sophistication possible in today's unmanned aircraft requires examination of major periods of technical advancement and operational expansion, from the neophyte years of development to the modern day.

■ LATE NINETEENTH CENTURY

The use of unmanned aircraft, albeit rudimentary, began long before the Wright brothers successfully introduced the world to powered flight. One of the first reports of utilitarian use of an unmanned aircraft was at the Battle of Fleurus in 1794. French forces used a simplistic balloon to observe the battle as it unfolded. It was soon realized that such aerial vehicles could do more than simply observe. At the siege of Venice by Austrian forces in 1849, the Austrians reportedly launched from offshore ships hundreds of balloons carrying shrapnel-filled bombs that were timed to explode when drifting over the besieged city. Although these efforts most likely caused more psychological harm than any sort of strategic value, it presented the potential value of employing such mechanisms. In the U.S. Civil War era, unmanned aerostats were launched to guide subsequent manned balloon reconnaissance flights used to support artillery fire sighting. In the 1870s, unmanned balloons were used to send mail and messages over the siege surrounding the city of Paris. Clearly, these examples demonstrated the usefulness of unmanned aircraft in a variety of venues.

---

[1] Per the FAA Modernization and Reform Act of 2012, a nationwide community-based organization is "a membership based association that represents the aeromodeling community within the United States; provides its members a comprehensive set of safety guidelines that underscores safe aeromodeling operations within the National Airspace System and the protection and safety of the general public on the ground; develops and maintains mutually supportive programming with educational institutions, government entities and other aviation associations; and acts as a liaison with government agencies as an advocate for its members."

FIGURE 1-11. Hewitt-Sperry Automatic Airplane.

Early iterations of heavier-than-air, unmanned aircraft became more commonplace in the mid-to-late 1800s. John Stringfellow successfully flew a steam-powered airplane with a ten-foot wingspan in 1848. Stringfellow then flew a tri-foil airplane in London's Crystal Palace in 1868. Samuel Langley flew his steam-powered, unmanned Aerodrome 5 down the Potomac River in 1896. These occurrences no doubt influenced how unmanned aircraft would be used in the future, in particular in upcoming military conflicts.

▌WORLD WAR I ERA

Archibald Low began work on a radio-controlled, unmanned aircraft in 1915, envisioning its use in defending against German aerial attacks. He could not perfect the design at that time because of radio interference from the engine ignition system. By 1916, Sopwith, a British aircraft company, had begun working on an unmanned aerial torpedo to engage Zeppelins and other targets. The first reliable success among radio-controlled aircraft was the Ruston Proctor Aerial Target, developed in 1916, which survived several remotely piloted test flights. The Ruston device was actually designed as a weapon, not a target, again envisioned to be used against Zeppelins and other enemy assets. In the same year, the Hewitt-Sperry Automatic Airplane was developed (credited as the predecessor of the modern day cruise missile) with control and stability provided by Sperry gyroscopes (*see* Figure 1-11).

In 1917, the U.S. Army commissioned an unmanned "flying bomb," the Kettering Aerial Torpedo (or Kettering "Bug"), which used a four-cylinder, 40-horsepower gas engine to deliver its payload approximately 40 miles at a speed of 50 miles per hour. Sperry gyros were used for guidance and the system was designed to measure its distance flown in terms of engine revolutions. Upon reaching the desired range (number of measured RPMs), the engine would shut

FIGURE 1-12. Kettering "Bug."

FIGURE 1-13. RAE Larynx.

off, leaving the craft to glide into its target area. The Bug (*see* Figure 1-12) was never used in combat because of its perceived unreliability. The U.S. Navy also experimented with the aerial torpedo concept in the form of the Curtiss N-9. With a 22-foot wingspan and a 90-horsepower engine, the N-9 would deliver a payload of TNT using a similar distance-measurement arrangement as the Bug. This system never was widely adopted, however.

▌1920s–1940s

Following World War I, experimentation with unmanned aircraft ramped up. In the United States, Standard E-1 aircraft were converted into unmanned test beds. By the late 1920s, the British Navy created the Larynx, an anti-ship "cruise missile," launched via catapult from destroyers (*see* Figure 1-13). This design was rather sophisticated, with a 200-horsepower engine providing a transit speed of 200 miles per hour. It was also successfully launched from land at sea targets. By the 1930s, it was determined that unmanned aircraft would be well suited for use as aerial practice targets. The Fairey Queen, a modified Fairey III seaplane, was developed in 1931 to act as target for gunnery training. A derivative of the De Havilland Tiger Moth (*see* Figure 1-14), the DH-82B "Queen Bee," flown in 1935, was novel in that it was the first system envisioned to be reusable. Used for anti-aircraft gunnery practice, the aircraft could be land or sea launched and could fly as high as 17,000 feet at 100 miles per hour with a range of 300 miles. A total of 380 Queen Bees were built and used in missions through the end of World War II. The Queen Bee is credited with introducing the name of "drone" (i.e., worker bee), which has since been used to describe subsequent unmanned aircraft.

By 1935, the use of aerial targets was well accepted, and in an effort to bolster the supply thereof, Radioplane Company was begun by ex-British Royal Flying Corpsman Reginald Denny. Radioplanes represent the first large-scale production line of target drones, the RP-1, which was adopted by the U.S. Army. This model was also marketed to hobbyists as a remote-controlled airplane.

The Germans were also very interested in remotely piloted aircraft. In 1937, Argus Motoren GmbH designed their model As-292, initially unguided, which served as an anti-aircraft gunnery

FIGURE 1-14. De Havilland Tiger Moth DH-82.

FIGURE 1-15. Radioplane OQ-2A.

target. A reconnaissance version was subsequently developed and by 1939, a remotely controlled version was made available. Some additional milestones in technological advances occurred during this period. Ross Hull, an Australian-American, discovered shortwave radio relays in which he could communicate over long distances (e.g., the United States to Australia). Further radio communication advances were made by Clinton DeSoto and fellow neophyte amateur radio hobbyists. These individuals experimented with radio components and frequencies, honing low frequencies for long-range communications. Radio repairman and amateur radio user Joseph Raspante was also a pioneer in radio control of model aircraft by advocating for micro-batteries, which were essential for the future development of these aircraft. His work even attracted the attention of Sperry for evaluation for applications involving the company's gyros. The work done by Walter and William Good, who designed and developed a working radio-controlled aircraft in 1937, was instrumental to the development of guided missiles. Walter refined the radio proximity fuse for use in World War II, which was considered a significant advance for military ordinance.

▮ WORLD WAR II ERA

The rapid escalation in technology among both Axis and Allied powers during World War II, such as advances in propulsion and air vehicle structure, led to a larger military investment, which supported the operation and experimentation involving unmanned aircraft. In particular, new purposes were envisioned for these systems. Most critically, this era brought forth many of the necessary technologies for guided and unguided systems that would later transition into today's cruise missiles and unmanned aircraft.

Radioplane further refined its products through various modified designs (RP-2 through RP-4), eventually producing the RP-5 in 1941, also known as the Radioplane OQ-2A (*see* Figure 1-15), of which approximately 15,000 were built for the U.S. Army. Showing similar interest, the U.S. Navy purchased a lighter, modified version of the RP-5, designated the TDD-1, which eliminated the landing gear. By 1943, a faster (over 100 miles per hour) and more powerful (8 horsepower) version, the OQ-3/TDD-2, was produced in large numbers.

FIGURE 1-16. TDR-1 Assault Drone.

FIGURE 1-17. V-1 (JB-2 Loon) on display.

In 1941, a significant advance came in the form of the Naval Aircraft Factory "Project Fox," which is credited with the first television camera installed on an unmanned aircraft allowing for remote visual control to be conducted from a "mother ship" TG-2 airplane. Following the successful attack on a destroyer at a range of 20 miles, the Navy envisioned boosting its use of unmanned vehicles. By the summer of 1941, radar guidance was tested on such unmanned vehicles to make them all-weather and night capable. The newer models, TDR-1s (see Figure 1-16), were initially planned to be adopted in large numbers with 162 TG-2 and 1,000 remote vehicles initially warranted, but these numbers were consistently revised lower (to below 400) and most of those built were left unused by the end of the war.

One of the most recognized unmanned aircraft of the World War II era was the German V-1 "Kirschkern," which was essentially an improved version of the As-292. The V-1 (see Figure 1-17) used a new type of propulsion, a pulsejet, which gave off a buzzing sound and thus was fearfully known as a "buzz bomb" by the Allied forces. Due to the nature of its engine, it had to be catapult or aerially launched, though typically the former. The V-1 used a simplified autopilot, which included a gyro-stabilized, weighted pendulum for attitude control, as well as a gyro-compass to assist in the yaw and roll control (although only yaw inputs were provided, which was deemed sufficient to maintain the proper direction). During the testing of the systems, a radio transmitter was installed to verify precision and functionality, but was not commonly used in general operations. An anemometer was used to count turns of the device, acting as a distance sensor that would trigger the warhead once safely away from the launch zone and would subsequently cause the vehicle to dive once reaching the designated target distance. The typical precision was within 20 miles of the target, with reports of instances when accuracy was as close as 7 miles. After test flights in 1942, the Germans would launch up to 18 a day, primarily at targets in the U.K. but also against Belgium. The V-1 campaign essentially ended by 1944, and only during the initial campaign did they have much effect because British countermeasures later improved (e.g., anti-aircraft gunfire, fighter intercepts, and barrage balloons[2]).

---

[2] Tethered balloons with thick cables meant to break up the aircraft in flight.

FIGURE 1-18. Project Aphrodite BQ-7 "Careful Virgin."

FIGURE 1-19. Northrop Ventura RP-71 "Falconer."

Another development of the World War II era that is still in effect today is the concept of the optionally piloted aircraft (OPA). Operation Aphrodite used modified B-17s, designated BQ-7s, to deliver high quantities of explosives to targets. These aircraft, designed to be flown by human pilots until set on target at which time crews abandoned the aircraft, had very limited success. Along similar lines, the BQ-8 Project Anvil used modified B-24s to achieve the same outcome using the same technique (*see* Figure 1-18). Joseph Kennedy, brother of late John F. Kennedy, was killed during an ill-fated Project Anvil flight in 1944.

Following the end of the war, the United States transformed a variety of aircraft for the purposes of radiological weapons data capture. In Operation Crossroads, a total of eight B-17s were used on Bikini Atoll to fly around the radioactive cloud following nuclear weapons tests. The U.S. Navy conducted similar tests with unmanned F6F Hellcats. Lastly, Lockheed P-80 Shooting Stars were also used for such purposes.

∎ 1950s–1960s

As the Cold War escalated, so did the use of unmanned aircraft. A family of Basic Target Training (BTT) aircraft ensued, which included the OQ-19 and the MQM-33/36 Shelduck. The MQM-33 was eventually converted into the RP-71 (*see* Figure 1-19), the first target drone to be used as an aerial observation platform. Due to the continuous pawn game played by both the U.S. and Soviet forces, a means to penetrate defenses though the use of decoys was envisioned. The ADM-20, carried by a B-52 Stratofortress, was specifically designed to throw Soviet defenses. Also, because aircraft speeds had increased dramatically and were by this time exceeding the speed of sound, faster targets were required. The Q-4 (AQM-35) was developed complete with the same engine as an F-5 fighter to provide supersonic target practice.

The Korean War era included a range of unmanned aircraft use. F6F-5K Hellcats were used to deliver 1,000-pound bombs in 1952, guided by a Douglas AD-4N Skyraider. Several missions were conducted that year targeting infrastructure in North Korea. Unfortunately, these systems were still relatively unreliable, with success rates of only around 50 percent. Following

FIGURE 1-20. Ryan BQM-34F "Firebee II" on display (*top*).

FIGURE 1-21. QH-50 DASH (*bottom left*).

FIGURE 1-22. Lockheed Martin D-21 on the back of a SR-71 (*bottom right*).

the success of various unmanned systems and in light of the downing of Francis Powers' U-2 reconnaissance plane in 1960, the push for more capable unmanned aircraft became more aggressive. The U.S. Army began work with their SD-2, a craft similar to the RP-71. The Ryan Firebee (*see* Figure 1-20) led to development of a family of reconnaissance vehicles including the "Lightning Bug" series, which were used to gather intelligence over Asian military targets.

The U.S. Navy developed the QH-50 (DASH) unmanned helicopter (*see* Figure 1-21) in response to the constant threat from Russian submarines. These systems could be fitted with torpedoes, depth charges, flares, sonobuoys, cargo, or smoke flares. QH-50s were later fitted with mini-bombs and would be used into the Vietnam War era.

It was around this time that more stealth techniques began to surface with advanced aircraft such as the Lockheed D-21, originally designed to be released from a piggyback position on a SR-71 (*see* Figure 1-22).

With the escalation of conflict in Vietnam, AQM-34s were developed to be launched from C-130 aircraft. These systems were capable of taking high-quality reconnaissance over enemy airspace. Unmanned aircraft began to be used more ubiquitously. During the Vietnam War, it has been reported that almost 3,500 unmanned missions were flown. Interestingly, to assist in the safe recovery of such vehicles, a mid-air retrieval system (MARS) was developed in which parachuted drones could be captured by a helicopter mid-descent. Due to the highly effective anti-aircraft capabilities of the North Vietnamese, the use of reconnaissance drones was reinforced, which led to the push for longer-range vehicles. One of the firsts of this type developed, the Ryan 154 "Compass Arrow," was designed to fly in excess of 70,000 feet and used primitive forms of stealth. Developing novel missions for drones was also a priority. The XQM-93 (*see* Figure 1-23) was designed specifically as a communications relay platform that was used during the Vietnam War to assist in keeping troops connected to command.

FIGURE 1-23. Ling-Temco-Vought XQM-93 (*top*). **FIGURE 1-25.** RQ-2 "Pioneer."
FIGURE 1-24. MQM-105 "Aquila" (*bottom*).

▌1970s–1980s

In the early 1970s, significant advances in unmanned aircraft technology took place. They were increasingly being used for intelligence and surveillance as well as being developed as offensive weapons. The BQM/SSM was tested in 1971 as an all-weather, anti-ship weapon system, although it eventually lost out to the Harpoon missile. In response to the conflict involving Israel, the BGM-34 was created as an air-to-surface weapon. Based on earlier "Lightning Bug" designs, the BQM-34 was used to engage Egyptian ground targets using guided air-to-surface missiles during the Yom Kippur War.

During this period, the paradigm shifted away from viewing unmanned aircraft as expendable, discardable tools toward viewing them as repeatedly recoverable and reusable. In addition, systems became more reliable, thus extending their longevity and utility. The MQM-105 "Aquila" (*see* Figure 1-24), first flown in 1983, was developed as a target designation system. The MQM-105 brought forth small-scale launch and recovery setups only requiring a 50-foot clearing to operate. Coupled with the launch and recovery equipment was a mobile ground station used to control the craft. This system also pioneered advances in secure data link transmission between the aircraft and the control station. Although the U.S. military reluctantly operated UAS because of high costs, the success of Israeli forces in the 1980s influenced the United States to begin investing an increasing amount in development of such systems.

By the mid-1980s, the United States had adopted the Israeli Aircraft Industry RQ-2 "Pioneer," which used a unique net recovery system still used in some systems today. The versatile RQ-2 (*see* Figure 1-25) could be launched and recovered by land (catapult and/or runway) and sea (rocket assist and netting). The system was both day and night capable and offered a gimbal stabilized optical and infrared camera with real-time video datalink. As unmanned aircraft became increasingly more sophisticated, the need for them to be capable to house the necessary sensors and avionics began to point to the need for larger platforms.

FIGURE 1-26. General Atomics ALTUS I (civilian variant of GNAT-750).

Aeronautical engineer Abraham Karem is credited with designing various platforms (Albatross and Amber) that laid the foundation for today's Predator. A simplified version of the Amber was evolved into the General Atomics GNAT-750 reconnaissance platform (and the civilian ALTUS used for NASA research and development) (*see* Figure 1-26).

The lighter weight of the GNAT allowed it to carry a higher payload, which was kept aloft by a Rotax 912, 95-horsepower engine. It was capable of flying over 1,200 miles and could stay aloft 12 hours before recovery. This precursor to the RQ-1 Predator entered service in 1989.

▮ 1990s–PRESENT

It was not until the 1990s that the widespread acquisition and use of unmanned aerial vehicles (UAVs) took place, at least for the United States. Following the successes of the Israeli forces in the 1980s, it was apparent that these vehicles offered significant promise for tactical use—in particular to view and strike remote locations without putting human lives in danger. Other applications quickly were identified and implemented. Micro systems, small enough for troops to carry with them on the battlefield, allowed for quick launch and recovery, which provided real-time observational intelligence to gain a tactical advantage over an enemy. These proved to be extremely helpful in rugged, difficult-to-reach locations, such as in Iraq and Afghanistan.

A significant development in military systems came in 1995 with the deployment of the RQ-1 Predator, a product of General Atomics, in the Balkan Conflict. It was quickly adopted for use in Iraq in 1996 and has continued to see service in subsequent conflicts. Different payloads were also developed to assist in military operations. In particular, by the mid-1990s, electronic countermeasures became more commonplace among unmanned vehicles. Classified as a medium-altitude, long-endurance (MALE) platform, the Predator was designed to collect intelligence and later was armed for target engagement. The Predator is easily mobilized through transport on typical U.S. Air Force aircraft (e.g., C-130) and is capable of operating from runways of 5,000 feet in length. It uses a Rotax 914, four-cylinder, piston engine, which provides 115 horsepower, similar to very small general aviation aircraft (e.g., C-162). It measures 55 x 27 x 7 feet and weighs 2,250 pounds at maximum gross weight. It cruises up to 135 miles per hour, can cover over 700 miles, and can fly up to 25,000 feet. The armed version, MQ-1[3] (*see* Figure 1-27), can carry two laser-guided Hellfire missiles.

As the utility of the Predator was quickly realized, a more capable version was introduced. The RQ-9 Reaper, previously referred to as the Predator B, was first flown in 2001 and put into service by 2007. Fulfilling similar missions as the Predator but with more sophisticated sensors and higher weight-carrying capacity, the Reaper was a welcome asset in recent conflicts. The MQ-9 includes a multi-spectral targeting system (MTS), which provides an infrared sensor, daylight video, image-intensified video, a laser range finder, as well as a laser illuminator for weapons targeting. The platform can be fitted with four AGM-114 Hellfire missiles. The Reaper has a much more powerful Honeywell TPE-331 turbopropeller engine providing 900 shaft horsepower. Its dimensions are 66 x 36 x 12.5 feet and it weighs 10,500 pounds with maximum payload. It can cruise at 230 miles per hour, has a range of 1,150 miles, and can fly up to 50,000 feet. Beyond the Hellfire missiles, the Reaper can also carry other guided weapons such as the GBU-12 Paveway bombs as well as GBU-38 Joint Direct Attack bombs.

A shift toward platforms with longer endurance was also sought. The concept of high-altitude long-endurance (HALE) vehicles came to fruition with the Insitu Aerosonde leading the way, successfully traversing the Atlantic Ocean in 1998 and demonstrating the significant capabilities of these types of vehicles. In this same year, a significant leap in unmanned aircraft was first flown, the Northrop Grumman RQ-4 Global Hawk (*see* Figure 1-28). Developed in collaboration with the Defense Advanced Research Projects Agency (DARPA), the RQ-4 was quickly implemented in operations in Afghanistan and subsequently in Operation Iraqi Freedom. Versions have been adopted by the U.S. Navy and Air Force, as well as the German Air Force (the German version is named the Euro Hawk). The most current version, the Block 30, has significant range and endurance, advertised at 12,300 miles and over 34 hours, respectively. The Global Hawk is very large, with a 130-foot wingspan, a length of more than 46 feet, and a

FIGURE 1-27. MQ-1 Predator.

FIGURE 1-28. RQ-4 Global Hawk.

[3] R designation is for "reconnaissance," M is for "multi-role," and Q is for "unmanned."

FIGURE 1-29. RQ-5 Hunter.

FIGURE 1-30. RQ-7A Shadow 200.

height just over 15 feet. To put this in perspective, the average modern Boeing 737 has a wingspan of around 115 feet, is more than 100 feet long, and is 20 feet high (fuselage). The RQ-4 is powered by a 7,600-pound thrust, Rolls Royce-North American F137-RR-100 turbofan engine. It has a maximum takeoff weight of 32,350 pounds, a fuel capacity of 17,300 pounds, and payload capability of 3,000 pounds. It cruises at 60,000 feet at 310 knots and although unmanned, it is crewed by three individuals—two pilots (one for the launch and recovery element [LRE] and one for the mission control element [MCE]) and a sensor operator. Payloads allow for persistent theater observation providing imagery intelligence (IMINT), signals intelligence (SIGINT), and moving target indication (MTI) through its sensor array. Additional sensor capabilities are being explored through the Universal Payload Adaptor program to potentially replace aircraft like the U-2 with unmanned types.

Although the Global Hawk has significant capabilities, it could not perform all observation functions required in battle due to extended mission times and substantial launch and recovery requirements. Shorter-range, lower-flying vehicles were needed to fill various operational niches. The RQ-5 Hunter (*see* Figure 1-29) was developed in 1989 through a collaboration between what today is Northrop Grumman and Israeli Aircraft Industries (IAI). It entered service in 1996 and was quickly put into use in Kosovo to support NATO operations in 1999. The two Moto Guzzi two-cylinder engine (push and pull types) Hunter is designed to serve a variety of theater-centric functions, including real-time imagery intelligence, artillery guidance, damage assessment, surveillance, and target identification. The Hunter is 1,600 pounds and has a 23-foot length and 29-foot wingspan. It has a payload capacity of just under 200 pounds, an 11.5 hour endurance capability at short range (around 150 miles), and a maximum altitude of just over 15,000 feet.

The move to more mobile and agile deployment and recovery of systems in the battlefield led to the procurement of the RQ-7 Shadow (*see* Figure 1-30). Launched by a mobile catapult, it is used for shorter-range reconnaissance, target acquisition, and damage assessment. First introduced for use in 2002, it has been adopted by a variety of military forces beyond the United States, including Swedish and Australian complements. These platforms provided a

FIGURE 1-31.
ScanEagle launch from mobile catapult system.

FIGURE 1-32. Hand launch of RQ-11B "Raven."

significant amount of support in recent Middle East conflicts, with over 200,000 hours of operation in 2007 alone. This platform (200 model) is around 11 feet long, has a 14-foot wingspan, and has a maximum weight of 375 pounds. It features a 38-horsepower Wankel engine to drive a propeller, which supports a maximum speed of 127 miles per hour and a range of just under 70 miles, with six to nine hours endurance at 15,000 feet.

One of the most widely used and robust small platform is the Insitu (Boeing) ScanEagle (*see* Figure 1-31). First envisioned as a platform to provide strategic locating of tuna schools (called SeaScan), its potential in other applications was rapidly realized. First flown in 2002 and later deployed by the U.S. military in 2005, the ScanEagle is equipped with stabilized electro-optical and/or infrared sensors. More advanced versions have improved nighttime capabilities and some configurations are equipped with lightweight synthetic aperture radar (SAR). It has a wingspan of just over 10 feet and is approximately five feet long (depending on the model) with a 48.5-pound maximum weight and a payload capacity of 7.5 pounds. The ScanEagle can loiter for 24 hours and cruises at around 60 miles per hour at altitudes of up to 19,500 feet. It also has two engine options, one using conventional fuel and the other using kerosene-like fuel (similar to jet fuel). The platform can be launched with a catapult system and uses a unique recovery system allowing for very easy use in remote locations and at sea. The ScanEagle actually seeks a signal generated by the recovery system (i.e., vertical wire), which it hits with a specialized hook attachment. The design has recently been undergoing testing using a multirotor carrier for aerial deployment and capture, without the need for significant physical infrastructure to be installed, configured, transported, or stored.

Reducing size further and expanding capabilities for individual troops or units to deploy systems in their immediate area, the RQ-11 Raven (*see* Figure 1-32) was first developed in 1999. The novel attribute of this vehicle is that it is small—only 4.2 pounds—and can be hand-launched. Recovery is automated and requires no special equipment. It provides video and night vision capabilities over a six-mile radius and can loiter for up to 90 minutes. These systems have seen widespread, global use, with most NATO countries and other U.S. allies utilizing them in various capacities.

FIGURE 1-34.
MQ-8 Fire Scout.

FIGURE 1-33. RQ-20 Puma.

Continuous improvements have been made to small unmanned platforms with the RQ-20 Puma (see Figure 1-33) entering service in 2007. Fulfilling similar roles as the RQ-11, it weighs 13 pounds and provides a nine-mile radius and two-hour endurance. The Puma boasts a more robust operating condition range with the capacity to operate at extreme temperatures and in rain rates of up to an inch per hour. Improvements to the Puma are ongoing, including capabilities for solar recharging of its batteries and enhanced batteries to provide better endurance.

The continuing push for ease in deployment and recovery of UAV led to the development of the MQ-8 Fire Scout (see Figure 1-34), which is a helicopter-type platform developed by Northrop Grumman. This system was of interest to the U.S. Navy as it identified a need for platform replacement and expansion that could easily be used at sea. The Fire Scout has offensive capabilities including the carriage of Hellfire missiles, laser-guided weapons, and Advanced Precision Kill Weapon Systems (APKWS). It also can provide anti-submarine operations support. Additionally, the MQ-8 can deliver supplies to troops while in theater. Fire Scouts are currently deployed on the U.S. Navy Littoral Combat ships and such use is planned to be expanded to other ship types.

It should not be surprising that, similar to manned military aircraft, there has been a movement toward stealth technology among unmanned military systems. The Lockheed Martin RQ-170 Sentinel (see Figure 1-35) was developed for the U.S. Air Force and the Central Intelligence Agency and appears markedly similar to the B-2 Stealth Bomber. This platform has reported been used in Operation Enduring Freedom in Afghanistan as well as in the Pakistan theater. It has also purportedly been used over Iran with a prominent claim that Iran had downed one for violating its airspace in 2011. It is reported that the Sentinel is able to provide video monitoring of targets of interest. Although specific details on the platform are currently unavailable, it is estimated to be just under 15 feet long, 6 feet high, with a wingspan of just over 65.5 feet and a service ceiling of 50,000 feet.

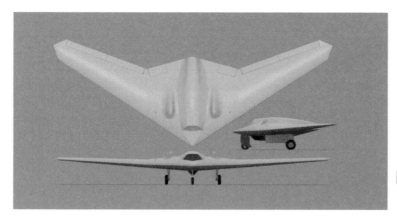

FIGURE 1-35.

Artist's rendition of the RQ-170 Sentinel.

FROM TACTICAL TO TRANSFORMATIONAL TECHNOLOGY

As the technologies associated with military UAVs became more sophisticated and proven, the interest of civilian innovators was peaked. As previously mentioned, ever since the initiation of manned flight, there has been an interest in flying model aircraft. Yet the capabilities of military platforms, supported through improvements in both civilian aircraft modeling and defense-specific research and development efforts, are what pushed civilians to contemplate the potential non-military uses. The civilian, hobbyist community has grown due to increased availability, which has transitioned from individually built and sourced kits featuring internal combustion glow engines to mass-produced, flight-ready electric systems available at affordable price points. These mass-produced, commercial off-the-shelf (COTS) options include almost ready-to-fly (ARF), ready-to-fly (RTF), and bind-and-fly (BNF) versions, which can be purchased online and from local retailers for as little as $20 or as much as $10,000.

Advances in reliability, miniaturization, batteries, components, and capabilities, along with the decreasing costs of the aforementioned, have taken something that was at one time only attainable by military and government entities and made it into a transformational technology available to the general public. The mechanical complexity and level of support required (e.g., setup, tuning, maintenance, and repair) of the civilian COTS options have also decreased through increased incorporation and availability of electric, battery-powered propulsion options. With the introduction of brushless motors, lithium-based batteries, and foam airframes into the aircraft modeling community, the usability of consumer model aircraft (sUAS) drastically increased. These civilian sUAS platforms have the capability to affect everyday citizens as well as impact industry on a wide-scale. These systems are being used now to assist in precision agriculture, communications, utilities inspection, firefighting, search and rescue, and even for delivery services.

Other government agencies, academic institutions, and private corporations are now utilizing unmanned airborne platforms.

FIGURE 1-36. NASA Helios solar-powered UAS.

FIGURE 1-37. TAM 5, "Spirit of Butts' Farm."

Examples of government research platforms include:

- RQ-3A Darkstar
- X-37B
- X-45A J-UCAS
- X-47B UCAS
- NASA Ikhana
- NASA Pathfinder
- NASA Helios (see Figure 1-36)

Example academic and private research platforms include:

- Astro Flight Sunrise I/II
- Zephyr
- SoLong Solar UAV
- Aerosonde "Laima"
- TAM 5 "Spirit of Butts Farm" (see Figure 1-37)
- Pterosoar

TRANSITION FROM UAV TO UAS

As unmanned aircraft have become increasingly complex, they have come to be described as a "system of systems." As such, the term **unmanned aerial vehicle (UAV)** no longer seemed to be representative of the level of sophistication and intricacy of these platforms; UAV came to be recognized as the **aerial element** of the overarching, unified system. As a result, the term **unmanned aerial system (UAS)** was adopted to describe the composite array of systems composing the total system (platform, payload, control and communication, and support equipment). Unfortunately, even following this paradigm shift, a lack of standardization remains (including among government entities), with the terms UAV, drone, remotely piloted aircraft (RPA), and remotely piloted vehicle (RPV) commonly used across the field. This inconsistent vernacular can be confusing to the public and in an effort to standardize the terminology, the FAA and industry have adopted the terms **unmanned** *aircraft* **system (UAS)** and *small* **unmanned aircraft system (sUAS)**, with the latter referring to platforms under 55 pounds. The FAA classifications and terminology are being used to delineate the regulatory requirements for certification and operation, applicable to each category.

OPEN SOURCE TO CROWDFUNDING

Further driving the expansion of platform design and construction is the fact that elements necessary to create reasonably priced, highly capable platforms have become more accessible and customizable. Electronic components, such as circuits, sensors, and controls, have become significantly less expensive, putting affordable, useful platforms within reach of the average consumer. Even more sophisticated platforms, although costing thousands of dollars, are still economically feasible for academic institutions and businesses. Moreover, the software and drivers in such platforms are often open source, allowing users to modify their capabilities for individual, custom purposes. The following activities have been instrumental in achieving this level of accessibility, customization, and affordability:

- Hobbyist construction and development (RC model aircraft and electronics)
- Do it yourself (DIY) community (e.g., DIY-drones.com, APM/ArduPilot)
- Crowdsourcing and crowdfunding (e.g., DARPA, Indiegogo, Kickstarter) (*see* Figure 1-38)

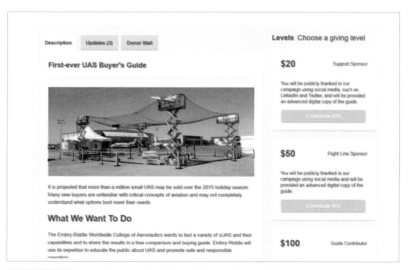

FIGURE 1-38. Example crowdfunding effort, Embry-Riddle Aeronautical University (ERAU) sUAS Buying Guide.

The impact these groups are having in transitioning what started as recreational devices to now encompass consumer and professional-grade products (prosumer) cannot be underestimated. Assisting in this process is innovation funded by collectives of investors, such as crowdfunding (when innovators seek investment from the public at large). This allows development of novel platforms and components without the inventor having to foot upstart and development costs. Furthermore, crowdsourcing has proven to help identify novel new concepts and support development of further capabilities and performance in unmanned system related technologies. One such example is the ArduPilot project, which features collaborative development and improvement of source code for the popular Arduino-based unmanned control system. Further examples of crowdsourcing and collaborative development of open-source designs include the MultiiWii (flight controller derived from Nintendo Wii controller hardware), Paparazzi UAV (autopilot), OpenPilot (autopilot), and OpenDroneMaps (imagery processing toolkit).

It is important to note that while these groups have extended technological capabilities, the results are not as thoroughly tested or always certified, relying on trial and error (multiplied across tens of thousands of users) rather than the procedural, quantitative analysis, testing, and certification typically used among certified aviation parts manufacturers. The results of such efforts can, of course, be very beneficial and innovative, especially when such economies of scale are employed. However, they can also be disastrous when they are untested and used in uncontrolled, safety-critical scenarios, such as among manned aircraft.

RELATED TECHNOLOGY AND INNOVATIVE DEVELOPMENT

Currently, advances in the following areas are pushing the industry forward and hold the potential to drastically change the technology to improve safety, decrease costs, and put platforms and their capabilities into the hands of those who can capitalize on them in an effective manner, such as entrepreneurs.

- *Computing*—Advances in microprocessors, portable computing, microcontrollers, machine code, algorithms, and applications occur on a constant basis. As components gain capability, become smaller and lighter, and continue to become increasingly affordable, the growth of UAS usage across the globe will continue.

- *Robotics*—UAS are considered aerial robotics, a subset of mobile robotics. As such, related technology development, as well as corollary technology and application, will bolster UAS development and use.

- *Microminiaturization*—Consider what has happened to cellphones in the last decade: they now have global positioning systems (GPS), inertial sensors, and a high level of computational power. At the same time, they have come at reduced costs and with increased sophistication and capabilities, smaller power

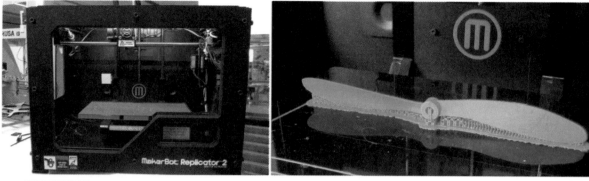

FIGURE 1-39. 3D printer (*left*) and printed propeller (*right*).

consumption, increased endurance, and improved fidelity and quality of data, as well as with improved survivability of components. The same has occurred and continues to occur among all aspects of UAS.

- *Materials Development and Manufacturing*—Just as the technology at the core of UAS are continuously improving, the same is occurring in the development of materials for the platforms. For example, carbon fiber, additive layer manufacturing, and the advent of 3D printing all have opened the door for just about anyone to build complex parts for their systems. As an example of how these technologies can assist the industry, it is not unusual for sUAS to sustain damage during use, which, in the past, may have resulted in a discarding of the platform. Now, 3D printing has allowed for easier repair and replacement for such systems (*see* Figure 1-39). Also, this type of activity has allowed for the customization of designs, such as fitting existing designs with altered landing gear. Such innovation can only be expected to continue with individuals being able to design, construct, and operate their own unique systems or market them freely across the globe.

- *Power Storage, Collection, and Distribution*—While larger UAS rely on fuels for operation, most sUAS use batteries. Not surprisingly, there have been drastic improvements in electrical storage capacity and reductions in weight. Battery use has also moved away from nickel–cadmium toward lithium types, which allow for increased power storage density. Additionally, efforts are being made to conserve available battery power through reductions in component power consumption and by employing alternative power storage mechanisms, such as fuel cells. Another technology on the horizon is the transfer of power from the ground to sUAS in flight, such as through the use of energy beams or lasers (e.g., Lockheed Martin and LaserMotive R&D using Stalker sUAS).

- *Handheld Electronics*—The various support and control devices used to interface with UAS, such as interconnected communications, smartphones, tablets, and ultraportable computers, have also become more commonplace. In fact, many sUAS on the market use Bluetooth technology to pair with a smartphone to provide first-person view (FPV) during flight. Similar adoptions of existing handheld devices as interfaces with UAS are likely to emerge.

REGULATIONS SET THE STAGE FOR THE (R)EVOLUTION

As military UAS came into the spotlight and with the subsequent rapid growth of civilian UAS use, civil aviation authorities began to realize that it was time to begin controlling and regulating such operations, as it quickly became apparent how much of an impact these operations might have on the National Airspace System (NAS) in the United States. (Similar actions have been taken by governments outside the U.S. for the same reasons.) Here are some of the noteworthy regulatory steps taken by the federal government:

- **Unmanned Aircraft Operations in the National Airspace System (Docket No. FAA-2006-25714)**—The FAA released this Federal Register notice in 2007 identifying that FAA Advisory Circular (AC) 91-57, Model Aircraft Operating Standards (1981), does not apply to commercial activities, which would require review and approval on a case-by-case basis. Such commercial operations would further require use of a certified aircraft, licensed pilot, and FAA operational approval (precursor to the certificate of waiver or authorization [COA] process).

- **FAA Modernization and Reform Act of 2012 (Public Law 112-095)**—In this Congressional action, the FAA was mandated to integrate UAS into the NAS. This prompted the FAA to begin taking actions to create standards, safeguards, and regulations concerning UAS use across the United States.

- **Public and Civil Certificates of Waiver or Authorization (COA)/Section 333 Petition for (Grant of) Exemption**—The FAA created a series of mechanisms, including the temporary Section 333 process, to provide review and approval of individual UAS operations, prior to the release of a formal regulatory structure. While initially an onerous, difficult, and lengthy process, the FAA has recently been more forthcoming with approvals through these processes.

- **Designation of six UAS Test Sites**—In 2014, a series of locations and entities that would support experimentation, testing, and flight operations of UAS were announced. The role of these sites is to conduct UAS testing activities that will assist in determining the necessary procedures and technologies to safely integrate UAS into the NAS.

- **Notice of Proposed Rulemaking (NPRM) for the Operation and Certification of sUAS**—In early 2015, the FAA sought to move forward with its regulation of UAS by specifically focusing on operational and certification criteria for sUAS (platforms under 55 pounds) (see Figure 1-40). At this time, the FAA sought

FIGURE 1-40. Example sUAS platforms.

comments on sUAS standards, requirements, and regulations. The final rules are still pending as of mid-2016.

- **Presidential Memorandum: Promoting Economic Competitiveness While Safeguarding Privacy, Civil Rights, and Civil Liberties in Domestic Use of Unmanned Aircraft Systems**—In response to concerns about domestic military UAS use as well as privacy issues, the U.S. President (Obama) issued a memorandum in February 2015 stating that "as UAS are integrated into the NAS, the Federal Government will take steps to ensure that the integration takes into account not only our economic competitiveness and public safety, but also the privacy, civil rights, and civil liberties concerns these systems may raise."

- **Designation of UAS Center of Excellence**—In May 2015, the FAA announced the creation of a Center of Excellence (COE) for UAS. Comprised of a team of universities, the Center is initially tasked with researching the following topics: detect and avoid technology; low-altitude operations safety; control and communications; spectrum management; human factors; compatibility with air traffic control operations; and training and certification of UAS pilots and other crewmembers, in addition to other areas.

- **Advisory Circular (AC) 91-57A, Model Aircraft Operating Standards**—This advisory circular released by the FAA in 2015 replaced a 34-year-old version (1981) that provided guidance for hobbyist use of model aircraft. This update provides a clearer delineation of how and where hobbyists can operate their models as well as the maximum allowable size of a hobbyist platform.

- **UAS Registration Requirements**—In late 2015, the U.S. Department of Transportation (DOT) announced the requirement to register recreational pilots intending to use an sUAS between 0.55 to 55 pounds within the U.S. National Airspace System.

- ***14 CFR Part 107—Operation and Certification of Small Unmanned Aircraft Systems***—The release of the formal rules identifying sUAS usage and certification requirements occurred in late June 2016, with the enactment and availability of testing in late August. This historic rule set changed the dynamics and tempo of civil sUAS application, providing a high degree of accommodation to support commercial operations by reducing certification requirements, expanding operational capabilities, and providing a set of waiverable conditions to further control and mitigate risk.

- ***Wide-Scale Integration of UAS into Global Airspace***—Once the technical and regulatory challenges of UAS integration—including detect, sense, and avoidance (DSA) and unmanned traffic management (UTM)—are addressed in the United States, it is envisioned that wide-scale implementation of these systems will take place. While other countries have exceeded the current airspace access capabilities of the United States, their integration efforts have mostly mirrored those being promoted by the FAA and they tend to have relatively lower aircraft operational density. While forecasts vary, all available research indicates the market for UAS will grow exponentially over the next 20 years, eventually reaching global values measured in billions of dollars.

It is important for all UAS stakeholders to be aware of the changing operational and regulatory landscape both to avoid unnecessary conflicts with local, state, and government authorities and to prevent upsetting neighbors or other aviation operators. Without such care, authorities will limit access and use, making the freedom to take UAS to their full potential much more difficult.

Chapter 4 will provide a more detailed review of the legislation and regulation issues surrounding UAS.

CHAPTER 2

APPLICATION OF sUAS: UNDERSTANDING USES

INTRODUCTION

Small unmanned aircraft systems (sUAS) can be used for a significant number of purposeful applications, providing benefits such as increased flexibility for capture of data on demand, decreased operational and support costs, and reduced risk. Their primary purpose can vary significantly, from remote sensing to transportation of cargo, as can the motivation behind their use, which may be driven by the need to improve safety, increase services and efficiency, supplement existing capabilities, or generate profit. These uses continue to grow as technological capabilities expand and the price point to acquire the technology decreases. Manufacturers have put a focused effort into making operations more intuitive, while increasing the features and level of support available to the community. While this technology is still highly prevalent in the recreational hobbyist segment, in part due to a wide variety of consumer platforms, specialized systems are available and in development to support the functions and tasks presented and discussed in this chapter.

COMMON USES

This section features the identification of documented and observed application of sUAS; it is not meant to serve as an all-inclusive list. Instead, consider this a guide to understanding many recent uses to help you conceptualize and ponder how to use sUAS to support anticipated activities or business ventures. By fully considering and comparing the exhibited capabilities and limitations of sUAS, in the context of the functions and tasks currently being performed, you will be better equipped to develop your own unique operational concepts and applications.

FIGURE 2-1. Example visual perspectives: manual (*top right*), aircraft (*bottom right*), and satellite (*left*).

Several important aspects of an effective sUAS application should be considered and defined early in your development process:

- *Satisfies needs*—Does the use of sUAS provide a feasible solution to solving an issue or challenge? Think about whether the options you are considering will be widely available and supported; intuitive and easy to operate; and affordable for the end user to accomplish the desired task

- *Provides benefit*—Does the conceptual solution establish greater advantages than it does limitations or problems? Consider if the solution supports covering vast areas from an elevated perspective; decreases costs; generates expedient, timely results where/when needed; grants access to hard-to-reach locations; improves precision in repetitive flight profiles (through autonomy).

- *Improvement*—Will the use of an sUAS result in a definable improvement compared to current methods? Consider if the solution is advantageous for performing a task (lower cost, better performance, and the ability to operate when/where others cannot) or can supplement (augment) current methods to provide further benefit and capability (e.g., reduced risk, greater situational awareness, improved effectiveness).

It is important to compare and contrast the intended use of sUAS to conventional methods of performing the task to identify the specific benefits, as well as the limitations. By identifying the comparable performance, cost, and support required among all the options, you will be better prepared to evaluate and determine which option provides the optimal solution to the challenge. Such comparison will require a detailed look at how these tasks and functions are currently performed—such as by manual survey (e.g., walking a field and surveying with equipment), purchase and review of data captured using satellites, or contracting and scheduling manned aircraft to perform the required flight operation. Remember, despite how interesting, novel, or exciting this technology may be to you personally, an sUAS is not always the best solution. The following represents some of the benefits and limitations of commonly used methods to perform tasks (see example perspectives shown in Figure 2-1):

- *Manual*
  — Improved observation for small areas; significantly decreases for large areas
  — Cost-dependent on size of workforce (scalable); typically requires a larger workforce for coverage of significant terrain
  — Workforce requires task training, specific to the function performed
  — Introduces inherent risk to personnel in the field
  — Mobilization costs, which can include transportation, lodging, and per diem
  — Greater potential for sensor occlusion
- *Manned aircraft*
  — Higher operating cost than sUAS; lower cost than satellites
  — Easier to re-task than satellites; slower to re-task than sUAS
  — Broader coverage area than sUAS (range, speed, and endurance); less than satellites
  — Higher resolution than satellite, but lower than some sUAS
  — Can carry multiple sensors, and payload can be customized to mission
  — Introduces inherent risk to flight crew
  — Requires scheduling of aircraft and pilot
- *Satellites*
  — Provides broad area coverage
  — Expensive to build, launch, operate, and access custom-captured data (countered by economies of scale)
  — Re-tasking takes significant planning, time, and effort
  — Limited to sensors included at launch
  — Data acquisition can be impacted by cloud cover
  — Resolution not as fine as from manned or unmanned aircraft, which are closer to ground and feature interchangeable payloads
  — Requires significant infrastructure to support (from launch to orbital operations supported by ground control)

When this book was written, more than 4,000 Section 333 Petition for Exemptions had been submitted to and approved (granted) by the FAA, exhibiting a significant interest in use of sUAS for non-recreational purposes by the civil-use community. The following represent the most common uses identified in the final approved applications[1]:

- Aerial filming (video and photography)
- Real estate
- General aerial surveying
- Agriculture
- Construction
- Utility inspection (*see* Figure 2-2)
- Environmental
- Search and rescue
- Emergency management
- Insurance
- Other

FIGURE 2-2. VTOL sUAS performing line inspection.

It is critical to note that any use cannot interfere with or obstruct emergency response operations and should not be conducted without appropriate approval or outside specified tolerances for environmental conditions. The safe operation of sUAS is highly dependent on weather, as they are significantly affected by wind, precipitation, and visibility. Any planned use should be conducted in accordance with federal, state, and local laws; community-based practices; and manufacturer requirements. Your use of sUAS as a solution must ensure regulatory/legal compliance; protect the safety of crewmembers, bystanders, and property; and address known limitations and constraints. Understanding the complexity of the application and technology used is critical to achieving success.

RECREATION AND HOBBY

Using sUAS for personal recreation or hobby (*see* Figure 2-3) remains the most widespread and recognizable application with numerous businesses—from online retailers to local hobby stores—as well as nonprofit organizations supporting this use. This community has easy access to components and parts, guidance, and detailed training and education to better understand responsible use, whether for the personal enjoyment of flight, competition, or scale modeling. Many of the products and underlying technology used in consumer sUAS have been developed and propagated with this community in mind. Additionally, many of the advances of sUAS-related technology have sprung from the minds and hands of model aircraft enthusi-

---

[1] As identified in the AUVSI 2015 report, *The First 1,000 Commercial UAS Exemptions.*

FIGURE 2-3. Example recreational model aircraft.

asts, including the development and use of glow-plug[2] and diesel engines,[3] access to radio frequencies,[4] first-person-view,[5] and antennae configurations (e.g., CloverLeaf circular polarized[6]). Recreational use of sUAS can be categorized into four areas: fun, competition, scale-realism, and uncompensated educational use.

▌FUN

This category represents the reason why many start using sUAS: the pure enjoyment of flight. This could range from building a model aircraft from a kit to purchasing a ready-to-fly (RTF) platform off the shelf and taking it to the local park (assuming sufficient distance from airports, heliports, or other prohibited areas). Sending an sUAS aloft for the afternoon provides enjoyment and evokes passion for the hobby. It also represents how many are introduced to the wider aviation community. Subsequently, this is one of the underlying reasons why hobbyist use has been so protected: it is a historical pastime that serves to excite and engage the next generation of pilots, engineers, and responsible citizens.

---

[2] Developed in the 1940s by Ray Arden (from George M. Myers, "One Man's View of How AMA History was Driven by Technology," 1991).
[3] In 1975, Bob Davis introduced the Davis Diesel Converters (Myers, 1991).
[4] The combined efforts of AMA leadership and members, including John Worth, Dr. Walter Good, Ed Lorenz, and Bob Aberle, lobbied the FCC for RC modeler access (Myers, 1991).
[5] While the model aircraft community was not the first to use FPV in aircraft, they worked to incorporate it into model aircraft, resulting in widespread inclusion in many consumer sUAS available today.
[6] Adapted from the skew planar wheel and introduced to the model aircraft FPV community by Alex Greve (IBCrazy) in 2011.

■ COMPETITION

Numerous types of model aircraft competitions and aircraft categories are found within recreational use. These events provide hobbyists the opportunity to showcase the build quality of their models, as well as demonstrate their proficiency at flying their specific category of aircraft. Common competition categories include nostalgia, scale, sport, soaring, free flight, and control line, as well as radio-control aircraft racing, combat, and aerobatic (precision and three-dimensional [3D]) flight. Competition events are held and judged at gatherings, such as fly-ins and shootouts. The latest example of competition use is first-person view (FPV) racing in which a pilot uses a helmet-mounted display (HMD) or video-goggles to fly a multirotor sUAS platform through a circuit, among other platforms, or independently (timed-trial). This use has gained substantial interest abroad and has recently begun to emerge in the United States with a number of proposed venues and events.

■ SCALE REALISM

A hobbyist does not need to limit their construction of scale model aircraft to competitions alone. Enthusiasts may be interested in the historical significance of specific platforms or enjoy building working models that appear and/or operate similarly to their manned counterparts. This category is focused on the creation and operation of realistic, scaled-down versions found throughout aviation, from historical to modern aircraft. There are a multitude of resources available in support of this category, from aviation museums to online profiles of aircraft.

■ UNCOMPENSATED EDUCATIONAL USE

In May of 2016, the FAA clarified that use of sUAS by students (and in a limited capacity, faculty) of accredited educational institutions is considered recreational, if used to perform uncompensated operations in support of course and research objectives. The defining characteristic of this category is confirming that such operations are secondary to the intent of the coursework. An example would be operations in engineering courses, where design and development represents the primary purpose of the course, with operation of the constructed platform being secondary. The FAA determined that such use qualifies as recreational and does not require specific operational approval. It is critical to note that this category does not include those academic programs or courses developed to specifically demonstrate or teach operation of UAS (i.e., UAS flight instruction). The following represent the specific elements of the FAA interpretation permitting such use:

- A person may operate an unmanned aircraft for hobby or recreation in accordance with Section 336 of the FAA Modernization and Reform Act of 2012 (FMRA) at educational institutions and community-sponsored events provided that person is (1) not compensated, or (2) any compensation received is neither directly nor indirectly related to that person's operation of the aircraft at such events.

- A student may conduct model aircraft operations in accordance with Section 336 of the FMRA in furtherance of his or her aviation-related education at an accredited educational institution.
- Faculty teaching aviation-related courses at accredited educational institutions may assist students who are operating model aircraft under Section 336 and in connection with a course that requires such operations, provided the student maintains operational control of the model aircraft such that a faculty member's manipulation of the model aircraft's controls is incidental and secondary to the student's (e.g., the faculty member steps in to regain control in the event the student begins to lose control, to terminate the flight, etc.).[7]

The following represents further details regarding operations under this category:

Students:

- Student use of UAS at accredited educational institutions as a component of science, technology, and aviation-related educational curricula or other coursework such as television and film production or the arts closely reflects and embodies the purposes of "hobby or recreational" use of model aircraft and is consistent with the intent of Section 336 of the FMRA.[8]
- Students are responsible for "meeting and complying with all other elements required for lawful model aircraft operations pursuant to Section 336 of the FMRA, including the student not receiving any form of compensation (including reimbursement of costs, honorarium, etc.) directly or incidentally to his or her operation of the model aircraft."[9]
- Student operation of UAS in support of faculty-led research is not considered recreational use.

Faculty (Instructors):

- Faculty operation of a UAS in support of instruction and research is not considered recreational use.
- "De minimis limited"[10] faculty participation (as an instructor) overseeing student operation would conform to recreational use.

Educational uses that do not meet the described requirements fall under either public or civil use of UAS, requiring FAA approval and/or appropriate certification to operate (for details, *see* Chapter 4).

---

[7] Federal Aviation Administration (FAA), *Memorandum: Educational Use of Unmanned Aircraft Systems (UAS)* (2016), pp. 1–2. Retrieved from http://www.faa.gov/uas/regulations_policies/media/Interpretation-Educational-Use-of-UAS.pdf
[8] FAA, *Memorandum: Educational Use of Unmanned Aircraft Systems*, p. 4.
[9] FAA, *Memorandum: Educational Use of Unmanned Aircraft Systems*, p. 4.
[10] Minimal operation associated with maintaining safety oversight.

U.S. Geological Survey

FIGURE 2-4. NDVI analysis, derived using data collected from UAS (*left*).

FIGURE 2-5. Full-spectrum georeferenced orthomosaic model (*right*).

PRECISION AGRICULTURE

Use of sUAS to support precision agriculture is one of the most rapidly growing operational segments. Low entry point and maintenance costs, combined with the wide variety in platforms and capabilities, make sUAS a desirable option for farmers and agricultural researchers to consider. Traditionally, farmers have relied on the use of manual survey, satellites, and manned aircraft to capture important data, as well as apply necessary treatments to their crops (e.g., crop dusting). While these conventional options have provided significant benefit, they are expensive and dependent on the availability of highly tasked resources. Unmanned aircraft, including sUAS, can be used as an alternative or in combination to supplement, improving the efficiency and effectiveness of agricultural management efforts. The use of sUAS in agricultural applications supports reduced risk by limiting operations to rural land with lower population, structural, and traffic density. It also supports the management of irrigation, crops, and live-stock through aerial inspection, as well as targeted application of pesticides, herbicides, fungicides, and fertilizers. The use of sUAS can help to determine when and where to apply critical resources to treat problems, at a reduced cost and improved level of efficiency.

■ CROP/LIVESTOCK MONITORING AND INSPECTION

When sUAS are used to perform monitoring and inspection, they are flown in a pattern or route over the subject environment. The aircraft is equipped with one or more sensors to capture environmental data—including color, infrared, or multi/hyperspectral imagery—which are sensed from an orthogonal (downward) or user-defined perspective (gimballed view). The remotely sensed data is stored on board or relayed down to the ground station for interpreta-

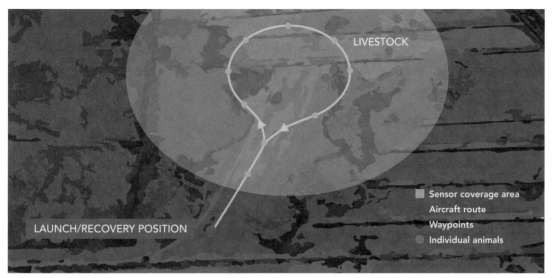

LIVESTOCK

LAUNCH/RECOVERY POSITION

■ Sensor coverage area
— Aircraft route
■ Waypoints
● Individual animals

FIGURE 2-6. Example livestock management flight.

tion using processes such as normalized difference vegetation index (NDVI[11]) comparison (*see* Figure 2-4) or georeferenced orthomosaic assembly[12] (*see* Figure 2-5). The results of the data analysis can be used to determine the following:

- Health of the crop (including livestock; monitor thermal signatures for signs of elevated temperature)
- Damage caused by storms, environmental conditions, and pests (invasive insects, competing plants, and fungus)
- Early detection of major crop impacts (disease, drought, flood)
- Water usage and need
- Maturity and estimated yield
- Soil composition (moisture and nutrients) and erosion
- Recurrent environmental conditions
- Location of herd members in large enclosures or pastoral lands
- Presence, categorization, and status of important terrain features

By better understanding the state of their crops and herds, farmers can better coordinate management of farming tools and assets, implement protective measures, treat problems, and plan for harvest. Figure 2-6 depicts an example sUAS flight over farmland in support of live-

---

[11] Remote sensing imaging processing method designed to indicate level and state of live vegetation.
[12] Combining multiple orthographic photographs (images) with the origin and bounding corners of each image identified and correlated to a specific three-dimensional reference position (e.g., x, y, and z, or latitude, longitude, and altitude).

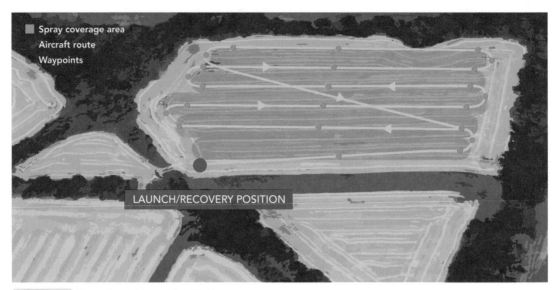

FIGURE 2-7. Example aerial spraying flight.

stock management; note the sensor coverage area (shaded orange), aircraft route (yellow line), waypoints (blue dots), and identification of specific animals in the field (orange dots).

Such an application could feature the use of optical sensors, coupled with automated object tagging (machine vision processing), or radio frequency identification (RFID) technology to determine the specific location of the animals within the environment. The data captured from a single flight could be used to locate lost animals, or if captured over a series of flights, analyzed to determine common livestock movement and grazing patterns.

■ CROP TREATMENT

There are several examples of how larger UAS platforms, such as the Yamaha RMAX, are currently being used to treat crops, including targeted application of pesticides and nutrients and frost mitigation. Once data regarding the state of the crop has been captured and used to identify problem areas (from monitoring and inspection) the necessary treatment can be applied aerially, with the UAS carrying and dispersing a subsequent treatment mixture over the affected areas of the crop. Aerial treatment can be performed over specific locations (spot treatment) or over the entire crop (blanket application) using preprogrammed flight patterns. Figure 2-7 depicts an example of such aerial application over a single field in a larger growing area; note the spray coverage area (orange), aircraft route (yellow line), and waypoints (blue dots).

While aerial crop treatment using UAS has been widely demonstrated using larger platforms 55 pounds and over, there have been a number of sUAS research and development efforts to better understand how the smaller platforms can best be applied or used to supplement conventional methods. It is important to note that due to their size (under 55 pounds) and the regulation limiting beyond visual line-of-sight (BVLOS) operations, a single sUAS may not be well suited to apply a significant quantity of treatment over an entire crop. Instead, they are most effective when coupled with aerially captured data identifying problem areas to spot targets and apply treatment (isolated crop areas) or used in combination with multiple sUAS to cover a larger area (multiple crop areas or multi-acre crops). However, this limitation may be addressed through future technology advancements, such as improved power storage and propulsion efficiency increases.

PUBLIC SAFETY AND SERVICE

Access to accurate and timely data has changed how tasks and projects are approached, from emergency response efforts to planning of infrastructure development. sUAS provide a new mechanism to obtain instrumental data as a situation unfolds, over the full duration of the event, whether in minutes or years. In support of public safety and service uses, an sUAS can be configured with a variety of payloads, including electro-optical (EO) imaging, signal emission and return measurement, or direct measurement sensors.[13] The platforms are used to perform or support the following functions:

- Observe localized environment
- Coordinate expedient responses
- Cover large expanses of territory
- Isolate and locate objects/persons of interest
- Reduce workload of response personnel
- Operate in dangerous environments
- Improve proximity and visibility
- Depict spatial relationship among object, terrain, and assets
- Inspect infrastructure
- Monitor traffic
- Incident response

By improving awareness of the interactions within the environment, public safety and service providers can better prepare contingencies or determine a more suitable course of action to take for a given scenario. The benefits include improved response, tasking or allocating specific assets to reach target areas, and improved use of resources. Use of sUAS also supports performing higher-risk operations without the potential loss of life, whether due to the nature of the environment or the required task.

▉ SEARCH AND RESCUE

UAS have been used in numerous military search and rescue operations over the last several decades. Recently, sUAS have begun to be applied in civilian environments and in support of wider tasks. Their portability, low cost, and performance (endurance, range, speed) make

---

[13] Details of various remote-sensing payload types can be found in Chapter 3 under Major Elements and Equipment.

sUAS well suited to support rapid response for time-critical actions, such as searching for lost and missing persons, disaster victims, or assets, or supporting pursuit of criminals. Figure 2-8 depicts an example search flight over a mountainous area; note the sensor coverage area (shaded yellow), aircraft route (yellow), and waypoints (blue dots).

Use of an sUAS, combined with high-definition visual optics, such as color and thermal sensors, can provide the ability to visually isolate and identify the position of a person or object in a remote and difficult-to-traverse area. While manned assets can cover wide search areas, they can be difficult to schedule and expensive to operate and maintain. Alternatively, a wide variety of sUAS can be employed, individually or in a coordinated effort, to provide a similar level of coverage with increased flexibility. These platforms, while range and endurance-limited, can be flown closer to areas of interest, along or under structures (e.g., bridges) from within the search area, and are typically less expensive, easier to operate, and flown on demand, as needed. One of the greatest challenges to their effectiveness is the regulatory limitation on BVLOS (expanded operations), which may soon be overcome through the employment and integration of innovative new detect, sense, and avoidance (DSA) technology.

▌INFRASTRUCTURE INSPECTION

Through consistent and thorough monitoring, it is possible to detect changes in critical infrastructure before they become significant problems or risks. By employing sUAS, it is possible to cover large expanses of terrain, access hard-to-reach locations, and detect leaks, cracks, and other factors leading to infrastructure failure or impacts to the surrounding environment (*see* Figure 2-9). In addition to the potential for cost savings, use of sUAS can simplify efforts and

FIGURE 2-8. Example search flight.

reduce risk by eliminating the need to erect scaffolding, scale great heights, or send humans into perilous situations. Example uses for this category include inspection of the following:

- Oil and gas pipelines
- Electrical transmission lines and substations (corona discharge and structural integrity)
- Bridges, overpasses, and roadways
- Construction sites
- Radio towers, windmills, refinery flare tips, smokestacks, and other structural inspection for hard-to-reach or high-risk inspection areas

Figure 2-10 depicts an example infrastructure inspection flight using an sUAS launched, operated, and recovered from onboard a ship to conduct detailed visual inspection of two breakwalls that support harbor protection; note the launch and recovery position (red), aircraft route (yellow), and waypoints (blue dots).

FIGURE 2-9.

Digital surface model of construction site derived from photogrammetric processing.

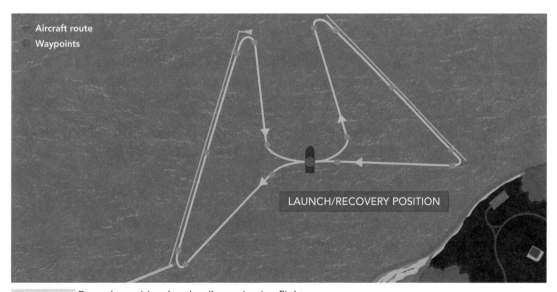

Aircraft route
Waypoints

LAUNCH/RECOVERY POSITION

FIGURE 2-10. Example maritime breakwall examination flight.

Figure 2-11 depicts an example of an sUAS being used to inspect two smokestacks, which otherwise would require human inspectors to climb the structures, resulting in an increased risk of injury or death; note the sensor coverage areas (shaded yellow), aircraft route (yellow line), and waypoints (blue dots).

▮ EMERGENCY RESPONSE

The need to capture accurate information as an emergency unfolds makes some small sUAS particularly well adapted to support emergency response efforts. By removing the pilot from the aircraft, sUAS can be used to support information-gathering operations in high-risk situations, such as monitoring contamination levels of nuclear, biological, and chemical (NBC) events; operating in closer proximity to fires; or flying into dangerous weather such as hurricanes. Responders are able to take advantage of the sUAS's unique capabilities—such as speed, range, endurance, easily manipulated aerial perspective, and rapid deployment—to capture useful information, as it is needed. With this information in hand, incident commanders and other management personnel are able to improve their decision making based on timely observation, rather than speculation or unreliable data. It is important to note that the use of sUAS should augment (enhance) the abilities of responders, without diminishing their capability or causing additional burden in their response. Otherwise, the use may result in the delay, distraction, or decreased safety of responders or overall diminished response effectiveness.

sUAS have been used in law enforcement, fire response, emergency management, security and safety, and military organizations to perform the following, in support of generating increased situational awareness:

- Gather intelligence as dynamic events unfold.
- Locate and identify critical factors that affect response efforts.
- Assess damage and manage personnel and assets in response to man-made disasters (major transportation accidents, oil spills, and acts of terrorism), as well as natural events (hurricanes, tornadoes, tsunamis, and fires).
- Monitor and support response to NBC contamination events.

Figure 2-12 depicts an example of an emergency response flight to capture information relating to the unfolding scene of a spreading fire. Note the launch and recovery position, fire spots (red), aircraft route (yellow line), waypoints (blue dots), response vehicles (orange) and potential routes (blue lines), relative to the city features.

▮ LAW ENFORCEMENT

A number of demonstrated uses of sUAS to support law enforcement operations have occurred, including the previously discussed search-and-recovery and emergency response applications. Law enforcement use is primarily focused on performing intelligence, surveillance, and reconnaissance (ISR) activities, but as the technology and regulations further develop, more uses can be expected to emerge. Such application reduces the risk to officers and agents in the field, while increasing both the volume and fidelity of information available to request warrants, investigate crime, issue warnings and citations, and engage

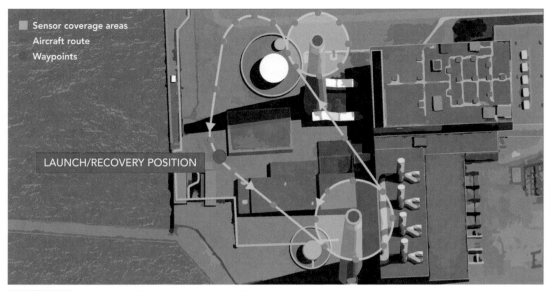

FIGURE 2-11. Example smokestack inspection flight.

FIGURE 2-12. Example emergency response support flight.

in the tracking of illegal activities and pursuit of criminals. The following represent the most common law enforcement uses of sUAS:

- Border protection
- Smuggling and poaching monitoring and prevention
- Security
- Stand-off situation support
- Traffic monitoring
- Emergency response

▌ MAPPING AND SURVEYING

The ability to overfly specific areas and terrain features, coupled with data capture combining high-resolution sensors and GPS coordinates, provides an effective method to capture accurate geographic, spatial information and observations quickly and at low cost. Using sUAS, it is possible for researchers, engineers, planners, and policymakers to obtain an aerial perspective of land to be developed, add increased fidelity and accuracy to three-dimensional maps and models, and examine the impact of specific man-made structures or naturally occurring features on the environment. Use of the data captured from these flights supports improved planning for future construction, infrastructure evaluation, and decreased aerial survey expense and risks. Typical mapping and surveying uses of sUAS include the following:

- Resource exploration
- Geographic information system (GIS) data capture (see Figure 2-13)
- Archeology
- Land development and construction monitoring
- Safety assessment
- Traffic and congestion analysis
- Research

FIGURE 2-13.
Geo-referenced point cloud from aerial data captured using sUAS.

COMMUNICATIONS

Unmanned aircraft can be used as a bridge to connect and network devices, such as radios, cellular phones, computers, and other UAS, in an environment lacking communication infrastructure or impacted by adverse events (e.g., cellular towers disabled by storms). Lightweight and portable sUAS, featuring long endurance, are well-suited to provide on-demand connectivity, including beyond line-of-sight transmission and receipt, for a variety of conditions and environments. By taking advantage of their elevated operating positions, these systems can be used to establish and maintain a large coverage envelope to support continued connectivity of local populations and assets. The communication relay functionality of sUAS is especially useful to augment emergency relief and support efforts or to provide internet access to regions that cannot support local communication infrastructure, such as transmission lines or towers.

Communication coverage envelope
Aircraft route
Waypoints

LAUNCH/
RECOVERY
POSITION

FIGURE 2-14. Example communications relay flight.

Figure 2-14 depicts an example of an sUAS flying an orbit pattern over an area after a power blackout and loss of critical infrastructure; note the communication coverage envelope (shaded yellow), aircraft route (yellow line), and waypoints (blue dots).

AERIAL FILMING

The use of sUAS as aerial camera platforms is significantly increasing, with a high degree of investment and interest from news gathering, television, filmmaking, marketing, and insurance organizations. They provide a cost-effective alternative to manned aircraft, which must be flown into the operational area and coordinated with the team on the ground. The use of sUAS lowers risk, increases flexibility in reshooting, supports closer and more customizable shots, and provides the ability to capture imagery quickly. Additionally, the programmability of many sUAS platforms supports pre-planned filming operations, which are highly dependent on light levels, smooth transitions, and perspective to create desired cinematic effects. `

The limiting factors of using sUAS for aerial filming include the requirement for the pilot-in-command (PIC) to be a certified airman; airspace restrictions; low endurance and payload capacity of stable platforms (e.g., multirotors); and unique features within the operational environment (e.g., guidewires, transmission lines, and buildings). With the availability of an sUAS remote pilot certificate (Part 107), one of the most significant barriers to entry has been reduced; however, the airspace limitations will still require coordination with local air traffic control (ATC). Technological developments may lead to lighter-weight cameras and sensors,

FIGURE 2-15. Example real estate flight.

while improvements to system efficiency and power storage may result in more capable plat-forms with longer endurance, range, and payload lifting ability. A detailed visual inspection of the operation area should be conducted to ensure possible issues and obstructions are noted and addressed. Figure 2-15 depicts an sUAS deployment and flight path over a suburban neighborhood to perform aerial filming in support of real estate; note the aircraft route (yellow line) and waypoints (blue dots), relative to the houses.

CARGO TRANSPORT

UAS, including sUAS, have demonstrated suitability to carry cargo, such as emergency supplies, over substantial distances, in dangerous environments, and over otherwise impassable terrain. They have been used to deliver materials to medical stations, emergency aid to soldiers in the field, and consumer goods in early prototype efforts. Despite their diminished size, sUAS with a maximum takeoff weight (MTOW) between 20 to 55 pounds (Group 2) can effectively carry an average of 12 pounds of cargo more than 200 miles, while those under 20 pounds (Group 1) can carry 2.5 pounds more than 33 miles.[14] This performance is heavily impacted by the type of aerial platform and propulsion source used, with fixed-wing and internal combus-tion providing the optimal effectiveness and efficiency; vertical takeoff and landing (VTOL) enabling improved site accessibility (smaller takeoff/landing footprint); and electric propulsion providing decreased complexity (rapid startup, deployment, recovery, and resupply/refueling).

---

[14] Presented average sUAS cargo transport capabilities are the result of UAS performance analysis research conducted by Terwilliger, Vincenzi, and Ison. References to the published results of this research are available in Chapter 6. At the time this text was written, 500 total Group 1–3 UAS were sampled to calculate average values, of which 379 were sUAS (175 fixed-wing sUAS, 204 VTOL sUAS, 110 group 1 fixed-wing, 147 group 1 VTOL, 65 group 2 fixed-wing, and 57 group 2 VTOL).

Transportation of goods and materials represents one of the more novel sUAS applications that has generated significant interest from large logistics firms, such as Amazon, DHL, Alibaba, and the U.S. Postal Service. Their efforts have been affected by several of the more pressing challenges, including regulatory, weather, safety, and performance limits. The current U.S. regulatory requirements to maintain VLOS between the remote pilot and the aircraft, as well as the prohibition of performing intrastate operations, without a waiver or exemption, presents a major barrier to effective use of sUAS for cargo transport. However, research being conducted by UAS stakeholders may assist in identifying potential procedures and technology to overcome and address risk in future operations. If such research and development efforts are successful, routine BVLOS, including transportation of cargo, may eventually become permissible using FAA-approved technology and operational methods. Weather and performance limits, such as wind and precipitation levels, payload capacity, and endurance, are specific to the platform and vary significantly among options. These items can be confirmed from the manufacturer and are expected to improve as technology advances.

ENVIRONMENTAL MONITORING

Environmental monitoring represents a broad application category, ranging from law enforcement use to aerial research. sUAS provide an unobtrusive (non-distracting or detectable) method to aerially surveil an environment using a variety of sensing mechanisms. The data collected through such flights can be used to monitor pollution, environmental impact, wildlife migration and behavior, poaching, weather, and vegetation, as well as map terrain features and perform natural resource exploration. In turn, the long-term results of monitoring can be used to support the development and execution of appropriate management strategies and policies, as well as criminal investigations. High-altitude long-endurance (HALE) platforms can provide broad data capture over a significant period of time, while smaller close-range platforms can be used to inspect and monitor specific objects or events. Use of low to no emission propulsion, such as electric motors, improve the accuracy of environmental atmospheric sampling and measurement, while use of internal combustion provides improved operational speed, endurance, and range to cover large areas.

TRAINING AND EDUCATION

Unmanned aircraft, including model aircraft, have long been used to introduce and exhibit academic concepts, such as aerodynamics, physics, chemistry, system design and engineering, mathematics, and other science and technology-related topics to students. The structured operation of these systems also helps to promote critical thinking, creative problem solving, teamwork, and career development. This use of this technology is also featured within higher education activities and curricula to support research, design, application, analysis, and specialized operational training to prepare students for career pursuit, development, and advancement. These academic programs include individual courses; certificates; associate, bachelor, master, and PhD degrees; and minor courses of study and graduate specializations within other degree programs. Academic degree topics include applied robotics, engineering and design, unmanned system science and application, computer science, aeronautical science (aviation), and human factors. Additionally, sUAS have been increasingly featured in specialized training programs designed to introduce students to the background, design composition, theory of operation, applications, and operation. Such specialized training may be focused on unique aspects, such as rules and regulations, or the operational requirements and capabilities of a specific platform or system.

Figure 2-16 depicts an example sUAS training flight over a model aircraft airfield; note the launch and recovery position (red), aircraft route (yellow line), and waypoints (blue dots).

RESEARCH

One of the most significant historical uses of UAS has been in support of increasing knowledge and capability, through experimentation and data capture. As research platforms, scaled-down aircraft can be used to determine the effectiveness of a design, while affixing specialized data collection mechanisms, such as sensors, can support the capture of specific data from various environments. They can be used to obtain direct measurements (sampling) from the atmosphere, use onboard telemetry to test suitability of components or designs for specific operational profiles or strategies, or discretely monitor wildlife without directly influencing their actions. Examples of uses include systems and aeronautical engineering design and evaluation, archeology, weather monitoring, environmental study, and wildlife monitoring.

Aircraft route
Waypoints

LAUNCH/RECOVERY POSITION

FIGURE 2-16. Example training flight.

FIGURE 2-17. Example archeological evidence-gathering flight.

Figure 2-17 depicts an example flight over an archeological site; note the sensor coverage areas (shaded yellow), aircraft route (yellow line), and waypoints (blue dots). Use of sUAS in this capacity can provide researchers with the ability to capture data without disturbing the ground or existing structures at the location.

EMERGING USES AND CHALLENGES

With the invention and refinement of technology comes the opportunity to develop new ways to use or adapt it to meet ever-changing needs. Examples include the development of private, wide-scale communications services; further supporting disaster recovery/relief efforts; investigating insurance claims; delivery of cargo/goods; advertising (e.g., banner towing); cloud seeding (production of rain/snow or hail mitigation); further research; and evaluation of safety to the certification level. Despite the numerous potential uses of this technology, a number of challenges must be addressed to ensure safety, effectiveness, and efficiency can be maintained. For example, the constantly changing legislation at the federal, state, and local levels affect how this technology can be used. In many cases, the underlying technology advances faster than the regulation and subsequent approval, which must be obtained prior to operation. This results from the need to ensure safety in the National Airspace System (NAS), which requires reduced risk compared to conventional application methods and sufficient separation from manned aircraft, bystanders, non-participants, and objects. The potential effectiveness must be demonstrated and well understood to confirm that the system performs better than conventional methods. Additionally, cost-efficiency must be realizable, meaning the use of sUAS should be affordable compared to conventional methods. Understanding the abilities and limitations of platforms (e.g., range, speed, endurance, and payload capacity) will help users to meet such requirements going forward.

ON THE HORIZON

A number of advances in technology may have significant impact on how sUAS are used in the future. Reduced latency communications delivery and processing (e.g., research into development of quantum communications, computing, and plasmonics) may help to ensure information is conveyed in a more effective and timely manner, when it is needed most. Power storage and distribution advances (solar/hybrid fuel cells, quantum energy transport, efficiency, energy density, electrical storage medium, and solid state electrolyte) coupled with new aerodynamic designs and materials may lead to UAS being utilized as ultra-long endurance platforms to support satellite replacement, and the development of airborne UAS carriers (e.g., DARPA Distributed Airborne Capabilities[15]). Additionally, the latest scientific research, sensor processing and categorizing algorithm improvements, microminiaturization, 3D printing of electronics, wearable technology, and regulatory proposals (such as those being proposed by technology companies Google and Amazon) to segregated airspace, hold the potential to radically transform how this technology can be applied. By continuing to explore the design and development of novel new technologies, strategies for implementation of sUAS, and how to meet specific needs within the field—such as DSA and integration; command, control, and communication (C3); autonomy; sensing and processing; and power, propulsion, and maneuvering—users will be better prepared to meet future challenges and identify potential solutions.

---

[15] DARPA-SN-15-06 Request for Information (RFI) on Distributed Airborne Capabilities: https://www.fbo.gov /index?s=opportunity&mode=form&id=a73e0ea615c675383c1529c5ad631249&tab=core&_cview=0

CHAPTER 3

VARIETY OF DESIGN: EXPLORING THE TECHNOLOGICAL POSSIBILITIES

INTRODUCTION

Understanding all of the elements of a small unmanned aircraft system (sUAS)—such as options available, why one is better suited to meet operational requirements, or how they may compliment or interfere with one another—represents a critical piece to determining what system can best support your intended use. By examining this information and increasing your knowledge about the unique advantages and limitations of different configurations, you will be better prepared to compare, select, and appropriately use sUAS. This chapter contains details and examples of various sUAS design configurations, architecture, and primary elements, as well as considerations and limitations for selection and use.

PLATFORM DESIGN CONFIGURATIONS

There is significant variation in types of sUAS platform design configurations, each with their own unique benefits, requirements, and limitations to be considered. The following subsections contain an overview of typical platforms, as well as descriptions of their unique attributes. Many critical aeronautical concepts are introduced, but not explored in detail, to provide an overview of these important items. You are encouraged to investigate and explore the concepts in-depth on your own, using resources identified throughout in footnotes, as well as in Chapter 6. Critical terms and concepts are identified and briefly described below to provide a contextual baseline.

IMPORTANT TERMS AND CONCEPTS

The following represent important terms and concepts used throughout this section.[1] This information is presented here to assist in understanding the concepts in the proper context, prior to review of the detailed descriptions of sUAS design and configuration elements (refer to this list as necessary):

- **Above ground level (AGL)**—the local vertical distance above the ground, regardless of the relationship to actual altitude as measured above mean sea level (MSL); typically important in determining relational position to terrain and ground-based objects/buildings.

- **Beyond visual line-of-sight (BVLOS)**—operational method in which the UAS is operated outside of the visual perception range of the remote pilot; in some cases this type of operation is supported through use of a chase plane or technology.

- **Center of gravity (CG)**—geometric property representing average location of weight; many attributes and characteristics are significantly affected by the location of CG in the aircraft design.

- **Commercial off-the-shelf (COTS)**—products ready-made and available for public purchase; typically hardware or software not requiring significant customization for end-use.

- **Directional stability**—property of an aircraft to maintain or resist rotational yaw displacement (about z-axis) or return to its original orientation, if displaced.

- **Drag**—a force opposing motion through the air and thrust.

- **Endurance**—the amount of time an aircraft can remain airborne, in powered flight (subject to efficiency of propulsion system, aerodynamic efficiency, lift generation, flight profile, amount of fuel, and environmental conditions).

- **Extended visual line-of-sight (EVLOS)**—operational method in which the UAS is operated on the edge of the visual perception range of the remote pilot (between BVLOS and within visual range); in some cases this type of operation is supported through use of a chase plane or technology.

- **First-person view (FPV)**—an egocentric perspective, replicating the view from within the aircraft.

- **Horizontal takeoff and landing (HTOL)**—platform requiring conventional launch and recovery with wings/fuselage parallel to the ground.

---

[1] Many of these concepts are also presented in further detail in Chapter 4.

- **Induced drag**—drag created as a wing moves through the air and generates lift; result of vortices generated at wing tips.
- **Interference drag**—drag created when airflow from multiple regions converge (e.g., where wing meets fuselage); results in creation of turbulence and increased form drag.
- **Knot (kt)**—standard measurement of aeronautical airspeed; 1 knot equates to flying one nautical mile in an hour; approximately 1.151 statute miles per hour (mph).
- **Lateral stability**—property of an aircraft to maintain or resist rotational roll displacement (about x-axis) or return to its original orientation, if displaced.
- **Lift**—upward force generated by movement of air around a wing.
- **Longitudinal stability**—property of an aircraft to maintain or resist rotational pitch displacement (about y-axis) or return to its original orientation, if displaced.
- **Mean sea level (MSL)**—"true altitude" above sea level; common reference frame for altitude measurement and indication.
- **Propeller (prop) wash**—a spiraling column of disturbed air generated by a propulsion source; thrusted air, propulsed by a propeller.
- **Range**—the cumulative distance a UAS can fly upon launch, based on endurance and speed (directly related to available fuel; not indicative of linear range from source, such as communication range, unless directly stated).
- **Short takeoff and landing (STOL)**—platform capable of performing launch and recovery within reduced distance with wings/fuselage remaining parallel to the ground.
- **Thrust**—force generated by the propulsion system of an aircraft that moves air in a specific direction; direction and magnitude can be varied.
- **Vertical takeoff and landing (VTOL)**—platform capable of achieving translational flight for launch/recovery.
- **Visual line-of-sight (VLOS)**[2]—operational method in which the UAS is kept within visual perception of a remote pilot/visual observer.

---

[2] Visual line-of-sight and beyond visual line-of-sight, as used in this context, differs from the subsequent linear pathway of radio waves as they perpetuate away from the source. These terms are differentiated throughout the text as LOS/BLOS and VLOS/BVLOS.

As with manned aircraft, the purpose of an sUAS is to achieve controllable and sustained flight in support of a specific application (task/purpose). However, unlike manned aircraft, design configurations of sUAS are not limited by the requirement to include elements to support a pilot aboard the aircraft. Accordingly, the size, weight, and complexity can be significantly reduced, which affords designers an opportunity to radically change the loadout and operational profiles of these platforms. There are three sUAS platform types commonly available as COTS: fixed-wing, VTOL, and miscellaneous. These are each discussed in detail in the following subsections.

■ FIXED-WING

Fixed-wing sUAS feature the use of a stationary wing[3] to generate lift as the aircraft gains forward speed, resulting in achievement of flight. Attainment (and sustainment) of forward flight is the common characteristic of fixed-wing platforms, whether achieved through use of a propulsion source (e.g., engine) for powered flight or through external environmental conditions, such as wind and gravity for gliding. Additionally, it should be noted that fixed-wing platforms use horizontal or short takeoff and landing (HTOL or STOL) for launch and recovery operations.

Benefits and advantages of fixed-wing sUAS:
- Higher operational efficiency and effectiveness
  — Longer endurance
  — Longer range
- Higher maximum and cruise speeds[4]
- Capable of higher operational altitude[5]

Limitations of fixed-wing sUAS:
- Require greater support for launch and recovery (equipment, crew, larger takeoff/landing area); some limitations can be mitigated using dedicated launch and recovery mechanisms
- Forward flight only (no translational or hovering); may require placing the aircraft into an orbit to consistently monitor an area or object

There are several key characteristics of fixed-wing design configurations that affect performance and handling, including placement and type of propulsion, wing(s), control surfaces, and landing gear.

---

[3] Stationary in a relative sense, as the wing can still be articulated or actuated in a manner to change pitch, sweep, or shape, as needed to introduce a desired benefit; characteristics do not constantly change as a means to produce lift as with a rotary-wing, in which circulator rotation of the lifting surface (i.e., rotor) creates thrust and lift.

[4] Speed capability over 87 kts (100 mph) is irrelevant under FAA provisions, unless such operation is directly approved by the FAA.

[5] Maximum altitude capability is irrelevant under FAA provisions, unless such operation is directly approved. sUAS operators must stay under maximum altitude permitted under regulation or exemption (e.g., 400 feet AGL or above the top of a structure, operational ceiling).

❱ Propulsion Configurations

The propulsion source is the mechanism used on an sUAS to generate thrust. It features the rotation of a propeller or shrouded impeller (turbine, jet, ducted fan) to manipulate and accelerate surrounding air into a circular air column (i.e., **prop wash**) used to propel the aircraft forward. In some cases, the prop wash can be used to provide moving air to control surfaces for enhanced control response in low-speed operations. There are three primary propulsion configurations used in fixed-wing sUAS: tractor, pusher, and push-pull.

Tractor—This is the most common and easily identified propulsion configuration, in which a propeller is situated at the front of the aircraft in the nose or wing and attached to the fore-end of a motor/engine (*see* Figure 3-1). In this configuration, the spinning propeller generates thrust and "pulls" the aircraft forward. Tractor configurations tend to produce less noise or vibration, while creating more thrust and improved directional stability than a pusher-driven propeller configuration. Thrust generated by this configuration is pushed (back) over the engine (providing improved cooling) as well as the control surfaces and wing, resulting in increased performance. This results in improved lift and maneuverability at low speeds, which also supports low-speed and STOL operations. Additionally, placement of the propeller at the front of the aircraft reduces the potential for **blade strike** with the ground during takeoff and landing (further supporting STOL operations). However, since the propulsion source is situated at the front of the aircraft, and the CG is further forward, this configuration can result in reduced longitudinal controllability compared to a pusher in which the CG is further aft.

Advantages of tractor propulsion configuration:
- Quieter operation (less audible)
- Improved maneuverability (for low-speed and STOL operations)
- Reduced blade strike potential (further supporting STOL operations)
- When used with forward FPV camera, provides a visual indication of propulsion system performance (e.g., free spinning, stopped/locked, or powered)

Disadvantages of tractor propulsion configuration:
- Spinning propeller can partially obstruct view
- Reduced longitudinal maneuverability (pitch)

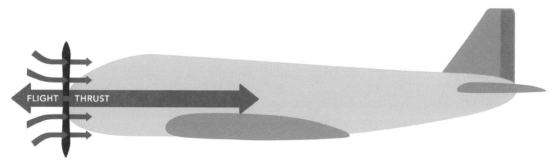

FIGURE 3-1. Fixed-wing sUAS tractor propulsion configuration.

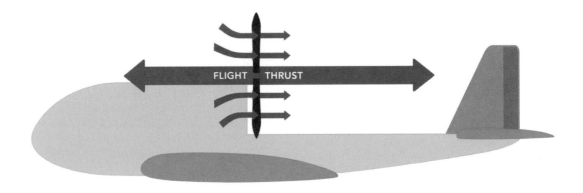

FIGURE 3-2. Fixed-wing sUAS pusher propulsion configuration.

Pusher—This configuration was used in many early aircraft designs, including the Wright Flyer. In a pusher configuration, the thrust-generating mechanism, such as the propeller, is situated behind the engine/motor and "pushes" the aircraft forward (*see* Figure 3-2). Pusher configurations typically offer improved longitudinal control, forward visibility, and space to mount payloads in the aircraft nose, as well as reduced fuselage length, elevator deflection during takeoff, and drag. However, the thrust efficiency and directional stability/maneuverability is lower due to fuselage/wing wake and the need for forward movement to generate airflow over control surfaces and wing (from prop wash).

Advantages of pusher propulsion configuration:

- Supports front mounting of payload (unobstructed view and CG balancing)
- Improved longitudinal control

Disadvantages of pusher propulsion configuration:

- Subject to higher potential for blade strike (when prop is positioned at rear of aircraft)
- Louder (audible noise)
- Difficult to cool engine (reduced airflow over engine)
- Less maneuverability at lower speeds

Push-Pull—This configuration combines the tractor and pusher into a single configuration to mitigate several issues and improve redundancy, should an engine fail. In a push-pull configuration, each engine is typically mounted along the aircraft's center line (tractor fore and pusher aft), which requires significant structural design consideration. While this configuration provides improved maneuverability and stability, it remains subject to several of the design limitations and issues of the other two configurations, such as louder (audible) noise, view obstruction, increased blade strike potential, and reduced efficiency. Additionally, due to increased complexity and use of two powerplants, it limits available space and requires additional structural support.

Advantages of push-pull propulsion configuration:
- Improved maneuverability at lower speeds (compared to pusher)
- Offers redundancy for loss of an engine

Disadvantages of push-pull propulsion configuration:
- Remains subject to some limitations and constraints of either configuration
- More complex structural support

❱ Wing Configurations

A wing (or wings) represents the primary structure(s) of a fixed-wing sUAS used to generate lift, which is necessary to achieve and maintain flight. Lift is created as the wing moves through the air; the shape and orientation deflects passing airflow downward to create a pressure difference, with lower pressure occurring over the wing and higher pressure below. This results in a greater upward-generated force that lifts the wing and attached structures. The amount of lift generated by the wing is affected by its placement, shape, and size, relative to the fuselage and incoming airflow, including propulsed airflow (prop wash). Three primary wing configurations are used in fixed-wing sUAS: high, low, and mid-wing placement.

High-Wing—A high-wing configuration is the most balanced of the three configurations commonly used in fixed-wing sUAS designs due to its stability. The high-wing configuration represents the majority of COTS sUAS options. In this configuration, the wing is mounted over the fuselage (*see* Figure 3-3) and may be supported with bracing (struts) beneath to lighten the structural weight and free up space within the fuselage for other equipment. It places the CG lower in the aircraft, providing increased gliding capability and dihedral effect, improving the lateral stability (roll) of the aircraft. With more surface area exposed and available to generate lift, a high-wing provides improved lift and a lower stall speed, which supports low-speed operations. However, use of this configuration results in reduced ground effect (less lift at takeoff/landing), requires increased structure for the mounting of wing and landing gear, produces greater drag, needs a larger tail surface, and produces less lateral control response, resulting in a higher weight and reduced maneuverability.

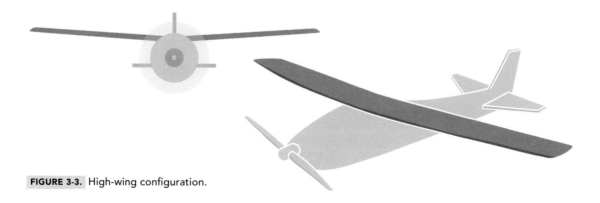

FIGURE 3-3. High-wing configuration.

Advantages of high-wing configuration:

- Better gliding capability
- Better lateral stability
- Better visibility below the aircraft
- More fuselage space to mount payload/avionics

Disadvantages of high-wing configuration:

- Less lift produced during takeoff/landing (less ground effect)
- Increased structure and weight (wing and landing gear)
- Higher induced drag
- Requires larger tail
- Less lateral maneuverability

Low-Wing—A low-wing configuration features a wing attached beneath the fuselage (*see* Figure 3-4) and is typically featured in higher-performance and more maneuverable platforms. The low placement supports a reduced structure for attachment of landing gear, improved ground effect, reduced drag, better longitudinal stability, and increased lateral maneuverability. However, the amount of lift and dihedral effect produced by a low-wing configuration is typically less than a high-wing, resulting in a higher stall speed, reduced lateral stability, and the need for a longer takeoff/landing area.

Advantages of low-wing configuration:

- Better longitudinal stability
- Better visibility above the aircraft
- Strong structural support for attachment of shorter, lighter-weight landing gear
- Increased ground effect
- Lighter aircraft
- Less drag
- Better maneuverability

Disadvantages of low-wing configuration:

- Less fuselage space to mount payload/avionics
- Reduced visibility below the aircraft

Mid-Wing—A mid-wing configuration features a wing attached to the sides of the fuselage (*see* Figure 3-5). The midpoint placement supports a more aerodynamically streamlined design with the lowest drag, including interference drag. However, this configuration is heavier and more complex, requiring reinforcement of the structure at the attachment joints.

Advantages of mid-wing configuration:

- More streamlined (less interference drag)
- Lowest drag

Disadvantages of mid-wing configuration:

- Less fuselage space to mount payload/avionics
- Heavier and more complex (reinforcement of structure required)

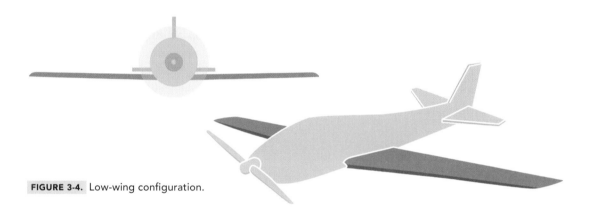

FIGURE 3-4. Low-wing configuration.

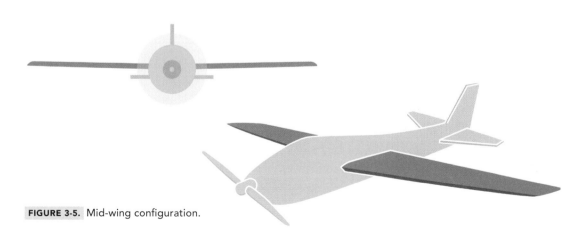

FIGURE 3-5. Mid-wing configuration.

Further Wing-Related Options—Several additional characteristics and attributes of wing designs also can impact the maneuverability and performance of a platform. The following represent common wing types, their characteristics, and their potential effects (*see* Figure 3-6):

- Shape
  - *Rectangular wings*—general purpose design ("jack of all trades, master of none")
  - *Elliptical wings*—generates improved lift at low speed
  - *Tapered wings*—generates greater efficiency than rectangular; simpler to manufacturer than elliptical
  - *Swept wings*—reduces drag at high speed, increases drag at lower speeds; drag reduction requires high speed, but can also provide enhanced longitudinal stability
  - *Delta wings*—reduces drag at extreme high speeds, increases drag at lower speeds; provides a larger structural area to better distribute loads and mount critical components
- Dihedral
  - Greater dihedral increases inherent stability and ground clearance of wing tips, but decreases lift and lateral responsiveness, while increasing drag.
  - Negative dihedral is referred to as **anhedral**.

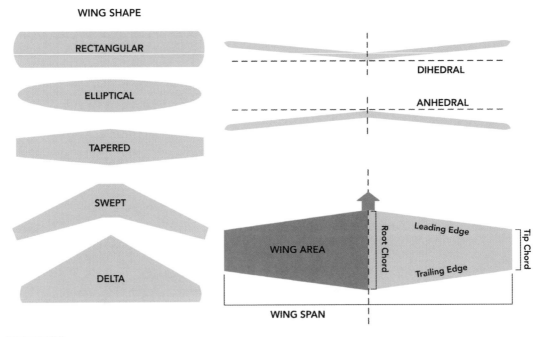

FIGURE 3-6. Example wing types and properties.

- Sweep
  — Increases weight
  — Subject to **pitchup**, an adverse effect

❭ Flight Control Surface Configurations

Flight control surfaces are used to deflect and disrupt the airflow by affecting the speed and direction of moving air over the aircraft to change the orientation (pitch, roll, and yaw) and flight performance characteristics (airspeed and stall speed). They are typically controlled in sUAS using electro-mechanical actuators, such as servos, through mechanical linkages (push-rods and rotational couplers) connected to the control surfaces. The effectiveness of controls to produce the desired orientation change is referred to as control response (directional, lateral, and longitudinal). There are several types of flight control surface configurations commonly used in fixed-wing sUAS: tail surfaces, ailerons, and secondary flight controls.

Tail Surfaces—These controls are used to change the pitch and yaw of an aircraft. sUAS designs feature several types of tail surfaces, including conventional, T-tail, V-tail, twin-boom, and tail-less (*see* Figure 3-7).

- *Conventional*—A typical fixed-wing aircraft incorporates a vertical stabilizer (with a rudder) and a horizontal stabilizer (and elevator). The rudder, which is connected to the vertical stabilizer via a hinge, provides directional stability and directional changes to yaw the aircraft by created sideways lift. The elevator, which is connected to the vertical stabilizer via a hinge, provides longitudinal stability and is used to make longitudinal changes to pitch by creating an upward or downward force at the rear of the aircraft.

- *T-Tail*—This tail configuration is similar to conventional, except that the horizontal stabilizer and elevator are moved to the top of the tail, which removes them from the propulsion downwash and disturbed air from fuselage/wing, providing consistent longitudinal control response. At low speeds, the elevator must be deflected further because the available airflow is reduced, offering little to no prop wash to manipulate.

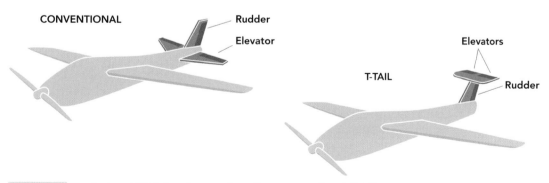

FIGURE 3-7. Fixed-wing sUAS tail surface configurations: conventional, T-tail.

- *V-tail*—This configuration mixes the functionality of the elevator and rudder into two equally sized and canted stabilizer structures using **ruddervators**. This design is lighter and produces less drag, but is more mechanically complex than other tail surface configurations.
- *Twin-boom*—This configuration is used significantly in conjunction with pusher propulsion systems and features the incorporation of two longitudinal structures that run parallel to the fuselage. The tail surfaces typically feature a vertical stabilizer and rudder mounted at the end of each boom, with a horizontal stabilizer and elevator, or V-tail or inverted V-tail, between. In some cases, the booms offer additional structure to mount propulsion systems and/or install equipment and fuel storage, while also enhancing the structural integrity of the aircraft.
- *Tailless*—Not all sUAS platforms feature use of tail controls; some remove or move one or more of the stabilizer/control components completely. The tailless configuration, which includes delta or flying wings, relies on use of alternative flight control surfaces, such as canards (fore-mounted on delta-wing designs) or those incorporated into the wing (**elevons, split ailerons, spoilers, or spoilerons**). It provides optimal aerodynamic efficiency to reduce parasitic drag, but can also suffer from directional instability and control issues that require augmented digital control to correct.

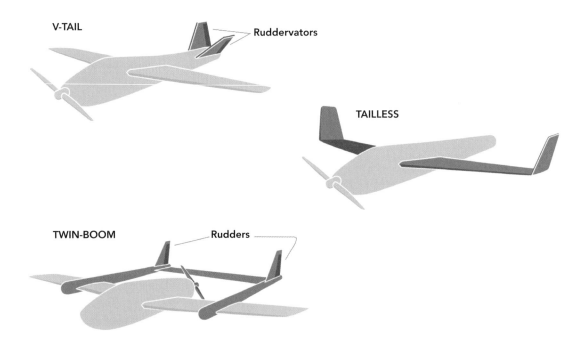

FIGURE 3-7. *(continued)* Fixed-wing sUAS tail surface configurations: V-tail, tailless, twin-boom.

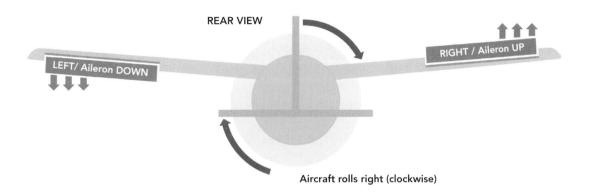

FIGURE 3-8. Effect of aileron movement on roll rotation of fixed-wing aircraft (as viewed from rear).

Ailerons—These control surfaces are used to manipulate the roll of an aircraft. Ailerons are attached to the rear edge of a wing (or wings) and are not typically used in smaller, simpler platforms due to the increased complexity and weight. When the right aileron is deflected up, the left deflects down, which decreases lift on the right side and increases lift on the left. Such control manipulation results in the aircraft rolling to the right (clockwise rotation) when viewed from the rear (*see* Figure 3-8).

Secondary—These flight controls are used to change flight performance characteristics of an aircraft. They typically are only used in more complex and larger sUAS platforms.

- *Flaps* are used to change the shape of the wing to increase both lift and drag to decrease the stall speed and slow the aircraft down, which supports STOL, low-speed operations, and landing. Flaps are attached to the rear (trailing) edge of a wing (or wings).

- *Spoilers* are similar to flaps, but are usually used on the upper wing surface to force flow separation and reduce lift production. Spoilers are used to control speed as well as the lift-to-drag (i.e., glide) ratio in platforms that feature attributes and characteristics of (powered) gliders.

- *Trim* is used to make small changes to flight controls to maintain the orientation and flight performance of an aircraft. They change the relative position of the control to the commanded center position mapped to the operator controls. Use of trim allows a remote pilot to take their hands off the controls and maintain straight-and-level flight (even with winds and other forces present; re-trimming is required when such forces dissipate). This capability supports reducing the task loading of a pilot by providing a mechanism to maintain a desired orientation, despite the presence of external environmental factors.

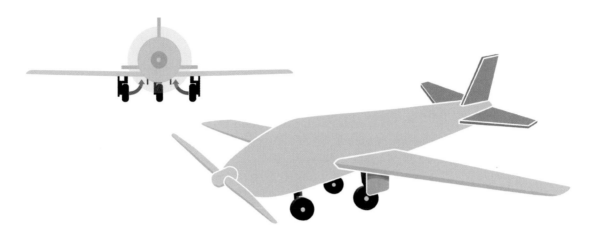

FIGURE 3-9. Retracting tricycle landing gear.

▶ Landing Gear Configurations

Landing gear are used to protect the primary aircraft structures and installed equipment, such as sensitive avionics and payload, from impact and to reduce friction between the takeoff/ landing surface and the aircraft during launch and/or recovery operations. Some sUAS platforms do not require any landing structure, while others feature the incorporation of wheels, floats, skids, or skis.

None—For purposes of simplicity and weight savings, some sUAS do not feature use of landing gear. These platforms typically belly land (on a reinforced bottom), use aerial retrieval or netting, deploy a parachute or cushion, reverse thrust prior to impact, or perform a deep stall and intentionally break apart at predetermined joints to dissipate impact energy.

Wheeled Gear—This provides support for taxiing from point to point, as well as rolling takeoffs and landings to achieve higher speed while absorbing shocks from uneven terrain or impacts.

- *Tricycle*—This configuration features a steerable nose wheel and set of rear gear that distribute the weight of the aircraft across a larger area and keep the aircraft in level orientation while on the ground (*see* Figure 3-9). The use of tricycle gear supports higher-speed landings by preventing nose over and ground-loop (uncontrolled yaw), while improving forward visibility as the aircraft remains level until climb. However, use of tricycle gear also increases aircraft weight and mechanical complexity, while reducing the clearance of nose-mounted propellers.

- *Taildragger (conventional gear)*—This configuration features a set of larger, forward landing gear, which are placed ahead of the CG, and a single, smaller, steerable gear attached to the tail (*see* Figure 3-10). The tail-wheel is linked to the rudder control to provide coordinated directional (yaw) control during taxi

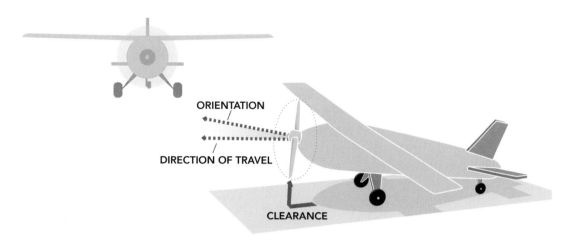

FIGURE 3-10. Taildragger landing gear, showing prop clearance and horizontal orientation.

and takeoff/landing. The use of conventional gear results in the nose of the aircraft facing further upwards (pitched up) during startup/shutdown and taxi, improving ground clearance for the propeller. This configuration reduces the weight of the aircraft, but also decreases visibility of forward-facing FPV cameras, unless attached to a movable gimbal. During takeoff and landing, once sufficient airspeed has been achieved, the nose is pitched down to improve visibility and performance; the nose is pitched upward again near the end of the takeoff process to achieve the desired attitude and generate sufficient lift.

- *Fixed*—This configuration is permanently affixed to the aircraft, exposing the wheels and the supporting struts to airflow. It results in simpler mechanical complexity, decreased weight, and reduced electrical power consumption (static position means no actuator to power), but also lowers the aerodynamic efficiency (higher drag). The fixed gear configuration can be used with both tricycle and taildragger (conventional) landing gear.

- *Retracting (retracts)*—This configuration features electro-mechanical actuation to lift or rotate the wheels and struts inside the landing gear attachment structure, such as wheel wells inside the fuselage or wing (*see* Figure 3-9), to reduce drag from airflow. The use of retracting gear increases the aerodynamic efficiency by decreasing the drag (when retracted), but also increases the mechanical complexity, power consumption, and weight. Additionally, if power loss occurs while the landing gear is retracted, the aircraft will be forced to belly-land, possibly resulting in significant damage to the aircraft and payload.[6] Retracts can be used with both tricycle and taildragger (conventional) landing gear.

---

[6] For this reason, it is highly suggested that a secondary, independent battery be used for retracts, which will also protect the primary power available to the propulsion and flight controls should a retract become stuck and subsequently drain critical power from the entire system.

Floats—This configuration is used to elevate an aircraft above water, while providing a stable, aquatic lift-generating and directional control mechanism (*see* Figure 3-11). Floats are typically interchanged with wheeled landing gear, specifically to support operation on the water. In some cases, floats can be equipped with retractable wheeled gear, making them amphibious. Use of floats provides maritime operational capability, but significantly decreases aerodynamic efficiency and maneuverability in the air.

Skid—This configuration provides a lightweight, unobtrusive, reinforced landing structure to protect the aircraft from ground impact during landing (*see* Figure 3-12). Use of a skid increases aerodynamic performance compared to platforms with fixed landing gear, and reduces weight, but such platforms cannot take off without a launching mechanism or maneuver once on the ground.

Skis—This configuration consists of a device that can be fitted over or in place of wheels to provide a larger surface for weight distribution on ice and snow (*see* Figure 3-13). Use of skis improves maneuverability while on the ground, but decreases aerodynamic efficiency and maneuverability in the air.

▶ Further Fixed-Wing Platform Variations

Additional variations in type and function of fixed-wing sUAS platforms exist that do not fully conform to the descriptions or categorizations described in the previous sections. While these types of configurations are not as common, COTS examples of each exist. These variations include amphibious, powered gliders, powered parachutes, and tube-launched platforms.

Amphibious (Seaplane)—These platforms are capable of launch and recovery on land or water, providing increased support for operations in maritime environments. This configuration is most commonly represented by flying boats, a platform featuring a single hull that floats on the water and a set of small **pontoons** or **sponsons**. Due to the corrosive and damaging nature of water (especially salt water) on sensitive aircraft components, significant protections must be implemented during the design and construction of amphibious sUAS, which increases both the complexity for maintenance and repair as well as the weight of the platform. Additionally, while the aerodynamic efficiency of an amphibious sUAS platform is typically lower than a conventional fixed-wing, it is usually higher than many rotary-wing VTOL platforms.

Powered (Motor) Glider—Many features of powered gliders have been incorporated into long-endurance sUAS platforms—including folding propellers; an aerodynamic fuselage; slender, high-efficiency wings; and a gliding flight profile—which can result in reduced power or even no power required in the presence of thermals or wind. These platforms provide high aerodynamic efficiency, such as low drag and long endurance, but they also offer reduced speed and less area available for installation of equipment, such as payload or avionics.

Powered Parachute (Paraglider)—These platforms, while rare, have been produced as COTS sUAS and recreational hobby platforms. They feature an elliptical parafoil, with a primary fuselage suspended beneath, containing a pusher propulsion configuration. The propulsion system is used to control thrust, which increases or decreases vertical climb rate. The parafoil is manipulated by deflecting the trailing edges to provide directional yaw control. Powered para-

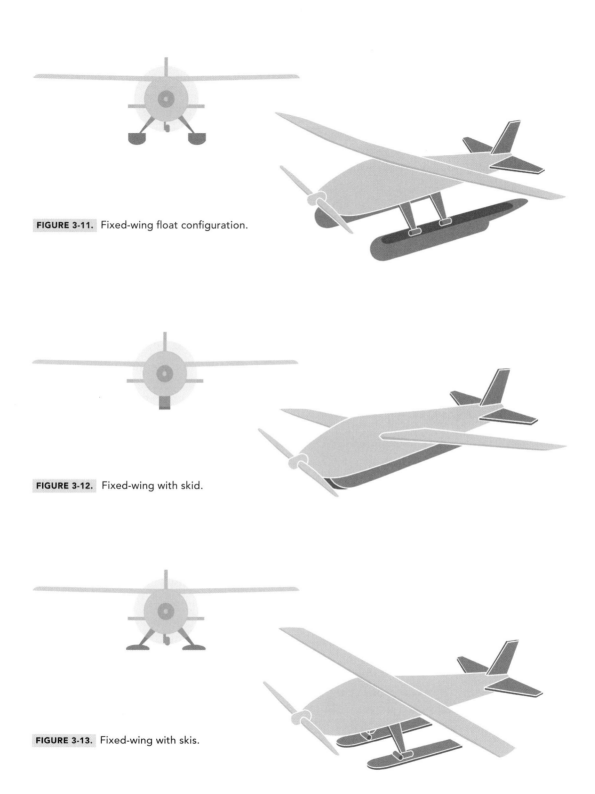

FIGURE 3-11. Fixed-wing float configuration.

FIGURE 3-12. Fixed-wing with skid.

FIGURE 3-13. Fixed-wing with skis.

chutes are typically deployed from the ground, which requires a short takeoff/landing area. However, some have been adapted for aerial deployment. This configuration is highly stable and provides limited control response, consistent maneuverability, and resistance to stall, but its resultant speed is low and highly susceptible to environmental wind conditions.

Tube-Launched—These configurations are a type of fixed-wing sUAS that can be loaded into a small, lightweight, tubular launching mechanism for quick, highly portable deployment. The wings fold or are wrapped around the fuselage in the tube for launch. Tube-launched platforms tend to primarily be used for tactical purposes, but their expedited operational readiness and portability could be useful to support future sUAS applications, such as emergency response, infrastructure inspection, search and rescue, and launch from under (through) foliage canopy. Some variants feature an electric propulsion system for sustained flight, while others rely on use of a short, propulsive booster and gliding profile. Future variants are expected to possibly include rotary-wing configurations.

▮ VERTICAL TAKEOFF AND LANDING (VTOL)

VTOL sUAS represent aircraft featuring use of rotary-wing flight mechanisms, fixed-wing aircraft capable of vertical operation, or hybrid systems incorporating both rotary and fixed-wing characteristics into a single platform. The attainment and sustainment of hovering and translational (longitudinal and lateral) flight is the common characteristic of VTOL platforms.

Benefits and Advantages of VTOL sUAS:

- Smaller launch/recovery area needed (no runway)
- Rapidly deployable
- Capable of translational flight (slow, fast, lateral, longitudinal, and hover; better low-speed maneuverability)

Limitations of VTOL sUAS:

- Less fuel efficient, reduced range
- Lower airspeed
- Lower operational altitude (irrelevant under FAA operational provisions: <400 feet AGL)

There are several key characteristics of VTOL design configurations that affect performance and handling, including the type of lift generation mechanisms and controls, as well as propulsion configurations.

▸ Lift Generation and Control Types

VTOL sUAS use dedicated mechanisms to generate thrust through the rotation of rotors or propellers in connection with a series of control options to manipulate the thrust both downwards (to counteract the effects of gravity) and in specific directions (to change orientation and position). There are several types of lift generation and control mechanisms commonly used in VTOL sUAS: collective rotor, variable-pitch propellers, and fixed-pitch propellers.

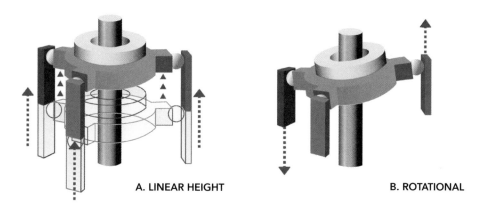

A. LINEAR HEIGHT   **B. ROTATIONAL**

FIGURE 3-14. Commanded CCPM swashplate movements: (A) linear height and (B) rotational.

Cyclic/Collective Pitch Mixing (CCPM, or collective rotor)—This mechanism features the use of two or more flat, variable-pitch rotor blades mounted to a rotor hub (rotorhead), which sits atop a shaft connected to the powerplant, swashplate, and cyclic control linkages. In this configuration, the swashplate is manipulated by three actuator servos, usually spaced at 120-degree intervals around the rotor mast,[7] which when mixed mechanically or through software change the pitch, roll, and/or height of the swashplate (*see* Figure 3-14). When this control manipulation is combined with a spinning rotor (disc), the magnitude and direction of thrust becomes controllable.

A commanded collective change, up or down, causes the three servos to work in coordination to adjust the height of the swashplate along the z-axis of the rotorhub (Figure 3-14A). A fore or aft cyclic change causes the three servos to change the pitch of the swashplate around its currently commanded height (collective position), which results in longitudinal pitched movement of the rotor disc about the y-axis of the rotor hub (Figure 3-14B).[8] Likewise, a commanded left or right cyclic changes swashplate roll around the currently commanded height, which results in lateral rolling movement of the rotor disc about the x-axis of the rotor hub. A commanded collective increase raises the swashplate on the rotor mast, in turn changing the pitch of the rotors relative to the rotor hub. The more rotor pitch that is introduced, the more the rotors deflect and generate thrust.[9] Some CCPM configurations feature incorporation of a **flybar** to add further stability to the main rotor and improve maneuverability, while others eliminate it using electronic stabilization, which increases complexity and requires use of a three-degrees of freedom (3-DOF) gyroscope (gyro).

---

[7] A 90-degree CCPM configuration is typically used with mechanical mixing.

[8] The coordinated CCPM servo movement must be calibrated to not pitch too far, or else the rear tail boom could be struck.

[9] A spinning rotor could be brought to full throttle and still not generate any usable thrust if the collective/swashplate is not raised. Additionally, a lateral swashplate movement results in further manipulation of the rotor pitch as the rotor approaches at 90 degrees to the desired rotor disc reorientation (fore or aft), while a longitudinal movement affects the rotor pitch at it approaches the left or right of the disc.

Typically, the powerplant revolutions per minute (RPMs) are paired to the collective control to match a predefined curve of correlated collective values; little to no operator control may be required beyond the initial calibration as the commanded throttle signal can be automatically sent to the powerplant. This configuration provides a high degree of control and maneuverability, but also presents significant mechanical complexity. CCPM components are designed to a specific size category (e.g., electric 175–700 class;[10] internal combustion .30–.90 cubic inch) and are readily available as COTS from a large number of vendors and retailers.

Variable-Pitch Propeller—This mechanism is similar in its basic concept to the collective aspect of CCPM, in which changing the pitch of the propeller controls the magnitude and direction of thrust generated. However, unlike CCPM, it does not provide the means to vector or manipulate the thrust about a point; there is no lateral or longitudinal control of a propeller disc about a rotor hub. Instead, the direction of the generated thrust is linear, forward to reverse. The mechanism is mechanically simpler than CCPM and is only used on fixed-wing (HTOL, STOL, or VTOL) or hybrid platforms. The pitch control can be passive and automatically adjusted as needed, or active and controlled by the remote pilot, which requires power. The propeller RPM is controlled by adjusting the powerplant throttle, either a mechanical throttle assembly for internal combustion/turbine engines or an electronic speed control (ESC) for electric motors.[11] Variable-pitch propellers are expensive and may only be available from a limited number of vendors. When mounted in a perpendicular orientation, upward or downward facing, they are commonly referred to as rotors (multirotors); otherwise they are referred to as propellers.

Fixed-Pitch Propeller—This mechanism is the simplest of the three propulsion and control options and is represented by the controlled rotation of a preformed, unadjustable propeller with the pitch determined when the propeller is manufactured. With this configuration, a remote pilot controls the magnitude of thrust generated by manipulating the powerplant RPMs, and in some cases, it is possible to generate reverse thrust. Some electric motors/ESCs are capable of reversing direction, while others feature a breaking mechanism. It works on the same principle as the variable-pitch propeller, except that the pitch cannot be changed. However, there are a number of pitch, direction, blade number, and construction material options to suit the desired performance and flight environment (e.g., a greater pitch for higher-altitude operations[12]). Options usually include specific diameters and pitch; pusher, tractor, folding, or matched pair; and wood, nylon, and glass-filled/composite. Fixed-pitch propeller mechanisms are typically only used in fixed-wing or multirotor configurations and are readily available from a large number of vendors and retailers. As with variable-pitch, when mounted in a perpendicular (upward or downward facing) orientation, they are commonly referred to as rotors (multirotors); otherwise, they are called propellers.

---

[10] Representative of physical motor and aircraft sizing, not power output or input requirements.
[11] Propeller RPM on internal combustion engines is also influenced by the selected pitch, which creates an input power requirement that is proportional to RPM.
[12] Operation at higher altitudes will result in an increase to airspeed and subsequent takeoff/landing speed due to lift differential.

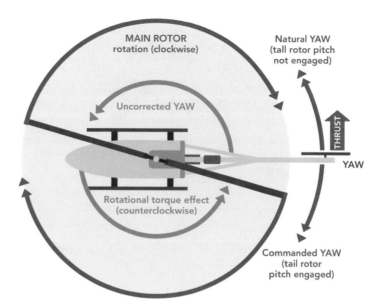

FIGURE 3-15.

The effects of rotational torque and a tail rotor with single-rotor CCPM.

❭ Rotary-Wing Propulsion Configuration

Rotary-wing sUAS designs represent the most prevalent and recognizable form of VTOL sUAS, featuring integration of one or more CCPM/collective rotors or multiple fixed-pitch propellers to both generate and manipulate thrust to achieve highly maneuverable operation.

Conventional Single-Rotor—This configuration represents the most common use of a CCPM/collective rotor to generate and manipulate thrust for the operation and control of a rotary-wing sUAS (helicopter). It features the high-speed rotation of a single rotor around a mast.[13] A tail rotor is used to counteract rotational torque by increasing or decreasing the pitch of its blades (angle of attack) (*see* Figure 3-15):

- *Increasing pitch*—generates an equal, opposing amount of thrust to maintain current yaw orientation with torque yaw in equilibrium
- *Maximum pitch*—generates excess thrust to yaw against the torque-induced rotation
- *No pitch*—prevents generation of any thrust to allow the aircraft to naturally yaw in the opposite direction of the main rotor spin

The lateral thrust generated using the tail rotor is directly connected to the commanded collective, with the output filtered through a small, electronic gyro mounted on the tail. The gyro monitors directional rotation (yaw about the z-axis) and sends a signal to the servo to vary tail-rotor pitch accordingly. Commanded yaw is sent through the gyro and processed to produce the desired yaw change with little to no operator control required beyond initial calibration. Commanded throttle signals are automatically sent to the tail rotor, but can be

---

[13] High-speed rotation of a single rotor induces rotational-torque effect, causing the main body to yaw in the opposite direction of rotor rotation.

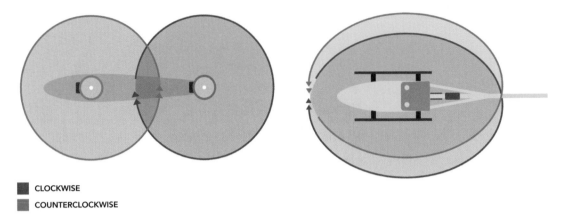

CLOCKWISE
COUNTERCLOCKWISE

FIGURE 3-16. Tandem rotors configuration.   **FIGURE 3-17.** Intermeshing rotors configuration.

trimmed using controls. There are two primary forms of gyros: yaw rate gyros, which dampen yaw to correctable levels, and heading hold gyros, which hold the yaw orientation in a specific direction. Some smaller platforms feature the integration of a small motor, instead of a mechanically linked tail rotor, to reduce mechanical complexity and weight.

Lateral and longitudinal control is accomplished through manipulation of the swashplate, as previously described. Lateral changes are performed by applying right or left cyclic, which causes a subsequent longitudinal orientation change of the swashplate,[14] to roll the rotor disc, resulting in roll of the aircraft. Longitudinal changes are performed by applying forward or rearward cyclic movement to laterally roll the swashplate, in turn pitching the rotor disc forward or aft and changing the pitch of the aircraft.

Dual-Rotor—Several types of dual-rotor configurations exist, and are often featured in popular hobby remote control[15] (RC) platforms. However, more of these platforms are being developed for use as sUAS platforms. The common features among the dual-rotor options are the use of a set of counter-rotating rotors and also that all available power from the powerplant(s) is available to generate lift; no power is diverted to counteract rotational torque. Additionally, hover and low-speed operations typically require less power than a single-rotor configuration. Dual-rotor configurations can feature tandem, intermeshing, or co-axial rotors:

- *Tandem rotors*—This configuration features the incorporation of two, counter-rotating CCPM (collective) rotors longitudinally mounted in series, with one fore and the other aft (*see* Figure 3-16). Gearing is used to prevent rotor strike during rotation and manipulation. Directional change is accomplished by applying opposing lateral cyclic to the two rotors. Longitudinal change is accomplished by varying the collective (rotor blade pitch) of each rotor. Lateral change is

---

[14] Due to gyroscopic precession, the respective input has to be accomplished 90 degrees ahead of where the desired result is achieved (longitudinal swashplate movement results in lateral rotor disc orientation changes; lateral swashplate movement results in longitudinal rotor disc changes).

[15] Also commonly defined as "radio controlled."

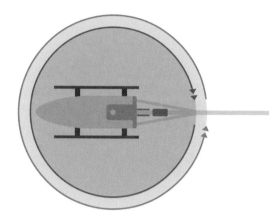

CLOCKWISE

COUNTERCLOCKWISE

FIGURE 3-18. Co-axial rotors configuration.

accomplished in the same manner as a single-rotor CCPM—by applying right/left cyclic to roll the rotor disc about the hub.

- *Intermeshing rotors*—This configuration features two counter-rotating CCPM (collective) rotors mounted transversely and symmetrically, at an angle (*see* Figure 3-17). Gearing is used to prevent rotor strike during rotation and manipulation. Directional change is accomplished by varying the collective (rotor pitch) between the rotors. Lateral and longitudinal change is accomplished in the same manner as a single-rotor CCPM, by applying right/left cyclic to roll the rotor disc and forward/rear cyclic to pitch the rotor disc.

- *Co-axial rotors*—This configuration features two counter-rotating rotors mounted along a common (single) axis, with concentric shafts (*see* Figure 3-18); the higher rotor shaft passes through the lower. Directional change is accomplished by varying the collective (rotor pitch) between the rotors. Lateral and longitudinal change is accomplished in the same manner as a single-rotor CCPM, by applying right/left cyclic to roll the rotor disc and forward/rear cyclic to pitch the rotor disc.

Multirotor—This configuration is relatively new compared to the other rotary-wing types, but it has seen significant development and use. Multirotors are one of the most popular forms of consumer sUAS, with a large number of platform and vendor options available. They feature the use of fixed-pitch blades attached in a variety of motor placement and rotation configurations to counteract rotational torque (*see* Figure 3-19). Some use motors and affixed propellers oriented upward in a perpendicular tractor or perpendicular pusher configuration, while others feature perpendicular push-pull. All orientation and translational movement is accomplished by varying the rotational speeds (thrust and torque) of the individual motor/propeller combinations, which requires the use of a multirotor flight controller to translate control commands into appropriate rotational speeds for each. This results in the need for complex programming to appropriately adjust the RPM of each rotor, but multirotors are also very mechani-

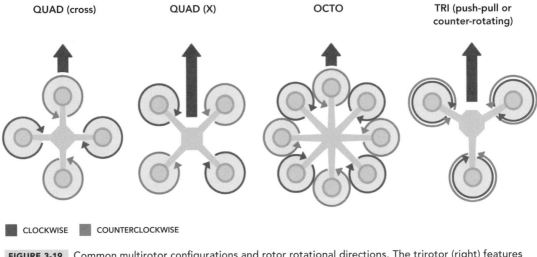

| QUAD (cross) | QUAD (X) | OCTO | TRI (push-pull or counter-rotating) |

■ CLOCKWISE   ■ COUNTERCLOCKWISE

FIGURE 3-19. Common multirotor configurations and rotor rotational directions. The trirotor (right) features coaxial rotor placement, above and below.

cally simplistic. A basic multirotor flight controller incorporates a gyroscope to maintain and manipulate yaw, while more advanced controllers feature sensors, such as global positioning system (GPS), inertial measurement units (IMUs), and ranging sensors to provide autonomous operational capabilities.[16]

As a rotary-wing aircraft performs straight-line longitudinal flight—forwards or backwards with no altitude change—the entire aircraft rotates about the CG's y-axis (pitch), resulting in the front of the aircraft pitching downward for forward flight and upward for backwards flight. Likewise, for straight-line lateral flight (left or right) the aircraft rotates about the CG's x-axis (roll), resulting in a left side drop for leftward flight and a right side drop for rightward flight.[17] The pronounced changes to aircraft orientation can obscure the visibility and usefulness of forward-facing cameras, especially when used for FPV. A 3-DOF gimbal can be used to keep a payload sensor pointed in a specific orientation, despite the aircraft's dynamic re-orientation that occurs from maneuvering.

▶ VTOL Fixed-Wing Propulsion Configuration

VTOL fixed-wing configurations, which include the tail-sitter and hybrid, feature the incorporation of the inherent advantages of fixed-wing designs while mitigating application-limiting issues, such as the inability to hover or operate in small launch/recovery areas.

Tail-Sitter—This configuration operates as the name implies—by launching and recovering in an upward orientation, with the rear of the aircraft (tail) facing the ground (*see Figure 3-20*).

---

[16] Many multirotor flight controllers consist of a basic microcontroller with inputs for sensors and control signals, output for command signals (to motors), and embedded algorithms to calculate appropriate engine RPM needed to achieve desired motion, based on platform configuration and layout.

[17] Tri-copter configurations (excluding push-pull) commonly rely on the use of a servo-steerable tail motor for maneuverability.

Upon launch, it hovers, applies thrust, and reorients horizontally (longitudinal transition) for forward flight, returning to the vertical orientation for subsequent landing. The majority of tail-sitter sUAS are technology evaluation platforms used for research and development, but a small number of COTS products have been developed in recent years.

Hybrid—These configurations combine several of the desirable characteristics of fixed-wing with those of rotary-wing to produce platforms that exceed the limited performance attributes of rota-

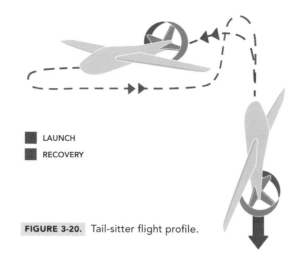

■ LAUNCH
■ RECOVERY

FIGURE 3-20. Tail-sitter flight profile.

ry-wing alone (reduced endurance, range, and speed). While these hybrid platforms are not typically capable of the same level of performance as fixed-wing configurations, the enhanced capabilities—including STOL/VTOL, forward flight, and increased altitude—may be considered worthwhile trade-offs for certain applications.

- *Tilt-rotor*—This hybrid configuration features the use of two counter-rotating, variable-pitch propellers mounted in a tractor configuration to longitudinally rotating nacelles (pods containing powerplants) at the wingtips (*see* Figure 3-21). The platform initiates launch with the propellers facing upward (thrusting down), and then transitions from a hover to translational flight, similar to a helicopter. Once a sufficient forward airspeed has been achieved, the nacelles (and attached propellers) are rotated longitudinally downward (toward the nose), transforming the aircraft to a fixed-wing tractor configuration. Landing follows the same process but in reverse. Tilt-rotors feature a high degree of control complexity, even compared to that of CCPM/collective rotors.

VTOL FLIGHT CONFIGURATION

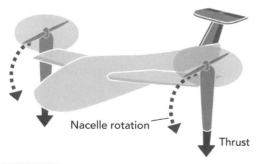

Nacelle rotation

Thrust

FIXED-WING FLIGHT CONFIGURATION

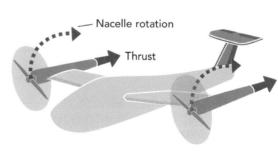

Nacelle rotation

Thrust

FIGURE 3-21. Tilt-rotor hybrid configuration.

VTOL FLIGHT CONFIGURATION

FIXED-WING FLIGHT CONFIGURATION

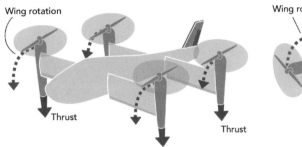

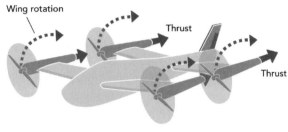

FIGURE 3-22. Tilt-wing hybrid configuration.

- *Tilt-wing*—This configuration is similar to tilt-rotors, but features longitudinal rotation of the entire wing structure with the powerplants and propellers/rotors (*see* Figure 3-22). By including the wing in the rotation, the aircraft is able to improve aerodynamic performance for STOL operations, but suffers reduced performance for hover compared to tilt-rotors and rotary-wing configurations, as the larger vertical surface area is also susceptible to the negative effects of crosswind. Tilt-wing platforms may feature a single or multiple sets of wings.

- *Fixed-wing with quadrotor lift*—This configuration represents the most recent form of fixed-wing/VTOL hybrid, in which a conventional fixed-wing design is outfitted with four perpendicular upward-facing tractor rotors (quadrotor) (*see* Figure 3-23). For launch, the upward-facing rotors are used to generate lift[18] and achieve hover or translational flight in the same manner as a quadrotor, but with reduced performance due to increased weight. To transition to forward flight, the primary fixed-wing propulsion system is engaged and the rotor lifting elements are disengaged. Landing is achieved through re-engagement of the rotor lifting elements and shutdown or reduction of the primary propulsion. In some systems, the primary propulsion source and flight control surfaces are also used in collaboration with the rotor lift element to perform low-speed longitudinal (forward or reverse) flight to maintain straight-and-level orientation. This is unlike a quadrotor, which tilts its entire body longitudinally in flight, thereby reducing forward visibility.

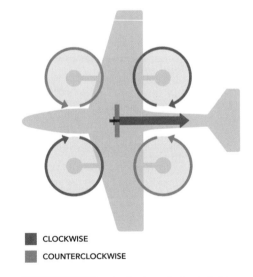

■ CLOCKWISE

■ COUNTERCLOCKWISE

FIGURE 3-23. Fixed-wing/quadrotor hybrid.

---

[18] Through production and control of downward thrust.

▐ MISCELLANEOUS

Not all sUAS platforms conform to the fixed-wing or VTOL designs and configurations described in the previous sections. There are cases in which developers have used biomimicry, adapted other manned aircraft designs (lifting envelopes), or proposed radical new designs to create these atypical sUAS platforms (not commonly available as COTS options). Examples of these miscellaneous configurations include ornithopters, hybrid airships, and transforming systems.

▶ Ornithopter

Ornithopters use **biomimicry** to replicate the flapping, lift-generation mechanisms found in nature to achieve controlled and sustained flight. This configuration is not new to the aeronautical world, but it has only recently become possible to accurately monitor and control such platforms for practical purposes. Potential uses include flight in small, enclosed areas and the ability to capture intelligence without notice, which is especially beneficial for tactical or conservation purposes. The size range of these sUAS platforms mirrors that of the creatures they emulate, from as small as an insect to as big as a large bird. The majority of these platforms have been designed as technology demonstrators used for research and development, but there are a limited number of toy manufacturers producing ornithopter designs (*see* Figure 3-24). Such designs may become more practical and widely available as the power density of electrical batteries improve.

▶ Lifting Body Airship

The lifting body airship (LBA) configuration represents a hybrid combination of **lighter-than-air** airship (dirigible) and conventional fixed-wing and VTOL designs. The result is a configuration capable of remaining aloft for significant periods of time (high endurance), achieving greater speed and range (improved efficiency), and carrying larger amounts of cargo (improved effectiveness). The LBA design uses a combination of body shape and movable propulsion to improve handling and flight performance in conditions that would otherwise render an airship unusable, such as high winds.[19] While slower and less maneuverable than conventional sUAS, this configuration can carry a significantly larger amount of cargo more efficiently and for a greater time. At this time, LBA sUAS designs have only been conceptual, but it is anticipated this configuration may eventually become advantageous for future applications.

FIGURE 3-24. Example remote control ornithopter.

---

[19] LBA envelope is buoyant and shaped to further generate lift in forward flight. Movable/vector-able propulsion is used to manipulate magnitude and orientation of thrust.

❱ Multi-Environment Transforming

The multi-environment transforming configuration has primarily been observed in technology demonstration platforms used for research and development, but a growing number of toy manufacturers are producing designs of this nature. As the name implies, these configurations are designed to transform to operate in more than one environment, such as air–water, air–ground, or air–water–ground. They differ from other examples, such as amphibious, because of the degree to which they adapt for operation in these other environments. Additionally, in some cases, once the platform undergoes a transformation, it may be unable to return to the other environment type; it sheds critical components for weight and performance gains. In many cases, these platforms tend to not produce exceptional performance results due to the unique requirements associated with the respective environments and technological limits. However, this configuration type is anticipated to show promise as technology further advances, in the same way smartphones are capable of providing a high degree of computation and usability, beyond simply making calls.

CATEGORIES AND DESIGNATIONS

There are a multitude of categories and designations used to classify UAS, beyond those presented in the Platform Types section earlier in this chapter. These categories and terms, including those specific to Department of Defense (DoD), industry, and governing regulatory bodies, are typically representative of capability, sizing, or unique features of the aircraft. Understanding how UAS are classified will help you to better understand the relationship among types and configurations as they relate to regulations, advisories, and information found through your own research. It should be noted that there are additional categories used to classify and describe UAS (such as optionally piloted aircraft [OPA], target and decoy drones, combat, hypersonic, or exo-atmospheric); however, their details are not presented here because they are not typically inclusive of the purpose or characteristics of sUAS platforms.

■ DOD CLASSIFICATIONS

The U.S. DoD uses an "unofficial" group classification schema, based on a combination of characteristics and functionality, to categorize UAS. This classification is the most commonly referenced categorization of UAS used within U.S. government documents. Please note that if a UAS is determined to have at least one characteristic of the next-level category, it is classified into the higher category.

FIGURE 3-25. Example Group 1 UAS platforms.

▶ Group 1

UAS in this group weigh 20 pounds or less, operate below 1,200 feet AGL, and fly under 100 knots. They are typically small, hand-launched, fixed-wing platforms or VTOL platforms that can also be classified as sUAS (*see* Figure 3-25), with the provision that operations are limited to below 400 feet AGL and under 87 knots (unless a specific waiver or exemption is granted by the FAA). Table 3-1 shows the average characteristics of Group 1 fixed-wing and VTOL platforms.

TABLE 3-1. GROUP 1 UAS—AVERAGE CHARACTERISTICS

	FIXED-WING PLATFORM	VTOL PLATFORM
Cruise speed	29.4 kts	18.3 kts
Maximum speed	53 kts	30.6 kts
Endurance	85.2 min (1.4 hr)	27.5 min (<0.5 hr)
Range (fuel)	48.8 SM	10 SM
Payload capacity	2 lb	3 lb
Sample size (number of systems)	110	147

FIGURE 3-26. Example Group 2 UAS platforms.

Group 2

UAS in this group weigh 21–55 pounds, operate below 3,500 feet AGL, and fly under 250 knots. They are fixed-wing or VTOL platforms that can also be categorized as sUAS (larger, more capable than Group 1) (*see* Figure 3-26), with the provision that operations are limited to below 400 feet AGL and under 87 knots (unless a specific waiver or exemption is granted by the FAA). Table 3-2 shows the average characteristics of Group 2 fixed-wing and VTOL platforms.

TABLE 3-2. GROUP 2 UAS—AVERAGE CHARACTERISTICS

	FIXED-WING PLATFORM	VTOL PLATFORM
Cruise speed	42.5 kts	27.4 kts
Maximum speed	75 kts	42.6 kts
Endurance	412.4 min (6.9 hr)	115.8 min (1.9 hr)
Range (fuel)	349.3 SM	99.1 SM
Payload capacity	11.4 lb	11.9 lb
Sample size (number of systems)	63	56

Group 3

UAS in this group weigh less than 1,320 pounds, operate below 18,000 feet MSL, and fly under 250 knots. These UAS are most often much larger than those in Group 1 or Group 2, requiring significant infrastructure and support for operation (*see* Figure 3-27). It is worth noting that Group 3 platforms that weigh under 55 pounds can be classified as sUAS with the provision

FIGURE 3-27. Example Group 3 UAS platforms.

that operations are limited to below 400 feet AGL and under 87 knots (unless a specific waiver or exemption is granted by the FAA).

▶ Group 4

UAS in this group weigh more than 1,320 pounds, operate below 18,000 feet MSL, and fly at any airspeed. These aircraft have the same size and complexity as manned aircraft and require significant infrastructure and support to operate.

▶ Group 5

UAS in this group weigh more than 1,320 pounds, operate over 18,000 feet MSL, and fly at any airspeed; the only difference from Group 4 is that the operational altitude is greater.

It should be noted that each of the respective military services (U.S. Air Force, Army, and Navy/Marines) also use their own, independent, tiered categorizations (e.g., I–III) representative of the functional roles of the UAS, in relation to the respective organization. There are also additional categorizations that describe the function and endurance/range of platforms. However, due to the lack of standardization among these classifications and their inapplicability to civilian applications and operations discussed in this text, they are not presented.

■ INDUSTRY AND REGULATORY

The use of UAS by non-military users—such as public (government) agencies and civil operators (non-government)—and the variety of options available has necessitated the creation and use of clarifying and descriptive terms, such as categories and nomenclature. Understanding the context and meaning of these classifications will help you to review regulations; locate, compare, and acquire COTS options; and devise a strategy to safely and appropriately use sUAS.

◗ Hobby

This category represents aircraft, including scale model aircraft, used for the purpose of recreation (hobby). It includes fixed-wing, VTOL, and many of the miscellaneous configurations, with platforms and equipment ranging from extremely low-cost toys to expensive, customized solutions. The equipment and components created for this segment are not subject to certification as a "standard part" by the FAA,[20] but may need to meet other regulatory compliance confirmation.[21]

As this segment of the industry is fairly unregulated, a number of non-standard or "unofficial" subcategories are used to classify hobby sUAS:

- Airplanes (fixed-wing)
  — Trainer
  — Sport
  — Aerobatic
  — Scale (visually representative model aircraft)
  — Jets (ducted fan or turbine)
- Gliders (fixed-wing)
  — Sailplanes
  — Powered
- Helicopter (rotary-wing)
  — Single-rotor
  — Co-axial
  — Scale (model aircraft)
- Multirotor (rotary-wing)
  — Trirotor
  — Quadrotor/copter
  — Hexrotor/copter
  — Octorotor/copter
- Blimps (dirigible)
- Miscellaneous (unique toys, novelty items, and models)

---

[20] Standard Parts must conform to either established industry or U.S. specifications.

[21] Electronics and communications equipment are typically subject to Federal Communications Commission (FCC) regulations and policies to limit the "radio noise" emitted or conducted by the device. For the introduction of new electronics into the U.S. market, the FCC requires devices to be tested and their compliance confirmed, prior to marketing and sale. The developers of these components also tend to apply for other product safety and electromagnetic compatibility evaluations and ratings from independent, industry certification organizations, such as Underwriters Laboratories (UL) or Applied Research Laboratories (ARL). After confirmation of standards compliance, the device is labeled as meeting the applicable standard(s) with the certification organization's designated mark.

FIGURE 3-28. Example sUAS platforms.

Each of these categories can be further subdivided by the following:
- Scale (model aircraft—e.g., 1/8th, 1/4th, or giant)
- Powerplant type and size
  - Electric motors (brushed or brushless—e.g., 175–700 class)
  - Internal combustion engines (also referred to as gas, nitro, or glow-fueled; e.g., 0.01–3.01+ cubic inches)
  - Turbines (e.g., 5.5–52 pounds of thrust)
- Construction material
  - Covered frame
  - Wood
  - Foam
  - Fiberglass
  - Carbon fiber
  - Plastic
- Preparation/construction effort required
  - Ready to fly (RTF)
  - Almost ready to fly (ARF)
  - Kit

❱ sUAS

The term **sUAS** is an industry term that has recently been adopted by the FAA for use in establishing regulations and policies. It is likely that the sUAS concept and nomenclature evolved from the earlier **small unmanned aerial vehicle (SUAV)**, which was a military term used to classify and describe the growing number of portable, hand-launched **unmanned aerial vehicles (UAVs)** used to perform intelligence, surveillance, and reconnaissance (ISR).[22]

The sUAS category represents any UAS that weighs less than 55 pounds and is capable of operation below 400 feet AGL at a speed less than 100 mph (87 knots; in accordance with FAA requirements) (*see* Figure 3-28). Table 3-3 shows the average characteristics of sUAS platforms as a whole, as well as of different types of platforms and powerplants (fixed-wing, VTOL, electric, and internal combustion).

TABLE 3-3. sUAS PLATFORMS—AVERAGE CHARACTERISTICS

	sUAS	FIXED-WING sUAS	VTOL sUAS	ELECTRIC sUAS*	INTERNAL COMBUSTION sUAS**
Cruise speed	28.5 kts	34.9 kts	21.8 kts	25.3 kts	42.2 kts
Maximum speed	49.1 kts	62.1 kts	35.3 kts	44 kts	71 kts
Endurance	129.7 min (2.2 hr)	217.7 min (3.6 hr)	58.7 min (0.9 hr)	67 min (1.1 hr)	494.2 min (7.4 hr)
Range (fuel)	112.9 SM	175.7 SM	44.9 SM	42.3 SM	408.5 SM
Payload capacity	6.8 lb	6.8 lb	6.9 lb	5.2 lb	13.1 lb
Sample size (number of systems)	376	173	203	321	55

* Includes fixed-wing and VTOL sUAS featuring use of electric propulsion.
** Includes fixed-wing and VTOL sUAS featuring use of internal combustion propulsion.

❱ Micro

Micro UAS is another industry term that evolved from previous military nomenclature (**micro unmanned aerial vehicle**, later shortened to **micro air vehicle** [MAV]). The FAA is exploring adoption of this category to provide an operational avenue featuring reduced regulatory requirements. Initially the proposed category was to represent any UAS weighing less than 4.4 pounds, constructed of frangible material (breaks into smaller fragments upon impact), and capable of operation below 400 feet AGL at a speed less than 100 mph (87 knots) (as identified in the FAA NPRM, *Operation and Certification of Small Unmanned Aircraft Systems*). However, in April 2016, an Aviation Rulemaking Committee (ARC), composed of members of industry

---

[22] The term UAV has historically been used to describe what is now referred to as a UAS (unified system); this term now typically connotes the Aerial Element of the unified UAS.

and the stakeholder community, recommended the creation of four categories of UAS (1–4) to support operations over people. The recommendations of the ARC were produced after reviewing information presented by UAS subject matter experts,[23] discussion, and deliberation. Their recommendations were to categorize platforms based on a set of performance-based standards, with category classification being used to determine permissibility of operations, including those close to or over people and crowds.

The following represent the specific Micro UAS ARC category recommendations.

Category 1 UAS—Unmanned aircraft that weigh 250 grams (0.55 pounds) or less and that do not need to meet any performance-based standards to fly over people.

Category 2 UAS—Unmanned aircraft weighing more than 250 grams that present less than a one-percent risk of causing serious injury to people, given impact. UAS in this category would require the manufacturer to self-certify that the energy impact would be less than a threshold amount (12 J/cm^2) for most probable failures, which would be confirmed through testing. Such testing would be conducted in accordance with a set of industry consensus testing standards. These platforms would also require the manufacturer to produce and include an operator manual with specific requirements to be met to operate over people and be labeled to identify successful compliance with the standard. Operation of such UAS would require compliance with manufacturer instructions and maintaining sufficient operational distances, including a minimum vertical distance of 20 feet from people's heads or 10 feet horizontal separation.

Category 3 UAS—Unmanned aircraft that present less than a 30-percent risk of causing serious injury to people, given impact. UAS in this category would also require testing, in accordance with industry consensus standards, to determine if they meet an impact energy threshold. These platforms would require inclusion of a manufacturer-produced operator manual and standard compliance labeling. Operation of such UAS could only be conducted within controlled (closed) environments with the permission of the landowner or operator (remote pilot) and in compliance with the same requirements as Category 2 UAS (following manufacturer instructions; maintaining safe separation). Flight over people could not be sustained; only transient or incidental overflight would be permissible.

Category 4 UAS—Unmanned aircraft that present less than a 30-percent risk of causing serious injury to people, but that are intended for sustained flight over crowds. UAS in this category would also require testing, in accordance with industry consensus standards, to determine if they meet an impact energy threshold. These platforms would require a risk mitigation plan, in accordance with an industry consensus standard and in addition to the manufacturer-produced operator manual and labeling. The risk mitigation plan is suggested to address operator (remote pilot) qualifications (to exceed enacted sUAS certification and operational requirements) and ensure compliance with the plan. Additionally, the constituent elements and construction materials of the platform should be considered in order to determine if they present an increased risk of collateral serious injury to members of the crowd. Operation of such

---

[23] Presenters included researchers from ASTM, FAA, Transport Canada, NASA, NIST, ASSURE, FAA Test Sites, RTCA, EASA, US Navy, CPSC, universities, and industry.

UAS could only be conducted with the same requirements as Categories 2 and 3 (following manufacturer instructions; maintaining safe separation with transient or incidental overflight).

Implementation of these recommendations from the Micro UAS ARC would require manufacturer self-certification and advertisement of aircraft weight, and the development of industry consensus standards for operation over people, a self-certification declaration form to submit to the FAA, and a labeling format.

PLATFORM SELECTION CONSIDERATIONS

As previously presented, fixed-wing sUAS can offer increased operational efficiency and effectiveness, longer endurance and range, greater speeds, and the ability to operate at higher operational altitudes. However, they tend to require greater support for launch and recovery and are only capable of forward flight. Alternatively, VTOL sUAS require a smaller launch and recovery area, are rapidly deployable from the operational locale, and provide translational flight and improved low-speed maneuverability. Their limitations are reduced fuel efficiency, range, airspeed, and operational altitude. Electric platforms tend to offer immediate power available (propulsion response), reduced vibration, and are significantly less mechanically complex, usually only requiring installation of a battery and data storage device (e.g., SD card) prior to launch. However, their endurance is reduced compared to internal combustion, unless supplemented by solar or more expensive advanced power supplies (e.g., fuel cells). Internal combustion platforms, on the other hand, provide greater power, but require increased infrastructure and support and are subject to increased vibration, which can impact the effectiveness of data collection sensors.

The selection of a platform will depend on your specific operational needs, including endurance, altitude, maneuverability, payload capacity, and complexity. If you will be looking to fly for extended periods of time, at greater speeds, and with no need to hover, then a fixed-wing platform may provide the desired capabilities to meet your requirements. However, if your intended operation requires hover or translational flight, then VTOL will be necessary. Choosing an appropriate platform requires identifying and weighing applicable performance capabilities as a series of trade-offs. Very rarely does a platform meet all requirements without some level of trade-off, even among similar options within the same category.

SYSTEM COMPOSITION

The architecture of UAS designs are scalable, with varying levels of complexity relating to performance or functionality. Typically, sUAS are less complicated than larger-sized UAS, such as the AAI RQ-7 Shadow 200 (fixed-wing) or Yamaha RMAX (rotary-wing). However, the overarching structure of an sUAS design, as a "system of systems," follows the same hierarchy as the larger UAS, which includes the following major elements (also referred to as subsystems) (see Figure 3-29):

- **Aerial Element**—the remotely or autonomously operated unmanned aircraft (UAV), designed to perform specific functions or provide broad support for multiple applications
- **Payload**—portable, remote-sensing apparatus or transported and deployable material (including supporting infrastructure) carried by the Aerial Element
- **Command, Control, and Communication (C3)**—interface and underlying infrastructure used to convey and translate information between remote pilot(s) on the ground and the Aerial Element
- **Human Element**—crew required for operation and support of the entire system
- **Support Equipment**—equipment and material required for operation and sustainment of the entire system

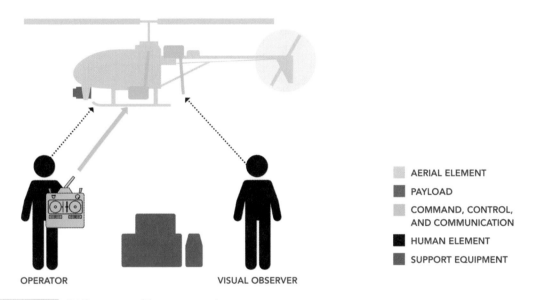

AERIAL ELEMENT
PAYLOAD
COMMAND, CONTROL, AND COMMUNICATION
HUMAN ELEMENT
SUPPORT EQUIPMENT

OPERATOR   VISUAL OBSERVER

FIGURE 3-29. sUAS system architecture overview.

MAJOR ELEMENTS AND EQUIPMENT

Understanding how the major elements or subsystems of an sUAS contribute to the total system functionality, as well as its inherent capabilities and limitations, will help you to evaluate options and configure your own system. Designing the loadout or composition requires a series of trade-off considerations in which cost, capability, and functional requirements of the task and available options must be compared and addressed. Such considerations are necessary to ensure safety can be maintained, while balancing system efficiency and effectiveness. The information in this section has been presented to assist with informed decision making as you explore potential sUAS configuration options. Detailed descriptions and common examples of major elements and components are presented and discussed.

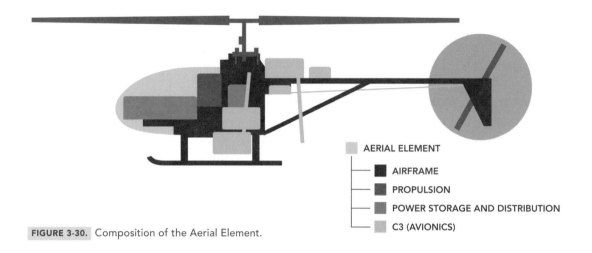

FIGURE 3-30. Composition of the Aerial Element.

AERIAL ELEMENT

The **Aerial Element** represents the airborne portion of the sUAS, which is used to perform the desired system function.[24] This element is commonly referred to as a UAV or the unmanned aircraft (UA), and its purpose ranges from serving as a training platform to the more common use of gathering data (imagery) from an elevated (aerial) perspective. The primary components—airframe, propulsion source, power storage and distribution, and avionics—are shown in Figure 3-30 and described in the following sections.

▌AIRFRAME

The airframe is the primary infrastructure component of the Aerial Element, providing the necessary strength and structural integrity to house, mount, and protect other critical components. This element is available in many options, with forms and functions as described in the Platform Types section earlier in this chapter. An airframe can be constructed using a variety and combination of materials, including wood, plastics, metal, composites, and/or foam.

▌PROPULSION SOURCE

The propulsion source is a combination of a thrust-generation mechanism and powerplant used to achieve airspeed and lift required for sustained flight.

---

[24] The owner must register the sUAS with the FAA either as a recreational user (owner receives a personal registration for use with all their sUAS) or as a non-recreational user (public or civil; required per individual sUAS). Non-recreational users receive an N-number, which must be displayed in accordance with 14 CFR Part 45. (If unable to comply with marking requirements due to the size or space available, the operator will need to apply to the FAA UAS Integration Office for alternative marking consideration.) To apply for N-number registration, submit a copy of the Aircraft Registration Application (AC Form 8050-1) with evidence of ownership to the Aircraft Registration Branch (AFS-750); see Unmanned Aircraft System (UAS) Registration (www.faa.gov/uas/registration/) for details.

FIGURE 3-31. Example sUAS featuring propellers.

▶ Thrust Generation

The primary thrust-generation mechanisms and their associated theories of operation were introduced in the Platform Types section earlier in this chapter. Common forms of thrust generation include propellers, rotors, ducted fans, and turbines.

Propeller—This mechanism uses a series of hub-mounted, rotating blades (wings) attached to a powerplant (*see* Figure 3-31). It is available in the three configurations introduced earlier (tractor, pusher, or push-pull) and generates thrust using a rotationally induced pressure difference and RPM. In simplified terms, propellers can be thought of as rotating wings. They are subcategorized into fixed-pitch and variable-pitch, and are available in a variety of construction materials (e.g., wood, plastic, glass-filled nylon, and composites). Additionally, there are specific types of propellers designed to dynamically improve aerodynamic efficiency, such as folding propellers (fixed-pitch[25]) or self-feathering (variable-pitch[26]).

Propeller sizing is traditionally depicted using a common format (e.g., 10 x 6), with the first number representing the diameter of the propeller disc (in inches; created by the propeller as it rotates) and the second number representing pitch (calculated distance the propeller will move through the air after completion of a single rotation; in inches). A propeller's performance (effectiveness) is affected by several factors, including integrity, density, weight, size, vibration, and number of blades, as well as environmental conditions (e.g., temperature, air density/altitude, and humidity). Larger diameter propellers require lower RPMs and a higher amount of torque than small propellers to generate the same amount of thrust. While using a small propeller requires less power for each rotation, generating higher RPMs increases the audible noise level. The number of blades also impacts performance, as the fewer number of blades used the more efficient the system performance. The reason that three or more

---

[25] Improves aerodynamics when the powerplant is not engaged.
[26] Passively adjusts pitch to the optimal angle of attack.

FIGURE 3-32. Example sUAS featuring rotors.

blades are typically used is to decrease the clearance of the propeller (produce a smaller rotational disc) or intentionally slow the flight of the aircraft, while retaining thrusting capability at higher RPMs, which can be beneficial for training. As more blades are added to a propeller, it becomes less efficient because the airflow each subsequent blade must pass through becomes increasingly more turbulent (disturbed).

Rotor—This mechanism, like propellers, features a series of hub-mounted, rotating blades attached to a powerplant. Rotors are mounted horizontally in one of the several configurations introduced earlier under Platform Types (see Figure 3-32), are available in lengths that match a specific powerplant/aircraft sizing, and are made from a variety of materials, including wood, plastic, and carbon fiber. In the case of CCPM/collective pitch, the rotor's angle of attack is changed during operation to increase or decrease thrust (correlated with powerplant RPM increases), while a multirotor relies on changing the RPMs of a fixed-pitch rotor (the same as a propeller).

Ducted Fan—This mechanism features the use of an impeller (fan rotor) mounted to a powerplant inside of a tubular enclosure (housing or "duct"), which is attached either outside the fuselage or wing, or within a channel inside the aircraft (between intake and exhaust) (see Figure 3-33). The impeller rotates at high RPMs,[27] pushing air over the powerplant (providing cooling), and out the rear, over an aft-mounted cone (which reduces turbulence) and set of stator blades (which reduce axial, rotating movement of thrust generated by the impeller).[28] Ducted fans can be powered using either an electric powerplant (electric ducted fan [EDF]) or internal combustion (glow-powered ducted fan [GDF]). Ducted fans can also be affixed with mechanisms, such as vanes or a flexible nozzle, or mounted in a manner so that the orientation

---

[27] Shorter, broader impeller blades improve efficiency by reducing loss generated by the tips of a propeller.

[28] The majority of ducted fans feature use of a tractor configuration, in which thrust is pushed back through the assembly and over the powerplant. However, there are cases of pusher configurations in which the powerplant is positioned in front of the impeller.

FIGURE 3-33.

Aircraft featuring incorporation of ducted fans.

FIGURE 3-34.

Turbine (jet) installed on top of an RC model aircraft.

of the entire assembly is controllable to vector the thrust, significantly improving maneuverability but at the cost of increased complexity and weight.

Turbine (Jet)—This mechanism is similar to the ducted fan, in which thrust is generated by the high speed rotation of an impeller. However, with a turbine the air is further compressed, mixed with liquid fuel, and then combusted; the exploding air/fuel mixture is exhausted over a turbine assembly and out the rear, producing the greatest amount of thrust of all discussed mechanisms (*see* Figure 3-34).[29]

Thrust Generation—Considerations and suggested practices:

- Always inspect the integrity of a propeller (including rotors/impellers) before use; if a blade is chipped or cracked, discard and replace it.
- The balance of a propeller and its components (entire propeller assembly, stand-alone hub, blades, and spinner) should be confirmed and corrected prior to mounting and use in a propulsion subsystem (accomplished using a prop balancer); otherwise, vibration can occur, resulting in detrimental performance or propulsion system failure.
- Propeller construction material affects durability, but it can also cause unanticipated injury or damage based on how easily the propeller breaks up upon impact (e.g., thrown splinters/shards or resistance against running powerplant/drive shaft upon impact with the ground). Examine and weigh this against how and where the sUAS will be operated.
- Treat spinning propellers with care; they rotate at extremely high RPMs. Do not try to stop a propeller using your hands or by placing an object into the spinning disc.

---

[29] The resulting rotation of the rear turbine assembly can be used to mechanically turn an electrical power-generating alternator or propeller (e.g., turboprop).

▶ Powerplant

The powerplant is used to convert stored energy, in the form of either electricity or liquid fuel, into desired mechanical motion or exhaust. For the majority of sUAS, this translates into rotation of a drive shaft connected to rotating elements (i.e., propellers, rotors, impeller). Powerplants typically also produce significant heat, and in the case of internal combustion, emissions and exhaust. Gearing (step-down/up) can also be incorporated into drive assemblies to change the RPMs of the propeller from that of the powerplant.

Electric—An electromagnetic motor is the mechanical power-producing element in electric propulsion systems. Direct current (DC) electrical power is provided to the motor, between a fixed range; varying the power increases or decreases the RPMs, providing control for the motor drive shaft RPM. Electric systems are significantly less mechanically complex than other powerplant configurations, featuring fewer moving parts, less adjustment, and simpler refueling (replacing the battery), but they tend to not produce the same level of speed, endurance, and range. Electric propulsion systems can be supplemented through integration of electrical energy-producing elements, such as photovoltaic (solar) films and cells. There are two primary types of electric motors used in sUAS designs: brushed and brushless.

Brushed (canned)—This motor type features the rotation of a centrally mounted, electromagnet (rotor) inside of a cylindrical housing (can) to which two opposing permanent magnets are attached (stator) (*see* Figure 3-35). A commutator (rotating mechanical switch and brushes) reverses the polarity of the rotor, causing it to repel (rotate) away from the identically charged magnet and attract toward the oppositely charged magnet. As electrical power is increasingly applied to the rotor, the strength of the rotational repulsion/attraction grows; the electromagnetic field effects are combined with the inertia of the spinning mass of the rotor, resulting in an increase in RPMs. Electrical power is provided through two wired connections (+/-) at variable

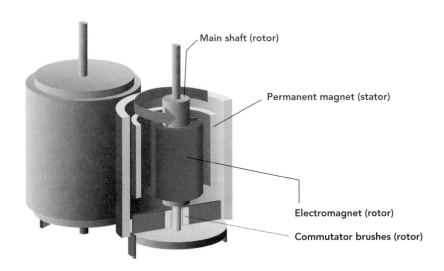

FIGURE 3-35. Brushed (canned) motor and cutaway details.

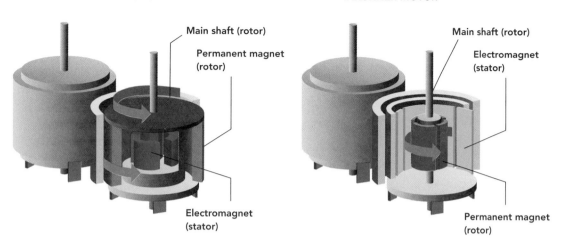

OUTRUNNER MOTOR

Main shaft (rotor)

Permanent magnet
(rotor)

Electromagnet
(stator)

INRUNNER MOTOR

Main shaft (rotor)

Electromagnet
(stator)

Permanent magnet
(rotor)

FIGURE 3-36. Outrunner and inrunner brushless motors with cutaways featuring details.

levels; a very simple electrical power controller (mechanical or electronic) is required to vary the power (current). Brushed motors are mechanically uncomplicated, inexpensive to produce, and can be refurbished. However, they require regular maintenance to replace commutator brushes, do not dissipate heat effectively, generate electrical magnetic interference (EMI), and are RPM limited.[30]

Brushless—This motor type reverses the rotor/stator configuration from brushed motors by rotating the permanent magnets (now the rotor) and fixing the position of three electromagnets (now the stator). It also replaces the commutator and brushes with an electronic circuit (controller) and rotational sensor to switch the current to the electromagnets. Brushless motors require less maintenance, are smaller and highly efficient, provide a high power-to-weight ratio, and do not generate EMI. However, they are more costly to produce and are subject to increased control complexity, which can require expensive components, such as a specific three-wire ESC.

Two primary configurations of brushless motors are used in sUAS: outer rotor and inner rotor (*see* Figure 3-36). In **outer rotor** (outrunner) motors, a fixed-position electromagnet (stator) is mounted in the center and permanent magnets are attached to a rotating outer element (rotor) to produce a large amount of torque and stable speed. They are subject to slower rotational speeds (low RPMs) and necessary safety provisions to protect the spinning rotor. **Inner rotor** (inrunner) motors centrally mount the permanent magnets on a rotating assembly (rotor) surrounded by three, fixed-position electromagnets (stator) to provide quick commanded responses and improved heat dissipation, but it becomes difficult to produce a large amount of torque, and centrifugal force can damage the permanent magnets.

---

[30] Brushed motors tend to produce less torque, provide a smaller RPM range, and reduced rotational speed.

Internal Combustion—Internal combustion powerplants rely on the combination, compression, and controlled explosive detonation of air and fuel within a reinforced chamber (or series of chambers). These powerplants feature the combination of air, drawn from outside the assembly, and atomized fuel (air-fuel mixture). When the proportional mixture contains less fuel, it is lean; when it contains more fuel, it is rich.[31] Internal combustion tends to produce a higher specific impulse and subsequent power-to-weight ratio than electric propulsion, but this result reduces significantly with the size of the powerplant.[32] When sUAS are configured with internal combustion propulsion, they must also use electric batteries and/or electrical generators (alternators) to provide electrical power for electronics and actuators. Internal combustion engines are categorized as intermittent or continuous, and sub-classified by fuel type (gas, glow/nitro, or diesel), engine displacement, and in some cases end-platform (e.g., helicopter).

Intermittent—This engine type represent those internal combustion configurations that use a periodic, repeating process to produce mechanical power for rotational drive shaft motion. The following represents the typical operational steps of an intermittent, reciprocating engine (*see* Figure 3-37):

1. Fuel is atomized and drawn into combustion chamber with air.
2. Air/fuel mixture is compressed (piston completes travel toward ignition source).
3. Compressed mixture is ignited (forces piston away from ignition source).
4. Detonated mixture is exhausted (piston completes travel; process repeats).

The resulting linear (upward/downward) piston motion is translated into rotational movement, which is used to turn the powerplant drive shaft. This operation occurs in a cycle that is repeated until the fuel is consumed or the fuel flow has been shut off.

The most common intermittent internal combustion engines used in sUAS are 2-stroke, 4-stroke (*see* Figure 3-38), and Wankel (rotary). **2-stroke** (two-cycle) reciprocating engines combusts once, per rotation of the drive shaft rotor and are simpler, less expensive, and offer an improved power to weight ratio. **4-stroke** (four-cycle) reciprocating engines combusts twice,

FIGURE 3-37.

Intermittent reciprocating engine operational cycle:

(1) intake

(2) compression

(3) ignition/combustion

(4) exhaust

---

[31] A lean mixture may be more fuel efficient, but requires higher combustion temperatures and produces less power than rich mixtures. The selection of an appropriate air-fuel ratio is dependent on several factors, including altitude, air density, temperature, and power required.

[32] Small electric powerplants require less infrastructure and mechanical complexity than internal combustion, decreasing subsystem weight.

FIGURE 3-38. Common intermittent internal combustion engines: 2-stroke glow *(right)* and 4-stroke rotary *(left)*.

per rotation and generates more low-end torque and less noise. **Wankel** engines feature rotational displacement of a rotor inside a housing; mechanical power is produced rotationally, which does not need to be translated from linear motion. However, while Wankel engines provide a high power output for their size, they are less efficient and more expensive and mechanically complex than other intermittent internal combustion options.

Continuous—This engine type, as the name implies, does not intermittently start/stop. Instead, it operates by consuming and igniting a constant air/fuel feed, resulting in the production of an unbroken volume of thrust as exhaust or mechanical turbine assembly rotation. The turbine powerplant is the only configuration of continuous internal combustion used in sUAS for practical applications. The following represents the typical operational steps of a turbine engine (*see* Figure 3-39):

1. Air is drawn through a compressor assembly (air is compressed).
2. Fuel is added to the compressed air (mixture combusts).
3. Combusted mixture is exhausted (the exhaust is used to directly generate thrust or rotate a rear turbine impeller assembly).

Turbine powerplants (introduced in the Thrust Generation section earlier in this chapter) tend to have the highest power-to-weight ratio of all the powerplant options, but are extremely expensive and complex, requiring fine adjustment, the use of compressed air to start the engine, and volatile liquid fuel to sustain operation.

FIGURE 3-39.

Turbine (jet) operation:
(1) intake and compression
(2) mixture and combustion
(3) exhaust/thrust generation

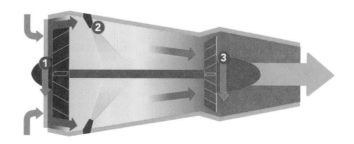

■ POWER STORAGE AND DISTRIBUTION

The power for operation of the Aerial Element must be self-contained (stored) and distributed to the powerplant, actuated components, and electronics (electricity and/or fuel) in the proper format and range. The type of storage and distribution depends on the category of propulsion: electrical or internal combustion.

▶ Types of Power Storage

This component provides the infrastructure and chemical medium used to store system power (energy). The primary mediums for energy storage are batteries, fuel cells, or liquid (combustible) fuel.

Batteries—This storage medium typically consists of a series of rechargeable, electrochemical voltaic cells that produce an electric current through an electrochemical reaction; recharging reverses the reaction. Batteries are used to provide power for system electronics, such as avionics and actuators/servos, and are available in a variety of cell configurations, connection types, and materials. The most common types of batteries used in sUAS are nickel or lithium-based options.

Nickel-based—Earlier RC model aircraft configurations tended to rely heavily on the use of nickel-based batteries, such as nickel-cadmium (NiCd) or nickel-metal hydride (NiMH). These inexpensive batteries support rapid charging with a low resultant temperature and reduced volatility (they rarely combust during charge/discharge), but they have a much lower power-to-weight ratio (lower energy density) and their performance can significantly degrade over time with inconsistent charging (memory effect). Each cell is rated at 1.2 V per cell, with cells combined in series to increase operating voltage (e.g., 6 cells for 7.2 V) and/or in parallel to increase capacity (milliampere hour [mAh][33]). With the availability of lithium-based options, nickel-based batteries have been relegated to providing power for non-propulsion related components, such as avionics and sensors, which do not place as heavy of a demand on the batteries.

Lithium-based—Many modern electronics, including sUAS, use lithium-based batteries, such as lithium-polymer (LiPo) or lithium-ion (Li-ion), to store and release electrical power. LiPo batteries tend to be used in propulsion systems, while Li-ion are used more commonly in avionics, tools, or other electronics (*see* Figure 3-40). Lithium batteries provide a significantly improved power-to-weight ratio (high energy density) and can be formed into custom shapes, while providing longer endurance under load and a higher discharge rate, which supports their use as a power source for electric powerplants and actuation. However, they are more expensive to produce, feature increased complexity, require specific charging equipment, have a shorter

FIGURE 3-40. Example of a COTS LiPo battery.

---

[33] mAh represents how much current is discharged over an hour.

lifespan, are subject to operational temperature effects, and are more volatile because components are pressurized and highly flammable.

There are several important identifiers used in lithium batteries: discharge rate (C), cell count (S), and capacity. The discharge rating of the battery (indicated by C) conveys how many times the battery can safely be continuously discharged; if a battery is rated as 10C, it can be safely discharged up to 10 times its capacity. Unlike nickel-based cells, lithium are rated at 3.7 V per cell, and the series combinations (to increase voltage) are designated using an S number to indicate cell count: 1S is 3.7 V, while 3S is equivalent to 11.1 V. The capacity of a lithium battery is identified in the same manner as a nickel battery, through identification of mAh. For example, the details of a 20C 2000 mAh 2S battery can be determined by examining each of the identifiers:

Voltage = 2S = 2 x 3.7 = 7.4 V
Capacity = 2000 mAh = 2 amps (1000mAh = 1 Ampere-hour [Ah])
Discharge rating = C-number x capacity = 20 x 2 = 40 amps of continuous discharge

Lithium batteries must be cared for and stored properly; charging/ discharging, storage temperature, and proper handling are all critical to properly maintaining the batteries.

Batteries—Considerations and suggested practices:
- Always follow the rules laid out by the manufacturer.
- Always inspect the integrity of a battery. If a battery has been dropped, a cell may have ruptured (and can catch fire when used); dispose of properly, as specified by the manufacturer.
- Always use a charger that matches the type of battery being charged (NiCd, NiMH, and Lithium all use different chargers; the majority of LiPos charge at 1C or 1 amp per hour).
- Never leave batteries to charge unattended.
- Place lithium batteries in a fire-proof pouch during recharging.
- Many airlines have policies regarding the transport of lithium-based batteries; it is suggested that such policies be reviewed prior to any planned travel and transportation of batteries.

Fuel Cells—Similar to batteries, fuel cells are used to produce electrical power for electronic components. Unlike batteries, they generate power using a finite fuel stored in the cell (e.g., solid or gaseous hydrogen). Their use and availability for incorporation into sUAS has increased in recent years. The use of this storage medium shows significant promise, with examples extending operational endurance of multirotor platforms substantially (from minutes to hours) and in the case of solid hydrogen fuel, improving the stability and safety of power storage.

Liquid Fuel—The controlled explosive detonation of the internal combustion process requires the combination of air and an atomized liquid fuel, which is available in several formats and matched to the specific engine type. Liquid fuel is stored in a pressurized tank, available in a variety of sizes and shapes (e.g., rectangular, slanted, round, and oval).[34] The most common types of liquid fuel used in sUAS are glow (nitro), gasoline, and diesel.

Glow (nitro)—This is the most common fuel used in smaller internal combustion propulsion systems, such as 2-stroke and 4-stroke engines. Glow fuel is a blend of methanol (58–88%) and oil (12–28%),[35] while nitro features the addition of nitromethane (0–30%) to the blend for additional power.[36] This fuel requires the use of a glow plug (ignition element) incorporated into the cylinder head of the engine to initiate combustion of the air/fuel mixture, and it is readily obtained from specialty stores, such as RC hobby retailers.

Gasoline (gas)—This inexpensive and readily available fuel is used in larger engines. Gasoline produces less emissions and residue than glow fuel and requires the use of a spark plug (ignition element) to initiate combustion of the air/fuel mixture. Some engines designed to operate using glow fuel can be converted to use gasoline.

Diesel—This fuel has been used in RC model aircraft, but is the least commonly used in sUAS. Diesel features the blend of ether, kerosene, and oil, which achieves combustion from compression pressure rather than an ignition element, such as a glow plug or spark plug. Engines that use diesel fuel tend to handle a wider range of operating factors, such as propeller diameter, temperature, and variety in fuel composition.

▶ Distribution and Control

The controlled distribution of fuel is dependent on the format of the propulsion system—electric or internal combustion. Stored energy (electrical power or liquid fuel) is released using mechanisms specific to the propulsion system format.

Electric—Electric controls regulate and modify the flow of electricity using either mechanical or electronic speed controls (ESCs). Some ESCs have been designed to cut off the flow of power to the propulsion system once a certain voltage threshold has been reached, using battery elimination circuitry (BEC). BECs support the use of a single battery to provide power to the entire Aerial Element, including regulated and reduced voltage for 6 V accessories, such as servos and communications components. Universal BECs (UBECs) are used to provide this capability, when not included in the ESC (this can also prevent the occurrence of ground loop). Additionally, battery monitors can be used in line with electrical distribution and storage to visually depict the power remaining in a battery and sound an audible alarm once a preset voltage threshold has been reached.

Internal Combustion—Fuel flow infrastructure is necessary to transport the combustible liquid fuel from the storage tank to the powerplant. Common components include a servo for mechanical control of the engine throttle body, fuel delivery lines, fueling valve, fuel filter, and air filter. The fuel flow system, which is pressurized using output of the engine muffler exhaust, moves from the tank, through the flexible tubing and filter, up to the mechanically actuated throttle body, and into the engine; flow increases or decreases as the throttle is opened or closed. Telemetry sensors can be attached to the storage tank to monitor pressure and volume.

---

[34] Fuel storage and distribution is pressurized through a connection to the engine muffler.
[35] Oil provides lubrication.
[36] Nitro increases the effect of oxidizer.

▮ AVIONICS

Avionics are those electronic components used to communicate and process commanded control and telemetry, providing C3 for the Aerial Element. Control commands from the remote pilot on the ground are sent wirelessly to the Aerial Element; upon receipt, the system interprets the commanded signals into appropriate actuated control responses and executes the commands. Those systems capable of sensor data capture and communication actively monitor critical operating parameters, such as airspeed, orientation, location, heading, powerplant RPM, temperature, and fuel remaining, and communicate this information back to the remote pilot as telemetry. Avionics provide communication, processing, and actuation capabilities.

▶ Communications

Communication between the remote pilot and the Aerial Element is, at a minimum, mono-directional[37] (**uplink**); commanded control is sent from the ground control station (GCS) up to the Aerial Element for execution (*see* Figure 3-41). However, more complex systems incorporate bi-directional communications or multiple communication lines, on differing frequencies, to also send telemetry and captured payload data back to the GCS (**downlink**) to improve remote pilot situational awareness and subsequent commanded control decisions.[38] The majority of communication is achieved using digital format, but some systems use an analog format for transmission of visual and audio data, which are subject to increased interference and noise, are less complex, and can be viewed with simpler devices.

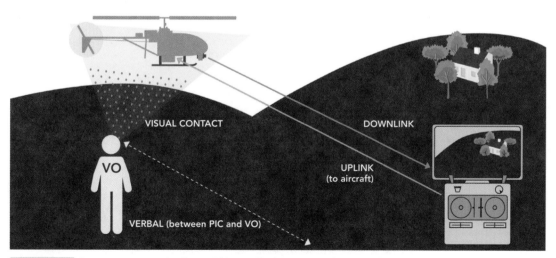

FIGURE 3-41. Common communications within an sUAS operational setting.

---

[37] One-way from ground up to aircraft.
[38] Telemetry: data reporting the state of the aircraft.

Important Concepts—Establishing and maintaining communication links is dependent on several important factors, which if not considered or properly addressed can lead to loss of signal and possibly loss of control.

Line of sight (propagation)[39]—Higher frequency radio waves (signal) follows a linear (straight line) pathway, which does not curve along the surface of the Earth. The resulting effect is referred to as radio horizon, where the signal is no longer able to maintain connection as it becomes blocked by the Earth. These signals can also be reflected or refracted by the atmosphere, further extending the range. Additionally, if the pathway between paired communication devices is blocked (occluded) by a terrain feature or object (including foliage), the signal may not be received (or will be degraded from such interference).

Beyond line-of-sight—Beyond line-of-sight (BLOS) communications and operations are possible using a repeater or relay affixed to another aircraft, vehicle, or fixed point to bridge the link around or over such features, including significant distances. Satellite communication systems represent a common BLOS communication mechanism to relay the transmitted signal from an orbital position. The use of a relay to maintain communications for BLOS is subject to the effects of **latency**, which may introduce significant delay into receipt of communicated messages. (A two-second delay or more is not uncommon for satellite communications.) A combination of localized, manual line-of-sight control to perform takeoff and recovery, and autonomy to automatically make flight corrections or follow preset instructions when communication is lost, is often used to overcome the detrimental effects of latency in long-distance BLOS operations.

Operational frequencies—Communication equipment used in the operation of sUAS in the United States typically uses 27 megahertz (MHz), 50 MHz (requires certification such as an Amateur Radio Operator License[40]), 53 MHz (requires certification), 72 MHz, and 2.4 GHz (using spread spectrum) frequency bands for control (uplink).[41] Those used for data, video, or audio (downlink) use industrial, scientific, and medical (ISM) bands, such as 900 MHz, 2.4 GHz, and 5.8 GHz.[42] Longer-wave (lower) frequencies (e.g., 900 MHz compared to 5.8 GHz) offer better penetration through foliage canopies, terrain features, and obstacles, but typically require use of a larger antenna.

---

[39] Line-of-sight and beyond line-of-sight, as used in this context, differs from the FAA requirement to maintain visual line-of-sight (VLOS) with the aircraft during operation, as this concept pertains to the subsequent linear pathway of radio waves as they perpetuate away from the source. These terms are differentiated throughout the text as LOS/BLOS and VLOS/BVLOS.

[40] In accordance with 47 Code of Federal Regulation (CFR) §97.215, Telecommand of model aircraft, an amateur station that is transmitting signals to control a model aircraft may be operated in the following manner: (1) Station identification is not required for transmissions directed only to the model aircraft; (2) if control signals are not considered to be codes or ciphers, intended to obscure the meaning of communication; and (3) the power of the TX does not exceed 1W. Many commonly available radio communications equipment may require an amateur radio operator's license to use.

[41] Note that 75 MHz is for use in surface models only. See the Academy of Model Aeronautics (AMA) Frequency Chart for Model Operation for further detail regarding available frequencies: www.modelaircraft.org/events/frequencies.aspx

[42] Operations on ISM bands commonly used for sUAS operations (902.0–928.0 MHz, 2.300–2.310 and 2.390–2.450 Ghz, and 5.650–5.925 GHz) are governed by FCC 47 CFR Part 15. See the National Association for Amateur Radio's comprehensive webpage, FCC Part-15 Rules: Unlicensed RF Devices, for further details: www.arrl.org/part-15-radio-frequency-devices

As dependence on wireless technology increases and a growing numbers of sUAS are introduced to the airspace, the amount of available frequencies and occurrence of EMI increases, while bandwidth decreases. This has been a well-publicized problem in the military UAS community, but has not received significant attention in domestic civil UAS discussions. The use of digital radios featuring spread spectrum and frequency hopping has helped to alleviate some of the problems encountered by the RC model aircraft community over the years, but this issue will need further consideration and mitigation in the future to prevent further complications and problems with the numerous anticipated sUAS operations.

Receiver—A receiver (RX) is a mono-directional, electronic communication device designed to wirelessly capture signals broadcast by a transmitter (TX) emitting a signal on the same frequency. It is coupled with an antenna or series of antennae (as a diversity receiver or through a multiplexer) and relies on use of a specific (discrete) frequency or range of frequencies. An RX installed in the Aerial Element is used to receive commanded actuation position, sensor manipulation, or autonomous operation parameters.[43] Paired combinations of TX/RX used in RC model aircraft operations are often referred to collectively as a radio.

Transmitter—A transmitter (TX) is an electronic communication device, paired with an RX or connected to multiple RXs on the same frequency, required to complete a mono-directional link. As with an RX, a TX also features coupling with an antenna (or multiple antennae) and reliance on a specific frequency or range of frequencies. A TX is typically used on the Aerial Element to broadcast telemetry and payload data (downlink) to a RX connected to the GCS. Use of a TX installed in the Aerial Element can improve situational awareness of the remote pilot by conveying critical aircraft state information; however, this comes at the cost of increased power consumption, weight, cost, and complexity.

Transceiver—A transceiver is a combination of a TX and RX that is capable of bidirectional communication with a TX, RX, or other transceivers. Transceivers are used to create and maintain either point-to-point or nodal mesh networked communications.[44] Mesh networks support expanded and redundant operations, reducing the potential for loss of signal and subsequent communications loss; they are typically used with multiple sUAS in BLOS operations to bridge communications over a terrain feature that would otherwise obscure line-of-sight between the GCS and the Aerial Element. A wireless RS-232 wireless serial data modem (*see* Figure 3-42) is an example of a transceiver commonly used to enable sUAS data communications.

FIGURE 3-42.
Example serial transceiver.

---

[43] Three-dimensional positional information, such as desired altitude, heading, and latitude/longitude.
[44] Point-to-point: Conventional bidirectional uplink/downlink between the aircraft and GCS.
Nodal mesh networked communication: Information is broadcast to nodes in range and then relayed throughout the entire network.

Multiplexer—A multiplexer is an electronic device that monitors the received signal strength indication (RSSI; signal strength) of several communication inputs (analog or digital) and selects the signal with the highest signal strength to forward onto the signal processing element (controller). A multiplexer is placed in-line between a group of RXs (each on differing frequencies or using different antenna types) and the signal processing element, or alternatively between a group of antennae and a single RX. The use of a multiplexer increases the likelihood of signal receipt, and subsequent prevention of loss of signal, but it increases power consumption, weight, cost, and complexity of the system.

Antennae—Antennae (or singular antenna) are used to receive and transmit information. An antenna captures and converts radio waves into an electrical signal, which, when connected to the input of a RX or transceiver (capture), provides critical information and commands to the onboard controller. Likewise, they can also be used to convert and broadcast electrical signals into radio waves when connected to the output of a TX or transceiver (broadcast). Antennae are available in a variety of configurations, designed to emit (radiate) and receive signals in specific directions and patterns.

Omnidirectional—This type of antenna emits a signal in multiple directions to provide broader coverage, at a cost of reduced strength and range. The conventional **whip** (vertical) antenna, used in the majority of RC model aircraft RXs, and the common **dipole** (horizontal) antenna are examples of omnidirectional antennae. The radiated signal patterns of omnidirectional tend to appear ovoid along several axes, producing a spherical, donut-shaped coverage area.[45] However, circular polarized antenna, such as cloverleaf, produce a helix-shaped pattern that rotates relative to a pronounced linear path, combining the beneficial attributes of conventional omnidirectional with directional.[46] Cloverleaf antennas have become very popular among sUAS users, especially for FPV.

Directional—This type of antenna emits a pronounced linear signal along a specific axis and within a focused beam pattern. A Yagi-uda, phased array (patch), and parabolic dish represent common forms of directional antennae used in sUAS communications. Due to the limited beamwidth, directional antennae are more effective when combined with a tracking base to orient the antenna broadcast/receipt axis in the direction corresponding to the alternate device (Aerial Element or GCS).[47]

❱ Processing

Commanded control parameters are typically communicated in a digital format that must be interpreted by a controller and conveyed to a specific component (actuation, internal sensor, or payload). Command of each component is tied to a specific channel or input/output pathway (command in, translated control out). Actuation components, such as servos, require a signal

---

[45] Shape of signal propagation can be more pronounced in one of the axes.

[46] Despite directional attributes, cloverleaf antenna are still classified as omnidirectional.

[47] The need to reorient the transmission axis tends to limit the use of most directional antennae to the GCS alone, due to size, power consumption, and weight gains. However, it is possible to use directional antenna featuring wider beam widths, such as a phased array, without a tracking base through integration with a multiplexer and other antennae. Such a combination would increase the ability to broadcast and receive critical communication signals. However, this approach may not be suitable for simple, low-cost, smaller sUAS.

in a specific format and range to move the component to a specific position (e.g., rotation of a servo arm to a position on its arc). Processing of inputs (commanded or captured values) and outputs (translated values) requires a controller (hardware), software, and the mapping of the input/output (I/O) structure.

Controller—The interpretation of commanded control signals requires the use of a specialized component, either a servo receiver or a microcontroller. These devices are designed to accept and read incoming commands and translate them into appropriate analog or digital outputs, sent to the actuation components to make applicable mechanical changes (e.g., control surface movements, powerplant RPM changes, or payload reorientation).

Servo receiver—This component, common in RC model aircraft platforms, is a combination RX and servo control board with a set number of actuator outputs (channels) used to support mono-directional communication on a specific frequency range. A servo RX (*see* Figure 3-43) features a series of three-pin servo output ports mapped to specific channels.[48] A two-pin power input port provides the electrical power required to operate the RX (communication and signal processing) and connected actuators. Servo RX are easy to configure, widely available, inexpensive, and feature relatively low power consumption, but their communication range is significantly limited without modification and they can only operate mono-directionally (receive only).

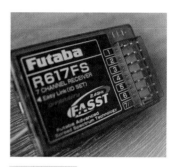

FIGURE 3-43.

Example COTS servo receiver.

Microcontroller—This small electronic computational device is designed to perform complex calculation, processing, and monitoring with low power consumption in an embeddable form factor (it can be integrated discreetly into complex devices). Microcontrollers have functionality that approaches that of a personal computer (PC), with some able to provide the same level as older, legacy PC systems (and their performance continues to increase with microminiaturization advances). They feature a CPU, memory (volatile and nonvolatile), a series of general-purpose input/output (GPIO; configurable as input or output), an analog-to-digital converter (ADC), and a serial communication port; more complex microcontrollers include electrical power conversion, a digital-to-analog converter (DAC), and additional communication ports, such as USB and I2C.

Microcontrollers have been used significantly in robotics as they provide the capability to monitor and process analog and digital sensor inputs, process commanded inputs, calculate responses, output analog or digital signals to control actuation, and communicate with other devices, such as the GCS and/or more complex sensors. To work effectively in the Aerial Element, these devices must be paired with a dedicated data communication component, such as a transceiver and a corresponding PC or microcontroller incorporated into the GCS. Even relatively simple-to-operate COTS sUAS commonly feature the integration of microcontrollers, but these systems tend to limit the programmability or reconfiguration to maintain an intuitive and simple operating paradigm. An autopilot is an example of a control system with a

---

[48] The interface between specific actuators on the aircraft and controls on the handheld TX.

FIGURE 3-44.

Arduino Uno microcontroller.

design architecture focused around a microcontroller, such as the Arduino Uno (*see* Figure 3-44), providing the ability to capture commanded (remote pilot) and perceived (sensor) inputs to build a dynamic model of the operating environment and state of the aircraft, which is used with programmed logical routines to determine and execute appropriate automatic (automated) responses.

Software—Software represents the logical programming developed and installed onto computational hardware, such as a microcontroller or PC, to provide functionality and support for the intended operation of the device. Software can be already loaded onto a device (with no user configuration required), require installation and setup, or be developed (programmed) specifically by the user to provide the desired functionality. Several designations of software are applicable to sUAS design.

Firmware—This lower-level software is stored on non-volatile memory and used to provide functionality for hardware, serving as a low-overhead operating system (OS). Firmware can also be executed on devices that run an alternative OS (e.g., BIOS on a PC during initialization) and is updateable with the proper interface (e.g., USB or RS-232 port). Firmware is common in sUAS electronics, such as servo RX, TX, ESCs, transceivers, and complex sensors, with the complexity varying significantly depending on the device and its inherent capabilities.

Embedded—This lower-level software is similar to firmware, but it is designed to be the only software loaded and executed on a device, serving as the sole real-time OS.

Proprietary—This license type for COTS software packages represents applications or code that is purchased for a fee and/or requires acceptance of an operational agreement limiting how the software is to be used. In most cases the software is already compiled and not editable, to protect the intellectual property of the manufacturer. However, some manufacturers create an application programming interface (API), software development kit (SDK), or link library that enables a programmer to develop their own code and import proprietary functionality, for a fee and/or acceptance of an operational agreement.[49] An example of proprietary software used in sUAS is the DJI **Onboard SDK** and associated **API**, which provides developers with the capability to access, monitor, and control a DJI sUAS using a PC running their own custom-developed software application.

Open source—This license type represents software packages or examples that are freely and widely distributed, developed collaboratively, and often available from repositories online. APIs, SDKs, and link libraries can also be produced as open source code. An example of open source software used commonly in sUAS is **ArduPilot**, which was collaboratively developed in 2007 by members of the **DIYdrones.com** online user forum; it can be downloaded for free and modified (as needed) by developers for use in their own sUAS designs.

---

[49] APIs, SDKs, and link libraries are programming language dependent. In most cases, an interface layer (wrapper) can be developed in that interface language to provide interoperability with an application written in another language. However, this may result in loss of fidelity or inability to replicate full functionality.

Custom developed—This designation represents software designed and written by an individual or group that does not conform to the proprietary or open source designations. It represents code or applications that have not been published or shared beyond the original developer or a customer, including collaborative group members or employees. Custom-developed software is commonly used in prototyping efforts to demonstrate a concept or build an application to achieve specific functionality. It can be interfaced with proprietary, open source, or other custom developed code. This level of programming typically requires in-depth knowledge of a coding language, system architecture, and operational constraints. Coding languages commonly used in custom-developed software for sUAS include Java, C, C++, C#, and Python.[50] Each language has its own set of semantics, applicable integrated development environment (IDE), and compiler.

Inputs/Outputs—I/O represents the directed flow of data signals or electrical current among the architected components, relative to the total system. Inputs are those pathways directed toward an assembly (e.g., commanded control signals to a microcontroller), while outputs are the resultant pathways out of the assembly (e.g., resultant control signals to servo). The typical inputs to a bidirectional Aerial Element-C3 subsystem include:

- commanded control (synchronous from GCS:[51] pitch, roll, yaw, powerplant RPM/collective, flaps, and gear retraction)
- automated response settings (asynchronous from GCS:[52] waypoint positions, altitude/heading hold, and geofencing parameters)
- internal sensor signals (orientation, airspeed, powerplant RPM, temperature, pressure altitude, three-dimensional position, and actuation positions)
- payload sensor signals depicting the operating environment (camera view, ultrasonic, or radar/LiDAR profile)[53]

The typical outputs include:

- actuation signals (synchronous, to servos/ESC; e.g., fixed-wing, changes to elevator, rudder, ailerons, flaps, powerplant RPM, and landing gear position)
- telemetry data (synchronous, to GCS; internal sensor values)
- payload data (synchronous or asynchronous, to GCS; payload sensor values).

Microcontrollers have a finite set of I/O ports used for digital or analog connections, with at least one connection for serial communications. In many cases these ports can be configured for either input or output (GPIO) to accommodate use with a variety of sensors and actuators.

---

[50] Microcontroller programming is typically written in an assembly language, C, or a C-derivative.
[51] Synchronous commands must be executed immediately, in real time due to the nature of commanded results. The introduction of latency into such commands could result in loss of control and subsequent crash or mishap.
[52] Asynchronous commands do not require immediate real-time execution.
[53] Payload sensor values are not typically routed as an input through a microcontroller, unless onboard processing and compression is required to reduce the size of the data packet.

▶ Actuation

Actuation represents the mechanical process to move a component, such as changing the deflection of a control surface or increasing the throttle of an internal combustion engine. Actuators are provided a command signal using a signal wire (third wire, in addition to +/- power connections), over which a pulse width modulation (PWM) signal is transmitted (every 20 milliseconds). Three types of actuators are used in sUAS: rotational servos, linear actuators, and electronic speed controls.

Rotational Servos—These are small, geared motor assemblies that provide up to a 180-degree rotation of a disc or control arm, which is connected to a push rod to achieve linear motion. While rotation is usually between 0 and 180 degrees (centered at 90 degrees), manufacturers have produced some continuous rotation servos, but these servos tend to be impractical for use in sUAS. The resting center position of the servo can be offset using trim controls, which change the relative center of the servo movement compared to the control input (TX joystick). Rotational servos are widely available in several sizes, including micro (*see* Figure 3-45), standard, and giant (1/4 scale).

Linear Actuators—Linear actuators are larger assemblies featuring the translation of a high RPM motor into linear motion (push-pull) using a screw-driven geared mechanism. Their use can reduce the mechanical complexity of linkages within the aircraft, improve mechanical efficiency, and provide a constant velocity, but the size of linear actuators is prohibitive to their use in smaller, lightweight platforms.

Electronic Speed Controls—ESCs were introduced previously in the Power Storage and Distribution section earlier in this chapter. While solid-state ESCs (*see* Figure 3-46) do not produce mechanical motion to change motor RPMs, the PWM signal sent to the ESC is the same used for all other actuators. Alternatively, there are instances of mechanically driven speed controls, which require the use of a servo to move a potentiometer governing current flow from the battery to the motor.

▶ Telemetry

Telemetry represents the data used to determine critical operational parameters of the Aerial Element, captured from sensors mounted throughout the airframe and within components. The processing of sensor data, including telemetry and payload, can be performed on the aircraft using the primary controller or a dedicated computational device, at the GCS, or after the flight; the approach is typically dependent on the volume and detail of data collected. When processed on board or at the GCS, synchronously, it is referred to as **real-time processing**. When data are stored on a data logger or processed asynchronously using further calibration, filtering, and categorization routines, it is referred to as **post-processing**. Post-processing tends to provide higher fidelity and accuracy based on the availability of computational resources, routines, and time to process.

If data are real-time processed on the Aerial Element, the size of the data stream sent to the GCS via downlink is smaller, but the resulting product may be limited due to the available computational power of the equipment. In some cases, it may be preferable to send the raw

FIGURE 3-45. Micro hobby servo.

FIGURE 3-46. 35A electronic speed control.

data directly to the GCS for processing to use the greater resources of equipment on the ground, or log and store the data for processing after the operation. An alternative strategy employed in many FPV configurations is to place an on-screen-display (OSD) board between the telemetry sensors and the visual sensor (FPV camera) TX; the OSD overlays the telemetry data overtop of the analog visual imagery stream, which is transmitted down to the GCS for display, reducing the need for a separate TX/RX pair. The disadvantage with this setup is that the data must be logged on board the Aerial Element or it may not be available for analysis later, since it was sent using an analog format (overtop of the visual imagery).

Sensors used to capture state, orientation, and location and are classified in accordance to purpose and format.

Proprioceptive—These sensors are used to measure the internal status and orientation of the Aerial Element and its components to determine the state of the system. The following are examples of proprioceptive sensors used in sUAS:[54]

- Encoder
- Gyro
- Accelerometer
- Inertial measurement unit (IMU)
- Strain gauge
- Flex gauge
- Vibration sensor
- Voltage/current sensor
- Magnetometer (compass)
- GPS
- Temperature sensor
- Contact sensor

---

[54] Some sensors can be designated as either proprioceptive or exteroceptive; the distinction is made in their application. If used for measuring the internal state of the system, they are designated as proprioceptive, but if used to determine the proximity or relationship to the external environment, they are exteroceptive.

FIGURE 3-48. Aerial imagery capture using IR sensor.

FIGURE 3-47. VTOL sUAS carrying payload.

Exteroceptive—These sensors are used to measure the relationship between the Aerial Element and the operational environment to determine the relative position (proximity) of the aircraft to the Earth and critical terrain features. Payload sensors are often exteroceptive sensors. The following are examples of exteroceptive sensors used in sUAS:

- Range (distance) sensor
- Visual sensor
- Contact sensor
- Environmental temperature sensor
- Pressure sensor
- Humidity sensor
- Geiger counter

Sensor Power and Format—Sensors used in sUAS can require varying degrees of power and can output their signals to convey results either in an analog or digital format. **Active sensors** require the emission of energy to operate,[55] and they tend to produce highly accurate readings, but increase power consumption, weight, cost, and complexity. **Passive sensors** are simpler and do not require emitted energy to make measurements (they use ambient energy in the environment), but can be subject to reduced accuracy and interference. **Analog sensors** convey information by varying signal voltage in a specific range, such as 0–5 V (e.g., potentiometer), and are connected to analog inputs on a microcontroller for conversion (ADC). Processing can convey a broad range of values, but producing an accurate and exact value can be difficult due to inherent noise and EMI (filters and shielding can help to reduce noise, but may not always eliminate it). **Digital sensors** convey information using discrete values, on or off (e.g., contact switch), and are connected to digital inputs on a microcontroller; they produce clean, easy-to-interpret results, but may not convey the same level of information (fidelity) as analog sensors.

---

[55] Reflection of propagated energy, such as heat, light, sound, or radio waves is measured.

PAYLOAD

Transport and operation of a payload (*see* Figure 3-47) represents one of the primary purposes of an sUAS, besides platform-specific training or familiarization. The configuration and balanced loading of the Aerial Element must account for the incorporation of the payload, whether to remotely capture imagery or disperse pesticides over a crop. While the payload is a critical component of the Aerial Element, it has been elevated to a standalone element in the total system architecture based on its complexity and specific alignment to the sUAS's application. An Aerial Element configuration does not always call for integration of the same payload for every function; as such, many payloads can be swapped for alternative assemblies or options.

The following subsections contain example payload options used in support of common sUAS operations, including remote sensing, aerial application, and cargo delivery missions. (Further detail regarding specific types of applications can be found in Chapter 2.)

■ REMOTE SENSING

Remote sensing represents the most common use of sUAS, including intelligence, surveillance, and reconnaissance (ISR); infrastructure inspection; mapping and surveying; and environmental/weather monitoring. These applications tend to require the unobtrusive gathering of exteroceptive data from a specific area or environment.

▶ Electro-optical

Electro-optical (EO) visual imaging sensors are used to capture various emitted, absorbed, or reflected energy across the electromagnetic spectrum, including visible, infrared (IR), and ultraviolet (UV). These sensors can be passive or active, and are typically categorized by the wavelength range captured. EO can be further subdivided and categorized by spectrum coverage provided.

Visual—These sensors are designed to capture red, green, and blue (RGB) light in the visual range (380–700 nanometers [nm]) and are the least complex and most widely available visual capture devices. They include passive standard and high definition cameras, such as charged coupled device (CCD) and complementary metal oxide semiconductor (CMOS) sensors. Visual sensors are useful in daytime applications to depict the scene (view) from the aircraft's elevated perspective.

Ultraviolet—These sensors are designed to capture imagery in the UV range (10–380 nm) to improve the resolution and depiction of surface topology or detect high-voltage (corona) discharge. UV sensors are especially useful to support infrastructure inspection and mapping and surveying applications.

IR—These sensors are designed to capture imagery in the IR range (700 nm–1 mm) to contrast thermal signatures of objects in view. IR sensors are especially useful in low light conditions to identify and track objects that do not visually contrast with the environment, and to locate thermally active (hot) spots (*see* Figure 3-48). The cost and size of IR sensors has decreased significantly in recent years, making them well-suited to integration and use in sUAS.

FIGURE 3-49. Imagery generated using SAR captured data.

Multi/Hyperspectral—Multispectral sensors are used to capture three to ten bands across the electromagnetic spectrum, with each band captured by a radiometer. Similarly, hyperspectral sensors use an imaging spectrometer for the capture of many narrower bands (200+, each 10–20 nm wide). The imagery captured using these tools are used to identify spectral signatures of objects, supporting applications such as natural resource exploration, environmental impact analysis, and nuclear, biological, and chemical (NBC) monitoring.

❯ Signal Emission and Return Measurement

These active sensors radiate energy, such as radio waves or light, and observe the subsequent reflection to generate an accurate rendering of the topology and spatial relationships (relative distances). They are commonplace in larger aircraft, but their availability and use in sUAS has begun increasing in recent years due to microminiaturization and technological advancements.

Radar—Radio detection and ranging (RADAR, or radar), including beam-scanning and synthetic aperture radar (SAR), relies on the controlled emission (continuous or pulsed) and observed reflection of radio waves (signal) as they interact with features and objects in an environment. It can be used to determine the range (linear distance), direction, shape, and speed of objects relative to the sensor (*see* Figure 3-49). Processing accounts for the inherent direction and speed of the aircraft using inertial navigation telemetry. Radar provides the ability to identify potential the trajectory and/or relative position (distance and direction) of objects, terrain, or weather, despite being visually occluded (unable to be seen). However, radar consumes significant power, requires processing, and adds considerable weight. Advances have been made to decrease the size and power requirements of radar for use in sUAS, with one such prototype weighing 0.33 pounds with a power consumption of 4.5 W (5–6 VDC).

LiDAR—Light detection and ranging (LiDAR) operates much like radar, except it uses pulsed light (generated using UV, visible, and near-IR lasers) instead of radio waves. The observed reflection of the light is captured and processed in combination with inertial navigation telemetry data to determine the relative position of sensed objects, including terrain features. The fidelity of LiDAR tends to be much greater than that of radar, making it well suited for the mapping of fixed objects and terrain.

▶ Direct Measurement

Direct measurement payloads are designed to sample the air of the operational environment to identify characteristics or determine the presence of specific traits. Unmanned aircraft platforms, such as sUAS, are well suited to performing direct measurement of atmospheric conditions based on their low risk profile, ability to stay aloft for significant periods, reduced volume of disturbed air, flexibility in re-tasking and reorientation, reduced cost and complexity, and low emissions. These payloads are useful in performing environmental observation, emergency response, weather monitoring, and research applications.

Gaseous—Air sampling sensors or instruments are used to capture and analyze gases from an environment, including the atmosphere. The sample is captured and either stored for later analysis (post-processed) or analyzed in real-time (processed) to determine the composition and presence of specific compounds, elements, or particles, such as ozone, carbon dioxide, or radiation.

Particulate Matter—These payloads work similarly to gaseous air sampling, but instead of gases, the sampling is focused on the capture of microscopic matter suspended in the atmosphere.

Meteorological—The study and analysis of weather phenomena features the use of specialized sensors to capture the temperature, pressure, and moisture content (humidity) of the atmosphere; visibility; and speed and direction of wind. The collected data tends to be smaller than that produced by complex sensors (visual or spectrometers), which supports incorporation into the telemetry data packet for communication to the GCS via downlink.[56] Unmanned aircraft have been used to fly through severe weather events, such as tropical storms and hurricanes, to gather data that otherwise would present a risk to manned operators.

▶ Related Components

There are several components useful to supplement or improve the operation of the described payloads. The addition of these components increases power consumption, weight, and complexity and may impact the air handling and performance characteristics of the Aerial Element.

---

[56] Complex sensors, such as radiometers, may require significantly more processing and therefore may not be suitable for integration of total output into communicated telemetry. Sampling may provide a valuable indication of observations that can be transmitted real-time to the GCS for display, reducing the total bandwidth needed.

FIGURE 3-50. sUAS platforms featuring incorporation of a gimbal.

Gimbal—A gimbal is used to stabilize, reorient (point), and house visual sensors (*see* Figure 3-50). In larger systems, it can provide mounting points for multiple sensors and typically features an aerodynamic covering, but in smaller systems the developer may limit mounting options to a single sensor and forgo the covering to simplify and reduce weight. Gimbals used in sUAS provide either 2-DOF (pitch and yaw) or 3-DOF (pitch, roll, and yaw) rotation using electric actuators.

Dedicated Power Source—An alternative power source, dedicated to the sensor or payload, may be included to reduce the potential draw on the critical power required for operation of the aircraft. While employing such a strategy adds more complexity and weight, it enables the Aerial Element to continue to maintain control and thrust generation capability after the payload has exhausted its power.

Dedicated Control—An alternative computation device dedicated to the control and processing of payload sensor data may be included to prevent further taxation of the primary controller. Use of such a device supports the separation of mission-critical calculations performed by the primary controller from non-critical payload processing requests, eliminating the need for a processing prioritization schema, increased computational resources, or use of an input connection to the primary controller.

▪ AERIAL APPLICATION

Aerial application represents a significantly growing use of sUAS. Supporting such use requires fitting specialized components on the Aerial Element to transport and control the release of consumable materials.

▶ Pesticide/Growing Agent Application

The application of pesticides and growing agents (fertilizers) using UAS (precision agriculture) has been widely demonstrated in other countries (such as Japan) where land and resources are scarce and the topography unlevel (e.g., terraced agricultural land or steep grades). However, such sUAS applications have only recently been undertaken domestically, in an exploratory (R&D) fashion. VTOL rotary-wing tend to represent the majority of sUAS platforms used for this purpose, due to the high lift-to-weight ratio, translation/hover flight ability, and generation of desirable downwash to further distribute spray mixture. These capabilities make such platforms well suited to covering smaller and/or difficult-to-reach tracts/plots. sUAS can provide improved cost-effectiveness for the targeted application of liquid mixtures, where and when needed, as opposed to large distribution over an entire crop (i.e., blanket spraying). Aerial spraying payloads include the mixture (water and chemical component), storage tank, spray pump and speed controller, delivery lines, multiple boom arms, and spray nozzles (multiple possible spray patterns).

◗ Cloud Seeding

Cloud seeding represents inducing cloud condensation and subsequent precipitation over a specific location using aerial dispersants (silver iodide or dry ice). It can be used to reduce the formation of fog or hail, or increase the formation of rain and snow (to combat the effects of drought), and it has been further postulated that cloud seeding may assist to counteract the effects of artificially induced climate change. Payloads supporting cloud seeding include dry ice dispensers, ejected flares, and miniaturized acetone generators (to burn silver iodide).

◗ Fuel Transfer

The transfer of fuel among manned aircraft has become commonplace in military operations and was first demonstrated between two large UAS (Global Hawks) in 2012. Aerial refueling of an electrically powered sUAS using a laser and a solar cell was also demonstrated in 2012, indicating the possibility for sustained operation up to 48 hours. Additionally, the docking of an sUAS with an aerial refueling system (using LEDs and IR sensors) was demonstrated in 2015. While there are no current examples of aerial fuel transfer from sUAS to sUAS, the further development of emissive and inductive power transfer technologies may make such applications practical in the near future.

◼ CARGO DELIVERY

The use of sUAS to deliver cargo has received significant attention, in large part because of the publicized efforts of companies such as Amazon (Prime Air), which are working to achieve the rapid delivery of purchased goods, autonomously, to a customer's home. Others, such as DHL, FedEx, and Google, are also exploring the use of sUAS to deliver critical supplies, tools, or materials rapidly, with reduced overhead and time constraints compared to conventional delivery. The capabilities of sUAS support a wide variety of cargo delivery applications, such as emergency response, logistics, search and rescue, and tactical resupply. The practical requirements lead many developers to consider larger (Group 2) platforms capable of VTOL flight, as they can carry a significant amount of weight; takeoff/land in small, enclosed areas; execute quick, precise maneuvers; and stay aloft for 30 or more minutes (endurance). Cargo delivery payload includes the transported cargo, as well as any mechanisms/sensors required to monitor, release, and confirm successful delivery.

GROUND-BASED COMMAND, CONTROL, AND COMMUNICATION (C3)

A remote pilot's interaction with controls on the ground determines the operational response of the Aerial Element and associated payload; the **Ground-based C3 Element** (i.e., GCS) provides the critical interface to support and maintain this control. Simple GCS options provide the infrastructure necessary to accept commanded control instructions, while more complex options also present aircraft orientation, state, and location information (telemetry); depict processed payload data (e.g., the visual scene); and convey important feedback to influence the remote pilot's future control commands. Ground-based C3 includes communications and controls, with integrated processing and power storage and distribution.

▌COMMUNICATION

Communication is the critical link between the remote pilot and the Aerial Element, used to convey executable control commands to the aircraft and receive state, orientation, location, and payload data from the aircraft.

▶ Communication Components

The assemblies, devices, and mechanisms used to support communications were presented and discussed earlier, as they relate to the Aerial Element. Those aircraft-based components have counterparts, integrated into the GCS, used to complete the connection with the remote pilot.

Receiver—A GCS RX receives telemetry and payload data (via downlink) from the Aerial Element. Use of a RX, coupled with appropriate GCS displays, can improve the situational awareness of the remote pilot by depicting critical aircraft state information as it is received (preferably in real-time). Simpler C3 options, such as handheld controls, may forgo the inclusion of a telemetry RX and display; instead, it may use a data logger on board the aircraft to store the information for later review, or rely solely on visual observation.

Transmitter—A GCS TX (or handheld control) is used to broadcast the commanded control instructions processed and executed by the Aerial Element (via uplink). The output power size, capabilities, and power consumption of a ground-based TX tend to be greater than that of the Aerial Element TX, based on the availability of greater resources at the GCS.

Transceiver—A transceiver is used in more complex systems to save power and weight, while reducing the footprint of the Ground-based C3 Element.

Multiplexer—A multiplexer is used in more complex and costly systems to improve the redundancy of the system design, reducing the potential for loss of signal.

Antennae—Antennae used for GCS communications can usually be much larger than their counterparts installed on the Aerial Element. Some systems use several in combination with a multiplexer and additional RXs. Additionally, it is much more practical to install a 3-DOF tracking base on a GCS than on the aircraft, based on the availability of greater resources and footprint area at the GCS.

FIGURE 3-51. Example handheld controls.

USER CONTROLS

The remote pilot user controls for sUAS vary significantly, including the form, purpose, and mapping schema used to correlate user inputs to commands, which are communicated to the Aerial Element. User controls provide the tangible connection between the remote pilot and total system (sUAS), feature a mix of physical components and software-based graphical user interfaces (GUIs), and are commonly referred to as a human-machine-interface (HMI). GCS and the associated HMI can be categorized as handheld, man-portable, trailerable, or fixed-base. In more complex systems, control can be transferred among control options as needed (e.g., handheld to fixed-base).

Handheld

Handheld controls provide extremely portable, lightweight options for manipulation and command of the Aerial Element, integrating the GCS TX with user controls into a single device. While such an option provides versatility and ease of transport, the use of handheld control produces inherent limitations that affect remote pilot interaction with the system, such as decreased manipulation (interoperability), reduced control fidelity, and limited to no data display or feedback. More complex handheld options replace the TX with a transceiver to also capture telemetry for limited display to the remote pilot, at the cost of increased controller complexity, weight, and power consumption. There are several types of handheld controls used for the operation of sUAS: conventional, FPV, and smart devices.

Conventional—Conventional handheld controls are commonly used for the operation of RC model aircraft or consumer sUAS and provide remote pilot control through manipulation of physical mechanisms, such as analog joysticks, knobs, buttons, switches, and sliders (*see* Figure 3-51). More complex options include very limited GUIs for display of calibration and configuration parameters for six or more channels (each mapped to a corresponding actuator installed

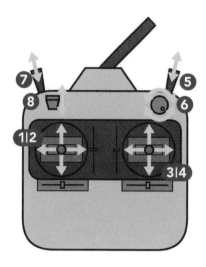

FIGURE 3-52.

Conventional flight control, depicting mapping for fixed-wing mode 1.

on the Aerial Element), while the simplest options are limited to three channels (pitch, yaw, and throttle). These controls are typically provided with entry-level, amateur-built, or non-commercially developed sUAS that do not require telemetry or feedback for operation.[57]

Control types—The following represent controls found on many conventional handheld controllers:

- *Analog joysticks*—Provides up/down and left/right motion; controlled with thumbs or fingertips
- *Momentary pushbuttons*—Activates when depressed, deactivates when released
- *Toggle switch*—Moves between set positions, and holds setting until manually changed; can be either two position (single pole single throw [SPST]) or three position (single pole double throw [SPDT])
- *Rotary switch*—Rotates to increase or decrease a commanded actuator position
- *Slider*—Slides up/down or left/right to increase or decrease a commanded actuator position

Control mapping—Each radio channel provides control for a specific actuated component; four common mapping modes (1–4) are used in conventional handheld controls.[58] Table 3-4 depicts common control maps, designated by modes, channels, and aircraft control type (*see* Figure 3-52):[59]

---

[57] Some handheld controls do feature telemetry or visualization; however, it is not necessarily required to operate the system.

[58] Modes 1 and 2 are the most prevalent in conventional handheld controls. Many TX manufacturers provide the capability to reconfigure the operational mode.

[59] While it is possible to use a conventional handheld helicopter radio (TX/RX) to operate a fixed-wing aircraft, it is not possible to use a fixed-wing radio with a helicopter. The helicopter-specific radio features unique control mapping (automatic mixing for the CCPM) and programmable functions that cannot be replicated in a fixed-wing controller. It is recommended that radios designed for specific aircraft types only be used with those configurations identified as supported by the manufacturer.

TABLE 3-4. CONTROL MAPPING FOR CONVENTIONAL HANDHELD CONTROLS (*see figure 3-52*)

MODE 1 (channels 1-4)		
	LEFT analog joystick	**RIGHT analog joystick**
UP / DOWN	pitch (elevator/longitudinal cyclic)	thrust generation (throttle/collective)[60]
LEFT / RIGHT	yaw (rudder/tail rotor)	roll (aileron/lateral cyclic)

MODE 2 (channels 1-4)		
	LEFT analog joystick	**RIGHT analog joystick**
UP / DOWN	thrust generation (throttle/collective)	pitch (elevator/longitudinal cyclic)
LEFT / RIGHT	yaw (rudder/tail rotor)	roll (aileron/lateral cyclic)

MODE 3 (channels 1-4)		
	LEFT analog joystick	**RIGHT analog joystick**
UP / DOWN	pitch (elevator/longitudinal cyclic)	thrust generation (throttle/collective)
LEFT / RIGHT	roll (aileron/lateral cyclic)	yaw (rudder/tail rotor)

MODE 4 (channels 1-4)		
	LEFT analog joystick	**RIGHT analog joystick**
UP / DOWN	thrust generation (throttle/collective)	pitch (elevator/longitudinal cyclic)
LEFT / RIGHT	roll (aileron/lateral cyclic)	yaw (rudder/tail rotor)

FIXED-WING (channels 5-8)[61]	
CHANNEL 5	(SPST switch, up/down)—retractable landing gear
CHANNEL 6	(rotary dial)—flaps (retracted/extended)
CHANNEL 7	(SPDT switch, up/center/down)—unused/custom
CHANNEL 8	(SPDT switch, up/center/down)—unused/custom

ROTARY-WING (channels 5-8)[62]	
CHANNEL 5	(SPST switch, up/down)—rate mode/heading hold
CHANNEL 6	(SPST switch, up/down)—throttle hold
CHANNEL 7	(SPDT switch, up/center/down)—unused/custom
CHANNEL 8	(SPDT switch, up/center/down)—unused/custom

---

[60] For CCPM rotary-wing, this channel is combined with a component channel (5 or 6) to provide separate, fine adjustment and control of powerplant RPMs during operation. The analog joystick is used to input the primary commanded response of collective/powerplant, while the component channel is for adjustment.

[61] Fixed-wing sUAS require at least three channels for operation: pitch, yaw, and throttle; all other channels (4+) are supplemental to improve maneuverability or increase functionality.

[62] Non-CCPM rotary-wing sUAS require at least four channels for operation: pitch, roll, collective, and yaw. All other channels (5+) are supplemental to improve performance or increase functionality. CCPM typically require at least six channels (separate controls for operation and adjustment of collective pitch, powerplant, and gyro).

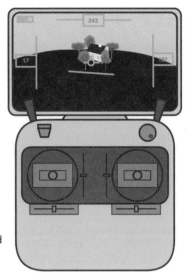

FIGURE 3-53. Smart device configurations: (A) standalone and (B) paired with conventional controls to provide FPV display.

Unused channels on a TX (those not required for flight operation) are often mapped to unique peripheral components or functions on the sUAS, such as pitch or yaw control of a payload camera or custom actuation.

FPV—FPV provides enhanced situational awareness through display of visual feedback and the environmental scene as viewed from the Aerial Element (*see* Figure 3-53A). The view, captured using visual sensors, is depicted either on a small monitor incorporated into the handheld control (built in or bolted on) or inside head-mounted displays (HMDs)/video-goggles.[63] Incorporating FPV into a handheld control can significantly increase its complexity, weight, and power consumption; many FPV controls also feature inclusion of an on-screen display (OSD), a dedicated battery to power the display, and a neck strap to offset and redistribute the increased weight.

Smart Device—This configuration builds on the FPV concept depicting the remote visual scene by also providing a high degree of customization and computational capability using portable electronics, such as smartphones and tablets. By taking advantage of the touchscreen display and computational resources, the GUI and HMI can be expanded to provide improved functionality and user interoperability. The device can be used standalone or combined with a dedicated handheld controller or conventional control to display FPV and telemetry information to the remote pilot (see Figure 3-53B). This control configuration is becoming more commonplace, increasingly featured in many "prosumer" multirotor sUAS options.

❱ Man-Portable

Man-portable controls represent small GCS easily transported and set up quickly (one to two-person lift) (*see* Figure 3-54). They often feature multiple assemblies, integrated to provide

---

[63] Used to improve visibility in bright environments; very difficult to perceive the environment outside the HMD.

FIGURE 3-54. Examples of man-portable UAS control equipment.

expanded and improved functionality compared to handheld controls. Man-portable GCS improve the interoperability between a remote pilot and the system, but they also are increasingly more complex, have a larger operational footprint, and consume greater power. These user controls are typically provided with higher-end COTS sUAS options or developed in connection to prototype technology demonstration systems that require more in-depth remote pilot interaction and depiction of feedback (payload sensors and telemetry) during operation. They feature the use of small handheld gaming controllers or more complex joysticks, throttles, and physical buttons/switches, combined with expanded GUIs.

▶ Trailerable GCS

Trailerable GCS represent a significantly larger C3 infrastructure with greater computational resources, display capabilities, power generation and storage, as well as seating, multiple-remote-pilot interfaces/stations, and ambient environmental controls (e.g., air conditioning and lighting) (see Figure 3-55). The HMI typically replicates capabilities of manned aircraft (flight stick/cyclic/yoke, pedals, and throttle quadrant with flaps and component controls). These Ground-based C3 options tend to be very expensive, produced and operated by government agencies or researchers, and paired with very complex platforms.

FIGURE 3-55. An example of a trailer-based GCS.

❯ Fixed-Base GCS

Fixed-base GCS are very similar to trailerable GCS; the primary differences are that fixed-base GCS lack portability, have no need for independent power generation (although backup, stored power is suggested), and have an increased footprint for antennae and other components. As with trailerable GCS, fixed-base GCS tend to be very expensive, produced and operated by government agencies or researchers, and paired with very complex platforms.

HUMAN ELEMENT

The **Human Element** plays an essential part of the successful operation and configuration of an sUAS. Before setting out to purchase a new sUAS or integrate a system already in inventory, it is crucial to understand how the operation will be performed and who will handle the various duties. Is the system simple and intuitive to operate, requiring minimal personnel to meet FAA regulations, or is it extremely complicated with components and functions that require multiple experts trained to handle various technical challenges that may arise? Will personnel perform the duties and responsibilities associated with several roles, or will someone be required to handle each independently? What level of training and experience should each crewmember have? For details regarding regulatory requirements for certification, operation, and training, see Chapter 4. Understanding the roles and responsibilities of typical crewmembers and how they relate to the operation requirements and limitations of an sUAS (as previously presented and discussed) will help you address these and other similar considerations.

◼ REMOTE PILOT(S) AND FLIGHT CREW

Remote pilot and flight crew roles represent crewmembers who monitor, control, support, and oversee the sUAS and all its various subsystem/elements throughout operation, from preflight inspection to recovery.

❯ Remote Pilot-in-Command (Remote PIC)

The remote pilot-in-command (remote PIC) is the primary pilot; he or she is *"directly responsible for, and is the final authority as to, the operation of [the] aircraft."*[64] The remote PIC:

- maintains and inspects the Aerial Element (prior to operation);
- interfaces with the Ground-based C3 Element HMI (controls and displays) to command the orientation and airspeed of the Aerial Element;
- reviews telemetry and sensor data to respond to dynamic conditions in the operating environment; and
- assigns (issues) duties, as necessary, to other crewmembers.[65]

---

[64] Taken from 14 CFR §91.3(a) and *Notice of Proposed Rulemaking for the Operation and Certification of Small Unmanned Aircraft Systems* (Docket No.: FAA-2015-0150; Notice No. 15-01, 2015, p. 61).
[65] Federal Aviation Administration, "Operation and Certification of Small Unmanned Aircraft Systems" (2016) (Docket No.: FAA-2015-0150; Amdt. Nos. 21-99, 43-48, 61-137, 91-343, 101-9, 107-1, 119-18, 133-15, and 183-16; RIN 2120–AJ60). Retrieved from www.faa.gov/uas/media/RIN_2120-AJ60_Clean_Signed.pdf

FIGURE 3-56. PICs operating sUAS platforms.

It is important to note that the remote PIC is responsible for ensuring the Aerial Element remains within VLOS distance (even when an observer is used) and away from bystanders and prohibited operational areas. The remote PIC (*see* Figure 3-56) is the only role required for operation, with all other roles subordinate and secondary (unless VLOS obscured, then an observer is required). At a minimum, an FAA-issued remote pilot **airman certificate** must be held for civil use sUAS. The remote PIC should not share duties with any other role and it is recommended that appropriate training, specific to the type and function of the sUAS, be satisfactorily completed prior to performance of any application/mission planning or actual operations.[66]

◗ Copilot/Secondary Operator

A copilot serves as a secondary, safety pilot, supporting instruction or operation of complicated systems. The role of the copilot is to assist the PIC with visual observation, command and control, navigation, and operation of specialized payloads. This crewmember is not required for operation of an sUAS.

◗ Visual Observer

A visual observer (VO) is used to support the PIC to ensure VLOS is maintained between the GCS and the Aerial Element, while communicating important observations such as hazards, conflicts, and changing conditions in the operating environment to the PIC. Communication between the PIC and VO is accomplished verbally, either unassisted or using radios. The VO is

---

[66] Certificates of waiver or authorization (COA)s and Section 333 petitions for exemption for operation of sUAS have been approved with non-sUAS rated pilots (category did not exist); instead, the PIC holds another airman certificate, such as a Private Pilot Certificate.

not required for operation of an sUAS, except in cases in which the PIC is unable to maintain VLOS, such as if the command and control is performed inside an enclosed GCS or when the PIC is using FPV.[67] The VO is not required to be co-located with the PIC, but both must remain within unassisted visual distance to the Aerial Element. Additionally, while multiple VOs can be employed, they are not permitted to be used in a manner in which the aircraft flies BVLOS of the PIC (e.g., daisy-chaining). The VO is commonly referred to as a "spotter" in the RC model aircraft community. The provisions of some certificates of waiver or authorization (COAs), such as those issued under an FAA designated test site, may require use of a VO with specific medical requirements (e.g., Class 3 medical certificate). In such cases, these VOs may also be responsible for logging critical operational details (e.g., flight conditions, airworthiness, actions, and accidents and mishaps), which are reported back to the test site and FAA.

▶ Payload Operator

A payload operator supports the operation of a complicated **Payload Element**, installed on the Aerial Element to perform the given application. A payload operator may control the visual sensor orientation, monitor payload status and settings, interpret data as it is received, and identify and track objects or hazards, as needed. Use of this role reduces the attentional load placed on the PIC, enabling each crewmember to focus on successful performance of their assigned critical duties, in turn increasing the safety and efficiency of the system. Increasing numbers of COTS sUAS feature complex controllable payload features; it is highly recommended that consideration be given to employing a dedicated payload operator to control and manage these functions, enabling the PIC to focus entirely on maintaining safe control of the aircraft.

▶ Additional Crewmembers

Additional crewmembers may include:

- Range safety officer
- Flight engineer
- Test engineer
- Maintenance/support technician
- Data analyst
- Operational subject matter expert (SME)

◼ OPERATIONAL SUPPORT

The successful and sustained operation of sUAS requires personnel well-versed in hardware, software, data, business operation and development, as well as regulatory compliance. These roles are needed to achieve continued system operation and generate the support necessary to obtain and maintain certification and funding/revenue.

---

[67] The Aerial Element must remain within VLOS distance to the PIC, even if their view of the aircraft is obstructed (using HMD or inside a GCS) and a VO is used to maintain visual contact.

◗ Maintenance and Repair

The maintenance and repair of sUAS is focused on preparing the system and confirming that it is suitable for operation, configured to achieve optimal efficiency, and meets airworthiness and operational provisions. These roles are responsible for ensuring components are properly repaired, replaced, and recalibrated; elements are properly configured; and the system has been repaired and maintained in accordance with best practices and regulatory requirements. **Technicians, specialists, or engineers** experienced with airframe and powerplant, avionics, composites, electronics, sensors, and networking are usually employed in these roles, in addition to a **maintenance coordinator** to provide scheduling and administrative support.

◗ Management and Organizational Support

Management and sustainment of sUAS operations (operational support) requires a wide variety of skills and knowledge. The personnel in these roles are responsible for the development and pursuit of business, recruitment, preparation of documentation, scheduling, acquisition, accounting, recordkeeping, instruction/training, licensure/certification, and management of organizational operations. The background and experience of these personnel vary widely, depending on their function and responsibility.

◗ Data Processing and Analysis

Processing of the data captured using the sUAS may require in-depth and time-consuming analysis, performed by experts trained in operation of specific tools or techniques. Such personnel tend to be experienced in the application of advanced mathematical and analytical methods. The results of their efforts include detailed descriptions and graphical depictions of findings, identification of issues and implications, and recommendations for capture of future data and use of findings.

SUPPORT EQUIPMENT

As with any complex system, there are conditions in which additional equipment is required to contend with complex issues or inherent limitations of the system that cannot be sufficiently addressed using self-contained capabilities. The **Support Equipment Element** represents those tools, components, and specialized materials used to operate, troubleshoot, repair, and maintain the sUAS in such conditions. This equipment has been categorized by environment and function: flightline operations, maintenance and repair, storage and transport, and training.

■ FLIGHTLINE OPERATIONS

Flightline (launch and recovery) operations are typically performed in close proximity to the GCS and, due to design decisions to limit aircraft weight (capabilities not included in the Aerial Element), require the use of specialized components to prepare for launch. Common components used to perform startup and fueling, launch, and recovery of the aircraft are described below.

❯ Fueling and Startup

Internal combustion engines require external assistance to initiate startup, which is accomplished using tools designed to provide electrical power, engine turnover, and transfer of fuel. If all of these capabilities were integrated into the propulsion system, the weight would increase dramatically, significantly reducing the endurance, speed, and range of the Aerial Element. Likewise, electric propulsion systems require external transfer of power to batteries. The following represent tools, equipment, and consumables commonly used to support flight-line fueling and startup:

- Engine starter (12 VDC)
- Glow plug ignition clip/adapter
- Power panel
- 12 VDC (sealed) battery
- Fuel pump (manual or electric)
- Liquid fuel
- Battery charger

❯ Launchers

In some instances, the Aerial Element of a fixed-wing sUAS might be loaded or configured in a manner that prevents conventional HTOL, or the operational environment may not support a runway (e.g., shipboard maritime operations). In such cases, a launching mechanism (see Figure 3-57) is used to propel the aircraft, at sufficient speed, to achieve sustainable flight. The following represent common types of launchers used with sUAS:

- Simple (handheld bungee cord; Hi-start)
- Car top
- Catapult

FIGURE 3-57. Gatewing X100 on a launcher.

❯ Recovery

Fixed-wing sUAS platforms configured for heavier operations or those requiring recovery in a constrained environment can be captured either using netting suspended vertically or through aerial snagging using a hook placed on the platform and a vertically oriented emplacement (e.g., Insitu SkyHook). These systems are designed to transfer and disperse the kinetic energy of the aircraft and bring it to a stop in a safe and effective manner. Alternative options can be integrated into the airframe, including deep stall dive, parachute deployment, and use of components designed to break apart upon impact (so that the aircraft is not damaged, joints are designed to release).

■ MAINTENANCE AND REPAIR

Performing routine, preventative, or unscheduled maintenance requires both commonly available tools, equipment, and materials and those created specifically for use with sUAS components. These items are used to diagnose and measure, as well as repair or replace time-limited, damaged, or malfunctioning elements or components.

▶ Diagnostic and Measurement Equipment

The following tools are useful to troubleshoot various issues and faults, as well as test replacement parts for installation:

- Multimeter
- Battery tester
- Blade balancer
- Propeller balancer
- Digital caliper
- Pitch gauge
- Digital scale
- Tachometer
- Temperature gauge

▶ Repair Equipment and Materials

The following tools and materials can be used to make repairs to sUAS elements/components or prepare new parts/assemblies for installation:

- Common handheld tools (screwdrivers; socket wrench and sockets; pliers)
- Battery balancer
- Aircraft stand/cradle
- Glow plug driver/wrench
- 4-way wrench
- Wiring, plugs, and connectors
- Propeller hub reamer
- Soldering iron and solder
- Binding agents/glues
- Double-sided tape
- Hook and loop fastener
- Zip ties
- Tubular shrink-wrap
- Covering
- Spares (washers, nuts, bolts, propellers/rotors, and other assemblies)

■ STORAGE AND TRANSPORT

Containers for the storage and transfer of elements and components come in a wide variety of shapes, sizes, and materials. They are used to protect sensitive and delicate components, improve material handling, separate volatile elements, and provide appropriate air pressure (a feature available in more expensive, sealed containers) (see Figure 3-58). Careful consideration of how often the system will travel, the ease of setup, and the method used to transport it (e.g., hand carried, commercially shipped, carry-on luggage) will help determine what option is most appropriate for your use. Common examples of storage and transport containers include soft-sided bags, hard cases, and field boxes/caddies.

FIGURE 3-58.
DJI Phantom with a hard-sided transport case.

■ TRAINING TOOLS

Building experience prior to actually performing an application under inherent pressures (such as environmental conditions, schedules, and pressing customer needs), as well as gaining critical insight regarding the handling characteristics and appropriate response maneuvers of a specific platform, can prove to be invaluable to a remote pilot. COTS RC model aircraft simulators can help increase familiarity with types of airframes and their unique operational characteristics, while devices such as a "buddy box" enable a new remote pilot to fly under the guidance of a more experienced instructor. Understanding what sUAS can or cannot do will help to define what applications can be undertaken with a specific platform.

The following represent a series of COTS RC flight simulation tools, available online, that can be used to build proficiency and experience with specific types of sUAS platforms:

- AccuRC: **www.accurc.com**
- aerofly: **www.aeroflyrc.com**
- AeroSimRC: **www.aerosimrc.com/en**
- ClearView RC Flight Simulator: **rcflightsim.com**
- Flying Model Simulator (free): **www.microflight.com/FMS-Flight-Simulator**
- Phoenix R/C: **www.phoenix-sim.com**
- RC-AirSim: **fabricated-reality.itch.io/rc-airsim-rc-model-airplane-flight-simulator**
- R/C Desk Pilot (free): **rcdeskpilot.com**
- RealFlight: **www.realflight.com**

While built for familiarization with RC hobbyist UAS (model aircraft), these software applications provide sufficient capability for exhibition of general flight dynamics, practice of maneuvers, and development of motor skills in realistic operational settings (see Figure 3-59).

Such tools are available as free/open-source, limited demonstration, or paid options and include physics-based performance calculations, multiple platform models, and a variety of scenery/environments. Use of a simulator is highly recommended prior to purchase and operation of your first sUAS.

Simulation can also be used to gain a better understanding of platform capabilities, as well as the environmental and configuration considerations affecting end performance. A number of COTS and custom-developed options are available to support detailed analysis of such factors, including weather present in a potential operational environment, LOS communication signal propagation, Aerial Element VLOS maintainability, and platform configuration performance. One such example of a UAS analysis software application is the Aerial Robotics Virtual Laboratory (ARVL), which was developed under partnership between Embry-Riddle Aeronautical University (ERAU)–Worldwide and Pinnacle Solutions. This software provides an interactive environment for assembling a UAS configuration from preset components (see Figure 3-60A) to determine operational performance values (Figure 3-60B). Once a system has been configured, a functional mission can be planned (see Figure 3-61A) and conducted to observe operational performance results in the simulated environment (see Figure 3-61B).

FIGURE 3-59.

Screen captures of RealFlight 7.5 with a quadrotor UAS in view.

(© 2016 Hobbico, Inc. Used with Permission.)

By critically examining and analyzing factors that potentially affect performance, you will be able to make more informed decisions regarding the acquisition and safe operation of sUAS technology. Furthermore, modeling and simulation tools can help you to build essential experience in tasks ranging from functional mission planning to practiced conduct of the planned operation with responses to potential issues or risks. As the sUAS market continues to grow, the availability and functionality of such tools can also be expected to increase, at a price point consistent with that of the operational hardware.

A   B

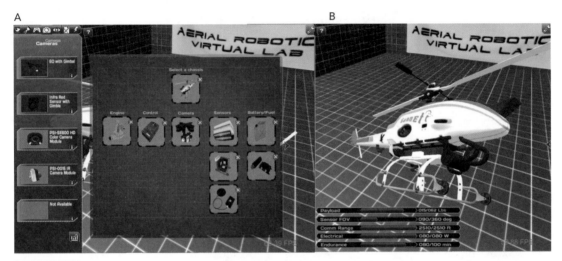

FIGURE 3-60. ERAU-Worldwide ARVL (A) UAS assembly (B) calculated configuration performance.

A   B

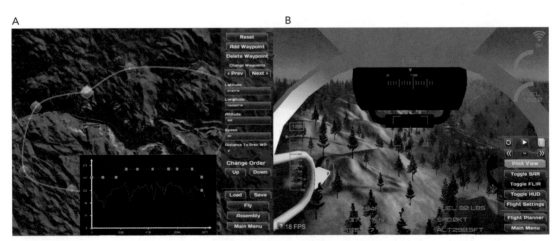

FIGURE 3-61. ERAU-Worldwide ARVL (A) flight route with height over terrain (B) operational scene.

CHAPTER 4

LEGAL, ENVIRONMENTAL, AND OPERATIONAL CONSIDERATIONS: A MAP TO NAVIGATE THE MAZE

INTRODUCTION

Over the past decade, unmanned aircraft systems (UAS) have become increasingly popular with hobbyists and professionals intending to use them for recreation or as viable tools supporting task completion or enhanced productivity. The miniaturization of technology, development of lightweight composites, and increased computing power of modern microchip processors and controls have supported the development of platforms that were once considered by many as unrealistic. The small UAS (sUAS) market has shown substantial growth, exceeding that of larger systems. With the growth of any widespread technology comes the need for not only regulation, but the enforcement of those policies, procedures, and protocols. This area of law is somewhat unestablished, but supported by regulation that may be similar in operational aspects to that of manned aircraft. This chapter will highlight operational considerations and guide you through the tide of evolving regulation necessary for any sUAS remote pilot, operator,[1] or entrepreneur to understand. It is your responsibility as a remote pilot to maintain a level of safety and operational knowledge consistent with those policies and regulations set forth by the Federal Aviation Administration (FAA).

REGULATORY FRAMEWORK

Aviation represents a unique operational setting; however, it does exhibit some similarities to other complex industries, such as maritime or rail. Many think of aviation as a form of transportation or as a subset of military technology, but it encompasses a much larger scope than

---

[1] The term "operator" can be used to indicate the role of aircraft pilot or the owner/lessee with right of legal control.

these two areas alone. Aviation also includes recreational flight, aerial photography and cine-matography, public safety and services, mapping and surveying, aerial inspection, and agricultural support—many of the same operational areas as sUAS.[2] The technical complexity and development of infrastructure in these areas may have significant impacts on public safety, supporting the necessity of a regulatory framework. This section has been presented in a manner designed to aid you in navigating the current regulatory environment and staying informed of regulatory changes.

Throughout history, the regulatory environment and infrastructure requirements of the aviation industry have required change to keep up with unbounded expansion and technological advancements. Since the Wright brothers' flight in 1903, significant progressive thought has been dedicated toward design of a framework to ensure the highest level of safety within the system. With aviation's progression, technological advancements introduced new capabilities and subsequent risks, including a greater number of aircraft and improved performance capabilities. For example, the "Jet Age" of the 1950s saw the introduction of more powerful aircraft capable of flying faster, at higher altitudes, and over further distances. Such changes resulted in the need for rapid infrastructure development, such as a robust air traffic control (ATC) system to ensure the efficient and safe flow of traffic within the National Airspace System (NAS). This expansion of infrastructure also brought about the necessity for federal oversight to support the regulatory and enforcement needs of the aviation industry.[3]

The growth and evolution of early aviation closely mirrors that of modern unmanned aviation, which has brought about significant changes to previous policy and regulation. In response to pressing concerns and need for regulatory change, Congress included UAS-specific content in the FAA Modernization and Reform Act of 2012 (Public Law 112-095). This legislation was designed to streamline programs, create efficiencies, reduce waste, and improve aviation safety and capacity; to provide stable funding for national aviation; and to support other required actions[4] (e.g., UAS traffic integration into the NAS). In response to the challenge issued by Congress, the FAA developed a UAS integration roadmap, which would be used to develop regulations, policy, procedures, guidance material, and training requirements to support safe and efficient UAS operations in the NAS.[5] This effort—which requires coordination with relevant departments and agencies to address related key policy areas of concern, such as privacy and national security—led to the development of the UAS Integration Office in the FAA. Under enacted legislation, the FAA has been authorized to use administrative action

---

[2] See Chapter 2 for detailed descriptions of sUAS applications.

[3] The Civil Aeronautics Authority (CAA) was established in 1938; in 1940, the CAA was split into the Civil Aeronautics Authority (CAA) and the Civil Aeronautics Board (CAB). In 1958, legislation was enacted to create the Federal Aviation Agency (FAA), and in 1967 the Department of Transportation (DOT) was created with the FAA renamed the Federal Aviation Administration and incorporated under the DOT. The CAB was subsequently established as an independent investigative agency, the National Transportation Safety Board (NTSB).

[4] FAA Modernization and Reform Act of 2012 (Public Law 112-095): www.congress.gov/112/plaws/publ95/PLAW-112publ95.pdf

[5] U.S. Department of Transportation, Federal Aviation Administration, *Integration of Civil Unmanned Aircraft Systems (UAS) in the National Airspace System (NAS) Roadmap* (Washington, DC: FAA, 2013).

or legal enforcement action to ensure compliance with regulation defining all model aircraft as "aircraft,"[6] requiring such aircraft be flown only for hobby or recreational purposes, and FAA approval for any other uses, including public agency and civil applications.

MAINTAINING SAFETY IN THE NATIONAL AIRSPACE SYSTEM

The integrity and safety of the NAS is paramount, as it provides the environment for operation and application of UAS, including sUAS. The previously mentioned UAS roadmap is an evolving document that is updated on an annual basis. Its primary function is to define areas of concern and provide forward strategy to mitigate these issues. The airspace overlying the United States is finite in dimensions and must be used in a way to maximize efficiency. With an increase in the number of aircraft operating in the NAS, it has become essential to identify appropriate and effective means to safely operate UAS in closer proximities and areas not proven by the operation of manned platforms. For instance, analysis indicates that the majority of sUAS operations will be confined to altitudes less than 400 feet above ground level (AGL) and speeds less than 100 miles per hour (87 knots), in most instances.[7] Historically, manned aircraft operations have not been highly used in these operational segments, so accommodations must be made to ensure UAS will not present undue hazards to persons or property both on the ground and in the air.

▮ FEDERAL AVIATION REGULATIONS AND PARTS

To develop an understanding of rules and regulations specific to any area of aircraft operation or airman certification, remote pilots must be familiar with the *parts* of the **Federal Aviation Regulations** (FARs) and how they apply to operation of UAS. The FARs are contained in a larger legislative document referred to as the Code of Federal Regulations (CFRs), specifically in Title 14 of the CFR, Aeronautics and Space. The FARs are subdivided into "parts" that deal with segregated components of the regulations; those applicable to sUAS are described in the following sections.

▶ Part 1: Definitions and Abbreviations

Aviation, as with most other industries, has a lexicon or language that may confine the usage of terms to different areas of meaning. 14 CFR Part 1 carries a number of terms that users must be familiar with to interpret the FARs, providing a listing of detailed definitions as they relate to areas of operation. It is common to refer to this part of the FARs to better understand the context or meaning of a specific rule or regulation.

---

[6] Per the FAA Modernization and Reform Act of 2012 (PL 112-95), Section 336, Special Rule for Model Aircraft, which defines model aircraft as aircraft.

[7] In accordance with proposed rulemaking relating to the certification and operation of sUAS; deviations will require FAA approval and exemption.

▶ Part 21: Certification Procedures for Products and Parts

14 CFR Part 21 contains the details of airworthiness and type certification of aircraft to include initial certification through modification and repair. Some aircraft may require special issuance of a type certificate based on a repair or alteration beyond the scope of what the aircraft was designed for. The UAS industry is evolving to support design and airworthiness standards still in development. This condition provides the remote pilot or builder leeway in design considerations and system complexity. An example of a repair or alteration to a UAS that may require special type certification is a modification to an existing power source. Future certification or airworthiness standards may only approve a given power system for a given platform—for example, a 2500 mAh lithium-polymer battery. The approval to change power sources (in this example, to a 5000 mAh lithium-polymer battery) may require the issuance of a new type certificate, because the aircraft was not initially certified to include that system component.

▶ Part 45: Identification and Registration Marking, and Part 47: Aircraft Registration

The pairing of 14 CFR Parts 45 and 47 implies that they are somewhat dependent on each other. The rules and regulations pertaining to the identification and registration of UAS, especially sUAS, are continually changing at the time of this publication. An important consideration is that the size of UAS, especially sUAS, may prohibit traditional documentation and visual identification requirements. In this case, it is common for a request of exemption in an effort to meet these requirements in another way.

▶ Part 60: Flight Simulation Training Device Initial and Continuing Qualification and Use

14 CFR Part 60 prescribes the rules pertaining to initial and continuing qualification and use of all aircraft flight simulation training devices (FSTD) to meet training, evaluation, or flight experience requirements. Simulation has become an accepted method to teach and assess performance in many disciplines and topics. Outside of aviation, industries such as medical, transportation, academia, and defense rely on the use of simulation to exhibit concepts and replicate dangerous or delicate scenarios in virtual environments, without the threat of danger. The UAS industry is also expected to heavily use simulation technologies to support detailed training within various operational scenarios, which will support the development of deeper skills in the cognitive and psychomotor domains. Simulation-based training mechanisms and methods will allow remote pilots to gain initial proficiency and re-currency without the cost, risk, or liability of operating an actual aircraft.

▶ Part 61: Certification of Pilots, Flight Instructors, and Ground Instructors

Historically, airmen have been required to obtain a category and class rating as designated by the FAA for operation of any air vehicle. The development and enactment of 14 CFR Part 107 defined operational and certification provisions for sUAS, including a simplified pathway for

Part 61 airmen certificate holders. However, the operation of larger UAS will likely require the user to hold an airman certificate and rating appropriate to the type of aircraft being operated.

▶ Part 65: Certification of Airman Other Than Flight Crewmembers

The certification of aviation users other than pilots is an important consideration with regard to UAS operations. Held under this part of the FARs are mechanics, repairman, aircraft dispatchers, and ATC tower operators. As regulation continues to define operational standards for UAS, the requirement for crewmembers other than pilots becomes viable, because these stakeholders will be an integral component of any given UAS operation and must meet the federal standard to maintain issuance and currency requirements.

▶ Part 67: Medical Standards and Certification

Medical standards are a very important consideration with regard to UAS operations and a topic for much debate. The current regulation requires UAS pilots operating outside of Part 107 (e.g., in accordance with a certificate of waiver or authorization) to have a minimum of a third-class medical certificate or valid U.S. driver's license issued by a state, the District of Columbia, Puerto Rico, a territory, a possession, or the federal government, but this may change with future regulation.[8] Many groups have petitioned the FAA to waive medical requirements for airmen in specific applications. Commercial operations have historically required airmen to hold a minimum of a second-class medical certificate, with the preference of a first-class. The issuance and duration of a medical certificate by a qualified Aviation Medical Examiner (AME) is a function of age, so it is imperative to discuss this with your doctor at the time of examination. Changes in effect under Part 107 do not require the holder of a Remote Pilot Certificate to acquire or maintain an Airman Medical Certificate.

▶ Part 91: General Operating and Flight Rules

14 CFR Part 91 details general operating and flight rules required for all types of operation. The sUAS remote pilot will rely heavily on this part for operational considerations and rules specific to a given flight profile. Each of the rules listed under Part 91 outline topics such as operations in certain types of airspace, right-of-way rules, speed limitations, and altitude limitations.

▶ 14 CFR Part 107: Operation and Certification of Small Unmanned Aircraft Systems

Part 107 represents the rules governing the non-recreational operation of sUAS in the U.S. National Airspace System and the certification of remote pilots. The rules and provisions identified under Part 107 include identification of operational limitations, remote pilot certification and responsibilities, aircraft requirements, and applicable waivers and exemption processes. This rule set is expected to substantially increase the volume and productivity of sUAS use in the United States.

---

[8] See the FAA's *Become a Pilot: Medical Certificate Requirements* for details relating to types of medical certificates: www.faa.gov/pilots/become/medical

▌ COMPOSITION OF THE NATIONAL AIRSPACE SYSTEM

Previous to the prolific growth of aviation in the early twentieth century, users had the ability to move through the nation's airspace with limited to no communication, primarily using visual separation as the only tool to avoid airborne collisions with other aircraft. As the aviation industry has continued to grow, more aircraft have been required to operate in closer proximity to each other in a finite amount of area. This continued growth eventually led to a unified airspace system over the United States, commonly referred to as the NAS.

The airspace overlying the United States is classified based on usability, interaction, and type of aircraft transiting each airspace type. Classes A, B, C, D, E, and G airspace are designators designed to aid all aviators in understanding the procedures required to traverse each invisible boundary. sUAS remote pilots are not immune to the responsibilities of understanding how aircraft, avionics, communications, and pilot requirements must be met to safely and efficiently use each airspace segment. It is important to consider that the airspace discussed in this section is specific to the United States. If operating in another country or nation, it is the responsibility of sUAS remote pilots, including recreational pilots, to abide by all laws and regulations specific to that area.

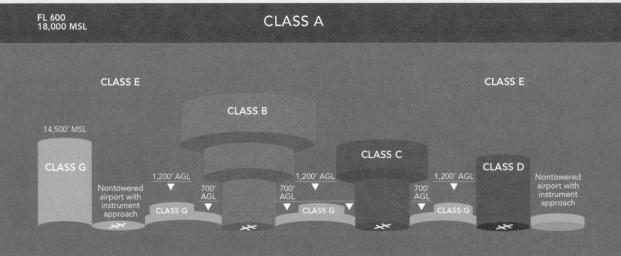

FIGURE 4-1. Airspace categories and altitudes.

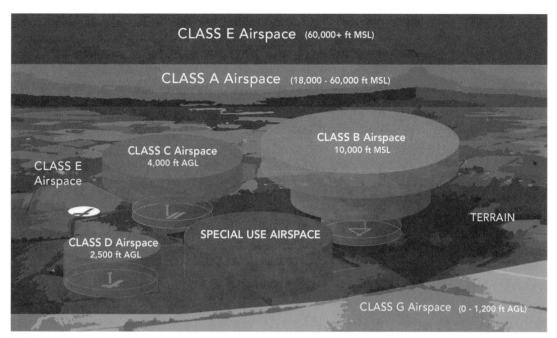

FIGURE 4-2. Airspace in relation to terrain.

▶ Visibility and the Flight Environment

Manned aircraft have specific visibility and cloud clearance requirements necessary to fly in each type of airspace, which are defined in 14 CFR Part 91. Operations in "good" weather are referred to as visual flight rules (VFR) while those in "poor" weather are referred to as instrument flight rules (IFR). Currently, these terms and associated regulations are not applicable to UAS flight. According to 14 CFR Part 107, the sole weather requirement for UAS operations (without waiver or exemption) is 3 miles of flight visibility and clearance of 500 feet below and 2,000 feet horizontal from all clouds. Unlike the rules applicable to manned aircraft, there are no defined differences in these requirements between airspace types. Hobby/recreational operations, dictated by 14 CFR Part 101, do not specifically call out weather requirements; instead, they refer operators to their applicable community-based safety program. Figure 4-1 depicts the arrangement and altitude requirements for each type of airspace, while Figure 4-2 depicts various classes of airspace as they relate to terrain.

▶ Class A Airspace

The operation of aircraft from Flight Level 180 (18,000 feet mean sea level [MSL]) to FL600 (60,000 feet MSL) over the majority of the United States, including territories, are in Class A airspace. This area of operation requires several conditions that few sUAS remote pilots will use on a regular basis, unless operating aircraft that fly at medium to high altitudes under a waiver or exemption. Class A airspace extends to 12 nautical miles (NM) off of the U.S. coast and is highly used by faster jet aircraft. Manned aircraft operations in Class A airspace are required to operate under IFR, the pilot must be instrument rated, and the aircraft must be equipped with a Mode C transponder.[9]

▶ Class B Airspace

This class of airspace overlies airports with very high traffic density and commercial operations. As the popularity and reliability of sUAS continue to grow, operations inside Class B airspace are expected to become more feasible. The shape of Class B airspace is often irregular in definition and is made up of multiple areas that usually extend to an altitude of 10,000 feet MSL. Manned aircraft operating in Class B must be "cleared" verbally into the airspace via two-way communication and must also have a Mode C transponder, which is required within 30 NM of the primary airport. Currently, there are no clearly defined requirements specific to UAS operations in Class B other than ATC permission prior to flight. The United States has a relatively high number of Class B terminal environments (e.g., Hartsfield–Jackson Atlanta International Airport [ATL], New York LaGuardia Airport [LGA], and Los Angeles International Airport [LAX]). As an sUAS remote pilot, you must remain cognizant not to penetrate this type of airspace unless the user has permission from ATC or an airspace waiver from the FAA.

▶ Class C Airspace

As with other types of controlled airspace, airman and aircraft requirements must be met for operations inside Class C airspace. This type of airspace overlies airports with commercial traffic and relatively high traffic densities, but is not considered to carry the same traffic volume as the busier Class B environment. Class C airspace is usually well-defined and similar in appearance to an upside down wedding cake, with the five-mile area surrounding the primary airport extending from the surface to 4,000 feet MSL. The next layer usually extends to 10 NM from the primary airport and vertically from 1,200 feet MSL up to 4,000 feet MSL. This type of airspace requires all manned aircraft operating inside to be equipped with a Mode C transponder and two-way (bi-directional) radio communication capabilities. Aircraft operating under the layer of Class C are neither required to communicate with ATC or meet transponder requirements. All sUAS operations require ATC permission or an airspace waiver from the FAA.

▶ Class D Airspace

Class D represents the airspace surrounding airports with control towers and traffic densities lower than Class C airports. Manned pilots are required to meet two-way radio communication requirements prior to entry, but unlike all other classes of controlled airspace, the aircraft is not typically required to be equipped with a Mode C transponder. Another condition of airports contained in Class D airspace is the intermittent or part-time operations of control towers.

---

[9] Mode C transponder: Device integrated into aircraft equipped with an altitude encoder that is designed to respond to an interrogation signal received from ATC. Conveys altitude and pressure altitude information back to ATC for use in combination with their radar to determine three-dimensional positioning of aircraft in the NAS.

In the event the control tower is closed, the airport may revert to either Class E or Class G operations (discussed in the following sections). Unmanned operations in Class D require ATC permission or FAA airspace waivers.

▶ Class E Airspace

The operational considerations of Class E airspace can be slightly complex, but it is the last type of "controlled" airspace. Airmen may operate inside Class E with no transponder or radio communication requirements, but certain ATC services may be requested for flight operations, such as flight following.[10] Most operations of manned aircraft outside of the other classes of airspace discussed are considered in Class E, which typically extends from 1,200 feet AGL to the base of overlying Class A airspace. This type of airspace also holds most of the airway system for the orderly flow of low-level traffic. In many cases, Class E will extend from 700 feet AGL or even the surface,[11] depending on the type of instrument flight procedures to a given airport. ATC permission or FAA airspace waiver is required for surface-based Class E (a location where Class E begins at the ground).

▶ Class G Airspace

This type of airspace is considered to be "uncontrolled" and typically extends from the surface to either 700 or 1,200 feet AGL, but may rise as high as 14,500 feet AGL. Airman and aircraft requirements are limited in Class G, but it is important to remain extremely vigilant, as aircraft may or may not be using two-way communication as a means for traffic separation. Radio communications in a Class G environment are usually noted by either a Unicom frequency or common traffic advisory frequency (CTAF). The majority of sUAS operations are conducted in Class G airspace.

▶ Special Use Airspace

The term "special use" implies that specialized aircraft operations may take place in this type of airspace. Warning areas, restricted areas, alert areas, military operations areas, prohibited areas, and controlled firing areas are all types of special use airspace that airmen must become familiar with prior to any flight. Some of these areas—such as warning areas, alert areas, and military operating areas—allow entry of aircraft; however, vigilance must be maintained with regard to the specific activity inside that airspace when it is in use. SUAS operations must remain clear of prohibited and restricted airspace, per 14 CFR Part 107, except when not in use or special approval has been issued by the controlling agency.

▶ Other Types of Airspace and Restrictions to Flight

As the density of aircraft operating over the United States increases, so do the requirements to prohibit overflights in specific areas. The issuance of a temporary flight restriction (TFR) may occur with a high population density event, such as a sporting event, or may be in relation to a public figure traveling through or staying in a given location. It is the responsibility of the sUAS

---

[10] Use of ATC radar advisories and communication to aid real-time navigation.
[11] In remote areas, Class E may have a floor of 14,500 feet.

remote pilot and all other aircraft to be aware of all TFRs in an area in order to avoid penetrating this type of airspace. The unapproved entrance into a TFR may lead to interception by military aircraft and heavy civil punishments or fines.

National security areas are other areas surrounding primarily governmental restrictions or installations where increased security is necessary. Voluntary avoidance of this type of airspace is necessary at all times. Many commercial applications are available to review airspace and the issuance of Notices to Airmen (NOTAMs). These notifications allow airmen the ability to review any special conditions or operational constraints along a given route of flight to better ensure safe and responsible operations.

■ AVOIDANCE OF VIOLATION AND REGULATORY ACTION

One of the most important aspects supporting responsible and lawful conduct in any industry is the notion of outreach and communication of regulations, guidance, and best practices. In support of changing UAS operational requirements and the rapid growth of this field (e.g., the availability and operation of a significant number of consumer sUAS), the FAA and its stakeholder partners have launched educational outreach campaigns, including **Know Before You Fly**[12] (*see* Figure 4-3) and **No Drone Zone** (*see* Figure 4-4), to increase awareness in the public sector regarding permissible sUAS operations. The need to operate in a regulated and responsible fashion is of utmost importance, yet the number of questionable and irresponsible operations being conducted by consumers new to aviation has continued to rise. Thus it is essential that such remote pilots, who may have limited background, ability, knowledge or experience with aviation, have access to the tools, resources, and training to help them become responsible aviators. It is your responsibility as an sUAS remote pilot to be aware of all regulations and policies necessary to operate your aircraft safely, including for recreational or commercial activity. The FAA continues to enforce illegal operations of UAS in collaboration with federal, state, and local law enforcement agencies through issuance of guidance, fines, and possible civil penalties.[13]

FIGURE 4-3.

Know Before You Fly UAS educational campaign logo.

FIGURE 4-4.

No Drone Zone signage, available from the FAA.

---

[12] The Know Before You Fly campaign was launched and is supported as a collaborative effort among AUVSI, the FAA, and the AMA.

[13] While the FAA must exercise caution not to mix criminal law enforcement with the FAA's administrative safety enforcement function, the public interest is best served by coordination and fostering mutual understanding and cooperation between governmental entities with law enforcement responsibilities. Although there are federal criminal statutes that may be implicated by some UAS operations (e.g., see 49 U.S.C. §46307), most violations of the FAA's regulations may be addressed through administrative enforcement measures.

In an effort to increase user responsibility and conformance to industry standards (e.g., ASTM International), the FAA has outlined the following strategies to ensure compliance with statutory and regulatory requirements:

- Public outreach and education to encourage voluntary compliance
- Administrative action or legal enforcement action
- Investigation of alleged violations
  - Evaluate safety risk to the NAS due to alleged UAS operational noncompliance.
  - Initiate contact with operator [remote pilot], and provide information and guidance regarding current regulatory requirements.
  - If necessary, send an administrative informational (advisory) letter to the operator [remote pilot] that includes addresses to applicable FAA UAS guidance and CFR provisions.
  - If operator [remote pilot] is uncooperative (remains intentionally noncompliant; repeats violations; presents a medium to high potential risk of endangering the NAS, or results in actual endangerment), initiate appropriate enforcement action.[14]
  - Enter the alleged activity into the FAA Program Tracking and Reporting Subsystem (PTRS) database in accordance with current guidance,[15] additionally documenting the operator's [remote pilot's] airman certificate number, or name (if not certified).

MODEL AIRCRAFT AND SUAS

Differentiating between a radio-controlled[16] (RC) model aircraft and an sUAS may be relatively difficult, but the core element of separation is the intent of the user. Any proprietary or commercial application of a powered and remotely controllable air vehicle will categorize it as a UAS, and both the remote pilot and aircraft will be confined by the most current regulation. It is important to also understand what constitutes a commercial application. If the output data or imagery collected from the UAS is sold or provides monetary benefit of any kind (e.g., exchanging services for goods), the operation will be considered commercial and is regulated by all applicable UAS guidance. Model aircraft are considered unmanned aircraft per Public Law 112-95 and Section 336 of Public Law 112-95, and therefore "aircraft" as defined by 49 USC §40102 and 14 CFR §1.1.

---

[14] As outlined in the FAA *Compliance and Enforcement Bulletin* No. 2014-2.
[15] As outlined in FAA Order 8900.1, *Flight Standards Information Management System (FSIMS), Volume 16.*
[16] Also commonly defined and referred to as "remote control (RC)."

◼ AC 91-57—MODEL AIRCRAFT OPERATING STANDARDS

The first accepted guidance, FAA Advisory Circular (AC) 91-57, *Model Aircraft Operating Standards*, was issued for the operation of model aircraft on June 9, 1981, and recommended safety standards and protocols for the most safe and efficient operation in a number of environments. The AC was intended to provide modelers with a "best practices" framework to safe operations, which was non-regulatory in nature. This document would later provide the structure and framework for sUAS regulations, including Part 107. An update on September 2, 2015, replaced AC 91-57 with AC 91-57A.

AC 91-57A (2015) covers the following topics:

- Potential for model aircraft to pose as hazards

  — Share airspace with manned operations

  — May endanger persons and property, if not operated safely

  — Those who operate UAS in an unsafe manner, including interference with or failure to yield to manned aircraft, may be subject to FAA enforcement action

- Permissible operations

  — UAS only used for recreation or hobby and flown within visual line-of-sight (VLOS) of the remote pilot (*see* Figure 4-5)

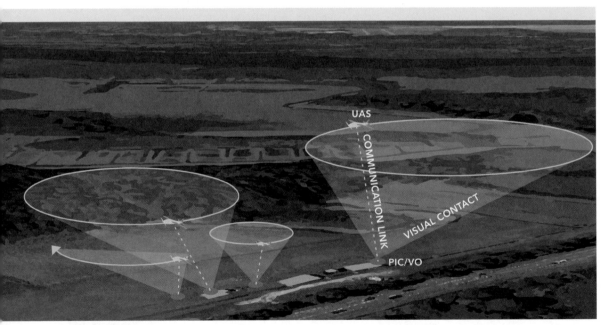

FIGURE 4-5. Flight tracks of several sUAS in close proximity and within VLOS at model aircraft airfield.[17]

---

[17] UAS operating areas, UAS Traffic Management (UTM), and other relevant flight planning resources can be found under the UAS tab of the *1800 Weather Brief* (www.1800wxbrief.com) and *Know Before You Fly* (knowbeforeyoufly.org) websites or the *B4UFly* mobile app (www.faa.gov/uas/b4ufly).

- Operations conform to a community-based set of safety guidelines, within an operational safety program of a nationwide community-based organization (CBO), including remaining under 400 feet AGL, in accordance with best practices (e.g., Academy of Model Aeronautics [AMA] *sUAS Flight Safety Guide*)
- UAS weight does not exceed 55 pounds, unless its design, construction, and operational airworthiness has been certified by a CBO-administered operational safety program
- Operation of the UAS does not interfere with the operation of manned aircraft, and the remote pilot yields the right-of-way to manned aircraft
- Planned operations to be conducted within five statute miles of an airport (two miles of heliport) are coordinated with airport operator or ATC (*see* Figure 4-6 and Figure 4-7)
- Prohibited operations
  - Recreational or hobby UAS operations are not to be conducted in Prohibited Areas, Special Flight Rule Areas, Flight Restricted Zones (e.g., Washington National Capital Region), TFR areas, or areas where NOTAMs prohibiting operation are in effect

An airport reference point (ARP) is used to identify the approximate geometric center of all usable runways, and is depicted on most airport diagrams. The ARP is computed using a windows-based software program, www.ngs.noaa.gov/AERO/FAQ.shtml, and is used to delineate the five-mile area for UAS operations.[18]

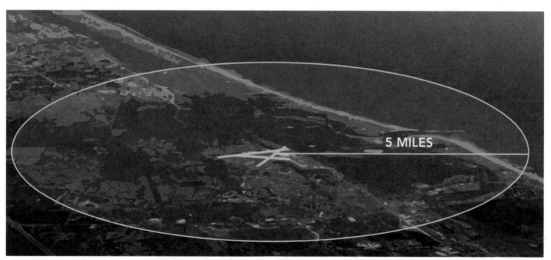

FIGURE 4-6. Example five-mile area surrounding an airport.

---

[18] The FAA interprets five miles to mean five statute miles (SM), as opposed to nautical miles (NM).

FOREIGN AIRSPACE

5 MILE AIRPORT ZONE

FIGURE 4-7. Environment featuring multiple airports, with five mile surrounds and foreign airspace delineated.

▌14 CFR PART 101—MOORED BALLOONS, KITES, AMATEUR ROCKETS, UNMANNED FREE BALLOONS, AND CERTAIN MODEL AIRCRAFT

This part of the regulations covers model aircraft (including what may be referred to as sUAS) that are operated for hobby or recreational use. Subpart E specifically addresses these aircraft and includes a "catch all" rule prohibiting endangerment of aviation safety.

Subpart E—Special Rule for Model Aircraft
§101.41   Applicability.
This subpart prescribes rules governing the operation of a model aircraft (or an aircraft being developed as a model aircraft) that meets all of the following conditions as set forth in section 336 of Public Law 112-95:

(a) The aircraft is flown strictly for hobby or recreational use;

(b) The aircraft is operated in accordance with a community-based set of safety guidelines and within the programming of a nationwide community-based organization;

(c) The aircraft is limited to not more than 55 pounds unless otherwise certified through a design, construction, inspection, flight test, and operational safety program administered by a community-based organization;

(d) The aircraft is operated in a manner that does not interfere with and gives way to any manned aircraft; and

(e) When flown within 5 miles of an airport, the operator of the aircraft provides the airport operator and the airport air traffic control tower (when an air traffic facility is located at the airport) with prior notice of the operation.

§101.43 Endangering the safety of the National Airspace System.
No person may operate model aircraft so as to endanger the safety of the national airspace system.

(14 CFR §101.41, §101.43)

■ SECTION 336 (PUBLIC LAW 112-95)—SPECIAL RULE FOR MODEL AIRCRAFT

Guidance under this section of regulation was signed in as part of the FAA Modernization and Reform Act of 2012 (FMRA) on February 14, 2012. The FMRA was created to address the understanding that the aviation system was changing rapidly and needed improvement consistent with these changes. One of the outcomes to this was defined as Section 336, Special Rule for Model Aircraft, which did not exclude model aircraft from being actual aircraft operating in the NAS, and prohibited the commercial use of UAS. It stated that model aircraft were to be flown strictly for hobby or recreational purposes and within the remote pilot's VLOS.

The following is a description of the rules defined under Section 336:

(a) In General—Notwithstanding any other provision of law relating to the incorporation of unmanned aircraft systems into Federal Aviation Administration plans and policies, including this subtitle, the Administrator of the Federal Aviation Administration may not promulgate any rule or regulation regarding a model aircraft, or an aircraft being developed as a model aircraft, if—

(1) the aircraft is flown strictly for hobby or recreational use;

(2) the aircraft is operated in accordance with a community-based set of safety guidelines and within the programming of a nationwide community-based organization;

(3) the aircraft is limited to not more than 55 pounds unless otherwise certified through a design, construction, inspection, flight test, and operational safety program administered by a community-based organization;

(4) the aircraft is operated in a manner that does not interfere with and gives way to any manned aircraft; and

(5) when flown within 5 miles of an airport, the operator of the aircraft provides the airport operator and the airport air traffic control tower (when an air traffic facility is located at the airport) with prior notice of the operation (model aircraft operators flying from a permanent location within 5 miles of an airport should establish a mutually-agreed upon operating procedure with the airport operator and the airport air traffic control tower (when an air traffic facility is located at the airport)).

(b) Statutory Construction—Nothing in this section shall be construed to limit the authority of the Administrator to pursue enforcement action against persons operating model aircraft who endanger the safety of the national airspace system.

(c) Model Aircraft Defined—In this section, the term "model aircraft" means an unmanned aircraft that is—

(1) capable of sustained flight in the atmosphere;

(2) flown within visual line-of-sight of the person operating the aircraft; and

(3) flown for hobby or recreational purposes.

This rule affords protection to recreational model aircraft remote pilots, including the ability to fly above 400 feet AGL, when operating within the safety guidelines of a community-based organization. An example is flying in accordance with the Academy of Model Aeronautics' *Safety Code* as a registered member of the AMA.[19]

APPROVED OPERATION OF UAS

Currently, there are several paths to gain federal (i.e., FAA) approval for operation of UAS in the NAS. The specific path best suited to your intended operation is dependent on what type of operator you are—public or civil (private). Part 107 has substantially reduced the burden to gain access to airspace, providing a clear set of provisions and requirements for the operation of sUAS in the NAS. Another option is the public **certificate of waiver or authorization (COA)**, which is meant for operators of public aircraft, such as federal, state, or local government agencies; public universities and colleges; and other public organizations. Alternatively, a **Section 333 Petition for Exemption application** is used to seek operational approval of civil UAS (privately owned) by individuals, companies, non-profits, private universities and colleges, and other private organizations seeking to conduct operations outside of the limits of Part 107. The awarding of a **Section 333 Grant of Exemption** by the FAA includes a "blanket" 400-foot nationwide COA, with certain restrictions around airports, restricted airspace, and other densely populated areas. Once a **Grant of Exemption** has been approved, the operator will be eligible to apply for individual COAs if they desire further operational exceptions *outside* the parameters of the blanket COA.[20]

Additionally, the FAA has worked to provide increased accommodation of access to the NAS for sUAS operators through **special airworthiness certificates** (SAC), **experimental** (SAC-EC) and **restricted** (SAC-RC) categories. This section outlines the processes you may use as tools to gain access to airspace and operate UAS within regulatory requirements and guidance.

---

[19] Academy of Model Aeronautics, *National Model Aircraft Safety Code* (Muncie, IN: AMA, 2014)

[20] For example, if operations are to be conducted at or within 5 NM of an airport or heliport, a COA application designating the specific location must be submitted.

◼ TYPE OF OPERATORS

The following subsections describe types of operations, and those conducting such operations, under federal approval. This information can provide a more thorough understanding of what type of UAS operational approval you need to solicit, based on your organizational structure.

◗ Public Aircraft Operations (Governmental)

This category represents public operators, such as federal, state, or local government agencies, departments, or organizations, including state colleges and universities, using public aircraft. FAA Advisory Circular (AC) 00-1.1A, *Public Aircraft Operations*, provides information to assist in determining whether government or government-contracted aircraft operations conducted within the United States are public or civil aircraft operations. Not all aircraft operations run by government agencies are public aircraft operations, and not all public aircraft operations are run by government agencies alone.

The definition of a "public aircraft" is found in Title 49 of the United States Code, Section 40102—Definitions, Subparagraph (a)(41), and means any of the following:

(A) Except with respect to an aircraft described in subparagraph (E), an aircraft used only for the United States Government, except as provided in section 40125(b).

(B) An aircraft owned by the Government and operated by any person for purposes related to crew training, equipment development, or demonstration, except as provided in section 40125(b).

(C) An aircraft owned and operated by the government of a State, the District of Columbia, or a territory or possession of the United States or a political subdivision of one of these governments, except as provided in section 40125(b).

(D) An aircraft exclusively leased for at least 90 continuous days by the government of a State, the District of Columbia, or a territory or possession of the United States or a political subdivision of one of these governments, except as provided in section 40125(b).

(E) An aircraft owned or operated by the armed forces or chartered to provide transportation or other commercial air service to the armed forces under the conditions specified by section 40125(c). In the preceding sentence, the term "other commercial air service" means an aircraft operation that (i) is conducted within the United States territorial airspace; (ii) the Administrator of the Federal Aviation Administration determines is available for compensation or hire to the public, and (iii) must comply with all applicable civil aircraft rules under title 14, Code of Federal Regulations.

(49 U.S.C. §40102[a][41])

Eligibility is further covered in 49 U.S.C. §40125, Qualifications for Public Aircraft Status. This section defines the type of operation each descriptor listed below applies to. It is important to understand how the intent to operate an aircraft may change, based on mission parameters defined by the operator or customer. Advisory Circular 00-1.1A further explains Public Aircraft Operations in accordance with Title 49 U.S.C. §§ 40102(a)(41) and 40125.[21]

---

(2) GOVERNMENTAL FUNCTION—The term "governmental function" means an activity undertaken by a government, such as national defense, intelligence missions, firefighting, search and rescue, law enforcement (including transport of prisoners, detainees, and illegal aliens), aeronautical research, or biological or geological resource management.

(3) QUALIFIED NON-CREWMEMBER—The term "qualified non-crewmember" means an individual, other than a member of the crew, aboard an aircraft—

(A) operated by the armed forces or an intelligence agency of the United States Government; or

(B) whose presence is required to perform, or is associated with the performance of, a governmental function.

(49 U.S.C. §40125[a][2] and [a][3])

(b) AIRCRAFT OWNED BY GOVERNMENTS—An aircraft described in subparagraph (A), (B), (C), or (D) of section 40102(a)(41) does not qualify as a public aircraft under such section when the aircraft is used for commercial purposes *[performing a non-governmental function]* or to carry an individual other than a crewmember or a qualified non-crewmember.

(49 U.S.C. §40125[b]

An aircraft that meets the criteria listed under 49 U.S.C. §40125(a)(3), (A) and (B) listed above, under the definition of public aircraft may or may not be classified as performing public aircraft operations for the federal government. Additionally, an aircraft that meets the criteria listed under (C) or (D) above under the definition of public aircraft may or may not be classified as performing public aircraft operations for state governments. The flow charts depicted in Figure 4-8 can help to determine if aircraft fall under either of these classifications.

The status of an aircraft operation as public is not automatic, as contracted aircraft operations are considered civil aircraft operations, until:

- The contracting government entity provides the operator with a written declaration of public aircraft status for applicable flights;

- The contracting government entity notifies the local FAA Flight Standards District Office (FSDO) having oversight of the operator (or operation) that they have contracted with the civil operator to conduct "eligible" public aircraft operations;

---

[21] FAA Advisory Circular (AC) 00-1.1A, *Public Aircraft Operations*, www.faa.gov/documentLibrary/media/Advisory_Circular/AC_00-1_1A.pdf

- The flights in question are determined to be legitimate public aircraft operations under the terms of the statute; and

- The above declarations are done in advance of the proposed public aircraft flight

NOTE: Declaration of public aircraft operation status must come from the contracting officer or higher level authority government official.[22]

◗ Civil Aircraft Operations (Non-Governmental)

Civil aircraft operations constitute any operation that does not meet the statutory criteria for a public aircraft operation. The FAA regulatory authority over a public aircraft operation might be limited (e.g., Department of Defense [DOD] operations in restricted airspace), other than those requirements that apply to all aircraft operating in the NAS; however, civil aircraft operations are different in that they are subject to a high degree of FAA oversight and restrictions. Additionally, any aircraft operation (including UAS operation) not meeting the statutory criteria for a public aircraft operation is considered a civil aircraft and must be conducted in accordance with all FAA regulations applicable to the operation.

▪ TYPES OF OPERATIONAL APPROVAL PROCESSES

There are several methods to gain FAA authorization to fly public (governmental) and civil (non-governmental) sUAS in the NAS. The following subsections describe the different types of federal approval processes that a potential user will apply for, or meet through certification,

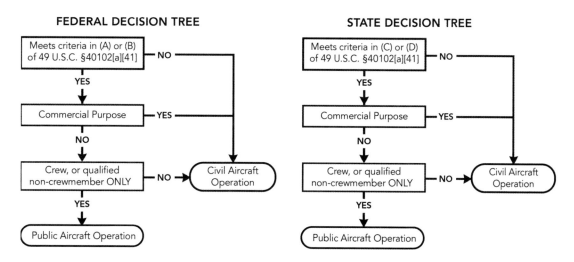

FIGURE 4-8. Decision flow charts for federal and state operations.[23]

---

[22] John Allen, *Public Aircraft Operations Forum* (Washington, DC: Federal Aviation Administration, 2011).
[23] Adapted from FAA Advisory Circular (AC) 00-1.1A, *Public Aircraft Operations*. www.faa.gov/documentLibrary/media /Advisory_Circular/AC_00-1_1A.pdf

prior to conducting operations. When combined with the previously presented type of organizational structure, this information will provide a more thorough understanding of the type of sUAS operational approval you will need to solicit or complete, based on your organizational structure and intended operational purpose.

▶ 14 CFR Part 107—Operation and Certification of sUAS

The FAA and other UAS stakeholders, supporting the development and application of unmanned aircraft technology, have recognized the potential benefits achievable through permitting controlled, responsible, and appropriate operations within the NAS. In February 2015, the FAA released the Notice of Proposed Rulemaking (NPRM), *Operation and Certification of Small Unmanned Aircraft Systems* (Docket No.: FAA-2015-0150; Notice No. 15-01). The NPRM contained the details of a proposed framework to support improved accommodation of civil small unmanned aircraft system (sUAS) access to the NAS, certification requirements (remote pilot and aircraft), and possible pathways for exemption or waiver in a manner supporting continued and enhanced safety, increased efficiency, and improved cost-effectiveness. Major provisions included identification of proposed sUAS operational limitations, remote pilot certification and responsibilities, aircraft requirements, impact to model aircraft operations, designation of a micro UAS category, and establishment of innovation zones.

In June 2016, the FAA released the rule set for 14 CFR Part 107 (enacted late August 2016). These rules are expected to increase access to airspace, spur innovation and entrepreneurial activity, and improve safety and system application, while minimizing and controlling risk among other aircraft and to those on the ground. The following represent an overview of Part 107 requirements:

- Operational limitations:[24]
  — Aircraft (sUAS—Aerial Element) must weigh less than 55 pounds (MTOW; including any loading, such as payload and/or fuel).
  — Limited to VLOS distance only; aircraft must remain within visual range so the operator (remote pilot) is able to see, unaided by any device other than corrective lenses (even when a visual observer [VO] is used; VO can be used as an alternative means to maintain VLOS).*
  — May not fly over any non-participants (those not directly involved in the operation), under a covered structure, or inside a stationary vehicle.
  — Daylight-only operations (official sunrise to sunset, local time) or within +/–30 minutes of civil twilight (with use of appropriate anti-collision lighting).*
  — Must yield right-of-way to other aircraft (manned or unmanned).
  — May use VO, but this crewmember is not required.

---

[24] Most of these restrictions (indicated with an asterisk [*] in the following list) are waivable, if the applicant demonstrates that operation can safely be conducted under the terms of a certificate of waiver; operations outside of non-waived requirements require a COA or Section 333 Grant of Approval from the FAA.

— First-person-view (FPV) cameras do not satisfy "see-and-avoid" requirement, but they can be used when requirement is fulfilled using other means (e.g., use of a VO).

— Maximum groundspeed of 100 mph (87 knots).*[25]

— Maximum altitude of 400 feet AGL, or within 400 feet from top of a structure (e.g., tower).*

— Minimum weather visibility of three miles from control station (remote PIC).*

— No sUAS operations are permitted in Class A airspace (18,000 feet MSL and above, including Flight Level [FL] 600)

— Operations in Class B, C, D and E airspace are allowed, with permission from FAA ATC (to be supported by application request through an online system).

— Operations in Class G airspace are allowed without ATC permission.

— Can only act as a remote PIC or VO for one UAS at one time.

— No operations from moving aircraft (e.g., chase plane).*

— No operations from moving vehicles (unless over sparsely populated areas).*

— No careless or reckless operations.

— No carriage of hazardous materials.

— A preflight inspection of the entire system, to be performed by the remote PIC, is required.

— A person may not operate an sUAS if he or she is aware of or suspects any physical or mental condition that would interfere with safe operation.

— Foreign-registered sUAS are permitted to operate under Part 107 if they satisfy the requirements of Part 375.

— External load operations (e.g., cargo carrying or transportation) are permitted if load is securely attached and does not adversely affect flight characteristics or controllability of the aircraft.

— Transportation of property for compensation (e.g., cargo carrying) is permissible if MTOW of aircraft is less than 55 pounds, flight is conducted VLOS and not from a moving vehicle, and is conducted intrastate.[26]

• Remote pilot certification and responsibilities:

— Pilots of an sUAS are considered "remote pilot-in-command (PIC)."

— Anyone operating an sUAS must either hold a Part 107 remote pilot airman certificate or be under the direct supervision of an FAA-certified remote pilot.

---

[25] True airspeed corrected for wind; horizontal speed relative to the ground.

[26] Flight occurs wholly within the bounds of a state and does not involve transport between (1) Hawaii and another place in Hawaii through airspace outside Hawaii; (2) the District of Columbia and another place in the District of Columbia; or (3) a territory or possession of the U.S. and another place in the same territory or possession.

- To qualify for the remote pilot certificate:
  - ▶ If a current Part 61 certificate holder (e.g., private pilot; does not include student pilots) with a review within the last 24 months, participate in an online course provided by the FAA.
  - ▶ All others must pass an initial aeronautical knowledge test at an FAA-approved knowledge testing center.
  - ▶ Must be vetted by the Transportation Security Administration (TSA).
  - ▶ Must be at least 16 years old.
- Remote PICs are required to:
  - ▶ Provide the FAA, upon request, the entire sUAS for inspection or testing, as well as any required documentation.
  - ▶ Report an accident to the FAA within 10 days of any operation that resulted in injury, loss of consciousness, or property damage ($500, not including damage to sUAS).
  - ▶ Conduct a preflight inspection, to include specific aircraft and control station systems checks, to ensure the small UAS is safe for operation.
  - ▶ Ensure sUAS complies with existing registration requirements specified in 14 CFR §91.203(a)(2).
- Aircraft requirements:
  - FAA airworthiness certification is not required for sUAS.
  - Remote PIC must maintain the sUAS in a condition for safe operation and conduct appropriate preflight inspection.
  - Aircraft registration is required (same requirements that apply to all other aircraft).
  - Aircraft markings are required (same requirements that apply to all other aircraft); if aircraft is too small to display standard-sized markings, markings will need to be displayed in the largest practicable manner.
- Model aircraft:
  - Part 107 does not apply to model aircraft that satisfy all of the criteria specified in Section 336 of FMRA (Public Law 112-95).
  - The rule codifies the FAA's enforcement authority in Part 101 by prohibiting model aircraft operators from endangering the safety of the NAS.

Part 107 is anticipated to support and accommodate substantially increased sUAS operations, while reducing the volume of Section 333 Petition for Exemption requests. While Section 333 Grants of Exemption will still be provided for those requests that can demonstrate maintenance of safety, the FAA expects the majority of past requests will be achievable using Part 107 and a series of waivable conditions.

▶ Certificate of Waiver or Authorization (COA)

A COA allows the approved operation of a specific type of UAS, within a laterally and vertically confined segment of airspace with very specific operational limitations, and it requires the filing of a Notice to Airmen (NOTAM) within 24 hours of operation to alert other aircraft in the area of operations within the COA area.[27] Once approved for operation within a COA, the FAA will issue a document outlining specific requirements, such as UAS registration requirements, identification by marking, flight time reporting, and incident reporting instructions, which in most cases must be filed on a monthly basis to the issuing agency.[28] COAs are categorized as **public use** (governmental) and **civil use** (non-government), with unique provisions applicable to type.

Public Use COAs—The FAA manages public-use aircraft COAs through its **COA Online system.** Before the FAA grants an agency access to COA Online, the agency (or proponent) will be asked to provide the FAA with a "declaration letter" from the city, county, or state attorney's office assuring the FAA that the proponent is recognized as a political subdivision of the government of the state under 49 U.S.C §40102(a)(41)(c) or (d), and that the proponent will operate its unmanned aircraft in accordance with 49 U.S.C. §40125(b) (not for commercial purposes). An agency's accountable executive *cannot* self-certify that their agency is a "public" agency.

COA applications need to describe the operations in a manner that supports the FAA's review, analysis, and assessment of safety. An application is necessary for the operation of each specific aircraft (which requires registration and display of N-number). The COA application should identify and address the following information:

1. *Applicant points of contact*—Identify those primary contacts within the organization supporting the planned use of the specific sUAS.
2. *Operational/executive summaries*—Describe the proposed operation that represents a narrative of the theory of operation (or multiple operations), including identification of methods to establish and maintain system guidance, navigation, and control (GNC); detect, sense, and avoid (DSA; or see and avoid); and safe operation.
3. *System design/configuration description*—Describe the platform and how it will be configured for planned operations, including identification of elements (aerial vehicle, payload, C3, human, and support).
4. *Air (aerial) vehicle performance characteristics*—Describe the unique performance attributes of the Aerial Element, including anticipated effects of operation with payloads.
5. *Air vehicle airworthiness*—Describe the characteristics of the Aerial Element as they relate to its suitability to fly as intended, without causing a hazard to crewmembers, bystanders, or property, including the construction/manufacturing process, maintenance plan, and those provisions that make the platform uniquely suited to the requested operation.

---

[27] The UAS operator must cancel NOTAMs when UAS operations are completed or will not be conducted.
[28] For further detail, see the FAA's Unmanned Aircraft Systems webpage: www.faa.gov/uas

6. *Planned contingencies*—Describe how operational issues will be addressed, including procedures for mitigating effects of lost link, system fault, or component failure.

7. *Avionics equipment*—Describe the avionic equipment used in the system.

8. *Lighting*—Describe how the system will remain visible and what modifications or configuration changes will be employed to improve visibility in operational settings.

9. *Frequency spectrum analysis*—Describe what communication frequencies will be used and what actions will be taken to monitor and prevent interference.

10. *Method of air traffic control (ATC) communications*—Describe how ATC communications will be supported.

11. *Surveillance capability*—Describe the electronic and visual data that will be captured, the technical capabilities of the sensing mechanisms, and how privacy regulations (e.g., state and local) will be met.

12. *System monitoring/recording capability*—Describe how data captured using the Aerial Element will be monitored and recorded, including any applicable policies for deletion, release, or long-term storage.

13. *Flight crew qualifications*—Describe the credentials, experience, and flight ratings of the crewmembers to operate the sUAS.

14. *Flight operations description*—Describe the proposed flight plan.

15. *Special circumstances*—Describe any special circumstances associated with the proposed operational plan.

16. *Reports of past incidents or accidents*—Identify details of any past incidents or accidents, under previously held operational approvals.

Note that per 14 CFR §61.3(a) and §91.203(a), public operators are able to self-certify pilots, as well as the airworthiness and maintenance of their aircraft, which should be taken into consideration when completing the COA application. Historically, the FAA has been successful in reviewing applications through an online process and issuing the corresponding COA within 60 days after application (not including the time to acquire the public declaration letter). It may be desirable for an issued COA to be used even after the regulation has been implemented because it may allow operations not readily defined by the new regulation.

Expedited applications (emergencies)—The FAA also provides a mechanism for review and approval of emergency use COAs, such as in support of law enforcement or emergency services. It is essential that such applications not propose a use that will result in reduced safety, as they will be denied. Such a COA application will be considered by the FAA when all of the following conditions are demonstrated:

1. A situation exists that is defined as a condition of distress or urgency.

2. The remote pilot and UAS are already approved under an existing COA (different purpose or location).

Expedited (emergency) COAs will not be approved for the following uses:

- UAS demonstration
- Capability testing
- Training (e.g., crew; integration with other assets)
- Operations in Class B airspace or populated areas
- Flights in populated (congested) areas (unless a suitable mitigation plan is proposed and approved)

Civil Use COAs—This COA type, applicable to non-governmental operators, requires that an accompanying Section 333 Grant of Exemption be awarded by the FAA before an application will be processed. It is important to note that each Section 333 Grant of Exemption also includes a nationwide civil use COA (nationwide blanket), with specific operational provisions (see details in the following subsection). Awarding of the Section 333 Grant further enables an operator to propose and apply for a civil use COA to perform operations outside provisions of the nationwide blanket COA. Such applications are submitted using the **UAS Civil COA Portal**.[29] Civil use COA applications, which should not be submitted through the public docket as with Section 333 applications, must include the awarded Section 333 Exemption number and aircraft N-number. This process differs from the Section 333 by informing applicable ATC facilities within the proposed area of proposed operations, as well as providing the FAA an opportunity to review and consider requested deviations from provisions afforded under the nationwide blanket COA.

▶ Section 333 Petition for Exemption

The FAA allows provisional operations in the form of a Section 333 Exemption. This exemption serves as a means for civil entities to "file in review of deviation" (i.e., request exception to requirement) from Federal Aviation Regulations that may be impossible or improbable for a UAS or remote pilot to meet. The main reason for establishment of this exemption was to permit operations in a safe manner under conditional guidance by the FAA. This process may be used to obtain permission to use UAS to perform commercial operations in low-risk, controlled environments.

The FAA has outlined the following conditions that must be met before the issuance of a Section 333 Exemption:

- The specific model of UAS is identified in application, is registered, and displays assigned N-number.
- The UAS is not operated from a moving vehicle (without special approval).
- The pilot-in-command (PIC) has an airman certificate (sport pilot or higher).
- The unmanned aircraft (Aerial Element) is operated in a manner ensuring a minimum of 500-foot separation (horizontal and vertical) from non-participants (bystanders) is maintained.
- UAS is flown during daylight hours only.

---

[29] See oeaaa.faa.gov/oeaaa/external/uas/portal.jsp

Civil Nationwide Blanket COA[30]—This COA is automatically included in the award of Section 333 Grants of Exemption to permit operations below 400 feet AGL[31] using the unmanned aircraft specified in the exemption (weighing less than 55 pounds), during daytime visual flight rules (VFR) conditions, and within VLOS of the pilot. Operational provisions require maintenance of the following distance requirements from public airports or heliports:

- Five (5) nautical miles (NM) from an airport having an operational control tower; or
- Three (3) NM from an airport with a published instrument flight procedure, but not an operational tower; or
- Two (2) NM from an airport without a published instrument flight procedure or an operational tower; or
- Two (2) NM from a heliport, gliderport, or seaplane base

If operations are to be conducted at or within these specified distances, a civil use COA application designating the specific location must also be submitted with a letter of agreement (LOA) from the airport (sponsor) and an existing Section 333 Grant of Exemption. By requiring application for a specific COA, the FAA can ensure that local airports are aware of the proposed operation to de-conflict with other aviation operations, while further coordinating and sharing unique operational provisions with the applicant.

The most common route to legally fly sUAS for civil operations is to complete the requirements for Part 107 remote pilot certification and carry out operations in accordance with the rule set. However, to conduct any operations that exceed the operational provisions contained within Part 107, a specific waiver to an operational limit or a Section 333 Grant of Exemption will be required. Because of the dynamic nature of sUAS technology and operational methods, the Section 333 Exemption process is anticipated to remain in place for the foreseeable future.

▶ Airworthiness Certificates/Type Rating

The operator of a civil aircraft may apply for a special airworthiness certificate–experimental category (SAC-EC), which permits operation of an aircraft in the experimental category for the following purposes:

- Research and development
- Showing compliance with regulations
- Crew training
- Exhibition
- Air racing
- Market surveys

UAS and optionally piloted aircraft (OPA) operators (including manufacturers) may apply for the issuance of this type of certificate, which defines a special class and category aircraft for the same purposes listed above. Additionally, an operator may also apply for type certification under 14 CFR §21.17(b) for a standard airworthiness certificate in the special class category or

---

[30] See the FAA's Unmanned Aircraft Systems webpage at www.faa.gov/uas
[31] Maximum permitted altitude increase from 200 to 400 feet AGL was approved by the FAA in March 2016.

under §21.25 for a SAC in the restricted category (SAC-RC). There are currently two sUAS that are type certified under 14 CFR §21.25: the AeroVironment Puma AE and Insitu ScanEagle. For more information on the application process for the issuance of a SAC, please consult your nearest Flight Standards District Office (FSDO) or the FAA website.[32]

REGULATORY POLICIES AND RESOURCES

Regulation for operational use of UAS has been at the forefront of the industry; however, other areas of concern have become apparent through the variable uses of UAS. Many will use this technology to benefit society and provide substantial gains in knowledge and economic viability to the system. On the other side of the equation, a minority of users will use UAS technologies to infringe or impede the constitutional rights of others. It is your responsibility as a UAS remote pilot to operate within the confines of the law and provide information to the appropriate authority regarding those who do not.

■ PRESIDENTIAL MEMORANDUM

A part of the forward movement resulting from the FAA Modernization and Reform Act of 2012 is the Presidential Memorandum, "Promoting Economic Competitiveness While Safeguarding Privacy, Civil Rights, and Civil Liberties in Domestic Use of Unmanned Aircraft Systems."[33] Through the integration of UAS into the NAS and the widespread capability of UAS, it has become apparent that they are a viable tool for positive economic impact. With benefit often comes a number of issues, however. At the forefront of policy regarding the use of UAS is privacy. Many have expressed extreme concern with regard to the illegal or improper use of UAS technologies to gather surveillance or disturb the system of law in place today. The presidential memorandum, released on February 15, 2015, was subdivided into several sections outlining the following:

- Section 1. UAS Policies and Procedures for Federal Government Use
    - (a) Privacy Protections (collection and use; retention; and dissemination)
    - (b) Civil Rights and Civil Liberties Protections (prohibit violations of First Amendment or discrimination; ensure use is consistent with laws, Executive Orders, and Presidential Directives; and provide procedures for review of complaints)
    - (c) Accountability (auditability; rules and training; policies and procedures; data use and dissemination; and federal funding requirements)
    - (d) Transparency (public notice; policy changes; and annual briefing)
    - (e) Reports

---

[32] FAA's websites for SAC-Experimental (www.faa.gov/aircraft/air_cert/airworthiness_certification/sp_awcert/experiment/) and SAC-Restricted (www.faa.gov/aircraft/air_cert/airworthiness_certification/sp_awcert/restrict/).
[33] The White House, Office of the Press Secretary, "Presidential Memorandum: Promoting Economic Competitiveness While Safeguarding Privacy, Civil Rights, and Civil Liberties in Domestic Use of Unmanned Aircraft Systems" (Washington, DC: The White House, 2015).

- Section 2. Multi-stakeholder Engagement Process
  - (a) Engagement process
  - (b) Department of Commerce/National Telecommunications and Information Administration initiation of engagement process
- Section 3. Definitions (terms used in memorandum)
- Section 4. General Provisions
  - (a) Memorandum will not supersede existing laws and policies for operation of UAS in the NAS
  - (b) Implementation of memorandum will be consistent with applicable laws and appropriations
  - (c) Will not impair or affect authority or function of departments/agencies
  - (d) Encouragement of independent agencies to comply
  - (e) Prevent benefit against U.S. government
  - (f) Authorize Secretary of Commerce to publish memorandum in Federal Register

■ sUAS REGISTRATION

Any sUAS operated under Part 107, a COA, Section 333, or SAC, must be registered prior to operations in the NAS. The owner or operator must register the sUAS with the FAA to receive an **N-number**, which must be displayed in accordance with 14 CFR Part 45. (If unable to comply with marking requirements due to the size or space available, the operator will need to apply to the FAA UAS Integration Office for alternative marking consideration.). To apply for N-number registration, submit a copy of the **Aircraft Registration Application** (AC Form 8050-1) with evidence of ownership to the Aircraft Registration Branch (AFS-750).[34]

As of December 21, 2015, the FAA also began requiring registration for all recreational remote pilots intending to fly sUAS weighing between 0.55 pounds (256 grams) and 55 pounds (25 kg). The method of registration does not require the individual sUAS platform to have an N-number; instead a unique registration identification number is assigned to the operator/remote pilot. This registration number must be affixed to each applicable sUAS in the operator/remote pilot's inventory.[35] To register, the owner must be 13 years of age or older and a U.S. citizen or legal permanent resident.[36] Registration of recreational sUAS costs five dollars, is available online, and is valid for up to three years.[37]

Platforms weighing more than 55 pounds cannot use the same process as those registering as a remote pilot of platforms weighing less than 55 pounds. They must apply for registration through the FAA Aircraft Registry and subsequently will receive an N-number. Those who fly their sUAS in the NAS without registration could face civil and criminal penalties.

---

[34] To register a commercial UAS, a platform larger than 55 pounds, or a UAS to be operated outside of the United States, see the FAA's Aircraft Registry.

[35] See FAA's "How to Label Your UAS" document, available on its "Fly for Fun" webpage: www.faa.gov/uas/getting_started/fly_for_fun

[36] If the owner is less than 13 years of age, a person 13 years of age or older must register the sUAS.

[37] FAA's Small Unmanned Aircraft System (sUAS) Registration Service: registermyuas.faa.gov

■ EXPORT CONTROLLED TECHNOLOGY

Some of the technology and data employed in modern UAS designs is protected by export control regulations, such as Export Administration Regulations (EARs)[38] and International Traffic in Arms Regulations (ITAR).[39] The majority of exports are defense/military-specific UAS technology and data, including but not limited to programming elements, performance data, payloads, and control components of commercially available products and resources. Responsibility for compliance with export control policies lies with the owner/operator. Deviations from these policies may lead to strict civil or criminal penalties with prison sentences or monetary fines.

■ TRANSPORTATION OF EQUIPMENT AND MATERIALS

Many of the items commonly used in the operation of UAS may be hazardous in certain environments. For instance, lithium-ion batteries, certain metals, or fuels may be considered hazardous material, so it is important to be familiar with the properties of all materials in use and also the responsibility to notify all appropriate parties prior to carriage of these materials. Many airlines have policies regarding transport of lithium-based batteries; it is suggested that such policies be reviewed prior to any planned travel and transportation of batteries.

The FAA requires the following be met, when any batteries are carried on commercial aircraft:[40]

- Brought in carry-on baggage only (cannot be checked).
- Battery terminals must be protected from short circuit (e.g., covered with electrical tape).
- Lithium-ion batteries are limited to a rating of 100 watt hours (Wh) per battery; with airline approval, passengers may also carry up to two spare larger lithium-ion batteries (101–160 Wh).[41]
- Must be for use by the passenger (not carried for sale or distribution).
- Must be protected from damage (a charge bag is recommended to limit fire potential).

Make sure to review federal, state, and local laws and guidance, including those issued by the DOT, prior to arranging for shipment or transportation of sUAS components and elements.

■ UAS TEST SITES AND COE DESIGNATIONS

In an effort to create a safe operational area for UAS, the FAA has established a series of Test Sites (see Figure 4-9) and a Center of Excellence (COE) to conduct operational research in support of its outlined UAS Integration Roadmap. These resources are being used to gain a

---

[38] Contact U.S. Department of Commerce for details.
[39] Contact U.S. Department of State for details.
[40] See the FAA's "Pack Safe: Lithium ion and lithium metal batteries, spare (uninstalled)," www.faa.gov/about/initiatives /hazmat_safety/more_info/?hazmat=7 .
[41] To calculate Wh, multiple voltage (V) by amp hours (Ah).

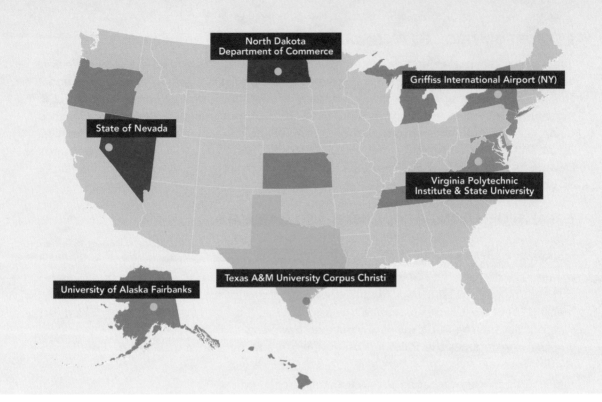

FIGURE 4-9. Map of FAA designated UAS Test Sites.

more thorough understanding of the limitations and capabilities of UAS technology; identify new technology, processes or methods to improve safety and efficiency; and expand public outreach and industry collaboration.

▶ Six FAA Designated Test Sites

New York's Griffiss International Airport—This site includes test range locations in New York, Massachusetts, and Michigan and was approved for operations on August 7, 2014. It is managed by the Northeast UAS Airspace Integration Research (NUAIR) Alliance.

North Dakota Department of Commerce—This site, covering most of northeastern North Dakota, was approved for operations on April 21, 2014. It is managed by the Northern Plains UAS Test Site.

State of Nevada—This site encompasses the entire State of Nevada and was approved for operations on June 9, 2014. It is managed by the Nevada Institute for Autonomous Systems (NIAS).

Texas A&M University-Corpus Christi—This site, featuring multiple locations across the state of Texas, was approved for operations on June 20, 2014. It is managed by the Lone Star UAS Center of Excellence & Innovation.

University of Alaska-Fairbanks—This site includes test ranges in Alaska, Hawaii, Oregon, Kansas, and Tennessee and was approved for operations on May 5, 2014. It is managed by the Alaska Center for Unmanned Aircraft Systems Integration (ACUASI).

Virginia Polytechnic Institute and State University—This site includes test ranges in Virginia, New Jersey, and Maryland and was approved for operations on August 13, 2014. It is managed by the Mid-Atlantic Aviation Partnership (MAAP).

❱ FAA UAS Center of Excellence

In an effort to achieve a viable research base, the FAA designated the Alliance for System Safety of UAS through Research Excellence (ASSURE) in May 2015. The creation of this COE was supported by a number of universities that provide UAS-related education, operation, or research, as well as private companies working in this field. The COE serves as a tool for both academic institutions and industry partners to work together to progress areas of UAS research by providing purpose, funding, and tasking to move issues affecting UAS operations, design, maintenance, ATC interoperability, and crew training. The potential opportunities among partners of this COE allows for the effective pairing of ventures between academic and industry experts to create solutions to both existing and future problems associated with multiple disciplines regarding UAS.

OPERATING ENVIRONMENT

Environmental conditions specific to the area where sUAS are to be operated must be considered to predict how the system will react and to further determine if the chosen platform will have success in a given mission profile. Previous chapters have outlined the definition of a UAS platform as a composition of systems (i.e., a collection of independent and unified subsystems). Each of these components has limits, which may inhibit use in certain conditions. It is also important to consider the human element in this discussion, as the majority of users are operating in VLOS conditions. The final and most considerable element to consider is how the aircraft will physically interact with the environment. This section will briefly outline environmental elements and discuss how each may generically interact with a UAS. Environmental conditions such as visibility, terrain, temperature, wind velocity/direction, and density altitude play a key role in the success of any particular sUAS mission.

VISIBILITY

Visibility may be defined either by what the airman would see on the ground or visibility in the air (*see* Figure 4-10). These may be substantially different when certain weather phenomena are introduced such as clouds, precipitation, or visible moisture in the form of fog. VMC and IMC were discussed previously in this chapter to give you an idea of cloud clearance and visibility requirements in controlled and uncontrolled airspace, but they play a significant role in the operational profile of a given mission. The human interactions between manned aircraft

FIGURE 4-10. Visibility in environments can range from obscured (*left*) to clear (*right*).

and unmanned aircraft are different in many cases, so operations with regard to sUAS are mostly considered to take place in solely VFR conditions conducted in VMC, at this time. As system reliability and user abilities to operate in complex environments continues to improve, operations outside of visual boundaries are likely to occur as a component of pilot interpretation of instrumentation and telemetry data through a suitable ground control interface. The interface for this type of interaction is more complex than rudimentary systems and is designed to give the user full control of the platform in beyond visual line-of-sight (BVLOS) or in IMC. VLOS conditions as previously discussed may also be inhibited by terrain elements, which will be discussed later in this section. Part 107 requirements identify a minimum of three-mile visibility between the remote pilot and aircraft must be maintained.

■ SEE AND AVOID

The term "see and avoid" has had many different variations based on the best interpretation of the term. It has been coined both "sense and avoid" and "detect and avoid" in past references, but essentially remains the same in context. As simply as it is stated, the term means identification and avoidance between UAS and any other flying object, to include manned aircraft and other UAS. A special review committee defined by the Radio Technical Commission for Aeronautics (RTCA 228) was formed to discuss and recommend the best system and procedures to successfully mitigate traffic incursions between UAS and all other aircraft.[42]

As see and avoid solutions continue to emerge, the most promising appears to be one based on Automatic Dependent Surveillance–Broadcast (ADS-B), which is a "cooperative" surveillance position reporting system that uses satellite navigation as a primary means for position reporting. The term *cooperative* defines the requirement for aircraft operating in controlled airspace to be equipped for safe operation within that airspace. ADS-B "out" is commonly used by aircraft to communicate position, and ADS-B "in" may be used for communication purposes between ATC and other cooperative aircraft. The FAA has mandated that all cooperative aircraft will be equipped with ADS-B by January 1, 2020, as this will serve as a primary tool for separation of aircraft in the Next Generation (NextGen) air traffic control system.[43]

---

[42] RTCA Special Committee 228, Minimum Operational Performance Standards (MOPS) for Unmanned Aircraft Systems, is working to develop MOPS for Detect-and-Avoid (DAA) equipment and a Command and Control (C2) Data Link.
[43] The regulatory requirement under 14 CFR §91.225 only applies to ADS-B(Out) and does not include ADS-B(In).

▌MAINTAINING VISUAL CONTACT

Maintaining visual contact between the remote pilot and the aircraft in VLOS application is the responsibility of the remote pilot. It is important not to allow the aircraft to fly outside of this boundary (typically one mile) because the remote pilot may lose visual and positional orientation. This loss of visual acuity may subsequently make successful recovery of the aircraft difficult or cause damage to persons or property in the event of a loss-of-control scenario. User experience may play a role in increasing the user's ability to recognize or maintain visual orientation, but it is purely at the discretion of the operator (owner/lessee) to define visual limits. Other factors such as distance, altitude, aircraft coloration, reflection, and background blending may cause gaps in visual acuity and lead to loss of visual orientation or control. It is important to assess these issues prior to flight to determine how each factor may affect the success of the operation.

An approximate calculation of VLOS can be made using Howett's equation by assuming that an object must subtend one minute of visual arc to be detectable by a human with normal 20/20 vision.[44] An estimate of the VLOS distance for operation of the sUAS, based on the distance in feet (ft) for identifying and detecting an object with the human eye, for a PIC or VO with 20/20 vision and typical visual acuity (see Figure 4-11), can be calculated with the following equation:

Visible Distance (ft) = 3,438 x Side View Height of sUAS (inches)

Example: An sUAS has a side view height (profile size) of 10 inches:
Visible distance = 3,438 x 10 = 34,380 ft[45]

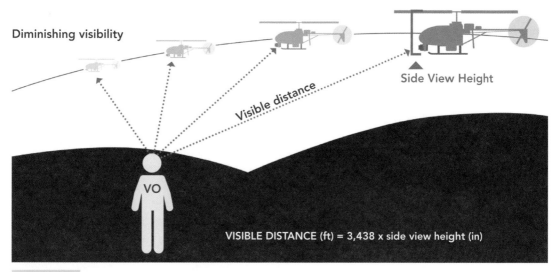

FIGURE 4-11. Visible distance calculation.

---

[44] Gerald L. Howett, "Size of letters required for visibility as a function of viewing distance and observer visual acuity," NBS Technical Note 1180 (Washington, DC: National Bureau of Standards, 1983).
[45] Any distance beyond this would render the platform non-visible to the PIC/VO, assuming optimal visibility conditions.

VLOS distances are also affected by a multitude of controllable and uncontrollable variables, including the general level of ambient natural and artificial illumination, angle of the sun or moon, meteorological conditions and transparency of the atmosphere, terrain masking, sUAS paint scheme and external lighting, and degree of contrast between the sUAS and the background.

▌ UNIMPEDED LINE OF SIGHT

Radio line of sight (LOS) operations differ from VLOS in reference to the ability for electromagnetic waves to propagate between the remote pilot and the aircraft or the aircraft and remote pilot. Radio signals operate over different frequencies with the most common control frequency in 2.4GHz. Other types of communications such as video or telemetry feeds may operate over a different spectrum, but all electromagnetic waves are susceptible to certain phenomena that may impede their transmission. Communications may be significantly impeded by factors such as terrain, scatter, absorption, power, free-space path loss, and the curvature of the earth. Radio waves are susceptible to a number of phenomena, which may be difficult to discern or calculate for every operation. Please refer to publications and manuals relevant to the equipment used in your sUAS for specific operational parameters.

▌ EXTENDED AND BEYOND VISUAL LINE-OF-SIGHT

UAS operations can be classified as VLOS, extended VLOS (EVLOS), or BVLOS.[46] The majority of civil non-VLOS operations are prohibited at this time,[47] but waivers and permitted use are expected to increase as user ability and aircraft technology progresses. EVLOS and BVLOS (E/BVLOS) application requires operation beyond the visual reference of the remote pilot, supported through daisy-chaining a series of VOs or using specialized equipment, such as a chase plane or antennas and arrays to propagate usable signals between the ground control and the aircraft. Larger public UAS (e.g., used by DOD and other agencies) have been operating using E/BVLOS for decades with applicable equipment and user requirements developed through airframe and system-specific training. It should be noted that the distance required for the signal to travel in BVLOS applications may cause issues in latency. Electromagnetic waves travel at the speed of light, in which very long-distance applications may cause "lags" or a lack of instant controllability to actuators, servos, and the relay of communication.

There are currently two FAA Pathfinder projects tasked with formally defining the requirements for civil EVLOS and BVLOS operations. One such project features the developer PrecisionHawk, which is exploring how UAS flights outside the pilot's direct vision might allow greater use of sUAS, including EVLOS operations to monitor crops (precision agriculture) in rural settings. The second project features BNSF Railroad's examination of the use of UAS to inspect rail system infrastructure BVLOS in rural or isolated areas. At the conclusion of the Path-

---

[46] The FAA has definitions for VLOS and BVLOS that have been published and are generally accepted; however, the definition of EVLOS has yet to be formalized. The European Organization for the Safety of Air Navigation (Eurocontrol) has published definitions for VLOS (<500 m), EVLOS (>500 m and supported by daisy-chained VOs), and BVLOS (>500 m, using technological support).

[47] Civil EVLOS/BVLOS requires FAA-approved exemption, such as has been provided to PrecisionHawk and BNSF Railroad under the FAA's Pathfinder program.

finder projects and subsequent development and issuance of formal guidance, civil EVLOS and BVLOS operations are anticipated to be approved. However, such operations may require a type certification (TC) under 14 CFR §21.17(b), rather than a Part 107 waiver or Section 333 Exemption. Currently the FAA is processing over a dozen 14 CFR §21.17(b) type certification projects for sUAS/UAS designed for EVLOS and BVLOS operations by a variety of aircraft types.

ALTITUDE

The height of the aircraft above the remote pilot is another important consideration. Current regulations prohibit flying sUAS at altitudes over 400 feet AGL unless special provisions or exemptions have been made. Visually judging altitude can be difficult, so it is important for the remote pilot to visually discern objects at a given fixed distance to build a reference to altitude. Telemetry data obtained from the aircraft through the user interface should aid the remote pilot in maintaining a given altitude in the form of a digital display. Considerations such as traversing air traffic, loss of visual reference, and radio line of sight must be well reviewed to maintain safety in the operation of any UAS. It is important to consider that air traffic in the area may be unaware or unable to see sUAS at low altitude. It is common for rotor wing aircraft to operate at altitudes less than 400 feet AGL, so the user must constantly remain aware and vigilant of any traffic in the area.

HAZARDS AND OBSTACLES

The flight environment contains a host of hazards related to terrain and other obstacles. Man-made structures (such as towers, buildings, and power lines), combined with natural structures (terrain, trees, and bodies of water) can be of significant concern to the sUAS remote pilot. Radio towers are usually accompanied by guidewires, which may be difficult or impossible to visually detect. Maintaining a safe operational area requires the user to be aware of all physical structures that may cause an impediment to the safety of the flight. Site surveys are a common component of pre-flight activity and will provide the user with an assessment of any existing structures that may cause concern.

Obstacles outside of the control of the remote pilot may come in the form of birds or other aircraft/vehicles traversing the operational boundaries of the site. Even though these types of obstacles may be unavoidable in some cases, it is the responsibility of the remote pilot to maintain vigilance and situational awareness of the entire operational area. Flight into obstacles is commonly referred to as controlled flight into terrain (CFIT) and accounts for a very high occurrence of aircraft accidents and incidents.

OPERATIONAL ENVIRONMENTS

The operational environment where primary sUAS operations will occur is important to consider when acquiring any type of platform. Some environmental factors may impede the user's or aircraft's ability to fulfill the operational goals of a given mission. Factors such as persistent

FIGURE 4-12. Examples of farmland/rural environments.

weather, moisture, visibility, hazards/obstacles, environmental impact regulations, and density altitude must all be considered to determine if the aircraft can maintain appropriate performance within its operational envelope. This section will briefly outline operational environments and special considerations to make note of prior to acquiring or operating any type of sUAS.

▌ FARMLAND/RURAL

An advantage of farmland or rural operations is that most operational areas are in sparsely populated environments that can be flat and spacious or elevated and compact (e.g., terraced) (see Figure 4-12). Conditions that may impede usability of a system are limited endurance capabilities to operate over large areas, or obstacles in the path of the aircraft. Agricultural communities often have a number of low-level obstacles (windmills, structures, and farming vehicles) and high wind levels, making a thorough site assessment necessary.

▌ MOUNTAINOUS

Mountainous environments (see Figure 4-13) often require special operational considerations. High levels of wind or mechanical turbulence associated with uneven terrain may require operational capabilities well beyond that of most commercial off-the-shelf (COTS) sUAS. Moun-

FIGURE 4-13. Examples of mountainous environments.

FIGURE 4-14. Examples of forested environments.

tainous environments can also vary in weather conditions with very little notice, as well as in topography and the availability of GPS and communication pathways, making pre-flight planning of weather conditions and performance capabilities very important considerations.

▌ FORESTED

Operations in dense forest areas may impede the remote pilot's ability to operate due to confinement, sporadic turbulence, or visibility issues (see Figure 4-14). Launch and recovery issues may also become apparent due to a lack of space, so systems must be chosen carefully to avoid operational issues. Depending on the type of data being gathered, fixed-wing platforms may provide longer endurance and better controllability than multirotor platforms.

▌ WETLANDS

Special considerations in wetlands (see Figure 4-15) include high levels of moisture content and oftentimes issues with accessibility. Environmental concerns may become an issue due to mechanical issues such as noise or, in the event of a system loss, the possible introduction of unrecoverable hazardous materials in sensitive environments.

FIGURE 4-15. Examples of wetland environments.

FIGURE 4-16. Examples of desert/arid environments.

▌ DESERT/ARID

Desert or arid (dry) environments (*see* Figure 4-16) may limit the life of certain components on the sUAS. For example, fine grain sands are usually set adrift and become suspended in the air relatively easily. Components, such as motors and other mechanical devices, may succumb to significant wear well below their respective designed failure limits. Operations in this type of environment are possible, but the remote pilot must take care to shield components that may be susceptible to foreign body intrusion and inspect the aircraft on intervals exceeding those for normal operations. Another consideration in desert or arid environments is the fluctuation in temperature. Certain components may be limited by high or low temperatures, so the aircraft may need to be modified with different components to operate successfully and remain viable in this type of environment.

▌ COASTAL

Operations in coastal environments have become increasingly more common with many remote pilots supplying videography from boats and beaches around the world (*see* Figure 4-17). Operations in this type of environment require special thought and planning. With any

FIGURE 4-17. Examples of coastal environments.

FIGURE 4-18. Examples of cold-weather environments.

environment consisting of large volumes of water, moisture intrusion into the aircraft and its components must be assessed to determine any special equipment requirements or modifications. As with desert environments, usability of the system may be severely impeded by lower-than-expected component life.

Winds may also become an issue in coastal environments, depending on where the primary operation is to occur. Large bodies of water are considered to have a large "fetch," which allows winds to blow in excess over large regions. Temperature fluctuations between day and night may also cause inconsistent weather patterns or strong winds, so the remote pilot must be vigilant of all meteorological conditions.

▮ ARCTIC/COLD-WEATHER

Arctic and cold weather environments often succumb to extreme environmental conditions (*see* Figure 4-18). In addition to temperature, high winds and turbulence are often associated with operations in this type of environment. Operational times on components of the aircraft may be significantly reduced, unless the aircraft was specifically designed for this type of operation. Icing may also be an issue in any type of visible moisture when temperatures are near or below freezing, which may reduce the aerodynamic capabilities of the system. Most COTS airframes will not meet the requirements of arctic or cold weather operations, unless they are significantly modified.

▮ MARITIME

The maritime environment is attractive to remote pilots because of a lack of regulation in warning areas, but it is important to consider that territorial sea, and subsequent airspace, extends out 12 miles from the shoreline,[48] making launch and recovery difficult for most systems. As with coastal environments, the use of aircraft in maritime environments may cause significant wear to

---

[48] Per *Presidential Proclamation No. 5928, December 27, 1988, 54 F.R. 777: Territorial Sea of the United States of America.*

FIGURE 4-19. Examples of populated areas, ranging from urban (*left*) to suburban (*right*).

components and lower the useful life of the system. Applications in this area are being tested for commercial fishing and other ventures such as census data gathering, but the acquisition costs of specialized equipment and the experience necessary to fulfill mission requirements is prohibitive for most users.

■ AVIATION/AIRPORT

Operations near terminal environments are possible, if special provisions or exemptions are allowed by the FAA or controlling agency, but it is important to consider other aircraft operating in or near terminal environments. It's predicted that operations will be given more leeway in this type of environment as regulation continues to mature and technology allows smaller platforms to safely operate in closer proximity to manned aircraft. Considerations that must be planned for are right-of-way procedures, communication protocols to include lost communications, and see-and-avoid protocols to effectively allow all stakeholders to monitor any and all air traffic in the area.

■ POPULATED AREAS

The use of sUAS in urban and suburban environments has become popular for gathering photography and videography of events in which the population density may be high (*see* Figure 4-19). It is important to avoid all areas that may place any risk to users or property, in case an aircraft becomes uncontrollable or loses communication with the remote pilot. Most regulatory policy limits the proximity of UAS near areas that may introduce undue risk to observers or other components of urban environments that may be adversely affected by the use of UAS. As with other environments discussed in this section, the regulatory policies and procedures in effect at the time of this publication are likely to change as more experience with UAS becomes commercially viable. It is important to consult all federal, state, and local regulations prior to any flight, as they may be prohibitive.

◼ INDOORS

Indoor operations of UAS are not regulated by the FAA; however, the use of UAS in such settings does fall under the liability requirements of a facility/property insurance provider, as well as safety rules and regulations established and administered by organizations such as the Occupational Safety and Health Administration (OSHA). There are many uses for sUAS within indoor environments, but it is important to consider risk and create a thorough understanding of procedures, protocols, liability and permissions. Examples of operations indoors may include supporting emergency response, public safety, marketing/filming, and exhibition. Prior to conducting indoor operations, the safety and facilities management personnel responsible for operation of the location, as well as the legal representative of the facility owner or administrator, should be consulted. The guidance outlined by these representatives will indicate whether the proposed operation is permissible or suitable, given organizational, legal, and facility requirements.

Indoor operations should be limited to large, open areas, without impediments or hazards such as ceiling fans, hanging lights, or tapestries. The platform should be operated with sufficient clearance to avoid potential mishaps and impacts with walls, ceilings, internal structures, and obstacles. Confined areas may cause undue risk to personnel, so it is important to understand how the aircraft will be managed in close proximity to those on the ground. Establishing and following proper procedures and protocols may prevent or limit both damage to property and harm to persons on the ground. The location of all crewmembers, observers, or non-participants should be known and communicated to the PIC, relative to the position and orientation of the sUAS. Furthermore, any personnel in the environment should wear appropriate protective clothing and apparel (e.g., safety glasses, non-slip shoes, and full-length garments), as well as be briefed on safety considerations and appropriate responses, prior to operation.

Note that some external reference sensors, such as global positioning system (GPS), may not work in an indoor environment. This may result in reduced maneuverability or controllability, including failure or inaccessible autonomous control functions. It is recommended that prior to indoor operations, the manufacturer's guidance be reviewed to determine if the system requires manual reconfiguration of modes, such as GPS, attitude and altitude hold, and stability assistance.

FIGURE 4-20. Examples of sUAS indoor flight.

■ NATIONAL PARKS (FEDERAL)

sUAS operations in National Parks is highly restrictive and severely limited in most cases. Consult the National Park Service Policy Memorandum 14-05, "Unmanned Aircraft—Interim Policy," for more information prior to any flight activity in this type of area.[49] In early 2016, the U.S. Forest Service published the following guidance relating to the use of UAS:

- Avoid operation in (including taking off from, flying over, or landing within) federally-designated wilderness, primitive, or noise-sensitive areas and populated sites, including rivers, campgrounds, trail heads and visitor centers.
- Do not disturb or harass wildlife.
- Do not interfere with official aerial activities over National Forests, such as wildfire detection and suppression.
- State privacy laws must be observed.

These guidelines are only applicable to recreational (hobby) sUAS operations. Civil operations, such as aerial filming, still photography, survey, or any application of sUAS, may still be performed with appropriate U.S. Forest Service approval (special use permit issued by the Forest Service).

■ ACCIDENT/EMERGENCY SCENES

The use of sUAS to support infrastructure needs for automobile and transportation accidents/incidents, fires, and manmade and natural disaster relief is becoming attractive to many federal, state, and municipality stakeholders (*see* Figure 4-21). This technology can provide viable, real-

FIGURE 4-21. Example accident/emergency scenes.

---

[49] See www.nps.gov/policy/PolMemos/PM_14-05.htm

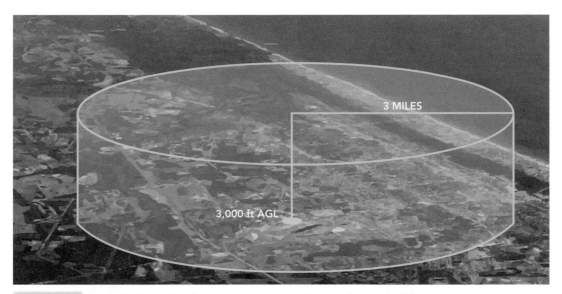

FIGURE 4-22. Example National Defense Airspace surrounding sporting event TFR.

time imagery and data; however, it is important to consider safe operations. The scene of an accident often requires rescue personnel to work as a unit to achieve positive outcomes, so it is important to mitigate any interference by sUAS in a safety or life-critical situation. You must also consider how equipment such as fire trucks, ambulances, and rescue helicopters may work seamlessly with sUAS in the air to avoid any type of incursion or incident from working in confined or high-risk areas.

▮ LARGE PUBLIC EVENTS

While the use of sUAS to provide news coverage or marketing for public events, such as Major League games, is appealing to many users, there are federal and local prohibitions that may prevent such operations. Federal prohibitions, in the form of a TFR, are intended to protect the public in the wake of the coordinated terrorist attacks of September 11, 2001. A TFR is automatically put in place for any event at a stadium featuring seating for 30,000 or more for a Major League Baseball, National Football League, or National Collegiate Athletics League Division I Football game, as well as NASCAR Sprint Cup, Indy Car, and Champ Series races. These TFRs begin one hour before the event and last until one hour after. The airspace for an area three nautical miles around the stadium and from the ground to 3,000 feet AGL is designated as National Defense Airspace (*see* Figure 4-22), which carries significant penalties if violated, including up to one year in prison. It is possible to request and receive FAA approval for specific operations within a TFR through an airspace waiver. However, any sUAS operations would also require the appropriate UAS operational approval, such as a COA or Section 333 Petition for Exemption. The restrictions imposed by the TFR are not applicable to ATC-directed, DOD, law enforcement, or air ambulance flight operations.

WEATHER

It is imperative for all sUAS remote pilots and users to understand how current or severe weather may impede flight capabilities. Pre-planning on the part of the remote pilot may determine risk associated with precipitation, wind, temperature (density altitude), visibility, or severe weather, which may change rapidly. Many commercially available applications to monitor weather meet FAA standards for pre-flight planning and can be acquired relatively easily with the use of portable devices. It is beyond the scope of most UAS users to be familiar with common aviation weather reports (METARS, TAFS, winds aloft forecasts, area forecasts, or PIREPS), but it is necessary to understand how current and predicted weather forecasts may affect the outcome of a given flight. For more information on types of aviation weather reports and how they may be interpreted, please consult the *Pilot's Handbook of Aeronautical Knowledge*, which is available for free from the FAA's website.[50] Part 107 requirements identify a minimum of three-mile visibility between the remote pilot and aircraft, as well as require that a separation of 500 feet below and 2,000 feet away (horizontally) from clouds be maintained.

ENVIRONMENTAL CONSIDERATIONS

The following are a list of environmental considerations recommended for review prior to any sUAS flight:

- Visual and communications line-of-sight (VLOS and LOS)
- GPS availability
- Geomagnetic events (solar storms)
- Sufficient room for takeoff/recovery (and normal and appropriate alternatives for emergencies)
- Foliage density
- Humidity (moisture levels)
- Temperature
- Non-participating persons, vehicles, or objects (e.g., livestock)
- Retention ponds, streams, canals, and bodies of water
- Operational boundaries and landholder permission to overfly
- Thermals and turbulent air
- Dynamic weather conditions
- Terrain features

---

[50] U.S. Department of Transportation, Federal Aviation Administration, *Pilot's Handbook of Aeronautical Knowledge*, FAA-H-8083-25A (Washington, DC: FAA, 2008).

SUAS OPERATION

SUAS are confined by the same physical properties as any other air vehicle, so users must become familiar with the terminology and principles that support flight. Basic knowledge of principles such as aerodynamics, weight and balance, aircraft performance, and aeronautical decision making (ADM) are elements necessary for the safe operation of any type of aircraft. This section will briefly outline these elements to provide you with a working knowledge of basic aircraft principles.

GENERAL AERONAUTICAL KNOWLEDGE

Since the beginning of human history, man has been fascinated with flight. Early writings of Leonardo da Vinci outlined the flight of birds, but it took centuries of forward thinking to come to the milestone of manned aviation, which was the first powered and controllable flight achieved by the Wright brothers in 1903. The advent of new materials and technologies in the twentieth century led to advancements well beyond that of previous generations and continues to grow at an unbounded rate with technologies such as 3D printing, composite structures, and lighter and more efficient powerplants.

This section begins with a fundamental overview of aerodynamic principles that you must be familiar with prior to becoming an sUAS remote pilot. The material in this section will not only aid you in becoming familiar with aerodynamic principles, but will also provide the framework for sound judgement when acquiring an sUAS for a given operational skill set. More detailed information regarding general aeronautical knowledge may be supplemented by the FAA *Pilot's Handbook of Aeronautical Knowledge*.[51]

■ FUNDAMENTALS OF FLIGHT

The fundamentals of flight fall into four basic elements: lift, thrust, weight, and drag (*see* Figure 4-23). As an aircraft maneuvers, each of these forces changes to compliment the others, resulting in a change in position. When all four forces of flight are in equilibrium, or the net resultant is equal to zero, the aircraft is said to be in "unaccelerated" flight. For instance, if

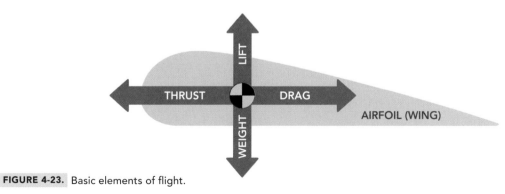

FIGURE 4-23. Basic elements of flight.

---

[51] U.S. DOT, FAA, *Pilot's Handbook of Aeronautical Knowledge*.

a multirotor system establishes a hover, the resultant or net sum of the upward forces to the downward forces—and forward forces to rearward forces—is zero. When a fixed-wing aircraft enters a climb, the lift is initially changed via pitching the nose upwards; however, it returns to equilibrium once in steady climbing flight.

▶ Lift

Lift is one of the primary factors in how aircraft fly and is relatively easy to understand if you think about it as a relationship of difference in pressure. Any time a pressure or temperature differential exists, some sort of energy transfer will occur to try to restore equilibrium. In the case of lift, the curved surface of a wing requires air molecules to move faster over the top surface, creating an area of low pressure. The air moving across the bottom of the wing will move slower and be at a higher pressure than the air moving across the top. This pressure differential causes the wing to create lift, or the primary upward force of flight. A downwash effect is also created, which is a downward and backward flow of air generated at the trailing edge, or rear, of the wing. Lift opposes the downward force of gravity and acts perpendicular to the center of the lifting surface (wing).

To understand how lift works, it's necessary to understand how wings are designed. An airfoil may be viewed as the cross-sectional area of a lifting surface, to include the conventional wing on a fixed-wing platform or rotor on a rotary-wing platform. Early airfoils were shaped much differently than those used today, which have been refined based on research and engineering design principles; however, the same relationship holds true. The curvature of the airfoil is referred to as "camber" and may be apparent on both the top and bottom to a point of symmetry when the top and bottom have equal curvature. In order for lift to be produced, the airfoil must form a pressure differential, which is controlled by what is called the **angle of attack**. This term refers to the angle of the chord line, or centerline of the airfoil, to the relative wind. Relative wind is defined as the airflow parallel and opposite to the flight path. When the angle of attack becomes excessive and the smooth airflow over the top of the lifting surface becomes disrupted or turbulent, the aircraft is said to be in a stalled condition. A stalled condition indicates that the lifting surface is creating little to no lift. In order for smooth airflow to be restored, the angle of attack must be reduced.

▶ Thrust

Thrust is a force that applies to the type of propulsion on your aircraft. It may act in different directions, based on the type of platform in use. This force may be considered to oppose drag in many cases, such as with a fixed-wing platform configured with a tractor propeller (discussed in Chapter 3). A rotor-wing platform, on the other hand, may produce thrust in a different vector when in a hover. In a rotor-wing platform in upward flight, thrust would oppose both weight and drag simultaneously in the same vector, but when a hover is maintained, no drag is placed on the aircraft, because it has no relative movement. In a fixed-wing platform, forward movement will be initiated when thrust exceeds drag; conversely, the aircraft will slow in level flight when thrust is reduced, because drag will overcome the forward movement produced by excess thrust.

❯ Weight and Balance

Weight and balance is very important in determining how well an aircraft will perform in all aspects of flight. Weight is the force that opposes lift and acts toward the center of the earth as a result of gravity. An imaginary point on every aircraft, referred to as its center of gravity (CG), is the point around which the aircraft would balance. Any movement of the CG fore or aft of its calculated CG envelope will cause either a desirable or undesirable flight effect. CG is affected by the placement, weight, and distance of items from a given point, referred to as a datum. The further items are placed aft of the datum, the more effect they will have on CG. Items placed nearest the datum will have less effect on CG. The distance an item is placed from the datum is referred to as an "arm." The arm multiplied by the weight provides a number referred to as "moment." If the total moment of all items is divided by the total weight, a calculated arm will be derived. This is important, because all aircraft have a CG limitation based on fore and aft arm limits. This envelope is graphically depicted in the Flight Operations Manual (FOM) of many aircraft, but may be omitted from some UAS platforms due to variability of system components. Refer to the operations manual for your specific aircraft to determine CG requirements.

❯ Drag

Drag is the force that resists forward movement in a conventional fixed-wing aircraft and may resist forward, rearward, sideward, upward, or downward movement in a rotor-wing aircraft, depending on the direction of flight. Drag may be broken into two types: parasite drag and induced drag.

Parasite drag is defined by the air resistance created by external components, skin friction, or the interference of airflow where certain components of the airframe come together. Parasite drag may be reduced by keeping all surfaces on the aircraft smooth and by removing any excess structures directly in the airstream. It is important to consider that parasite drag increases as velocity increases in the direction of movement.

Induced drag is the result of airflow around a wing and the differential of air pressure that meets at the wing tips. Greater induced drag will be created as the pressure differential between the top and bottom surfaces of the wing increases (i.e., becomes farther apart). For instance, high angles of attack will produce greater amounts of lift. As lift becomes greater with an increasing angle of attack, so does the pressure gradient; therefore, induced drag will increase. In more technical terms, induced drag is inversely proportional to the square of speed. The airflow that meets at the wing tip produces a phenomena referred to as vortices, which represent cyclonic air rotation just beyond the trailing edge of the wing and that become larger as lift generation increases. A reduction in the size of vortices will also cause a reduction in induced drag; therefore, if the pressure gradient is reduced at the wing tip, induced drag will be reduced. A common design remedy for the reduction of vortices and induced drag is referred to as a winglet, which is a vertical projection attached to the wing tip of an aircraft.

The relationship of induced drag to parasite drag is important in the understanding of how total drag affects an aircraft. The point at which the parasite drag curve and induced drag curve meet is where minimum drag occurs. This point is referred to as the L/D$_{MAX}$, or the point at which lift is greatest and drag is lowest. This point will give the aircraft the best glide speed and minimum sink rate, assuming powerplant failure (complete loss of thrust) in a single-engine aircraft.

▌AIRCRAFT AXES AND REFERENCE FRAME

Orientation and controllability of an aircraft may be referred to by the position of the axis that passes through it at different points. The three axes that pass through an aircraft are referred to as the longitudinal axis (x), lateral axis (y), and vertical axis (z) (*see* Figure 4-24). Flight control surfaces disturbing air flow result in aircraft movement about each axis (for fixed-wing aircraft).

- *Longitudinal axis*—Rotational changes about the aircraft's x-axis, which passes through a conventional aircraft from nose to tail, are referred to as "roll." It is typically controlled through deflection of ailerons.
- *Lateral axis*—The y-axis passes through both wing tips of the plane, perpendicular to the longitudinal axis. Rotational changes about the y-axis are referred to as "pitch" and are typically controlled through deflection of the elevator.
- *Vertical axis*—The z-axis passes vertically through the center of the aircraft. Rotational changes about the z-axis are referred to "yaw" and are controlled by deflection of the rudder.

It is important to understand that all aircraft are defined by these axes, but control surfaces can differ significantly. For instance, multirotor platforms achieve maneuverability by varying

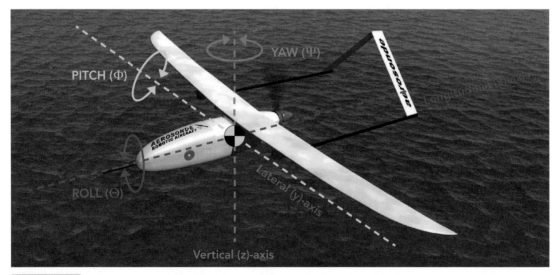

FIGURE 4-24. Reference axes and rotational movements overlaid on a fixed-wing UAS.

the speed of each rotor, so control surfaces are not present. Some fixed-wing aircraft may use "mixing," such as delta wing designs (featuring a combination of aileron and elevator control surfaces referred to as an elevon).

■ AIRCRAFT PERFORMANCE

Aircraft performance dictates how well your aircraft will maneuver, climb, and endure. It is a result of a number of factors such as powerplant selection, propulsion, weight, materials, temperature, and environmental conditions. Almost everything you equip your aircraft with will produce either a positive or negative effect on performance. Please consult your aircraft's flight operations manual to determine performance.

■ AERONAUTICAL DECISION MAKING (ADM)

The art of making appropriate decisions at the appropriate time is a result of experience, in many cases. The flight environment can be very unforgiving when issues arise outside of the capabilities of the remote pilot or crew. sUAS operations will probably require you to work with a VO or other crewmembers. Your ability to work cohesively as a group will determine how capable you are of handling a given situation.

Traditional aeronautical decision making (ADM) models suggest ways to mitigate issues based on elements such as attitudes, experience, group dynamics, or situations. The sUAS remote pilot will be required to understand how proper ADM allows for better decision making from case studies of past incidents; however, the use of automation may cause some different interactions based on unique operations of sUAS platforms. Some elements of ADM are the sole responsibility of the remote pilot, but when working with a crew, shared responsibility and team dynamics come into place. One component of responsible decision making is remaining calm and aware of what is going on around you at all times. This is referred to as situational awareness and can be severely impacted by workload. Higher tasking or workload may take up a remote pilot's attention and decrease his or her ability to properly monitor a given situation. The use of automation has become common for many operations and may also impede situational awareness if used improperly.

The following elements relate to ADM and may be explored in the *Pilot's Handbook of Aeronautical Knowledge* to further understand how technology, crew interactions, and awareness affect aviation operations:[52]

- Crew resource management (CRM)
- Risk management
- Task management
- Situational awareness
- Environmental awareness (controlled flight into terrain [CFIT] and other hazards)
- Automation management

---

[52] U.S. DOT, FAA, *Pilot's Handbook of Aeronautical Knowledge.*

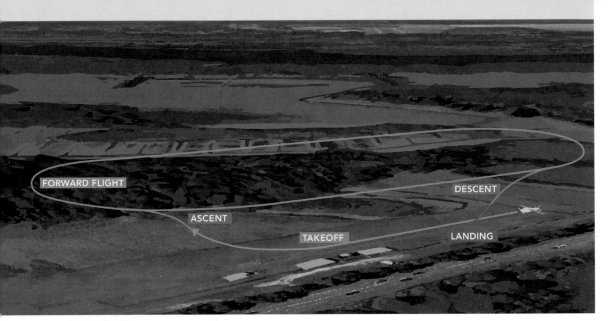

FIGURE 4-25. Example fixed-wing, simple flight profile.

FIXED-WING FLIGHT

Operations specific to fixed-wing flight may vary slightly, but aviators generally follow a set of standardized procedures to enhance safety and efficiency. Fixed-wing aircraft will usually have more endurance and operate in different missions than their vertical takeoff or landing (VTOL) counterparts. Many UAS operations will be conducted in airspace with high volumes of traffic, making it the responsibility of the remote pilot to determine procedures before flight to properly plan. An understanding of operations around airport terminal areas is imperative. Figure 4-25 indicates a "normal" traffic pattern, assuming the aircraft is taking off into the wind. Consult appropriate regulations and procedures at airports or RC model airfields, prior to flight.

▮ LAUNCH

Typical launch profiles for fixed-wing aircraft are horizontal takeoff and landing (HTOL), catapult launch, or hand launch (see Figure 4-26). Depending on the size, weight, speed, and power-plant, each sUAS manufacturer will define the appropriate method for launching your platform.

- *HTOL*—This type of launch requires substantial amounts of open space and the use of a runway environment, which may or may not be hard surfaced.
- *Catapult launch*—This type of launch mechanism may be heavy or bulky for transport, but may be required for certain sUAS applications. Catapult launches propel the sUAS from a fixed position to a rate of velocity required for flight in a short distance.
- *Hand launch*—Launching by hand is very common for sUAS applications, because of its ease and lack of space requirements. Consult your sUAS flight operations manual for a further description of how to hand launch safely.

FIGURE 4-26. Examples of sUAS platform launches.

▌RECOVERY

The methods for recovery of fixed-wing aircraft may vary significantly based on the operational environment. The amount of space required for successful recovery is contingent on factors synonymous with launch such as size, weight, speed, and powerplant. Common types of recovery mechanisms for UAS are HTOL or skid recovery, but some specialized aircraft will use nets or other devices to "catch" the aircraft in flight (*see* Figure 4-27).

- *HTOL*—Recovery in this manner requires significant amounts of space, which may affect your ability to operate in a given location.

- *Skid recovery*—This type of recovery is accomplished by simply landing the aircraft on a skid plate or hard-surfaced accessory on the bottom of the aircraft.

- *Netted or catch devices*—Recovery in this manner requires specialized airframes and equipment, due to high levels of force. In a recovery in which the aircraft is caught, it simply flies into a barrier designed for recovery.

FIGURE 4-27. Examples of UAS recovery: (A) net, (B) Insitu SkyHook, and (C) conventional HTOL.

VTOL FLIGHT

VTOL capability is desirable in many applications, because it does not require the same level of infrastructure as fixed-wing platforms. Many applications use VTOL technology because operations require the aircraft to maintain a fixed position, or hover. From an operational standpoint, it is important to consider that VTOL aircraft may have interactions with fixed-wing aircraft, so it is essential to understand all regulations and procedures for the airspace you are operating in. Launch and recovery of VTOL aircraft is much simpler than that of its fixed-wing counterparts, because it requires much less space.

Manufacturers have also developed hybrid aircraft options that combine the utility of both VTOL and fixed-wing platforms. These aircraft are becoming more popular because of their respective operational capabilities. For instance, fixed-wing aircraft usually have higher levels of endurance than VTOL aircraft, and conversely, VTOL aircraft require much less space for launch and recovery. A combination of these elements provides significant benefit to both users and industry in an effort to better support UAS applications.

REMOTE OPERATION

Operations of sUAS are limited to daytime VLOS at this time, but the regulation is likely to change to support industry growth. The remote pilot, in many cases, will operate the aircraft from a ground control station (GCS) that allows the remote pilot and VO to coordinate with visual reference to the aircraft. In other cases, such as waivered E/BVLOS applications, the user may be required to operate using an interface of displays and incoming data from the aircraft. The study of human factors defines many areas of operational difference between exocentric (external; e.g., chase plane view) versus egocentric (internal; pilot or first-person view) operations. For instance, maintaining visual contact with the aircraft allows the remote pilot to coordinate flight maneuvers by visual reference and orientation (see Figure 4-28A), whereas BVLOS applications rely on the pilot to interpret flight dynamics by the use of instrumentation and visual display from the onboard camera feed (see Figure 4-28B).

FIGURE 4-28. Examples of (A) exocentric and (B) egocentric sUAS operations.

FPV (egocentric) operations:

- Increased ability to determine the orientation of the aircraft, relative to commanded control responses (pitch, roll, yaw)
- Decreased situational awareness of the environment
- Operations can be supplemented with information presented through an onscreen display (OSD)

VLOS (exocentric) operations:

- Provides improved situational awareness of the vehicle relative to other objects in the environment
- Reduces the capability to determine the orientation of the aircraft, relative to commanded control (e.g., nose-in flight)
- Can be supplemented with telemetry display, which may be distracting to the remote pilot

REMOTE PILOT-IN-COMMAND AND VISUAL OBSERVER COORDINATION

There are two different aspects of verbal communication essential to successful (effective) and safe operation of an sUAS. The first aspect is communication among crewmembers, including the remote PIC, the VO, sensor operator, and ground/support crew (see Figure 4-29). The second is communication with outside parties, such as ATC, other aircrew (manned and unmanned) operating in the area, and bystanders. The complexity of the format and methods of communication exchange is highly dependent on a number of factors, including system design (architecture), quality of the human-machine interface (HMI), and operational process (simple to complex). For example, simple operation of a small, micro UAS (less than 4.4 pounds) may only require communication among the remote PIC and any bystanders that wander into the operation area (e.g., "Be aware I'm flying in the area; please stay behind that line."). Alternatively, a highly complex operation performed at an airfield will require verbal

FIGURE 4-29. A PIC using FPV, with a VO aiming the directional antenna.

communication among the PIC, all crewmembers, bystanders, and local ATC (takeoff, landing, routing, and de-confliction). Such complex operational cases may require the ability to make announcements on the common traffic advisory frequency (CTAF) using applicable VHF radio equipment.

At a minimum, the remote PIC and VO should agree, prior to operation, upon a clear and concise method to communicate critical instructions and observations. Such a communication strategy should account for the limited ability of the remote PIC to perceive exterior conditions or risks while focused on performing the task at hand. Units of measurement and a specific frame of reference should be determined and used consistently in all communication. Conditions should be announced in a manner easily understood, with receipt acknowledged by the opposing party. If no confirmation is given, repeat the message. When warranted (such as in situations needing immediate action), a required operational response (i.e., an alternative action to perform) should be identified by the VO in the message, using a directive-descriptive format:

Required action identified first (*directive*), followed with supplemental information (*description*)

The following represent a series of example exchanges between a PIC and VO:

Remote PIC: "Launching aircraft, clear area."
VO: "Confirmed, area clear." *or* "Hold fast, area insecure."

VO: "Adjust position left, five feet right of guide wire."
Remote PIC: "Acknowledged, adjusting position left." *or* "Acknowledged, close proximity to obstacle right."

VO: "Increase altitude, imminent contact forward."
Remote PIC: "Acknowledged, increasing altitude; advise when clear."

VO: "Continue to next position, airspace clear."
Remote PIC: "Acknowledged, continuing to next position."

VO: "Hold position, non-participant RC entering from left."
Remote PIC; "Acknowledged, holding position; advise when clear."

VO: "Reorient south, flight approaching northern visual observation range limit."
Remote PIC: "Acknowledged, heading south."

VO: "Turn right, approaching southern visual limit."
Remote PIC: "Acknowledged, coming around right and heading north."

Remote PIC: "Flight inbound for landing, from heading 270."
VO: "Confirmed, path clear."

Remote PIC: "Touching down."
VO: "Confirmed, flight on ground."

Remote PIC: "Engine[s] off."
VO: "Confirmed, props stopped; safe to approach."

AUTONOMOUS (AUTOMATIC) OPERATION

The use of automation and automatic functionality in UAS, including the smaller systems on the market, is become more commonplace and standard among some configurations (e.g., consumer multirotor platforms). Automation provides precision in control, navigation, and support in the case of a failure, while allowing the remote pilot to put less effort into aircraft control and more into the actual application of the mission. Many aircraft are equipped with unique equipment and technologies that support user needs. For instance, some sUAS are equipped with point-and-click waypoint navigation, autopilot, automatic landing, return to home, and follow me functions. As the industry continues to grow and users discover the unique requirements and capabilities of systems, automation will lead to increasing levels of autonomy for automatic operations.[53]

GEOFENCING

Geofencing is becoming a standard in the manufacture of sUAS and is defined by the creation of invisible barriers to prevent the aircraft from flying into non-specified areas. Many manufacturers have enlisted geofencing technology to keep sUAS away from prohibitive operational environments. It is suggested that prior to planning operational flights in specific areas, the manufacturer's geofencing documentation be reviewed to ensure the system is not subject to a "no fly zone" limitation where the system software/firmware may prevent operation, even if performed in a lawful and approved manner.

DATA CAPTURE AND PROCESSING

Methods for data capture vary by operation. Live video or telemetry may allow for the use of "real-time" streaming, in which larger applications may require the user to retrieve data from the remote sensing device after the flight is complete. The desired result and calculation of post-processed data sets may require not only high levels of computing power and time to achieve a final result, but expertise in the subject matter. Many UAS manufacturers have formed partnerships with software providers to supply a "one-stop" solution for operations. For instance, SenseFly has paired with Pix4D to allow the remote pilot to fly a mission profile, gather, and post-process data without using any external services. This fusion of technology allows users and remote pilots to be highly efficient without subjecting them to steep learning curves.

OPERATIONAL PLANNING AND PREPARATION

Responsible engagement in unmanned flight operations requires the use of consistent, methodical, and repeatable processes, designed to confirm appropriate use in an operational environment, airworthiness of a configured platform, and proper operation of system elements.

---

[53] The International Civil Aviation Organization (ICAO), *Unmanned Aircraft Systems* (Cir 328 AN/90), defines autonomous operation as an operation during which an unmanned aircraft is operating without pilot intervention in the management of the flight.

Identifying factors that affect operational performance, analyzing platform abilities, and developing strategies for managing contingencies from potential hazards and risks are all critical to effective application of sUAS. Operational planning should feature the development and mapping of operational requirements to system capabilities and limitations, environmental considerations, and regulatory compliance. Policies, plans, and procedures should also be developed to address and maintain safety and to ensure the accuracy and retention of records.

■ DEVELOPING AN OPERATIONAL CONCEPT (OPSCON)

An OpsCon (historically referred to as a ConOps[54]) represents a theory of operation describing *what a system is to be used for*, including identifying and confirming applicable operational criteria, supporting rationale, and dependencies. It is used to refine and document an initial concept into a mature strategy supporting the creation of detailed operational plans, specific to an application, environment, system configuration, and crew. Once you have identified or devised an application that an sUAS would be well suited to support or perform, it will be necessary to examine the underlying details of such use, committing the details to an OpsCon. This will require research to determine how such an application is currently performed (conventional methods or systems used); the policies, regulations, and limitations that govern performance of such a task; and the rationale supporting replacement with the conceptual idea. When drafting an initial OpsCon, it is important to remember to capture relevant conceptual details, such as the following:[55]

- Description of the remote pilot, operator, or organization (who you are)
- Overview of scenario or legacy system (option to be replaced using sUAS)
  - Perceived need (exhibited need the system fulfills)
  - Objective (purpose or intent)
  - Operational policies and constraints (limits)
  - Description of current application method
- Change rationale
  - New needs or factors
  - Deficiencies or limitations of current method(s)
  - Justification for new system or change
- Overview of sUAS concept
  - Objective (purpose or intent)
  - Operational policies and constraints (limits)
  - Description of new application

---

[54] The term ConOps was replaced by OpsCon in the IEEE (2011) document, *International Standard—Systems and software engineering—Life cycle processes—Requirements engineering*, ISO/IEC/IEEE 29148:2011 (E).

[55] Suggested OpsCon element list was adapted by simplifying and isolating critical elements provided in the system operation concept (Annex A, pp. 62–73) in the IEEE (2011) *International Standard—Systems and software engineering—Life cycle processes—Requirements engineering*, International Standard (ISO/IEC/IEEE 29148:2011[E]).

- Operational scenarios
  — Unique operational situations
  — Description of how system should work
  — Operational sequence
  — Identification of dependencies
- Effects of system use
  — Anticipated results
  — Required changes
- Proposed solution analysis
  — Benefits (pros)
  — Limitations (cons)
  — Alternative options

■ DEVELOPING AN OPERATIONAL PLAN

Once the initial concept has been researched and documented in the OpsCon, it will be necessary to examine and address all the requirements needed to make it a practical reality. This is accomplished through development of an operational plan, which details *how the system is operated*. An operational plan is used as a flexible and reusable framework, supporting identification and development of future operations and documenting the specific details of a planned activity. It evolves through the development process, being revised as needed. The information detailed in the plan can be used to support regulatory applications, such as a Part 107 waiver, COA, or Section 333 Petition for Exemption, as well as an internal operational guide to ensure consistency for safety and cost planning activities. The plan should contain a series of requirements, outlining the known operational needs and compliance items to be satisfied during operation.

Developing an effective operational plan requires identification of critical factors, analysis of potential effects, and consideration of and planned responses to potential events. A series of steps are recommended to create an effective operational plan:[56]

1. *Identify* the following:
   a. *Objective*—The purpose of the planned application, including measures of success
   b. *Threats*—The potential internal and external risks to the operation, likelihood of occurrence, and methods to mitigate
   c. *Resources*—The personnel, capabilities, materials, and financial assets available for use to address threats and support completion of the objective
2. *Evaluate Related Experience*—Examine and incorporate lessons learned from personal past experience and observations of others in the operational community.

---

[56] Suggested operational plan steps were adapted by simplifying and isolating critical elements identified in *Six-steps to Mission Planning* from James D. Murphy, *Flawless Execution: Use the Techniques and Systems of America's Fighter Pilots to Perform at Your Peak and Win Battles in the Business World* (New York: HarperCollins, 2010).

3. *Define Appropriate Course of Action*—Document the specifics of how resources will be used to complete the objective, in a manner that addresses lessons learned and threats.
4. *Evaluate Hypothetical Situations*—Examine potential scenarios and determine appropriate response contingencies to threats using lessons learned and resources.

As you formulate your operational plan, consider and address the following questions:

- Is your planned operation fully contained within permitted operational parameters (400 feet AGL, inside controlled airspace, etc.)?
- How do you plan to launch/recover and what equipment is necessary to support the operation?
- What registration, certification, and insurance is required?
- How far will the Aerial Element need to travel?
- Have you identified the following?
  - Types of flight profiles typical for the task/application (forward flight, translational flight, hover, and altitude/positional changes)
  - Flight path and maneuver requirements of planned operations (speed, distance, bank angles/coordinated turns, latitude, longitude, and altitude; may require several examples)
  - Linear distance ranges of Aerial Element from the GCS, remote pilots, and visual observer(s)
  - Limitations or constraints that need to be met (e.g., keeping flight altitude under 400 feet AGL and speeds under 100 mph)
  - Measures of success (define what constitutes declaring operational objectives achieved)
  - Situations that would prevent or halt operations
  - Personnel and support necessary
  - Regulatory and insurance compliance requirements

▮ RISK IDENTIFICATION AND MINIMIZATION

Risks can range from loss of component functionality, such as GPS failure, to complete loss of aircraft control and subsequent death of a group of unaffiliated bystanders. Development and use of a **safety risk management process (SRMP)** and incorporation into an overarching **safety management system (SMS)** will support the decision making process to determine viability of planned operations and improve the likelihood of sustainable operational success. After examining and analyzing the operational environment and sUAS platform configuration, you should have a clearer image of the potential risks. Your findings and observations will be useful to analyze, isolate, prioritize and treat potential risks.

◗ Operational Environment Analysis

Gaining a thorough understanding of the environment where operations are to be conducted is critical to minimizing risk, increasing efficiency, and maximizing the potential for task success (completion of the objective). Researching the area where operations are to be conducted can help uncover the presence and potential impact of unique environmental characteristics, potential hazards or risks, important geographic landmarks, and specific regulatory compliance requirements. A wide variety of resources and tools are available to help with preparation and familiarization for operations in new locations, including websites and software that provide the following:

- Maps, surveys, and visualization
- Line-of-sight, elevation, and electromagnetic signal propagation mapping and analysis
- Weather forecasting and reporting
- Flight planning calculators
- TFR alerts and notices (e.g., NOTAMs)

Tools such as the FAA's **B4UFly** mobile app (*see* Figure 4-30) and the **Know Before You Fly** U.S. Air Space web tool (*see* Figure 4-31) represent tools that can be used to identify if sUAS operations can be conducted in specific locations. However, confirming final operational suitability by using VFR sectional charts is recommended.

FIGURE 4-30.

Screenshots of the FAA's B4UFLY app.

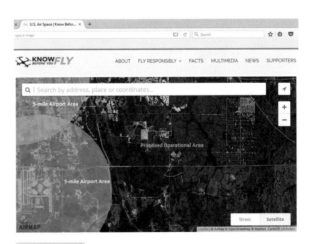

FIGURE 4-31.

Know Before You Fly U.S. Air Space web tool showing proposed operational area (green) in relation to local airports (orange).[57]

---

[57] Adapted using *Know Before You Fly, U.S. Air Space* web tool, with proposed operational area and labels added for improved clarity.

When performing an environmental analysis, it is important to thoroughly review the area to confirm it is suitable for sUAS operations and to identify any potential issues that must be further examined or considered. At a minimum, the following steps are suggested:

1. Confirm the proposed operational environment is not within a prohibited area (*see* Figure 4-31).
2. Visually examine the area, from multiple perspectives, to identify potential VLOS issues and other concerns (e.g., close proximity to high capacity motorway) (*see* Figure 4-32).
3. Measure distances to features and objects for use in platform application analysis and risk identification and mitigation (*see* Figure 4-33).

NORTHERN VIEW

WESTERN VIEW

SOUTHERN VIEW

EASTERN VIEW

FIGURE 4-32.
Rendered views of the proposed operational environment.

4. Layout possible flight paths and measure distances between segments to determine the total distance (*see* Figure 4-34A); confirm maintenance of VLOS will be possible, given the greatest distance between the remote PIC and aircraft (*see* Figure 4-34B).

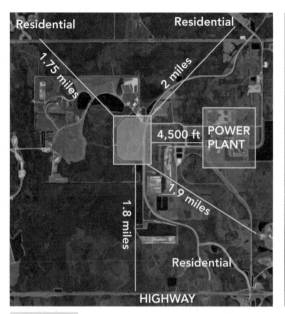

FIGURE 4-33. Distances to features (*left*) and potential risk areas (*right*).

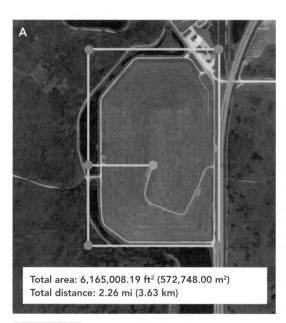

FIGURE 4-34. (A) Potential flight path and (B) VLOS distance.

5. Identify the sensor coverage area to confirm the proposed path will be sufficient to captured desired data or imagery (*see* Figure 4-35) and whether sensor coverage will capture information from adjacent properties; determine if permission from landowners will be required and specifically who it will need to be secured from.
6. Investigate weather for the area to identify wind, precipitation, temperature, and visibility conditions.

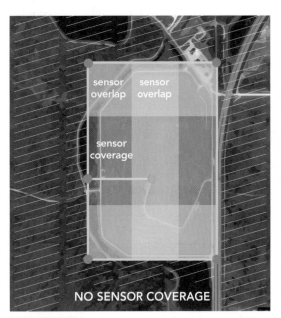 

FIGURE 4-35. Sensor coverage areas (*left*) and property-ownership (*right*).

After performing a detailed environmental analysis, consider the following questions:

- Is the operational environment subject to unique weather patterns or other phenomena? If so, how will conditions be verified?
- Is permission from a landowner or residents for overflight and data collection necessary, and how will permission be secured?
- Does the planned operation take place within five miles of an airport, in prohibited airspace, or over an area where UAS operations are not permitted?
- How will compliance with 14 CFR §91.119 (500 foot separation from non-participating persons, vehicles, structures, and objects) be maintained?
- Is there sufficient room for the operation, including launch and recovery?
- How will emergencies be handled in this environment?
- Are there obstacles or hazards to contend with and how might they affect operation?

◗ Platform Application Analysis

After creating a detailed picture of the operational environment, it may be necessary to revise your initial operational plan to incorporate new requirements. These requirements can then be mapped to confirm the ability of a specific sUAS to meet the needs of the customer, operation, and environment. A detailed and well-constructed analysis will indicate the suitability of a platform to operate (i.e., feasibility of performing application), as intended, in worst-case conditions, as well as help to identify any risks or concerns that will need be addressed. The operational performance details of sUAS platforms are often available from manufacturers.

It is recommended that a platform application analysis incorporate the following:

- Required operational performance
  - Altitude (under maximum allowable)
  - Speed
  - Endurance (with applicable power in reserve)
  - Range (for both cumulative distance flown and communications)
  - Payload capacity
  - Electrical power (format, load, and capacity)
- Environmental factors
  - Wind speed and direction
  - Precipitation level
  - Visibility (distance and potential occlusion due to objects/terrain)
  - Atmospheric conditions (air density, temperature, and humidity)
  - Traffic
- Functionality
  - Optimal operating altitude (minimum and maximum)
  - Routing (flight path) and distance
  - Data capture resolution and storage
  - Sensor fidelity
  - Communication strength and range
  - Crewmembers required
  - Alternative options
- Economic drivers
  - System acquisition cost
  - Operational cost
  - Maintenance and repair cost

Understanding how a system will perform, prior to use, will support the development of plans and procedures to minimize risk. It will also help a remote pilot identify traits of the system well suited to specific types of functions or tasks. It is suggested that multiple options for performing the given application, including non-sUAS methods, be examined and compared prior to selection and acquisition of an sUAS platform. This will help to ensure the optimal solution has been identified for the given task. While it may not always be possible to purchase new systems because of acquisition cost or availability of inventory options, it is highly recommended that this step still be performed, prior to operation, to identify any potential issues, risks, or concerns. At a minimum, any system being considered should be evaluated and analyzed against the specific application and environment to confirm it is capable of supporting safe operations, when used as identified in the operational plan.

After performing a thorough platform application analysis, consider the following questions:

- Can the system perform the intended function?
- Does the platform, as configured, provide sufficient power, endurance, range, speed, and payload capacity to meet operational requirements? What are the maximums and minimums supported?
- Will it be possible to maintain a sufficient power reserve, and what should the reserve be (5–20%)?
- What are the potential effects of weather (wind, precipitation, visibility, etc.)?
- What environmental factors may impact performance of the platform, including powerplant operation and visibility of sensors?
- What conditions would prevent or halt operations?
- What steps are necessary to minimize risk and maximize safety of personnel, bystanders, and property?
- What steps have been taken to confirm the sUAS is the most suitable solution for the given application (i.e., is use of an sUAS justified)?
- What alternative options have been considered and ruled out? What was the rationale?

▶ Minimizing Risk

Minimizing the adverse effects of risks is a critical element to maintaining safe operations and ensuring continued availability and use of this technology. Strategies to mitigate risks should be examined as they relate to potential effectiveness, efficiency, costs, and implementation trade-offs. The following mapping structure is suggested to examine, identify, and outline potential risks and their potential treatments:

- Identify
  - Vulnerability
  - Prompt (triggers events or conditions)
  - Result(s)
- Priority
- Constraints
- Treatments

The following represents an example of operational risk mapping and treatment strategies to mitigate effects, based on the scenario of fixed-wing platform power loss during flight:

- Risk Identification
  - Vulnerabilities
    A: Powerplant
    B: Propeller integrity or attachment
    C: Power supply/fuel
    D: Lack of remote pilot attention
  - Prompts
    A: Powerplant shuts down, mechanical failure
    B: Propeller detaches from powerplant
    C: Power/fuel supply exhausted
    D: Remote pilot does not set timer or review telemetry feedback
  - Results
    A–D: Aerial Element loses ability to produce thrust; forward airspeed diminishes
    B only: Propeller strikes a bystander
    A–D: Aerial Element crashes
- Priority
  - **A:** low potential; undamaged recovery to full loss of aircraft and injury or death possible
  - **B:** medium potential; no to high degree of damage, injury, or death possible
  - **C:** high potential without telemetry and low potential with telemetry; no to high degree of damage, injury, or death possible
  - **D:** low potential; no to high degree of damage, injury, or death possible
- Constraints
  - Powerplant removed and inspected only after every 25 hours of operation
  - Visibility inside powerplant difficult without disassembly
  - Occurrence of unforeseen circumstances
  - Damage not perceivable
  - No ability to monitor power/fuel level during operation (no telemetry)
- Treatments
  - **A:** Include applicable propulsion (powerplant) verification steps in pre-flight inspection procedures; properly perform routine and recommended maintenance on propulsion system.
  - **B:** Include applicable propulsion (propeller attachment) verification steps in the pre-flight inspection procedures; ensure Aerial Element is not operated over or toward bystanders; maintain sufficient clearance from bystanders and crewmembers.

— **C–D:** Set up a timer to audibly warn the remote pilot when approaching 25 percent of power remaining (assuming maximum consumption rate), return to landing location, and recover aircraft before power/fuel supply is exhausted; include telemetry feedback with power monitoring and depiction of power remaining in system configuration; train remote pilot to consistently verify power remaining.

— **A–D:** Train remote pilot for use of emergency gliding profile; identify suitable alternative landing area; ensure crewmembers are on standby to redirect bystanders from alternative area and assist with recovery.

Other potential risks to consider in the development of your own SRMP include the following:

- Loss of communication (to ATC tower or other parties) or lost link (from GCS to aircraft)
- Loss of visual contact
- Onboard fire (fuel, batteries, or other)
- Failure of visual, GPS, inertial navigation, or other telemetry sensors
- Collision with another aircraft
- Collision with a crewmember or bystander
- Collision with terrain or fixed object
- Onset of inclement weather (gusting wind, precipitation, loss of visibility)

Once the operational plan has been revised to address review of the operational environment, platform suitability, and any new developments, it is highly recommended that it be peer reviewed thoroughly and collaboratively by other experienced operators/pilots to identify any potential issues, concerns, or inconsistencies. This process can improve the functionality, alignment, and coverage of the plan, while ensuring required information and rationale has been documented in sufficient detail. The subsequent review comments and recommendations should be examined and addressed, when appropriate. Any revisions to the operational plan should be documented in a change matrix placed in the front of the document, along with the version and dates of the change.

SCHEDULE, COORDINATE, AND CONDUCT OPERATIONS

As with any aviation application, it is important to be prepared for issues that may arise when operating in a complex environment. The following are some questions to consider prior to any flight:

- Are all required assets, crewmembers, and other required elements available?
- Are there any limitations that prevent availability and use?
- Are all crewmembers sufficiently trained and experienced in their respective roles?

- Has permission been obtained from local FAA ATC for any portion of the operation that may occur within five miles of an airport?
- Has risk properly been assessed?
- Given an in-flight failure, what protocols have been set?
- Have proper notifications been issued?

▌ BRIEFING

Briefings are a common element in the aviation industry. They are necessary to define the current operational task, with any limitations, responsibilities, risks, or concerns among everyone involved with the operation. It is important that everyone understand what role they will play in the operational dynamic of the mission. It's recommended that the following points be identified and communicated for an effective sUAS operational briefing:

- Operational plan and expectations (under both normal and abnormal conditions)
- Roles and responsibilities of all involved parties, including crewmembers
- Operational objectives
- Known issues, risks, and contingency plans
- Details of the environmental, platform, and other factors potentially affecting operations (e.g., availability of on-site maintenance for diagnosis and repair)

▌ OPERATIONAL AREA PREPARATION

Once you have completed all necessary planning activities, including development and review of the operational plan, received appropriate approval for operations, coordinated scheduling, and briefed all those involved, you will be ready to begin final preparations for conducting the specific task. Confirming the suitability of the operational environment, on the given day and time, is crucial to reducing potential risk and optimizing the potential for success of the application. The following represent important actions to take prior to initiation of operations:

- Check weather forecast for the area.
- Confirm that visibility and weather is acceptable for planned flight operations.
- Note direction and speed of wind.
- Confirm that the planned operational area is clear of traffic and debris; establish a sufficient perimeter to ensure maintenance of safety.
- Identify and determine the risk of obstacles and hazards present in the area, such as buildings, power lines, and foliage.
- Identify the planned recovery location and an alternate location, as a contingency; confirm with all crewmembers.
- Ensure bystanders are located at a sufficient distance from startup, launch, operational, and recovery locations.

- Confirm that appropriate permission for the planned operation has been obtained from the FAA (including ATC coordination, if necessary), landowner, property management, insurance provider, and any individuals who may be affected by the flight (e.g., privacy) and that an applicable NOTAM has been filed (24–48 hours prior to flight).
- If possible, use a spectrum analyzer to identify the potential presence of conflicting signals or interference in the operational area.

■ PRE-FLIGHT SYSTEM INSPECTION

System inspection procedures should be customized to address specific features and requirements of the sUAS being operated. The following represent suggested steps and actions to serve as a starting point in the development or adaptation of a pre-flight and startup inspection checklist for your own operations:[58]

- Support equipment
  - All components and supplies necessary to support operation are available and ready for use at the flightline.
  - All support equipment is secure and undamaged.
- Human element
  - All crewmembers have been briefed on planned operations, including applicable contingencies and potential risks and hazards that could result in the following occurrences (and ensure that the operational plan addresses these potential occurrences and identifies appropriate responses):
    ‣ Crash/accident
    ‣ Injury/mishap
    ‣ Fire
    ‣ Loss of propulsion, power, communication, FPV/telemetry, or visual contact
  - All crewmembers have confirmed an understanding of their roles and responsibilities.
  - Any required operational credentials are current and valid, including airman certificate, medical, and radio operator licenses.
  - Perform an operational check of verbal communication among crewmembers, at respective locations, to ensure instructions and warnings can be heard in the case of handheld radio failure.
- Aerial Element
  - Ensure primary batteries are installed, but not connected.
  - Conduct visual inspection, looking for signs of wear or damage.
  - Place Aerial Element in cradle or on level surface.

---

[58] Requirements and steps identified by the manufacturer should always supersede these suggested actions and their order.

— Propulsion system:
  ▸ All connections, including power, actuation, and linkages, are connected and secure (excluding the primary connection to the battery).
  ▸ All propulsion system components, including propeller/rotor/impeller, powerplant, drive shaft, and power distribution, are undamaged and secure.
  ▸ Attachment components are secure and tightened to appropriate levels.
  ▸ For internal combustion, starting components (glow plug, clip, and connections) are in place and secure (power should not be applied).
— Power distribution and supply
  ▸ Batteries are fully charged and undamaged; replace as needed.
  ▸ Fuel tank is filled.
  ▸ No evidence of leakage in batteries, fuel tank, or lines is present.
— Onboard command, control, and communication (C3)
  ▸ All connections, including power, actuation, and signal linkages, are connected and secure (excluding the primary connection to the battery).
  ▸ All C3 components, including control receiver (RX), telemetry and sensor data transmitters (TXs), antennae, servo controller, and data logging mechanisms, are undamaged and secure.
  ▸ Antennae are in the proper orientation.
— Actuation
  ▸ All moving components are unobstructed in full range of motion.
  ▸ All actuation connections, including power cabling and physical linkages, are attached and secure (excluding the primary connection to the battery).
  ▸ All actuation components, including control arms, pushrods, and servos, are undamaged and secure.
— Payload
  ▸ All connections, including power, actuation, and signal linkages, are connected and secure.
  ▸ All payload components, including sensors, mounting assemblies, power supply and distribution, and actuation mechanisms, are undamaged and secure.
  ▸ Dedicated battery, if applicable, is connected. (Installing a switch to turn off and save power during system checks is suggested.)
  ▸ Storage media has been installed, if applicable.
  ▸ All lenses are free from debris and clean.
— Center of gravity (CG) is correct for payload and operational flight profile.

- Ground-based C3 (GCS) element
  — Batteries are appropriately charged and undamaged; replace as needed.
  — All connections, including power cabling and signal linkages, are attached and secure.
  — All components are secure and undamaged, including control TX, telemetry and data RXs, antennae, displays, power source, and command input devices.
  — Any applicable actuated components, such as the tracking antenna base, are free to move without obstruction.
  — The controls move as expected, with throttle position at the minimum position (no throttle).
  — Automatic (autonomy) features are properly configured and loaded into the GCS, if supported:
    ‣ Home location (launch position) and altitude
    ‣ Waypoints appropriate for operational location
    ‣ Geofence range and altitude
  — Perform an operational check of verbal communication radios to ensure that instructions and warnings can be heard and that equipment works appropriately during operation.
  — Timer is prepared and ready for engagement (e.g., alarm to coincide with appropriate power-remaining setting, if system is to be operated at maximum power consumption).
- Integrated system check
  — Remove Aerial Element from its cradle and locate a sufficient distance from the remote pilot, other crewmembers, bystanders, and obstacles in preparation of startup.
  — Power-on C3 equipment, such as TX, RXs, displays, and controllers (and ensure controls are in appropriate positions, including no throttle).
  — Install battery in the Aerial Element and engage electrical power (no throttle).
  — Verify communication has been properly established (all applicable channels/frequencies) between the Aerial and Ground-based C3 (GCS) elements
  — Calibrate any sensors, such as GPS, magnetometer/compass, inertial measurement unit (IMU)/inertial navigation components, altimeters, pressure sensors, or barometers.
  — Verify receipt and display of telemetry and visual sensor data, if applicable.

— Verify that proper waypoints, including the home position, have been uploaded to the Aerial Element, if supported by automatic features.

— Verify appropriate actuation of control surfaces and other moving components.[59]

— Visually re-confirm that the startup and launch area is free from traffic, bystanders, debris, obstacles, or hazards.

— Announce the commencement of startup to all crewmembers and bystanders (e.g., "starting engine[s]" or "clear prop").

— Start propulsion system.

— Keep throttle at a minimum setting for several seconds and confirm that propulsion system operation is as expected.

— Verify that the propulsion system responds appropriately to commanded throttle changes. (Do not fully engage throttles to generate sufficient lift to launch; confirm any delay present is within acceptable tolerances.)

— Verify the following before proceeding:

  ▸ Communication signal strength (received signal strength indication [RSSI])

  ▸ GPS status and report

  ▸ Battery level

  ▸ Home position

  ▸ Control mode state (manual, semi-auto, automatic)

— Prepare for launch by announcing to crewmembers and bystanders (e.g., "launching aircraft, clear area" or "taking off").

— Operate as planned (including emergency responses).

— Recover the Aerial Element as defined in the operational plan and announce major actions to crew and bystanders prior to performance (e.g., "flight inbound for landing," "touching down," and "engine[s] off").

■ POST-FLIGHT SYSTEM INSPECTION

It is imperative to perform a thorough post-flight system inspection after all flights to assess any mechanical issues that may have occurred during flight. Use of a checklist is necessary for each phase of operation to provide a systematic flow to each procedure, to ensure items are not left out or deferred. The following are some elements that may be components of a post-flight system inspection.

• Shutdown propulsion system.

• Confirm all propellers/rotors have fully stopped rotating.

• Disconnect the battery in the Aerial Element.

---

[59] For this step, some users elect to disconnect a motor lead of electrical propulsion systems to prevent accidental engagement of the powerplant while verifying control surface responses. If this action is taken, remember to reattach and confirm motor response at conclusion.

- Disconnect any additional power (e.g., dedicated payload battery), if applicable.
- Turn off Ground-based C3, if appropriate.
- Visually re-inspect the Aerial Element, looking for signs of wear or damage.
- Verify that all elements and components are secure and free from damage.
- Identify any observed issues, including performance or handling experienced during flight, and document for diagnosis, repair, and future reference; report any accidents or mishaps, as required.
- Note the time and duration of flight and fuel consumed; log hours appropriately, including time on components, such as the engine/motor.
- If applicable, analyze logged or transmitted telemetry or sensor data.

■ DEBRIEFING

A proper debriefing will allow all participants of the operation to understand the level of success of the mission and any areas available for improvement. The following are a list of items typically discussed as part of a standard debriefing:

- Introduction
- Results (successes, issues, and failures)
- Goals
- Assessment/strategy
- Risks
- Assignment of action items
- Closing

HOUR LOGGING AND REPORTING

FAA COA operational provisions require tracking and monthly reporting of the following, even if no flights were conducted:[60]

- Identification
  — Name of remote pilot
  — Exemption number
  — Aircraft registration number
- UAS type and model
- All operating locations
  — Location city/name
  — Latitude/longitude coordinates
- Number of flights (per location, per aircraft)
- Total aircraft operational hours

---

[60] UAS operators must submit the following information, on a monthly basis.

- Takeoff or landing damage
- Equipment malfunctions (reportable malfunctions)
  — Onboard flight control system
  — Navigation system
  — Powerplant failure in flight
  — Fuel system failure
  — Electrical system failure
  — Control station failure
- Number and duration of lost link events per UAS, per flight
  — Control, performance and health monitoring
  — Communications

It is recommended that Remote Pilots and Visual Observers flying under Part 107 also log their hours using a similar schema (see ASA's Remote Pilot logbook, www.asa2fly.com).

MAINTENANCE, CALIBRATION, AND DIAGNOSIS

Maintenance of airframes, motors, electronics, and other components vary by the size and classification of airframes. Researchers are currently working on methods to better define maintenance, modification, repair, and inspection issues that may or may not be similar to that of manned aircraft.

■ IN-THE-FIELD VERSUS PROFESSIONAL SERVICING

It may be necessary to maintain your aircraft in the field, which may or may not require specialized tooling or knowledge. Many of the electronic elements on your aircraft may require diagnosis or replacement by the manufacturer, so it is important to consult your operations manual prior to any repair.

■ PREVENTATIVE MAINTENANCE

Keeping your aircraft in flying condition will require the periodical inspection and replacement of components. Please consult your operations manual for any scheduled or preventative maintenance required on your platform or its components.

sUAS OPERATIONAL CONSIDERATIONS

As regulation and policy continue to meld with the operations and use of sUAS, it is important to consider how the legal and business environment will affect how you plan on doing business. Factors such as privacy, liability, and insurance are a component of the UAS industry as with any other. Having the proper background and knowledge going into this profession will aid you in decision making to allow your business to grow and prosper.

CHAPTER 5

BUSINESS OF UNMANNED AVIATION: FROM AGENCIES TO STARTUPS

INTRODUCTION

There are a growing number of organizations and individuals invested in the development, manufacture, and operation of unmanned aviation technology, ranging from personal hobbyists enjoying an afternoon of flight in the park to multi-departmental government agencies overseeing the integration and safe operation on the national scale. The unifying factor linking all of these parties is the pursuit of successful and maintainable application of UAS across the United States. Without UAS, there would be no market in the United States for related goods, services, or uses. UAS technology—specifically sUAS with their widespread availability, low cost, and ease of use—have provided opportunities for the development of new capabilities and products to support both public and civil (personal and commercial) use.

UAS STAKEHOLDERS

This section presents an overview of public and civil organizations with a vested interest in the success of this field and related industries. UAS stakeholders are entities whose duties and functions are enhanced through the manufacture, service, management, or use of such platforms to achieve their operational goals and objectives. This community is composed of private companies and industry members; academia; and federal, state, and local government agencies charged with the protection, safety, or oversight for the benefit of the public. Understanding the involvement, role, and possible functions of stakeholders can help you to better prepare for future collaboration, business pursuits, or technology development opportunities. At this point in your own journey, and after review of the prior chapters ranging from UAS history to operations, you are now a part of this stakeholder community.

ORGANIZATIONAL STRUCTURES

The organizations outlined and described in this section represent those that are currently using or that may be well suited to use sUAS. Important concepts and the related potential benefits to organizations are identified, when possible.

■ PUBLIC AIRCRAFT OPERATIONS (GOVERNMENTAL)

Government agencies have benefited from the availability of UAS platforms, loosening of restrictions within the National Airspace System (NAS), and an improved definition of who may fly, when, and for what purpose. When the label of a "government" agency is used, people typically think of local, county, state, and federal law enforcement (e.g., Federal Bureau of Investigation [FBI], Customs and Border Protection [CBP], etc.). However, a wide range of government agencies, beyond law enforcement, could use and are considering future use of this technology.

Several forms of operational approval must be obtained prior to conducting flight operations. These approvals are dependent on the type and format of the organization (i.e., public versus civil). As discussed in Chapter 4, for public UAS operations the FAA issues a Certificate of Waiver or Authorization (COA) that permits public agencies and organizations to operate a particular aircraft, for a particular purpose, in a particular area. The COA represents federal approval for an operator to use a defined block of airspace and includes special safety provisions unique to the proposed operation. The FAA works with these organizations to develop conditions and limitations for UAS operations to ensure they do not jeopardize the safety of other aviation operations. The objective is to issue a COA with parameters that ensure a level of safety equivalent to manned aircraft. This usually entails making sure that the UAS does not operate in a populated area and that the aircraft is observed, either by someone in a manned aircraft or someone on the ground, to ensure separation from other aircraft in accordance with right-of-way rules. Additionally, public operators can conduct operations under Part 107, given their operations can be performed within the requirements of the rule set. Common public uses today include law enforcement, firefighting, border patrol, disaster relief, search and rescue, military training, and other government operational missions.

▶ Local City and County Government Application and Uses

Local government agencies at the city and county level provide law enforcement and first responder services, but they also provide many other municipal services, which can benefit from the capabilities of sUAS platforms. Obvious uses that have been at the forefront of the news in the past few years include sUAS operations performed by local law enforcement for observation and monitoring of traffic flow on roads and highways, as well as providing assistance with search and rescue activity. Larger municipal law enforcement agencies and most county law enforcement agencies already have fleets of helicopters to augment ground units in situations that require a bird's-eye view (e.g., criminal pursuit, search and rescue using visual and/or infrared [IR] capability, or emergency operations in disaster situations), but these are typically large, expensive units that require extensive maintenance, fuel, and manned pilot services.

Many of these services can be easily replaced with less expensive, unmanned units at a fraction of the cost. The same requirements for needing a certified civilian pilot and maintenance of the aircraft still exist in the domain of unmanned aircraft, but these services can be obtained and provided at a much lower cost than is currently available for larger, manned aircraft.

Other services that local and county agencies have responsibility for include civil engineering planning; development services related to planning and zoning; public works and infrastructure inspection and maintenance; taxation; and disaster/emergency management. Having an inexpensive, on-demand system to obtain aerial observations to provide support for these municipal services would be extremely valuable. Current methods for execution of these duties involve personnel, ground vehicles, or manned aircraft for inspection of property and infrastructure. Many of these traditional methods are expensive and can easily be replaced or augmented using UAS technology with a variety of payloads and software. Table 5-1 (*see* next page) shows common uses of UAS by both local and county governmental departments.

▶ **State Government Applications and Uses**

Many of the functions provided by state governments mirror what is offered on a more local level (city and county governments), but state jurisdiction often encompass a much larger area and scale of operation. Functions such as law enforcement often include state police, with jurisdiction over state roads and highways, and state wildlife management, which monitors and maintains large expanses of wildlife preserves and environmentally sensitive areas, as well as large areas of state parks and recreational areas. To adjust to the ever-expanding need to monitor and survey increasingly large areas, selection of a more capable sUAS with different capabilities may be warranted. For example, while a capable multirotor might be sufficient for local use, encompassing distances of a few miles and periods of use less than one hour, this type of unit would be absolutely inadequate for longer distances and durations. Uses involving longer distances and greater endurance might require a fixed-wing, internal combustion unit capable of flying hundreds of miles over multiple hours of use. Along with greater capability, increases in costs for maintenance, control stations, and pilots can be expected if units are intended to fly multiple hours and beyond visual line-of-sight (BVLOS). Table 5-2 (*see* page 207) represents an overview of common state governmental departments and their potential uses of UAS.

▶ **Federal Government Applications and Uses**

Duties and responsibilities of the federal government differ significantly from those of city, county, and state governments. Many of the duties and responsibilities of the federal government revolve around protection of U.S. citizens. What started out as a simple "protection" mandate in the most direct sense and meaning has evolved into protection defined in a number of areas, including environmental, agriculture, commerce, health, and transportation, to name a few. These combined duties cover virtually every aspect of the lives of American citizens.

Typical uses for UAS by the federal government include those by law enforcement, border patrol, and the Department of Defense. These uses range from intelligence, surveillance, and reconnaissance (ISR), to long-range border patrol, to weaponized drones in foreign countries

TABLE 5-1. POTENTIAL UAS USES BY CITY AND COUNTY GOVERNMENT AGENCIES

DEPARTMENT / Purpose	UAS USAGE BY GOV. AGENCIES: ● by city ● by county				
	Visual survey	Search & rescue	Data gathering	Property inspection	Civil engineering & inspection
ENGINEERING Maintenance of roads, drainage, infrastructure	● ●		● ●	● ●	● ●
FIRE Emergency response to specific accidents and incidents	● ●	● ●	● ●		● ●
POLICE Emergency response to specific accidents and incidents	● ●	● ●	● ●		
PLANNING & ZONING Maintenance and inspection of current and future growth	● ●			● ●	● ●
PUBLIC WORKS Maintenance and inspection of infrastructure	● ●		● ●		● ●
TAX ASSESSMENT Inspection of buildings and property for taxation purposes	●			●	●
EMERGENCY MANAGEMENT Surveillance and recon of disaster areas for asset deployment	● ●	● ●	● ●	● ●	● ●
EDUCATION Monitoring of school property and activities	●		●	●	●
ENVIRONMENTAL PROTECTION Surveying and monitoring of environmentally sensitive areas	●		●	●	●

NOTE: This is not a complete list of city and county government departments and agencies; applications are not necessarily in use.

TABLE 5-2. POTENTIAL UAS USES BY STATE GOVERNMENT AGENCIES

DEPARTMENT Purpose	UAS USAGE				
	Visual survey	Search & rescue	Data gathering	Property inspection	Civil engineering & inspection
WORKFORCE INNOVATION Help maintain employment and reduce unemployment	●	●	●	●	●
AGRICULTURE & CONSUMER SERVICES Surveying and monitoring of agricultural areas and farmlands	●		●	●	●
BUSINESS & PROFESSIONAL REGULATION Reviews policy and regulations pertaining to business & licensing	●			●	●
COMMUNITY AFFAIRS Maintenance and inspection of current and future growth	●			●	●
CORRECTIONS Prison/prisoner inspection and monitoring	●	●	●		●
ECONOMIC DEVELOPMENT Inspection of buildings and property	●			●	●
EMERGENCY MANAGEMENT Surveillance and recon of disaster areas for asset deployment	●	●	●	●	●
EDUCATION Monitoring of school property and activities	●		●	●	●
ENVIRONMENTAL PROTECTION Surveying and monitoring of environmentally sensitive areas	●		●	●	●

(continued)

TABLE 5-2. *(continued)*

DEPARTMENT Purpose	UAS USAGE				
	Visual survey	Search & rescue	Data gathering	Property inspection	Civil engineering & inspection
GEOLOGICAL SURVEY Surveying and monitoring of the Earth, natural resources and phenomena	●			●	
INSURANCE Reviews and oversees insurance regulations	●		●	●	●
POLICE Emergency response to specific accidents and incidents	●	●	●		
LEGAL AFFAIRS Reviews policy and regulations	●				
MANAGEMENT SERVICES HR and vendor services for state-related business	●				
REVENUE/TAXATION Inspection of buildings and property for taxation purposes	●			●	●
TRANSPORTATION Surveying and monitoring of transportation infrastructure	●		●	●	●
WILDLIFE CONSERVATION Surveying and monitoring of natural fauna, animals and ecosystems	●		●		

NOTE: This is not a complete list of state government departments and agencies; applications are not necessarily in use.

used to engage and destroy enemy targets and terrorist leaders. Other domestic uses have been described and encouraged, but many have not been employed due to slow development of rules and regulations by the FAA pertaining to UAS use within the NAS. Table 5-3 (*see next page*) outlines potential uses by a number of federal government agencies that may come into play in the near future.

▌ CIVIL AIRCRAFT OPERATIONS (NON-GOVERNMENTAL)

Civil entities can also benefit from the availability of sUAS technology and the potential opportunities afforded by integration. In the civilian sector, using sUAS to perform operations and applications currently performed by costly manned aircraft will result in potential efficiency gains in the near future as these technologies become widely available. Civil aircraft operations constitute any operation that does not meet the statutory criteria for a public aircraft operation. As described in Chapter 4, there are currently three approved methods to gain FAA authorization to fly civil (non-governmental) aircraft operations utilizing UAS in the NAS: (1) in accordance with 14 CFR Part 107; (2) apply for and obtain a Section 333 Exemption (with subsequent COA being obtained), or (3) apply for and obtain a special airworthiness certificate (SAC). The most suitable route to legally fly sUAS for civil operations is to complete the requirements for Part 107 remote pilot certification and carry out operations in accordance with the rule set. Any operations that exceed the operational provisions contained within Part 107 can be addressed through either a specific waiver to an operational limit or Section 333 Petition for Exemption application.

▶ Companies and Entrepreneurs

Commercial uses of sUAS are currently being pursued and evaluated by companies across the world. This category represents the industry contingent that is helping to advance technology and potential application through its research and development efforts. It is composed of a diverse set of organizations and individuals looking to derive economic advantage and opportunity through the use of UAS technology. Companies and entrepreneurs will be instrumental in establishing the economic viability of sUAS operations and support by providing the financial capital, expertise, and business opportunities required to achieve sustainable growth. Those able to quickly adapt and respond to changing regulatory conditions, apply resources to current challenges and issues, and effectively meet market demands and consumer needs will have improved potential for success in this field.

Private entities and small businesses are already using this technology to assist in tasks such as viniculture, surveying construction sites, or monitoring property (e.g., livestock, fences, erosion evaluation). Large firms and publicly traded companies have been more visible in the media in regards to their plans for the utilization of sUAS. Amazon and Google have made it well known that they intend to implement sUAS for delivery and other purposes, while Domino's Pizza has envisioned a potential pizza delivery platform. Service providers (both public and private) have also shown interest in or are currently using sUAS to support their businesses. Examples include evaluation of post-catastrophe damage by insurance companies, photographic documentation of properties by real estate companies, and a wide range of filming projects for movies and television. Peripheral businesses—such as consultants, legal

TABLE 5-3. POTENTIAL UAS USES BY FEDERAL GOVERNMENT INDEPENDENT DEPARTMENTS AND AGENCIES

DEPARTMENT / AGENCY Purpose	UAS USAGE				
	Visual survey	Search & rescue	Data gathering	ISR	Civil engineering & inspection
DEPT. OF AGRICULTURE (USDA) Provide stability to agriculture economy	●		●		●
FEDERAL BUREAU OF INVESTIGATION (FBI) Federal law enforcement	●	●	●	●	
U.S. IMMIGRATION & CUSTOMS ENFORCEMENT (ICE) Customs and immigration enforcement	●	●	●	●	
U.S. CUSTOMS & BORDER PROTECTION (CBP) Customs and border protection and patrol	●	●	●	●	
U.S. MARSHALS SERVICE (USMS) Protection of courts, judges, and apprehension of fugitives	●	●		●	
DEPT. OF COMMERCE (DOC) Job creation	●	●	●	●	●
DEPT. OF DEFENSE (DOD) Protection and security of the United States	●	●	●	●	●
DEPT. OF EDUCATION (ED) Promote student achievement and equal access	●	●	●		●
DEPT. OF ENERGY (DOE) Address energy, environmental, and nuclear challenges	●		●	●	●
DEPT. OF HEALTH & HUMAN SERVICES (HHS) Enhance and protect the well-being of Americans	●	●	●	●	●
DEPT. OF HOMELAND SECURITY (DHS) Ensure all areas of homeland security	●	●	●	●	●

TABLE 5-3. *(continued)*

DEPARTMENT / AGENCY Purpose	UAS USAGE				
	Visual survey	Search & rescue	Data gathering	ISR	Civil engineering & inspection
DEPT. OF HOUSING & URBAN DEVELOPMENT (HUD) Create strong, sustainable, inclusive communities	●	●	●		●
DEPT. OF LABOR (DOL) Develop the welfare of wage earners	●	●	●		●
DEPT. OF TRANSPORTATION (DOT) Ensuring a safe, fast, convenient transportation system	●	●			●
ENVIRONMENTAL PROTECTION AGENCY (EPA) Protect human health and the environment	●		●		●

NOTE: This is not a complete list of state government departments and agencies; applications are not necessarily in use.

guides, training providers, and data analysts—have also come to fruition to support the varied unmanned aircraft applications. Other types of civilian UAS operations are conducted by systems integrators and developers. Many of these users are defense contractors working on improving UAS technologies through testing and demonstration. UAS manufacturers also have the need to operate their UAS during development, testing, training, and marketing. Without being able to conduct these critical tasks, it would be virtually impossible to continue expansion and advancement of the UAS industry

▶ Non-Profit—501(c)(3)

Civil applications of sUAS are also conducted by a variety of non-profit entities and organizations.[1] Some of the primary users in this category are institutions of education, typically at the postsecondary level. Higher education institutions generally conduct research and development activities, as well as provide an array of training. Related to this type of activity are operations conducted by scientific research entities. For example, operators can use sUAS to gain

[1] Organizations classified by the Internal Revenue Service (IRS) in *Tax-Exempt Status for Your Organization* (Publication No. 557) as Religious, Educational, Charitable, Scientific, Literary, Testing for Public Safety, to Foster National or International Amateur Sports Competition, or Prevention of Cruelty to Children or Animals Organizations

access for up-close imagery of volcanic eruptions or to monitor oil spill flows. Environmental monitoring, tangential to the aforementioned scientific efforts, is being conducted with sUAS to monitor endangered species and illegal deforestation. Even health and human services efforts are being supported by this technology. In 2015, the FAA approved the first medicine delivery by sUAS to a rural Virginia clinic. The Bill & Melinda Gates Foundation has provided funding for delivery of vaccines to remote locations, which could possibly be supported using sUAS. Other options for public benefit are being explored, such as delivery of emergency supplies following disaster events. A Swiss company currently has the capacity to deliver medical supplies to trapped skiers and hikers. Contrary to many of the concerns about sUAS operations, there are certainly many philanthropic and altruistic uses being executed across the globe.

STAKEHOLDER ROLES AND COLLABORATION

While each UAS stakeholder individually contributes to the innovation and advancement of the industry, collaboration among stakeholders is critical to its combined success. Examples of this cooperation can be seen in numerous agreements, organizations, and partnerships. The establishment of the FAA UAS Test Site Program brought together states, government agencies and departments, universities, airports, and companies to foster flight operations for research and development of UAS. The FAA's Center of Excellence for UAS, a team of U.S. colleges and universities, was created to conduct research, education, and training to support safe integration of UAS. Industry partnerships also bring together various stakeholders to work toward advancing UAS. Examples of such alliances are the Northern Plains UAS, a group of 20 companies and education institutions in or around North Dakota; the Desert Research Institute Wildfire-Fighting Drone Research Partnership; and FAA partnerships with CNN and BNSF Railway. Advocacy and policy review occur through the participation of a range of stakeholders, including colleges and universities as well as hobby and industry representative organizations. Lastly, the collaboration among researchers in the production of publications and presentations provide insight into cutting-edge technologies and concepts critical to advancing UAS adoption and utilization. Through the peer-review process, in which experts provide unbiased assessments of this research and related findings, the best and most relevant data is disseminated to stakeholders through conferences, journals, and other outlets. Clearly, it is in the best interests of all involved with UAS to proactively support such collaborative efforts, which result in mutually beneficial innovations and improvements.

BUSINESS OPPORTUNITY AND DEVELOPMENT

From an economic perspective, there are at least two paths to apply personal knowledge and experience to this field. First is the possibility of pursuing the entrepreneurial route: defining a new concept, starting up a business, and bringing derived services or products to market. Alternatively, the more conventional path is to work for others, collaborating and leveraging an organization's resources to address challenges or generate new business for the company.

Success in business is dependent on many factors, including establishing brand and reputation, networking among fellow stakeholders and potential customers, marketing services and products, and—in the case of sUAS activities—aligning planned sUAS pursuits and actions with your core business model. Whether setting out to start up a new business enterprise or proposing a new division within a larger business structure, it is imperative to obtain a solid understanding of the needs of clientele, as well as the requirements of the business. Before committing to either path, reflect on your personal goals and consider the path more likely to bring you closer to achievement.

STARTING A BUSINESS

Creating a new business can represent an exciting endeavor, providing the opportunity to be your own boss and develop innovative and interesting new technology. The guidance presented here is not meant to serve as an in-depth plan, but instead to serve as an introduction to concepts and considerations. If this path is one you are interested in pursuing, it is highly recommended that you perform independent research to better understand the expectations, needs, and requirements (federal, state, and local) of starting a business in your area. A number of detailed, well-presented overviews of the business startup process are available online, including those created by the economic development agencies of specific states and local governments, thoroughly describing the process and responsibilities of the potential business owner.

One of the first items to consider is what the purpose of the business will be. What unique capability will be provided, challenge solved, or market demand/consumer need fulfilled? Will you employ a service-based approach to perform work on behalf of a client (intangible), or will you be developing a specific product or suite of tools to address a need (tangible)? Conventional business guidance relates that for an economic enterprise to succeed it must provide two or more of the following benefits:

- *Cheaper*—a lower-cost (not lower-quality) alternative to current products or services (offerings) that provides efficiency and/or productivity gains
- *Better*—a preferable option that provides improved operational execution, enhanced safety, and/or greater profitability
- *Faster*—provides expedited results or improved time to market

The value proposition for use of sUAS is not always fiscally driven. Is it faster, cheaper, or better than alternative options? If the use of sUAS is faster and better (higher quality), then it may be justifiable to pay a premium (more expensive). Likewise, if it is cheaper and faster, then reduced performance may be acceptable, as long as baseline requirements are still met. Finally, if an sUAS provides a cheaper and better option, then it may be worth the extra time to conduct the operation or process the data. All of these factors are driven by the specifics of each use scenario and the associated requirements that must be satisfied to fulfill a perceived need in the market. Otherwise, it may be necessary to invest significant capital in a marketing campaign to educate potential users on why they need the offering. However, if the need is already established, then pursuit may be sufficiently justified, improving the potential of obtaining outside investment and critical startup capital early in the venture. Development and delivery of the offering should also be feasible and practical given other alternatives, and the potential benefits achievable through its use should be sustainable.

A critical element of a startup is the development of a clear and accurate business plan. The plan should be dynamic and subject to consistent updates to reflect changing conditions, the state of the market, and the business's mission. The business plan should clearly articulate the following:

- *Organizational structure*—Define ownership and management, including roles, responsibilities, percentages, and format (e.g., partnership, sole proprietorship, limited liability corporation [LLC], or corporation)
- *Purpose*—The overview identifying the objectives (what is intended), mission (goals), and vision (where the business is heading)
- *Target customers*—Who the offering will be created for and their important attributes, characteristics, needs, or strategic information that can help prepare the offering
- *Problem or challenge addressed*—The perceived need that will be addressed through the offering
- *Value proposition*—Why the business is worth developing or investing in, including details of planned offerings
- *Business development strategy*—How the business will be established, grown, and supported to ensure sustainability and profitability
- *Competitive differentiation*—Identification of competitor's offerings and detail regarding how your offerings differ (e.g., competitive advantage: how your offerings will be cheaper, better, and/or faster)
- *Business model*—How cost, revenue, and profit will be treated, including reinvestment, acquisition, product and intellectual property development, and strategic planning

The business should be supported by the following:

- Clearly defined goals and measures of success
- Consistent access to needed resources
- Definable user/customer base (demographics and needs should be well understood)
- Skilled labor and expertise
- Competitive advantage (cheaper, better, and/or faster)
- Strong networking and mentoring
- Marketing (creating public awareness of product offerings)
- Feedback capture and improvement mechanism (agile, scrum, lean, or six sigma)
- Incorporation of new/other technology and methodologies
- Well-defined product development lifecycle

One method to decrease the time to market or increase exposure is to partner with other organizations, sharing the business capture and risk while taking advantage of each other's unique capabilities and experience (i.e., apply specialized knowledge/skills and complimentary abilities). Partnerships are common among businesses, individuals, academia, government, and industries. Obtaining legal counsel and guidance is recommended before entering into a partnership, as this can affect potential profit, intellectual property, and permissible disclosure of information.

IN FIELD EMPLOYMENT

As a growing industry, there are numerous career opportunities involving sUAS technology, which may be lucrative to those with specialized, in-demand knowledge or skills (e.g., programming, data analysis, engineering, and operational certification or training completion) (see Figure 5-1). Before applying for positions, ensure you have an up-to-date and accurate resume with applicable references. If possible, create a digital portfolio highlighting applicable work to share with potential employers. Consider if you have any network connections working in the industry or within a specific company and solicit their guidance. Take full advantage of social media outlets, such as LinkedIn and other professional networking sites, to search for and learn more about positions. Additionally, get involved with local area clubs, organizations, and competitions associated with model aircraft, robotics, or unmanned systems, which can help to both build practical experience and establish further networking connections.

FIGURE 5-1. Examples of employee roles within organizations utilizing unmanned system technology.

Employment opportunities in the unmanned aviation field include the following:

- **Business Development**
  — Acquisition/contracts specialists
  — Analysts
  — Managers
  — Planners
  — Proposal specialists
- **Analysis, design, and development**
  — Analysts
  — Engineers
  — Research scientists
  — Specialists
- **Operations (including training)**
  — Instructors
  — Managers
  — Operators/pilots
  — Specialists
- **Assembly/manufacturing**
  — Schedulers
  — Specialists
  — Technicians
- **Support**
  — Analysts
  — Artists/drafters
  — Managers
  — Planners
  — Purchasers
  — Specialists
  — System administrators
  — Training developers
  — Writers
- **Management**
  — Executives
  — Leads
  — Managers

ACQUISITION, SUPPORT, AND COST PLANNING

When exploring how sUAS technology can be used to enhance the performance of an organization, many new users tend to focus on the benefits without considering the limitations or total investments required. This can be a costly misstep that may result in the purchase of equipment unable to meet intended operational requirements or ensure necessary levels of safety. Prior to purchase, it is recommended that you clearly define the operational requirements of the system and compare these to available platforms, based on their identified performance attributes (e.g., payload capacity, endurance, range, speed, and environmental limitations). A clear understanding regarding reoccurring support costs—such as maintenance, consumables, registration, training and certification, and insurance—should also be obtained and incorporated into budgetary planning. Additionally, you should be aware of what crewmembers and personnel will be needed to operate and maintain the platform, annually and throughout its intended lifecycle, with these costs included in budgetary planning.

Before purchasing an sUAS, it will be necessary to do some homework. To research options, use online guides, articles, and discussions with network contacts to better understand the capabilities and drawbacks of platforms. Read reviews from other users and resellers, taking note of the issues and concerns they express regarding the systems. Price compare from multiple vendors, making sure to carefully review what is included with each package, as

FIGURE 5-2. Example conventional manned aviation aircraft: (A) crop dusting, (B) law enforcement helicopter, (C) firefighting, and (D) U.S. Customs and Border Protection.

many may include additional components or "add-ons" to entice the buyer. Closely compare cost, capabilities, and requirements for operation and maintenance. Before committing to the purchase and use of an sUAS, make sure to confirm the value proposition (what value does investment and continued support provide, especially compared to conventional options currently employed?). Existing government resources, such as UAS test sites, state and regional UAS centers, colleges and universities, as well as state and local technology incubators, can provide expert guidance to further explore the possible benefits and considerations associated with the responsible and effective use of sUAS technology. To reiterate the guidance provided in the "Starting a Business" section earlier in this chapter, the use of sUAS for any purpose besides recreational should result in a solution that is cheaper, better, and/or faster than existing options (see Figure 5-2). The low-entry cost of consumer-level systems makes their use very appealing; however, costs and support requirements can ramp up quickly. It is very important to understand the total picture and to research and consider all of the tools available to help you get started. The following subsections provide insight and detail for further consideration to help you determine if sUAS can provide you or your organization with sufficient value given the expected level of investment and sustainment.

■ CONSIDER USE AND LEVEL OF EXPERIENCE

The level of experience of a remote pilot (or employees within an organization) plays a key role in selection of a platform, as many sUAS have integrated features and unique handling properties that require a significant amount of practice and practical experience to operate effectively. Use of simulation tools can help to build experience, but should not be the sole source of experience. Consider gaining practical, hands-on experience under the guidance of an experienced instructor. The following sections provide details regarding experience level categories and applicable consideration points regarding complexity of platforms and recommended experience-building actions.[2]

▶ Novice

This category represents users with little to no experience (e.g., first-time remote pilots), exploring the capabilities and operations of sUAS. Such users should be focused on building the requisite motor skills and knowledge, including aeronautical decision making, theory of flight and operations, awareness of platform options, and implications of sUAS operations (potential risks and effects). It is recommended that users at this level focus on building experience with small, forgiving training platforms (i.e., less expensive with minimum performance capability), such as indoor or electric recreational aircraft. It is highly suggested that novice users do not overbuy or purchase a system beyond their capabilities and consider purchase of flight simulation tools to further build and refine their experience. Focusing on improving understanding of the technology and its use, while building critical operational experience, will better prepare novice remote pilots for use of more complex aircraft that match their capabilities.

▶ Limited

This category represents those users who have completed a familiarization program and built minor experience through simulation and instructed flight. These users should be focused on further expanding their experience and understanding of critical operational requirements of more complex systems, which will better prepare them for operation of specialized and diverse sUAS platforms. It is recommended that such users consider entry-level application-specific or increased-complexity training platforms (providing an improved performance capability compared to baseline training platforms). Such users may also be prepared to operate more capable systems under the guidance of an experienced instructor and/or pilot-in-command.

▶ Experienced

This category represents established remote pilots who have mastered simulated sUAS flight and have built years of experience with operation and support of recreational model aircraft or sUAS. Consideration of complex consumer systems to simplistic commercial systems, requiring review of unique operational parameters and functions, as well as complex commercial systems

---

[2] Experience should be specific to type of aircraft being considered. For example, if you are an experienced model aircraft operator with hundreds of hours on fixed-wing aircraft and are looking to fly rotary-wing for the first time, you are considered a novice in the new category.

with appropriate training, is warranted for this level. However, it is recommended that such users continue to practice with specific systems to understand their complexities and unique attributes before using any system in a formal manner in the field, and also complete applicable training and certification programs, when available.

▶ Expert

This final category represents remote pilots who have mastered sUAS flight on multiple types and models of platforms, with significant experience responding to unforeseen issues and emergencies, managing flight operations, and conducting complex applications in the field. These users typically have received formal training from a vendor, institution, or national community-based organization (e.g., Academy of Model Aeronautics [AMA]). These remote pilots may be well suited to serve as a PIC and/or instructor to oversee other user's operations, as well as develop and lead training and familiarization programs. This experience level warrants consideration of complex systems, requiring review of unique operational parameters and functions, as well as specialized training.

■ LEVEL OF SUPPORT REQUIRED

Determining what will be required to operate the sUAS in a safe and responsible manner is a necessary element of receiving and maintaining federal operational approval, while understanding what is needed for your operation to remain effective is required to address the economic side. The success of your operation will depend on your ability to account for the level of support necessary, with appropriate planning, scheduling, and financial coverage.

▶ Setup and Configuration

As discussed in Chapter 3, platforms are available in many levels of operational readiness, from kit to ready-to-fly (RTF); make sure you select an option that matches your support capability. Examine the equipment and actions necessary to prepare the aircraft for flight. From simple battery insertion and startup to complex refueling, engine priming, and tuning, your experience and level of knowledge should match the platform requirements.

▶ Documentation

FAA operational approval requires submission of applicable documentation (e.g., operation, maintenance, and calibration instructions), much of which can be supplemented using vendor or manufacturer-provided materials. These materials can also provide detailed insight into the capabilities and expectations associated with a platform, which can assist in selection and use. Evaluate the level and quality of documentation provided for a system. (Acquiring documentation may require contacting the manufacturer.)

▶ Training and Education

Some vendors provide specialized training (simulated or actual) to help users become familiar with the unique capabilities and characteristics of their platforms. Such training can also improve the safety and effectiveness of operations and subsequently lower the cost of insurance. A wide variety of professional training and safety courses are available, designed to help potential users—including pilots, business developers, managers, and engineers—better understand how this technology can be used within their discipline or market. The level of training necessary to support sUAS application is dependent on several factors, including the previously discussed organizational type (public or civil), insurance requirements, internal organizational policies, regulations, and the role of the individual in the organization.

Prior to individually enrolling in any training or education program, identify what specific knowledge, skills, or abilities (KSAs) are needed and confirm they can be acquired within the available options. Some vendors and educational institutions may be willing to adapt or build custom content to support your needs. If you are exploring certification, be mindful of whether the FAA has established the criteria required to properly train and assess performance. Additionally, it is important to note that in order for credits to transfer among academic institutions (colleges and universities), the institution should be regionally accredited (a license to operate is not the same as accreditation). There are a significant number of associate, bachelor, graduate, and professional education programs relating to unmanned system design, operation, and application across the United States.[3] To support the dynamic needs of students, these programs are also available in multiple learning modalities: synchronous (e.g., face-to-face or supported through telecommunication technology), asynchronous (online), or hybrid (synchronous supported with asynchronous).

▶ Repair and Maintenance

Some vendors only support use of their own parts (i.e., original equipment manufacturer [OEM]), while others may provide specifications indicating the format and requirements of alternative components (aftermarket or add-on parts). As such, systems relying on proprietary OEM designs may need to be serviced at a dedicated vendor location or center, while others can be performed by the owner or a third party. The maintenance and repair expectations associated with a platform should be clearly understood prior to purchase.

▶ Regulatory Application-Specific Materials and Guidance

An increasing number of sUAS platforms have been developed and marketed to support specific applications, such as precision agriculture crop monitoring. As configured, these systems may not be well suited for alternative uses without modification or reconfiguration. Additionally, a platform's capabilities are highly dependent on the underlying integrated technology, which may require specific certification, registration, or approval to use (e.g., high-powered communication radios and radio operator certification, platforms greater than 0.55 pounds, or non-recreational operation). Carefully review system descriptions and documentation to determine if a system meets regulatory requirements or if additional paperwork (i.e., registration) or certification is necessary to operate, as configured.

---

[3] "Professional education" courses and programs typically award a certificate upon completion, as well as continuing education units (CEUs) used to confirm currency in a field/discipline.

❱ User Community

A strong, supportive community of users can help to troubleshoot issues, generate solutions, provide insight, and share observations from the field. This community exists through hobby shops and recreational flying clubs, as well as online through websites and user groups that can be platform- or vendor-specific and that provide interactive and collaborative resources through blogs, message boards, document hosting, FAQs, and messaging. It is highly suggested that new users connect with local and online organizations for guidance and mentorship with this complex and dynamic technology.

■ PROVEN PERFORMANCE

It is useful to examine if the platforms under consideration have been used previously by others in a similar manner. Have these users shared their experience or observations in reports, articles, or blogs? Has the vendor identified the performance capabilities of their platform and detailed how the values were calculated or determined? Researching and reviewing such information prior to purchase is recommended to better understand the platform's capabilities and the accuracy of published performance.

❱ Reported Metrics

Important values such as reliability (i.e., mean time between failure [MTBF]), performance, and operational limits play an important role in the comparison and selection of platforms. Understanding how systems perform relative to other options, as well as the methods used to determine these values, are important as they indicate quality and the level of forethought on the part of the manufacturer. Locating this information may be straightforward, as the manufacturer might present the data in a performance specification on their website, or it may require investigation and directly contacting the manufacturer or user.

❱ Documented Performance Testing and Analysis

If a system was created for a government user, the manufacturer is generally required to document the results of detailed requirements testing (e.g., acceptance testing). Alternatively, as a cost-saving measure or for simplicity and reduced time to market, less complex systems (e.g., recreational hobby platforms) may forgo detailed performance analysis and testing and instead rely on the use of calculated estimates. Examine available documentation regarding acceptance testing or evaluation that may be contained within performance specifications, research articles, reports, or presentations. These materials and the results of testing and/or analysis will provide insight into the operation and potential suitability of a platform.

❱ Larger User Population

Larger user groups tend to result in the publication and availability of an increased amount of data regarding the platform, both from observations across the population and in response to their needs, as well as an increased availability of parts and support. Likewise, newer platforms with fewer users tend to have less documented information regarding their capabilities, limitations, and unique traits. Examine the user community and online forums to determine the size of the population and availability of information to consider how access to this information, parts, and services may support your organizational needs.

■ COST AND AVAILABILITY

The price point of the system, including necessary support equipment, can drive selection of the platform. However, it is also necessary to consider the wider availability and market demand to ensure replacement parts, spares, and future upgrade components can be obtained, given their potential need in subsequent years. Additionally, it might be warranted to consider the health and viability of an organization you plan to purchase from to ensure the continued availability of support and components, in accordance with your long-term business plans.

▶ Wide Availability

Ensuring a system and its components are not limited to a single source can help to prevent delay or significant price increases due to changing demand. By confirming that the system and needed parts can be procured from a number of vendors, it may be possible to alleviate or prevent potential logistical and acquisition issues. Any delays in acquisition of parts or services can translate to delays in or prevention of your own business pursuits; plan accordingly and ensure you have created sufficient contingencies to mitigate possible issues.

▶ Consistent Pricing

The pricing of purchased systems, components, and services should be representative of market demands, not undercutting by lower-price imitation or counterfeit units lacking in quality or functionality. Some variation is to be expected, due to competition and availability. However, be wary of deals too good to be true; ensure the reputation of the seller before committing to a purchase.

▶ Within Allocated Budget

Make sure to consider the pricing of all components and services, including consumables and the required level of support (e.g., access to documentation, provision of training, technical support, and troubleshooting). Not all systems are created equal or provide the same level of support after purchase. Pay close attention to warranty provisions and advertised service or maintenance costs, and make sure not to spend your entire budget on the up-front cost without considering long-term operation and maintenance costs.

▶ Negotiable Pricing and Support

Many commercial off-the-shelf (COTS) systems (e.g., recreational hobby or consumer platforms, under $5,000) will be subject to the manufacturer's suggested retail price (MSRP), with some room for resellers to reduce the price based on their inventory and number of sales. However, as the price and complexity of systems increase, so does the ability of a buyer to negotiate. Many custom developers and government vendors start with a "catalog price," which can be negotiated down based on a number of factors including the level of support provided (ranging from "as is" purchase to full-system training and troubleshooting, after sale), the number of units purchased, and your type of organization (donations to non-profit 503(c) organizations are tax-deductible). Before committing, it is highly recommended that you research what others have paid for identical or similar systems or configurations.

▌ BUDGETING

Planning for the long-term operation and support of purchased systems is critical to achieving success. There are a myriad of ways to spend money in this field, but it would be to your benefit to thoroughly consider and plan for what will be necessary to meet your organizational and business goals. Instead of spending as you go, evaluate and consider how you can best forecast and allocate financial resources, prior to integrating sUAS into your organizational structure.

❯ Purchase and Acquisition

Purchase of this technology can represent a significant investment in time and money. Consider estimating the cost to research, evaluate, test, and acquire the sUAS that meets your goals. If you are an individual, this cost may only represent time. However, if you are a company representative, that time must be accounted for and budgeted financially (i.e., man hour loading). These costs may also include travel expenditures to meet with companies, observe demonstrations, and negotiate pricing, or materials and equipment to test and evaluate a system in a laboratory. Once a system has been selected, you may also need to consider the cost to transport it to your location (i.e., shipping and handling), as well as to pay any import taxes or duties owed if it is sourced from a vendor outside the United States. Pay close attention to the total cost of acquisition, not just the MSRP.

❯ Operations

The operational costs of a system can also be significant, depending on how the sUAS will be used, including the number and duration of anticipated flights. You will need to estimate and account for the cost to operate your sUAS as intended. This may require performing an analysis of expected use to calculate consumable costs, such as fuel, lubricant, scheduled maintenance, and time-limited part replacement (e.g., rechargeable batteries usable for a finite number of charges); man hour loading (hourly or salaried cost of crewmembers); equipment transport to operational sites; and reoccurring fees or charges, such as certification, registration, or insurance premiums. This estimate can help to guide future decisions and determine what your "breakeven point" will be for annual business capture.

❯ Internal Support

Identifying opportunities to leverage knowledge, skills, and abilities, as well as equipment and products, from within an organization can help to reduce costs, secure or protect sensitive business plans, provide expedited response, and establish further institutional buy-in for the pursuit of related technology or business development. This requires coordination among business units, departments, managers, and human resources to appropriately allocate resources and personnel. In cases of organizations with an existing flight department, coordinating the acquisition, certification, operation, and support of sUAS through this department is recommended, as they typically have a high degree of related aeronautical experience and knowledge (i.e., FAA regulations, safety management, aeronautical decision making, scheduling, and requisite FAA airman and maintenance certification and ratings). Make sure to determine the costs of using internal assets and resources so they can be compared to alternatives, such as external consultation, and incorporated into your operational budget. In some cases, it may be more cost-effective to use external support.

▶ External Support

In some instances, required capabilities or services are not available within an organization. For these cases, it may be necessary to contract with an outside party. Common examples in which such outside services are used include specialized consultation, taxation, documentation, registration, certification, training, and insurance coverage. Perform due diligence when hiring an outside firm, making sure to ask for and review applicable references and examples of work (e.g., portfolio). Determine the costs of using such services and incorporate those costs into your operational budget.

▶ Cost Estimation Example

Estimating the potential costs of acquiring, operating, and supporting the use of an sUAS can be a complex process. An example is provided to exhibit high-level guidance and narrative relating to the purchase and operation of a single COTS sUAS within a large business organization, over a five-year period. While this example does not cover all potential scenarios or possible variables, it does provide sufficient detail to assist in the creation of your own budget and estimation analysis. The example is broken down into several distinct sets of calculations, including acquisition costs, lifecycle sustainment costs, per hour calculations, and effectiveness determination.

Scenario

An engineer at a large business (500+ employees and multiple business units) has examined the potential use of sUAS to replace costly manned aircraft flights over their property. Conventional manned flights are conducted several times a year to visually inspect and document the state of large earthwork berms used to store the byproduct of production processes. Due to their remote location, the cost to conduct such manned flights is approximately $75,000 annually (24 flights at $3,125 per flight), requiring aircraft to transit to the Class G airspace over their facility. The engineer consulted with the company's flight department manager to research, analyze, and determine the suitability of a specific sUAS platform to conduct the necessary flights from the property (to be launched and recovered on site). Their combined effort, which included inspection of the platform, meeting with vendor representatives, and survey of the operational environment, has cost approximately $2,500, which will need to be accounted for in the potential acquisition cost of the platform, should the cost estimation serve to indicate that the proposition is worth pursuing.

Their analysis—which included a thorough review of the performance capabilities of a series of platforms, and development of an operational concept (OpsCon) and plan—indicated an improved level of safety and efficiency could be achieved. During development of the OpsCon, it was determined that a single, one-hour flight could cover the entire area to be visually inspected. Furthermore, having access to a platform in house would support the performance of an increased number of annual flights (250), which would provide enhanced information for the engineer to determine the effectiveness and state of the storage berms, as well as meet other company goals. It was also determined that operations could be conducted under Part 107 rules, with the flight department manager serving as the remote PIC (assuming acquisition of a remote pilot certificate). Additionally, the flight department manager suggested using internal aviation resources and personnel to support the potential operations, including associated inspections, maintenance, and support.

Acquisition Costs

Based on the analysis, the engineer and flight department manager were able to identify a platform and payload suitable to perform the intended operations. The platform requires specialized equipment and must be shipped from a vendor outside the state, incurring a shipping and handling cost. As the engineer and maintenance personnel are familiar with the materials and construction of the platform, no service support was purchased. However, spares, including propellers, motors, and chassis elements, were purchased to address potential mishaps, failures, or operational time limits. No unique or specialized configuration or construction would be needed for this platform.

The following represents the estimated costs and calculations associated with acquisition of the COTS sUAS platform and payload, resulting in a total of $7,500.

Analysis and evaluation (labor, travel, testing)	$2,500
Equipment	
Air vehicle element	$2,000
Payload	$500
Ground-based C3	$1,500
Support equipment	$225
Spares (*propellers, motors, chassis elements*)	$300
Service support (*none purchased*)	$0
Transportation	$200
Taxes and/or duties	$275
Construction or development costs (*labor*)	$0
Formula: ∑ all items	
Total Acquisition Cost	**$7,500**

Lifecycle Sustainment Costs

After review of internal resources and personnel, it was determined that a data analyst would be necessary, which would require the involvement of human resources personnel to hire this new employee (who would be partially assigned to the sUAS project, with remaining time supporting other departments). The company's legal representative would be needed to review the operations and subsequent safety management plan annually. The flight department manager proposed including business development to determine, on an annual basis, if there would be external opportunities to generate further revenue using the sUAS. After a detailed review of other operators' experiences with the platform, it was also determined that 40 hours per year of maintenance activity would provide sufficient coverage, including potential repairs from mishaps or accidents. No external consultation would be needed for preparation of registration or operational approval applications, but inclusion of the sUAS on the existing aviation insurance policy would increase the premium by approximately $250 per year.

The following represents the estimated overhead costs and calculations associated with supporting the use of the COTS sUAS platform throughout the anticipated lifecycle (performance period of five years), resulting in a total of $43,475, or $8,695 per year.

Internal support (labor)	
Human resources (one-time; *4 hrs @ $50 per hour*)	$200
Data analysis ($2,000 per year; *40 hrs @ $50 per hour*)	$10,000
Legal ($400 per year; *2 hrs @ $200 per hour*)	$2,000
Management ($4,000 per year; *40 hrs @ $100 per hour*)	$20,000
Business development ($1,000 per year; *10 hrs @ $100 per hour*)	$5,000
Maintenance ($1,000 per year; *40 hrs @ $25 per hour*)	$5,000
External support (labor and services)	
Consultation	$0
Insurance ($250 per year)	$1,250
Fees	
Registration ($5/year)	$25
Certification	$0
Formula: Σ all items	
Total Lifecycle Sustainment Cost (5 years)	**$43,475**
Lifecycle Sustainment Cost (annual)	**$8,695**

Calculation of Per-Hour Costs

The operational concept and plan indicated that a single, one-hour flight would be sufficient to cover the subject area for visual inspection, with approximately 250 such flights planned annually. A performance period of five years was selected to provide sufficient time to determine the long-term effectiveness of the new method, as well as recoup the significant investment costs.

The following represents the estimated costs and calculations associated with hourly operational costs of the COTS sUAS platform, resulting in a total per-hour cost of $162.53, including acquisition, sustainment, and operation.

1. Per Hour Acquisition and Sustainment Cost

Total Acquisition Cost..	$7,500
Lifecycle sustainment (non-operational labor)	$43,475
Number of estimated flights per year (N).................................	250
Estimated average duration of each flight (T; in hours)..................	1
Performance period (in years; time to cover cost of acquisition)........	5

Formula
(Total Acquisition Cost + Lifecycle Sustainment Cost) ÷ N ÷ T ÷ Performance Period

Per-Hour Acquisition Cost... **$40.78**[4]

2. Per Hour Operational Cost

Operational personnel (per hour)

PIC	$50
Visual Observer...	$35
Safety Officer..	$35

Consumables

Fuel	$1.75

Formula: Σ all items
Per Hour Operational Cost... **$121.75**

3. Total Per Hour Cost

Per Hour Acquisition Cost..	$40.78
Per Hour Operational Cost...	$121.75

Formula: Σ all items
Total Per Hour Cost... **$162.53**

Determining Effectiveness

The effectiveness of sUAS operations will be dependent on several factors, including determining whether the operation is meant to be used to generate external business and build profit or to replace a costly conventional method of performing a task. As is observable in this example, the costs to sustain the use of the sUAS ($43,475) far exceed the acquisition cost ($7,500). However, when cost is viewed hourly or in comparison to an external cost (e.g., contracting conventional manned aircraft), sUAS use may represent a competitive option. The

[4] Assuming the sUAS is used to fly 250 or more annual flights, lasting at least one hour, over a five-year period.

question will be whether you are able to accurately estimate the number and duration of flights within the year and performance period. These estimations are much more accurate when used in comparison to known costs within an organization, as opposed to when estimating the potential capability to generate external business. This is one reason why businesses are considering internal use of sUAS to replace conventional methods of performing aerial tasks, as the cost savings can be fairly apparent when analyzed. The following represents a series of calculations to determine both potential revenue, as well as cost savings (effectiveness), of using the example sUAS compared to the conventional method.

1. Revenue Potential

Charge Rate (per hour)[5]...	$175
Total Per Hour Cost	$162.53

Formula: *Charge Rate – Total Per Hour Cost*

Revenue (per hour)...	*$12.47*
Revenue (per flight) *(per hour x T)*..	*$12.47*
Revenue (annual) *(per flight x N)*	*$3,117.50*
Revenue (performance period)...	***$15,587.50***

2. Revenue-based Return on Investment (ROI)

Revenue (performance period)...	$15,587.50
Total Acquisition Cost...	$7,500
Lifecycle Sustainment Cost..	$43,475

Formula: *Revenue ÷ (Total Acquisition Cost + Lifecycle Sustainment Cost) x 100*

Revenue-based ROI...	***30.58%***

3. sUAS to Conventional Comparison

sUAS Operational Cost (annual) *(Charge Rate x N x T)*	*$43,750*
Conventional Cost (annual; externally contracted)	*$75,000*

Formula: *Conventional Cost – sUAS Operation Costs*

Potential Savings (annual)..	*$31,250*
Potential Savings (performance period).................................	***$156,250***
(annual x 5) (41.67% savings)	
Cost-savings ROI (performance period).................................	***306.52%***

---

[5] This value represents the cost to charge for use of the sUAS, which is greater than the actual operational costs of $163.53 per hour to create profit and expedite recuperation of acquisition and sustainment costs in the performance period. This value is to be set by the user at a sufficient level to support generation of profit. However, it may be warranted to create distinct charge rates for providing support of tasks within the organization (internal rate), as opposed to those requiring external billing of clients (customer rate).

4. Total Value Calculation

Revenue (performance period)...	$15,587.50
Potential Savings (performance period)............................	$156,250

Formula: *Revenue + Potential Savings*

Total Value (performance period)	**$171,837.50**

Upon review of the final analysis and calculations, the engineer and flight department manager concluded that the acquisition and operation of an sUAS, instead of manned over-flight, was warranted and highly supportable. With the ability to perform almost daily flights (250 per year), the engineer would be able to capture significantly enhanced data regarding the state of the berms and their gradual change, while the flight department manager could support other aviation activities for the company (e.g., media capture, marketing development, external business generation, safety inspection, and security). The potential annual savings of $31,250 would justify the hiring of a new employee (data analyst), as well as the possible purchase of additional platforms, which would provide benefit to other departments and increase the flexibility of the flight department to respond to other company needs. With a potential value of $171,837.50 over the five-year performance period, use of an sUAS in this example would merit consideration.

It should be noted that this scenario was created to exhibit an example of when the use of an sUAS is justified. It featured the development of an operational concept and plan, thorough evaluation of potential platforms, and replacement of a costly conventional method. Not all evaluations will be subject to the same conditions and decisions. It's important to carefully consider, based on the information presented in this section and in the various chapters of this textbook, if use of an sUAS would be merited for your potential concept. Weigh the pros and cons, assigning a value to each that will help you evaluate if use of sUAS technology is truly suitable. Do not purchase or use sUAS because of the "wow" factor (unless you are focused on marketing and that is your intent). Instead, critically compare and evaluate, choosing the option that results in the highest levels of safety, efficiency, and effectiveness.

INCORPORATING SUAS OPERATIONS

A growing number of businesses are exploring the use of sUAS across their enterprises. As discussed earlier, the technology has the potential to offer substantial gains in safety, efficiency, and effectiveness, which can translate to improved service, increased profitability, decreased risk, and enhanced response to customer needs. However, its use is also governed by complex regulatory and operational requirements, such as federal approval and oversight; registration; operational provisions and prohibitions; and insurance. With the recent advancement and accessibility of sUAS as tools to support business pursuits and services, the desire of engineers, technicians, marketing personnel, and other company employees to use this technology continues to increase. However, such individuals may not have received the appropriate aviation training, certification, or practical experience to safely and effectively operate these platforms, in accordance with operational requirements.

Aviation and flight departments are well versed in ensuring compliance with requirements, while also offering a wealth of KSAs garnered from their extensive training and experience in this safety-critical field. Integrating the responsibility for management and oversight of all sUAS operations in a company under an existing flight department can provide improved compliance, operational safety and effectiveness, standardization, economies of scale, and collaborative benefit. Likewise, creation of such a unit within an organization that does not currently employ aviation assets may be worth exploring to ensure consistent management and oversight of sUAS use across the organization. The following are potential benefits of integrating any sUAS operations under such a department:

- *Improved regulatory compliance*—With sUAS defined as "aircraft," the technology falls under federal regulations and guidelines (e.g., CFRs, FARs, and advisory circulars). Aviation professionals understand and are experienced with interpreting, assessing, and confirming compliance with such requirements. When a unit within an organization fails to meet requirements, whether intentionally or inadvertently, it has the potential to adversely affect all current and future aviation operations within the organization.

- *Increased safety and effectiveness*—Involving flight departments in proposed operations from the beginning improves the potential for successful task completion and continued operational safety. As professionals in aviation, they are well versed in best practices and potential implications associated with the operation of aircraft in specific environments and conditions (e.g., degraded visual conditions, precipitation, wind, and performance limitations). They can assist engineers and subject matter experts (SMEs), who are well versed in the technology or infrastructure, to appropriately apply aviation assets such as sUAS in a manner ensuring that requirements, beyond technical implementation alone, are met. This can in turn help prevent mishaps, accidents, undesirable exposure or embarrassment, fines, or prohibition of aviation operations.

- *Standardization across organization*—sUAS offer many technological capabilities that differ from manned aircraft, but they still must conform to a number of operational and support requirements (e.g., insurance, internal company policies, and federal/state/local regulations). Integration into a flight department ensures different cases of use from across the enterprise can be managed, in a consistent and reliable manner and in accordance with such requirements, further improving the safety, efficiency, and effectiveness of application.

- *Realizing economies of scale*—Managing all aviation assets under a flight department supports expanded capability and sustainment. All operations of the sUAS platform can be conducted nationwide and across the organization under Part 107; insurance can be purchased for a fleet, rather than individual platforms; observations from the field can be captured and used to generate lessons learned and improved policies for all operations (or unique exemptions); captured data can be managed and stored for the entire enterprise, supporting wider analysis and discovery; and platforms, maintenance, and other service contracts can be acquired for the fleet, rather than for individual units (resulting in improved pricing and coverage).

- **Collaborative gains**—By working together, SMEs and flight departments can better understand the potential for applying UAS technology to safely meet the evolving needs of the organization. The unique perspective each can provide, as UAS stakeholders, will help to address challenges, risks, and cost-effectiveness concerns, while identifying new and novel ways UAS can be used in the future. Achievable benefits will be applied beyond a single site to the entire operation, while ensuring risks and issues are identified early and communicated out to all potential users within the organization.

GROWTH AREAS AND CHALLENGES

There are number of industries, fields, and technologies connected to unmanned aviation. While the UAS industry has made significant strides in technology, adoption, and application, substantial opportunity for growth still exists in these areas. Advances in materials is occurring rapidly, with the use of composites and 3D-printed/additive-layer manufacturing parts becoming commonplace. Power density augmentation has also been at the forefront of sUAS technological improvements, with increased battery life (endurance) and/or lighter-weight batteries becoming available. Communications and networking enhancements have also been forthcoming, including the use of WiFi and Bluetooth communication, and the capability of drones to "swarm" to provide a network of sensors working collaboratively. This technology will also benefit from upgrades in computation and processing with the continuing dramatic improvements in the quality, cost, and sizing of computer components, processors, and sensors, as well as the development of improved sensor processing and algorithm/classification routines. All of these advancements and improvements translate to improved access for users, increased manufacturer and developer opportunities, and increased possibilities for entrepreneurship and innovation (*see* Figure 5-3).

Service providers, such as telecommunications, are another area of potential growth in which sUAS have been used to augment coverage across the globe. One such example is Facebook's desire to use various types of UAS to blanket the planet with Internet coverage. The need for training and education of remote pilots, designers, and maintenance personnel will continue to grow along with the industry as a whole. With the enactment of Part 107, and subsequent evolution of the UAS operational framework, training and education entities will need to closely examine the needs of their clients (e.g., students and professionals) to provide the necessary regulatory-compliant services. Another service that has great potential is consulting. With many potential users unaware or unknowledgeable about all that is necessary to operate sUAS, consultants can assist in addressing the relevant knowledge gaps. They can

FIGURE 5-3. Example commercial sUAS platforms.

also act as the bridge between manufacturer and user, matching the two together to optimize the relationship between parties. By taking a detailed look at these fields and technologies by reviewing trade and scientific publications, attending conferences, trade shows, and symposiums, and networking with leading companies, you will be better prepared to pursue opportunities as they arise.

Despite the growing opportunities in this field, challenges still exist that may hamper or prevent the level of growth forecasted by industry experts. These challenges can be partially mitigated within your own business plans and may help to set you apart from competitors, especially if you address the challenges using novel technology or methods. Some of the most significant challenges to the economic development of this field include:

- Ensuring widescale compliance with regulations
- Maintaining an equivalent level of safety (ELOS) in operation of sUAS
- Anticipating and incorporating technological advancements
- The need for agility and responsiveness to constantly changing conditions
- Cooperation in a competitive landscape (UAS stakeholders working toward sustainability of the industry)
- Uneven competition (small firms against large firms with vast resources)
- Uninformed public, including organizations and businesses unaware of or intentionally disregarding federal regulations and guidance
- Inconsistent regulation (from federal down to local level)
- The need for specialized support (training, development, analysis, and insurance)

CHAPTER 6

PREPARING FOR THE FUTURE: ACCURATE INFORMATION MAKES ALL THE DIFFERENCE

INTRODUCTION

After reviewing and considering the history and evolution of UAS technology, its future potential, the significant number of options and requirements, and its varying levels of complexities, you are better prepared to tackle the challenges and opportunities for its profitable and gainful use. However, even after review of the information presented, your work is far from over. The message reiterated throughout these chapters bears repeating—that the technology, regulations, and needs associated with the application of UAS are far from stationary and will continue to evolve to achieve greater safety, efficiency, and effectiveness. For this field and its stakeholders to continue significant forward progress, collaboration and diligent pursuit of knowledge must be a primary goal. By applying what you have learned about sUAS and actively contributing as a fellow stakeholder, you will be a part of the sustainable success of this technology.

FINDING INFORMATION

This section contains a detailed list of resources and reference materials, categorized by topic, to assist your continuing exploratory pursuits. These materials include websites, documents, articles, and other publications relating to regulations; the UAS Test Sites and Center of Excellence; advocacy and public outreach organizations; news resources; online user communities; insurance providers; legal counsel; publications; events; and research. The resources and materials provided here represent those available at the time of this writing. As the industry continues to develop, website addresses may change and new resources will emerge; you can use the information in this section as a starting point to conduct your own search for relevant, up-to-date materials and resources.

NOTE: *To support usability of these resources, formal documents, reports, or articles are presented using the American Psychological Association (APA) reference citation format, while websites are identified in a simplified manner (organization, page title: web address). It is highly recommended that you use due diligence in the review, corroboration, and acceptance of any guidance found using these sources; if in doubt, contact a representative from the FAA, your state or local government, a lawyer, or a subject matter expert to confirm the accuracy and relevance of presented information. Identification of an individual, company, or firm in any of these lists does not equate to author endorsement, but is provided as an example to assist readers in exploring options that may support their specific needs and requirements. It is suggested that multiple options be considered, thoroughly reviewed, and compared before final selection, contracting, use, attendance, or commitment of resources or funding.*

REGULATORY INFORMATION

The following resources contain information regarding U.S. federal regulations for the operation and certification of sUAS:

- FAA, *Unmanned Aircraft Systems*:
  www.faa.gov/uas
- U.S. Federal Register, *Electronic Code of Federal Regulations*
  (see Title 14— Aeronautics and Space):
  www.ecfr.gov
- FAA, *FAA Safety Team (FAASTeam)*:
  www.faasafety.gov

▌ PART 107 RESOURCES

These resources contain information relating to operation and certification of sUAS under Part 107:

- FAA, *Becoming a Pilot*:
  www.faa.gov/uas/getting_started/fly_for_work_business/becoming_a_pilot
- FAA, *Fly for Work/Business*:
  www.faa.gov/uas/getting_started/fly_for_work_business
- FAA, *Beyond the Basics*:
  www.faa.gov/uas/getting_started/fly_for_work_business/beyond_the_basics

▌ UAS AUTHORIZATION RESOURCES

These resources contain information relating to operation and certification of UAS:

- FAA, *UAS Resources*:
  www.faa.gov/uas/resources
- FAA, *Certificate of Waiver or Authorization (COA)*:
  www.faa.gov/about/office_org/headquarters_offices/ato/service_units/systemops/aaim/organizations/uas/coa

- FAA, *Special Airworthiness Certification: Certification for Civil Operated Unmanned Aircraft Systems (UAS) and Optionally Piloted Aircraft (OPA)*: www.faa.gov/aircraft/air_cert/airworthiness_certification/sp_awcert/experiment/sac

▌REGISTRATION RESOURCES

These resources contain information relating to registration of UAS:

- FAA, *Aircraft Registry*: www.faa.gov/licenses_certificates/aircraft_certification/aircraft_registry
- FAA, *How to Label Your UAS document*: www.faa.gov/uas/getting_started/fly_for_fun/media/uas_how_to_label_infographic.pdf
- FAA, *Small Unmanned Aircraft System (sUAS) Registration Service*: registermyuas.faa.gov

▌STATE AND LOCAL REGULATIONS

These resources contain information relating to state and local regulations affecting the operation of UAS:

- FAA, *State and Local Regulation of Unmanned Aircraft Systems (UAS) Fact Sheet*: www.faa.gov/uas/resources/uas_regulations_policy/media/uas_fact_sheet_final.pdf
- National Conference of State Legislatures, *Current Unmanned Aircraft State Law Landscape*: www.ncsl.org/research/transportation/current-unmanned-aircraft-state-law-landscape.aspx
- Syracuse University's Institute for National Security and Counterterrorism (INSCT), *Local Regulation*: uavs.insct.org/local-regulation

▌EXPORT CONTROL RESOURCES

These resources contain information relating to export control restrictions and requirements that may affect the acquisition, sale, and transport of sUAS technology:

- U.S. Department of Commerce, Bureau of Industry and Security, *Export Administration Regulation Downloadable Files*: www.bis.doc.gov/index.php/regulations/export-administration-regulations-ear
- U.S. Department of State, Directorate of Defense Trade Controls, *The International Traffic in Arms Regulations (ITAR)*: www.pmddtc.state.gov/regulations_laws/itar.html

▌UAS STANDARDS RESOURCES

These resources contain information relating to industry standards that are used to evaluate possible changes to regulations and guidance:

- ASTM International, *Subcommittee F38.01 on Airworthiness*: www.astm.org/COMMIT/SUBCOMMIT/F3801.htm

- Active Standards, ASTM International, Subcommittee F38.01 on Airworthiness:
  — F2585-08, *Standard Specification for Design and Performance of Pneumatic-Hydraulic Unmanned Aircraft System (UAS) Launch System*
  — F2851-10, *Standard Practice for UAS Registration and Marking (Excluding Small Unmanned Aircraft Systems)*
  — F2910-14, *Standard Specification for Design and Construction of a Small Unmanned Aircraft System (sUAS)*
  — F2911-14e1, *Standard Practice for Production Acceptance of Small Unmanned Aircraft System (sUAS)*
  — F3002-14a, *Standard Specification for Design of the Command and Control System for Small Unmanned Aircraft Systems (sUAS)*
  — F3003-14, *Standard Specification for Quality Assurance of a Small Unmanned Aircraft System (sUAS)*
  — F3005-14a, *Standard Specification for Batteries for Use in Small Unmanned Aircraft Systems (sUAS)*
  — F3201-16, *Standard Practice for Ensuring Dependability of Software Used in Unmanned Aircraft Systems (UAS)*
- Proposed New Standards, ASTM International, Subcommittee F38.01 on Airworthiness: www.astm.org/COMMIT/SUBCOMMIT/F3801.htm

UAS TEST SITES AND CENTER OF EXCELLENCE

These resources contain information relating to the six FAA designated Test Sites and the Center of Excellence, which may be useful to better understand the technological advances and research being undertaken to support further integration of UAS into the National Airspace System:

- FAA-Designated Test Sites:
  — Griffiss International Airport/Northeast UAS Airspace Integration Research (NUAIR) Alliance: www.nuairalliance.org
  — North Dakota Department of Commerce/Northern Plains UAS Test Site: www.npuasts.com
  — State of Nevada/Nevada Institute for Autonomous Systems (NIAS): www.nias-uas.com
  — Texas A&M University-Corpus Christi/Lone Star UAS Center of Excellence & Innovation: www.lsuasc.tamucc.edu
  — University of Alaska-Fairbanks/Alaska Center for Unmanned Aircraft Systems Integration (ACUASI): acuasi.alaska.edu

— Virginia Polytechnic Institute & State University/Mid-Atlantic Aviation Partnership (MAAP):
www.maap.ictas.vt.edu

- FAA-Designated Center of Excellence for UAS Research:
  — Alliance for System Safety of UAS through Research Excellence (ASSURE):
  www.assureuas.org/index.php

GOVERNMENT-SPONSORED, ADVOCACY, AND PUBLIC OUTREACH ORGANIZATIONS

These resources represent examples of government-sponsored, advocacy, and public outreach organizations working on behalf of their local residents, members, and the general public to align permitted UAS use with their individual missions/charters, as well as improve perception of how this technology can be applied.

NOTE: *Many of these organizations provide guidance, briefings, documents, and tutorials that may be useful in the development of your own strategies or to further explore the capabilities, benefits, and limitations of this technology.*

- Academy of Model Aeronautics (AMA):
  www.modelaircraft.org
- Aerospace Industries Association (AIA):
  www.aia-aerospace.org
- Aircraft Owners and Pilots Association (AOPA):
  www.aopa.org
- American Civil Liberties Union (ACLU), Domestic Drones:
  www.aclu.org/issues/privacy-technology/surveillance-technologies/domestic-drones
- Association for Unmanned Vehicle Systems International (AUVSI):
  www.auvsi.org
- Know Before You Fly campaign:
  www.knowbeforeyoufly.org
- National Business Aviation Association (NBAA), Unmanned Aircraft Systems (UAS):
  www.nbaa.org/ops/uas
- Ohio/Indiana UAS Center:
  www.dot.state.oh.us/divisions/uas
- Small UAV Coalition:
  www.smalluavcoalition.org
- Washington State, Department of Transportation, Unmanned Aerial Vehicle Systems:
  www.wsdot.wa.gov/business/visualcommunications/UAV.htm

These resources present recent news regarding UAS designs, technology advancements, regulations, applications, and business developments, which are useful in staying informed of the changing UAS landscape:

- Aviation International News (AIN), *Unmanned Aerial Vehicles News*:
  www.ainonline.com/aviation-news/unmanned-aerial-vehicles
- Discovery Communications, Seeker, *Unmanned Autonomous Vehicles*:
  www.seeker.com/tag/unmanned-autonomous-vehicles
- DIY Drones, *News*:
  diydrones.com/profiles/blog/list
- FAA, *News*:
  www.faa.gov/news
- FlightGlobal, *UAV*:
  www.flightglobal.com/news/aircraft/uavs
- Inside Unmanned Systems:
  www.insideunmannedsystems.com
- Military & Aerospace Electronics, *Unmanned Vehicles*:
  www.militaryaerospace.com/unmanned-vehicles.html
- Popular Science, *Rise of the Drones*:
  www.popsci.com/drones
- sUAS News:
  www.suasnews.com
- Unmanned Aerial Online:
  www.unmanned-aerial.com
- *UAS Magazine*:
  www.uasmagazine.com
- Unmanned Systems Technology (UST):
  www.unmannedsystemstechnology.com

USER COMMUNITIES AND NETWORKS

The following resources represent various user groups and forums relating to UAS:

- ArduPilot:
  ardupilot.com
- DIY Drones, *Discussion Forum*:
  diydrones.com/forum
- DJI, *Forum*:
  forum.dji.com

- Drone User Group Network, *Group Forums*:
  www.dugn.org/groups.html
- RCgroups.com, *UAV—Unmanned Aerial Vehicles Forums*:
  www.rcgroups.com/uav-unmanned-aerial-vehicles-238/
- WattFlyer RC Network, *Group Forums*:
  www.wattflyer.com/forums

NOTE: *Please keep in mind that materials found in online user/group forums are not always supported with citation or applicable evidence of assertions, nor are they peer-reviewed and revised based on new knowledge discovery. It is highly suggested that you not accept information presented in such sources as fact, without sufficient corroboration. Instead, consider using these sources as a starting point for your own independent investigation and research. Any legal/regulatory or technical guidance should be confirmed from an original (seminal/ foundational) source, government representative, legal counsel, or subject matter expert, prior to incorporation into your own operational strategies or plans. However, despite these cautions, insightful information, tutorials, and narratives can be found within these forums from others' experiences relating to construction, assembly, exhibition, and other UAS or RC model aircraft-related activities.*

JOURNALS/SCIENTIFIC PUBLISHING

These resources represent sources for scholarly, academic research papers and presentations relating to UAS and can be useful to obtaining in-depth descriptions of how UAS are being used (use cases), underlying details of technological development, and the impact of business and regulatory changes that affect the community:

- *Embry-Riddle Aeronautical University (ERAU) Scholarly Commons*:
  commons.erau.edu
- *International Journal of Advanced Robotic Systems*:
  www.intechopen.com/journals/articles/
  international_journal_of_advanced_robotic_systems/51/all/1
- *International Journal of Aviation, Aeronautics, and Aerospace*:
  commons.erau.edu/ijaaa/
- *International Journal of Intelligent Unmanned Systems*:
  www.emeraldgrouppublishing.com/products/journals/journals.htm?id=IJIUS
- *IEEE Unmanned Aerial Vehicles*:
  technav.ieee.org/tag/1935/unmanned-aerial-vehicles
- *Journal of Automation, Mobile Robotics & Intelligent Systems*:
  www.jamris.org
- *Journal of Intelligent & Robotic Systems*:
  www.springer.com/engineering/robotics/journal/10846

- *Journal of Unmanned Aerial Systems:*
  www.uasjournal.org
- *Journal of Unmanned System Technology:*
  ojs.unsysdigital.com/index.php/just
- *Journal of Unmanned Vehicle Systems:*
  www.cdnsciencepub.com/_email/_email08251401.aspx
- *ResearchGate:*
  www.researchgate.net
- *Robotics and Autonomous Systems:*
  www.journals.elsevier.com/robotics-and-autonomous-systems
- *The American Institute of Aeronautics and Astronautics:*
  www.aiaa.org
- *Unmanned Systems:*
  www.worldscientific.com/worldscinet/us

CONFERENCES, SYMPOSIUMS, AND EVENTS

These resources represent academic, scholarly, scientific, technical, or industry events where the advancement and application of UAS are highlighted. They provide excellent opportunities to meet and attend briefings from experts, policy makers, manufacturers, and industry representatives, as well as observe demonstrations of the latest generation of UAS technology:

- *Aviation/Aeronautics/Aerospace International Research Conference (A3IRCon):*
  commons.erau.edu/aircon/
- Association for Unmanned Vehicle Systems (AUVSI), *Chapters*
  (look for a chapter in your location):
  www.auvsi.org/membershipandchapters/chapters
- AUVSI, *Events* (check for events in your area):
  www.auvsi.org/events1aa/events
- AUVSI, *XPONENTIAL:*
  www.xponential.org
- *International Conference on Unmanned Aircraft Systems (ICUAS):*
  www.uasconferences.com
- *Small Unmanned Systems Business Exposition:*
  susbexpo.com
- *The International Drone Conference and Exposition (InterDrone):*
  www.interdrone.com
- *The UAS Midwest Conference:*
  www.ohiouasconference.com
- *UAS Commercialization Industry Conference:*
  www.uascommercialization.com

- *UAS Technical Analysis and Application Conference (TAAC)*:
  taac.psl.nmsu.edu
- *UAS West Symposium*:
  www.uaswest.com

INSURANCE PROVIDERS

These resources represent insurance carriers that specialize or offer services specifically related to the operation of UAS:

- AIG, *Unmanned Aircraft Solutions*:
  www.aig.com/business/insurance/specialty/unmanned-aircraft-solutions
- AMA, *Membership Enrollment Center* (only applicable to recreational hobbyists):
  www.modelaircraft.org/joinrenew.aspx
- Aviation Insurance Resources, *UAS/UAV Insurance*:
  www.air-pros.com/uas.php
- Coverdrone:
  www.coverdrone.com
- LeClairRyan, *Unmanned Aircraft Systems*:
  www.leclairryan.com/unmanned-aircraft-systems-groups
- Sutton James Incorporated, *Insurance for Unmanned Aircraft Systems*:
  www.suttonjames.com/unmanned-aerial-systems.aspx?id=536
- Transport Risk, *UAS UAV Drone Insurance*:
  www.transportrisk.com/uavrcfilm.html
- Unmanned Risk Management:
  unmannedrisk.com

LEGAL SUPPORT AND REPRESENTATION

These resources represent firms or individuals that provide specialized legal services specifically related to UAS:

- Antonelli Law, *Drone/UAS Practice Group*:
  www.antonelli-law.com/Drone_UAS_Practice_Group.php
- Dentons:
  www.dentons.com
- Eckert Seamans, *Unmanned Aircraft Systems*:
  www.eckertseamans.com/our-practices/unmanned-aircraft-systems
- HCH Legal:
  www.hchlegal.com
- Hogan Lovells:
  www.hoganlovells.com

- Jackson Walker:
  www.jw.com
- Kramer Levin:
  www.kramerlevin.com
- Lewis Roca Rothgerber, *Unmanned Aircraft Systems*:
  www.lrrc.com/unmanned-aircraft-systems-1
- Pillsbury Winthrop Shaw Pittman, *Unmanned Aircraft Systems*:
  www.pillsburylaw.com/unmanned-aircraft-systems
- Ravich Law Firm:
  www.ravichlawfirm.com
- Rupprecht Law:
  www.jrupprechtlaw.com/about-jonathan

OTHER WEB-BASED RESOURCES

These online resources provide additional information that may assist in your further exploration of UAS technology, application, regulatory policies, and guidance:

- FAA, *B4UFly* (mobile application):
  www.faa.gov/uas/b4ufly
- FAA, *Become a Pilot: Medical Certificate Requirements*:
  www.faa.gov/pilots/become/medical
- FAA, *Pack Safe: Lithium ion and lithium metal batteries, spare (uninstalled)*:
  www.faa.gov/about/initiatives/hazmat_safety/more_info/?hazmat=7
- FAA, *Fly for Fun*:
  www.faa.gov/uas/getting_started/fly_for_fun
- NASA, *Unmanned Aircraft System (UAS) Traffic Management (UTM)*:
  utm.arc.nasa.gov
- National Oceanic and Atmospheric Association (NOAA),
  Unmanned Aircraft Systems (UAS) Programs:
  uas.noaa.gov
- RAND Corporation, *Unmanned Aerial Vehicles*:
  www.rand.org/topics/unmanned-aerial-vehicles.html
- FlightService, *1800 Weather Brief (wx)* (UAS tab):
  www.1800wxbrief.com

UAS REPORTS AND DOCUMENTS

These published materials (cited in accordance with APA and presented in order of publication) provide additional details regarding the benefits, advantages, potential applications, and anticipated business opportunities associated with the use of UAS:

Contract Services Administration Trust Fund, Industry Wide Labor-Management Safety Committee. (2015). *Safety Bulletin #36: Recommended Guidelines for Safely Working Around Unmanned Aircraft Systems (UAS)*. Retrieved from www.csatf.org/pdf/36UAS.pdf

The White House, Office of the Press Secretary. (2015). *Presidential Memorandum: Promoting Economic Competitiveness While Safeguarding Privacy, Civil Rights, and Civil Liberties in Domestic Use of Unmanned Aircraft Systems*. Retrieved from www.whitehouse.gov/the-press-office/2015/02/15 /presidential-memorandum-promoting-economic-competitiveness-while-safegua

U.S. Department of Justice, Office of the Inspector General. (2015). *Audit of the Department of Justice's Use and Support of Unmanned Aircraft Systems*. Retrieved from oig.justice.gov/reports/2015/a1511.pdf

U.S. Department of Transportation, Federal Aviation Administration. (2015). *Overview of Small UAS Notice of Proposed Rulemaking*. Retrieved from www.faa.gov/regulations_ policies/rulemaking/media/021515_sUAS_Summary.pdf

U.S. Department of Transportation, Federal Aviation Administration. (2015). *Operation and Certification of Small Unmanned Aircraft Systems* (Docket No.: FAA-2015-0150; Notice No. 15-01). Retrieved from www.faa.gov/regulations_policies/rulemaking /recently_published/media/2120-AJ60_NPRM_2-15-2015_joint_signature.pdf

U.S. Department of the Interior. (2015). *Department of the Interior Unmanned Aircraft Systems (UAS) Integration Strategy (2015–2020)*. Retrieved from www.doi.gov /sites/doi.gov/files/uploads/DOI_UAS_Integration_Strategy_2015-2020.pdf

U.S. Government Accountability Office. (2015). *Report to Congressional Committees, Unmanned Aerial Systems: Actions Needed to Improve DOD Pilot Training* (Report No. GAO-15-461). Retrieved from www.gao.gov/assets/680/670225.pdf

Academy of Model Aeronautics. (2014). *Academy of Model Aeronautics National Model Aircraft Safety Code*. Retrieved from www.modelaircraft.org/files/105.PDF

National Aeronautics and Space Administration. (2014). *NASA Armstrong Fact Sheet: Unmanned Aircraft Systems Integration in the National Airspace System*. Retrieved from www.nasa.gov/centers/armstrong/news/FactSheets/FS-075-DFRC.html

U.S. Department of Transportation, Federal Aviation Administration. (2013). *Integration of Civil Unmanned Aircraft Systems (UAS) in the National Airspace System (NAS) Roadmap*. Retrieved from www.faa.gov/uas/media/UAS_Roadmap_2013.pdf

U.S. Department of Transportation, John A. Volpe National Transportation Systems Center. (2013). *Unmanned Aircraft System (UAS) Service Demand 2015–2035: Literature Review & Projections of Future Usage* (Report No. DOT-VNTSC-DoD-13-01). Retrieved from ntl.bts.gov/lib/48000/48200/48226/UAS_Service_Demand.pdf

Gertler, J. (2012). *Report for Congress: U.S. Unmanned Aerial Systems* (Report No. R42136). Retrieved from www.fas.org/sgp/crs/natsec/R42136.pdf

International Association of Chiefs of Police, Aviation Committee. (2012). *Recommended Guidelines for the Use of Unmanned Aircraft.* Retrieved from www.theiacp.org /portals/0/pdfs/IACP_UAGuidelines.pdf

Blom, J.D. (2010). *Unmanned Aerial Systems: A Historical Perspective* (Occasional Paper No. 37). Retrieved from usacac.army.mil/cac2/cgsc/carl/download/csipubs/OP37.pdf

U.S. Department of Transportation, Federal Aviation Administration. (2016). *Pilot's Handbook of Aeronautical Knowledge* (FAA-H-8083-25B). Retrieved from www.faa.gov /regulations_policies/handbooks_manuals/aviation/media/pilot_handbook.pdf

Aerospace Industries Association. (n.d.). *Unmanned Aircraft Systems: Perceptions & Potential.* Retrieved from www.aia-aerospace.org/assets/AIA_UAS_Report_small.pdf

AUTHOR-PRODUCED UAS MATERIALS

These articles and documents (cited in APA format and presented in order of publication) were developed by the authors (Terwilliger, Vincenzi, Robbins, and Ison) to describe their various UAS-related research and may provide further insight and details to support your personal exploration (including materials cited):

Terwilliger, B., Thirtyacre, D., Ison, D., Kleinke, S., Burgess, S., Cerreta, J.S., & Walach, C. (2016). Consumer Multirotor sUAS Evaluation and Training. *International Journal of Unmanned Systems Engineering*, 4(2), 1-18. doi: 10.14323/ijuseng.2016.5

Thirtyacre, D., Goldfein, M., Hunter, D., Brents, R., Ison, D., & Terwilliger, B. (2016). Standardization of Human-Computer-Interface for Geo-Fencing in Small Unmanned Aircraft Systems. In Goonetilleke, R. & Karwowski, W. (Eds.), *Advances in Physical Ergonomics and Human Factors. Proceedings of the AHFE 2016 International Conference on Physical Ergonomics and Human Factors, 489* (pp. 761-771). New York, NY: Springer International Publishing. doi: 10.1007/978-3-319-41694-6_73

Balog, C., Terwilliger, B., Vincenzi, D., & Ison, D. (2016). Examining Human Factors Challenges of Sustainable Small Unmanned Aircraft (sUAS) System Operations. In Savage-Knepshield, P. & Chen, J. (Eds.), *Advances in Human Factors in Robots and Unmanned Systems. Proceedings of the AHFE 2016 International Conference on Human Factors in Robots and Unmanned Systems, 499* (pp. 61-74). New York, NY: Springer International Publishing. doi: 10.1007/978-3-319-41959-6

Robbins, J., Terwilliger, B., Ison, D., & Vincenzi, D. (2016). Wide-Scale Small Unmanned Aircraft System Access to the National Airspace System. In *Proceedings of the Association for Unmanned Vehicle Systems International 43rd Annual Symposium*. Arlington, VA: Association of Unmanned Vehicle Systems International.

Terwilliger, B., Vincenzi, D., Ison, D., Liu, D., & Kleinke, S. (2016). Selection of Optimal UAS Using Task Requirements and Platform Parameters to Optimize Operational Performance. In *Proceedings of the 2016 Industrial and Systems Engineering Research Conference*. Norcross, GA: Institute of Industrial Engineers.

Sanders, B., Terwilliger, B., Witcher, K., Leary, M., Ohlman, J., & Tucker, C. (2015). Design of an Educational Tool for Unmanned Aerial Vehicle Design and Analysis (Paper No. 15086). In Volume 2015: *Proceedings of the 2015 Interservice/Industry Training, Simulation, and Education Conference (I/ITSEC)*. Arlington, VA: National Training and Simulation Association.

Terwilliger, B., Vincenzi, D., Ison, D., & Smith, T. (2015). Assessment of Unmanned Aircraft Platform Performance Using Modeling and Simulation (Paper No. 15006). In Volume 2015: *Proceedings of the 2015 Interservice/Industry Training, Simulation, and Education Conference (I/ITSEC)*. Arlington, VA: National Training and Simulation Association.

Vincenzi, D., Terwilliger, B., & Ison, D. (2015). Unmanned aerial system (UAS) human-machine interfaces: New paradigms in command and control. In *Proceedings of the 6th International Conference on Applied Human Factors and Ergonomics (AHFE 2015) and the Affiliated Conferences*. doi:10.1016/j.promfg.2015.07.139

Terwilliger, B., Vincenzi, D., Ison, D., Herron, R., & Smith, T. (2015). UAS Capabilities and Performance Modeling for Application Analysis. In *Proceedings of the Association for Unmanned Vehicle Systems International 42nd Annual Symposium*. Arlington, VA: Association of Unmanned Vehicle Systems International.

Stansbury, R., Robbins, J., Towhidnejad, M., Terwilliger, B., Moallemi, M., & Clifford, J. (2015). Modeling and Simulation for UAS Integration into the United States National Airspace System and NextGen. In Hodicky, J. (Ed.), *Modelling and Simulation for Autonomous Systems, Information Systems and Applications, incl. Internet/Web, and HCI, 9055* (pp. 40–59). New York, NY: Springer International Publishing. doi: 10.1007/978-3-319-22383-4

Terwilliger, B. (2015). *ERAU-Worldwide Unmanned System Related Career Opportunities: 2015*. Retrieved from http://assets.erau.edu/cm1/Assets/worldwide/forms/ERAU%20 Unmanned%20System%20Graduates%20Potential%20Job%20Opportunities%202015b. pdf

Terwilliger, B., Vincenzi, D., & Ison, D. (2015). Unmanned Aerial Systems: Collaborative Innovation to Support Emergency Response. *Journal of Unmanned Vehicle Systems*. doi: 10.1139/juvs-2015-0004

Terwilliger, B. Vincenzi, D., Ison, D., Witcher, K., Thirtyacre, D., & Khalid, A. (2015). Influencing Factors for Use of Unmanned Aerial Systems in Support of Aviation Accident and Emergency Response. *Journal of Automation and Control Engineering, 3*(3), 246–252. doi: 10.12720/joace.3.3.246-252

Ison, D.C., Terwilliger, B., & Vincenzi, D. (2014). Privacy, Restriction, and Regulation Involving Federal, State and Local Legislation: More Hurdles for Unmanned Aerial Systems (UAS) integration? *The Journal of Aviation/Aerospace Education & Research, 24*(1), 41–80. Retrieved from http://commons.erau.edu/jaaer/vol24/iss1/3

Terwilliger, B., Ison, D., Vincenzi, D., & Liu, D. (2014). Advancement and Application of Unmanned Aerial System Human-Machine-Interface (HMI) Technology. In Yamamoto, S. (Ed.), *Human Interface and the Management of Information. Information and Knowledge in Applications and Services, Lecture Notes in Computer Science, 8522* (pp. 273–283). New York, NY: Springer International Publishing. doi: 10.1007/978-3-319-07863-2_27

Vincenzi, D., Ison, D., & Terwilliger, B. (2014). The Role of Unmanned Aircraft Systems (UAS) in Disaster Response and Recovery Efforts: Historical, Current, and Future. In *Proceedings of the Association for Unmanned Vehicle Systems International 41st Annual Symposium.* Arlington, VA: Association of Unmanned Vehicle Systems International.

Terwilliger, B.A., & Ison, D. (2014). Implementing Low Cost Two-Person Supervisory Control for Small Unmanned Aerial Systems. *Journal of Unmanned Vehicle Systems, 902*(2), 1–16. doi: 10.1139/juvs-2013-0020

Khalid, A., Terwilliger, B., Coppola, A., Marion, J., Ison, D., Shepherd, A., & Sanders, B. (2014). Real World Design Challenge (RWDC)—An Overview. *Advanced Materials Research, 902*, 437–447. doi: 10.4028/www.scientific.net/AMR.902.437

Ison, D., Terwilliger, B., & Vincenzi, D. (2013). Designing Simulation to Meet UAS Training Needs. In Yamamoto, S. (Ed.), *Human Interface and the Management of Information. Information and Interaction for Health, Safety, Mobility and Complex Environments* (Part IV, pp. 585–595). doi: 10.1007/978-3-642-39215-3_67

Terwilliger, B. (2012). Effects of Visual Interaction Methods on Simulated Unmanned Aircraft Operator Situational Awareness (Paper No. 12435). In Volume 2012: *Proceedings of the 2015 Interservice/Industry Training, Simulation, and Education Conference (I/ITSEC).* Arlington, VA: National Training and Simulation Association.

Terwilliger, B. (2012). *Examining Effects of Visual Interaction Methods on Unmanned Aircraft Operator Situational Awareness* (Doctoral Dissertation). Retrieved from ProQuest Dissertations and Theses database. (UMI No. 3516061; ISBN: 9781267488626).

FIGURE CREDITS

Following is the credit information for figures used in this book. Figures not listed here are © Aviation Supplies & Academics, Inc.

For images from Wikimedia Commons (commons.wikimedia.org) used as figures in this textbook, the attribution for each is provided. All of these images are either in the public domain, or under one or more type of "Wikimedia Creative Commons" license ("Attribution 2.0, or "CC BY 2.0," among others), which allow for commercial usage for the material licensed in this manner. Wikimedia Commons images are indicated below with "WC" plus the relevant Creative Commons license code. For more information about Creative Commons licenses, see www.creativecommons.org/licenses.

Figure 1-1: Sir George Cayley's Governable Parachutes; Mechanics Magazine (1852, no. 1520); scanned and uploaded by Michael32710 (commons.wikimedia.org/wiki/File:Governableparachute.jpg); Public domain, WC / CC-PD-Mark; PD-1923.

Figure 1-2: Stringfellow's Flying Machine; Popular Science Monthly (1886, v. 25); scanned and uploaded by Ineuw (commons.wikimedia.org/wiki/File:PSM_V28_D025_Stringfellow_flying_machine.jpg); Public domain, WC / CC-PD-Mark; PD-1923.

Figure 1-3: Alphonse Penaud's 1870 Model Helicopter; Tissandier, G., La Navigation Aerrienne, 1886 (commons.wikimedia.org/wiki/File:Helicopter_of_Penaud.jpg); Public domain, WC / CC-PD-Mark; PD-1923.

Figure 1-4: Otto Lilienthal gliding experiment, 1895; U.S. Library of Congress, Digital ID: ppmsca 02546 (www.loc.gov/item/2002722087); Public domain.

Figure 1-5: Guglielmo Marconi 1901 wireless signal; LIFE|id= 4a204d82f07524bd, 1901 (commons.wikimedia.org/wiki/File:Guglielmo_Marconi_1901_wireless_signal.jpg); Public domain / PD-1923.

Figure 1-6: Photo of replica Chanute Biplane Glider—Warner Robins, taken by Alan Wilson (uploaded 18 April 2013) (www.flickr.com/photos/65001151@N03/11340513273); CC-BY-SA-2.0.

Figure 1-7: Langley Aerodrome and launching platform; Popular Science Monthly (1904, vol. 64) (commons.wikimedia.org/wiki/File:PSM_V64_D099_The_aerodrome_ready_for_launching.png); Public domain, WC / PD-1923.

Figure 1-8: Wright Brothers first flight; U.S. Library of Congress Prints and Photographs Division, Digital ID: cph 3a53266 (commons.wikimedia.org/wiki/File:Wrightflyer.jpg); Public domain, WC / PD-US.

Figure 1-9: *Left:* Woodblock print of kite flying by Japanese artist Suzuki Harunobu (1766); Metropolitan Museum of Art, online collection, entry 54541 (commons.wikimedia.org/wiki/File:Kite_Flying_by_Suzuki_Harunobu_%28%E9%88%B4%E6%9C%A8_%E6%98%A5%E4%BF%A1%29.jpg); Public domain, WC / PD-1923. *Center:* Watercolour painting by an unknown Burmese artist depicting 19th century Burmese life (1897); The Bodleian Library, University of Oxford (commons.wikimedia.org/wiki/File:Bodleian_Ms._Burm._a._5_fol_155.jpg); WC / CC-BY-4.0. *Right top:* First known depiction of a parachute (1470s); Lynn White, Technology and Culture (vol. 9, 1968) (commons.wikimedia.org/wiki/File:Conical_Parachute,_1470s,_British_Museum_Add._MSS_34,113,_fol._200v.jpg); Public domain, WC / CC-PD-Mark; PD-1923. *Right bottom:* Takembo, by Haragayato (commons.wikimedia.org/wiki/File:Taketombo.JPG); WC / CC-BY-SA-2.5.

Figure 1-10: *Left to right:* *(1)* Radio control model Bell 222 in flight, taken by Barfisch (commons.wikimedia.org/wiki/File:RC_Helicopter_Bell222_with_Pilot.png); WC / CC BY-SA 3.0. *(2)* Shinden Pattern aircraft, by Mjfrederick (en.wikipedia.org/wiki/File:Shinden_001.jpg); WC / CC BY-SA 2.5. *(3)* Large radio control model J-3 Cub, by Airplanespotter15 (en.wikipedia.org/wiki/File:Large_scale_J-3_Cub_Remote_Control_aircraft.jpg); WC / CC BY-SA 3.0. *(4)* Electric model airplane, by Tony Speer (commons.wikimedia.org/wiki/File:Parkzone-slov.jpg); WC / CC BY-SA 3.0.

Figure 1-11: Hewitt-Sperry Automatic Airplane in 1918 (commons.wikimedia.org/wiki/File:Hewitt-Sperry_Automatic_Airplane_1918.jpg); Public domain, WC / PD-1923.

Figure 1-12: Kettering Aerial Torpedo "Bug"; Courtesy of the U.S. Air Force (www.nationalmuseum.af.mil/Upcoming/Photos.aspx?igphoto=2000129297).

Figure 1-13: The RAE Larynx, 1927, Wsacul on English Wikipedia (commons.wikimedia.org/wiki/File:Larynx.png); Public domain, WC / PD-USGov.

Figure 1-14: The de Havilland DH-82B Queen Bee, taken by Adrian Pingstone (commons.wikimedia.org/wiki/File:De_havilland_dh-82b_queen_bee_lf858_arp.jpg); Public domain, WC / PD-user.

Figure 1-15: OQ-2A on display at the National Museum of the Air Force; U.S. Air Force photo (commons.wikimedia.org/wiki/File:Radioplane_OQ-2A_USAF.jpg); Public domain; WC / PD-USGov.

Figure 1-16: Interstate TDR-1 "assault drone" at National Naval Aviation Museum; Greg Goebel (commons.wikimedia.org/wiki/File:Interstate_TDR-1_on_display_at_Naval_Aviation_Museum.jpg); Public domain, WC / PD-user.

Figure 1-17: JB-2 Loon (German V-1) on display at the National Museum of the Air Force; Courtesy of the U.S. Air Force.

Figure 1-18: BQ-7 "Careful Virgin" in flight; Courtesy of the U.S. Air Force.

Figure 1-19: RP-71 Falconer; Courtesy of the U.S. Air Force.

Figure 1-20: Ryan BQM-34F Firebee II on display at the National Museum of the Air Force; Courtesy of the U.S. Air Force.

Figure 1-21: QH-50 DASH in flight; U.S. Navy Naval Aviation News (Jan/Feb 1988) (commons.wikimedia.org/wiki/File:QH-50_DASH_over_USS_Hazelwood.jpg); Public domain, WC / PD-USGov.

Figure 1-22: D-21 mounted atop SR-71 and in flight; Courtesy of the U.S. Air Force.

Figure 1-23: XQM-93A Compass Dwell in flight, USAF photograph (commons.wikimedia.org/wiki/File:XQM-93A.jpg); Public domain, WC / PD-USGov.

Figure 1-24: Lockhead MQM-105 Aquila; U.S. Army (commons.wikimedia.org/wiki/File:Aquila_02.jpg); Public domain, WC / PD-USGov.

Figure 1-25: Photo of RQ-2 Pioneer in flight, taken by Photographers Mate 2nd Class Daniel J. McLain; Courtesy of the U.S. Navy.

Figure 1-26: Photo of the General Atomics Altus I in flight, taken by Carla Thomas; Courtesy of NASA.

Figure 1-27: Photo of MQ-1 Predator in operation, taken by Staff Sgt. Brian Ferguson; Courtesy of the U.S. Air Force.

Figure 1-28: Photo of RQ-4 Global Hawk, taken by Senior Airman Nichelle Anderson; Courtesy of the U.S. Air Force.

Figure 1-29: RQ-5 Hunter on display at Hatzerim Israeli Air Force Museum; by Yossifoon (commons.wikimedia.org/wiki/File:Hunter_RQ-5_UAV.jpg); WC / CC BY-SA 4.0.

Figure 1-30: Photo of RQ-7A Shadow 200 on the ground; Courtesy of the U.S. Army.

Figure 1-31: Photo of ScanEagle launch, taken by John F. Williams; Courtesy of the U.S. Navy.

Figure 1-32: Photo of hand launch of RQ-11B Raven, taken by Sgt. 1st Class Michael Guillory (22 November 2006); Courtesy of the U.S. Army.

Figure 1-33: Photo of the hand-launch of RQ-20 Puma, taken by Sgt. Bobby Yarbrough; Courtesy of the U.S. Marine Corp.

Figure 1-34: Photo of MQ-8 Fire Scout in hover, taken by Kelly Schindler; Courtesy of the U.S. Navy.

Figure 1-35: Artist rendition of RQ-170 Sentinel, created by Mark Schierbecker, updated by Truthdowser at English Wikipedia (commons.wikimedia.org/wiki/File:RQ-170_Sentinel_impression_3-view.png); WC / CC BY-SA 3.0.

Figure 1-36: Photo of NASA Helios in flight, taken by Nick Galante/PMRF (Photo No. ED01-0209-3); Courtesy of NASA.

Figure 1-37: TAM 5, Mannin Beach, Ireland, by Ronan Coyle (commons.wikimedia.org/wiki/File:Tam5.jpg); WC / CC BY-SA 3.0.

Figure 1-38: Provided by and used with the permission of Embry-Riddle Aeronautical University, all rights are reserved.

Figure 1-39: *Left:* MakerBot Replicator 2 3D printer; Peabodybore (en.m.wikipedia.org/wiki/File:MakerBot_Replicator_2.jpg); Public domain, WC / CC0 1.0. *Right:* 3D printed propeller; Creative Tools (www.flickr.com/photos/creative_tools/9135607252); CC BY 2.0.

Figure 1-40: *Left:* ZALA 421 in flight; QwasERqwasER at English Wikipedia (commons.wikimedia.org/wiki/File:ZALA_421-12.jpg); WC / CC BY-SA 3.0. *Center:* pixabay.com/13082; Public domain / CC0 1.0. Right: pixabay.com/lucrus91; Public domain / CC0 1.0.

Figure 2-1: *Left:* Satellite imagery of crops in Kansas, by NASA (commons.wikimedia.org/wiki/File:Crops_Kansas_AST_20010624.jpg); Public domain, WC / PD-USGov. *Right top:* Crops, Riverford, UK (SX7765), taken by Derek Harper (www.geograph.org.uk/photo/1074475); CC BY-SA 2.0. *Right bottom:* Aerial photo of GREZAC, by Cliché J. Dassié (commons.wikimedia.org/wiki/File:Grezac.jpg); WC / CC BY-SA 3.0.

Figure 2-2: Camclone T21 UAS fitted with CSIRO guidance system, uploaded by CSIRO (www.scienceimage.csiro.au/image/10876); CC BY 3.0.

Figure 2-3: *Left:* Carl Goldberg Products Yak-54 radio control model airplane; PMDrive1061 (en.wikipedia.org/wiki/File:Yak_beauty1.jpg); WC / CC BY-SA 3.0. *Right top:* TREX 600 radio control helicopter in flight; Paul Chapman (en.wikipedia.org/wiki/File:TREX_600_NSP.jpg); WC / CC BY-SA 3.0. *Right bottom:* SQuiRT in flight; Wings Across America (commons.wikimedia.org/wiki/File:SQuiRT_in_flight.jpg); WC / CC BY 3.0.

Figure 2-4: from U.S. Geological Survey, National Unmanned Aircraft Systems (UAS) Project Office, UAS Derived Data Products (rmgsc.cr.usgs.gov/UAS/images/imageProcessing/products/Color%20NDVI_400.jpg).

Figure 2-5: Full Spectrum Geo-Referenced Orthomosaic (RGB+NIR) processed by DroneMapper obtained with Pteryx UAV; Stoermerjp (commons.wikimedia.org/wiki/File:Full_Spectrum_Geo-Referenced_Orthomosaic_%28RGB%2BNIR%29.JPG); WC / CC BY-SA 3.0.

Figure 2-9: Digital Surface Model of motorway construction site obtained from aerial photoset using Pteryx UAV; Kbosak (commons.wikimedia.org/wiki/File:DSM_construction_site.jpg); WC / CC BY 3.0.

Figure 2-13: Red Rocks UAV Photogrammetry Mission. Geo-referenced point cloud generated by DroneMapper; Stoermerjp (commons.wikimedia.org/wiki/File:Geo-Referenced_Point_Cloud.JPG); WC / CC BY-SA 3.0.

Figure 3-24: FlyTech Dragonfly ornithopter; Fred Hsu (commons.wikimedia.org/wiki/File:FlyTech_Dragonfly_1.jpg); WC / CC BY-SA 3.0.

Figure 3-25: *Left:* pixabay.com/Flyingbikie; Public domain / CC0 1.0. *Right:* Falken SUAV; Stefan Sundkvist (www.flickr.com/photos/stefansundkvist/4697864162); CC BY 2.0.

Figure 3-26: *Left:* Orbiter UAS on launcher; Alexmilt at Serbian Wikipedia (commons.wikimedia.org/wiki/File:Bespilotna_letelica_Orbiter_VS.JPG); Public domain, WC / PD-user. *Right:* ShadowHawk Mk-II in flight; Unmannedldr (commons.wikimedia.org/wiki/File:ShadowHawk_in_flight.JPG); WC / CC BY-SA 3.0.

Figure 3-27: *Left:* RQ-7B Shadow 200 in flight; U.S. Marine Corp (commons.wikimedia.org/wiki/File:USMC-01522.jpg); Public domain / PD-USGov. *Right:* Yamaha R-Max unmanned helicopter; Gtuav (commons.wikimedia.org/wiki/File:YamahaRMax.jpg); WC / CC BY-SA 3.0.

Figure 3-28: *Left:* Pixabay.com/PIX1861; Public domain CC0 1.0. *Right top:* Stardust II UAS landing; Jf.sainz (commons.wikimedia.org/wiki/File:MOV034_20100815213239%28s%29.jpg); Public domain, WC / PD-self. *Right bottom:* Aerovision Fulmar UAV in flight; Txema1 (commons.wikimedia.org/wiki/File:Fulmar_Flight.JPG); Public domain, WC / PD-self.

Figure 3-31: *Left:* Pixabay.com/fill; Public domain / CC0 1.0. *Right top:* German Army EMT Aladin; KrisfromGermany (commons.wikimedia.org/wiki/File:AladinDrohne.jpg); Public domain, WC / PD-self. *Right bottom:* Zala 421-08 on display; Vitaly V. Kuzmin (commons.wikimedia.org/wiki/File:ZALA_421-08_ISSE-2012.jpg); WC / CC BY-SA 4.0.

Figure 3-32: *Left:* Pixabay.com/Robzor; Public domain / CC0 1.0. *Right:* Align T-Rex 450SE; Mike Lehmann (commons.wikimedia.org/wiki/File:Align_T-REX_2386.jpg); WC / CC BY-SA 3.0.

Figure 3-33: *Top:* Pixabay.com/haraldbendschneider; Public domain / CC0 1.0.
Bottom: Skyship 600 dirigible ducted fans; Luftschiffseiten.de (commons.wikimedia.org/wiki/File:GR_SK_Propeller.jpg); WC / CC BY-SA 3.0.

Figure 3-34: Turbine engine mounted on radio control model airplane; The ball-commonswiki (commons.wikimedia.org/wiki/File:PST_Model_Airplane_Jet_Trainer.png); WC / CC BY-SA 3.0.

Figure 3-38: *Left:* Four stroke aircraft radial engine; MedniLedved (commons.wikimedia.org/wiki/File:Scarlett_mini_5.png); WC / CC BY-SA 3.0. *Right:* Taipan 2.5cc 1968 Glowplug model aeroplane engine; Warren Leadbeatter (commons.wikimedia.org/wiki/File:Taipan_2.5cc_1968_Glowplug_model_aeroplane_engine.jpg); WC / CC BY-SA 3.0.

Figure 3-40: AR Drone LiPo battery; Chaagii 0817 (commons.wikimedia.org/wiki/File:AR_Drone_Battery.jpg); WC / CC BY-SA 3.0.

Figure 3-42: Xbee transceiver; Mark Fickett (commons.wikimedia.org/wiki/File:XBee_Series_2_with_Whip_Antenna.jpg); WC / CC BY 3.0.

Figure 3-43: Futaba receiver; Daniel van den Ouden (www.flickr.com/photos/38831547@N04/4278638483); CC BY 2.0.

Figure 3-44: Arduino Uno microcontroller; SparkFun Electronics (www.flickr.com/photos/sparkfun/8406865680/); CC BY 2.0.

Figure 3-45: micro servo; oomlout (www.flickr.com/photos/snazzyguy/3632893840/); CC BY-SA 2.0.

Figure 3-46: 35A electronic speed control; Avsar Aras (commons.wikimedia.org/wiki/File:ESC_35A.jpg); WC / CC BY-SA 3.0.

Figure 3-47: Rotary-wing UAS carrying sensor payload; CSIRO (www.scienceimage.csiro.au/image/2346); CC BY 3.0.

Figure 3-48: Infrared imagery captured from helicopter; courtesy of the U.S. Navy.

Figure 3-49: Radar imagery captured and processed by NASA-JPL depicting Death Valley; Public domain (NASA image PIA01349); courtesy of NASA/JPL.

Figure 3-50: *Left:* Skylark UAS; taken by Photographer's Mate 2nd Class Daniel J. McLain; courtesy of the U.S. Navy; Public domain / PD-USGov. *Right:* Fox-C8 XT drone; ZullyC3P (commons.wikimedia.org/wiki/File:Onyxstar_Fox-C8_XT_xender_360.jpg); WC / CC BY-SA 4.0.

Figure 3:51: *Left:* DX6i Spektrum DX6i transmitter; SayCheese! and Ken Alan (commons. wikimedia.org/wiki/File:Spektrumdx6i.jpg); WC / CC BY-SA 3.0. *Right:* DJI Phantom 3 Professional Drohne; Marco Verch (commons.wikimedia.org/wiki/File:DJI_Phantom_3_Professional_Drohne_(23453843212).jpg); WC / CC BY 2.0.

Figure 3-54: *Left:* Photo of command and control of RQ-11B Raven; photo by Staff Sgt. Noel Gerig; courtesy of the U.S. Army. Center: Vrabac mini UAV control panel; Proka89 (commons. wikimedia.org/wiki/File:Vrabac_mini_UAV_control_panel.jpg); WC / CC BY-SA 4.0. *Right:* Kale Baykar GCS; Bayhaluk (commons.wikimedia.org/wiki/File:MobileGCSsun.jpg); WC / CC BY-SA 4.0.

Figure 3-55: Bayraktar Tactical UAS GCS; Bayhaluk (commons.wikimedia.org/wiki/File:Bayraktar_Tactical_UAS_GCS.JPG); WC / CC BY-SA 4.0.

Figure 3-56: *Left:* Pixabay.com/MemoryCatcher; Public domain / CC0 1.0. Center: RC wing and pilot in Kolomenskoe; Okorok (commons.wikimedia.org/wiki/File:RC_wing_and_pilot_in_Kolomenskoe.JPG); WC / CC BY-SA 3.0. *Right:* Pixabay.com/Robzor; Public domain / CC0 1.0.

Figure 3-57: Gatewing X100; Alainq (commons.wikimedia.org/wiki/File:GatewingX100.jpg); WC / CC BY-SA 3.0.

Figure 3-58: AC-DJI-I Action Case with DJI Phantom UAS; Frankly PM (www.flickr.com/photos/franklyrichmond/8637772670); CC BY-ND 2.0.

Figure 3-59: Screen captures of RealFlight 7.5; © 2016 Hobbico, Inc. Used with Permission.

Figure 3-60: Figure provided by and used with the permission of Embry-Riddle Aeronautical University, all rights are reserved.

Figure 3-61: Figure provided by and used with the permission of Embry-Riddle Aeronautical University, all rights are reserved.

Figure 4-1: FAA *Pilot's Handbook of Aeronautical Knowledge.*

Figure 4-3: From knowbeforeyoufly.org.

Figure 4-4: Federal Aviation Administration.

Figure 4-10: *Left:* Fog over mountain in South India; Brandvenkatr (en.wikipedia.org/wiki/File:Fog_over_mountain.jpg); CC BY-SA 3.0. *Center:* Haze over Singapore; Oliverlyc (commons.wikimedia.org/wiki/File:Effects_of_2013_Southeast_Asian_haze_on_Singapore.jpg); WC / CC0 1.0. *Right:* Pixabay.com/Bluesnap; Public domain / CC0 1.0.

Figure 4-12: *Left:* Banaue Rice Terraces in the Philippines; McCouch S (2004) Diversifying Selection in Plant Breeding. PLoS Biol 2(10): e347. doi:10.1371/journal.pbio.0020347; CC BY 2.5. *Center:* Murray grey cows and calves; Cgoodwin (commons.wikimedia.org/wiki/File:Murray_Grey_cows_and_calves.JPG); WC / CC BY-SA 4.0. *Right:* Farming near Klingerstown, PA (Image No. K5052-5); photo by Scott Bauer; courtesy of the USDA.

Figure 4-13: *Left:* Tilted sandstone in Roxborough State Park; Montano336 at the English language Wikipedia (commons.wikimedia.org/wiki/File:Roxborough.jpg); WC / CC BY-SA 3.0. *Center:* Kings Canyon; Crd637 (commons.wikimedia.org/wiki/File:KingsCanyonNP.JPG); WC / CC BY-SA 3.0. *Right:* The Breaks; Reggie Tiller/00squirrel (commons.wikimedia.org/wiki/File:Breaks.jpg); Public domain, WC / PD-user.

Figure 4-14: *Left:* Utah mountain tree; DR04 (commons.wikimedia.org/wiki/File:09272008_BrightonUT.JPG); WC / CC BY 3.0. *Center:* Simpson-Reed Grove of Coast redwoods; Acroterion (commons.wikimedia.org/wiki/File:US_199_Redwood_Highway.jpg); WC / CC BY-SA 3.0. *Right:* Old-growth forest, Opal Creek Wilderness; Nickpdx (commons.wikimedia.org/wiki/File:Opal_creek_old_growth_2.JPG); Public domain, WC / PD-user.

Figure 4-15: *Left:* Wye Marsh; Óðinn (commons.wikimedia.org/wiki/File:Wye_Marsh_panorama1.jpg); WC / CC BY-SA 3.0. *Center:* Sawgrass prairie, Everglades; Moni3 (commons.wikimedia.org/wiki/File:Everglades_Sawgrass_Prairie_Moni3.JPG); WC / CC BY 3.0. *Right:* Bald cypress swamp, southern Louisiana; Jan Kronsell (commons.wikimedia.org/wiki/File:Cypresses.jpg); WC / CC BY-SA 3.0.

Figure 4-16: *Left:* Virgin Peak, Nevada; Stan Shebs (commons.wikimedia.org/wiki/File:Virgin_Peak_approach_3.jpg); WC / CC BY-SA 3.0. *Right top:* Ash Meadows National Wildlife Refuge, Nevada; Stan Shebs (commons.wikimedia.org/wiki/File:Ash_Meadows_1.jpg); WC / CC BY-SA 3.0. *Right bottom:* Calico Basin, Red Rock National Conservation Area; Fred Morledge (commons.wikimedia.org/wiki/File:Calico_basin_red_rock_cumulus_mediocris.jpg); WC / CC BY-SA 2.5.

Figure 4-17: *Left:* Beach, Road's End State Park, Lincoln City, OR; Justin Lonas, Moviegoer84 at English Wikipedia (commons.wikimedia.org/wiki/File:Beach_at_Road%27s_End_State_Park_(Lincoln_City,_Oregon_-_June_2007).jpg); WC / CC BY-SA 3.0. *Center:* Waves in Lake Ontario; SYSS Mouse (commons.wikimedia.org/wiki/File:Wave_in_Lake_Ontario.jpg); WC / CC BY-SA 3.0. *Right:* Bahia Honda, Florida Keys; Mwanner (commons.wikimedia.org/wiki/File:BahiaHonda.jpg); WC / CC BY-SA 3.0.

Figure 4-18: *Left top:* Snow on Southern California mountains; Zink Dawg at English Wikipedia (commons.wikimedia.org/wiki/File:Snow_on_the_mountains_of_Southern_California.jpg); WC / CC BY 3.0. *Left bottom:* Veteran's Day storm 1996, Snow removal Cleveland (commons.wikimedia.org/wiki/File:Snow-removal-cleveland-4.jpg); WC / GNU FDL. *Right:* Air hoar frost; Jim Hammer (www.flickr.com/photos/7365168@N03/2249025124); CC BY-SA 2.0.

Figure 4-19: *Left:* Los Angeles skyline and mountains; Nserrano (commons.wikimedia.org/wiki/File:LA_Skyline_Mountains2.jpg); WC / CC BY-SA 3.0. *Center:* Aerial view of Orlando, FL; Michael Adams (commons.wikimedia.org/wiki/File:Orlando_downtown_2011.jpg); WC / CC BY-SA 3.0. *Right:* Suburban development, Colorado Springs, CO; David Shankbone (commons.wikimedia.org/wiki/File:Suburbia_by_David_Shankbone.jpg); WC / CC BY-SA 3.0.

Figure 4-20: *Left:* AirRobot AR-100B; Padeluun (commons.wikimedia.org/wiki/File:AirRobot_AR-100B.jpg); Public domain, WC / PD-self. *Right:* American Venue, International Aerial Robotics Competition; Firewall (en.wikipedia.org/wiki/File:Michigan_Aerial_Robot-2014.JPG); WC / CC BY-SA 3.0.

Figure 4-21: *Left:* Fire in Massueville, Quebec, Canada; Sylvain Pedneault (commons.wikimedia.org/wiki/File:FirePhotography.jpg); WC / CC BY-SA 3.0. *Center:* Maracaibo car crash; Giancarlo Rossi (commons.wikimedia.org/wiki/File:Maracaibo_car_crash_scene.jpg); WC / CC BY-SA 3.0. *Right:* Graniteville Train Wreck; Eddie George/Techcop50 (commons.wikimedia.org/wiki/File:SLED_Helicopter_View.JPG); WC / CC BY-SA 4.0.

Figure 4-24: Base photograph—Aerosonde UAV; Aerosonde Ltd (commons.wikimedia.org/wiki/File:Aerosonde.jpg); WC / CC BY-SA 3.0. Additions to original—overlaid labels added.

Figure 4-26: *Left:* RQ-11 Raven handlaunch; photo by Sgt. 1st Class Michael Guillory; courtesy of the U.S. Army. *Center:* ScanEagle launch in Yuma, AZ; photo by Cpl. Michael P. Snody; courtesy of U.S. Marine Corps (ID #060619-M-8788S-004). *Right:* Storekeeper 1st Class Michael Lake prepares to launch UAV; photo by Mass Communication Specialist 3rd Class Daisy Abonza; courtesy of U.S. Navy.

Figure 4-27: *Left:* UAV recovery; photo by Photographer's Mate 1st Class Ted Banks; courtesy of the U.S. Navy (ID# 020106-N-3236B-032). *Center:* ScanEagle recovery using Skyhook; photo by Mass Communication Specialist Seaman Patrick W. Mullen III; courtesy of U.S. Navy (ID# 060818-N-8547M-001). *Right:* Bayraktar Mini UAVS3; Bayhaluk (commons.wikimedia.org/wiki/File:Mini3.jpg); WC / CC BY-SA 3.0.

Figure 4-28: *Left:* Exocentric, line-of-sight operation of a tethered sUAS; photo by Rose Moskowitz. *Right:* FPV video feed with an OSD readout; Patrick McKay (commons.wikimedia.org/wiki/File:FPV_OSD.png); WC / CC BY-SA 3.0.

Figure 4-29: FPV pilot flying RC aircraft, with spotter; Patrick McKay (commons.wikimedia.org/wiki/File:FPV_Pilot.JPG); WC / CC BY-SA 3.0.

Figure 4-30: From www.faa.gov/uas/b4ufly

Figure 4-31: Airspace Map Images Courtesy of AirMap.com.

Figure 5-1: *Left:* Underwater unmanned vehicle maintenance; photo by Petty Officer 3rd Class Jumar Balacy; courtesy of the U.S. Navy (ID# 130429-N-GG400-043) *Right top:* NASA aerospace engineer in a wind tunnel with a Large-Scale Low-Boom supersonic inlet model; photo by Bridget R. Caswell; courtesy of NASA. *Right bottom:* Readying a UAV for test flight, Naval Air Station Key West; photo by Mass Communication Specialist 2nd Class Timothy Cox; courtesy of the U.S. Navy.

Figure 5-2: *Left:* Agricultural pilot applying a low-insecticide bait; photo by Ken Hammond; courtesy of the USDA (ID# K7803-2). *Right top:* LAPD Bell 206 Jetranger helicopter; Matthew Field (commons.wikimedia.org/wiki/File:LAPD_Bell_206_Jetranger.jpg); WC / CC BY-SA 3.0. *Right center:* Kern County Fire Department Bell 205 dropping water; Alan Radecki (commons. wikimedia.org/wiki/File:Kfd-205-N408KC-050428-26cr.jpg); WC / CC BY-SA 3.0. *Right bottom:* U.S. Customs and Border Protection Beechcraft King Air (Beechcraft King Air Series 200 and C-12C Fact Sheet, 2101-1015); courtesy of U.S. Customs and Border Protection.

Figure 5-3: *Left:* DJI Phantom 4 drone; Andri Koolme (www.flickr.com/photos/ andrikoolme/26306004826); CC BY 2.0. *Right top:* German Deutsche Post AG microdrones md4-1000; Frankhöffner (commons.wikimedia.org/wiki/File:Package_copter_microdrones_ dhl.jpg); WC / CC BY-SA 3.0. *Right bottom:* Aeryon Scout UAV in flight; Dkroetsch (commons.wikimedia.org/wiki/File:Aeryon_Scout_In_Flight.jpg); Public domain, WC / PD-self.

INDEX

attractive intermolecular interactions between the ester groups of neigh-
ring molecules.

A prominent feature of the preceding results is that the virtual bond
nning the benzene ring and connecting the carbonyl carbons should
have as a statistical freely rotating link[39] in polyesters based on terephthal-
acid. This model of the terephthaloyl residue yields chain dimensions in
stantial accord with the values deduced from experiments.[83]

The effect of reversing ester groups should be mentioned here (compare
nd **6**, below). Conformational energies have been calculated for phenylac-
te. An empirical force field (6-exp type) supplemented by terms for frame
tortion and electron delocalization was used for this purpose.[42] Bond
gles and bond lengths were adjusted to values that minimize the total
ergy at each value of the torsion angle. Conformational energy calculated
this molecule exhibits maximum at coplanarity of the ester group with
enyl, owing to steric repulsions involving orthohydrogens. The stable
nformations of phenyl acetate are those in which the plane of the ester
up is rotated $58 \pm 10°$ from the phenyl plane. Accordingly, four conforma-
ns representing combination of rotations ϕ_1 and $\phi_2 = 58 \pm 10°$ about the
enylene axis are accessible to the *p*-diacetoxy benzene[80]:

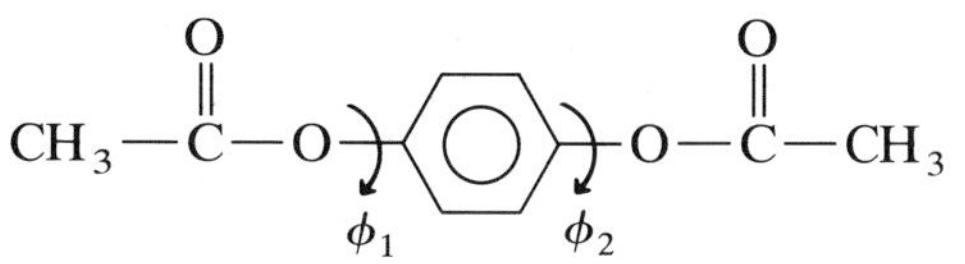

6

For biphenyl (**2**), values of the conformational energy, taken relative to
at for the coplanar form, are plotted versus Ψ_1 in Fig. 4. The PCILO
lculations give an absolute conformational energy minimum at $\Psi_1 = 40°$,
ich is in good agreement with the torsional angle of approximately 42–45°
tween the planes of the rings in the vapor state.[84] The height of the energy
rrier is 1.9 kcal mol^{-1}. It is worth noting that the dihedral angle Ψ_1 lies in
e range 20–25° in solution[85, 86] and in the melt,[87] while biphenyl is planar
nearly so in the crystalline state[88–92] at room temperature. This planar
nformation, however, has been claimed[91, 93] to be the result of a statistically
ntered arrangement with large oscillations around the inter-ring bond. The
planar conformation is hindered by steric interferences involving the ortho
drogen. However, in the crystalline state intermolecular interactions favor
e coplanar form by its more efficient packing and, in so doing, counteract
e intramolecular steric hindrance, especially since the barriers to planarity
e relatively low.[94]

Bastiansen and Samdal[95] and Häfelinger and Regelmann[96] summarized
e theoretical calculations of different degrees of sophistication carried out
biphenyl. Calculations by molecular mechanics[97–100] with separate consid-

segments can give rise to different conformations. Since from Fourier transform infra-red (FTIR) spectroscopy, electron spin resonance (ESR), and
NMR investigations the thermal behavior of these polymers appears to be a
sequence of changes from the solid state to the isotropic liquid phase,
gradually liberating one degree of freedom after another, this flexibility may
be important in this regard. The present section is not intended to be an
updated comprehensive collection of conformational characteristics of the
mesogenic moieties and disruptors currently used to synthesize LCP's. Some
examples have been chosen to show how conformational analysis can be used
to predict the way in which changes in molecular structure affect the
properties of LC's induced by heating LCP's.

3.2. Mesogenic Core

A number of theoretical calculations have been devoted to LCP's, but most
of them have been applied to the chemical units listed in Table 1. Their main
first objective was to evaluate conformational energy maps, indicating the
molecular energy as a function of the internal rotation angles.

PCILO calculations were carried out to obtain conformational energy
profiles of molecules **1**–**5**[78]:

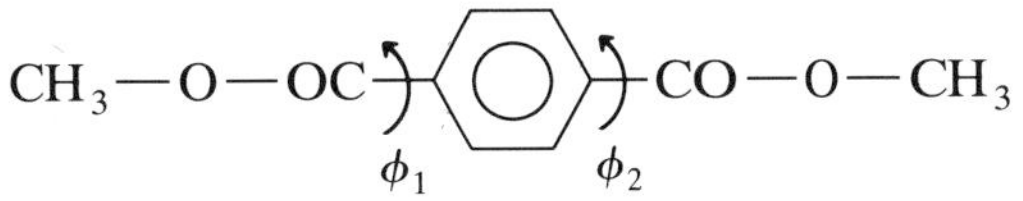

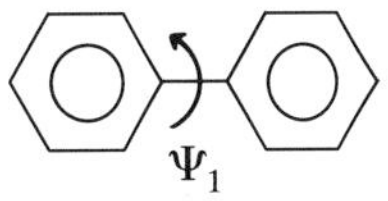

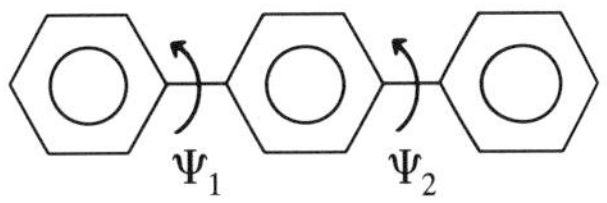

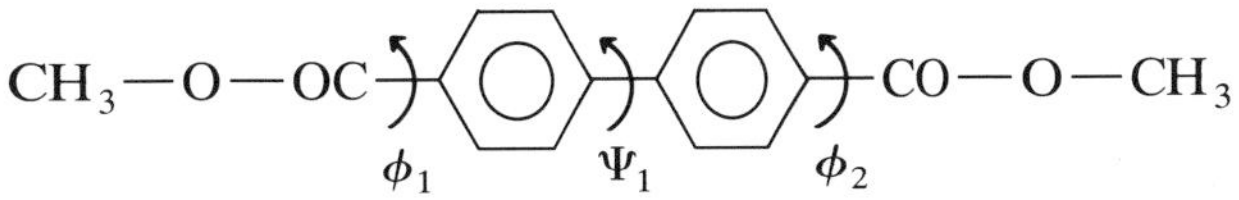

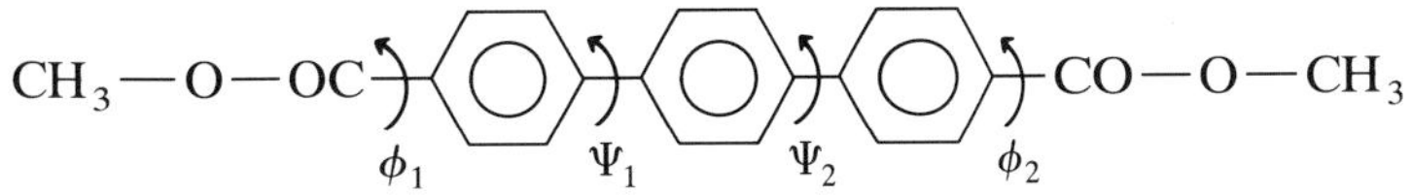

Table 1
Common Thermotropic Systems

Rigid core				Disruptor
Cyclic unit	Linkage group	Functional group	Flexible segment	Rigid kink

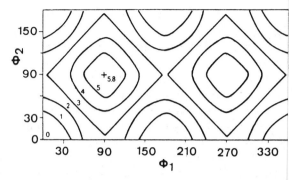

FIGURE 3
Conformational energy map (ϕ_1, ϕ_2) of methylterephthalate.
(Reproduced with permission from Ref. 78. Copyright Gordc
Breach Science Publ.)

The internal rotation angles ϕ_i define the orientation of an
with respect to the adjacent carboxyl group. The angles Ψ_i ch
relative orientation of two adjacent rings.

The conformational energy map of methyl terephthalate (
Fig. 3. Two energy minima are found at $\phi_1 = \phi_2 = 0°$ and $\phi_1 =$
The former corresponds to the cis configuration of the ca
relative to the central ring and the latter coincides with the tr
tion. Coplanarity of the carboxyl group with the benzene ri
maximum overlapping of electrons of the participating atoms.
the energy barrier is 2.9 kcal mol^{-1}. The energy maximum is (
$\phi_1 = \phi_2 = 90°$. Besides, ϕ_1 and ϕ_2 rotations are independent.

For comparison it is useful to cite earlier empirical calcu
out by Hummel and Flory[42] and by Tonelli[79] in an attempt to
preferred angles and evaluate the energy barriers for methy
terephthalate moiety, respectively. Very similar potential enei
obtained. The equilibrium conformations also correspond to
and trans configurations. Only the height of the energy b
5 kcal mol^{-1} and 3 kcal mol^{-1} according to Hummel and
Tonelli,[79] respectively. Such discrepancies may be due to th
evaluating conjugation energy in empirical calculations.

These results are in reasonable agreement with experim
tions on dimethyl terephthalate. Indeed, the energy differenc
cis and trans isomers was found to be 0.05 kcal mol^{-1} from c
measurements in solution.[80] Besides, infrared and Raman stud
that the populations of the cis and trans conformers are near
the melt. Finally, the molecular conformation in the crystal
found to be the trans one, the phenyl ring standing at an angl
plane of the carboxyl group.[82] The nearly planar conformatic
phthaloyl residue favors the molecular packing in the crystal

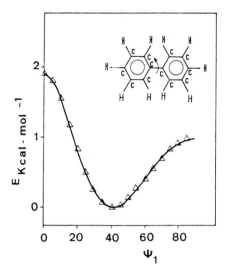

FIGURE 4
Conformational energy shown as a function of torsional angle Ψ_1
for biphenyl. (Reproduced with permission from Ref. 78. Copyright
Gordon & Breach Science Publ.)

eration of the π-electron system by HMO or PPP theories lead to reasonable
values for both torsional energy barriers and $\Psi_{1\,min}$ (26–40°). Also good
results are derived by use of hybrid atomic orbitals with modified INDO
calculations ($\Psi_{1\,min} = 36$–37°),[101] and reasonable values for energy barriers
are calculated by NDDO[102] and PCILO[78] methods with $\Psi_{1\,min} = 45°$ and
30–40°. Quite recently, the complete molecular structure of biphenyl was
derived by ab initio calculations.[96, 103, 104] All give a nonplanar structure but
differ somewhat in the torsional angle and greatly in the barrier height.

It should be noted that the torsional angle in biphenyls is strongly
dependent on substitution in the positions ortho to the inter-ring bond. The
equilibrium torsional angles of 2′,6′-dihalogenated biphenyl derivatives (X =
F, Cl, Br, I) were determined from the NMR spectra of these compounds
dissolved in nematic LC solvents.[105] The equilibrium torsional angles in this
series were found to be a smooth monotonic function of the size of the
halogens at C2 and C6 (Fig. 5). There are indications that through conjugation plays a very minor role in determining the torsional angles.

For *p*-terphenyl (**3**), PCILO calculations[78] give an absolute conformational energy minimum at $\Psi_1 = \Psi_2 = 40°$, in agreement with previous theoretical calculations.[106–108] The height of the energy barrier for the rotation of
the central ring relative to the adjacent rings is twice that determined for the
rotation of the rings about the 1,1′-bond in biphenyl, which has been found
experimentally.[109]

The crystal structure of *p*-terphenyl and its molecular conformations in
the crystalline state are now well understood. Neutron and x-ray diffraction

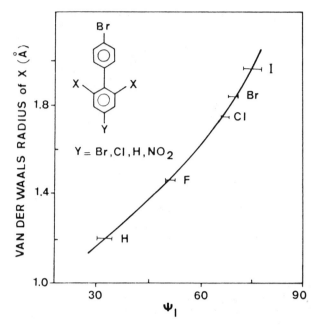

FIGURE 5
The correlation between the torsional angle Ψ_1 and the van der Waals radius of the substituents X in 2′,6′-dihalogenated biphenyl derivatives. (Reproduced with permission from Ref. 105. Copyright Am. Chem. Soc.)

studies[106, 109] show that, in the disordered high-temperature phase, the p-terphenyl molecule exhibits a mean planar conformation, the librations of the central ring ($\pm 16°$) being governed by a double-well flat potential. Incoherent neutron-scattering studies led to a value of 1.0 kcal mol^{-1} for the height of the potential barrier,[110] a value that has been confirmed by proton spin–lattice relaxation measurements.[111] On lowering the temperature, second-order order–disorder phase transition takes place at 193 K, in which the central ring and the outer ones twist in opposite directions from the mean planar configuration and occupy one of the two possible wells of the potential. The molecules take two kinds of nonplanar conformations in which the dihedral angles between the central ring and the outer ones are equal to about 16° and 25°.

The molecular structure of p-terphenyl in the liquid state and in solution is still lacking certainty. Most probably, p-terphenyl has nonplanar conformations in solution. The infrared spectrum[112] and its band intensities,[113] the shift of the longest wavelength UV band on going from the pressed KCl disk spectrum to the hexane solution spectrum,[114] the diffuseness of the solution fluorescence spectrum,[115] and its dependence on the excitation wavelength at 77 K,[116] all support this idea. A measurement of the bathochromic shift between the origins of the fluorescence spectra of nonplanar p-terphenyl in solution and in the low-temperature crystalline phase led Williams[117] to suggest that there should be no difference in the molecular conformation of p-terphenyl in these two phases; therefore in solution, as in the low-temperature crystalline phase, the outer rings should be twisted by 16–25° relative to the middle one. Rather interestingly, the analysis of molar Kerr constants for infinitely diluted benzene solutions of terphenyls does not exclude the possibility of the existence of two conformers in p-terphenyl solutions: good agreement between the calculated and measured Kerr constants is obtained for both a D_2 and a C_{2h} geometry with twist angles of 20°.[118]

The nonplanarity of p-terphenyl in the gas phase is supported by photoelectron spectroscopy studies[119]; the experimental results combined with CNDO/S calculations show that p-terphenyl may be present in two conformers. p-Terphenyl molecules may assume D_2 and C_{2h} symmetries, with inter-ring angles of 42 and 43°, respectively. A potential curve model is used by Wakayama[120] for explaining his $T \leftarrow S_0$ absorption spectrum of 77 K and room-temperature crystal. The S_0 potential curve is given a minimum, corresponding to the equilibrium geometry of the gas-phase molecule, at a torsion angle of ca. 35°. The nonplanarity of gaseous p-terphenyl is also the qualitative conclusion of a comparison of the vacuum UV absorption spectra of the vapor and of the low-temperature crystalline phase[121] and of the analysis of the multiphoton ionization spectrum of p-terphenyl in a supersonic free jet.[122]

Quite recently, Fourier transform infrared spectroscopy was used for studying the conformational changes occurring in the crystalline, smectic, and isotropic phases of diethyl-p-terphenyl-4,4″-dicarboxylate (DETC) and di-n-propyl-p-terphenyl-4,4″-dicarboxylate (DPTC)[123]:

$$C_nH_{2n+1}-O-OC-\!\!\left\langle\bigcirc\right\rangle\!\!-\!\!\left\langle\bigcirc\right\rangle\!\!-\!\!\left\langle\bigcirc\right\rangle\!\!-CO-O-C_nH_{2n+1}$$

$n = 2$ (DETC) $K_1 \xleftrightarrow{154°C} K_2 \xleftrightarrow{177°C} S_E \xleftrightarrow{191°C} S_A \xleftrightarrow{263°C} I$

$n = 3$ (DPTC) $K \xleftrightarrow{123°C} S_E \xleftrightarrow{139°C} S_A \xleftrightarrow{240.8°C} I$

Of special interest is the band at 463 cm^{-1}, which has been assigned to out-of-plane vibrations implying[124] a ν_{CC} 16b mode. This band shifts toward higher frequencies with increasing temperature (Fig. 6). The same effect has been observed for biphenyl[124] and p-terphenyl[112] upon melting. Frequency calculations[124, 125] have shown an extreme sensitivity of this mode to changes in the dihedral angles between the planes of the adjacent rings. On the basis of these calculations and previous observations, the frequency rise was interpreted as an increase in the dihedral angles of the p-terphenyl moiety upon heating, passing through abrupt changes at phase transitions.

Values of the conformational energy, taken relative to that for the coplanar form, are plotted versus Ψ_1 in Fig. 7 for the planar conformation of

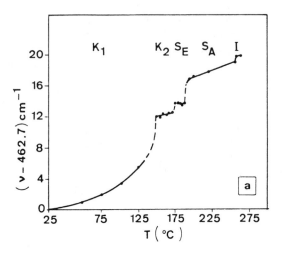

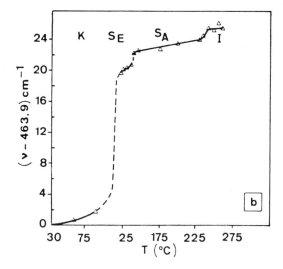

FIGURE 6
Frequency changes observed for the out-of-plane ring mode in
DETC (a) and DPTC (b).

the ϕ — CO — O groups in molecule **4**. As observed for biphenyl (Fig. 4), the
energy minimum is obtained when $\Psi_1 = 40°$. Experimental evidence indicates values of approximately 40° in the crystalline state[126] and 30° in the LC
state[127] for 4,4′-disubstituted biphenyls. Indeed, in these compounds intermolecular interactions are reduced compared with biphenyl and the crystalline form is closely related to the vapor form. On the other hand, the
conformational energy contour for the phenyl ring rotation about the
C_{ar} — CO adjacent bond is shown in Fig. 8 for $\Psi_1 = 40°$. As observed for

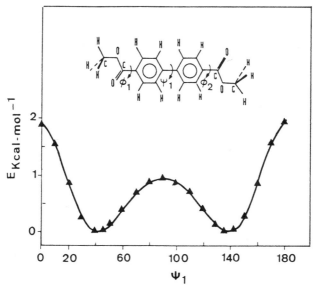

FIGURE 7

Conformational energy shown as a function of torsional angle Ψ_1 for molecule **4** ($\phi_1 = \phi_2 = 0°$). PCILO calculations. (Reproduced with permission from Ref. 78. Copyright Gordon & Breach Science Publ.)

methylterephthalate, two energy minima are found at $\phi_1 = \phi_2 = 0°$ and $\phi_1 = 0°$, $\phi_2 = 180°$. It appears from these results that the most stable conformations of molecule **4** can be deduced from the studies of methyl terephthalate and biphenyl. Besides, the heights of the energy barriers for each of the rotations ϕ_1, ϕ_2, and Ψ_1 are the same as those determined for these two simpler model compounds.

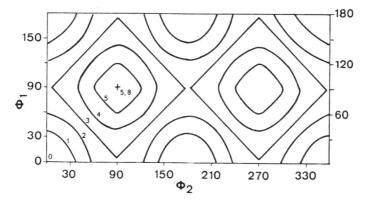

FIGURE 8

Conformational energy map (ϕ_1, ϕ_2) of molecule **4** ($\Psi_1 = 40°$). PCILO calculations. (Reproduced with permission from Ref. 78. Copyright Gordon & Breach Science Publ.)

The replacement of biphenyl by terphenyl, as occurs in molecule **5**, is of interest in this study particularly with regard to the extent to which lengthening of the mesogenic moiety affects the conformational characteristics. Again, the energy minima are found at $\phi_1 = \phi_2 = 0°$ or $\phi_1 = 0°$, $\phi_2 = 180°$ and $\Psi_1 = 40°$, $\Psi_2 = \pm 40°$. Besides, as observed for molecule **4**, the heights of the energy barriers for each of the elementary rotations are the same as those determined for methyl terephthalate and *p*-terphenyl. The 4.8 kcal mol^{-1} energy barrier derived from PCILO calculations[78] for the internal rotation of the outer rings, assuming independent rotation of each of the three rings of the terphenyl unit, is in close agreement with the 5 kcal mol^{-1} deduced from ^{1}H and ^{13}C NMR relaxation data for polyester[128]:

$$\left[OC - \langle O \rangle - \langle O \rangle - \langle O \rangle - CO-O-(CH_2-CH_2-O)_4 \right]$$

In the same way, the 3.8 kcal mol^{-1} barrier height calculated under the same assumption is consistent with the 3–3.5 kcal mol^{-1} experimental activation energy for the internal inner ring rotation about the long axis of the *p*-terphenyl moiety.[128]

A prominent feature of the preceding PCILO calculations is that the conformational characteristics of the carboxyl groups are independent of the number of phenyl rings. In other words, the main consequence of the replacement of a phenyl ring by biphenyl or *p*-terphenyl is to extend the linearity, the rigidity, and anisotropy of the system. The theory of LCP's attaches great importance to these geometrical factors.[7] For instance, according to Flory and Ronca,[129] for an undiluted system, there exists a critical value of the axial ratio (length to diameter) for LC formation. Thus, polyesters $\left[OC - R_1 - COO - R_2 - O \right]$, with $R_1 = $ *p*-terphenyl, provide a rich source of LC's that are more thermally stable than those of the biphenyl analogs.[130–133] On the other hand, polyalkylene terephthalates do not form LC's.

The molecular conformations of *trans*-stilbene (**7**)[134–137] and *trans*-azobenzene (**8**)[138] in the crystalline state were found to be nearly planar, while a torsional angle of $\Theta \simeq 55°$ was reported for benzylidene aniline (**9**).[139]

7   8

9

Such conformational differences were also deduced from ultraviolet

(UV),[140–143] infrared (IR),[144–146] and NMR[144, 146, 147] studies performed in solution. However, the dihedral angle Θ was lacking certainty, lying in the range 30–90°. According to Traetteberg et al.[148] the dihedral angle Θ of benzylidene aniline determined in the gas phase is 52°. For both *trans*-stilbene and *trans*-azobenzene under the same conditions they found $\phi \simeq 30°$.[149, 150]

Perrin and Berges[151] summarized the theoretical calculations of different degrees of sophistication carried out on these molecules. Good results are obtained by NDDO and PCILO calculations. In particular, reasonable values for bond lengths, valence angles, and torsional angles are calculated by the PCILO method.

Information about the effects of the mesogenic moiety on liquid crystal properties can be illustrated by reference to polyesters[130] of general formula:

$$+OC-R_1-COO-R_2-O+$$

where R_1 = biphenyl, *p*-terphenyl, stilbene, and $R_2 = +CH_2\,)_n$.

In accordance with the general requirement of an elongated and fairly rigid molecular structure, derivatives of *p*-terphenyl provide liquid crystals that are much more thermally stable than those of the biphenyl and stilbene analogs. The effects of biphenyl and stilbene groups are similar, although mesophases of slightly lower thermal stability are formed by biphenyls. This points out the importance of extending the length of the rigid core. Indeed, the linking unit CH=CH contains a double bond about which freedom of rotation is restricted, so preserving the rigidity and elongation of the molecules. However, other considerations are important and affect the thermal stability of mesophases: *trans*-stilbene is not linear and its anisotropy is much smaller than that of *p*-terphenyl.

Examples of highly extended structures in which small differences in valence angles in conjunction with alternative rotations about skeletal bonds conspire to conduce departures from rectilinearity are furnished by poly(*p*-hydroxybenzoic acid):

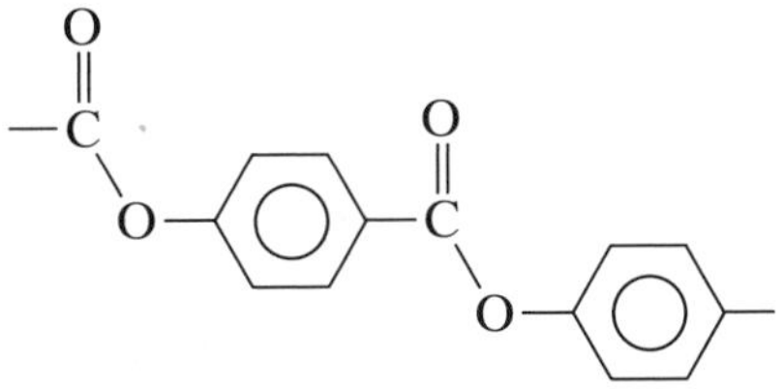

and the corresponding polyamide, poly(*p*-aminobenzoic acid). Recently, quantum mechanical calculations utilizing an approximate ab initio technique (PRDDO) were used to characterize intrachain rotations in phenylbenzoate:

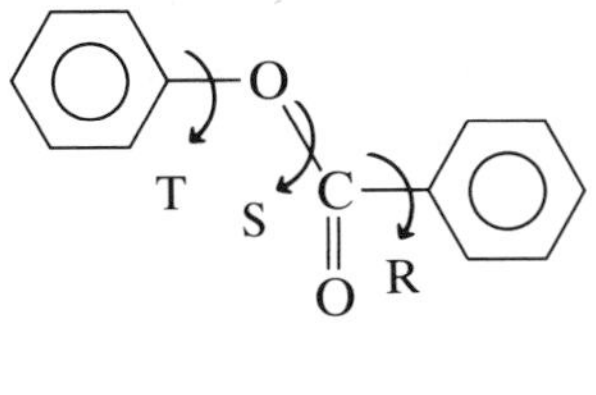

which is representative of short chain segments.[152] The ester linkage and the phenyl ring directly attached to the ester carbon are found to be at an angle of 0.2° relative to one another: i.e., they are coplanar within the limits of numerical accuracy of the calculations. In crystalline phenylbenzoate, the — COO group is twisted 9.8° out of the plane of the benzene ring to which it is attached.[153] This near coplanarity is caused by the stabilization resulting from resonance between the electrons in the phenyl ring and in the ester linkage when the planes of these two groups are coplanar with each other. The other phenyl ring, which is attached to an oxygen atom, is calculated to have a torsional angle of 46.4° relative to the plane of the ester linkage. This torsional angle is 65.1° in crystalline phenylbenzoate,[153] substantially larger than the calculated angle. There are two possible explanations for this difference. First of all, the potential surface is very flat for this particular torsion motion, resulting in a very broad minimum. Second, the geometry that allows for optimum packing in the crystalline state is not necessarily the same as the most stable geometry of the "isolated" molecule.

Quite recently, Coulter and Windle[154] deduced geometries and rotational parameters appropriate for the molecular modeling of aromatic polyesters by combining a study of published crystal, experimental and theoretical data, and conformational computations of their own. From their results they inferred an "idealized" geometry for the $-\phi-COO-\phi-$ moiety in crystal structure. According to these authors, for the R bond there is a region of low energy $\pm 10°$ around 0°, the energy minima being ca. 6° either side of 0°. A value of 0° can be assigned to the S bond dihedral angle. The π dihedral angle deviates from 0° by between 33° and 90°. However, experimental evidence suggests that the energy minimum is around 67°. The central C—O bond of conjugated esters was estimated to be somewhat less rigid than generally imagined (barrier at 90° of about 7 kcal mol^{-1}), a finding of particular relevance to mesogenicity of aromatic polyesters.

For comparison, it is interesting to summarize the theoretical calculations carried out on diphenyl carbonate[152, 155, 156]:

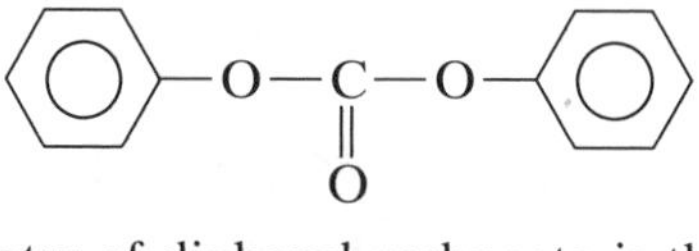

The optimized geometry of diphenyl carbonate is the trans,trans conformation,[152] which has a mirror plane of symmetry perpendicular to the plane of the carbonate linkage. The two phenyl rings are both at an angle of 44° relative to the plane of the carbonate linkage, in agreement with the torsional angle of 45° determined by Yoon and Flory[157] in crystalline diphenyl carbonate. This angle is just a little smaller than the 46.4° value calculated for the equivalent torsional angle in phenylbenzoate. This is not surprising since the second phenyl ring of phenylbenzoate lies on the same plane as the plane of the ester linkage and is therefore closer to the phenyl ring bonded to the oxygen atom than in diphenyl carbonate. It should be noted that since

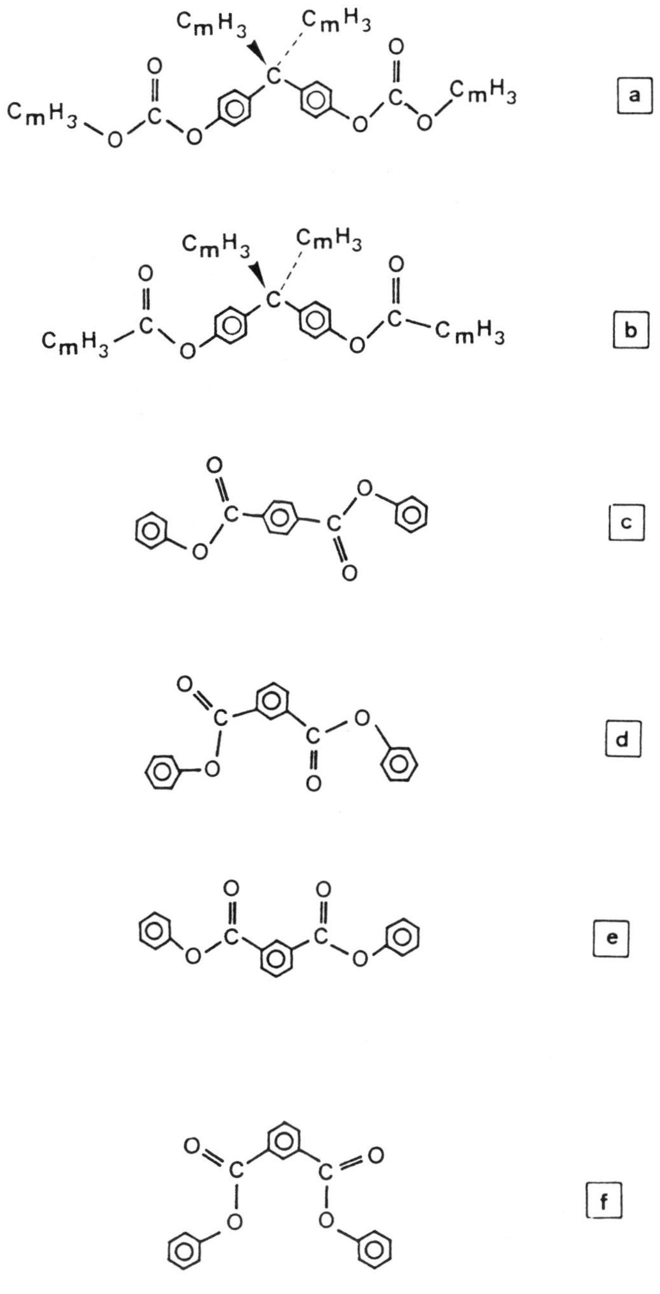

FIGURE 9
Schematic drawings of the (a) large carbonate (LC) molecule,
(b) large ester molecule (LE), (c) terephthalic structure (T),
(d) isophthalic structure (I), (e) isophthalic, linear structure (IL), and
(f) isophthalic, kink (IK) structure. (Reproduced with permission
from Ref. 152. Copyright Am. Chem. Soc.)

rotations of the phenyl rings about $O-C_{ar}$ bonds are almost free rotations, diphenyl carbonate does not have a strong preference for the trans,trans conformation described above.

There are also a low-lying trans,cis and an equivalent cis, trans conformation. The lack of a low-lying cis,cis conformation is due to the severe steric overlaps between adjoining phenyl rings, as pointed out by Williams and Flory.[158]

Intrachain rotations and rocking motions of the phenyl rings were studied by means of detailed calculations on several large molecules (Fig. 9) that represent different types of phenyl ring environment.[152] The barriers estimated for the 180° flip of the phenyl rings attached to an isopropylidene group are 9.9 and 10.4 kcal mol^{-1} when the phenyl rings are attached to a carbonate or to an ester linkage, respectively, at the para position. The ester phenyl ring in terephthalic structure has a rotation barrier of 13.1 kcal mol^{-1} as well as a large-amplitude low-energy oscillation range of $\pm 30°$ about its equilibrium position. There is no simple or cooperative low-barrier flipping motion for the ester phenyl ring in the isophthalic structure, where the low-energy oscillation or rocking motion range is also much more restricted ($\pm 15°$). These results are highly encouraging for further applications of quantum chemical calculations to other compounds in order to characterize the molecular motions associated with secondary relaxations observed below the glass transition in LCP's.

3.3. Disruptors

As discussed in the introduction of this section kinks or flexible segments may be introduced to offset the linearity of the rigid mainchain of simple but intractable paralinked aromatic polymers. The related disrupting effects will be illustrated by reference to bridged aromatic compounds $\phi-X-\phi$, where X = O, CH$_2$, CO, S in Section 3.3.1, and by reference to polymethylene and poly(ethylene oxide) spacers in Section 3.3.2.

3.3.1. BRIDGED AROMATIC COMPOUNDS $\phi-X-\phi$

where X = O, CH$_2$, CO, S.

According to the classical scheme, $E(\varphi, \Psi)$ is determined mainly by steric interactions between nonbonded atom pairs and torsional potentials about the $O-C_{ar}$ bonds. The clear physical meaning of these separate contributions to the conformational energy allows easy interpretation of the results obtained by classical calculations.[159, 160] For $\phi-O-\phi$ the increase in the height of the torsional barrier, U_0, about the $O-C_{ar}$ bond from 0 to

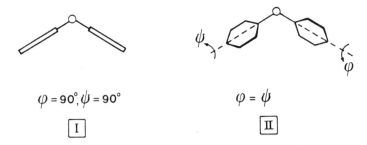

$\varphi = 90°, \psi = 90°$ $\varphi = \psi$

$\boxed{\text{I}}$ $\boxed{\text{II}}$

FIGURE 10
Typical conformations for $\phi — X — \phi$ molecules.

10 kcal mol^{-1} leads to a displacement of the energy minimum from the conformation I with $\varphi = \Psi = 90°$ to the "skew" form II with $\varphi = \Psi \cong 30–40°$ (Fig. 10). From these results it is clear that the nonbonded interactions, which are the only contributions to the conformational energy when $U_0 = 0$, stabilize conformation I. This is due to van der Waals attractions between phenyl rings. In phenol, the height of the torsional barrier about the $O—C_{ar}$ bond is close to 3.2 kcal mol^{-1}.[161] This comparatively large value is caused by interaction of the π electrons of the phenyl ring with the lone-pair electrons of the O atom. The classical calculations with $U_0 = 3$ kcal mol^{-1} give a minimum energy conformation at $\varphi = \Psi = 37°$, which is in good agreement with x-ray data for polyphenylene oxide.[162] Indeed, the most probable conformation was found to be the "skew" one with $\varphi = \Psi = 40°$. The conformational energy maps calculated by different quantum chemical methods are substantially different.[160, 163] Comparison with the results of classical calculations and with experimental data shows that the EHT and CNDO/2 methods give satisfactory results. It should be noted that the conformational maps do not change when the valence angle ξ is varied from 120° to 124°.

In the bridged aromatic compound $\phi—CH_2—\phi$, where the torsional barrier is small because of the lack of conjugation between the methylene group and the phenyl ring, the conformational energy minimum was found at $\varphi = \Psi = 90°$.[160] However, in the crystalline state intermolecular interactions favor the "skew" form with $\varphi = \Psi = 52°$,[164] which is in the low-energy region of the conformational map. The torsional barrier in $\phi—CO—\phi$ is larger than in $\phi—CH_2—\phi$ since the π electrons of the carbonyl group interact with the π electrons of the phenyl ring. As a consequence, the conformational energy minimum is found for the "skew" form with $\varphi = \Psi = 30°$. For $\phi—S—\phi$ the equilibrium conformation is also a skew one with $\varphi = \Psi = 35°$ which is rather close to the experimental values $\varphi = \Psi = 45°$.[165] An alteration of ξ has significance only for $\phi—CH_2—\phi$ where the increase of ξ from 111° to 119° diminishes the value of the maximum of conformational energy by 2 kcal mol^{-1}.

The analysis of the conformational energy maps[159, 160] allows some conclusions to be drawn about the main features of the internal rotation in ϕ—X—ϕ systems. Broadly speaking, there is a large portion of conformation space that lies in the 1 kcal mol^{-1} region. This implies a comparatively unrestricted internal rotation which manifests itself in the rather small dielectric relaxation times (2 × 10^{-12} to 12 × 10^{-12} s^{-1}).[166]

The heights of the barrier between the low-energy regions are another important feature of the conformational energy maps. For ϕ—O—ϕ and ϕ—CH$_2$—ϕ, the barrier between any of the low-energy regions does not exceed 1–2 kcal mol^{-1}; i.e., the molecule can easily go from one conformation to any other. Both ϕ—S—ϕ and ϕ—CO—ϕ are characterized by two sets of low-energy regions. In each set, again, the barriers do not exceed 2 kcal mol^{-1}, but to go from one set to the other it is necessary to overcome much higher barriers.

At this stage of the discussion, we would like to comment on the properties of macromolecules containing ϕ—X—ϕ groups in their backbones. The conformational energy maps are characterized by a highly symmetric distribution of low-energy regions.[159] This fact, together with the independence of rotations about neighboring ϕ—X—ϕ groups allows one to consider these macromolecules as freely rotating chains.[167] The characteristic ratios of such macromolecules calculated with this assumption are in good agreement with experimental data.[168]

3.3.2. FLEXIBLE SEGMENTS

Conformation-dependent properties of polyoxide chains $+(CH_2)_m\,O+_n$ were intensively investigated in the framework of the rotational isomeric state approximation.[39, 169–174] Rotational energies of the rotational states adopted by the skeletal bonds of the chains were determined through comparisons of calculated and experimental values of some configuration-dependent properties. In addition, conformational energy calculations were carried out to obtain information regarding the energy associated with the conformations of minimum and higher intramolecular energies.[39]

The most characteristic feature of polyoxide chains, in contrast to polymethylene chains,[175] $+CH_2+_n$, is a decisive preference for the gauche conformation over the trans around certain skeletal bonds: gauche states about CH$_2$—CH$_2$ bonds have an energy ca. 0.5 kcal mol^{-1} below the alternative trans state. This result was recently confirmed by Tasaki and Abe.[176] It should be noted, however, that the conformational properties of polyoxide chains vary markedly with the number of methylene groups in the repeat unit[170, 177] and the presence of sidegroups.[78, 178–182] In polyoxymethylene, gauche states about the central bond in the sequence

$$\underset{CH_2}{\nearrow}\overset{O}{\underset{\searrow CH_2}{\diagup}}\overset{O}{\diagup}$$

bring CH$_2$ groups and O atoms to a relatively small distance of separation; such states are found to be ca. 1.5 kcal mol^{-1} lower in energy than the alternative trans states. For bonds of the type

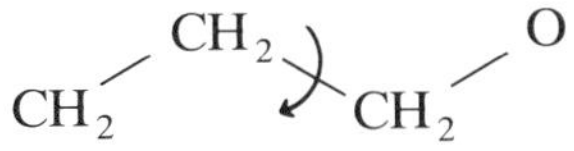

in $\mathrm{+(CH_2)_m\text{-}O+_n}$ chains having $m > 2$, the groups brought into proximity are again CH_2 groups and O atoms, but the preference for gauche states in these cases is only ca. 0.2 kcal mol^{-1}. In the polymer chains of general formula $\mathrm{+CH_2{-}C(R)(R'){-}O+_n}$ where R and R′ may be a proton atom or a methyl group, the conformational flexibility of a given (skeletal) bond varies with the degree of methyl substitution. The bond rotation around the skeletal C—C bond tends to be more restricted in the order polyoxyethylene, polyoxypropylene, and poly(oxy-1,1-dimethylethylene). The rotameric probability about $CH_2{-}CH_2$ bonds also depends on the nature of the environment.[183, 184] For example, the gauche states about $CH_2{-}CH_2$ bonds in both poly(diethylene glycol terephthalate) and poly(thiodiethylene glycol terephthalate) have an energy ca. 0.5 kcal mol^{-1} lower than similar states about these bonds in polyoxyethylene and poly(thiodiethylene glycol), respectively.[183] It seems that the presence of neighboring carbonyl groups enhances the gauche population about $CH_2{-}CH_2$ bonds.

Of special interest is the fact that the configuration-dependent properties of polyesters with repeating unit $\mathrm{CO{-}\phi{-}COO{-}(CH_2)_m{-}O{-}}$ are strongly dependent not only on the number of methylene groups of the glycol residue but also on the nature of the acid (terephthalic, isophthalic, or phthalic). Large repulsive intramolecular interactions between two ester groups of the phthaloyl residue overcome the stabilizing effects of the coplanarity between the carbonyl and phenyl groups, and the critical interpretation of conformation-dependent properties of polyesters based on phthalic acid[184] suggests that the rotational angle about $C_{ar}{-}CO$ bonds are $\pm 90°$. Consequently, the molecular packing of the chains in the crystal seems to be disfavored, hindering the possibility that crystallinity is developed in phthalate-based polyesters in which the number of methylene groups in the glycol residue is small. These conformational characteristics also explain that the phthaloyl residue is commonly incorporated in LCP's to reduce the transition temperatures to a reasonable range. In contrast, in polyesters based respectively on terephthalic and isophthalic acids, coplanarity between the carbonyl and phenyl groups guarantees maximum overlapping of electrons of these groups[42] and consequently the rotational angles about $C_{ar}{-}CO$ bonds are restricted to 0 and 180°.[80] The planar conformation of the terephthaloyl and isophthaloyl residues favors the molecular packing of the chains in the crystal and enhances the attractive intermolecular interactions between the ester groups and neighboring chains. As a result, the polyesters exhibit high melting points whose values decrease as the number of methylene groups in the glycol residue increases,[185] reaching a minimum, and then increase eventually reaching the T_m of polyethylene for $n \to \infty$. The same factors are of importance for LC formation.

For the same mesogenic unit, the length of the flexible spacer influences both the nature of the mesophase and the thermal transitions. As shown in Chapter 7, for many series,[132, 186–195] as the polymethylene chain is extended, the transition temperatures decrease while showing a typical even–odd alternation. At the same time, the tendency for predominantly (or purely) nematic behavior gives way to purely smectic behavior in the higher homologs.

It should be pointed out that when the polymethylene spacers are attached to the rigid moieties (RM) by $RM-O-(CH_2)_m$ or $RM-O(O{=})C{+}CH_2{+}_m$ linkage, the nematic states occur readily and the enthalpies and entropies of nematic–isotropic transitions are much larger than those of LMWLC's.[186, 193] Moreover, the enthalpy and entropy changes are much higher for the chains with even-numbered methylene spacers than those with odd-numbered spacers.[186, 187, 190, 193, 195, 196] An alternation of the order parameter is also observed.[197, 198] On the other hand, when the polymethylene spacers are attached by $RM-C({=}O)O{+}CH_2{+}_m$ linkage, the tendency to form a nematic state is significantly suppressed.[132, 199] When a nematic state occurs, the enthalpies and entropies of nematic–isotropic transitions of polymers with even-numbered spacers are smaller than those for the chains with odd-numbered spacers.[194]

It is difficult to explain the observed trends in LC thermal stability with increasing length of the flexible segment, particularly the even–odd alternation, if the flexible segment is free to adopt completely random conformations through flexing of the chain and rotation about carbon–carbon bonds. Interesting results showing that the spacers cannot adopt a single elongated conformation have been reported.[197, 200–203] However, the parallel alignment of rigid core parts of the repeating units constrains movement within the spacers to some extent, and although the spacers are not restricted to the all-trans conformation, the conformations that are adopted are rather extended.[197, 200, 204–206] It is of interest to compare these experimental results with the predictions of conformational energy calculations,[207–210] which have pointed out the influence, on the conformational order of the spacer units, of the spacer length (even–odd effect) and the nature of the functional groups that link the polymethylene segments to the mesogenic core. When the spacers are attached to the mesogenic cores by an oxygen atom or an $O(O{=}C)$ group, spacers that have an even number of methylene units exhibit a significant population of highly extended conformations which allow nearly parallel alignment of the rigid cores along the major extension axis (Fig. 11). The presence of these conformers, which offer high chain extension and parallel alignment of rigid groups without incurring excessive reduction in the configurational partition function, helps to promote a stable nematic state. These conformers are also most likely to be preferred over the others in the nematic state. The enthalpy of the resulting isotropic–nematic transition of the polymer will then have a significant contribution from this conformational selection owing to the large change in the internal (conforma-

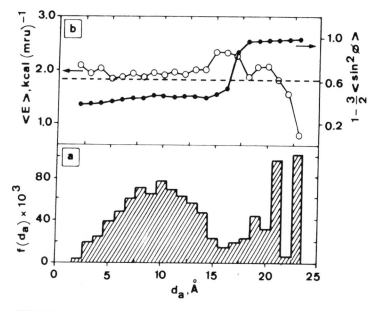

FIGURE 11

(a) Distribution of chain sequence extensions calculated when the polymethylene segments —(CH$_2$)$_{10}$— are attached by —O— linkage to the rigid moiety. (b) Orientational correlations of rigid units with the major extension axis and average internal energy as a function of chain sequence extension; the dotted line denotes the average energy of all conformers. (Reproduced with permission from Ref. 208. Copyright Am. Chem. Soc.)

tional) energy of the polymethylene segments. Consequently, the transition enthalpy of the polymer will be considerably larger than that of the corresponding LMWLC, which is found experimentally. On the other hand, for an odd number of spacer carbons, the number of highly extended chains is much smaller, the mesogenic cores are tilted by an angle of about 30° from the major extension axis, and the order parameter is smaller. The strong dependence of the transition enthalpy on the even–odd character of the polymethylene segment is matched closely by the characteristics of the extended conformers, i.e., the energies of those extended conformers relative to the average energy, as well as the orientational correlations of rigid units with respect to the chain extension (or alignment) axis that determine the anisotropic attractions.[129] When the polymethylene spacers are attached to the mesogenic core by a (C=O)O group, the population of extended conformers is reduced significantly for the chains with even-numbered methylene spacers. When compared with those of odd-numbered methylene spacers linked in the same way, they exhibit even smaller fractions of extended conformers.[208] Lack of an appreciable population of highly extended conformers suggests that it will be less likely to form a nematic state of this type of polymer. Furthermore, when a nematic state occurs, the transition enthalpy will have a very small contribution from the conformational energy of the polymethylene segment.

4. CONFORMATIONAL ANALYSIS OF SOME LYOTROPIC SYSTEMS

4.1. Introduction

Theoretical studies[211,212] predicted that rigid, rodlike polymers should undergo a spontaneous transformation from an isotropic to an anisotropic ordered solution above a threshold concentration, which in turn is an explicit function of the molecular axial ratio (Length L to diameter d).

Semirigid or semiflexible polymers, which although highly extended compared to conventional random coiling polymers nevertheless possess a significant flexibility may also impart liquid crystallinity to their solutions. Calculations suggested that the theory for rigid rods may be adapted to

Table 2
Some Lyotropic Polymers (Continued)

Polyamide hydrazide-type polymers:

Polyterephthalamide of p-amino benzhydrazide

Cellulose derivatives:

Hydroxypropylcellulose (HPC)
Cellulose acetate (CA)

(continued)

Table 2
Some Lyotropic Polymers (Continued)

Aromatic polyamides:

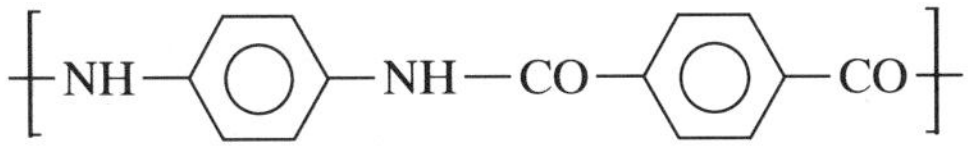

Poly(p-phenylene terephthalamide) (PPDT)

Poly(p-benzamide) (PBA)

Poly(N-alkylisocyanates)

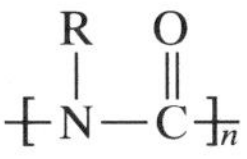

R = n-hexyl (PHIC)

Nucleic acids (double-helical conformation)
DNA, RNA

α-Helical polypeptides

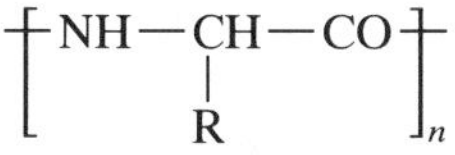

Poly(γ-benzyl-L-glutamate) (PBLG)

Polysaccharides
Xylan (bacterial polysaccharide)
Schizophyllan (extracellular fungal polysaccharide)

Aromatic heterocyclic polymers

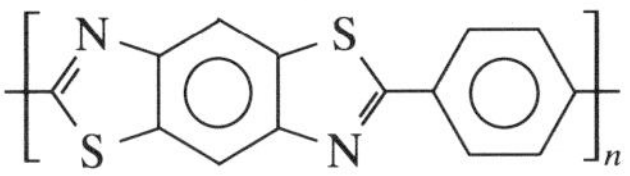

Poly(p-phenylene benzo-bis-thiazole) (PBT)

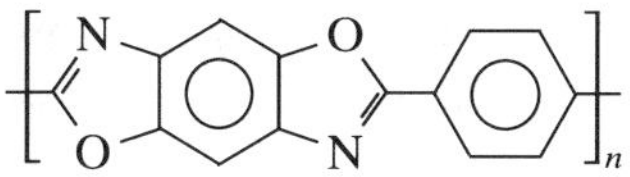

Poly(p-phenylene benzo-bis-oxazole) (PBO)

*As a result of rotation about the N—N bond, this polymer is relatively flexible. In solution it is not anisotropic at rest but becomes so under shear.

semirigid chains by the simple device of replacing the molecular axial ratio by the axial ratio X of the Kuhn segment. More sophisticated models are described in other chapters of this book.

From these results it appears that there are two prerequisites for LC formation in polymer solutions: (1) sufficient inherent rigidity of the molecular structure and (2) sufficient solubility (polymer concentration > threshold concentration). Table 2 shows typical polymers that meet these requirements. Corresponding persistence lengths, q,[213–222] are analyzed in Chapter 2.

As indicated in Table 2, sidechain polymers may fulfill the above conditions. As an example, conformational characteristics of poly(γ-benzyl-L-glutamate) have been determined by Abe and Yamazaki.[223] However, this section concentrates only upon materials based on aromatic and aryl-aliphatic polyamides and on polymers consisting solely of ring structures: poly(p-phenylenebenzo-*bis*-oxazole) (PBO) and poly(p-phenylenebenzo-*bis*-thiazole) (PBT). These materials are primarily intended to satisfy the demands of industry for light-weight, high-performance materials suitable for reinforcement purpose, especially in composites. Their properties and applications were recently reviewed.[224–226]

4.2. Aromatic and Aryl-aliphatic Polyamides

4.2.1. CONFORMATIONAL ENERGY CALCULATIONS

As noted by Tsvetkov and Shtennikova,[227] aromatic polyamides containing phenyl rings substituted in the para position, such as poly(p-phenylene terephthalamide) (PPDT) or poly(p-benzamide) (PBA), are characterized by a succession of bonds that are successively relatively free to rotate, such as ϕ—CO and ϕ—NH, and constrained to a fixed coplanar trans structure as the CO—NH group is. According to Tsvetkov and Shtennikova,[227] this very regular structure ensures an extremely high equilibrium rigidity of the chain skeleton, which is responsible for the ability of these polymers to yield lyotropic liquid crystals.

To get a deeper insight into the relationship between the chemical nature of the constitutive units of the para-aromatic or aryl-aliphatic polyamides and their mesomorphic character in solution, conformational energy calculations of model compounds have been performed by several authors.[40, 42, 228, 229] Hummel and Flory[42] used empirical force field methods to evaluate the conformational energy. However, the main unknown in this technique is the value of the energy of electron delocalization and conjugative effects between the phenylene ring and the amide or ester group. In the latter work,[42] the energy of electron delocalization was chosen as optimizing agreement of the torsional minima with torsion angles observed in the crystals of parent molecules. The approach of Lauprêtre and Monnerie[228, 229] was somewhat different: the evaluation of the conformational energies of model compounds was performed by the PCILO method,[20] which accounts

Ph—$\overset{\alpha_1}{|}$—CONH$_2$	

Structures:

$\text{(ring)} \overset{\alpha_1}{\text{—}} \text{CONH}_2$

$\text{NH}_2\text{CO} \overset{\alpha_1}{\text{—}} \text{(ring)} \overset{\alpha_2}{\text{—}} \text{CONH}_2$

$\text{(ring)} \overset{\beta_1}{\text{—}} \text{NHCHO}$

$\text{(ring)} \overset{\beta_1}{\text{—}} \text{NH} - \text{C(CH}_3)\text{O}$

$\text{(ring)} \overset{\alpha_1}{\text{—}} \text{CONH} \overset{\beta_1}{\text{—}} \text{(ring)}$

$\text{(ring)} \overset{\alpha_1}{\text{—}} \text{CONH} \overset{\beta_1}{\text{—}} \text{(ring)} \overset{\alpha_2}{\text{—}} \text{CONH}_2$

$\text{(ring)} \overset{\beta_1}{\text{—}} \text{NHCO} \overset{\alpha_1}{\text{—}} \text{(ring)} \overset{\alpha_2}{\text{—}} \text{CONH}_2$

$\text{(ring)} \overset{\alpha_1}{\text{—}} \text{CONH} \overset{\beta_1}{\text{—}} \text{(ring)} \overset{\alpha_2}{\text{—}} \text{CONH} \overset{\beta_2}{\text{—}} \text{(ring)} \overset{\alpha_3}{\text{—}} \text{CONH}_2$

$\text{COHNH} \overset{\beta_1}{\text{—}} \text{(ring)} \overset{\beta_2}{\text{—}} \text{NHCO} \overset{\alpha_2}{\text{—}} \text{(ring)} \overset{\alpha_3}{\text{—}} \text{CONH} \overset{\beta_3}{\text{—}} \text{(ring)} \overset{\beta_4}{\text{—}} \text{NHCOH}$

$\text{NH}_2\text{CO} \overset{\alpha_1}{\text{—}} \text{(ring)} \overset{\alpha_2}{\text{—}} \text{CONH} \overset{\beta_2}{\text{—}} \text{(ring)} \overset{\beta_3}{\text{—}} \text{NHCO} \overset{\alpha_3}{\text{—}} \text{(ring)} \overset{\alpha_4}{\text{—}} \text{CONH}_2$

*Reproduced by permission from Ref. 228.

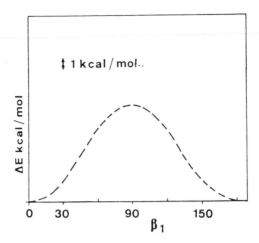

FIGURE 12
Conformational energy for rotation of the NHCO group about the
C_{ar}—N bond. β_1 is defined in Table 3. (Reproduced with permission
from Ref. 229.)

for both steric and conjugative effects and had already given satisfactory
results for nicotinamides,[230] nucleic acids, and a number of aminoacid
residues of proteins.[11]

The model molecules used to infer the conformational properties of
PPDT and PBA in Ref. 228 are listed in Table 3. Of course, in agreement
with Tsvetkov and Shtennikova,[227] from an equilibrium point of view, PCILO
conformational calculations on isolated molecules gave evidence of rigid
units in the chain, such as CO—NH, whereas ϕ—CO and ϕ—NH were
found to obey free-rotation statistics. The latter result is due to the symmetry
of the potentials affecting rotations about the phenylene axes, with respect to
the conformation in which the phenylene ring and the adjacent amide group
are coplanar, and to the fact that alteration of these rotations by 180° entails
only a negligible change in the potential. On the other hand, PCILO
calculations revealed some different characteristics of the ϕ—CO and
ϕ—NH bonds: with regard to internal rotation about the C_{ar}—N bond, as
shown in Fig. 12, the minimum-energy geometry is sharply defined; the ability
of the phenyl ring to oscillate about its equilibrium conformation is low and
the energy barrier is high (9 kcal mol^{-1}). In the case of the internal rotation
about the C_{ar}—CO bond, the shape of the conformational energy curve
(Fig. 13) is much flatter; thus, the phenyl ring may adopt a large number of
equilibrium conformations and is characterized by a higher entropy. The
ability of the phenyl ring to oscillate is thus greater, and the height of the
energy barrier is only 2 kcal mol^{-1}. Therefore, on an equilibrium basis, the
main difference between these two units originates from their entropies. One

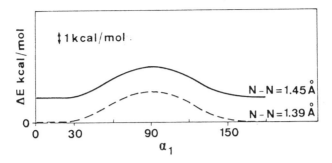

FIGURE 13

Conformational energy, calculated for two values of the N—N bond length, for rotation of the CONH group about the C_{ar}—CO bond. α_1 is defined in Table 3. (Reproduced with permission from Ref. 229.)

Table 4

Model Molecules Used to Infer the Conformational Properties of Aromatic Polyamide Oxamides and Polyamide Hydrazides*

$$\langle \bigcirc \rangle\!\!-\!\!\underset{\beta_1}{NHCO}\!\!-\!\!\underset{\gamma_1}{CONH_2}$$

$$\langle \bigcirc \rangle\!\!-\!\!\underset{\beta_1}{NHCO}\!\!-\!\!\underset{\gamma_1}{CONH}\!\!-\!\!\underset{\beta_2}{\langle \bigcirc \rangle}$$

$$NH_2CO\!\!-\!\!\underset{\gamma_1}{CONH}\!\!-\!\!\underset{\beta_1}{\langle \bigcirc \rangle}\!\!-\!\!\underset{\beta_2}{NHCO}\!\!-\!\!\underset{\gamma_2}{CONH_2}$$

$$\langle \bigcirc \rangle\!\!-\!\!\underset{\alpha_1}{CONH}\!\!-\!\!\underset{\delta_1}{NHCOCH_3}$$

$$\langle \bigcirc \rangle\!\!-\!\!\underset{\alpha_1}{CONH}\!\!-\!\!\underset{\delta_1}{NHCO}\!\!-\!\!\underset{\alpha_2}{\langle \bigcirc \rangle}$$

$$CH_3CONH\!\!-\!\!\underset{\delta_1}{NHCO}\!\!-\!\!\underset{\alpha_1}{\langle \bigcirc \rangle}\!\!-\!\!\underset{\alpha_2}{CONH}\!\!-\!\!\underset{\delta_2}{NHCOCH_3}$$

*Reproduced by permission from Ref. 229.

41

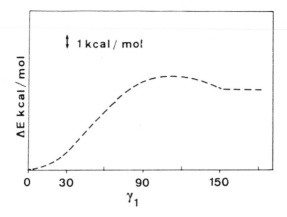

FIGURE 14
Conformational energy for rotation about the oxamide linkage. γ_1 is defined in Table 4. (Reproduced with permission from Ref. 229.)

can thus expect the two moieties ϕ—CO and ϕ—NH not to play the same role in the polymers in which they are found.

These PCILO calculations have been extended to aromatic polyamide oxamides and polyamide hydrazides.[229] The model molecules studied in Ref. 229 are listed in Table 4. Apart from the ϕ—CO and ϕ—NH units, they also contain NH—NH and CO—CO linkages. The energy curve for torsion about the oxamide bond in the planar conformation of the ϕ—NH—C=O unit is given in Fig. 14. The CO—CO group is confined to a single conformation, which is responsible for the rigidity; the equilibrium geometry is well-defined, and the calculated energy barrier is 7.0 kcal mol^{-1}. Therefore, the oxamide linkage appears as a rigid segment. This result is in contrast with that obtained from the NH—NH unit (Fig. 15), which shows a flat minimum. Hence, the NH—NH group can adopt numerous conformations and oscillations are likely to occur. The energy barrier for the torsion about the NH—NH bond is relatively low: it lies in the range 3–5 kcal mol^{-1} according to the value assumed for the N—N bond length.

Therefore, results derived from conformational energy calculations on isolated molecules tend to indicate that the constitutive units of aromatic polyamides, polyamide hydrazides, and polyamide oxamides may be classified into rigid groups, such as CO—NH and CO—CO, and flexible ones, either of low entropy, such as NH—ϕ—NH, or of higher entropy, such as NH—NH and ϕ—CO. When intermolecular interactions are present, as shown by the example of the benzanilide–water system, also studied by the PCILO method,[229] one observes a sharpening of the potential energy wells together with an increase of the energy barriers. However, the C_{ar}—CO bond is still characterized by a relatively low entropy, compared to the C_{ar}—N bond.

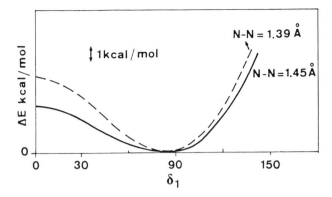

FIGURE 15
Conformational energy, calculated for two values of the N—N
bond length, for rotation about the N—N bond in
$C_6H_5CONH—NHCOCH_3$. δ_1 is defined in Table 4; α_1 is taken as
zero. (Reproduced with permission from Ref. 229.)

4.2.2. RELATION TO MESOGENIC CHARACTER IN SOLUTION

Results reported above have shown that the terephthaloyl unit is a
high-entropy group. Since the CO—ϕ—CO segments are not chiefly responsible for the chain stiffness, they can be replaced to a large extent by
CO—R—CO units having the same length and a high entropy without
destroying the ability of the polymers to yield liquid-crystalline solutions. For
example, when R is the flexible tetramethylene unit $(CH_2)_4$, the ordered
copolyamide with the recurring unit:

$$-CO-\langle\bigcirc\rangle-CO-NH-\langle\bigcirc\rangle-NH-CO$$

$$-(CH_2)_4-CO-NH-\langle\bigcirc\rangle-NH-$$

and the statistical copolyamides with the recurring units:

$$\left[CO-\langle\bigcirc\rangle-CO\right]_a \quad \left[NH-\langle\bigcirc\rangle-NH\right]_b$$

$$\left[NH-\langle\bigcirc\rangle-NH-CO-(CH_2)_4-CO-NH-\langle\bigcirc\rangle-NH\right]_c$$

where $a + b + 3c = 0.1$, and:

$$+CO-(CH_2\ _4-CO+_a$$

$$\left[CO-\left\langle\bigcirc\right\rangle-CO\right]_b \quad \left[NH-\left\langle\bigcirc\right\rangle-NH\right]_c$$

with $a/b < 2$, all yield mesomorphic solutions in H_2SO_4 when the polymer concentration is 15 to 20% (w/w).[231] Similarly, when R is $(CH_2)_4$ or the *trans*-cyclohexane group in the copolyamides containing the recurring units:

$$+CO-(CH_2)_4-CO+_a$$

$$\left[CO-\left\langle tH\right\rangle-CO\right]_b \quad \left[NH-\left\langle\bigcirc\right\rangle-NH\right]_c$$

the critical concentration C_p^* at which anisotropic solutions are first observed increases with the amount of flexible tetramethylene units: $C_p^* = 14\%$ (w/w) for $a/(a + b + c) = 0.1$ and $C_p^* = 17\%$ (w/w) for $a/(a + b + c) = 0.25$.[231] Thus, the presence of numerous high-entropy units does not prevent these copolyamides from yielding anisotropic phases. However, it must be noted that the different R groups exhibit comparable geometries so that, to a first approximation, intermolecular hydrogen bonding is a nearly constant parameter.

On the other hand, from the low entropy of the *p*-phenylenediamine units compared with that of the terephthaloyl group, one can expect modifications on exchanging such groups with groups of higher entropy. For example, the ordered copolyamide with the recurring unit[231]:

$$-CO-(CH_2)_4-CO-NH-\left\langle\bigcirc\right\rangle-CO$$

$$-NH-\left\langle\bigcirc\right\rangle-NH-CO-\left\langle\bigcirc\right\rangle-NH-$$

in which $(CH_2)_4$ replaces high-entropy units, is optically anisotropic in solution, whereas the ordered copolymer with the recurring unit:

$$-CO-\left\langle\bigcirc\right\rangle-CO-NH-\left\langle\bigcirc\right\rangle-CO-NH$$

$$-(CH_2)_4-NH-CO-\left\langle\bigcirc\right\rangle-NH-$$

which is identical to the previous one except for the introduction of the flexible $(CH_2)_4$ groups in place of low-entropy segments, exhibits no mesogenic character under comparable experimental conditions. The role of the $NH—\phi—NH$ groups is emphasized by the example of the copolyamide of the previous polymer and PPDT, whose recurring units are:

$$\left[CO-\bigcirc-CO\right]_a$$

$$\left[NH-\bigcirc-CO-NH-(CH_2)_4-NH-CO-\bigcirc-NH\right]_b$$

$$\left[NH-\bigcirc-NH\right]_c$$

The presence of 10–40% of low-entropy $NH—\phi—NH$ segments restores the mesogenic property.[231] Other examples underlining the role of low-entropy $NH—\phi—NH$ units in relation with the mesogenic character can be found in Ref. 229.

The $NH—NH$ bond is characterized by a relatively high entropy and flexibility. At the same time, it does not seem to favor the formation of liquid-crystalline solutions. For example, unlike PBA, PPDT, and other polyamides, the polyterephthalamide of p-amino benzhydrazide[232]:

$$-NH-\bigcirc-CO-NH-NH-CO-\bigcirc-CO-$$

does not yield anisotropic solutions at rest at the expected concentrations.[233] This failure, observed by Ciferri, is not entirely corroborated by recent values of persistence lengths (Chapter 2). On the other hand, polyamides containing the rigid $CO—CO$ unit, such as the polymers having the repeating units:

$$-NH-\bigcirc-NH-CO-CO-NH-\bigcirc-NH-$$

$$-CO-\bigcirc-NH-CO-CO-NH-\bigcirc-CO-$$

and:

$$-NH-\bigcirc-NH-CO-\bigcirc-NH-CO-CO-NH-\bigcirc-CO-$$

yield mesomorphic phases above rather low critical polymer concentration.[234]

Although very qualitative and limited to the specific series of aromatic and aryl-aliphatic polyamides, results reported in Ref. 229 indicate that there exists a relationship between the amount of low-entropy units and the mesogenic character of the solutions.

4.2.3. MOMENTS OF THE END-TO-END VECTORS FOR AROMATIC AND ARYL-ALIPHATIC POLYAMIDES

On the basis of structural data on model compounds and torsional potentials used for conformational energy calculations, Erman et al.[43] have calculated the moments of the end-to-end vector of PBA and PPDT as a function of chain length. The persistence vector has been found to be dominated by its component along the phenylene axis. The transverse component in the plane of this axis and the amide group is negligible owing to the approximate mutual independence of torsions about a given phenylene axis. The third component is equal to zero from symmetry considerations. For an infinite chain, these calculations gave a magnitude of the persistence vector on the order of 400 Å for both PBA and PPDT. Using light scattering and viscosity techniques, Arpin and Strazielle found persistence lengths in the range 400–600 Å and 150–200 Å for PBA and PPDT in 96% sulfuric acid, respectively.[216, 217] Flow birefringence studies by Tsvetkov and Shtennikova[227] yielded persistence lengths of 320 and 200 Å for the corresponding systems. It must be noted that more recent data (Chapter 2) do not show good agreement between calculated and measured values, and that theory fails to account for the differences between the persistence lengths observed for PBA and PPDT.[43]

4.3. Poly(*p*-phenylene Benzo-*bis*-oxazole) and Poly(*p*-phenylene Benzo-*bis*-thiazole) Chains

Energy calculations have also been used by Welsch et al.[94, 235–245] to investigate the conformational properties of poly(*p*-phenylene benzo-*bis*-oxazole) (PBO) and poly(*p*-phenylene benzo-*bis*-thiazole) (PBT) chains. Results obtained on this series of polymers have already been reviewed by Welsch.[245]

4.3.1. ISOLATED MODEL COMPOUNDS OF PBO AND PBT

The first step of these studies was to consider the cis and trans forms of isolated model compounds of PBO and PBT:

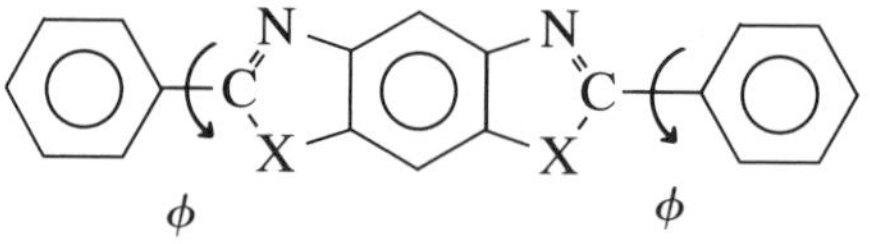

with X = O (PBO model compound) or X = S (PBT model compound).[236, 240] In these molecules, the conformational flexibility about the phenylene group

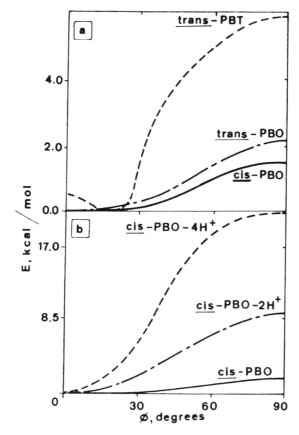

FIGURE 16
Dependence of the CNDO/2 calculated conformational energy on
the torsional angle ϕ. (a) cis-PBO, trans-PBO and trans-PBT model
compounds. (Reproduced with permission from Ref. 245.) (b)
Unprotonated form and the diprotonated and tetraprotonated ions
of the cis-PBO model compound. (Reproduced with permission
from Ref. 245.)

was described by the internal rotation angles ϕ. Intramolecular conformational energy calculations using standard semiempirical potential energy
functions performed on the cis and trans segments[236] have shown that the
lowest energy conformations of cis- and trans-PBO correspond to the coplanar geometry ($\phi = 0°$), in agreement with experiments on the corresponding
model compounds in the crystalline state.[246] As shown in Fig. 16a, similar
results have been found by using CNDO/2 calculations.[240] Besides, the
barriers to rotation away from coplanarity evidenced by the CNDO/2 method
reflect the importance of the conjugation effects between the aromatic
moieties that dominate the steric repulsions between the o-hydrogen atom
on the phenylene group and nearby atoms within the heterocyclic part.[240] In

the case of the *trans*-PBT model, whereas there is a lack of quantitative agreement between experimental data and results derived from empirical calculations,[236] which do not account for conjugative effects, the CNDO/2 calculations[240] yield a preferred angle $\phi = 20°$ (Fig. 16a) in good agreement with experiment.[247] As also shown in Fig. 16a, the barrier to rotation is quite high. However, it must be considered as an upper estimate since geometry optimization was not available for sulfur-containing molecules.[240]

Model compounds of the *cis*-PBT polymer have been shown to assume a slightly "bowed" geometry in the crystalline state.[247] Total energy CNDO/2 calculations performed on both the bowed and planar conformations of the *cis*-PBT model yielded a large energy difference in favor of the bowed form, indicating that energy decreases are realized as a result of bowing.[240]

4.3.2. INTERMOLECULAR INTERACTIONS IN PBO AND PBT MODEL COMPOUNDS: CRYSTALLINE STATE AND ACIDIC SOLUTIONS

In a second step, intermolecular interactions have been taken into account to describe both the crystalline state[237] and the solutions of PBO and PBT in very strong acids.[237,238] To get a deeper understanding of the crystalline chain packing, calculations were carried out on a pair of chains of a given type oriented in either their planar (*cis*- and *trans*-PBO) or nonplanar (*trans*-PBT) conformations.[237] The first chain was one repeat unit long, and the second one was assigned a series of lengths in an attempt to make the interaction energies as realistic as possible. Four repeat units were found appropriate in this regard. Semiempirical conformational energy calculations including both intramolecular and intermolecular interactions have shown that, for pairs of chains above one another, the chains are out of register by 3.0 Å in the case of the two PBO polymers (which would place a phenylene group of the upper chain over the bond bridging the two ring systems of the repeat unit of the lower chain) and by 1.5 Å in the case of *trans*-PBT.[237] Although approximate, these results are in at least qualitative agreement with x-ray data.[247] For the vertical spacings, the calculated results are in excellent agreement with the experimental value of 3.5 Å for the three model compounds.[247,248] Densities of the PBO and PBT polymers in the crystalline state estimated from the chain packing derived from these calculations[237] were also found to be in good agreement with data obtained on the model compounds.[247,248] The way they depend on the structure of the repeat unit indicates that the higher density of the PBT polymer is due to the higher atomic weight of S relative to O, rather than to more efficient chain packing.

When these polymers are dissolved in the very strong acids that are their only solvents, protonation of the chains must be considered. To account for such a phenomenon, the CNDO/2 method was used to derive charge distributions for protonated segments, whereas semiempirical potential functions were used to estimate the magnitudes of the interchain coulombic repulsions.[237] Results obtained from these calculations indicated that protonation of the chains should greatly decrease the intermolecular attractions, in agreement with the fact that only very strong acids can solubilize these polymers.[249, 250] The effects of protonation on the conformations of the PBO chain were investigated by using geometry-optimized CNDO/2 calculations.[238] For all the chains under study, i.e., the unprotonated chain, the diprotonated and tetraprotonated ions of the *cis*-PBO model compound, the preferred conformations were found identical. They correspond to $\phi = 0°$. However, as shown in Fig. 16b, the barrier to rotation away from the coplanar geometry increases on increasing protonation.[238] These results are in striking agreement with those obtained by the PCILO method.[229] The order of protonation within the *cis*-PBO model compound was also predicted by using geometry-optimized CNDO/2 calculations.[239] Protonation should occur in the order N, N, O, O, consistent with the greater basicity of nitrogen relative to oxygen.

4.3.3. INSERTION OF "SWIVELS"

As mentioned above, PBO and PBT polymers are soluble only in the strongest acids, and therefore they are very difficult to process into usable films and fibers. However, they can be rendered more tractable by the insertion of a limited number of units, or "swivels," which impart some flexibility to the chains. As an example, the "double-oxygen swivel" shown below:

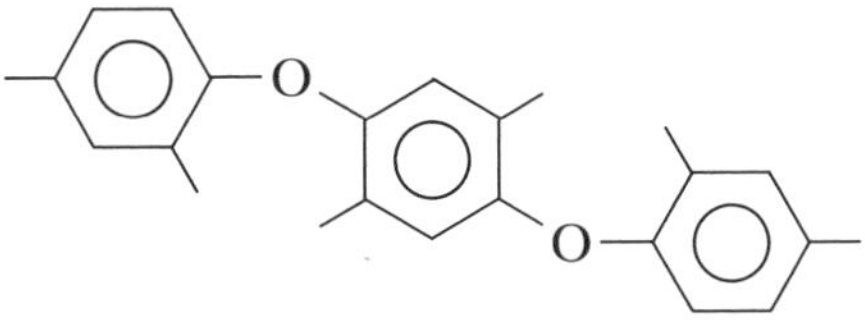

when inserted in a PBO or PBT chain, should decrease the rigidity of the chain but still permit occurrences of nearly parallel arrangements of the remaining PBO and PBT chains.[94, 235] With the same swivel and rotation about one of the C—O bond, a colinear continuation of the chain could also be realized. Intramolecular conformational energy calculations using standard semiempirical potential energy functions performed on swivels of the type $\phi—X—\phi—X—\phi$, where X is either O, S, Se, or Te, have shown that the sulfur swivel has the advantage both in terms of equilibrium flexibility (lower energy and thus more accessible conformations) and of dynamic flexibility (lower barriers between energy minima).[235] Similar studies were performed with X = CO, SO$_2$, CH$_2$, C(CF$_3$)$_2$.[235] In terms of both thermal stability[251] and conformational flexibility,[235] the most interesting units should be O, S, C(CF$_3$)$_2$, and CO.

In some of the above swivels, interactions between the aromatic hydrogen atoms α to the swivel linkage can force the swivel out of the coplanar conformation. These interactions are strongly reduced when one or both of the phenylenes in the swivel is replaced by a pyridylene group with the nitrogen in the ring α to the swivel linkage.[245] Such swivels have been shown to have an increased flexibility.

The protonation of nitrogen-containing swivels has also been investigated by CNDO/2 calculations. Large effects on the conformational characteristics have been evidenced by this method.[94]

4.3.4. THE AAPBO AND ABPBO POLYMERS

Recently, interest has been paid to more flexible analogs of PBO and PBT, such as poly(5,5'-bibenzoxazole-2,2'-diyl-1,4-phenylene) (AAPBO):

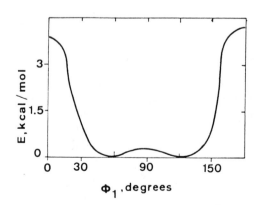

and poly(2,5-benzoxazole) (ABPBO):

Geometry-optimized CNDO/2 calculations have been carried out on AAPBO and ABPBO chain segments.[242, 243] Conformational energies as a function of ϕ_1 and ϕ_2 in AAPBO are plotted in Figs. 17 and 18. Concerning the internal rotation about ϕ_1, a broad energy minimum is observed in the

FIGURE 17
Dependence of the CNDO/2 calculated conformational energy on the torsional angle ϕ_1 in AAPBO. (Reproduced with permission from Ref. 245.)

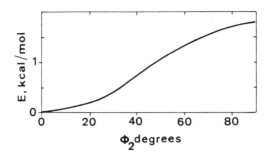

FIGURE 18
Dependence of the CNDO/2 calculated conformational energy on
the torsional angle ϕ_2 in AAPBO. (Reproduced with permission
from Ref. 245.)

region 60–120° (within the 0–180° conformational energy space). On either
side of this minimum, the energy rises sharply and continuously, reaching an
energy barrier of 3.6 kcal mol^{-1}. As expected from the environment in which
the ϕ_1 rotation takes place, some similarities with the conformational energy
map of biphenyl can be noted.[94] For the ϕ_2 rotation, calculations have
indicated a preference for the coplanar conformations with a maximum value
of the conformational energy of 1.8 kcal mol^{-1} at $\phi_2 = 90°$, in agreement
with results obtained on the PBO unit. Taking into account the values of
both ϕ_1 and ϕ_2 angles, the AAPBO molecule is predicted to prefer a
nonplanar conformation.[242, 243]

Dependence of the CNDO/2 calculated conformational energy on the
angle ϕ of ABPBO is shown in Fig. 19.[242, 243] The preferred conformation is
the coplanar one, with a maximum energy of 1.6 kcal mol^{-1} for the perpen-

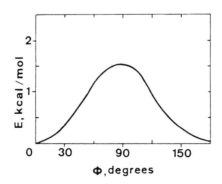

FIGURE 19
Dependence of the CNDO/2 calculated conformational energy on
the torsional angle ϕ in ABPBO. (Reproduced with permission from
Ref. 245.)

dicular form. Again, these results are in agreement with those obtained from both theoretical[241] and x-ray crystallographic[248] studies of the analogous PBO polymer model compounds. They are also consistent with the coplanarity or near coplanarity observed for the ABPBO in the crystalline state.[252]

The conformational differences between the AAPBO and ABPBO are satisfactorily reproduced by these calculations. The AAPBO molecule should take a nonplanar conformation, whereas the ABPBO assumes a coplanar one. Interestingly enough, the liquid crystalline behavior is observed for solutions of ABPBO but not for those of AAPBO.[253, 254]

5. CONCLUDING REMARKS

Selected examples presented in this chapter have clearly shown that conformational energy calculations can be considered a powerful tool for predicting the dependence of a number of properties of LCP's on their chemical structure. In this regard, it is of interest to distinguish effects that are mainly due to the very nature of the chain and can be dealt with, at least as a first approximation, by conformational energy calculations on isolated model compounds, and effects related to packing properties for which intermolecular interactions have to be taken into account in the energy evaluation.

In spite of their relative simplicity, conformational energy calculations on isolated molecules have proved most useful for investigating the ability of aromatic polyamides, polyamide hydrazides, and polyamide oxamides to yield lyotropic phases in acidic solutions. In the particular example of this series, in which intermolecular interactions are a nearly constant parameter, the lyotropic character of the solutions has been shown to be related to the amount of low-entropy constitutive units.[229] In the case of thermotropic polymers, the approach developed by Yoon and Brückner[208] is of special interest. By examining the distribution of chain sequence extension for three types of MP's, they found that characteristics of chain sequence extension and extended conformers relate very closely to the experimental results of isotropic–nematic transitions of the polymers. Moreover, detailed conformational order of flexible segments in nematic states can be deduced by matching the experimental results of enthalpy and entropy changes with those estimated from the conformational selection on the basis of chain sequence extension. The simple conclusion which can be reached from these studies is that the mesomorphic character of the polymers is clearly associated with the existence of low-energy extended conformations of the flexible units. Further investigation in this direction would likely lead to a deeper understanding of the phenomena responsible for the existence, nature, and stability of mesomorphic states in polymers.

Among the numerous data that can be derived from single-chain conformational energy calculations, the end-to-end distances and persistence vectors are of particular interest in the case of LCP's. Calculated and experimental data emphasizing the relation between the persistence length and the liquid crystal formation are found in this chapter and other chapters of this volume. The paper by Coulter and Windle[255] is one of the most recent examples of such studies. It defines a "rodlikeness" parameter (persistence length to diameter ratio, the persistence length being defined as the mean distance the chain travels in its mean direction from a mean position on the chain), which is shown to correlate with LC phase formation in the bulk for a variety of polymers. Although one may expect some uncertainty as to the prediction capacity in the "borderline" region, the results obtained by Coulter and Windle suggest that this method can be used as a tool for screening formulation for polymers with LC properties. Another very recent approach is due to Jung and Schürmann,[256, 257] who calculated the radius of gyration and persistence length of some polyesters on the basis of two different theoretical methods: the classical rotational isomeric model of Williams and Flory[158] described in this chapter, and the new technique of molecular dynamics. The results obtained by molecular dynamics agree acceptably with experimental data.

While such calculations on isolated molecules are fruitful points of departure, further studies are needed to describe the solution, melt or crystalline states in which intermolecular forces compete with the intramolecular forces. As reported in this chapter, the crystalline chain packing and protonation in strong acids were successfully investigated by Welsh et al.[237–239] for heterocyclic MP's. Quite recently, Rutledge and Suter[258] realized a simulation of potentially near-crystalline materials with a model built upon the packing of conformationally flexible chains on a regular array. Again, the energy is composed of two parts: the predominant term focuses on the short-range distortion effects characteristic of local chain packing, with the superposition of a correction term that assumes perfect crystal periodicities to reflect the compressive effects of long-range interactions. The total potential energy of the system is minimized simultaneously with respect to both intra- and intermolecular degrees of freedom. Analysis of poly(p-phenylene terephthalamide) by this method points out the existence of a number of polymorphs of comparable potential energy, each realizing the highly correlated orientation of chains into hydrogen-bonded sheets but differing significantly in the packing of sheets into three-dimensional structures. It would be of interest to develop this stimulating technique in order to investigate the elastic moduli of LCP's and complement the simpler method of Tashiro et al.[240] and Northolt and Van Aartsen.[259]

Finally, although they are beyond the scope of this chapter, it should be noted that Monte Carlo simulations of the rod–coil transitions in semiflexible linear sequences have been reported.[260, 261] They accounted for the transition from the coil to the fully extended rod state with increasing concentration. However, up to now, little attention[262] has been given to estimating the mean-square end-to-end length of the sequence, the mean-square radius of gyration, the orientational distributions, the development of hairpins, and length and flexibility dependence, all of which being of considerable theoretical interest: the study of these aspects represents one of the principal motivations for future investigations.

REFERENCES

1. G.W. Gray, in *Liquid Crystals and Plastic Crystals*, Vol. 1, G.W. Gray, P.A. Winsor, eds., Horwood, Chichester, 1974, p. 103.
2. G.W. Gray, in *The Molecular Physics of Liquid Crystals*, G.R. Luckhurst, G.W. Gray, eds., Academic Press, New York, 1979, Ch. 12, p. 263.
3. S. Marcelja, *J. Chem. Phys.*, **1974**, *60*, 3599.
4. P.J. Flory, A. Abe, *Macromolecules*, **1978**, *11*, 1119, 1122.
5. P.J. Flory, R.S. Frost, *Macromolecules*, **1978**, *11*, 1126, 1134.
6. P.J. Flory, *Macromolecules*, **1978**, *11*, 1138, 1141.
7. R.R. Matheson Jr., P.J. Flory, *Macromolecules*, **1981**, *14*, 954.
8. A. Yu Grosberg, A.R. Khokhlov, *Adv. Polym. Sci.*, **1981**, *4*, 53.
9. A.R. Khokhlov, A.N. Semenov, *Physica*, **1981**, *108A*, 546.
10. A. Golebiewski, A. Parczewski, *Chem. Rev.*, **1974**, *74*, 519.
11. O. Sinanoglu, *Modern Quantum Chemistry*, Academic Press, London, 1965; L. Salem, *The Molecular Orbital Theory of Conjugated Systems*, W.A. Benjamen, New York, 1966; B. Pullman, *Quantum Mechanics of Molecular Conformations*, Wiley-Interscience, New York, 1975.
12. G.H.F. Diercksen, ed., *Computational Technics in Quantum Chemistry and Molecular Physics*, NATO A.S.I. Series, Reidel, Dordrecht (Holland), 1975.
13. R. Hoffmann, *J. Chem. Phys.*, **1963**, *39*, 1397.
14. M. Wolfsberg, L. Helmholtz, *J. Chem. Phys.*, **1952**, *20*, 837.
15. J.A. Pople, D.L. Beveridge, *Approximate Molecular Orbital Theory*, McGraw-Hill, New York, 1970; R. Daudel, C. Sandorfy, *Semiempirical Wave-Mechanical Calculations on Polyatomic Molecules*, Yale University Press, New Haven, 1971; J.N. Murrell, A.J. Harget, *Semiempirical Self-consistent-field Molecular Orbital Theory of Molecules*, Wiley-Interscience, London, 1972.
16. R.J. Boyd, M.A. Whitehead, *J. Chem. Soc.*, **1972**, 82.
17. B. Tinland, *Theoret. Chim. Acta*, **1968**, *11*, 452.
18. S. Ljünggren, G. Wettermark, *Theoret. Chim. Acta*, **1970**, *19*, 326.
19. S. Diner, J.P. Malrieu, P. Claverie, *Theoret. Chim. Acta*, **1969**, *13*, 1, 18.
20. S. Diner, J.P. Malrieu, F. Jordan, M. Gilbert, *Theoret. Chim. Acta*, **1969**, *15*, 100.
21. F. Jordan, M. Gilbert, J.P. Malrieu, U. Pincelli, *Theoret. Chim. Acta*, **1969**, *15*, 211.
22. (a) I. Amdur, E.A. Mason, A.L. Harkness, *J. Chem. Phys.*, **1954**, *22*, 1071; (b) E.A. Mason, *J. Chem. Phys.*, **1955**, *23*, 49.
23. T.L. Hill, *J. Chem. Phys.*, **1946**, *14*, 465; **1948**, *16*, 938.
24. F.H. Westheimer, *J. Chem. Phys.*, **1947**, *15*, 252.
25. A.I. Kitaygorodsky, V.G. Dashevsky, *Teor. Eksp. Khim.*, **1967**, *3*, 35, 43.
26. C.A. Coulson, S. Senent, *J. Chem. Soc.*, **1955**, 1813.
27. C.A. Coulson, C.W. Haigh, *Tetrahedron*, **1963**, *19*, 527.
28. F.J. Adrian, *J. Chem. Phys.*, **1958**, *28*, 608.
29. T.H. Goodwin, D.A. Morton-Blake, *Theoret. Chim. Acta*, **1963**, *1*, 458.
30. D.E. Polansky, *Monatsh. Chem.*, **1963**, *94*, 22.
31. A. Golebiewski, A. Parczewski, *Z. Naturforsch.*, **1970**, *A25*, 1710; **1971**, *A26*, 180.

32. A. Golebiewski, A. Parczewski, *Acta Phys. Pol.*, *A*, **1970**, *37*, 879; **1972**, *41*, 727.
33. R. Pariser, R.G. Parr, *J. Chem. Phys.*, **1953**, *21*, 466, 767.
34. J.A. Pople, *Trans. Faraday Soc.*, **1953**, *49*, 1375.
35. I. Fischer-Hjalmars, *Tetrahedron*, **1963**, *19*, 1805.
36. M.J.S. Dewar, A.J. Harget, *Proc. Roy. Soc. Lond.*, *Ser. A*, **1970**, *315*, 443; M.J.S. Dewar, C. de Llano, *J. Am. Chem. Soc.*, **1969**, *91*, 789; M.J.S. Dewar, T. Morita, *J. Am. Chem. Soc.*, **1969**, *91*, 796.
37. A.J. Hopfinger, *Conformational Properties of Macromolecules*, Academic Press, New York, 1973.
38. M.V. Volkenstein, *Configurational Statistics of Polymeric Chains*, Interscience, New York, 1963.
39. P.J. Flory, *Statistical Mechanics of Chain Molecules*, Interscience, New York, 1969.
40. K. Tashiro, M. Kobayashi, H. Tadokoro, *Macromolecules*, **1977**, *10*, 413.
41. H. Tadokoro, *Structure of Crystalline Polymers*, Wiley, New York 1979, Ch. 7, section 7.10.2.
42. J.P. Hummel, P.J. Flory, *Macromolecules*, **1980**, *13*, 479.
43. B. Erman, P.J. Flory, J.P. Hummel, *Macromolecules*, **1980**, *13*, 484.
44. D. Rigby, R.J. Roe, *J. Chem. Phys.*, **1987**, *87*, 7285.
45. D. Rigby, R.J. Roe, *J. Chem. Phys.*, **1988**, *89*, 5280.
46. P.R. Sundararajan, *Macromolecules*, **1978**, *11*, 256.
47. P. Corradini, V. Petraccone, B. Pirozzi, *Eur. Polym. J.*, **1986**, *19*, 235.
48. S.K. Tripathy, A.J. Hopfinger, P.L. Taylor, *J. Phys. Chem.*, **1981**, *85*, 1371.
49. H. Kusanagi, H. Tadokoro, Y. Chatani, K. Suehiro, *Macromolecules*, **1977**, *10*, 405.
50. D.R. Ferro, S. Brückner, *Macromolecules*, **1989**, *22*, 2359.
51. D.R. Ferro, S. Brückner, S.V. Meille, M. Ragazzi, *Macromolecules*, **1990**, *23*, 1676.
52. R.A. Sorensen, W.B. Liau, R.H. Boyd, *Macromolecules*, **1988**, *21*, 194.
53. R.A. Sorensen, W.B. Liau, L. Kesner, R.H. Boyd, *Macromolecules*, **1988**, *21*, 200.
54. B. Reck, H. Ringsdorf, *Makromol. Chem. Rapid Commun.*, **1985**, *6*, 291.
55. B. Reck, H. Ringsdorf, *Makromol. Chem. Rapid Commun.*, **1986**, *7*, 389.
56. J. Watanabe, M. Goto, T. Nagase, *Macromolecules*, **1987**, *20*, 298.
57. A. Blumstein, *Liquid Crystalline Order in Polymers*, Academic Press, New York, 1978.
58. A. Blumstein, *Polymeric Liquid Crystals*, Plenum, New York, 1985.
59. L. Chapoy, *Recent Advances in Liquid Crystalline Polymers*, Elsevier Applied Science, London, 1985.
60. A. Ciferri, W. Krigbaum, R. Meyer, *Polymer Liquid Crystals*, Academic Press, New York, 1982.
61. S.K. Varshney, *Rev. Macromol. Chem. Phys.*, **1986**, *C26*, 551.
62. N. Koide, *Mol. Cryst. Liq. Cryst.*, **1986**, *139*, 47.
63. T.S. Chung, *Polym. Eng. Sci.*, **1986**, *26*, 901.
64. H. Finkelmann, *Angew. Chem., Int. Ed. Engl.*, **1987**, *26*, 816.
65. D. Sek, *Acta Polym.*, **1988**, *39*, 599.
66. C. Noël, *Makromol. Chem. Macromol. Symp.*, **1988**, *22*, 95.
67. H. Hinov, *Mol. Cryst. Liq. Cryst.*, **1986**, *136*, 221.
68. C.K. Ober, J.I. Jin, R.W. Lenz, *Adv. Polym. Sci.*, **1984**, *59*, 103.
69. K.F. Wissbrun, *J. Rheol.*, **1981**, *25*, 619.
70. C.E. Chaffey, R.S. Porter, *J. Rheol.*, **1984**, *28*, 249; **1985**, *29*, 281.
71. M. Cox, in *Liquid Crystal Polymers*, R. Meredith, ed., RAPRA Report No. 4, Pergamon, Oxford, 1987.
72. H. Finkelmann, G. Rehage, *Adv. Polym. Sci.*, **1984**, *60/61*, 99.

73. V. Shibaev, N.A. Plate, *Adv. Polym. Sci.*, **1984**, *60/61*, 173.
74. H.J. Coles, in *Developments in Crystalline Polymers*, D.C. Bassett, ed., Elsevier Applied Science, Amsterdam, 1988, pp. 297–340.
75. C.B. McArdle, *Side Chain Liquid Crystal Polymers*, Blackie, Glasgow, 1989.
76. J. Preston, *Angew. Makromol. Chem.*, **1982**, *109/110*, 1.
77. W.J. Jackson, *Br. Polym. J.*, **1980**, *12*, 154; in *Contemporary Topics in Polymer Science*, Vol. 5, E.J. Vandenberg, ed., Plenum, New York, 1984, p. 177.
78. P. Meurisse, F. Lauprêtre, C. Noël, *Mol. Cryst. Liq. Cryst.*, **1984**, *110*, 41.
79. A.E. Tonelli, *J. Polym. Sci. Polym. Lett. Ed.*, **1973**, *11*, 441.
80. E. Saiz, J.P. Hummel, P.J. Flory, M. Plavsic, *J. Phys. Chem.*, **1981**, *85*, 3211.
81. P. Sedlacek, J. Stokr, B. Schneider, *Coll. Czech. Chem. Commun.*, **1981**, *46*, 1646.
82. F. Brisse, S. Perez, *Acta Crystallogr.*, *B*, **1976**, *32*, 2110.
83. A.D. Williams, P.J. Flory, *J. Polym. Sci.*, *A-2*, **1967**, *5*, 417.
84. A. Almenningen, O. Bastiansen, *Skr.*, *K. Nor. Vidensk. Selsk*, **1958**, *4*, 1; A. Almenningen, O. Bastiansen, L. Fernholt, B.N. Cyvin, S.J. Cyvin, S. Samdal, *J. Mol. Struct.*, **1985**, *128*, 59.
85. H. Suzuki, *Bull. Chem. Soc. Jpn.*, **1959**, *32*, 1340.
86. E.D. Schmid, B. Brosa, *J. Chem. Phys.*, **1972**, *56*, 6267.
87. O. Bastiansen, M. Traetteberg, *Tetrahedron*, **1962**, *17*, 147.
88. G. Robertson, *Nature (London)*, **1961**, *191*, 593.
89. J. Trotter, *Acta Crystallogr.*, **1961**, *14*, 1135.
90. A. Hargreaves, S.H. Rizvi, *Acta Crystallogr.*, **1962**, *15*, 365.
91. G.P. Charbonneau, Y. Delugeard, *Acta Crystallogr.*, *Sect. B*, **1976**, *32*, 1420.
92. H. Cailleau, J.L. Baudour, C.M.E. Zeyen, *Acta. Crystallogr.*, *Sect. B*, **1979**, *35*, 426.
93. H. Bonadeo, E. Burgos, *Acta Crystallogr.*, *Sect. A*, **1982**, *38*, 29.
94. W.J. Welsh, H.H. Jaffe, N. Kondo, J.E. Mark, *Makromol. Chem.*, **1982**, *183*, 801.
95. O. Bastiansen, S. Samdal, *J. Mol. Struct.*, **1985**, *128*, 115.
96. G. Häfelinger, C. Regelmann, *J. Comput. Chem.*, **1985**, *6*, 368.
97. G.L. Casalone, C. Mariani, A. Mugnoli, M. Simonetta, *Mol. Phys.*, **1968**, *15*, 339.
98. R. Stolevik, Ø. Thingstad, *J. Mol. Struct.*, **1984**, *106*, 333.
99. J. Kao, N.L. Allinger, *J. Am. Chem. Soc.*, **1977**, *99*, 975.
100. H.L. Lindner, *Tetrahedron*, **1974**, *30*, 1127.
101. F. Momicchioli, I. Baraldi, M.C. Bruni, *Chem. Phys.*, **1982**, *70*, 161.
102. H.J. Hofmann, P. Birner, *Z. Chem.*, **1975**, *15*, 23.
103. J.D. McKinney, K.E. Gottschalk, L. Pedersen, *J. Mol. Struct.*, *Theochem.*, **1983**, *104*, 445.
104. G.H. Penner, *J. Mol. Struct.*, *Theochem.*, **1986**, *137*, 191.
105. L.D. Field, S. Sternhell, *J. Am. Chem. Soc.*, **1981**, *103*, 738.
106. H.M. Rietveld, E.N. Maslen, C.J.B. Clews, *Acta Crystallogr.*, *Sect. B*, **1970**, *26*, 693.
107. I. Baraldi, G. Ponterini, *J. Mol. Struct.*, **1985**, *122*, 287.
108. A. Gamba, G.F. Tandardini, M. Simonetta, *Theoret. Chim. Acta*, **1973**, *29*, 335.
109. J.L. Baudour, H. Cailleau, W.B. Yelon, *Acta Crystallogr.*, *Sect. B*, **1977**, *33*, 1773.
110. B. Toudic, *Thèse de Doctorat de 3ème cycle*, Rennes, 1981.
111. B. Toudic, J. Gallier, P. Rivet, H. Cailleau, *Solid State Commun.*, **1983**, *47*, 291.
112. A. Ghanem, L. Bokobza, C. Noël, B. Marchon, *J. Mol. Struct.*, **1987**, *159*, 47.
113. M. Akiyama, *Spectrochim. Acta*, *A*, **1984**, *40*, 367.
114. J. Dale, *Acta Chem. Scand.*, **1957**, *11*, 650.
115. I.B. Berlman, H.O. Wirth, O.J. Steingraber, *J. Phys. Chem.*, **1971**, *75*, 318.
116. K. Razi Naqvi, J. Donatsch, U.P. Wild, *Chem. Phys. Lett.*, **1975**, *34*, 285.
117. O. Williams, *Chem. Phys. Lett.*, **1976**, *42*, 171.
118. R.J.W. Le Fèvre, A. Sundaram, K.M.S. Sundaram, *J. Chem. Soc.*, **1963**, 3180.

119. T. Kobayashi, *Bull. Chem. Soc. Jpn.*, **1983**, *56*, 3224.
120. N.I. Wakayama, *Chem. Phys. Lett.*, **1980**, *70*, 397.
121. S. Hino, T. Veszprémi, K. Ohno, H. Inokuchi, K. Seki, *Chem. Phys.*, **1982**, *71*, 135.
122. J. Murakami, K. Okuyama, M. Ito, *Bull. Chem. Soc. Jpn.*, **1982**, *55*, 3422.
123. A. Ghanem, C. Noël, *Mol. Cryst. Liq. Cryst.*, **1987**, *150B*, 447.
124. G. Zerbi, S. Sandroni, *Spectrochim. Acta*, **1968**, *24A*, 483.
125. G. Zannoni, G. Zerbi, *J. Chem. Phys.*, **1985**, *82*, 31.
126. C.P. Brock, M.S. Kuo, H.A. Levy, *Acta Crystallogr.*, *Sect. B*, **1978**, *34*, 981.
127. E.M. Aveyanov, V.A. Zhulkov, P.V. Adomenas, *J.E.T.P. Lett.*, **1981**, *33*, 249.
128. P. Tekely, F. Lauprêtre, L. Monnerie, *Macromolecules*, **1983**, *16*, 415.
129. P.J. Flory, G. Ronca, *Mol. Cryst. Liq. Cryst.*, **1979**, *54*, 289, 311
130. P. Meurisse, C. Noël, L. Monnerie, B. Fayolle, *Br. Polym. J.*, **1981**, *13*, 55.
131. L. Bosio, B. Fayolle, C. Friedrich, F. Lauprêtre, P. Meurisse, C. Noël, J. Virlet, in *Liquid Crystals and Ordered Fluids*, Vol. 4, A. Griffin, J. Johnson, eds., Plenum Press, New York, 1984, pp. 407–427.
132. W.R. Krigbaum, J. Asrar, H. Toriumi, A. Ciferri, J. Preston, *J. Polym. Sci., Polym. Lett. Ed.*, **1982**, *20*, 109.
133. W.R. Krigbaum, J. Watanabe, *Polymer*, **1983**, *24*, 1299.
134. C.J. Finder, M.G. Newton, N.L. Allinger, *Acta Crystallogr.*, *Sect. B*, **1974**, *30*, 411.
135. A. Hoekstra, P. Meertens, A. Vos, *Acta Crystallogr.*, *Sect. B*, **1975**, *31*, 2813.
136. J. Bernstein, K. Mirsky, *Acta Crystallogr.*, *Sect. A*, **1978**, *34*, 161.
137. J.A. Bouwstra, A. Schouter, J. Kroon, *Acta Crystallogr.*, *Sect. C*, **1984**, *40*, 428.
138. C.J. Brown, *Acta Crystallogr.*, *Sect. B*, **1966**, *21*, 146.
139. H.B. Bürgi, J.D. Dunitz, *Helv. Chim. Acta*, **1970**, *53*, 1747.
140. E. Haselbach, E. Heilbronner, *Helv. Chim. Acta*, **1975**, *58*, 800.
141. B. Scheuer-Lamalle, G. Durocher, *Can. J. Spectrosc.*, **1976**, *21*, 165.
142. H.B. Bürgi, J.D. Dunitz, *Chem. Commun.*, **1969**, 472.
143. G. Favini, D. Pitea, F. Zuccarello, *J. Chim. Phys.*, **1972**, *69*, 9.
144. H. Van Putten, J.W. Pavlik, *Tetrahedron*, **1971**, *27*, 3007.
145. D. Pitea, D. Grasso, G. Favini, *J. Mol. Struct.*, **1974**, *10*, 101.
146. K. Tabei, E. Saitou, *Bull. Chem. Soc. Jpn.*, **1969**, *42*, 1440.
147. N. Inamoto, *Tetrahedron Lett.*, **1974**, *41*, 3617.
148. M. Traetteberg, I. Hilmo, R.J. Abraham, S. Ljunggren, *J. Mol. Struct.*, **1978**, *48*, 395.
149. M. Traetteberg, E.B. Frantsen, F.C. Mijlhoff, A. Hoekstra, *J. Mol. Struct.*, **1975**, *26*, 57.
150. M. Traetteberg, I. Hilmo, K. Hagen, *J. Mol. Struct.*, **1977**, *39*, 231.
151. H. Perrin, J. Bergès, *J. Mol. Struct.*, *Theochem.*, **1981**, *76*, 299, 375.
152. J. Bicerano, H.A. Clark, *Macromolecules*, **1988**, *21*, 585, 597.
153. J.M. Adams, S.E. Morsi, *Acta Crystallogr.*, *Sect. B*, **1976**, *32*, 1345.
154. P. Coulter, A.H. Windle, *Macromolecules*, **1989**, *22*, 1129.
155. B.C. Laskowski, D. Y. Yoon, D. McLean, R.L. Jaffe, *Macromolecules*, **1988**, *21*, 1629.
156. P.R. Sundararajan, *Macromolecules*, **1989**, *22*, 2149.
157. D.Y. Yoon, P.J. Flory, unpublished work referred to by B. Erman, D.C. Marvin, P.A. Irvine and P.J. Flory, *Macromolecules*, **1982**, *15*, 664.
158. A.D. Williams, P.J. Flory, *J. Polym. Sci., Polym. Phys. Ed.*, **1968**, *6*, 1945.
159. F. Lauprêtre, L. Monnerie, *Eur. Polym. J.*, **1974**, *10*, 21.
160. V.A. Zubkov, T.M. Birshtein, I.S. Mileskaya, *J. Mol. Struct.*, **1975**, *27*, 139.
161. T. Kojima, *J. Phys. Soc. Jpn.*, **1960**, *15*, 284.
162. J. Boon, E.P. Magre, *Makromol. Chem.*, **1969**, *126*, 130.
163. V. Galasso, G. De Alti, A. Bigotto, *Tetrahedron*, **1971**, *27*, 6151.

164. E.S.W. Whittaker, *Acta Crystallogr.*, **1953**, *6*, 714.
165. B.J. Tabor, E.P. Magre, J. Boon, *Eur. Polym. J.*, **1971**, *7*, 1127.
166. F.K. Fong, *J. Chem. Phys.*, **1964**, *40*, 132.
167. A.E. Tonelli, *Macromolecules*, **1973**, *6*, 503; **1972**, *5*, 558.
168. V.A. Zubkov, T.M. Birshtein, I.S. Milevskaya, *Vysokom. Soedin, Ser. A*, **1974**, *16*, 16.
169. G.D. Patterson, P.J. Flory, *J. Chem. Soc., Faraday Trans 2*, **1972**, *68*, 1111.
170. A. Abe, J.E. Mark, *J. Am. Chem. Soc.*, **1976**, *98*, 6468.
171. E. Riande, *J. Polym. Sci., Polym. Phys. Ed.*, **1976**, *14*, 2231.
172. E. Riande, *Makromol. Chem.*, **1977**, *178*, 2001.
173. K.M. Kelly, G.D. Patterson, A.E. Tonelli, *Macromolecules*, **1977**, *10*, 859.
174. J.E. Mark, *J. Chem. Phys.*, **1977**, *67*, 3300.
175. A. Abe, R.L. Jernigan, P.J. Flory, *J. Am. Chem. Soc.*, **1966**, *88*, 631.
176. K. Tasaki, A. Abe, *Polymer J.*, **1985**, *17*, 641.
177. C.C. Gonzalez, E. Riande, A. Bello, J.M. Perena, *Macromolecules*, **1988**, *21*, 3230.
178. A. Ghanem, P. Meurisse, F. Lauprêtre, C. Noël, *Mol. Cryst. Liq. Cryst.*, **1985**, *122*, 339.
179. E. Perez, M.A. Gomez, A. Bello, J.G. Fatou, *Colloid Polymer Sci.*, **1983**, *261*, 571.
180. Y. Takahashi, Y. Osaki, H. Tadokoro, *J. Polym. Sci., Polym. Phys. Ed.*, **1980**, *18*, 1863.
181. A. Abe, T. Hirano, T. Tsuruta, *Macromolecules*, **1979**, *12*, 1092.
182. A. Abe, I. Ando, K. Kato, I. Uematsu, *Polymer J.*, **1981**, *13*, 1069.
183. J.S. Roman, J. Guzman, E. Riande, J. Santoro, M. Rico, *Macromolecules*, **1982**, *15*, 609.
184. E. Riande, J.G. de la Campa, D.D. Schlereth, J. de Abajo, J. Guzman, *Macromolecules*, **1987**, *20*, 1641.
185. H.K. Yip, H.L. Williams, *J. Appl. Polym. Sci.*, **1976**, *20*, 1209.
186. A.C. Griffin, S.J. Havens, *J. Polym. Sci., Polym. Phys. Ed.*, **1981**, *19*, 951.
187. S. Antoun, R.W. Lenz, J.I. Jin, *J. Polym. Sci., Polym. Chem. Ed.*, **1981**, *19*, 1901.
188. R.W. Lenz, *Pure Appl. Chem.*, **1985**, *57*, 1537; *Polymer J.*, **1985**, *17*, 105.
189. A.C. Griffin, S.J. Havens, *Mol. Cryst. Liq. Cryst. Lett.*, **1979**, *49*, 239.
190. A. Roviello, A. Sirigu, *Makromol. Chem.*, **1982**, *183*, 895.
191. L. Strzelecki, D. Van Luyen, *Eur. Polym. J.*, **1980**, *16*, 299.
192. L. Strzelecki, L. Liebert, *Eur. Polym. J.*, **1981**, *17*, 1271.
193. A. Blumstein, O. Thomas, *Macromolecules*, **1982**, *15*, 1264.
194. C. Ober, J.I. Jin, R.W. Lenz, *Polymer J.*, **1982**, *14*, 9.
195. J.I. Jin, E.J. Choi, S.C. Ryu, R.W. Lenz, *Polymer J.*, **1986**, *18*, 63.
196. A.C. Griffin, T.R. Britt, *Mol. Cryst. Liq. Cryst. Lett.*, **1983**, *92*, 149.
197. K. Müller, G. Kothe, *Ber. Bunsenges. Phys. Chem.*, **1985**, *89*, 1214.
198. A. Blumstein, R.B. Blumstein, M.M. Gauthier, O. Thomas, J. Asrar, *Mol. Cryst. Liq. Cryst. Lett.*, **1983**, *92*, 87.
199. A. Blumstein, S. Vilasagar, S. Ponrathnam, S.B. Clough, R.B. Blumstein, G. Maret, *J. Polym. Sci., Polymer Phys. Ed.*, **1982**, *20*, 877.
200. E.T. Samulski, M.M. Gauthier, R. Blumstein, A. Blumstein, *Macromolecules*, **1984**, *17*, 479.
201. A. Ghanem, Thèse de Doctorat és-Sciences, Université Pierre et Marie Curie, Septembre, 1987.
202. P.P. Wu, S.L. Hsu, O. Thomas, A. Blumstein, *J. Polym. Sci., Part B, Polym. Phys.*, **1986**, *24*, 827.
203. Z. Jedlinski, J. Franek, A. Kulczycki, A. Sirigu, C. Carfagna, *Macromolecules*, **1989**, *22*, 1600.

204. S. Bruckner, J.C. Scott, D. Y. Yoon, A.C. Griffin, *Macromolecules*, **1985**, *18*, 2709.
205. A.F. Martins, J.B. Ferreira, F. Volino, A. Blumstein, R.B. Blumstein, *Macromolecules*, **1983**, *16*, 279.
206. H. Furuya, A. Abe, *Polym. Bull.*, **1988**, *20*, 467.
207. A. Abe, *Macromolecules*, **1984**, *17*, 2280.
208. D. Y. Yoon, S. Bruckner, *Macromolecules*, **1985**, *18*, 651.
209. R. Napolitano, B. Pirozzi, A. Tuzi, *Eur. Polym. J.*, **1988**, *24*, 103.
210. F. Auriemma, P. Corradini, A. Tuzi, *Macromolecules*, **1987**, *20*, 293.
211. P.J. Flory, *Proc. R. Soc. London, Ser. A*, **1956**, *234*, 60, 73.
212. P.J. Flory, *Adv. Polym. Sci.*, **1984**, *59*, 1.
213. E. Bianchi, A. Ciferri, J. Preston, W.R. Krigbaum, *J. Polym. Sci., Polym. Phys. Ed.*, **1981**, *19*, 863.
214. M.A. Aden, E. Bianchi, A. Ciferri, G. Conio, A. Tealdi, *Macromolecules*, **1984**, *17*, 2010.
215. E. Bianchi, A. Ciferri, G. Conio, L. Lanzavecchia, M. Terbojevich, *Macromolecules*, **1986** *19*, 630.
216. M. Arpin, C. Strazielle, *Polymer*, **1977**, *18*, 591; *Makromol. Chem.*, **1976**, *177*, 581.
217. M. Arpin, F. Debeauvais, C. Strazielle, *Makromol. Chem.*, **1976**, *177*, 585.
218. W.R. Krigbaum, H. Hakemi, A. Ciferri, G. Conio, *Macromolecules*, **1985**, *18*, 973.
219. P. Moha, G. Weill, H. Benoit, *J. Chim. Phys.*, **1964**, *61*, 1240.
220. G.M. Holtzer, in *Solution Properties of Polysaccharides*, D.A. Brant, ed., A.C.S. Symp. Series 150, Am. Chem. Soc., Washington, D.C., Chap. 2.
221. E.D.T. Atkins, K.D. Parker, *J. Polym. Sci., C*, **1969**, *28*, 69; *Proc. R. Soc. London, Ser. B*, **1969**, *173*, 209.
222. H.T. Norisuye, T. Yanaki, H. Fujita, *J. Polym. Sci., Polym. Phys. Ed.*, **1980**, *18*, 547.
223. A. Abe, T. Yamazaki, *Macromolecules*, **1989**, *22*, 2138.
224. M.G. Dobb, J.E. Mc Intyre, *Adv. Polym. Sci.*, **1984**, *60/61*, 61.
225. S.P. Papkov, *Adv. Polym. Sci.*, **1984**, *59*, 75.
226. M. Jaffe, R. Sidney Jones, in *High Technology Fibers*, Part A, A.M. Lewin, J. Preston, eds., Marcel Dekker, New York, 1985.
227. V.N. Tsvetkov, I.N. Shtennikova, *Macromolecules*, **1978**, *11*, 306.
228. F. Lauprêtre, L. Monnerie, *Eur. Polym. J.*, **1978**, *14*, 415.
229. F. Lauprêtre, L. Monnerie, B. Fayolle, *J. Polym. Sci., Polym. Phys. Ed.*, **1980**, *18*, 2243.
230. J.L. Coubeils, B. Pullman, P. Courrière, *Biochem. Biophys. Res. Commun.*, **1971**, *44*, 1131.
231. J. Kyritosos, J. Sacco, F. Patent 2,272,118 (May 24, 1974), Rhône-Poulenc.
232. J. Preston, *Polym. Eng. Sci.*, **1975**, *15*, 199.
233. A. Ciferri, *Polym. Eng. Sci.*, **1975**, *15*, 191.
234. B. Fayolle, personal communication.
235. W.J. Welsh, D. Bhaumik, J.E. Mark, *J. Macromol. Sci. Phys.*, **1981**, *B20*, 59.
236. W.J. Welsh, D. Bhaumik, J.E. Mark, *Macromolecules*, **1981**, *14*, 947.
237. D. Bhaumik, W.J. Welsh, H.H. Jaffe, J.E. Mark, *Macromolecules*, **1981**, *14*, 951.
238. W.J. Welsh, J.E. Mark, *Polym. Eng. Sci.*, **1983**, *23*, 140.
239. W.J. Welsh, J.E. Mark, *Polym. Bull.*, **1982**, *8*, 21.
240. W.J. Welsh, J.E. Mark, *J. Mater. Sci.*, **1983**, *18*, 1119.
241. W.J. Welsh, D. Bhaumik, H.H. Jaffe, J.E. Mark, *Polym. Eng. Sci.*, **1984**, *24*, 218.
242. W.J. Welsh, J.E. Mark, *Polym. Eng. Sci.*, **1985**, *25*, 965.
243. W.J. Welsh, J.E. Mark, *Prepr. Am. Chem. Soc., Div. Polym. Chem.*, **1983**, *24*, 315.

244. H. Kondo, H.H. Jaffe, H.Y. Lee, W.J. Welsh, *J. Comp. Chem.*, **1984**, *5*, 84.
245. W.J. Welsh, in *Current Topics in Polymer Science*, R. Ottenbrite, L.A. Utracki, S. Inoue, eds., Hanser Verlag, Munich, 1987, p. 217–234.
246. A. Bondi, *J. Phys. Chem.*, **1964**, *68*, 441.
247. M.W. Wellman, W.W. Adams, R.A. Wolff, D.R. Wiff, A.V. Fratini, *Macromolecules*, **1981**, *14*, 935.
248. M.W. Wellman, W.W. Adams, D.R. Wiff, A.V. Fratini, Air Force Technical Report AFML-TR-79-4184, Part I; private communications cited in Ref. 245.
249. G.C. Berry, P. Metzger Cotts, S.G. Chu, *Br. Polym. J.*, **1981**, *13*, 47.
250. J.C. Holste, C.J. Glover, D.T. Magnuson, K.C.B. Dangayach, T.A. Powell, D.W. Ching, D.R. Person, Air Force Technical Report AFML-TR-79-4107.
251. C. Arnold, Jr., *Macromol. Rev.*, **1979**, *14*, 265.
252. A.V. Fratini, E.M. Cross, J.F. O'Brien, W.W. Adams, *J. Macromol. Sci. Phys.*, **1985–86**, *B24*, 159.
253. J.F. Wolfe, private communication cited in Ref. 245.
254. E.L. Thomas, private communications cited in Ref. 245.
255. P. Coulter, A. Windle, *Am. Chem. Soc., Polym. Prepr.*, **1989**, *30*, 67.
256. B. Jung, B.L. Schürmann, *Macromolecules*, **1989**, *22*, 477.
257. B. Jung, B.L. Schürmann, *Makromol. Chem., Rapid Commun.*, **1989**, *10*, 419.
258. G.C. Rutledge, U.W. Suter, *Am. Chem. Soc., Polym. Prepr.* **1989**, *30*, 71.
259. M.G. Northolt, J.J. Van Aartsen, *J. Polym. Sci., Polym. Symp.*, **1977**, *58*, 283.
260. E. de Vos, A. Bellemans, *Macromolecules*, **1974**, *7*, 809.
261. A. Baumgartner, D.Y. Yoon, *J. Chem. Phys.*, **1983**, *79*, 521.
262. C.A. Croxton, *Am. Chem. Soc., Polym. Prepr.*, **1989**, *30*, 65.

CHAPTER 2

Experimental Evaluation of the Persistence Length for Mesogenic Polymers

GREGG L. BRELSFORD

Westvāco Research, Westvāco Corporation,
North Charleston, SC 29411-2905 USA

and

WILLIAM R. KRIGBAUM

Department of Chemistry, Duke University, Durham,
NC 27706 USA

CONTENTS

1. INTRODUCTION

The Kratky-Porod (KP) wormlike chain model is employed most often in characterizing polymers having an extended conformation.[1] The wormlike chain conveniently bridges two extremes encountered when studying macromolecules, the random coil and the rigid rod. Several theories utilize the wormlike chain model to relate experimental quantities to the parameter that characterizes the degree of chain extension. The unique parameter of the wormlike chain is the persistence length, q. This chapter focuses on the experimental methods that provide evidence of chain extension and permit the evaluation of q in *dilute* solution. In this introduction, we describe the

KP model. Section 2 considers the influence of excluded volume effects on wormlike chains. Frictional properties are detailed in Section 3. Scattering techniques used to determine q are described in Section 4. The latter section includes neutron scattering techniques, which also permit the determination of chain extension in the mesophase and in the bulk. Other elaborations on the wormlike chain are discussed in Chapter 5.

Experimental values of q or the Kuhn statistical segment length[2] are used to test and refine theories for liquid crystalline behavior which are considered in Chapters 3–5. High geometrical asymmetry, i.e., the ratio of the extended portion of the chain to its cross-sectional diameter distinguishes many polymers that form mesophases from coiling polymers, which do not.[3] Chemical structures and conformational characteristics known to influence mesogenic behavior are reviewed in Chapter 1. Ballauf[4] has also reviewed the "architecture" of liquid-crystalline polymers.

1.1. The Kratky-Porod Wormlike Chain Model

Kratky and Porod[1] define a discrete chain having n segments with segment length l and bond angle ϕ; ϕ is not necessarily the valence angle. The contour length $L = nl$ is the total length of the chain in its most extended form. The first segment is arbitrarily fixed at the origin in the z direction of an x, y, z coordinate system. The degree to which the remaining segments persist in the z direction is depicted by the average z component of the end-to-end distance, $\langle R_z \rangle$. We shall see that as $n \to \infty$, $\langle R_z \rangle \to 9$ yielding the KP result.

The discrete chain above is then redefined as a continuous chain. The chain is divided into a larger number of shorter segments having smaller ϕ between them, while holding q and L constant. The mean-square end-to-end distance is defined in the limit as $n \to \infty$, $l \to 0$ and $\phi \to 0$ by Eq. (1):

$$\langle R^2 \rangle = 2qL - 2q^2[1 - \exp(-N)] \tag{1}$$

where $N = L/q$. Note that N represents the number of persistence lengths in the chain.

Equation (1) has two limits. If $L \gg q$, or $N \to \infty$, the familiar result for random coils or that of the Kuhn chain is obtained:

$$\lim_{N \to \infty} \langle R^2 \rangle = 2qL \tag{2}$$

where $2q = \lambda$, λ being the length of the Kuhn link.[2] Alternatively, if N approaches zero, the value of $\langle R^2 \rangle$ in Eq. (2) approaches $(qN)^2$ or L^2, which corresponds to that of a rigid rod.

The average z component of the end-to-end distance for the continuous chain also has limiting forms. The result as $N \to \infty$ is:

$$\lim_{N \to \infty} \langle R_z \rangle = q(1 - \exp(N)) \tag{3}$$

When $N \to \infty$, we arrive at the wormlike chain result where $\langle R_z \rangle = q$. As $N \to 0$ we obtain the result for rods by expanding the exponential term in Eq. (3) to get $\langle R_z \rangle = qN = L$. Thus, we are able to model a polymer that at low molecular weight maintains some degree of correlation between end bonds and gradually begins to wander as the molecular weight increases.

The KP chain cannot describe the exact dimensional characteristics of all real chains.[5] The wormlike chain was modified by Yamakawa and Shimada to mimic chains possessing helical conformations.[6] The helical wormlike chain model (HW) explains the behavior of some polymers having characteristic ratios that increase faster than the KP model predicts, exhibit a maximum, or decrease toward the coil limiting value.[7] Alternatively, the rotational isomeric state model uses conformational energies and torsional angles to predict chain conformation.[5] The model of a randomly broken wormlike chain having sharp bends at particular sites has also been considered (cf. Chapter 6).

As we discuss the theories and experimental results that follow, two circumstances must be kept in mind. First, the theories derive quantities for monodisperse specimens. Therefore, the study of well-fractionated samples is preferred. If this is not possible, knowledge of the molecular weight distribution is helpful. Otherwise, the effects of an assumed form for the distribution on values derived for q should be considered. Polydispersity has the largest effect on the radius of gyration measured by scattering techniques.[8] This will be described in Section 4.

Second, the study of extended-chain polymers in dilute solution usually requires solvents that strongly interact with the polymer to achieve total molecular dispersion. If a sample is not totally dissolved, aggregation influences frictional properties and interferes with scattering techniques, particularly at higher molecular weight.[9] For systems where aggregation is not operative, experimental values of q can depend on the solvent. Cellulose, cellulose derivatives, and poly(n-alkyl isocyanates) are well-known examples.[10-12]

2. EXCLUDED VOLUME EFFECTS IN WORMLIKE CHAINS

2.1. Expansion Factor

The theory of Yamakawa and Stockmayer (YS)[13] utilizes a wire-bead model obeying wormlike statistics to calculate the intramolecular chain expansion factor, α_R^2:

$$\frac{\langle R^2 \rangle}{\langle R_0^2 \rangle} = \alpha_R^2 = 1 + K(N')z \qquad (4)$$

The unperturbed mean-square end-to-end distance is designated as $\langle R_0^2 \rangle$. The coefficient $K(N')$ is an increasing function of the number of Kuhn segment lengths in the chain, $N' = L/2q$; $K(N')$ is approximately zero at $N' < 1$ and equals $4/3$ in the Kuhn chain limit (see Equation 83 of Ref. 13). The excluded volume parameter z is given by:

$$z = \left(\frac{3}{2\pi}\right)^{3/2} B' N'^{1/2} \tag{5}$$

where B' is the dimensionless, reduced binary cluster parameter and is usually treated as a data-fitting variable. These theoretical relationships are presented to demonstrate the interplay between z and its coefficient, $K(N')$. For wormlike chains, α_R^2 is expected to be ~ 1 due to a small coefficient compared to the value $4/3$ for Gaussian coils and/or a small z due to a smaller number of statistical segments of relatively longer length.

Experimentally, these expectations are tested by measuring the radius of gyration $\langle R_G^2 \rangle$ in a good solvent and finding the ratio of $\langle R_G^2 \rangle$ to its unperturbed value $\langle R_{G,0}^2 \rangle$ under conditions where chain expansion due to long-range effects is counterbalanced by intermolecular interactions. This ratio gives $\alpha_{R_G}^2$. However, Flory theta conditions are rare for extended chains and most solvents which dissolve these polymers yield large second virial coefficients A_2.[14] Since we are unable to measure z directly, and in spite of nonvanishing A_2, we consider an application of the YS result to show that $\alpha_{R_G}^2 \simeq 1$.

For coiling molecules, α_{R_G} is related to z by[15]:

$$\alpha_{R_G}^2 - 1 = \frac{134}{105} z \tag{6}$$

when $\alpha_{R_G}^2$ is close to unity. Assuming that the coefficient of z for $\alpha_{R_G}^2$ behaves similarly to that of z for α_R^2 (Eq. 4), we have a relationship for wormlike chains[13]:

$$\alpha_{R_G, \text{worm}}^2 - 1 = \frac{67}{70} K(N') z \tag{7}$$

By taking the ratio of Eq. (7) to Eq. (6), we see that z cancels and $3K(N')/4$ approaches unity as the coefficient $K(N')$ approaches its coil-limiting value, $4/3$. Likewise, the ratio of $\langle R_G^2 \rangle$ for wormlike chains[16] to $\langle R_G^2 \rangle$ for coils, $3\langle R_G^2 \rangle_{\text{worm}}/Lq$, approaches unity. Therefore, a plot of $3\langle R_G^2 \rangle_{\text{worm}}/Lq$ and $3K(N')/4$ versus N' should reach a value of 1 at $N' = \infty$.

Experimental values of $\langle R_G^2 \rangle_w$ for 19 fractions of the polyterephthalamide of 4-aminobenzhydrazide (PABH-T)[17, 18] in dimethyl sulfoxide (DMSO), along with an estimate of q ($q = 115$ Å), were used to construct Fig. 1. The subscript w denotes that an estimate was applied to correct measured $\langle R_G^2 \rangle_z$

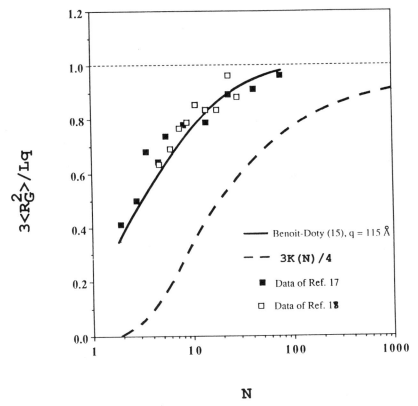

FIGURE 1
The ratio of experimental $\langle R_G^2 \rangle_w$ for PABH-T in DMSO at 25°C to $\langle R_G^2 \rangle$ for random coils, $3\langle R_G^2 \rangle_w / Lq$, plotted against number of persistence lengths in the chain, N. The heavy dashed curve represents the coefficient, $3K(N) / 4$. The solid curve is the Benoit-Doty equation for $\langle R_G^2 \rangle_w$ with $q = 115$ Å and $M_L = 18.2$ daltons Å^{-1}. A value of unity on the vertical axis represents the random coil limit. Adapted with permission from Ref. 17 (Copyright Am. Chem. Soc.) and Ref. 18.

values to weight-average values. The contour length L was calculated by dividing the weight-average molecular weight M_w by the molar mass per unit length M_L. M_L for PABH-T is 18.2 daltons Å^{-1}. Instead of plotting the data against N', we have used N, where $N = 2N'$ and corresponds to the number of persistence lengths in the chain. The coil limit for PAH is approached at $N \simeq 40$ or $M_w \simeq 8 \times 10^4$ daltons. The function $3K(N)/4$ is also plotted in Fig. 1. The coefficient $K(N)$ is well below the coil-limiting value 4/3 over the range of M_w studied indicating that $\alpha_{R_G}^2$ is near unity. The small values of N, with a value of q roughly an order of magnitude larger than those found for flexible polymers, also indicates that z is small. The solid line through the

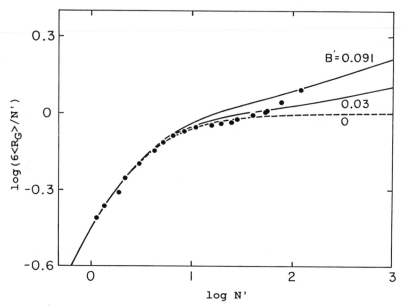

FIGURE 2
Double logarithmic plots of the reduced ratio $6\langle R_G^2 \rangle / N'$ against the reduced contour length N' for PHIC. The points represent experimental data in hexane at 25°C (Ref. 22). The curves are theoretical values using the YS scheme[13] and the indicated values of B'. (Reprinted with permission from Ref. 23.)

data points was calculated using the Benoit-Doty[16] equation (see Section 4, Eq. 23) and $q = 115$ Å. Tsvetkov and Tsepelevich[19] calculated α_s using the YS theory, their light-scattering data, and two extreme values of q, namely 35 Å[20] and 220 Å[21] for PABH-T in DMSO. The α_s values were < 1.012 in the range of M_w studied ($M_w < 48 \times 10^3$ daltons). These considerations show that excluded volume corrections made based on Gaussian coils[20] resulted in underestimating q. The expansion effect is negligible in this case in spite of large A_2.

We turn now to an example where deviation from unperturbed wormlike chain dimensions was detected at very high M_w. The case of poly(n-hexyl isocyanate) (PHIC) in hexane at 25°C was studied by Murakami et al.[22] Their 19 narrow fractions ranged between 6.8×10^4 and 7.24×10^6 daltons. Experimental values of $\langle R_G^2 \rangle$ begin to deviate above the theoretical curve at approximately 3×10^6 daltons. An expansion factor of 1.11 was calculated from the measured $\langle R_G^2 \rangle$ divided by its unperturbed theoretical value for the highest fraction using $q = 420$ Å and $M_L = 71.5$ daltons Å^{-1}.[22] Subsequently, Yamakawa and Shimada[23] attempted to fit the measured trend of $\langle R_G^2 \rangle$ versus M_w using the YS scheme to calculate $\alpha_{R_G}^2$. The attempt is shown by the log–log plot of $6\langle R_G^2 \rangle / N'$ against N' in Fig. 2. Again, N'

$(= L/2q)$ corresponds to the dimensionless, reduced contour length or number of Kuhn segments.

The solid curves were calculated using an improved relationship for α_{R_G},[24] $3K(N')z/4$, the Benoit-Doty equation and the corresponding values of B' indicated in Fig. 2. We note that the coil limit is attained at approximately $\log N' = 1.3$ or 1.2×10^6 daltons. PHIC contains roughly 40 Kuhn segments at this molecular weight. At higher M_w, the expansion effect becomes appreciable and the YS treatment fails to predict the measured trend adequately. Although the YS theory works remarkably well for short, non-Gaussian flexible chains, Yamakawa and Shimada conclude that the YS scheme for stiff chains should be reconsidered.[23] For most semiflexible polymers, however, the expansion effect does not seriously hinder reliable estimates of the persistence length, particularly when chains are below the coil limit. Kamide and Saito have performed extensive analysis on several cellulose derivatives and arrived at similar conclusions.[25]

2.2. Second Virial Coefficient

The YS scheme also treats the effect of chain extension on A_2 using a double-contact approximation for intermolecular interactions.[13] The scheme relates A_2 to a theoretical interpenetration function h without intramolecular excluded volume interactions:

$$A_2 = \left(\frac{N_A N'^2 B'}{16q^3 M_w^2} \right) h \qquad (8)$$

N_A is Avogadro's number and h is a function of N' and d':

$$h = 1 - Q(N', d')z \qquad (9)$$

where d' is the reduced diameter. The parameters B', N', and d' represent reduced quantities given by $B' = B/2q$, $N' = L/2q$, and $d' = d/2q$. The parameter B is related to the binary cluster integral β (see below). The coefficient $Q(N', d')$ is calculated using Equations 96 and 119 of Ref. 13 and approaches the Gaussian limiting value 2.865. Yamakawa and Stockmayer note that their double-contact approximation underestimates the classical result obtained for rods as $N' \to 0$, where $A_{2, \text{rod}} = \pi N_A dL^2/4M_w^2$ (unreduced).[26]

Despite this limitation, Huber and Stockmayer[27] were able to interpret the trend observed for the experimental interpenetration function (Ψ) of very low molecular weight polystyrene fractions in toluene ($M_w < 2.9 \times 10^4$ daltons) using the YS scheme. In this range of M_w, α_s approaches unity. Values of Ψ are dimensionless and given by:

$$\Psi = A_2 M_w^2/4\pi^{3/2} N_A \langle R_G^2 \rangle^{3/2} \qquad (10)$$

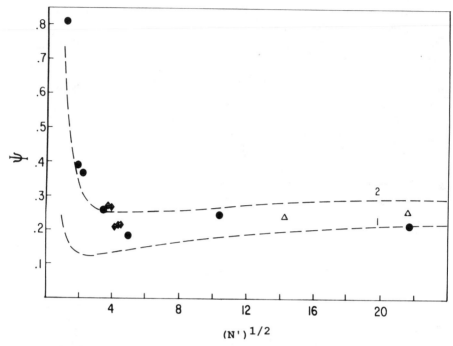

FIGURE 3
Literature data for Ψ plotted against the square root of number of Kuhn segments for polystyrene in toluene: ($\bigcirc$) Ref. 28, ($\triangle$) Ref. 29, ($\boxtimes$) Ref. 30. The dashed curves are theoretical values according to the YS scheme using $B' = 0.0656$ (1) and $B' = 0.273$ (2). (Reprinted with permission from Ref. 27. Copyright American Chemical Society.)

The A_2 were measured by light scattering[27] and $\langle R_G^2 \rangle$ were measured in deuterated toluene by neutron scattering.[28] The results for Ψ, including data from Refs. 29 and 30, were plotted versus the square root of the number of Kuhn segments $(N')^{1/2}$ in Fig. 3. Literature values[28] of $A = 29$ Å and $M_L = 45.0$ daltons Å^{-1} were used to calculate the coefficients $Q(N', d')$ and $K(N')$, which were incorporated in self-consistent relationships for $\alpha_{R_G}^2$ and Ψ (see Equations 3a, b and 3a', b' of Ref. 27). The z parameter was calculated using two values of B' ($= \beta/A^3$) to generate the dashed curves, where β is the unreduced binary cluster integral. Curve 1 was calculated with $B' = 0.0656$ and curve 2 with $B' = 0.273$. The higher value of B' must be used to achieve agreement with the Ψ data at $(N')^{1/2} < 4$. The same is true for the A_2 data, which decrease as M_w increases. Aside from these facts, the remarkable result is that the increase of Ψ with decreasing M_w can only be predicted by applying a theory that takes chain extension into account.[27] Without the YS modification, the predicted values of Ψ for coiling polymers increase as M_w increases.

We note that A_2 for rodlike solutes is independent of M_w,[26] whereas A_2 for some wormlike chains decrease slightly as M_w increases.[17, 22, 31] These considerations on finite chain flexibility should be relevant to theories utilizing the virial coefficient[32] to predict mesogenic phase behavior of wormlike chains.

3. FRICTIONAL PROPERTIES

3.1. Intrinsic Viscosity

The relationship between intrinsic viscosity, $[\eta]$, and molar mass is used most routinely to determine the degree of chain extension of linear polymers in dilute solution. We first mention the earlier theoretical work, which facilitated estimates of the Kuhn segment or persistence length and hydrodynamic diameter, d. Their limitations are briefly cited before moving on to later developments. The reader is referred to Yamakawa's book for more complete details.[15] If we accept the wormlike chain model, the ideal theoretical tool would allow us to determine q and d while accurately describing excluded volume, polydispersity, chain-end effects, and hydrodynamic draining across the entire range of molecular weights of interest.

Hearst et al.[33] extended an earlier touched-bead chain obeying the wormlike model to include hydrodynamic interaction between segments and excluded volume. Their results, however, apply only to the limiting cases of rods and coils. The treatment of Eizner and Ptitsyn[34] is based on the semiempirical approach of Peterlin.[35] It provides for interpolation between rod and coil limits but does not treat the excluded volume effect. The treatment has tended to yield smaller values for the Kuhn segment length and larger hydrodynamic diameters compared to those found from sedimentation data.[20] A similar situation exists with the Sharp and Bloomfield[36] scheme, which also utilizes the Peterlin relation while treating the excluded volume effect with the Ptitsyn-Eizner approximation.[37]

The more recent theories of Yamakawa and co-workers[7, 38, 39] for $[\eta]$ became popular during the mid to late 1970's. Their approach utilizes the Oseen-Burgers procedure for continuous cylinders behaving like the wormlike chain model. Hydrodynamic interactions between segments are introduced via preaveraging the Oseen tensor.[15] Excluded volume effects are neglected, however.

According to Yamakawa and Fujii (YF)[40]:

$$[\eta] = \frac{\Phi N'^{3/2}}{\lambda^{-3} M_w} \tag{11}$$

where $N' = M_w/M_L\lambda$ is the reduced contour length, with M_L being the shift factor, having units of molar mass per unit length, and $\lambda = 2q$; Φ is a function of N' and the reduced cylinder diameter d' $(= d/\lambda)$. The best fit of experimental data for $[\eta]$ and M_w using analytical expressions for Φ permit an estimate of q, d, and M_L (see Equations 23 and 25 of Ref. 41).

Equation (12) is often used to estimate d:

$$d = \left(\frac{4M_L}{\pi \rho_2 N_A} \right)^{1/2} \tag{12}$$

where d is the diameter of a circular cross section for the wormlike cylinder, ρ_2 is the polymer density, and N_A is Avogadro's number. If the number of fractions studied or the range of molecular weight is limited, M_L is found by dividing the molecular weight of the repeat unit M_0 by its projection length. The estimates of d and M_L reduce the fitting procedure to one variable, q. Caution must be observed using this estimate for M_L. Chain substituents and/or helicogenic solvents can alter the conformation or projection of the chain, and hence the assumed value of M_L. An underestimation of M_L will result in a correspondingly low value for q. Yamakawa demonstrated this effect with cellulose acetate in trifluoroethanol and amylose in dimethyl sulfoxide using the helical wormlike chain model.[41]

The Yamakawa treatment for $[\eta]$ serves as the basis for a convenient method for estimating the wormlike chain parameters. Bohdanecký[42] found a simple relationship for Φ that is valid over a broad, practical range of N':

$$\Phi = \Phi_\infty \left[B_0 + A_0(N')^{-1/2} \right]^{-3} \tag{13}$$

where B_0 is nearly constant and given as 1.05, A_0 is a function of d', and Φ_∞ $(= 2.87 \times 10^{23})$ is the limiting value of Φ for nondraining Gaussian coils at infinite M_w. A plot of $(M_w^2/[\eta])^{1/3}$ versus $M_w^{1/2}$ yields a slope B_η and intercept A_η. M_L is obtained from A_η and A_0 using Eq. (14) (and Equations 24 and 25 for d'^2/A_0 in Ref. 42):

$$A_\eta = A_0 M_L \Phi_\infty^{-1/3} \tag{14}$$

With M_L in hand, q is evaluated using Eq. (15):

$$B_\eta = 1.05\Phi^{-1/3}(2q/M_L)^{-1/2} \tag{15}$$

Note that $(2q/M_L)^{-1/2}$ equals $(6\langle R_{G,0}^2 \rangle/M_w)_\infty^{-1/2}$. $(6\langle R_{G,0}^2 \rangle/M_w)$ is the fundamental conformational characteristic ratio of polymers at the unperturbed coil limit.[15]

Results for q from $[\eta]$ are often lower than values derived from $\langle R_G^2 \rangle$. As Bohdanecký suggests, a lower value of Φ_∞ alleviates this discrepancy.[42] Saito has observed a dependence of Φ upon M_w for certain cellulose derivatives.[10] This is known as the draining effect. Recall that hydrodynamic

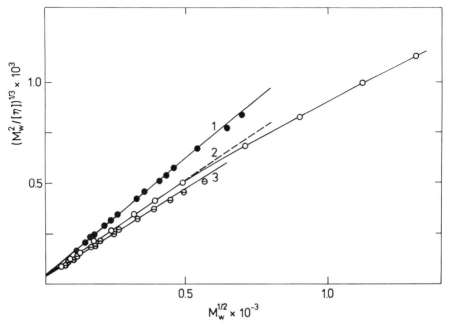

FIGURE 4
Bohdanecký plot of isomeric poly(phthaolyl-trans-2,5-dimethyl-piperazines) in m-cresol at 25°C: Curve 1, PPDP[44]; Curve 2, PIDP[44]; Curve 3, PTDP.[45] (Reprinted with permission from Ref. 42. Copyright American Chemical Society.)

interactions are preaveraged in the Yamakawa theory, so the discrepancy may result from this approximation.

Another interesting feature of the Bohdanecký plot manifests itself when used with the data of less extended polymers, such as the polyamide piperazines.[43,44] These polymers are not mesogenic and exhibit relatively small excluded volume effects. Values of q for poly(terephthaloyl-*trans*-2,5-dimethylpiperazine) (PTDP), poly(o-phthaloyl-*trans*-2,5-dimethylpiperazine) (PPDP), and poly(isophthaloyl-*trans*-2,5-dimethylpiperazine) (PIDP) depend mostly on the phthalic acid isomer and to a lesser extent upon solvent. The data in Fig. 4 are linear below $M_w \sim 2 \times 10^5$ daltons but exhibit downward deviations above that value.[42] This is attributed to the excluded volume effect. Chain expansion for these polymers is also evident in the data for $\langle R_G^2 \rangle$ as discussed by Norisuye and Fujita.[45] However, the neglect of excluded volume seems justified for the purpose of evaluating q from $[\eta]$ since the agreement between theory and experiment over a significant range of M_w below the coil limit is observed.

Another precaution with the Bohdanecký plot are upward deviations at high M_w. This artifact can occur with incomplete molecular dispersion in dilute solutions which results in measuring relatively higher M_w values and corresponding lower values for $[\eta]$. In contrast, deviations from linearity at low M_w for stiff chains, such as helical polypeptides, can occur.[42] Bohdanecký cites upper and lower limits for N' when using his plot (Table 1 of Ref. 42). At low N', hydrodynamic end effects may contribute to $[\eta]$.[46] Alternatively, the discrepancy may arise from the fact that the Kratky-Porod chain may not mimic real chains at low M_w.[23] For these reasons, evaluation of model parameters is best when made from only the linear portions of the Bohdanecký plot.

Despite these precautions, the Bohdanecký plot is preferred over the familiar Stockmayer-Fixman (SF) extrapolation, i.e., $(M_w/[\eta])^{1/2}$ vs. $M_w^{1/2}$. The latter is useful for flexible polymers in good solvents.[47] The intercept at $M_w^{1/2} = 0$ provides an estimate of K in the relation:

$$[\eta] = KM_w^{1/2}\alpha_\eta^3 \tag{16}$$

here $K = \Phi_\infty(6\langle R_{G,0}^2\rangle/M_w)^{3/2}$ and α_η is the viscosity expansion factor. When values of the Mark-Houwink exponent, $\nu = d\log[\eta]/d\log M_w$, exceed 0.7 for extended-chain polymers, particularly at $M_w < 10^4$ daltons, use of this extrapolation will result in an underestimation of $6\langle R_{G,0}^2\rangle/M_w$ and hence q.[48]

Stockmayer demonstrated this effect with data for cis-syndiotactic poly(phenylsilsesquioxane) in ethylene chloride.[48] At 50.5°C, A_2 values are zero ($\alpha_\eta = 1$), and $\nu = 0.89$.[49] The value of K from the (SF) plot led to $6\langle R_{G,0}^2\rangle/M_w = 3.2 \times 10^{-17}$ cm^2 mol g^{-1} or $q = 16.5$ Å which effectively treats the system as an unperturbed Gaussian chain. In contrast, a Bohdanecký plot using the data from Ref. 50 is shown in Fig. 5. The line through the data is a least-squares fit. The slope of this line is 1.39 from which a value of 68 Å is calculated for q using $M_L = 103$ daltons Å^{-1} in Eq. (15). This value of q agrees well with the value Stockmayer obtained by fitting the $[\eta]$ data with the theory of Ptitsyn and Eizner ($q = 70$ Å) and that of Helminiak and Berry from YF and $\langle R_{G,0}^2\rangle$ ($q = 74$ Å).[50] The larger value of ν is therefore due to chain extension, not the excluded volume effect.[48]

As noted earlier, the limited solubility of highly chain-extended polymers usually prevents a comparison of wormlike chain parameters under good solvent conditions with those under unperturbed, theta conditions. The finding that different values of q occur for the same polymer in different solvents demonstrates that chain conformation is influenced to varying degrees by polymer–solvent interactions. These interactions may be expected to be temperature dependent. The YF and Bohdanecký methods were used to evaluate q for various polymer–solvent pairs at several temperatures. Results are collected in Table 1.

To develop a better understanding of the mesogenic nature of these materials, Aden et al.[51] first proposed the inclusion of the temperature coefficient ($d\ln q/dT$) in the theory for thermotropic phase behavior. Abso-

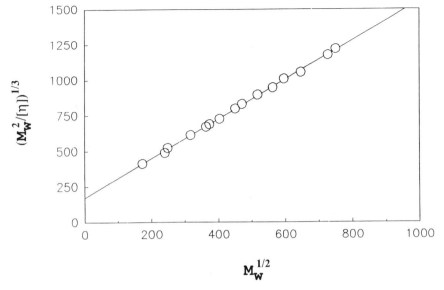

FIGURE 5

Bohdanecký plot of cis-syndiotactic poly(phenylsilsesquioxane) in ethylene chloride at 50.5°C. The slope β_η of the line in 1.39. (The plot was constructed with data from Ref. 50. Copyright J. Wiley & Sons, Inc.)

lute values of $Td \ln q/dT$ reported in Table 1 are larger than those observed for flexible polymers, e.g., polyethylene (-0.46).[59] A value of -1 is predicted for the wormlike chain.[1] It is likely that the solvent influences the chain bending force constant as T is increased and solvent binding is altered.[60] It should be interesting to perform calculations of q based on computer simulation or on bond force constants to separate the initrinsic chain contribution from that of solvent interaction.

In the case of polyelectrolytes, an electrostatic contribution q_{el} (defined by $q = q_0 + q_{el}$ where q_0 is the intrinsic chain contribution at high ionic strength) is operative. For Xanthan, however, q_{el} was found[61] to be rather small ($< 10\%$), a finding attributed to the rigidity of its double helical conformation.

3.2. Translational Friction Coefficient

The theoretical companion of $[\eta]$ produced by Yamakawa and co-workers[7] is the theoretical treatment for the translational friction coefficient, f_0. The f_0 were originally calculated for cylindrical wormlike chains.[62a] The treatment was later extended to treat helical wormlike chains[62b] and straight cylinders having hemispherical caps.[46] These treatments permit comparisons with

Table 1
Persistence Lengths for Chain-Extended Polymers from Intrinsic Viscosity

System	$q_{25°}$ (Å)	$Td \ln q/dT$	Ref.
PPHT–DB + CP[a]	72	−1.35	52
PHIC–1 − CN[b]	95	−3.7	53
PHIC–toluene	375	−3.6	54, 12
PHIC–hexane	420	—	22
PHIC–THF[b]	305	—	54
PHIC–DCM[b]	185	—	55
HPC–DMAc[c]	70	−1.7	51
HPC–DCA[c]	100	—	51
APC–DMPh[d]	60	−1.6	56
CA–DMAc[e]	70	−2.6	57
Cellulose–DMAc + 5%LiCl	110	—	58
PABH-T–DMSO[f]	70[g]	—	20
	80	—	17
	112	—	18
	90–100	—	19
Xanthan–1.0 M NaCl	1060	—	61

[a]PPHT = poly(phenylhydroquinone terephthalate), DB = σ-dichlorobenzene CP = p-chlorophenol.

[b]PHIC = poly(n-hexyl isocyanate), 1-CN = 1-chloronaphthalene, THF = tetrahydrofuran, DCM = dichloromethane.

[c]HPC = (hydroxypropyl)cellulose, DMAc = N,N-dimethylacetamide, DCA = dichloroacetic acid.

[d]APC = (acetoxypropyl)cellulose, DMPh = dimethylphthalate.

[e]CA = cellulose acetate.

[f]PABH-T = polyterephthalamide of 4-aminobenzhydrazide, DMSO-dimethyl-sulfoxide.

[g]Without correction for excluded volume.

experimental values of sedimentation coefficients (s_0) and diffusion coefficients (D_0) in the limit of infinite dilution. Again, hydrodynamic interactions are preaveraged and excluded volume effects are neglected. The transport coefficients are related through the Svedberg equation and the Einstein equation, respectively:

$$s_0 = \frac{M_w(1 - \bar{v}\rho_0)}{N_A f_0} \quad \text{and} \quad D_0 = \frac{kT}{f_0} \quad (17)$$

where $\bar{v}$ is the partial specific volume of the polymer, ρ_0 is the solvent density, k is the Boltzmann constant, and T is the absolute temperature. Plots of s_0 or D_0 versus M_w permit a fit of the data using the analytical expressions for f_0, which are a function of L, d, and q (see Equations 49 and 51 of Ref. 62a, Equation 28 of Ref. 62b, and Equation 116 of Ref. 46).

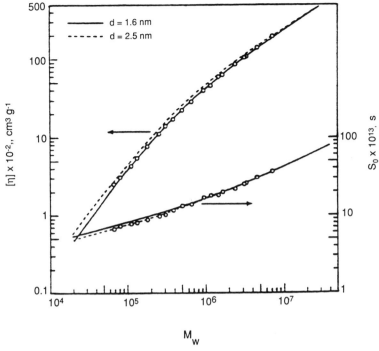

FIGURE 6

Comparison of experimental $[\eta]$ and s_0 for PHIC in hexane with YF theories; the solid and dashed lines are calculated, respectively, with $d = 16$ Å and 25 Å while $q = 420$ Å and $M_L = 71.5$ daltons Å remain fixed. (Reprinted with permission from Ref. 22. Copyright American Chemical Society.)

Workers have experienced difficulty discerning precise values of q having measured trends in s_0 or D_0. Vitovskaya et al.[63] studied poly(1,4-benzamide) (PBA) in concentrated H_2SO_4 and N,N-dimethylacetamide (DMAc). Their data show that q could be between 150 to 1500 Å. The theory for f_0 is not as sensitive to q as it is to L. This fact makes narrow molecular weight fractions necessary for purposes of evaluating q and comparing with other methods.

A thorough study by Murakami et al.[22] of PHIC in hexane demonstrates this point. $[\eta]$ and s_0 data on narrow fractions between 6.8×10^4 and 7.2×10^6 daltons were fitted to the corresponding relationships of Yamakawa and Fujii and co-workers[41, 46, 62a, b] as shown in Fig. 6. Values of q, M_L, and d were chosen on a trial and error basis until a fit to the data was obtained. The solid lines were generated using $q = 420$ Å, $M_L = 71.5$ Å^{-1}, and $d = 16$ Å. The agreement is good for both $[\eta]$ and s_0 over a broad range of M_w. The dashed line was calculated with a larger $d = 25$ Å to obtain even better agreement with s_0. Yanaki et al.[64] used this procedure for triple

Table 2
Values of q Evaluated from Sedimentation Data

System	q (Å)	M_L (Å^{-1})	d (Å)	Ref.
PHIC–hexane	420	71.5	16	22
Schizophyllan–H$_2$O	2000	2150	26	64
PBLG–DMF	1565	146	18.8	7
DNA–0.2 M NaCl	660	195	26.4	65

helical schizophyllan in H$_2$O. The persistence length that allowed a fit of [η] and s_0 data with the theoretical expressions for wormlike cylinders was 2000 ± 300 Å with the assignment $M_L = 2150$ Å^{-1} and $d = 26$ Å. Similar approaches were followed for poly(α-benzyl-L-glutamate) (PBLG)[7] and for DNA.[65] Data are collected in Table 2.

3.3. Dynamic Light Scattering

Dynamic light scattering (DLS) detects other features of chain-extended polymers using photon correlation spectroscopy.[66] Time-dependent fluctuations in light scattered from polymer solutions yield a characteristic, average relaxation time Γ^{-1}; Γ is also referred to as the first cumulant of an expansion about the average decay rate.[67] Scattering element displacements with respect to the effective wavelength of scattered light are related to Γ^{-1} as polymer molecules undergo Brownian motion.[68, 69] The translation diffusion coefficient D_0 is determined by extrapolating Γ/k^2, measured at several concentrations and scattering angles, to the limit of infinite dilution and zero scattering angle. The magnitude of the scattering vector, k_1, is given by $k_1 = 4\pi n_s \sin(\theta/2)/\lambda_0$, where n_s is the refractive index of the solvent, θ is the scattering angle, and λ_0 is the wavelength of incident light in vacuo. To determine q using DLS measurements, the data in a plot of D_0 against M_w are fit using the YF theory for f_0 as described in Section 3.2.[46, 62a, b] Alternatively, when only a few samples are available for study, measured and calculated D_0 for each specimen have been used to assess q.[70–72] Values of q derived from DLS measurements are reported in Table 3.

In addition to larger q values, extended-chain polymers exhibit larger absolute values for exponents in the relation $D_0 = K_D M_w^{-a_D}$ compared to coiling polymers. For example, flexible poly(α-methylstyrene) in toluene has a $-a_D$ value of 0.5 up to $M_w \sim 10^5$ daltons.[77] The value increases to ~ 0.6 in good solvents at higher M_w due to chain expansion. The higher values of $-a_D$ observed for several semiflexible polymers are given in Table 3. The $-a_D$ values approach the value expected for infinitely long rods, $-a_D = 1$.[15]

Effective hydrodynamic radii can be calculated from the Stokes-Einstein equation:

$$R_H = kT/6\pi\eta_0 D_0 \tag{18}$$

Table 3
Values of q and of a_D for Chain Extended Polymers Studied by DLS

System[a]	q (Å)	Literature M_w range	$-a_D$	ξ	Ref.
PABH-T–DMSO	105	$< 2 \times 10^4$	0.73		17
		$3.8 \times 10^3 < M_w < 1.6 \times 10^5$	0.62	0.45	
PPHT–DB + CP	100	1.6×10^4–5.0×10^4	0.73		73
PPTA–H$_2$SO$_4$[b]	290	1.4×10^4–4.8×10^4	0.77	0.43	74
PHIC–hexane	420	5.0×10^4–7.0×10^6	0.68	0.75	70
PBA–DMAc					
+3% LiCl[c]	750	2.8×10^4–2.3×10^5	0.89		75
PBLG–DMF[d]	875	9.0×10^4–2.7×10^5	0.88	0.37	71
	1565				72
Cellulose–DMAc					
+9% LiCl	250	1.25×10^5–7.0×10^5	0.73	0.336	76

[a]See abbreviations in Table 1.
[b]PPTA = poly(1,4-pheneleneterephthalamide),
[c]PBA = poly(1,4-benzamide),
[d]PBLG = poly(γ-benzyl-L-glutamate), DMF = dimethylformamide.

where η_0 is the solvent viscosity. McCormick et al.[76] used the proportionality:

$$R_H = \xi \langle R_G^2 \rangle_z \tag{19}$$

as the basis of another estimate of q for cellulose in DMAc + 9% LiCl by DLS. These workers used the relation:

$$D_0 = (kT/6\pi\eta_0\xi)(\Phi/M_w[\eta])^{1/3} \tag{20}$$

to evaluate ξ from the slope of a plot of D_0 against $(kT/6\pi\eta_0)(M_w[\eta])^{1/3}$ with $\Phi = 1.13 \times 10^{23}$ mol^{-1}. The $\langle R_G^2 \rangle$ values for several cellulose samples between 125,000 and 700,000 daltons were then calculated from $\xi = 0.336$ and the measured R_H with Eq. (19). The calculated value of $\langle R_G^2 \rangle$ at $M_w = 700,000$ daltons was then used to estimate $q = 252$ Å at the coil limit. This result is included in Table 3.

For comparison, ξ were estimated from literature data of R_H versus $\langle R_G^2 \rangle_z^{1/2}$ for several polymers in Table 3. The experimental values of ξ are well below values for typical flexible polymers in theta solvents or good solvents which range between 0.55 and 0.75.[78] It is interesting that the ξ for PHIC–hexane falls in the range observed for flexible polymers. The higher ξ may result from the relatively higher density within the domain of a molecule due to the n-hexyl branches on PHIC (see Ref. 79, page 405). We note that $\langle R_G^2 \rangle_z$ and $[\eta]$ are smaller for PHIC–hexane compared to PABH-T in DMSO and PPTA in H$_2$SO$_4$, whereas the R_H are similar in magnitude within a similar range of M_w. This observation is most likely associated with the higher molar mass per unit length of PHIC ($M_L = 71.5$ daltons Å^{-1}).[22]

Table 4
Values of q and C for Chain-Extended Polymers

System	q (Å)	L (Å)	C	Ref.
PPTA–H_2SO_4 + 0.05 M K_2SO_4	290	1200	0.29	74
		2030	0.21	
		2430	0.30	
PHIC–hexane	420	282	0.13	70
		575	0.14	
PBLG–DMF	700	1440	0.15	85
		3840	0.19	
	1565	2050	0.10	72
		2550	0.11	
	875	1840	0.11–0.12	71
Tobaco Mosaic Virus	3000	3000	~ 0.042	81, 83

Burchard et al.,[80] Meada and Fujime,[81, 82] Wilcoxon and Schurr,[83] and Kubota et al.[72] have attempted to evaluate chain stiffness from the angular dependence of Γ/k_1^2:

$$\Gamma/k_1^2 = D_0\left(1 + C\langle R_G^2\rangle k_1^2\right) \tag{21}$$

The dimensionless parameter C becomes measurable when $\langle R_G^2\rangle k_1^2 > 1$,[84] C depends on hydrodynamic interactions, chain structure, and polydispersity. It is not necessarily constant. Kubota et al.[72] applied a modification of Meada-Fujime (MF) theory in a study of PBLG in DMF. The measured trend in the Γ/k_1^2 versus k_1^2 was consistent using their relations, $q = 1565$ Å and $d = 22$ Å. The use of a smaller value for q, namely 700 Å,[85] produced a theoretical curve that was higher in magnitude than the measured Γ/k_1^2.[72] This work lends support to the higher q found from s_0 and $[\eta]$.[7] Kubota and Chu[70] also applied the MF treatment to study PHIC in hexane. Reasonable agreement was obtained for the angular dependence of Γ/k_1^2 with $q = 420$ Å. For comparison, initial slopes C for polymers studied by DLS, including rodlike Tobacco Mosaic Virus, are collected in Table 4. The q values reported were obtained by various means. It is seen that C values tend to be higher for polymers having smaller q.

3.4. Flow Birefringence

The ratio of birefringence Δn induced by shear flow to the intrinsic viscosity is related to q.[21, 86] The expression for the reduced birefringence in the zero shear, infinite dilution limit takes the form:

$$\frac{(\Delta n/c\dot{\gamma})c, \dot{\gamma} \to 0}{[\eta]} = \frac{4\pi\eta_0(n_s^2 + 2)^2}{45n_s kT}\left[(\alpha_\parallel - \alpha_\perp) + \frac{M_0(dn/dc)^2}{2\pi N_A \bar{v}}\right]\left(\frac{2q}{l}\right) \tag{22}$$

Table 5
Values of q Determined by Flow Birefringence

System	q (Å)	Ref.
DNA–0.005 M NaCl	1540	86
DNA–0.1 M NaCl[a]	740	86
DNA–0.6 M NaCl[a]	450	86
PBA–96% H_2SO_4	1000	87
PPTA–96% H_2SO_4	650	88
PABH-T–DMSO	400	89
PABH-T–DMSO	125	90
ATPE–TCE[b]	90	91

[a]$M_w = 1.3 \times 10^8$ g/mole.
[b]ATPE = Aromatic terephthalic acid copolyester;
TCE = Tetrachloroethane.

where $\dot{\gamma}$ is the shear rate, η_0 and n_s are the solvent viscosity and refractive index, respectively. The symbols $(\alpha_\parallel - \alpha_\perp)$, M_0, and l are the repeat unit anisotropy of polarizability, molecular weight, and repeat unit length, respectively. The polymer partial specific volume and concentration are represented by $\bar{\nu}$ and c. The ability to evaluate q by flow birefringence depends critically upon the geometrical asymmetry and optical anisotropy of the polymer under investigation. The absence of either factor makes the assessment of q impossible using this technique.[21] Some results are collected in Table 5.

Harrington[86] determined the variation of q with ionic strength for high MW DNA. Although molecular dimensions appeared affected by ionic strength, this was later shown to be a result of excluded volume effects at high molar mass instead of a change in rigidity with ionic strength.[92]

Several values for the aromatic polyamides reported by Russian workers tend to be larger than values obtained with other techniques. However, in later work, a lower q was determined for PABH-T/DMSO.[90] The reader is referred to the original literature for details pertaining to the experimental refinements that produced results in agreement with light scattering and viscosity measurement.[19, 90, 93]

Tsvetkov et al.[91] studied the flow birefringence of copolyesters consisting of terephthalic acid TA, 4,4'-dihydroxy-1,1-dinaphthoyl (DN), and a 2,2-propanediol PD. The persistence length found for the copolymer having a DN : D : T = 0.7 : 0.3 : 1 mole ratio was 90 Å.[91] The birefringence was also measured as a function of the mole fraction (0–0.7) of the most rigid monomer, DN. The reduced birefringence increased as a higher fraction of DN was incorporated in the chain. Polymer with DN > 0.7 was insoluble. Therefore, the experimental trend was extrapolated to the DN = 1 limit. The estimate for q was within the range 250–400 Å.[91] Although the estimate assumed that the optical anisotropy per unit length remained constant with varying composition, it does provide interesting experimental insight regarding the degree of chain extension of insoluble, wholly aromatic polyesters.

4. SCATTERING TECHNIQUES

4.1. Radius of Gyration, $\langle R_G^2 \rangle$

While examining $\langle R_G^2 \rangle$ data in Section 2 for the excluded volume effect, we utilized the Benoit-Doty[16] equation for monodisperse, unperturbed wormlike chains:

$$\langle R_G^2 \rangle = \frac{Lq}{3} - q^2 + \frac{2q^3}{L} - \frac{2q^4}{L^2}\left[1 - \exp\left(\frac{-L}{q}\right)\right] \qquad (23)$$

The scattering angle θ dependence of scattered radiation is related to the intramolecular interference factor $P^{-1}(k_1)$. The value of $\langle R_G^2 \rangle$ is evaluated from the scattering curve at the infinite dilution limit when $k_1\langle R_G^2 \rangle^{1/2} \ll 1$ using:

$$P^{-1}(k_1) = 1 + \tfrac{1}{3}k_1^2\langle R_G^2 \rangle_z \qquad (24)$$

where k_1 is the magnitude of the scattering wave vector (see Section 3.3) and the subscript z denotes the z-average value of $\langle R_G^2 \rangle$ for polydisperse specimens. The excess scattered intensity $I(k_1)$ is related to $P(k_1)$ and M_w by:

$$\lim_{c \to 0} \frac{K^*c}{I(k_1)} = \frac{1}{M_w P(k_1)} \qquad (25)$$

where c is the mass concentration and the parameter K^* is the contrast factor.

Table 6
Definitions of Contrast Factors for Scattering Techniques

Technique	K^*	Definitions	Ref.
Light scattering (vertically polarized incident light)	$\dfrac{4\pi^2 n_s^2 (dn/dc)^2}{\lambda_0^4 N_A}$	Refractive index increment: (dn/dc) Solvent refractive index: n_s Wavelength of light in vacuo: λ_0 Avogadro's number: N_A	94
Small-angle x-ray scattering	$N_A i_e \left(\dfrac{d\rho_e}{dc}\right)^2$	Molar excess of electrons per gram of solute: $(d\rho_e/dc)$ Thomson scattering factor for a single electron: i_e	95
Neutron scattering	$\dfrac{N_A(\alpha_H - \alpha_D)^2}{M_0^2}$	Monomer molar mass: M_0 Excess coherent scattering length: $(\alpha_H - \alpha_D)^2$	96

Contrast factors are defined for each scattering technique in Table 6. We mention the contrast factors to point out considerations that can influence the detection of scattered radiation from chain-extended polymers.

Scattered light intensity from dilute polymer solutions depends on the rate of change of solution refractive index with solute concentration, squared, $(dn/dc)^2$. Solutions of wormlike chain polymers are considered dilute in the absence of chain overlaps. The overlap concentration c^* (g mL^{-1}) is $c^* = 2^{3/2}M_w/N_A(qL)^{3/2}$.[97] Since the scattered intensity is inversely proportional to λ_0^4, significant corrections for light absorption may be necessary at lower wavelengths. Ying et al.[98] encountered an attenuation correction of $\sim 15\%$ at $\lambda_0 = 488$ nm and $c \approx 10^{-3}$ g mL^{-1} for PPTA in concentrated H_2SO_4. This difficulty can sometimes be circumvented by using incident light of longer wavelength at the expense of lower scattered intensity.

Extended chain polymers are often composed of optically anisotropic scattering elements that depolarize incident light.[99] The corrections to apparent values of M_{app}, $\langle R_G^2 \rangle_{z, app}$, and $A_{2, app}$ are made using the depolarization ratio ρ_v defined by:

$$\rho_v = \lim_{c, \theta \to 0} \frac{I_{vh}}{I_{vv}} = \frac{3\partial^2}{5 + 4\partial^2} \tag{26}$$

$$M_w = \frac{M_{app}}{1 + 4\partial^2/5} \tag{27}$$

$$\langle R_G^2 \rangle_z = \langle R_G^2 \rangle_{z, app} \frac{1 + 4\partial^2/5}{1 - 4f_1\partial/5 + 4(f_2\partial)^2/7} \tag{28}$$

$$A_2 = A_{2, app} \left(1 + \frac{4\partial^2}{5}\right)^2 \tag{29}$$

where I_{vh} and I_{vv} are the excess horizontally polarized and vertically polarized scattered light measured using vertically polarized incident light, respectively. The factor ∂^2 in Eq. (26) is the molecular optical anisotropy. Although the factors f_1 and f_2 range from 1 for totally anisotropic rods to 0 for optically isotropic random coils, Berry[9] has shown that they may be set equal to 1 with negligible error relative to experimental uncertainty. The depolarization correlation reduces apparent M_w values and increases $\langle R_G^2 \rangle_{app}$. Recall that the correction for polydispersity reduces $\langle R_G^2 \rangle_{z, app}$.[8] Depending on their magnitudes, corrections for depolarization and polydispersity may compensate for each other with respect to apparent values measured for $\langle R_G^2 \rangle$, and hence values derived for q using Eq. (23). Values of q derived for several polymers by light scattering are in Table 7.

Table 7
Values of q Derived from $\langle R_G^2 \rangle$ Measured by Light Scattering

Polymer–Solvent	q (Å)	Ref.
PBA–H$_2$SO$_4$	600	100
PPTA–H$_2$SO$_4$	200	100
PABH-T–DMSO	120	17
	112	18
	120	19
PBLG–DMF	700	85
DNA–0.2 M NaCl	540	65, 101a, b
BBL–MSA[a]	1500	9
Native xanthan–0.1 M NaCl	1270	102
Cellulose–8% NaOH (25°C)	110	60
Cellulose–DMAc + 5% LiCl	140	58

[a] Poly[(17-oxo-7,10-H-benz[de]-imidazo[4',5' : 5,6]benzimidazo [2,1-a]isoquinoline-3,4 : 10,11-tetrayl]-10-carbonyl]; MSA = methane sulfonic acid.

The value $q = 700$ Å for PBLG in DMF (obtained by simultaneous DLS and static light scattering, accounting for polydispersity[85]) is also included in Table 7. It is about the lowest limit for PBLG, the upper limit reaching 1800 Å.[7, 71, 72, 85, 103–105] We note that the effect of ionic strength on q for lower molar mass DNA was found to be quite small ($< 5\%$) owing to its rigid double-helix conformation.[101b]

4.2. Molecular Optical Anisotropy

The depolarization ratio ρ_v is used not only to correct apparent light-scattering values, but also provides another means to evaluate q. By modeling anisotropic scattering elements as ellipsoids, Arpin et al.[106] calculated the total chain anisotropy ∂^2 as a function of the segment anisotropy and the number of persistence lengths in the chain:

$$\partial^2 = \partial_0^2 \left(\frac{2}{3N} - \frac{2}{3N^2} [1 - \exp(-3N)] \right) \tag{30}$$

where $N = L/q$. Values of ∂_0^2 are estimated from measurements on model compounds or low molecular weight oligomers. Alternatively, ∂_0^2 may be estimated by extrapolating values of ∂^2 to the value expected for one scattering element in the chain.

An important advantage to the technique is that the measured trend in ∂^2 can be extended to a range in molecular weight below that required to

Table 8

Repeat Units of Aromatic Polyamides

Polymer–Solvent	Repeat unit	Refs.
PBA–DMAC + 3% LiCl	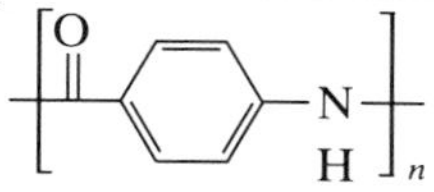	75
PPTA–H$_2$SO$_4$	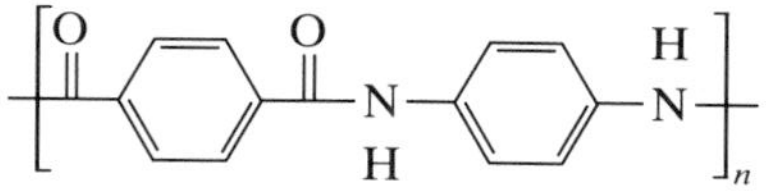	74, 100, 106
PBT–H$_2$SO$_4$	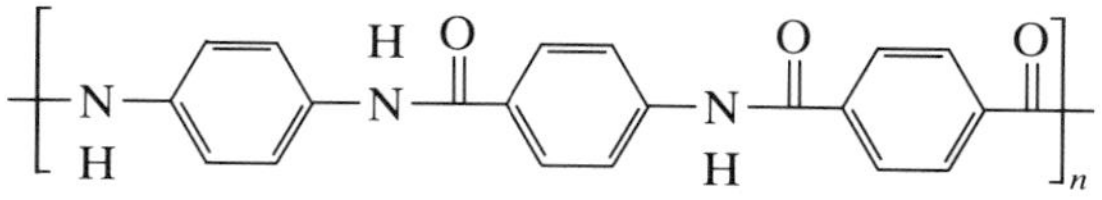	107
PA-2–DMAc + 1% LiCl	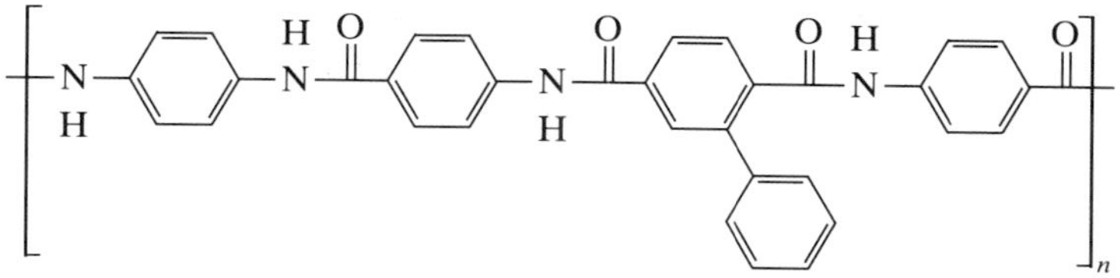	108
PA-4–DMAc + 4% LiCl	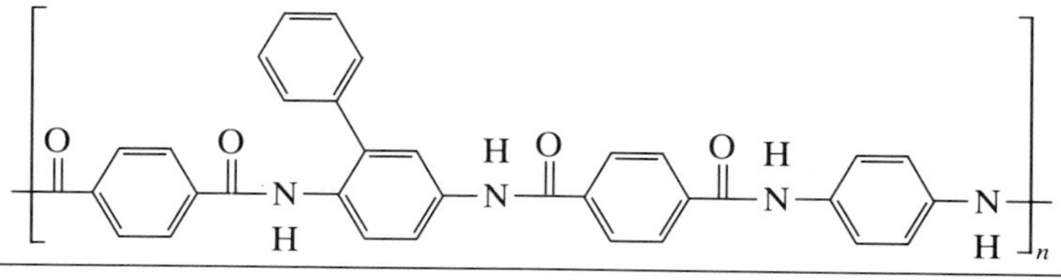	108

83

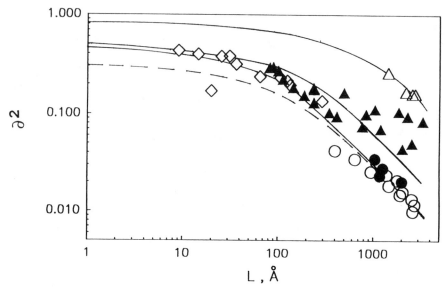

FIGURE 7

Chain optical anisotropy measured for aromatic polyamides against L. Values of ∂_0^2 and q used to calculate the solid curves are next to their respective symbols. The dashed line was calculated using $\partial_0^2 = 0.30$ and $q = 160$. The curve for $\partial_0^2 = 0.43$ and $q = 113$ Å is not shown for reasons of clarity. Adapted with permission from Ref. 74, 75, 106, 107, 108 (Copyright Am. Chem. Soc.) and Ref. 100, 106 (Butterworth-Heinemann Ltd. C).

Sample		∂_0^2	$q(A)$	Ref.
○	PA-2	0.43	110	108
●	PA-4	(0.30)	(160)	108
△	PBA	0.81	750	75
▲	PPTA	0.49	200	74, 100, 106
◇	PBT	0.43	113	107

measure $\langle R_G^2 \rangle$ by light scattering. However, deciding on a best fit of q to the data at low M_w alone may be difficult since Eq. (30) is not as sensitive to q as it is to ∂_0^2. Therefore, a fairly broad molecular weight range of fractionated specimens should be investigated, particularly since $\partial^2 \sim M_w^{-1}$ at high M_w.

With these considerations in mind, we summarize much of the ∂^2 data available for the aromatic polyamides. The repeat units of the polymers and the solvents in which they were studied are shown in Table 8. The two phenyl-substituted polyamides are highly soluble inorganic solvents compared to the unsubstituted analogues.[109]

The experimental ∂^2 are plotted against L for each polymer in Fig. 7. The variability in the data for PPTA compared to PBT may be due to the

Table 9
Persistence Lengths of Aromatic Polyamides Evaluated
by Total Chain Optical Anisotropy

Polymer–Solvent	q (Å)	∂_0^2	M_L (Daltons/Å)	Ref.
PBA–DMAc + 3% LiCl	750	0.81	21.6	75
PPTA–H$_2$SO$_4$	200	0.49	18.9	74, 100, 106
PBT–H$_2$SO$_4$	113	0.43^a	21.6	107
PA-2–DMAC + 1% LiCl PA-4–DMAC + 4% LiCl	110 (160)^b	0.43^a (0.30)^b	21.2	108

^{a}Measured for benzanilide.[107]

^{b}Alternative estimate.

polydispersity of several of the samples at higher M_w as noted by Zero and Aharoni.[107] The PBA samples are also unfractionated. The data for PA-2 and PA-4 were obtained on fractions prepared by successive precipitation.[108] The values of q and ∂_0^2 used in Eq. (30) to construct the solid curves are given in Table 9 along with the values of M_L used to calculate L from M_w for each sample. (None of the data are corrected for polydispersity here; the curve obtained with $q = 113$ Å and $\partial_0^2 = 0.43$ for PBT is not shown for reasons of clarity.)

At $L > 500$ Å the data show a marked difference between PBA, PPTA, and the phenyl-substituted polymers that may not be due to polydispersity alone. For instance, in order to assess the lower limit of q obtained by this technique for PPTA, Krigbaum and Brelsford[17] applied a correction to ∂^2 measured on polydisperse PPTA samples[74] using the weight to number average ratio of 1.8 determined by Chu et al.[110] The corrected PPTA data were fit with a q of 150 Å and compared to the value of 110 Å obtained on narrow fractions of PABH-T in DMSO. The difference in magnitude between the ∂^2 data after the correction was attributed to different degrees of chain extension and not entirely due to polydispersity.

Due to the phenyl substitutents on PA-2 and PA-4, a question arises as to what the best value for ∂_0^2 is. Two values of ∂_0^2 were used in attempts to fit the data. The dashed line in Fig. 7 represents the curve calculated for the q of 160 Å and $\partial_0^2 = 0.30$ (see values in parentheses in Table 9 and Fig. 7). Better agreement with [η] data was obtained with the lower value of $q = 110$ Å and $\partial_0^2 = 0.43$ (solid curve).

The q value for PA-2 and PA-4 is approximately two times smaller than PPTA and several times smaller than PBA. After examining space filling models, Krigbaum et al.[108] conclude that the phenyl substituent forces neighboring carbonyl groups out of the plane of the ring. This prevents a higher degree of chain extension by reducing amide bond conjugation. Aharoni[111] noted a similar effect with nitro-substituted polyamides. Admittedly, a more convincing comparison should be made by studying well-fractionated polymers in the same solvent before true differences in chain extension between the aromatic polyamides, or any other series of optically anisotropic polymers in solution, is definitely assessed.

4.3. Small-Angle x-Ray Scattering

Small-angle x-ray (SAXS) studies on synthetic extended-chain polymers are less numerous. The choice of solvents is limited not only by the lower solubility of these polymers, but also by the necessity of a sufficient electron density difference between the solute and solvent ($d\rho_e/dc$) (see Table 6). Adequate scattered x-ray transmission must also be achieved. When adequate contrast and transmission are achieved, more structural information in $P(k)$ is attainable with SAXS. Typical distances measured can range between several angstroms and a few hundred angstroms. Therefore, local conformation is probed in addition to measuring $\langle R_G^2 \rangle$.[95]

Regions of scattered x-ray intensity $I(k_1)$ depend on values of k_1 [$= 4\pi \sin(\theta/2)/\lambda_0$] relative to $\langle R_G^2 \rangle^{1/2}$. When $k_1 \leq \langle R_G^2 \rangle^{-1/2}$, the radius of gyration is determined from a plot of $\log I(k_1)$ against k_1^2. As k_1 increases, such that $\langle R_G^2 \rangle^{-1/2} \leq k_1 \leq q^{-1}$ and $\langle R_G^2 \rangle^{1/2}$ is significantly larger than q, the intensity approaches a horizontal asymptote when plotted versus k_1^2. At still larger k_1 ($k_1 > q^{-1}$), the intensity detects shorter segments of the chain and rodlike scattering behavior is observed.

These regions of scattered intensity form the basis of the Kratky plot, where $k_1^2 I(k_1)$ is plotted against k_1.[95] A reduced Kratky plot, normalized to the molar mass, is shown in Fig. 8.[95] Details of the scattering curves calculated for chains having various degrees of chain extension are in Chapter 12 of Ref. 95. Higher values of N' ($N' > 50$) correspond to flexible polymers. Curves labeled $N' \approx 1$ correspond to rodlike molecules.

Flexible chains exhibit a marked initial increase in $I(2k_1q)$ before approaching the expected asymptotic behavior. A linear increase is seen at larger $2k_1q$. In contrast, rodlike molecules show a weak initial trend followed by a linear region. The plot in Fig. 8 permits a comparison with experimental data to estimate the persistence length. A q of 490 Å for DNA in 0.2 M NaCl from light scattering and SAXS data was evaluated using this approach.[95]

Ballauff[4] has cited a limitation to this method encountered when studying chains with large diameters or pendent groups. As $d \sim k_1^{-1}$, interference results in an observed *decrease* in $I(2k_1q)$ at higher k_1. Although this effect is not accounted for in the wormlike chain model,[1] further work is expected to facilitate the evaluation of q despite interference of this nature.

Kratky and Porod[1] noted that if a transition between coil and rodlike scattering is observed, q can be evaluated from the value of k_1 at the transition (k_1^*) and the constant K_q. The constant K_q was found by equating the limiting intensities calculated for coils and rods at high k_1. Their value for K_q is 1.91. The persistence length is simply calculated from the relation: $q = K_q/k_1^*$. Krigbaum and Sasaki[112] studied PABH-T in DMAc using this

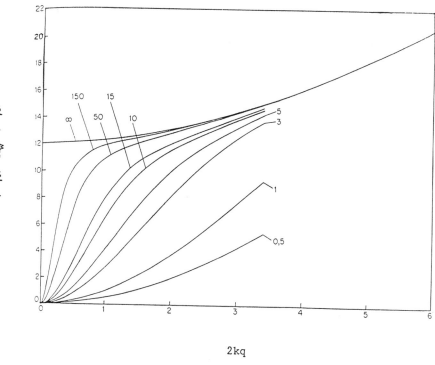

FIGURE 8

Normalized Kratky plot for wormlike chains. The number of Kuhn segment lengths per molecule N' is attached to each scattering curve: rods $N' \approx 1$ and coils $N' > 50$. The curve for an infinitely long chain is indicated by $N' = \infty$. (Reprinted with permission from Ref. 95.)

method and observed that k_1^* for two unfractionated samples and one narrow fraction were identical. Although theoretical values of K_q range between 1.7 and 2.87,[113] using $K_q = 2.0$ these workers obtained a q of 90–98 Å before applying a correction for chain expansion. In another study using SAXS, Burchard and Kajiwara[114] found $q = 108$ Å for cellulose tricarbanilate in acetone with $K_q = 1.91$ from the observed k_1^* transition. The limitation of this method might be inferred from Fig. 8. A sharp transition may be difficult to discern. This is particularly true when $\langle R_G^2 \rangle^{1/2}$ is not sufficiently larger than q.

Since an accurate determination of the transition between coil and rodlike scattering is frequently difficult, Schmidt et al.[8] recommend plotting $k_1 \cdot I(k_1)/\pi K^* c$ against $k_1 \langle R_G^2 \rangle^{1/2}$. This plot is referred to as the Holtzer plot. The scattering function for rods in this plot curves upward at low $k_1 \langle R_G^2 \rangle^{1/2}$ and reaches a horizontal asymptote. Flexible and semiflexible chains of sufficient length also reach asymptotic behavior when $2qk_1 \gg 1$, except that the scattering curve passes through a maximum. The position of the maximum depends on polydispersity. The maximum height is a function of the number of Kuhn segments or persistence lengths in the chain.[8] The utility of the Holtzer plot was demonstrated with scattering data obtained from aqueous solutions of xanthan. The Koyama theory[115] of $P(k_1)$ for Kuhn chains was used to fit the measured $k_1 \cdot I(k_1)/\pi K^* c$ trend with $2q = 150$ nm and a weight to number average ratio of 2.

4.4. Small-Angle Neutron Scattering

Neutron scattering studies of polymers in solution require either deuterium-labeled polymer in an unlabeled solvent or protonated polymer in a deuterated solvent. Studies in bulk phases are performed on a mixture of deuterated and protonated polymer having similar molar mass. Deuterium has a larger coherent scattering length and a smaller incoherent scattering length compared to hydrogen. These differences provide the contrast required to measure $P(k_1)$ in solution, melt, or bulk phases. The contrast or excess coherent scattering length $(\alpha_H - \alpha_D)^2$ (see Table 6) is calculated between the unlabeled and labeled molecules, where $\alpha_D = \Sigma_i b_i$ is the sum of coherent scattering lengths b_i of atoms in the labeled molecule and $\alpha_H = \Sigma_i b_i$ is the sum for unlabeled molecules.[96] The incoherent scattering is a spatially uncorrelated background signal and does not contribute to $P(k_1)$.

D'Allest[116] used neutron scattering to study the segmented liquid crystalline polyesters (P-7 and P-10) shown below.

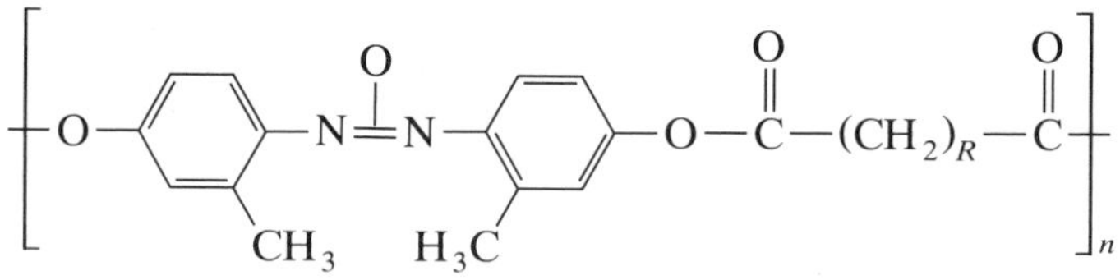

P-7: $R = 7$
P-10: $R = 10$

These polymers are well suited for neutron-scattering studies. The contrast required to detect scattered neutrons is achievable since the percentage of hydrogen atoms in the repeat units is high and highly deuterated polymers are readily prepared. The protonated polymers are also soluble in highly deuterated solvents. Isotropization temperatures depend upon M_w and range between 100°C and 160°C.[117]

The polymers were studied in isotropic and liquid-crystalline solutions and in bulk melts. Undeuterated polymer was dissolved in deuterated p-azoxyanisole (PAA) for the dilute solution studies. Average values of $\langle R_G^2 \rangle_z^{1/2}$ at the infinite dilution limit in unoriented solutions for two P-10 specimens and one P-7 sample are given in Table 10. Calculated values of $\langle R_G^2 \rangle_{calc}^{1/2}$

Table 10
Radius of Gyration Data for Segmented Polyesters Measured
by Neutron Scattering.[116]

Sample	M_w	$\langle R_G^2 \rangle_z^{1/2}$ (Å)[a]	$\langle R_G^2 \rangle_{calc}^{1/2}$ (Å)	
			Coil	Worm
P-10	6,000	50.0 ± 3.0	35	45
P-10	18,100	74.5 ± 4.0	60	85
P-7	36,000	90.0 ± 7.0	81	122

[a]Extrapolated at infinite dilution in PAA. Unoriented samples, no effect of temperature.

using the Gaussian chain model, $\langle R_G^2 \rangle_{coil} = nl^2/6$, and the wormlike chain model [Eq. (23), $q = 25$ Å] are shown for comparison in columns 4 and 5, respectively. Repeat unit projection lengths l and molar masses are 23.3 Å and 452.5 daltons for P-10 and 21.1 Å and 410.4 daltons for P-7, respectively.

The experimental $\langle R_G^2 \rangle_z^{1/2}$ values for P-10 are in fair agreement with the wormlike chain model using $q = 25$ Å. The degree of chain extension is similar to the repeat unit projection length. However, the result for the P-7 sample agrees more closely with the Gaussian chain model.

Dilute isotropic and nematic solutions of these samples were also investigated in an applied magnetic field.[118] The magnetic field served to orient the nematic phase. Scattered intensity at the detector was recorded as a function of position in two perpendicular directions relative to the applied field. This technique permitted the measurement of characteristic polymer size ($R_\parallel$ and $R_\perp$) relative to the direction of molecular order in the nematic (cf. Section 2.4, Chapter 5).

Strong anisotropic scattering was observed for both of the P-10 samples near the nematic–isotropic transition temperature of PAA ($\sim 135°C$). The anisotropy, $R_\parallel / R_\perp$, was largest for the P-10 (18,100 daltons) sample. By comparison, the anisotropy of the P-7 (36,000 daltons) sample was significantly lower than the P-10 (18,100 daltons) sample due to higher molecular weight and lower chain extension.

Mixtures (1 : 1 by weight) of deuterated polymer with protonated polymer having similar molar mass were also studied in isotropic and nematic melts under the applied magnetic field. Anisotropic chain dimensions increased as the temperature was lowered from the isotropic to nematic phases for a P-7 (6000 daltons) sample and the P-10 (6000 daltons) sample. Data for the two polymers were difficult to compare directly as a result of the wider biphasic gap and onset of crystallization for P-10 compared to P-7.[118] Nevertheless, these measurements provide direct evidence of higher chain extension as the temperature decreases in the nematic phase near the transition temperature.

Neutron-scattering studies on another segmented thermotropic copolyester based on 4,4'-dihydroxy-α,α'-dimethylbenzalazine and a 50/50 molar composition of sebacoyl and dodecanedioyl dichlorides are forthcoming.[119] A persistence length of ~ 27 Å was estimated from intrinsic viscosity measurements in chloroform at 25°C.[120] Measurements on solutions of polymers such as deuterated PPDT are also anticipated, once adequate contrast is achieved. Analysis of neutron-scattering data with plots such as those described in Section 4.3 should provide a more detailed assessment of conformations preferred by these polymers in the anisotropic phase.

5. CONCLUDING REMARKS

Analysis of the tables reveal a considerable scatter of persistence lengths in a given solvent observed with different techniques and sometimes the same technique but different investigators. Reports of persistence lengths differing even by a factor of 2 from existing data are not uncommon. It is not simple to derive general patterns for these deviations. Often,[10,51,58] q obtained by the Yamakawa-Fujii (YF), the Benoit-Doty (BD), and the coil-limit (CL) expressions fall in the order $q_{YF} < q_{BD} < q_{CL}$, and intrinsic differences in the approaches may be invoked (e.g., neglect of free-draining effect in the YF theory[10]). The above trend, however, is not generally valid. In the case of DNA, rather close values of q from sedimentation, light scattering, and intrinsic viscosity were obtained by the same group of investigators working on well-characterized fractions.[65] Fractionation is obviously preferred. However, little difference in the q values reported for unfractionated[54] and fractionated[12] PHIC in toluene was reported.

Assignment of parameters entering the theories may be critical. For instance, using the YF theory for $[\eta]$, a change in diameter of PHIC from 10 to 16 Å[54] entails a corresponding decrease of q from 375 to 310 Å. Aggregation may result in lower q values. However, situations in which aggregation is occurring may be easily detected[58,100] and avoided.

It appears that due to a number of theoretical and experimental problems which may affect the result to various extents, the assessment of q is a rather delicate task. At the present time it is felt that values of q of 750 Å for PBA in DMAc + 3% LiCl,[75] 300 Å for PPTA in H_2SO_4,[74] 1500 Å for PBLG in DMF,[103] 400 Å for PHIC in toluene,[54,12] 2000 Å for schizophyllan in H_2O,[64] and 660 Å for DNA in 0.2 M NaCl[86,92] are reliable ones.

Attention is currently expanding to the problems of more specialized conformations (i.e., broken worms), and to the effect of the nematic field on the conformation prevailing in dilute solutions. The occurrence of broken worms may be suspected in cases such as nicked DNA[121] (single-strand breaks along the double helix), or whenever occasional special bonds occur along the chain. The occurrence of flexible ether linkages[122] along the PHIC chain:

$$-C-O- \atop \underset{N-R}{\|}$$

may be sites for helix reversal.[123, 124] Mansfield[125] has treated a wormlike chain including random breaks characterized by an angle ϕ between consecutive breaks and a mean length b between breaks. His conclusions are that $\langle R_G^2 \rangle$, R_H, and the static structure factor are rather similar for the broken and the conventional wormlike chain. Thus, it may be difficult to characterize the behavior of the broken worm from dilute solution studies.

However, Khokhlov and Semenov[126] have compared the orientational behavior of the wormlike chain and of a chain incorporating rotational isomerism which may occur at predetermined sites. The inclusion of breaks substantially increases the order parameter and the orientation in an external field. Thus, the behavior of broken worms could be more easily detected in mesophases than in dilute solutions. There is indeed an indication that the broken worm model may explain some features of mesophase formation better than the classical persistent chain (cf. Chapter 6).

The above considerations add further interest to neutron scattering studies which can measure the effect of concentration on the radius of gyration in the anisotropic phase. For a Kuhn chain, orientation of segments is predicted, but no stretching of the macromolecule should occur (cf. Chapter 3). However, for persistent and broken worm models significant chain extension is expected.

ACKNOWLEDGMENTS

The copy of Ref. 116 provided by A. Ten Bosch and a preprint of Ref. 120 provided by R. A. Weiss are greatly appreciated.

REFERENCES

1. O. Kratky and G. Porod, *Recl. Trav. Chim., Pays-Bas*, **1949**, *68*, 1106.
2. W. Kuhn, *Kolloid*, **1936**, *76*, 2586; **1939**, *87*, 3.
3. P.J. Flory, *Adv. Polym. Sci.*, **1984**, *59*, 1.
4. M. Ballauf, *Angew. Chem. Int. Ed. Engl.*, **1989**, *28*, 253.
5. P.J. Flory, *Statistical Mechanics of Chain Molecules*, Interscience, New York, Chapter VII, 1969.
6. H. Yamakawa and J. Shimada, *J. Chem. Phys.*, **1978**, *68*, 4722.
7. H. Yamakawa, *Ann. Rev. Phys. Chem.*, **1984**, *35*, 23.
8. M. Schmidt, G. Paradossi, and W. Burchard, *Makromol. Chem. Rapid Commun.*, **1985**, *6*, 767.
9. G.C. Berry, *J. Polym. Sci., Polym. Symp.*, **1978**, *65*, 143.
10. M. Saito, *Polymer J.*, **1982**, *15*, 213.
11. A. Ciferri and E. Marsano, *Gazz. Chim. Ital.*, **1987**, *117*, 567.
12. T. Itou, H. Chikiri, A. Teramoto, and S.M. Aharoni, *Polymer J.*, **1988**, *20*, 143.
13. H. Yamakawa and W.H. Stockmayer, *J. Chem. Phys.*, **1972**, *57*, 2843.
14. T.M. Birshtein, A.M. Skvortsov, and A.A. Sariban, *Macromolecules*, **1976**, *9*, 892.
15. H. Yamakawa, *Modern Theory of Polymer Solutions*, Harper & Row, New York, 1971.

16. H. Benoit and P. Doty, *J. Chem. Phys.*, **1953**, *57*, 958.
17. W.R. Krigbaum and G. Brelsford, *Macromolecules*, **1988**, *21*, 2502.
18. K. Sakurai, K. Ochi, T. Norisuye, and H. Fujita, *Polymer J.*, **1983**, *16*, 559.
19. V.N. Tsvetkov and S.O. Tsepelevich, *Eur. Polym. J.*, **1983**, *19*, 267.
20. E. Bianchi, C. Ciferri, J. Preston, and W.R. Krigbaum, *J. Polym. Sci., Polym. Phys. Ed.*, **1981**, *19*, 863.
21. V. Tsvetkov and L. Andreeva, *Adv. Polym. Sci.*, **1981**, *39*, 95.
22. H. Murakami, T. Norisuye, and H. Fujita, *Macromolecules*, **1980**, *13*, 345.
23. H. Yamakawa and J. Shimada, *J. Chem. Phys.*, **1985**, *83*, 2607; **1986**, *85*, 591.
24. C. Domb and A.J. Barrett, *Polymer*, **1976**, *17*, 179.
25. K. Kamide and M. Saito, *Eur. Polym. J.*, **1983**, *19*, 507.
26. B.H. Zimm, *J. Chem. Phys.*, **1946**, *14*, 164.
27. K. Huber and W.H. Stockmayer, *Macromolecules*, **1987**, *20*, 1400.
28. K. Huber, W. Burchard, and Z.A. Akcasu, *Macromolecules*, **1985**, *18*, 2743.
29. B.K. Varma, H. Fujita, M. Takahashi, and T. Nose, *J. Polym. Sci., Polym. Phys. Ed.*, **1984**, *22*, 1718.
30. M. Ragnetti, D. Geiser, H. Hocker, and R.G. Oberthür, *Makromol. Chem.*, **1985**, *186*, 1701.
31. S. Itou, N. Nishioka, T. Norisuye, and A. Teramoto, *Macromolecules*, **1981**, *14*, 904.
32. T. Itou, T. Sato, A. Teramoto, and S.M. Aharoni, *Polymer J.*, **1988**, *20*, 1049.
33. J.E. Hearst, E. Beals, and R.A. Harris, *J. Chem. Phys.*, **1968**, *48*, 5371.
34. E.Y. Eizner and O.B. Ptitsyn, *Vysokomol. Soedin.*, **1962**, *4*, 1725; *Dokl. Akad. Nauk SSSR*, **1962**, *142*, 134.
35. A. Peterlin, *J. Polym. Sci.*, **1952**, *8*, 173.
36. P. Sharp and V.A. Bloomfield, *J. Chem. Phys.*, **1968**, *48*, 2149.
37. O.B. Ptitsyn and E.Y. Eizner, *Zh. Fiz. Khim.*, **1958**, *32*, 2464.
38. H. Yamakawa, *Ann. Rev. Phys. Chem.*, **1974**, *25*, 179.
39. H. Yamakawa, *Pure Appl. Chem.*, **1976**, *46*, 135.
40. H. Yamakawa and M. Fujii, *Macromolecules*, **1974**, *7*, 128.
41. H. Yamakawa and T. Yoshizaki, *Macromolecules*, **1980**, *13*, 633.
42. M. Bohdanecký, *Macromolecules*, **1983**, *16*, 1483.
43. M. Motowoka, T. Norisuye, and H. Fujita, *Polym. J.*, **1977**, *9*, 613; *Polym. J.*, **1978**, *10*, 331.
44. J. Sadanobu, T. Norisuye, and H. Fujita, *Polym. J.*, **1981**, *13*, 75.
45. T. Norisuye and H. Fujita, *Polymer J.*, **1982**, *14*, 143.
46. T. Yoshizaki and H. Yamakawa, *J. Chem. Phys.*, **1980**, *72*, 57.
47. W.H. Stockmayer and M. Fixman, *J. Polym. Sci.*, **1963**, *C1*, 137.
48. W.H. Stockmayer, *Br. Polym. J.*, **1977**, *9*, 89.
49. T.E. Helminiak, C.L. Benner, and W.E. Gibbs, *Am. Chem. Soc., Polymer Chem. Div., Prepr.*, **1967**, *8*, 284.
50. T.E. Helminiak and G.C. Berry, *J. Polym.Sci., Polym. Symp.*, **1978**, *65*, 107.
51. T.A. Aden, E. Bianchi, A. Ciferri, and G. Conio, *Macromolecules*, **1984**, *17*, 2010.
52. W.R. Krigbaum, G. Brelsford, and A. Ciferri, *Macromolecules*, **1989**, *22*, 2487.
53. E. Bianchi, A. Ciferri, G. Conio, and W.R. Krigbaum, *Polymer*, **1987**, *28*, 813.
54. W.R. Krigbaum, H. Hakemi, A. Ciferri, and G. Conio, *Macromolecules*, **1985**, *18*, 973.
55. G. Conio, E. Bianchi, A. Ciferri, and W.R. Krigbaum, *Macromolecules*, **1984**, *17*, 856.
56. G.V. Laivens and D.G. Gray, *Macromolecules*, **1986**, *18*, 1746.
57. E. Bianchi, A. Ciferri, G. Conio, L. Lanzavecchia, and M. Terbojevich, *Macromolecules*, **1986**, *19*, 630.
58. E. Bianchi, A. Ciferri, G. Conio, A. Cosani, and M. Terbojevich, *Macromolecules*, **1985**, *18*, 646.

59. A. Ciferri, C.A. Hoeve, and P.J. Flory, *J. Am. Chem. Soc.*, **1961**, *83*, 1015.
60. K. Kamide, M. Saito, and K. Kowasa, *Polymer J.*, **1987**, *19*, 1173.
61. C.T. Sho, T. Sato, and T. Norisuye, *Biophysical Chem.*, **1986**, *25*, 307.
62a. H. Yamakawa and M. Fujii, *Macromolecules*, **1973**, *6*, 407.
62b. H. Yamakawa and T. Yoshizaki, *Macromolecules*, **1977**, *12*, 32.
63. M.G. Vitovskaya, P.N. Lavrenko, O.V. Okatova, E.P. Estapento, V.Y. Nikolayev, V.D. Kal'mykova, A.V. Volokhina, G.I. Kudryavtsev, and V.N. Tstvetkov, *Vysokomol. Soyed.*, **1977**, *A19*, 1966.
64. T. Yanaki, T. Norisuye, and H. Fujita, *Macromolecules*, **1980**, *13*, 1462.
65. J.E. Godfrey and H. Eisenberg, *Biophys. Chem.*, **1976**, *5*, 301.
66. B. Chu, *Laser Light Scattering*, Academic Press, New York, 1974.
67. D.E. Koppel, *J. Chem. Phys.*, **1972**, *57*, 4814.
68. B.J. Berne and R. Pecora, *Dynamic Light Scattering with Applications to Chemistry, Biology and Physics*, John Wiley & Sons, New York, 1976.
69. J.M. Schurr, *CRC Crit. Rev. Biochem.*, **1977**, *4*, 371.
70. K. Kubota and B. Chu, *Macromolecules*, **1983**, *16*, 105.
71. K. Kubota and B. Chu, *Biopolymers*, **1983**, *22*, 1461.
72. K. Kubota, Y. Tominaga, and S. Fujime, *Macromolecules*, **1986**, *19*, 1604.
73. W.R. Krigbaum and T. Tanaka, *Macromolecules*, **1988**, *21*, 743.
74. Q. Ying and B. Chu, *Macromolecules*, **1986**, *19*, 1580.
75. Q. Ying and B. Chu, *Macromolecules*, **1987**, *20*, 871.
76. C.L. McCormick, P.A. Callais, and B.H. Hutchinson, Jr., *Macromolecules*, **1985**, *18*, 2394.
77. J.C. Selser, *Macromolecules*, **1981**, *14*, 346.
78. L. Mandlekern, W.R. Krigbaum, H.A. Scheraga, and P.J. Flory, *J. Chem. Phys.*, **1952**, *20*, 1392.
79. C. Tanford, *Physical Chemistry of Macromolecules*, John Wiley & Sons, New York, 1960.
80. W. Burchard, M. Schmidt, and W.H. Stockmayer, *Macromolecules*, **1980**, *13*, 1265.
81. T. Maeda and S. Fujime, *Macromolecules*, **1985**, *18*, 2430.
82. T. Maeda and S. Fujime, *Macromolecules*, **1984**, *17*, 2381.
83. J. Wilcoxon and J.M. Schurr, *Biopolymers*, **1983**, 22, 849.
84. M. Schmidt and W.H. Stockmayer, *Macromolecules*, **1984**, *17*, 509.
85. M. Schmidt, *Macromolecules*, **1984**, *17*, 533.
86. R.E. Harrington, *Biopolymers*, **1978**, *17*, 919.
87. V.N. Tsvetkov, G.I. Kudriatsev, I.N. Shtennikova, T.V. Peker, E.N. Zamarova, V.D. Kalmykova, and A.V. Volokhina, *Eur. Polym. J.*, **1976**, *12*, 517.
88. V.N. Tsvetkov, I.N. Shtennikova, T.V. Peker, G.I. Kudriavtsev, A.V. Volkhina, and V.D. Kalmykova, *Eur. Polym. J.*, **1977**, *13*, 455.
89. V.N. Tsvetkov, G.I. Kudriatsev, N.A. Nikhailova, A.V. Volokhina, and V.D. Kalmykova, *Dokl. Phys. Chem.*, **1977**, *235*, 817.
90. N.V. Pogodina, L.V. Starchenko, A.Z. Khrustalev, and V.N. Tsvetkov, *Polym. Sci. USSR*, **1984**, *26*, 2300.
91. V.N. Tsvetkov, L.N. Andreeva, S.V. Bushin, A.I. Mashoshin, V.A. Cherkasov, Z. Yedlinski, and D. Sek, *Polym. Sci. USSR*, **1984**, *26*, 2569.
92. T. Odijk, *Biopolymers*, **1979**, 18, 3111.
93. V.N. Tsvetkov, *Rigid Chain Polymers*, Plenum Press, New York, 1989.
94. M.B. Huglin, Ed., *Light Scattering from Polymer Solutions*, Academic Press, New York, 1972.
95. O. Glatter and O. Kratky, *Small Angle X-ray Scattering*, Academic Press, London, Chapter *12*, 1982.
96. G.D. Wignall, H.F. Mark, N.M. Bikales, C.G. Overberger, and G. Menges, Eds., *Encyclopedia of Polymer Science and Engineering*, Wiley, New York, Vol. 10, p. 112, 1987.

97. Q. Ying and B. Chu, *Macromolecules*, **1987**, *20*, 362.
98. Q. Ying, B. Chu, R. Qian, J. Bao, Z. Zhang, and C. Xu, *Polymer*, **1985**, *26*, 1401.
99. K. Nagai, *Polymer J.*, **1972**, *3*, 67.
100. M. Arpin and C. Strazielle, *Polymer*, **1977**, *18*, 591.
101a. H. Yamakawa and M. Fujii, *Macromolecules*, **1974**, *7*, 649.
101b. M. Mandel and J. Schouten, *Macromolecules*, **1980**, *13*, 1247.
102. T. Coviello, K. Kajiwara, W. Burchard, M. Dentini, and V. Crescenzi, *Macromolecules*, **1986**, *19*, 2826.
103. T. Sato and A. Teramoto, *Kobunshi*, **1988**, *37*, 278.
104. K. Tsuji, H. Ohe, and H. Watanabe, *Polym. J.*, **1973**, *4*, 553.
105. N. Ookubo, M. Komatsubara, H. Nakajiama, and Y. Wada, *Biopolymers*, **1976**, *15*, 929.
106. M. Arpin, C. Strazielle, G. Weill, and H. Benoit, *Polymer*, **1977**, *18*, 262.
107. K. Zero and S.M. Aharoni, *Macromolecules*, **1987**, *20*, 1957.
108. W.R. Krigbaum, T. Tanaka, G. Brelsford, and A. Ciferri, *Macromolecules*, accepted for publication.
109. W.R. Krigbaum, J. Preston, and J.Y. Jadhav, *Macromolecules*, **1988**, *21*, 538.
110. B. Chu, Q. Ying, C. Wu, J.R. Ford, and H.S. Dhadal, *Polymer*, **1985**, *26*, 140.
111. S.M. Aharoni, *Macromolecules*, **1987**, *20*, 2010.
112. W.R. Krigbaum and S. Sasaki, *J. Polym. Sci., Polym. Phys. Ed.*, **1981**, *19*, 1339.
113. A.K. Gupta, J.P. Cotton, E. Marchal, W. Burchard, and H. Benoit, *Polymer*, **1976**, *17*, 363.
114. W. Burchard and K. Kajiwara, *Proc. R. Soc. (London) (A)*, **1970**, *311*, 185.
115. R. Koyama, *Phys. Soc. Jpn.*, **1973**, *34*, 1029.
116. J.F. D'Allest, *Propertietes Des Polymeres Mesomorphes A Chaine Principale A La Transition Anisotrope-Isotrope*, Ph.D. Dissertation, University of Nice, 1988.
117. R.B. Blumstein, E.M. Stickels, M.M. Gauthier, A. Blumstein, and F. Volino, *Macromolecules*, **1984**, *17*, 177.
118. J.F. D'Allest, A. Maïssa, A. Ten Bosch, P. Sixou, A. Blumstein, R. Blumstein, J. Teixeira, and L. Noirez, *Phys. Rev. Lett.*, **1988**, *61*, 2562.
119. R.A. Weiss, personal communication.
120. A.L. Cimecioglu, H. Fruitais and R.A. Weiss, *Makromol. Chem.*, in press.
121. J.B. Hays and B.H. Zimm, *J. Mol. Biol.*, **1970**, *48*, 297.
122. N.S. Schneider, S. Furasaki and R.W. Lenz, *J. Polym. Sci., Part A*, **1965**, *3*, 933.
123. A. Tonelli, *Macromolecules*, **1974**, *7*, 628.
124. M.R. Ambler, D. McIntyre, and L.J. Felters, *Macromolecules*, **1978**, *11*, 300.
125. M.L. Mansfield, *Macromolecules*, **1986**, *19*, 854.
126. A.R. Khokhlov and A.N. Semenov, *Macromolecules*, **1984**, *17*, 2678.

PART II

Molecular Theories

CHAPTER 3

Theories Based on the Onsager Approach

A.R. KHOKHLOV

Physics Department, Moscow State University, Moscow 117234, USSR

CONTENTS

1. INTRODUCTION

The first molecular theory of liquid-crystalline ordering was proposed by Onsager,[1] who described a nematic ordering in a solution of cylindrical, long, rigid rods. Although this model is very convenient for application to stiff-chain polymers, the Onsager approach was rarely used for polymer problems until recently. Apparently this is because an alternative approach, based on the lattice model, was proposed by Flory (Ref. 2; see also Chapter 4), who was one of the leaders of polymer scientific community. Nevertheless, during the last 10 years the Onsager approach has been applied to many aspects of liquid-crystalline ordering in polymer systems and for many problems this approach has turned out a most useful one. In this chapter we will outline the main ideas of the Onsager method and its generalizations, as well as the applications of this method to various specific problems.

Only theoretical aspects will be covered in this chapter; comparison of theories and experiments will be given in Chapter 6. We shall limit ourselves only to the analysis of the theory of liquid crystals in systems of stiff-chain polymers. Properties of the orientational ordering in melts or solutions of macromolecules containing both stiff (mesogen) and flexible segments are considered in Chapter 7.

2. ONSAGER THEORY FOR THE NEMATIC ORDERING IN A SOLUTION OF RIGID RODS

Let us consider a solution of cylindrical, long, rigid rods of length L and diameter d ($L \gg d$). In polymer language this system is a model for a solution of extremely stiff-chain macromolecules, whose flexibility is so insignificant that it cannot be manifested in the length L. Let us assume further that the only forces of interaction of rods are due to their mutual impenetrability (steric interactions), i.e., that the solution of rods is athermal.

The basic steps in considering the isotropic–nematic transition for the system described by Onsager[1] are the following. Let N_2 rods lie in the volume V so that their concentration is $c = N_2/V$, while the volume fraction of rods in the solution is $v_2 = \pi c L d^2/4$. Let us introduce the orientational distribution function $f(\mathbf{n})$ for the rods; $cf(\mathbf{n}) \, d\Omega_\mathbf{n}$ is the number of rods per unit volume with directions lying within the bounds of the small solid angle $d\Omega_\mathbf{n}$ about the direction $\mathbf{n}$. In the isotropic state $f(\mathbf{n}) = \text{const} = 1/4\pi$; in a liquid-crystalline nematic phase $f(\mathbf{n})$ is a function with a maximum along the anisotropy axis.

The main approximation introduced by Onsager consists in writing the free energy of the solution of rods as a function of f in the form

$$F = N_2 T \left[\ln c + \int f(\mathbf{n}) \ln[4\pi f(\mathbf{n})] \, d\Omega_\mathbf{n} + \frac{c}{2} \int f(\mathbf{n}_1) f(\mathbf{n}_2) B(\gamma) \, d\Omega_{\mathbf{n}_1} \, d\Omega_{\mathbf{n}_2} \right]$$

$$(1)$$

The first term in Eq. (1) is the free energy of the translational motion of the rods; the second term describes the loss of orientational entropy due to nematic ordering; the third term is the free energy of interaction of the rods in the second virial approximation. In this last term $B(\gamma)$ is the second virial coefficient of interaction of rods, whose long axes (specified by the unit vectors n_1 and n_2) form an angle γ with each other. When only steric interactions of the rods are present we have[1]

$$B(\gamma) = 2L^2 d \sin \gamma \qquad (2)$$

Thus the fundamental approximation of the Onsager method is that the interaction of the rods is taken into account in the second virial approximation. Hence this method is directly applicable only at a low enough concentration of the solution of rods. Estimations of the virial coefficients of steric interaction of rods [the second virial coefficient is $B \approx L^2 d$ and the third is $C \approx L^3 d^3 \ln(L/d)]^3$ show that the second virial approximation ($cB \gg c^2 C$) is valid if $c \ll 1/L^2 d$ or $v_2 \ll 1$. We will see below that in the limit $L \gg d$ an isotropic–nematic transition in a solution of rods takes place precisely at $v_2 \ll 1$. Therefore, for studying this transition and the properties of the anisotropic phase in the limit $L \gg d$ (which is most interesting from the standpoint of application to stiff-chain polymers), the Onsager method is exact.[4,5]

If the L/d ratio is not very large, the next term of the virial expansion connected with the third virial coefficient, as well as the corrections to $B(\gamma)$ of relative order d/L should be taken into account. The corresponding corrections to formulas (4)–(6) were evaluated by Straley[3] and Odijk.[6]

The next step in the Onsager method is to find the equilibrium distribution function $f(n)$, which minimizes the functional Eq. (1). Direct minimization leads to an integral equation that can be solved only numerically. Therefore Onsager used an approximate variational method with the trial function

$$f(n) = \text{const } ch(\alpha \cos \Theta), \qquad \int f(n)\, d\Omega_n = 1 \qquad (3)$$

Here θ is the angle between the vector n and the direction of the anisotropy axis, while α is the variational parameter. The trial function (Eq. 3) was substituted in expression (1), which was then minimized with respect to α. The minima correspond to possible phases (isotropic and nematic). It is possible to study the properties of the transition between these phases by the usual method by equating the pressures $\Pi = (c^2/N_2)\partial F/\partial c$ and chemical potentials $\mu = (F + c\,\partial F/\partial c)/N_2$ of the two phases.

As a result it turned out that[1]:

1. The orientational ordering in a solution of long rigid rods is a first-order phase transition that occurs at low rod concentration ($v_2 \sim d/L \ll 1$) so that the second virial approximation is applicable.

2. At $v_2 < v_2^i$ the solution is isotropic, at $v_2 > v_2^a$ it is anisotropic, and at $v_2^i < v_2 < v_2^a$ the solution separates into isotropic and anisotropic phases, the values of v_2^i and v_2^a being

$$v_2^i = 3.34d/L; \qquad v_2^a = 4.49d/L; \qquad w = v_2^a/v_2^i - 1 = 0.34 \quad (4)$$

3. The order parameter $S = \langle 3\cos^2\Theta - 1 \rangle/2$ [the averaging is performed by using the equilibrium function $f(\mathbf{n})$] at the point of appearance of the liquid-crystalline phase (i.e., when $v_2^i = v_2^a$) is equal to

$$S_0 = 0.84 \qquad\qquad\qquad (5)$$

It is to be emphasized that the only fundamental physical restriction of the Onsager method is connected with the second virial approximation, i.e., with the condition $v_2 \ll 1$. The use of variational procedure is simply a method of simplifying the calculation. The integral equations that arise upon exact minimization of the functional Eq. (1) can be solved numerically to a high degree of accuracy[7-10]; the result is

$$v_2^i = 3.290d/L; \qquad v_2^a = 4.191d/L; \qquad w = 0.274; \qquad S_0 = 0.792 \quad (6)$$

This shows that the use of variational method leads to a very small error ($\sim 5\%$) in determining the characteristics of the liquid-crystalline transition.

3. GENERALIZATION FOR HIGH CONCENTRATIONS

Thus the Onsager method in the form presented above is valid only at low concentrations of the solution of rods, $v_2 \ll 1$. Many publications have been devoted to attempts to generalize this method to high concentrations.[3,7,11-14] Such generalization is necessary for considering many problems, for example, to study orientational ordering in the system of stiff-chain macromolecules in the presence of attractive forces between them.

The approach of Parsons[11] is distinguished by the greatest simplicity and generality from the standpoint of application to solutions of stiff-chain macromolecules. The essence of this approach consists in the following. The internal energy of the system of rods, U, can be related to the pair correlation function $g(\mathbf{r}, \mathbf{n}_1, \mathbf{n}_2)$ of two rods having the orientations $\mathbf{n}_1$ and $\mathbf{n}_2$ ($\mathbf{r}$ is the vector joining their centers) by means of the relation

$$U = \frac{N_2^2}{2V} \int f(\mathbf{n}_1) f(\mathbf{n}_2) g(\mathbf{r}, \mathbf{n}_1, \mathbf{n}_2) h(\mathbf{r}, \mathbf{n}_1, \mathbf{n}_2)\, d^3r\, d\Omega_{\mathbf{n}_1}\, d\Omega_{\mathbf{n}_2} \quad (7)$$

Here $h(\mathbf{r}, \mathbf{n}_1, \mathbf{n}_2)$ is the energy of pairwise interaction of the rods. If the interaction is determined only by the shape of the rods, the function h can be represented in the form

$$h(\mathbf{r}, \mathbf{n}_1, \mathbf{n}_2) = \mathbf{h}(r/\rho) \tag{8}$$

where $\rho = \rho(\mathbf{n}_1, \mathbf{n}_2, \mathbf{r}/r)$ is the minimum distance to which rods having the given orientations can approach. The central approximation of the approach by Parsons consists in writing the function g in the same form:

$$g(\mathbf{r}, \mathbf{n}_1, \mathbf{n}_2) = g(\mathbf{r}/\rho; v_2) \tag{9}$$

Approximation (9) is exact at low concentrations of the solution; at higher concentrations it is essentially an approximation of the mean-field type, which separates the translational degrees of freedom from the orientational ones (decoupling approximation). If we adopt assumption (9), then we can write the free energy of steric interaction of the rods F_{ster} in the form [cf. the last term in Eq. (1)][11]:

$$F_{\text{ster}} = N_2 TJ(v_2) \frac{2}{\pi d^2 L} \int f(\mathbf{n}_1) f(\mathbf{n}_2) B(\gamma) \, d\Omega_{\mathbf{n}_1} \, d\Omega_{\mathbf{n}_2} \tag{10}$$

$$J(v_2) = \int_0^{v_2} g(1; v_2) \, dv_2 \tag{11}$$

At low concentrations of the solution of rods ($v_2 \ll 1$) we have $g(1; v_2) \approx 1$. Therefore $J(v_2) \approx v_2$ and Eq. (10) reduces to the third term in Eq. (1).

The generality of Eq. (10) consists in the fact that it describes the results of many other studies dealing with the calculation of the free energy in a concentrated solution of rigid rods.[7, 12-14] Thus it can be concluded that the Onsager method can be consistently generalized for describing solutions of any arbitrary concentration and even melts of polymer chains. Below we will use this generalization (decoupling approximation) in the theories of liquid-crystalline ordering in concentrated polymer systems.

4. COMPARISON OF THE ONSAGER AND FLORY APPROACHES

Another approach to solving the problem of liquid-crystalline ordering in a solution of rigid rods was developed by Flory.[2] Flory's method is based on the lattice model and it is considered in detail in Chapter 4. Here we restrict ourselves only to the discussion of relative merits and disadvantages of both approaches.

It is clear from the above consideration that Onsager's approach is exact for the solution of rods of low concentration ($v_2 \ll 1$); for higher concentrations it can be approximately generalized. At the same time, Flory's method is based on some assumptions, among the most serious of which is that spatial positions of monomeric links and solvent molecules are related to a predetermined space lattice.

Thus, it is natural that the results obtained in the framework of the Flory model for the properties of nematic ordering in solutions of long rigid rods differ from the exact results [Eqs. (4)–(6)] of the Onsager approach. Indeed, the results of the Flory theory[15] analogous to Eqs. (4)–(6) are (see Chapter 4)

$$v_2^i = 7.89d/L; \qquad v_2^a = 11.57d/L; \qquad w = 0.47; \qquad S_0 = 0.92 \quad (12)$$

The lattice method faces even greater difficulties in treating nematic ordering in solutions of stiff-chain macromolecules having partial flexibility. In this case the presence of the fixed-space lattice places substantial restrictions on the flexibility mechanism of the polymer chain, many of which (e.g., the persistent mechanism) cannot be represented within the framework of the lattice model.

Therefore we think that it is the continuum Onsager approach that is most promising from the standpoint of studying liquid-crystalline order in polymeric systems. Within the framework of this approach it is possible to take into account in a natural way the presence of partial flexibility of a chain of arbitrary nature.

As regards the lattice model, it can be successfully applied to solving a number of specific problems in those cases in which the continuum approach leads to too complicated calculations. Moreover, it might be somewhat more directly applied to concentrated solutions and melts. Problems such as polydispersity, effect of flow fields, and nonsteric interaction between the molecules have been handled within the framework of both approaches.

A separate question is the account of the role of solvent molecules in the theory of nematic ordering in polymer solutions. Flory and Ronca[15] asserted that a serious disadvantage of the Onsager approach lay in the fact that the discrete structure of the solvent was not taken into account explicitly. In connection with this statement the following remarks can be made. First, for many polymers able to form a nematic solution the characteristic width of the chain is in fact much larger than the characteristic size of solvent molecules (e.g., for aqueous DNA solutions). Second, in Onsager's theory it is possible to indicate a limiting case (continuum solvent) for which this theory is asymptotically exact. Starting from this limiting case one can try to generalize the theory to the case of a discrete solvent (accounting the discrete nature of a solvent within the framework of the virial expansion is in principle possible), whereas no such limiting case exists in the Flory theory. Finally, in many cases the discreteness of the solvent should lead simply to the renormalization of the diameter of the rods; the renormalized diameter is directly connected with the osmotic second virial coefficient of the interaction of rods, so it can be determined directly from the experimental data.

It should be noted that a number of other lattice theories of nematic ordering of rigid rods have been proposed besides the Flory theory.[16-20] These theories retain all the merits and disadvantages of the lattice approaches, which have been discussed above. In particular, a series of papers by Dowell (Ref. 20 and references cited therein) deals with the development of lattice conformational statistics for melts and solutions of polymers, which are able to form a liquid-crystalline phase. The main assumptions used by Dowell are the following: (1) the relation of the spatial positions of constituents to a predetermined lattice; (2) self-consistent field arguments throughout the consideration; and (3) factorization of the contribution to a partition function due to steric interaction (i.e., it is supposed that this contribution is a product of factors related to different species or to different parts of chain). Thus the results obtained using this approach should not be very accurate. Nevertheless, in Ref. 20 impressive correlation between theory and experiment for some polymer systems is claimed. This problem deserves further analysis.

5. THE PROBLEM OF POLYDISPERSITY

Up to now we have assumed that all the rods have the same length. This situation is characteristic of polymers of biological origin. However, most often polymer solutions are polydisperse, i.e., they contain macromolecules of differing molecular masses. The generalization of the Onsager theory presented in Section 2 to this general case presents no difficulties in principle. The effect of polydispersity on a nematic phase transition has been analyzed using Onsager's method in a number of studies.[6, 9, 21-25] Below we present characteristic results for the simplest polydisperse system—a mixture of two kinds of rods of lengths L_a and L_b with $m = L_b/L_a > 1$.

Let $v_{2,a}$ and $v_{2,b}$ be the volume fractions in the solution of rods of length L_a and L_b, respectively; $v_2 = v_{2,a} + v_{2,b}$. In this case $z = v_{2,b}/v_2$ is the weight fraction of the long rods and

$$\bar{L} = L_a(1 - z) + L_b z \tag{13}$$

is the weight-average length of the rods. We can expect that, just as in the case of a monodisperse system, the nematic transition occurs at $v_2 \sim d/\bar{L}$. Therefore it is natural to introduce the reduced volume fraction

$$\vartheta = v_2 \bar{L}/d \tag{14}$$

The results obtained for the system described using the Onsager method by a computer calculation[9] are shown in Figs. 1 and 2 for $m = L_b/L_a = 2$. Analogous results have been obtained purely analytically.[6, 22]

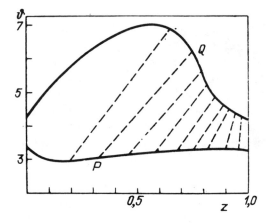

FIGURE 1
Phase diagram of a solution or rods having the length ratio
$L_b / L_a = 2$. z is the weight fraction of the longer rods; ϑ is defined
by Eq. (14). The curves surround the phase-separation region. The
ends of the broken lines correspond to coexisting phases.
(Reproduced with permission from Ref. 9.)

Figure 1 is the phase diagram of the system. Solid lines surround the
region of separation into two phases. In the monodisperse case, $L_a = L_b$,
these curves would be converted into parallel straight lines $\vartheta^i = 3.29$, $\vartheta^a =$
4.22. We see that polydispersity leads to a small decrease of ϑ^i and to a
strong increase of ϑ^a. Consequently the relative width of the separation
region substantially increases as compared with the monodisperse case (by a
factor of 4.7 for $z = 0.5$ and $q = 2$).

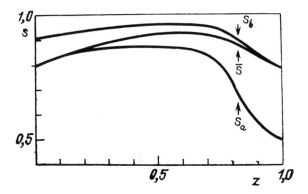

FIGURE 2
Dependence of the orientational order parameters of the short (S_a)
and long (S_b) rods, and of the average order parameters $\bar{S}$ [Eq.
(15)] on the weight fraction of long rods. (Reproduced with
permission from Ref. 9.)

The dotted lines in Fig. 1 join points that correspond to coexistent phases (e.g., the points P and Q). The volume fraction of the longer rods in the anisotropic phase (point Q) is considerably greater than in the isotropic phase (point P); for these two points $v_{2,b}^a/v_{2,b}^i = 3.7$. Thus the phase separation in the course of the isotropic–nematic transition is accompanied by a strong fractionation effect, which can be used to diminish the degree of polydispersity of a system. With the increase in the parameter $m = L_b/L_a$, the ratio $v_{2,b}^a/v_{2,b}^i$ increases approximately according to an exponential law, i.e., the fractionation effect becomes more pronounced.

The dependence of the order parameters S_a and S_b (corresponding to the two types of rods) and of the average order parameter

$$\bar{S} = (1 - z)S_a + zS_b \tag{15}$$

on the weight fraction z of the long rods at $\vartheta = \vartheta^a$ is shown in Fig. 2. We see that at $z \approx 0.5$ the average order parameter at $\vartheta = \vartheta^a$ is $\bar{S} = 0.92$, i.e., appreciably higher than in the monodisperse case ($S = 0.80$). It is worthwhile to note also that the order parameter of the shorter rods S_a decreases essentially as the fraction of these rods becomes smaller (i.e., $z \to 1$).

6. MODELS OF STIFF POLYMER CHAINS WITH SOME DEGREE OF FLEXIBILITY

Having considered the problem of nematic ordering of a simplest system—an athermal solution of rigid rods—we now proceed to the more realistic case in which stiff polymer chains have some finite degree of flexibility. In this section we will describe models of polymer chains with different mechanisms of flexibility that will be used in later discussion.

From the standpoint of theoretical description, the simplest flexibility mechanism is realized for a freely jointed chain, which can be represented as a sequence of rigid rods of length λ and diameter d (for stiff chains $\lambda \gg d$)

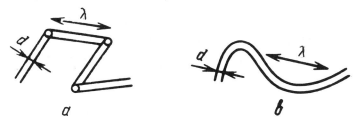

FIGURE 3
Freely jointed (a) and persistent (b) chain.

connected by freely rotating joints (Fig. 3a). The orientation of each successive rod does not depend on the orientation of the previous ones. For this
reason the mean-square distance between the ends of the chain $\langle R^2 \rangle$ equals

$$\langle R^2 \rangle = L\lambda, \qquad L \gg \lambda \qquad\qquad (16)$$

where L is the total contour length of the chain.

If the polymer chain has any other mechanism of flexibility (e.g., if the
orientations of adjacent links are correlated) then Eq. (16) is still satisfied,
but with a renormalized length λ. In the general case this renormalized
length is called the effective (Kuhn) segment length of the polymer chain.[26]

Most stiff-chain macromolecules are characterized not by the freely
jointed, but by the so-called persistent flexibility mechanism, in which the
flexibility arises from the accumulated effect of small oscillations in the
valence angles. Persistent macromolecule can be represented in the form of a
homogeneous cylindrical elastic filament of diameter d (Fig. 3b). The elasticity of the filament is such that in the state of thermal equilibrium it can be
substantially bent only on scales of the order of λ.

Another type of flexibility originates from the so-called rotational-iso-
meric flexibility mechanism.[26] Nematic ordering of polymer chains with this
type of flexibility has many specific features.[27, 28] However the corresponding
problems will not be discussed in the present chapter.

Depending on the relationship of the total contour length L of the
macromolecule to the length λ of the effective Kuhn segment, stiff-chain
macromolecules can belong to one of the three following fundamental
classes:

1. If the length of the Kuhn segment is so large that $\lambda \gg L \gg d$, then
   we can neglect the flexibility of the polymer chain and we arrive at the
   case of completely rigid rods treated above.
2. If $L \gg \lambda \gg d$, the stiff-chain macromolecule includes many Kuhn
   segments and from the global point of view its conformation in the
   isotropic state corresponds to a random coil. Such macromolecules are
   called semiflexible.
3. Of course, intermediate cases are possible in which the contour length
   of the macromolecule and the length of the Kuhn segment are of the
   same order of magnitude: $L \approx \lambda$. In real experiments this type of
   macromolecule is found rather often.

The nematic–isotropic transition in the solutions of partially flexible
polymer chains of the types described above has been studied using the
Onsager approach.[6, 27–32] Below we shall present some results of these

studies and briefly characterize the method by which these results were obtained.

7. NEMATIC ORDERING IN AN ATHERMAL SOLUTION OF SEMIFLEXIBLE CHAINS

Let us start with the case of semiflexible macromolecules ($L \gg \lambda \gg d$) which interact only by means of the forces of steric repulsion (athermal solution). By analogy with the treatment given in Section 2, we can conclude that the free energy of a solution of these macromolecules in the Onsager approximation must consist of the contribution F_{conf} describing the entropy losses due to the orientational ordering and the free energy F_{ster} of steric interaction of the macromolecules in the second virial approximation (the translational free energy for long polymer chains is usually inessential[29]).

To write the expression for F_{ster} we note that, since $\lambda \gg d$ for semiflexible macromolecules, one can always divide the polymer chains into elements (elementary links) of length l so that $d \ll l \ll \lambda$. The elements thus defined are long rigid rods; therefore, the second virial coefficient of interaction of two elements having the orientations $\mathbf{n}_1$ and $\mathbf{n}_2$ is $B(\gamma) = 2l^2 d \sin \gamma$ [cf. Eq. (2)]. Taking into account this fact, we can write the expression for F_{ster} in the form [cf. the third term in Eq. (1)]:

$$F_{ster} = \frac{1}{2} N_2 \frac{L}{l} T \frac{4v_2}{\pi l d^2} \int f(\mathbf{n}_1) f(\mathbf{n}_2) 2l^2 d \sin \gamma \, d\Omega_{\mathbf{n}_1} d\Omega_{\mathbf{n}_2} \qquad (17)$$

where N_2 is the total number of macromolecules in the solution, and $f(\mathbf{n})$ is the orientational distribution function for the unit vectors $\mathbf{n}$ tangential to the chain. The free energy F_{ster} is written in the form of Eq. (17) because L/l is the number of elementary links (of length l) in the macromolecule, while $4v_2/\pi l d^2$ is their concentration in the solution. We see that the quantity l in Eq. (17) drops out (as it should), so that finally we have[31]

$$F_{ster} = N_2 T L \frac{4v_2}{\pi d^2} \int f(\mathbf{n}_1) f(\mathbf{n}_2) \sin \gamma \, d\Omega_{\mathbf{n}_1} d\Omega_{\mathbf{n}_2} \qquad (18)$$

To determine the entropy contribution F_{conf} Khokhlov and Semenov[28,31] proposed that the dependence of the unit vector $\mathbf{n}$ on the consecutive number of a link along the chain could be treated as a realization of a discrete random walk of a point on the unit sphere (the number of the link plays the role of time, while the position of the point on the sphere is given by the vector $\mathbf{n}$). The function $f(\mathbf{n})$ in this case amounts to a somehow normalized "concentration" of links at the "point" $\mathbf{n}$. Thus the problem of calculating the orientational entropy reduces to the following: to find for the described random walk the entropy corresponding to the given "concentration" distribution $f(\mathbf{n})$ of links (with the entropy of an isotropic distribution taken as a zero point). In such a form this problem is fully analogous to the problem of calculating the conformational entropy of a polymer globule with a given distribution of the spatial concentration $n(\mathbf{r})$ of links, which was solved by I.M. Lifshitz[33] (see also Refs. 34, 35). The only difference is that now we deal with the space of orientation of links, rather than with the real three-dimensional space. Upon rewriting I.M. Lifshitz's result for this case Khokhlov and Semenov[31] obtained the following expressions for semiflexible freely jointed macromolecules (Fig. 3a):

$$F_{\text{conf}} = N_2 T \frac{L}{\lambda} \int f(\mathbf{n}) \ln(4\pi f(\mathbf{n})) \, d\Omega_{\mathbf{n}} \qquad (19)$$

and for semiflexible persistent macromolecules (Fig. 3b):

$$F_{\text{conf}} = N_2 T \frac{L}{\lambda} \int \left[\frac{(\nabla_{\mathbf{n}} f)^2}{4f} \right] d\Omega_{\mathbf{n}} \qquad (20)$$

Equations (18)–(20) fully determine the free energy $F = F_{\text{conf}} + F_{\text{ster}}$ of a solution of semiflexible molecules for the models shown in Fig. 3. In full analogy with the Onsager method (see Section 2) further calculations lead to the conclusions outlined below.[6, 29, 31]

The orientational ordering of the athermal solution has the character of a first-order phase transition and occurs at low polymer concentrations. Again, when $v_2 < v_2^i$ the solution is homogeneous and isotropic; when $v_2 > v_2^a$ it is homogeneous and anisotropic; and when $v_2^i < v_2 < v_2^a$ it separates into isotropic and nematic phases; for both models shown in Fig. 3 $v_2^i \sim v_2^a \sim d/\lambda \ll 1$.

For an athermal solution of freely jointed semiflexible chains minimizing the free energy $F = F_{\text{conf}} + F_{\text{ster}}$ [Eqs. (18)–(19)] with the trial function (3) we have[29]:

$$v_2^i = 3.25 d/\lambda; \qquad v_2^a = 4.86 d/\lambda; \qquad w = 0.50; \qquad S_0 = 0.87 \quad (21)$$

On comparing results (21) with Eqs. (4) and (5) we conclude that freely jointed connection of the rods in long chains leads to insignificant changes in the characteristics of the isotropic–nematic phase transition: the region of phase separation becomes somewhat wider, while the order parameter of the orientationally ordered phase at the transition point is slightly increased (a similar trend is obtained within the context of a lattice theory; cf. Chapter 4).

For an athermal solution of persistent semiflexible chains the characteristics of the liquid-crystalline transition obtained by minimizing F (Refs.

18–20) with the trial function (3) are[6, 31]

$$v_2^i = 10.48d/\lambda; \quad v_2^a = 11.39d/\lambda; \quad w = 0.09; \quad S_0 = 0.49 \quad (22a)$$

Vroege and Odijk[36] have solved numerically the integrodifferential equation, that appears as a result of the exact minimization of the free energy for this case. They obtained

$$v_2^i = 10.25d/\lambda; \quad v_2^a = 11.02d/\lambda; \quad w = 0.075; \quad S_0 = 0.46 \quad (22b)$$

We can see that orientational ordering in a solution of persistent chains occurs at essentially larger concentrations than in a solution of freely jointed macromolecules (with the same ratio d/λ). Moreover, the relative jump of polymer concentration at the transition, as well as the order parameter at the transition point, are considerably smaller for this case. Analysis shows[31] that these results arise from the fact that the entropy loss in the case of strong orientational ordering is substantially larger for the persistent flexibility mechanism than for the freely jointed model (see also the paper by Odijk,[37] where a scaling approach to this problem was formulated). Comparing results (21) and (22a), we can also draw the important conclusion that the character of orientational ordering depends substantially upon the magnitude of the Kuhn segment, and also upon the distribution of flexibility along the contour of the polymer chain, i.e., upon the flexibility mechanism.

This conclusion was further confirmed in studies of orientational ordering in solutions of polymer chains having other flexibility mechanisms.[27, 28, 38]

8. DEPENDENCE OF THE CHARACTERISTICS OF NEMATIC ORDERING ON THE LENGTH OF THE MACROMOLECULE

Now let us proceed to analyze nematic ordering in solutions of partially flexible macromolecules with $L \sim \lambda$. In this case the problem is substantially complicated in comparison with the semiflexible limit ($L \gg \lambda$) treated above. Actually, when $L \sim \lambda$ we cannot introduce a single distribution function $f(\mathbf{n})$ for all points of the polymer chain: it is essential to take into account the fact that the degree of orientational ordering depends on the position of the unit vector $\mathbf{n}$ on the chain (e.g., the end links of the chain must generally be more disordered than the middle links).[32] However, it turns out that the method of Lifshitz[33] can be used for this case as well; the corresponding theory is developed by Khokhlov and Semenov.[32] Here we shall present the results obtained only for the persistent flexibility mechanism, which is most often encountered for real stiff-chain polymers.

The following interpolation formulas were obtained for the characteristics of the nematic transition in a solution of macromolecules with persistent

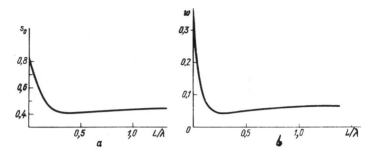

FIGURE 4
(a) Dependence of S_0 on L / λ for a solution of long persistent chains. (b) Dependence of w on L / λ for a solution of long persistent chains. (Reproduced with permission from Ref. 32.)

flexibility for an arbitrary relation between L and $\lambda^{6, 32}$:

$$\frac{v_2^i \lambda}{d} = \frac{3.34 + 11.3L/\lambda + 4.06L^2/\lambda^2}{(1 + 0.387L/\lambda)L/\lambda} \tag{23}$$

$$\ln w = -\frac{1.07 + 14.4L/\lambda + 84.1L^2/\lambda^2}{1 + 34.5L^2/\lambda^2} \tag{24}$$

$$\ln S_0 = -\frac{0.166 + 3.56L/\lambda + 15.9L^2/\lambda^2}{1 + 22.5L^2/\lambda^2} \tag{25}$$

Figure 4 shows the dependence of w and S_0 on L/λ calculated by Eqs. (23)–(25). The order parameter reaches a minimum equal to $S_0 = 0.41$ at $L/\lambda = 0.4$, while the relative width of the separation region has a minimum $w = 0.043$ at $L/\lambda = 0.3$.

The fundamental conclusion that we can draw from analyzing the results presented in Fig. 4 is the following. Only very stiff or rather short macromolecules behave like rigid rods. Even a small flexibility of the persistent-type chain (say, $L/\lambda \approx 0.1$) suffices to make the properties of the liquid-crystalline transition closer to those obtained in the limit of semiflexible chains $L/\lambda \gg 1$ than to those using the limit of absolutely rigid rods $L/\lambda \ll 1$ (despite the fact that the geometric shape of macromolecules with $L/\lambda \approx 0.1$ is far closer to rodlike). In particular, such high values of the order parameter at the point S_0, as in the Onsager theory for rigid rods ($S_0 = 0.84$), are possible only for very rigid and not too long chains. Even at $L/\lambda \approx 0.1$, the magnitude of S_0 is substantially smaller (see Fig. 4a)—approximately on the same order as is obtained in the self-consistent field theory of Maier and Saupe.[39]

9. CONFORMATION OF POLYMER CHAINS IN THE NEMATIC PHASE

The dependence of the properties of orientational ordering on the flexibility mechanism of polymer chains is manifested not only in the thermodynamic characteristics of isotropic–nematic phase transition, but also in the macromolecular conformations in the liquid-crystalline phase. For example, in Fig. 5 we show the dependences of the mean square end-to-end distance of a polymer chain, $\langle R^2 \rangle$, on polymer concentration in the solution for semiflexible freely jointed and persistent chains.[40] We see that for freely jointed model the value of $\langle R^2 \rangle$ is practically independent of c in the anisotropic phase; i.e., in this case we have orientation of segments, but not stretching of macromolecules. At the same time, for solution of persistent chains the increase of $\langle R^2 \rangle$ in the anisotropic phase with the increase in concentration is very essential (exponential increase[36,40]), i.e., anisotropic self-consistent field, which acts on persistent macromolecules in the nematic phase, leads to its significant stretching along the director (although the proportionality $\langle R^2 \rangle \approx L$ remains valid for semiflexible chains). The effect described can be called (in a certain sense) the stiffening of persistent macromolecules in the liquid-crystalline state. This result has been confirmed further in a set of recent papers.[41–43]

The physical meaning of the differences found between persistent and freely jointed macromolecules consist in the following. In both cases the distribution function in the anisotropic state, $f(\mathbf{n})$, has two sharp maxima along two opposite orientations parallel to the director. The orientation of each segment of the freely jointed chain belongs to one of these maxima with the same probability $\approx 1/2$, independently of the orientation of adjacent

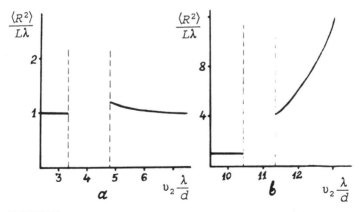

FIGURE 5
Dependence of the value of $\langle R^2 \rangle / L\lambda$ on $\upsilon_2 \lambda / d$ for semiflexible macromolecules with freely jointed (a) and persistent (b) flexibility mechanism. (Reproduced with permission from Ref. 40.)

segments. For persistent chains the situation differs: upon increasing the orientational order (with increasing concentration) a change in the orientation of the chain to the opposite one requires more and more expenditures of free energy. Therefore the average distance along the chain between adjacent jumps in orientation increases very rapidly (exponentially); it can be easily shown that this average distance is directly connected with $\langle R^2 \rangle$. Most accurate quantitative analysis of this effect can be found in the paper by Vroege and Odijk.[36]

10. NEMATIC ORDERING IN NONATHERMAL POLYMER SOLUTIONS

Up to now we have discussed exclusively athermal polymer solutions. In this case the nematic ordering takes place at low concentrations of stiff-chain polymer in the solution. In trying to take into account the influence of attractive forces between the macromolecules a serious difficulty immediately arises. The latter is connected with the fact that the anisotropic phase coexisting with the isotropic one can be very concentrated, and thus the second virial approximation of Onsager is not valid for describing isotropic–nematic transitions.

For this reason the liquid-crystalline nematic ordering with the formation of concentrated anisotropic phase usually has been studied in the framework of the lattice approach.[2, 30, 44–46] The shortcomings of this approach have been outlined in Section 4.

The first consistent analysis of this problem on the basis of the continuum approach was performed by Khokhlov and Semenov.[47–49] We shall present below the fundamental ideas and results of this study for the cases of solutions of completely stiff rods ($L \ll \lambda$) and semiflexible macromolecules ($L \gg \lambda$).

To describe the properties of the nematic ordering in a polymer solution in the presence of attractive forces and to construct the corresponding phase diagrams, we must first of all generalize expression (18) for the free energy F of steric interaction of macromolecules to the region of high concentration of the polymer in solution. To do this Khokhlov and Semenov[47] proposed to use the approach of Parsons (decoupling approximation; see Section 3), in which F_{ster} is defined by Eq. (10) and the function $J(v_2)$ in Eq. (10) is defined by the following relationship:

$$J(v_2) = -\ln(1 - v_2) \qquad (26)$$

It was shown that Eq. (26) is a very reasonable interpolation formula approximately valid at all concentrations. Thus we have [cf. Eqs. (10) and (18)]

$$F_{ster} = \frac{4N_2TL}{\pi d}\left|\ln(1 - v_2)\right|\left|\int f(\mathbf{n}_1)f(\mathbf{n}_2)\sin\gamma\,d\Omega_{\mathbf{n}_1}\,d\Omega_{\mathbf{n}_2}\right. \tag{27}$$

In the limit $v_2 \ll 1$ Eq. (27) reduces to Eq. (18), which is valid for a dilute solution. Moreover, this expression is essentially a continuum analog of the corresponding expression used in the lattice theory of Flory (see Eq. (11) of Chapter 4 and Ref. 47). Thus, Eq. (27), while retaining all the merits of the corresponding relationship in the Flory theory, is free from the disadvantages of that theory, which are mentioned in Section 4. Another variant of interpolation formula for $J(v_2)$ is considered in Ref. 49a.

Further, in the case under consideration we must add to the free energy the term F_{int} associated with the forces of intermolecular attraction. It was shown[47] that in most cases it is possible to write with good accuracy

$$F_{int} = -\frac{LN_2v_2}{2d}\left(u_i + u_a S^2\right) \tag{28}$$

Here u_i and u_a are constants characterizing, respectively, the isotropic and anisotropic components of the attractive forces, and $S = \langle 3\cos^2\Theta - 1\rangle/2$ is the order parameter. Formula (28) corresponds to the Maier-Saupe approximation in the theory of low molecular weight liquid crystals. The order of magnitude of the constants u_i and u_a is u_i, $u_a \approx u(r_a/d)^3$, where u is the characteristic energy of intermolecular interaction and r_a is the characteristic radius of the attractive forces.

Nyrkova et al.[50] have considered explicitly the contribution of Van der Waals attraction forces between the macromolecules to the free energy F_{int}. It was shown that the results for the properties of the isotropic–nematic transition obtained using this exact expression for F_{int} are essentially the same as the results derived with the help of a simplified expression (28).

Equation (28) can be also rewritten in the form

$$F_{int} = -\frac{LN_2v_2\theta}{d}(1 + \varkappa S^2) \tag{29}$$

where $\theta = u_i/2$ is the theta temperature of the polymer solution (the temperature at which the osmotic second virial coefficient vanishes), while $\varkappa = u_a/u_i$. As a rule, the anisotropic component of the attractive forces is substantially weaker than the isotropic component[51]; in the specific calculation Khokhlov and Semenov[47] assumed that $\varkappa = 0.1$ as a reasonable estimate. (It turned out that the properties of the liquid-crystalline transition depend only very weakly on $\varkappa$; therefore an exact specification of this quantity is inessential).

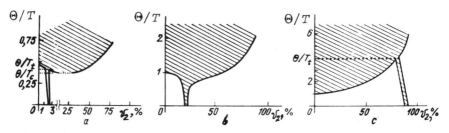

FIGURE 6

Phase diagrams for nematic ordering in solutions of semiflexible persistent macromolecules with $\lambda / d = 500$ (a), 50 (b), and 5 (c). The phase separation region is shaded. The critical point in Fig. 6c corresponds to the intersection point of the boundary line of the phase separation region with the θ / T axis. (Reproduced with permission from Ref. 47.)

Formulas (19)–(20), (27), and (29) fully determine the free energy of a polymer solution of arbitrary concentration in the presence of attractive forces between the macromolecules. For a solution of persistent semiflexible macromolecules the phase diagrams for the liquid-crystalline transition calculated using these formulas in the variables v_2 and θ/T for several values of the asymmetry parameter λ/d are shown in Fig. 6.[47] For large λ/d the phase diagram has the characteristic form shown in Fig. 6a, which is similar to that obtained by Flory[2] for rigid rods using the lattice method. In the region of relatively high temperatures we have a narrow corridor of phase separation into isotropic and anisotropic phases lying in the dilute solution region. Conversely, at low temperatures the region of phase separation is very broad, the coexisting phases being an isotropic very dilute phase and an anisotropic very concentrated one. These two regimes are separated by the interval between the triple-point temperature T_t and the critical temperature T_c ($T_c > T > T_t$), in which there are two regions of phase separation: between isotropic and anisotropic phases and between two anisotropic phases having different degrees of anisotropy. The temperatures T_t and T_c substantially exceed the θ temperature.

With decrease in the ratio λ/d the interval between T_c and T_t becomes narrower and disappears when $(\lambda/d)_{c1} = 125$. When $\lambda/d < 125$ there are neither critical nor triple points on the diagram (see Fig. 6b), and one can speak only of the crossover temperature T_{cr} between the narrow high-temperature corridor of phase separation and very broad low-temperature region of separation.

The temperature T_{cr} decreases with decreasing λ/d; for $(\lambda/d)_{c2} \approx 50$, when this temperature becomes lower than the θ point the situation qualitatively changes again: now we have triple and critical points corresponding to an additional phase transition between two isotropic phases (see Fig. 6c). The

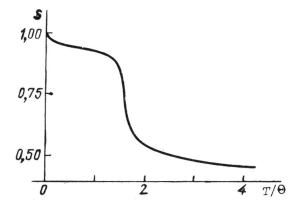

FIGURE 7
Dependence of the order parameter S_0 of a nematic solution of semiflexible persistent macromolecules at the transition point on the reduced temperature T / θ for $\lambda / d = 100$.

concentration of one of these phases is extremely low, hence the left-hand boundary of the separation region in Fig. 6c merges with the coordinate axis.

The phase diagrams of nonathermal solutions of semiflexible freely jointed chains (or rigid rods) undergo a sequence of changes with decreasing ratio λ/d similar to that shown in Fig. 6. For a solution of freely jointed chains we have $(\lambda/d)_{c1} \approx 20$, $(\lambda/d)_{c2} \approx 6.8$; for a solution of rigid rods the corresponding values are $(L/d)_{c1} \approx 15$, $(L/d)_{c2} \approx 3.5$.[47]

The dependence of the order parameter S of a nematic solution of semiflexible persistent macromolecules at the transition point on the reduced temperature T/θ is shown in Fig. 7 for $\lambda/d = 100$. We see that the attractive forces affect the value of S very substantially when $T/\theta \leq 2$.

The increase of the order parameter at the transition point due to the presence of attraction forces is one of the possible reasons for the fact that Eq. (25) predicts much lower values of S than are observed experimentally (cf. Chapter 6). Other factors that lead to the increase of the order parameter are (1) the presence of the flexibility component of rotational–isomeric character (sharp bends at occasional places), in which case according to Ref. 28 the order parameter at the transition point is much larger, and (2) the polydispersity of the solution (cf. Section 5). Experimentally observed high values of S can be due to the simultaneous influence of all the three factors.

11. NEMATIC ORDERING IN THE MELTS OF STIFF-CHAIN MACROMOLECULES

The formulas derived above for different contributions to the free energy, Eqs. (19)–(20), (27), and (29), can also be used to analyze nematic ordering in thermotropic systems—melts of stiff-chain macromolecules with different types of partial flexibility (with the understanding that v_2 is the degree of packing of the polymer in the melt as compared with the maximally dense packing). This has been done by Khokhlov and Semenov[48]; in this section we shall briefly present some of the results of this study and compare them with the conclusions of other theories of polymeric nematics based on stiff-chain macromolecules.

First of all, it should be noted that in thermotropic systems we must use as external parameter not the concentration c (or volume fraction v_2) of the polymer (as in solutions), but the pressure Π. The role of the external pressure has been studied in detail,[48] and it has been shown that: (1) from the point of view of the thermodynamics of liquid-crystalline ordering, the normal atmospheric pressure can be treated as a negligibly small quantity; (2) at high enough external pressure, $\Pi \geq 10^3$ atm, we should expect a substantial increase in the region of stability of the nematic phase; (3) as $\Pi \to \infty$ in melts of any particles that are anisodiametric and have a rigid steric core of interaction (in particular, in polymer melts), a liquid-crystalline phase should be observed.

Figure 8a shows the phase diagram obtained by Khokhlov and Semenov[48] for a melt of long persistent chains in the variables T/θ and λ/d for $\varkappa = 0.1$ under the assumption of minimal (or atmospheric) external pressure. Analo-

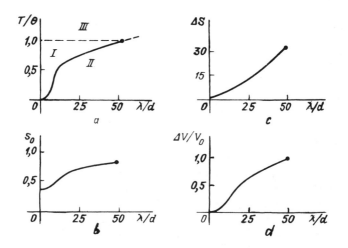

FIGURE 8
(a) Phase diagram of a melt of long persistent chains (I), isotropic melt; (II), nematic melt; (III), high-temperature gaslike phase. (b)–(d) Dependence of the order parameter at the nematic ordering point (b), transition entropy per effective segment (c), and relative volume change in the transition (d) on the parameter λ / d for a melt of long persistent chains. (Reproduced with permission from Ref. 48. Copyright Am. Chem. Soc.)

gous diagrams were obtained for melts of rigid rods, and also for semiflexible molecules with other mechanisms of flexibility. We see that, within the framework of the theory under consideration, it is possible to describe three phases—isotropic and anisotropic melts, and also a gaslike phase (at high temperature). Of course, primarily the curve describing the coexistence of the isotropic and nematic melt has physical meaning. It can be seen from Fig. 8a that the isotropic–nematic transition can take place only if the asymmetry parameter λ/d is smaller than the critical value $(\lambda/d)^c \approx 50$. When $\lambda/d > (\lambda/d)^c$ the melt in the equilibrium state is always a nematic (at any temperature). This result becomes quite understandable if one takes account of the fact that a polymer melt is a dense system; therefore, if the chain stiffness is high enough, liquid-crystalline ordering in it must occur solely as a consequence of the anisotropy of the steric interactions. The critical value $(\lambda/d)^c$ depends on the mechanism of flexibility of the chain. For example,[48] for freely jointed chain flexibility $(\lambda/d)^c \approx 7$, while for a melt of rigid rods $(L/d)^c \approx 3.5$. The latter result can be compared with the prediction obtained by Flory and Ronca[15] on the basis of the lattice approach that a nematic phase must arise in a melt of rigid rods when $L/d < 6.4$ (even in an athermal melt without any attractive forces).

Figure 8 shows also other characteristics of the nematic ordering in a melt of persistent chains (as a function of the asymmetry parameter λ/d): the order parameter S_0 at the transition point (Fig. 8b), the entropy of the transition per effective segment Δs (Fig. 8c), and the relative volume change in the transition $\Delta V/V$ (Fig. 8d). For melts of rigid rods and freely jointed semiflexible chains all these characteristics are larger than in Fig. 8; however, even a small component of flexibility in the persistence character suffices to make the quantities S_0, Δs, and $\Delta V/V$ close to the values characteristic of persistent chains.[48]

The results of Fig. 8 are valid for semiflexible persistent chains irrespective of the length L of the chain. This means in particular that for all values of the asymmetry parameter λ/d the temperature of the isotropic–nematic transition should level off as the length L increases.

The effect of stretching persistent chains in a nematic phase described in Section 9 remains for this case as well; this effect is taken into account in the results shown in Fig. 8. Stretching is not complete: for long enough chains the relation $\langle R^2 \rangle \approx L$ holds (cf. Section 9).

Of course, the results shown in Fig. 8 are applicable only for physically reasonable values of the asymmetry parameter λ/d: as a minimum, we must have $\lambda/d \geq 1$. Nevertheless the curves in Fig. 8 are extended down to $\lambda/d = 0$. Within the framework of the model the formal limit $\lambda/d \to 0$ corresponds to the situation in which the steric interactions (the term F_{ster}) are inessential, and liquid-crystalline ordering occurs only because of anisotropy of the attractive forces (theory of the Maier-Saupe type). In this limit liquid-crystalline ordering has also been treated by Ten Bosch with co-workers (see Chapter 5 and references cited therein) and by Rusakov and

Shliomis.[52, 53] The results of these studies are close to those obtained[48] for $\lambda/d = 0$. We see from Fig. 8, however, that these results are exact to any extent only at small values of λ/d, while in the most interesting region $\lambda/d \gg 1$ the steric interactions always dominate and the anisotropy of the attractive forces is a secondary factor.

Some additional conclusions[52, 53] should be mentioned here (compare with analogous results described in Chapter 5); these conclusions do not depend on whether steric forces are taken into account. First of all, it is found that the order parameter at the transition point S_0 depends on the length of the persistent macromolecules L as follows. When $L \ll \lambda$ the order parameter is $S_0 = 0.43$ (the Maier-Saupe result[39]); with increasing L the value of S_0 decreases to a minimum $S_0 = 0.34$ when $L \le \lambda$; then S_0 slightly increases to the value $S_0 = 0.36$ characteristic of very long macromolecules [compare this dependence $S_0(L)$ with the analogous dependence for a polymer solution shown in Fig. 4a].

The macromolecular conformations in polymer melts under consideration were also studied[52, 53] (cf. Chapter 5). It was shown that in the nematic phase the macromolecules were stretched along the ordering axis (the z axis). The degree of stretching can be characterized by the parameter $y = \langle R_z^2 \rangle / \langle R_x^2 \rangle$, where R_x and R_z are the projections of the end-to-end vector of a polymer chain. The value of this parameter (at the transition point) depends on the length of the macromolecules: $y = 3.25$ when $L \ll \lambda$; as L increases the value of y first decreases slightly to the value $y = 2.77$, and then increases substantially, reaching $y = 14.4$ in the limit of very long persistent chains ($L \gg \lambda$). With decreasing temperature of the nematic melt in the case $L \gg \lambda$ the polymer chains "unfold" further: the value of y rapidly increases exponentially (cf. the analogous conclusion for a solution with increase in concentration in Fig. 5).

References 43 and 54 contain the analysis of essentially the same problem as in Refs. 52 and 53 and the results obtained are similar.

12. INFLUENCE OF EXTERNAL FIELDS ON THE ISOTROPIC-NEMATIC TRANSITION

The study of the behavior of polymeric systems, that are capable of liquid-crystalline ordering in external orientational fields is of both fundamental and great practical interest, since the external field can serve to enhance the degree of orientational order and, thus, to improve the physicomechanical characteristics of a polymer material.

The influence of external orientational field on solution of stiff-chain macromolecules was analyzed within the framework of the Onsager method by Khokhlov and Semenov.[55] If $TU(\mathbf{n})$ is the potential energy acquired in the external field by a rectilinear part of a polymer molecule of length λ having orientation $\mathbf{n}$, then we must add the following term to the free energy of the solution of these molecules:

$$F_{\text{ext}} = N_2 T \frac{L}{\lambda} \int U(\mathbf{n}) f(\mathbf{n}) \, d\Omega_\mathbf{n} \tag{30}$$

(In the case of a solution of rigid rods we should omit the factor L/λ before the integral). Then the total free energy should be minimized as usual.

The following fundamental types of orientational fields should be distinguished: a field of dipole type

$$U(\mathbf{n}) = -G \cos \theta \tag{31}$$

(θ is the angle between the vector $\mathbf{n}$ and the anisotropy axis), and a field of quadrupole type

$$U(\mathbf{n}) = -\frac{3}{2} G \cos^2 \theta \tag{32}$$

For example, a dipole field can be an external magnetic (or electric) field in the case in which the links of the macromolecule have a constant magnetic (or electric) dipole moment directed along the chain. If the constant dipole moment is absent, but the links possess an anisotropy of susceptibility, then these same fields play the role of quadrupole fields. In this case it is necessary to distinguish between an orientational quadrupole field ($G > 0$; this corresponds to the situation when the susceptibility along the chain is greater than in the transverse direction) and a "disorientational" field ($G < 0$; opposite situation). An external quadrupole field can also be caused by a laminar hydrodynamic flow of the "longitudinal shear" type.[56] Figure 9 shows flows corresponding to an orientational (a) and disorientational (b) quadrupole field.

Phase diagrams of athermal solutions of rigid rods and semiflexible persistent chains in an external dipole-type field, which were calculated in

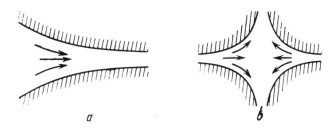

FIGURE 9
Hydrodynamic flows corresponding to an orientational (a) and a disorientational (b) quadrupole field.

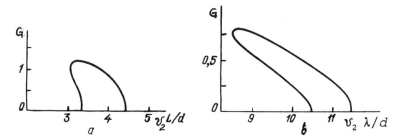

FIGURE 10
Phase diagrams (in the variables of concentration and field) of
athermal solutions of rigid rods (a) and long persistent chains (b) in
an external dipole-type field. (Reproduced with permission from Ref.
55. Copyright Am. Chem. Soc.)

Ref. 55, are shown in Fig. 10. The corresponding diagrams for quadrupole-
type fields are presented in Fig. 11.

From Fig. 10 it can be seen that the phase diagrams (for both rigid rods
and semiflexible persistent chains) are qualitatively similar. In the presence
of a weak enough external field, as before, a first-order phase transition
occurs in the system as the concentration of the solution increases. However,
it is important to stress that when $G \neq 0$ this is a transition between two
anisotropic phases with different degrees of anisotropy. With increasing G
the region of phase separation becomes narrower and is shifted toward lower

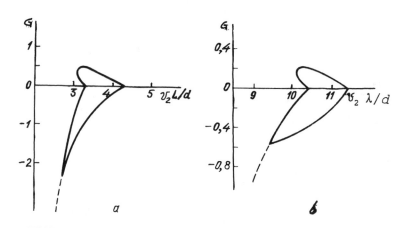

FIGURE 11
Phase diagrams of athermal solutions of rigid rods (a) and long
persistent chains (b) in an external quadrupole-type field. The
orientational field corresponds to the half-plane $G > 0$, and the
disorientational field — to $G < 0$. (Reproduced with permission from
Ref. 55. Copyright Am. Chem. Soc.)

concentrations. Finally, at a certain critical value of the external orientational field the interaction of links responsible for the phase transition is effectively suppressed (the segments are "sufficiently" oriented by the external field already in the dilute solution, and they have no need to be additionally rearranged by means of a phase transition upon concentrating the solution), and the region of phase separation disappears. We note also that, since the curves in Fig. 10 are shifted to the left with increasing G, in a certain concentration range a field-induced phase transition can occur. This concentration region is much broader for semiflexible persistent macromolecules than for rigid rods.

By comparing Figs. 10 and 11 it can be concluded that the influence of orientational quadrupole-type field ($G > 0$) leads fundamentally to the same qualitative effects as for the dipole field. On the other hand, the action of a "disorientational" quadrupole field ($G < 0$) requires separate discussion.

In the isotropic phase a weak field of this type induces an anisotropy of the "easy-plane" type with symmetrical distribution $f(\mathbf{n})$ with respect to the field direction. However, it turns out that for a nematic phase such a state is unstable even for extremely weak quadrupole field. A stable state corresponds to the situation when the orientation of the director lies in the "easy plane," i.e., it is perpendicular to the field direction. Thus, if $G < 0$ a transition that occurs as the concentration of the solution increases is a transition between phases of different symmetry and, therefore, must necessarily be a phase transition.

In a weak enough field this is a first-order phase transition; as $|G|$ is increased the corresponding phase separation region becomes noticeably narrower (see Fig. 11, lower half-phase). In a strong disorientational field the transition between the low- and high-concentration state of the solution becomes a second-order phase transition (dotted line in Fig. 11). As $G \to -\infty$ this transition occurs at

$$v_2^* = \frac{3\pi^2}{16} \frac{d}{L} \tag{33}$$

for a solution of rigid rods and at

$$v_2^* = \frac{3\pi^2}{8} \frac{d}{l} \tag{34}$$

for a solution of semiflexible persistent macromolecules. The line of the second-order phase transitions joins the boundaries of the phase separation region at a tricritical point.

13. NEMATIC ORDERING IN SOLUTIONS OF POLYELECTROLYTES

Many stiff-chain polymers, including most polymers of biological origin (DNA, α-helical proteins) acquire charges in solution. The influence of the Coulomb interaction of the links of a polymer on the isotropic–nematic transition was first treated[57,58] for the nonrealistic case of infinitely thin rods. The Onsager theory was systematically generalized to the case of a salt solution of charged rigid rods by Nyrkova and Khokhlov[59] and by Odijk and co-workers.[6,60] Below we shall discuss the fundamental ideas and results of these studies.

The electrostatic interaction potential of two cylindrical rods (of length L and diameter d) charged with the linear density σ has the following form in the Debye-Huckel approximation:

$$U_{el} = \frac{\sigma^2}{\varepsilon} \int \frac{\exp(-r(s_1, s_2)/r_D)}{r(s_1, s_2)} \, ds_1 \, ds_2 \tag{35}$$

Here $r(s_1, s_2)$ is the distance between the points having the coordinates (along the rods) s_1 and s_2 (Fig. 12), ε is the dielectric constant of the solvent, and the Debye radius is

$$r_D = \left(\frac{4\pi e^2}{\varepsilon T} \sum_a z_a^2 n_a \right)^{-1/2} \tag{36}$$

In Eq. (36) n_a and $z_a e$ are, respectively, the average concentration and the charge of the ion of type a (including the counterions). Approximation (35) is valid if $r_D \gg d$ and if the electrostatic potential ϕ_{el} throughout the region accessible to the ions satisfies the condition $e\phi_{el}/T \ll 1$. In the most realistic

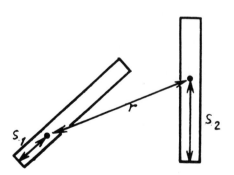

FIGURE 12
Two interacting rods. The distance between the points with coordinates s_1 and s_2 is r.

case $L \gg r_D$ we can write this latter condition in the form (omitting the logarithmic factors)

$$\frac{\sigma e}{\varepsilon T} \ll 1, \qquad \frac{\sigma e r_D^2 Lc}{\varepsilon T} \ll 1 \qquad (37)$$

where c is the concentration of rods.

The second virial coefficient of interaction of two rods whose axes ($\mathbf{n}_1$ and $\mathbf{n}_2$) form the angle γ equals

$$B(\gamma) = \int \left[1 - \exp\left(-\frac{U(\mathbf{r}, \mathbf{n}_1, \mathbf{n}_2)}{T} \right) \right] d^3r \qquad (38)$$

where

$$U(\mathbf{r}, \mathbf{n}_1, \mathbf{n}_2) = U_{st} + U_{el} \qquad (39)$$

is the interaction potential of the rods, which is equal to the sum of steric and electrostatic contributions; $\mathbf{r}$ is the radius vector joining the centers of the rods.

Stroobants et al.[60] have calculated the coefficient $B(\gamma)$ under the assumption that the integration in Eq. (35) over s_1 and s_2 is performed in the infinite limits. In this case U_{el} is equal to

$$U_{el} = \frac{2\pi\sigma^2 r_D}{\varepsilon \sin \gamma} \exp\left(-\frac{R}{r_D} \right) \qquad (40)$$

where R is the closest distance between infinite rods. Substituting Eq. (40) into Eqs. (38) and (39) we obtain

$$B(\gamma) = 2L^2 d \sin \gamma + 2L^2 r_D \sin \gamma \left\{ \ln\left[\left(\frac{2\pi\sigma^2 r_D}{\varepsilon T} \right) \exp\left(-\frac{d}{r_D} \right) \right] + C - \ln \sin \gamma \right\}$$

$$(41)$$

where $C = -\Gamma'(1) \approx 0.5772$, Euler's constant. From Eq. (41) it can be seen that Coulomb interaction leads in the region of validity of Eq. (40) to two main effects. First, due to the first two terms in braces in Eq. (41), the diameter of the rods is effectively renormalized

$$d_{eff} = d + r_D \left\{ \ln\left[\left(\frac{2\pi\sigma^2 r_D}{\varepsilon T} \right) \exp\left(-\frac{d}{r_D} \right) \right] + C \right\} \qquad (42)$$

and this leads to corresponding changes in the properties of the isotropic–nematic transition. Second, owing to the last term proportional to ln sin γ, an additional effect arises, which is called the "twisting effect." The origin of this effect is the factor $(\sin \gamma)^{-1}$ in Eq. (40), which makes unfavorable parallel orientations and stimulates perpendicular orientations of rods. The influence of the twisting effect is characterized by the parameter h

$$h = (d_{\text{eff}}/r_D)^{-1} \tag{43}$$

For the case of small values of h the authors of Ref. 60 have obtained corrections for the characteristics of the isotropic–nematic transition in the form of the expansion in the powers of h. For example,

$$w = 0.27 - 0.045h + 0.5h^2, \qquad S_0 = 0.79 + 0.13h + 0.6h^2 \tag{44}$$

The corresponding results for semiflexible persistent macromolecules were obtained by Vroege.[61]

However the expansions of the type in Eq. (44) can be used only for $h \leq 0.3$, i.e., for strongly charged rods. With decreasing charge on the rods the parameter h increases and finally the twisting effect becomes so strong that the nematic phase loses stability.

The origin of this artifact is the following. In fact, the limits of the integration over s_1 and s_2 in Eq. (35) are finite, so expression (40) is not always valid. The full problem of minimizing the function (1) with $B(\gamma)$ given by Eqs. (38), (39), and (35) is considered in Ref. 59, where possible qualitatively different regimes for the properties of the isotropic–nematic transition have been determined. Below we present some of the results obtained in the latter paper.

Dimensionless parameters, which govern the behavior of the system under consideration, are:

$$p = d/L, \qquad q = r_D/L, \qquad \Lambda = \sigma^2 L/\varepsilon T, (—)cL^3 \tag{45}$$

In Fig. 13, we show schematically qualitative forms of phase diagrams for solutions of charged rods in the variables (cL^3, q) for different values of Λ, i.e., for different linear charge densities of the rods, and possible regimes indicated by the letters in the right part of the diagrams in Fig. 13.

Formal limit $q = 0$ corresponds to the complete screening of electrostatic interaction; for this case properties of isotropic–nematic transition were described in Section 2: there is a relatively narrow region of phase separation at $cL^3 \approx p^{-1}$. The regime corresponding to the effective screening of the Coulomb interactions, denoted as St in Fig. 13, is characteristic for low q values independently of the magnitude of Λ. However, the evolution of the transition properties with the increase in q (decrease of the salt concentration in the solution) does depend on Λ.

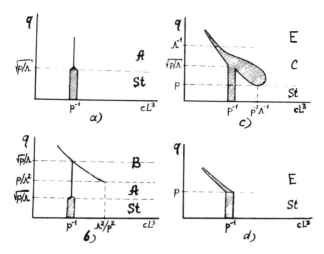

FIGURE 13

Schematic representation of the phase diagrams for solutions of charged rods corresponding to different linear charge densities of the rods ($\Lambda = \sigma^2 L / \varepsilon T$). (a) $\Lambda < p^{1/2}$; (b) $p^{1/2} < \Lambda < 1$; (c) $1 < \Lambda < p^{-1}$; (d) $p^{-1} < \Lambda$. Phase separation regions are shaded. Letters in the right part of the diagrams correspond to possible regimes of the behavior of the system. St, charges not important; A, narrowing of biphasic region; B, two phase transitions with narrow biphasic region; C, two phase transitions with relatively wide biphasic region; E, renormalization of the rod diameter.

For very low charge densities $\Lambda < p^{1/2}$ at $q > (p/\Lambda)^{1/2}$ we have essential narrowing of the phase separation region (regime A); in this regime we have

$$w \sim \Lambda q^2/p \ll 1 \qquad (46)$$

instead of $w \approx 1$ [see Eq. (4)]. The reason for this effect is the following: in regime A the electrostatic interaction gives a large, but effectively isotropic contribution to the second virial coefficient, thus making unfavorable a large concentration jump at the isotropic–nematic transition.

In the interval $p^{1/2} < \Lambda < 1$ regime A still exists (Fig. 13b), but with the increase in q we reach a new situation, regime B, at which a second phase transition between two anisotropic phases takes place at high concentration (cf. with the corresponding effect in Fig. 6). The phase separation region for this transition is extremely narrow ($w \ll 1$) in regime B, but the order parameters in coexisting phases differ considerably—in the more concentrated phase $1 - S \ll 1$, so that this phase can be called a strongly anisotropic phase. At $q \approx p^{1/2}/\Lambda$ the phase diagram exhibits a triple point, at larger values of q the direct transition between isotropic and strongly anisotropic

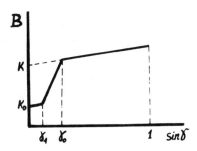

FIGURE 14
Qualitative form of the dependence $B(\gamma)$ in regime B.

phases takes place. The origin of these effects is the following: at small values of γ the increase of U_{el} with the decrease in γ, as predicted by Eq. (40), is no longer valid because the rods are finite. This leads to a very fast decrease of $B(\gamma)$ at small γ (Fig. 14), thus making small values of γ (or strongly anisotropic phases) favorable from the standpoint of free energy.

At $1 < \Lambda < p^{-1}$ the situation changes once more (see Fig. 13c): regime A of the isotropic–nematic transition disappears and, simultaneously, the width of the second phase transition becomes much larger (regime C). At $q > \Lambda^{-1}$ we finally reach regime E, where parameter h [Eq. (43)] is smaller than unity. It is this regime that is discussed in detail in Ref. 60. In this regime the effect of electrostatic interactions manifests in the effective renormalization of the diameter of the rod [Eq. (42)] and in the "twisting effect."

Finally, at $\Lambda > p^{-1}$ (strongly charged rods), with increasing q we pass directly from regime St to regime E (Fig. 13d).

Estimates of the characteristic parameters show that such highly charged polymers as DNA are usually described by regimes St and E. At the same time, the degree of charging of α-helical polypeptides can vary over a very broad range, so that it is possible to realize any of the regimes discussed. Many qualitatively new features of the liquid-crystalline transition in the solutions of stiff-chain polyelectrolytes renders the experimental study of this transition of great interest.

14. OTHER PROBLEMS SOLVED USING THE ONSAGER APPROACH

There are several other problems involving the statistical physics of liquid-crystalline ordering in polymer systems whose solutions have been reached on the basis of Onsager's approach described above. These problems are partially covered in other chapters of this book; here we shall only outline the corresponding references.

Elastic constants for splay, twist, and bend deformations of a polymer nematic, which is formed in a solution of rigid rods, were calculated using Onsager's method (cf. also Chapter 9).[62-65] In particular, Refs. 64 and 65 contain a generalization to the solutions of semiflexible (persistent and freely jointed) macromolecules (see also Ref. 36). The corresponding studies for nematic solutions of polyelectrolytes are performed in Refs. 61 and 66.

The Onsager approach was used to analyze the rheological properties of nematic solutions of rigid rods by Semenov[67] and Kuzuu and Doi.[68,69] In particular, the values of Leslie coefficients and Miezowicz viscosities, which determine the rheological behavior of nematic solution,[56] are calculated in these papers. The generalization of the method in these papers to the case of semiflexible persistent macromolecules has been performed in Ref. 70.

Elastic scattering and fluctuations of polymer concentration and anisotropy in isotropic solutions near the isotropic–nematic phase transition were calculated by Ivanov and Semenov.[71]

Surface properties of a polymer nematic were studied by Onsager's method.[72-73] The Onsager approach has been applied[76] to the study of nematic order in a layer of rods grafted on a flat surface.

If a stiff-chain macromolecule undergoes an intramolecular collapse (or coil–globule transition) in poor solvents, an orientational ordering can be simultaneously established in the globular phase. Such a globule has been called an "intramolecular liquid crystal." The statistical physics of this interesting polymer object have been studied.[5,77-81]

In this chapter we have considered in detail only the application of the Onsager approach to the study of nematic ordering in polymer systems. It should be noted that there are some papers in which similar approaches are used also to describe cholesteric ordering.[82-85] However, the theory of polymer cholesterics has been developed far less than for nematics.

REFERENCES

1. L. Onsager, *Ann. NY Acad. Sci.*, **1949**, *51*, 627.
2. P.J. Flory, *Proc. R. Soc. London*, *A*, **1956**, *234*, 73.
3. J.P. Straley, *Mol. Cryst. Liq. Cryst.*, **1973**, *24*, 7.
4. J.P. Straley, *Mol. Cryst. Liq. Cryst.*, **1973**, *22*, 333.
5. A.Yu. Grosberg and A.R. Khokhlov, *Adv. Polym. Sci.*, **1981**, *41*, 53.
6. T. Odijk, *Macromolecules*, **1986**, *19*, 2313.
7. G. Lasher, *J. Chem. Phys.*, **1970**, *53*, 4141.
8. R.F. Kayser and H.J. Raveche, *Phys. Rev.*, *A*, **1978**, *17*, 2067.
9. H. Lekkerkerker, P. Coulon, R. Van der Haegen, and R. Deblieck, *J. Chem. Phys.*, **1984**, *80*, 3427.
10. J. Hezfeld, A.E. Berger, and J.W. Wingate, *Macromolecules*, **1984**, *17*, 1718.
11. J.D. Parsons, *Phys. Rev.*, *A*, **1979**, *19*, 1225.
12. R. Alben, *Mol. Cryst. Liq. Cryst.*, **1971**, *13*, 193.
13. M.A. Cotter, *J. Chem. Phys.*, **1977**, *66*, 1098.
14. M.A. Cotter, *J. Chem. Phys.*, **1977**, *66*, 4710.

15. P.J. Flory and G. Ronca, *Mol. Cryst. Liq. Cryst.*, **1979**, *54*, 289, 311.
16. E.A. Di Marzio, *J. Chem. Phys.*, **1961**, *35*, 658.
17. R. Zwanzig, *J. Chem. Phys.*, **1963**, *39*, 1714.
18. M.A. Cotter, *Mol. Cryst. Liq. Cryst.*, **1976**, *35*, 33.
19. O.J. Heilmann and E.H. Lieb, *J. Stat. Phys.*, **1979**, *20*, 679.
20. F. Dowell, *J. Chem. Phys.*, **1989**, *91*, 1316.
21. R. Deblieck and H. Lekkerkerker, *J. Phys. Lett.*, **1980**, *41*, 351.
22. T. Odijk and H. Lekkerkerker, *J. Chem. Phys.*, **1985**, *89*, 2090.
23. W.E. McMullen, W.M. Gelbart, and A. Ben-Shaul, *J. Chem. Phys.*, **1985**, *82*, 5616.
24. T. Odijk, *Liq. Cryst.*, **1986**, *1*, 97.
25. T.M. Birshtein, B.A. Kolegov, and V.I. Pryamitzin, *Vysokomol. Soedin. Ser. A*, **1988**, *30*, 348.
26. A.Yu. Grosberg and A.R. Khokhlov, *Statistical Physics of Macromolecules*, Nauka, Moscow, 1989.
27. S.K. Nechaev, A.N. Semenov, and A.R. Khokhlov, *Vysokomol. Soedin. Ser. A*, **1983**, *25*, 1063.
28. A.R. Khokhlov and A.N. Semenov, *Macromolecules*, **1984**, *17*, 2678.
29. A.R. Khokhlov, *Phys. Lett.*, *A*, **1978**, *68*, 135.
30. A.R. Khokhlov, *Vysokomol. Soedin.*, *Ser. B*, **1979**, *21*, 201.
31. A.R. Khokhlov and A.N. Semenov, *Physica*, *A*, **1981**, *108*, 546.
32. A.R. Khokhlov and A.N. Semenov, *Physica*, *A*, **1982**, *112*, 605.
33. I.M. Lifshitz, *Zh. Eksp. Teor. Fiz.*, **1968**, *55*, 2408.
34. I.M. Lifshitz, A.Yu. Grosberg, and A.R. Khokhlov, *Usp. Fiz. Nauk.*, **1979**, *127*, 353.
35. A.Yu. Grosberg and A.R. Khokhlov, *Sov. Sci. Rev.*, *Sect. A*, *Phys. Rev.*, **1987**, *8*, 147.
36. G.J. Vroege and T. Odijk, *Macromolecules*, **1988**, *21*, 2848.
37. T. Odijk, *Macromolecules*, **1983**, *16*, 1340.
38. T.M. Birshtein and A.A. Merkureva, *Vysokomol. Soedin.*, *Ser. A*, **1985**, *27*, 1208.
39. P.G. de Gennes, *The Physics of Liquid Crystals*, Clarendon Press, Oxford, 1974.
40. A.R. Khokhlov and A.N. Semenov, *J. Phys.*, *A*, **1982**, *15*, 1361.
41. S.G. Pletneva, G.N. Marchenko, A.S. Pavlov, Yu.G. Papulov, P.G. Khalatur, and G.M. Khrapkovsky, *Dokl. Akad. Nauk SSSR*, **1982**, *264*, 109.
42. P.G. Khalatur, Yu.G. Papulov, and S.G. Pletneva, *Mol. Cryst. Liq. Cryst.*, **1985**, *130*, 195.
43. M. Warner, J.M. Gunn, and A. Baumgartner, *J. Phys.*, *A*, **1985**, *18*, 3007.
44. A.R. Khokhlov, *Vysokomol. Soedin.*, *Ser. A*, **1979**, *21*, 1981.
45. A.R. Khokhlov, *Int. J. Quant. Chem.*, **1979**, *16*, 853.
46. M. Warner and P.J. Flory, *J. Chem. Phys.*, **1980**, *73*, 6327.
47. A.R. Khokhlov and A.N. Semenov, *J. Stat. Phys.*, **1985**, *38*, 161.
48. A.R. Khokhlov and A.N. Semenov, *Macromolecules*, **1986**, *19*, 373.
49. A.N. Semenov and A.R. Khokhlov, *Vysokomol. Soedin.*, *Ser. A*, **1986**, *28*, 125, 132.
49a. R. Hentschke, *Macromolecules*, **1990**, *23*, 1192.
50. I.A. Nyrkova, M.A. Osipov, and A.R. Khokhlov, *Kristallographia*, **1988**, *33*, 957.
51. M.A. Cotter and D.C. Wacker, *Phys. Rev.*, *A*, **1978**, *18*, 2669.
52. V.V. Rusakov and M.I. Shliomis, *Preprint of the Ural Scientific Center of the USSR Academy of Sciences*, No. 42/83, Sverdlovsk, 1983.
53. V.V. Rusakov and M.I. Shliomis, *J. Phys. Lett.*, **1985**, *46*, 935.
54. X.L. Wang and M. Warner, *J. Phys.*, *A*, **1986**, *19*, 2215.
55. A.R. Khokhlov and A.N. Semenov, *Macromolecules*, **1982**, *15*, 1272.
56. P.G. de Gennes, *Scaling Concepts in Polymer Physics*, Cornell University Press, Ithaca, NY, 1979.

57. J.M. Deutch and N.D. Goldenfeld, *J. Phys., A*, **1982**, *15*, L71.
58. J.M. Deutch and N.D. Goldenfeld, *J. Phys.*, **1982**, *43*, 651.
59. I.A. Nyrkova and A.R. Khokhlov, *Biofizika*, **1986**, *31*, 771.
60. A. Stroobants, H. Lekkerkerker, and T. Odijk, *Macromolecules*, **1986**, *19*, 2232.
61. G.J. Vroege, *J. Chem. Phys.*, **1989**, *90*, 4560.
62. R.G. Priest, *Phys. Rev., A*, **1973**, *7*, 720.
63. J.P. Straley, *Phys. Rev., A*, **1973**, *7*, 720.
64. A.Yu. Grosberg and A.V. Zhestkov, *Vysokomol. Soedin, Ser. A*, **1986**, *28*, 86.
65. T. Odijk, *Liq. Cryst.*, **1986**, *1*, 553.
66. G.J. Vroege and T. Odijk, *J. Chem. Phys.*, **1987**, *87*, 4223.
67. A.N. Semenov, *Zh. Eksp. Teor. Fiz.*, **1983**, *85*, 549.
68. N. Kuzuu and M. Doi, *J. Phys. Soc. Jpn.*, **1983**, *52*, 3486.
69. N. Kuzuu and M. Doi, *J. Phys. Soc. Jpn.*, **1984**, *53*, 1031.
70. A.N. Semenov, *Zh. Eksp. Teor. Fiz.*, **1987**, *93*, 1260.
71. V.A. Ivanov and A.N. Semenov, *Vysokomol. Soedin., Ser. A*, **1988**, *30*, 1723.
72. M. Doi and N. Kuzuu, *J. Appl. Polym. Sci., Appl. Polym. Symp.*, **1985**, *41*, 65.
73. T. Odijk, *Macromolecules*, **1987**, *20*, 1423.
74. A.Yu. Grosberg and D.V. Pakhomov, *Dokl. Akad. Nauk SSSR*, **1989**, *308*, 92.
75. A.Yu. Grosberg and D.V. Pakhomov, *Kristallografia*, **1989**, *34*, 1534.
76. A. Halperin, S. Alexander, and I. Schechter, *J. Chem. Phys.*, **1987**, *86*, 6550.
77. A.Yu. Grosberg, *Biofizika*, **1979**, *24*, 32.
78. A.Yu. Grosberg, *Vysokomol. Soedin., Ser. A*, **1980**, *22*, 90, 96, 100.
79. A.Yu. Grosberg and A.V. Zhestkov, *Biofizika*, **1986**, *30*, 233.
80. A.Yu. Grosberg and A.V. Zhestkov, *J. Biomol. Struct. Dynam.*, **1986**, *3*, 859.
81. R.B. Boehm and D.E. Martire, *Macromolecules*, **1986**, *19*, 89.
82. J.P. Straley, *Phys. Rev., A*, **1976**, *14*, 1835.
83. A.Yu. Grosberg, *Dokl. Akad. Nauk SSSR*, **1980**, *253*, 1370.
84. M.A. Osipov, *Chem. Phys.*, **1985**, *96*, 259.
85. M.A. Osipov, A.N. Semenov, and A.R. Khokhlov, *Khim. Fiz.*, **1987**, *6*, 1312.

The Flory Lattice Model

A. ABE

Department of Polymer Chemistry, Tokyo Institute of Technology, Tokyo 152, Japan

and

M. BALLAUFF

Polymer-Institut, Universität Karlsruhe (TH), 76 Karlsruhe, Germany

CONTENTS

1. INTRODUCTION

In this chapter, the ordering transition of a system of rodlike particles from an isotropic state to an ordered nematic one is considered in terms of lattice models. Among the treatments based on evaluation of the partition function by lattice methods, the Flory theory[1] has found widespread use when dealing with liquid-crystalline polymers (LCP).[2,3] By the ease of its applicability, it turned out to be highly useful to understanding the nematic to isotropic transition for a manifold of systems, in particular for mixtures. In describing this model here, the theoretical framework is outlined in the following section. Section 3 is devoted to the application of the model to various aspects of LCP's. In Section 3.2 we shall deal extensively with low molecular weight liquid crystals (LMWLC) since these systems can serve as model compounds for the respective LCP. A brief comparison of the prediction of the lattice theory for LMWLC with some selected experimental data will show the usefulness of the lattice theory. In all other cases this chapter is confined to the development of the basic ideas; a comparison with experimental data is given in Chapter 6.

2. FRAMEWORK OF THE FLORY THEORY FOR NEMATIC FLUIDS

2.1. General Considerations

According to Flory, steric repulsions between the anisotropic particles are principally responsible for order in liquid-crystalline systems. At the high density and close packing prevailing in the liquid state, these molecules, at least as a first approximation, can be represented by "hard" bodies of appropriate size and shape whose only interactions are the insurmountable repulsions that would be incurred if one of them should overlap another.[4] Lattice treatments are well suited to the calculation of the configuration partition function for such a system. The effects of intermolecular attractions may be considered as a perturbation within the framework of the thermodynamic functions thus derived.[5]

Evaluation of the partition function by lattice methods necessitates subdividing the molecule into a succession of structural entities, usually called segments, each of which occupies one cell of the lattice. Despite of the inherent artificialities of this procedural device, the application of lattice methods to polymeric systems has met with gratifying success, especially in the deduction of the combinatorial contribution of mixtures to the partition function.[3,6]

The principal step for evaluating the partition function is estimating the expectation ν_{j+1} that a sequence of empty lattice sites is vacant when j molecules have already been inserted into the lattice containing n_0 sites. To calculate ν_{j+1} for disordered systems, it is sufficient in most cases to identify the expectation that a given site is vacant with the a priori probability p_{ji}

$$p_{ji} = (n_0 - xj - i)/n_0 \qquad (1)$$

of a vacancy in the system. Here x is the number of segments in the chain and i is the number of segments of particle $j + 1$ already assigned to the lattice.[7,8] The partition function for a system consisting of n_2 molecules then follows as

$$Z = (Z_c/n_2!) \prod_1^{n_2} \nu_j \qquad (2)$$

where Z_c is the intramolecular chain configuration partition function. In the

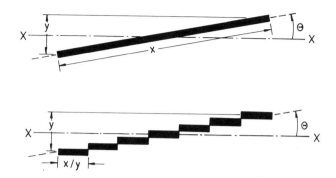

FIGURE 1
Rendition of a rod in a lattice. The angle Θ describes the inclination toward the preferred axis. (Reproduced with permission from Ref. 9. Copyright Gordon and Breach Science Publishers.)

absence of solvent molecules and for large x, we obtain[7,8]

$$Z = (z_c/e)^{xn_2} \tag{3}$$

with z_c being the factor contributed per segment to the intramolecular partition function. From Eq. (3), it is evident that Z may become much smaller than 1 if the effective number z_c per segment is less than e as may occur in relatively stiff chains. Thus the total number of accessible configurations is less than unity, a situation that is physically unacceptable ("entropy catastrophe," cf. Ref. 8) since there will be at least one totally ordered configuration being available for the system. This argument clearly demonstrates that the treatment of stiff-chain systems has to proceed in a different way by directly evaluating the partition function for ordered systems of rigid rods; i.e., the existence of a stable ordered state has to be assumed first.

2.2. Flory-Ronca Theory: Athermal Systems

Consider a system of rods having an orientation with regard to a preferred axis measured by an angle of inclination Θ (see Fig. 1). The essential step in the Flory model[1] consists of breaking up the rods into a sequence of y consecutive submolecules. In this two-dimensional rendition, the relation of the "disorder index" y to the number of segments x and the angle Θ may be written

$$y = x \sin \Theta \tag{4}$$

The exact relationship between y and Θ will be discussed in more detail below.

The calculation of v_{i+1} of situations accessible to the $i + 1$th rod after i particles have been assigned to the lattice now proceeds as follows[1]: For the first segment of the first submolecule, there are $n_0 - ix$ empty cells. In the mean-field treatment of a nematic phase, it may be assumed that the sequences of segments occurring in a given row of cells parallel to the preferred axis are uncorrelated with those in adjacent rows. Hence, the expectation of vacancy at the site required for an initial segment of the remaining $y_{i+1} - 1$ submolecules is the volume fraction of vacancies $(n_0 - ix)/n_0$. Having established that one of these sites is vacant, we require the conditional probability that the next sites in this row are vacant to be occupied by the remaining segments of the submolecule. This conditional probability is given by the number fraction of vacancies in the rows parallel to the preferred axis, which is in turn given by the ratio of the number of vacancies to the sum of vacancies and submolecules. Thus the required expectation that all the segments of rod $i + 1$ are arranged in y_{i+1} submolecules is

$$v_{i+1} = (n_0 - ix)\left(\frac{n_0 - ix}{n_0}\right)^{y_{i+1}-1}\left(\frac{n_0 - ix}{n_0 - ix + \Sigma_{j=1}^{i} y_j}\right)^{x - y_{i+1}} \tag{5}$$

It should be emphasized that a priori probabilities are employed for propagation along the direction perpendicular to the preferred axis, i.e., for placement of the first segments of the submolecules, whereas insertion of the remaining $x/y - 1$ segments requires the probability of finding a vacant pair of lattice cells. Use of a priori probabilities for the former process eventually leads to the Flory-Huggins result for the isotropic system.

The partition function Z consists of a combinatorial part responsible for the excluded volume and an orientational part referring to an ideal gas of cylinders with restricted orientations:

$$Z = Z_{comb} Z_{orient} \tag{6}$$

Insertion of Eq. (5) into Eq. (2) and subsequent consolidation leads to the first factor[1,9]

$$Z_{comb} = \frac{(n_s + n_x \bar{y})!}{n_s! n_x!} n_0^{n_x(1-\bar{y})} \tag{7}$$

Here n_s and n_x are the number of solvent molecules and rodlike particles, respectively; $\bar{y}$ is the mean value of the disorder index y defined by

$$\bar{y} = \Sigma n_{xy} y / n_x \tag{8}$$

where n_{xy}/n_x is the orientational distribution specifying the fraction of the molecules with disorientation y. The orientational part Z_{orient} follows as[9]

$$Z_{orient} = \prod_y (\sigma \omega_y n_x / n_{xy})^{n_{xy}} \tag{9}$$

with σ being an arbitrary constant. Because of the spherical symmetry of the problem, the statistical weight ω_y results to

$$\omega_y = \sin \Theta_y \tag{10}$$

Substitution of Eqs. (7) and (9) into Eq. (6), followed by introduction of Stirling's approximation for the factorials, gives

$$-\ln Z = n_s \ln v_s + n_x \ln(v_x/x) - (n_s + n_x \bar{y}) \ln[1 - v_x(1 - \bar{y}/x)]$$

$$+ n_x(\bar{y} - 1) + n_x \sum_y \frac{n_{xy}}{n_x} \ln\left(\frac{n_{xy}}{n_x \omega_y}\right) - n_x \ln \sigma \tag{11}$$

where $v_s = n_s/(n_s + n_x x)$ and $v_x = n_x x/(n_s + n_x x)$ are the volume fractions of the respective components.

There are two limiting cases of Eq. (11) to be considered: (1) For perfect alignment, each rod only consists of one submolecule, thus $\bar{y} = y = 1$. In this case, Eq. (11) must be reduced to the ideal mixing law, a requirement being fulfilled if

$$\sigma = 1/\omega_1 \tag{12}$$

(2) Random disorder requires $n_{xy}/n_x = \omega_y$. Then with $x = \bar{y}$, Eq. (11) reduces to the well-known Flory-Huggins expression for the free energy of mixing:[6]

$$-\ln Z = n_s \ln v_s + n_x \ln(v_x/x) + n_x(x - 1) - n_x \ln \sigma \tag{13}$$

The distribution function n_{xy}/n_x at equilibrium disorder may be derived in the following manner[9]: The last molecule inserted into the lattice may be taken as a probe for estimating the expected number of situations available to a particle, the disorder of which is specified by y. Since

$$v_y = n_0 \left\{ \frac{(1 - v_x)}{[1 - v_x(1 - \bar{y}/x)]} \right\}^x \left[1 - v_x \left(1 - \frac{\bar{y}}{x} \right) \right]^y \tag{14}$$

we have

$$n_{xy}/n_x = f_1^{-1} \omega_y \exp(-ay) \tag{15}$$

where

$$a = -\ln\left[1 - v_x(1 - \bar{y}/x)\right] \tag{16}$$

and f_1 is the normalization factor. The orientational part then follows as

$$\ln Z_{\text{orient}} = n_x\left[\ln(f_1\sigma) + a\bar{y}\right] \tag{17}$$

and, after insertion into Eq. (11),

$$-\ln Z = n_s \ln v_s + n_x \ln(v_x/x) - n_s \ln\left[1 - v_x(1 - \bar{y}/x)\right]$$
$$+ n_x(\bar{y} - 1) - n_x \ln(f_1\sigma) \tag{18}$$

The equation is only valid, of course, if $\bar{y}$ is assigned its equilibrium value. Alternatively, the orientational distribution function at equilibrium may be derived by taking the variation of Eq. (11) with regard to n_{xy}/n_x.

Equation (18) gives the free energy of a system of n_x rigid rods immersed in a solvent containing n_s molecules at orientational equilibrium with the order being measured by the disorder index y. At orientational equilibrium

$$\left[\partial \ln Z / \partial\left(\frac{n_{xy}}{n_x}\right)\right]_{n_s, n_x} = 0 \tag{19}$$

For calculating the concentrations in the coexisting isotropic phases, the chemical potentials have to be determined by partial differentiation of Eq. (18) with respect to n_s and n_x. The corresponding expressions for the random solution may be obtained from Eq. (13). Then the equilibrium conditions, $\mu_i^i = \mu_i^a$ with subscript $i = s$ or x, leads to

$$\ln\left(\frac{v_s^a}{v_s^i}\right) = \left(1 - \frac{1}{x}\right)v_x^i - \frac{(\bar{y} - 1)v_x^a}{x} + \ln\left[1 - v_x^a\left(1 - \frac{\bar{y}}{x}\right)\right] \tag{20}$$

and

$$\ln\left(\frac{v_x^a}{v_x^i}\right) = (x - 1)v_x^i - (\bar{y} - 1)v_x^a + \ln f_1 \tag{21}$$

It remains to evaluate the spatial relation of the disorder index y and the orientation angle Θ. This can be devised by considering the projection of a rod on a cross section of the cubic lattice perpendicular to the preferred direction (Fig. 2).[9] The transverse axes are labeled Y_1 and Y_2, respectively, and as shown in Fig. 1, Θ is the azimuthal angle between the axis of the rod and the preferred axis. The angle φ denotes the rotation of the projection in the plane perpendicular to the domain axis. It is apparent that the number of

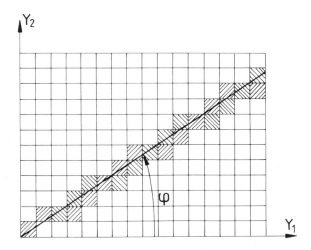

FIGURE 2
Projection of a rod in a plane perpendicular to the domain axis.
(Reproduced with permission from Ref. 9. Copyright Gordon and
Breach Science Publishers.)

lattice cells required for the representation of the projection of the rod on
the Y_1–Y_2 plane is given by the sum of the magnitudes of the components y_1
and y_2 of the length of the rod on the axes Y_1 and Y_2. Hence,

$$y = |y_1| + |y_2| = x \sin \Theta (|\cos \varphi| + |\sin \varphi|) \tag{22}$$

Averaging over φ, one obtains

$$y = \frac{4}{\pi} x \sin \Theta \tag{23}$$

Then

$$n_{xy}/n_x = f_1^{-1} \sin \Theta \exp(-\alpha \sin \Theta) \tag{24}$$

with

$$\alpha = (4/\pi) ax \tag{25}$$

where the quantity a is defined by Eq. (16). The integral f_1 now may be
evaluated according to

$$f_p = \int_0^{\pi/2} \sin^p \Theta \exp(-\alpha \sin \Theta) \, d\Theta \tag{26}$$

with $p = 1$. The average values of y and the nematic order parameter S are consequently given by

$$\bar{y} = (4/\pi)xf_2/f_1 \tag{27}$$

and

$$\langle \sin^2 \Theta \rangle = \frac{f_3}{f_1} = \frac{2}{3}(1 - S) \tag{28}$$

The self-consistency relations, Eq. (26) and Eq. (27), together with the equilibrium condition, Eqs. (20) and (21), now furnish a complete set of equations that, when solved numerically, lead to the concentrations in the respective phases as well as to the disorder index $\bar{y}$ at equilibrium.

2.3. The "1956" Approximation

Significant simplification of the above treatment of the angular distribution function can be achieved by assuming n_{xy}/n_x to be uniform out to a certain angle Θ_m and zero beyond that value. Then the orientational part Z_{orient} will be proportional to $(\omega)^{n_x}$ with ω being the solid angle within $\Theta \le \Theta_m$. In good approximation, ω is proportional to $\bar{y}^2$, leading to the expression[1]

$$Z_{\text{orient}} = \bar{y}^{2n_x} \tag{29}$$

The "1956" approximation can be derived from the Flory-Ronca theory by developing the integrals f_p into powers of α; i.e., omission of higher terms in α leads to the following expression for Z_{orient} (cf. Eq. 17),

$$\ln Z_{\text{orient}} = n_x \left[2 \ln \bar{y} + \ln(\sigma/x^2) + C \right] \tag{30}$$

where C is a small constant; $C = 2\ln(\pi e/8)$. The formulation set forth above can be recovered by adopting further simplifications, such as $C = 0$ and $\sigma = x^2$. Equations 20 and 21 for equilibrium become

$$\ln\left(\frac{v_s^a}{v_s^i}\right) = \left(1 - \frac{1}{x}\right)v_x^i - \frac{(\bar{y} - 1)v_x^a}{x} - \frac{2}{\bar{y}} \tag{31}$$

and

$$\ln\left(\frac{v_x^a}{v_x^i}\right) = (x - 1)v_x^i - (\bar{y} - 1)v_x^a - 2\left[1 - \ln\left(\frac{\bar{y}}{x}\right)\right] \tag{32}$$

It has been shown that this approximation leads to quite accurate results in the limit of high axial ratios.[9]

Straley[10] has concluded that the Flory model in this "1956" approximation gives unphysical results because of the problems originating from Eq. (4). In its original derivation,[1] the disorder index y [cf. Eq. (4)] was defined on the basis of a two-dimensional model. Direct application of Eq. (4) for the calculation of the orientational part of the partition function would indeed be followed by a finite degree of ordering at all concentrations. The need for the replacement of Eq. (4) by Eq. (23) has been advocated in the Flory-Ronca paper.[9]

In the Flory lattice treatment, the parameter $\bar{y}$ gives the average value of the projection of the rods onto the plane defined by the preferred axis. This parameter is thus a direct measure of the steric hindrance exerted by the assembly of densely packed rods on a probe rod. When specifying the relation of y to the angle of inclination Θ, however, some implications become apparent that may be traced back to the inherently discontinuous character of the lattice rendition. From $y = (4/\pi)x \sin \Theta$, it is obvious that in fully aligned systems y should vanish, whereas the lattice meaning of this parameter requires $y = 1$ in that case. Thus a small fraction of angles referring to values of y smaller than 1 is excluded.[11] As is evident from the above relation [cf. Eq. (23)], however, this problem only comes into play for very small axial ratios hardly exceeding unity or for highly anisotropic rods packed densely in the nematic state. Since real liquid crystal systems consist of molecules with x much greater than unity, the former condition is of minor importance. The physically unacceptable situation ($y < 1$) may be encountered in the calculation of the lyotropic system comprising rods of very large axial ratios x, which upon phase separation yields a highly ordered phase in equilibrium with a very dilute isotropic solution.[12] In those cases, the partitioning of the solute components may be calculated assuming ideal mixing in the anisotropic phase, in keeping with the reduction of the mixing partition function to the ideal mixing low for $y = 1$. The effect of restricting y to the range $y \geq 1$ has been found to be practically insignificant.

Another problem arises when the average of y is taken over Θ in the isotropic phase, yielding $\bar{y}_{iso} = x$. This requires values of y exceeding x, a condition difficult to reconcile with the lattice model (cf. Fig. 1). However, the free energy of the isotropic phase is essentially given by the Flory-Huggins expression, thus obviating the need for a description of a disordered system in terms of the parameter y. The order in the nematic phase, on the other hand, is usually quite high and $\bar{y}$ is much smaller than x and the lattice calculation should yield valid conclusions.

A criticism has been raised concerning the free energy of the isotropic phase.[13, 14] As pointed out in Section 2.2, the free energy reduces to an expression similar to the Flory-Huggins result for polymers in the isotropic state [cf. Eq. (13)]. In absence of a solvent, we obtain

$$-n_x^{-1} \ln Z = -\ln x + (x - 1) \tag{33}$$

In the theory of Warner,[13] the steric hindrance in the system is calculated by projecting the rods onto the probe rod. In the limit of high ordering, both treatments come to similar conclusions. In the isotropic phase, the free energy derived by Warner takes the form

$$-n_x^{-1} \ln Z = -\ln x - \left(\frac{(x-1)\pi/4 + 1}{1 - \pi/4} \right) \ln \left(\frac{x-1}{x} \frac{\pi}{4} + \frac{1}{x} \right) \quad (34)$$

Considering systems of rather short rods, both Eq. (33) and Eq. (34) come to comparable entropies in the isotropic state. With high axial ratios the difference in $-n_x^{-1} \ln Z$ for the isotropic state becomes significant, but these systems only exhibit a transition into the disordered state upon dilution where entropy is dominated by the solvent contribution. However, the proper evaluation of the free energy of a disordered system is certainly a problem in need of further elucidation.

The preceding discussion has shown that the Flory lattice theory furnishes a self-consistent treatment of the nematic ordering transition. There are problems, however, as discussed in the foregoing section, that may be traced back to the inherently discontinuous character of the model. Therefore a comparison with other theories starting from a continuum approach may be highly useful. A most significant contribution to the latter field has been made by Parsons, who introduced the decoupling approximation.[15] This theory has been augmented by Khokhlov and Semenov[16] (cf. Chapter 3 and Ref. 17). Its principal assumption is the replacement of the pair correlation $g(\mathbf{r}, \Omega_{12})$ by an expression of the type $g(r/\sigma)$, with $\mathbf{r}$ being the vector joining the centers of the molecules, Ω_{12} the mutual angle, r the magnitude of $\mathbf{r}$, and σ a parameter depending on Ω_{12} and a unit vector $\mathbf{r}/r$. As shown by Khokhlov and Semenov,[16] this assumption leads to an integral equation which in high dilution reduces to the result of the Onsager theory. For a certain choice of the pair correlation function the resulting integral equation for the free energy is identical to the result of the Flory approach at high orientations. For details the reader is referred to Chapter 3. The correspondence of these quite different approaches at least under special circumstances is interesting to note and worth pursuing further for development of a unified treatment of LCP.

2.4. Thermotropic Systems

Thermotropic nematic liquid crystals and semiflexible polymers transform into the isotropic state at a well-defined transition temperature T_{NI}. Experimental observations imply that the transition is of the first order. The concomitant latent volume change is usually too small to account for the latent heat of transition, which in consequence must be traced back to an increase or decrease of the intermolecular cohesion energy. At constant volume, such a change in the interaction energy cannot be caused by isotropic dispersion forces; in a dense liquid the overall number of mutual contacts between the rods should not change upon ordering. Hence, the dependence of the intermolecular energy on the degree of order must be attributed to the anisotropic dispersion forces.[18, 19] Isotropic dispersion forces promote the ordering transition only in an indirect manner by adjusting the density. This difference between the molar hard core volume V^* of the molecules and the observed volume V may be treated in terms of the lattice representation as unoccupied sites. In this approach akin to the mean-field lattice gas model,[20] the empty sites play a similar role as the solvent molecules in lyotropic systems [cf. Eq. (11)]. In both cases, a decrease of the volume fraction of rods will give rise to a lowering of the transition temperature.[21]

Accordingly, the lattice treatment of lyotropic systems outlined in Section 2.2 may be extended to thermotropic liquid crystals as follows[21]: The unoccupied space present in the system is taken into account[22] in terms of the reduced volume $\tilde{V} = V/V^*$. Assuming the additivity in volumes, the total number of lattice sties is

$$n_0 = \tilde{V}xn_x \qquad (35)$$

and the volume fraction of unoccupied sites follows as $1 - 1/\tilde{V}$. Now, we require the anisotropic dispersion interaction energy of a rod at inclination Θ with respect to the domain axis in the mean-field of all other rods. The quantity relevant to the transition is the difference between the energies attributable to the anisotropy of the polarizability in the isotropic and anisotropic state. According to Irvine and Flory,[14]

$$\epsilon_{an}(\Theta) = \sigma SP_2(\cos \Theta)(\Delta\alpha/\bar{\alpha})^2 \epsilon_{iso} \qquad (36)$$

where $\epsilon_{an}(\Theta)$ and ϵ_{iso} designate an orientation-dependent (or anisotropic) and isotropic part of the mean-field energy, respectively; S is the mean order parameter of the fluid, $P_2(\cos \Theta)$ the second Legendre polynomial, and $\Delta\alpha/\bar{\alpha}$ is the ratio of the anisotropic part of the polarizability tensor to the mean polarizability. The constant σ is located between $1/45$, calculated for a spherical distribution of segments, and $1/6$, found by fixing the neighboring molecule at a location r in a direction perpendicular to the long axis. The orientation-dependent energy for a segment is given by[21]

$$\epsilon_{an}(\Theta) = -(kT^*/\tilde{V})SP_2(\cos \Theta) \qquad (37)$$

where T^* is the characteristic temperature of anisotropic interaction.

With an identification $\epsilon_{iso} = -2p^*V_s^*/\tilde{V}$, where p^* denotes the characteristic pressure of the fluid and V_s^* the hard core volume of one segment of the molecule,[22] we have

$$kT^* = 2\sigma p^*V_s^*(\Delta\alpha/\bar{\alpha})^2 \qquad (38)$$

Equation (38) demonstrates that the characteristic temperature T^* measuring the strength of anisotropic interaction may be correlated to thermodynamic and optical data through a purely geometric constant σ. Adoption of the orientation-dependent energy

$$E_{orient}/kT = -(1/2)xn_pS^2/\tilde{V}\tilde{T} \tag{39}$$

($\tilde{T} = T/T^*$) in the previous formulation of the configuration partition function based on the lattice model leads to a revised expression for the integral[21, 23] [cf. Eq. (26)]:

$$f_p = \int_0^{\pi/2} \sin^p \Theta \exp\left[-(4ax/\pi)\sin \Theta - (3/2)(xS/\tilde{V}\tilde{T})\sin^2 \Theta\right] d\Theta \tag{40}$$

with

$$a = -\ln\left[1 - \tilde{V}^{-1}(1 - \bar{y}/x)\right] \tag{41}$$

From the coexisting condition at the biphasic equilibrium, we obtain[21]

$$x(\tilde{V} - 1)a - \ln f_1 - (x - \bar{y}) - (xS/\tilde{V}\tilde{T})(1 - S/2) = 0 \tag{42}$$

To calculate the characteristic temperature T^* from experimental data for a given axial ratio the reduced volume $\tilde{V}$ must be known as function of temperature.[22] Equation (42), together with the self-consistency relations (27) and (28), can be solved numerically. The integrals f_p, necessary for Eqs. (27) and (28), are calculated by numerical integration of Eq. (40). The resulting reduced temperature $\tilde{T}$ may be converted to T^* by the relation $T^* = T_{NI}/\tilde{T}$. Values of T^* thus obtained may serve for calculation of the constant σ through (38) if p^*, V_s^*, $\Delta\alpha$, and $\bar{\alpha}$ are known with sufficient accuracy at T_{NI}. The details of such a comparison for selected model systems are given in Section 3.2.1.

3. ADAPTATIONS OF THE FLORY THEORY TO VARIOUS ASPECTS OF LIQUID CRYSTALS AND LIQUID-CRYSTALLINE POLYMERS

3.1. Lyotropic Systems

3.1.1. MONODISPERSE SYSTEMS

We consider a system of rigid rods dispersed in a solvent. By definition the net interaction between solvent and solute are null, i.e., the familiar interaction parameter[6] χ is set equal to zero. Numerical solution of Eqs. (20) and (21) together with the self-consistency relation [Eq. (27)] leads to the concentration of the rods in the anisotropic phase (v_p^a) and in the isotropic phase (v_p^i). Figure 3 shows both v_p^a and v_p^i calculated by the Flory-Ronca theory (solid curve) and by the "1956" approximation as a function of axial

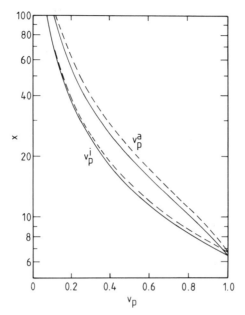

FIGURE 3

Volume fraction v_p^i (lower curves) and v_p^a (upper curves) in the isotropic and anisotropic phases, respectively, coexisting at equilibrium as functions of the axial ratio x (log scale). Solid curves were calculated according to the exact treatment (see text). Dashed curves represent the "1956" approximation. (Reproduced with permission from Ref. 9. Copyright Gordon and Breach Science Publishers.)

ratio x. It is obvious that the difference between the two treatments diminishes with higher axial ratios. The principal result deduced from Fig. 3 is a sharp decrease of v_p^a and v_p^i with increase of x. In the first approximation[1] v_p scales as $1/x$ in accord with deductions of the Onsager treatment (cf. Chapter 3). Using the "1956" approximation (cf. Section 2.3) Flory[1] derived the relation $v_p = 8/x(1 - 2/x)$, where v_p is the polymer concentration at incipient ordering. This expression has very often served for an estimate of the concentration where the ordered phase appears (cf. Chapter 6). For a quantitative comparison, however, the values v_p^i and v_p^a derived from the Flory-Ronca treatment (Fig. 3) should be used.

Another important result directly obvious from Fig. 3 is the prediction of an athermal limit x^{crit} of x, i.e., a minimum axial ratio necessary to produce an ordered phase when the system is fully occupied by the rods. From the Flory-Ronca treatment $x^{\text{crit}} = 6.42$. Special caution has to be exerted when comparing this much-quoted value to experimental data. From its derivation it is obvious that it only holds true for systems without free volume (see below) and without net interaction energy between the rods. Since these

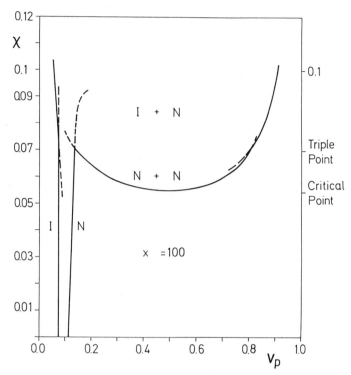

FIGURE 4
Composition of phases in equilibrium for rods with axial ratio 100
immersed in a solvent and values of the interaction parameter χ
plotted on the ordinate. The curve for isotropic solutions is on the
left and that for the ordered phases on the right, with the range of
heterogeneity occupying the region in between. The phase diagram
has been calculated using the Flory-Ronca treatment. (Reproduced
with permission from Ref. 27. Copyright American Chemical
Society.)

conditions are hardly fulfilled for any experimental system, the value of x^{crit}
does not bear direct importance to a comparison to liquid-crystalline polymers.

Net interactions between solvent and solute can be introduced[6] easily in
terms of the interaction parameter χ. The resulting phase diagram for rods
of axial ratio 100 is displayed in Fig. 4. This well-known phase diagram was
first calculated by Flory using the "1956" approximation. The main prediction of the theory was examined later by experiment, especially by Nakajima
et al.,[24] and Miller and co-workers,[25, 26] for lyotropic systems comprising
poly(γ-benzyl-L-glutamate) (PBLG), leading to a confirmation of the main
features.

The result given in Fig. 4 has been obtained using the Flory-Ronca treatment.[27] At small values of χ, v_p^i and v_p^a coincide with the data in Fig. 3. When the axial ratio x is sufficiently large, a nematic–nematic equilibrium region appears with certain values of χ. A wide biphasic gap follows at further deterioration of solvent quality. The characteristic features of the phase diagram are in qualitative agreement with various experimental findings. However, association often imposes severe problems in solutions of rodlike polymers in poor solvents. Hence, special care must be taken for a quantitative comparison (for an extended comparison of theory and experiment see Refs. 27 and 28).

Semiflexibility inherent to real molecular systems is also a problem that eludes an exact treatment by the lattice theory. The persistence length should provide a measure of the stiffness intrinsic to given rodlike molecules. An attempt along this line has been put forward by Ronca and Yoon,[29] who developed a theory by adopting a wormlike chain model conventionally defined in terms of a bending force constant, the contour length of the polymer chain, and the unit tangent vector at a given site. The essential step of this theory rests on the derivation of the configurational partition function for a wormlike chain[30] whose overall orientation is constrained under a nematic environment. The steric interactions are considered within the framework of the lattice theory, and thus the free energy expression reduces to the Flory rodlike theory in the limit of completely rigid chain. On the other hand, Khokhlov and Semenov[31] have introduced an entropy term to take account of such semiflexibility in the Onsager theory. The latter theory has been further elaborated by Odijk.[32] These theories have been extensively tested against phase equilibrium data by Teramoto and his group[33,34] and by Ciferri and co-workers[35] (cf. Chapter 6).

Another aspect of lyotropic solutions of rodlike polymers that merits investigation is the degree of order in the nematic phase. In the Flory-Ronca theory, explicit expressions are given both in terms of the disorder index $\bar{y}$ [Eq. (27)] and of the conventional order parameter $S = (3\langle\cos^2\Theta\rangle - 1)/2$ [Eq. (28)]. For a given concentration v_p, these quantities can be calculated by an iterative process. As shown in Fig. 5, the orientational order parameter decreases gradually by dilution and S–v_p curve terminates as the critical concentration (B point) is reached. The Flory-Ronca theory predicts $S_0 = 0.9$ over a wide range of x, being somewhat higher than those ($S_0 = 0.8$) derived from the Lee-Meyer treatment[36] of the Onsager theory.[37] On the other hand, if a persistence length of 150 nm is tentatively adopted in the Khokhlov-Semenov-Odijk expression,[37] the value of S_0 decreases to ca. 0.55 (or even lower value, ca. 0.41, by using the Khokhlov-Semenov expression[31]). In the latter theory, the semiflexibility of polymeric chains is considered in the Onsager scheme. The disparity among various theories is significant. Relevant experimental data have been reported for α-helical PBLG in the lyotropic liquid-crystalline state by using spectroscopic techniques such as IR[38] and deuterium NMR.[39,40] For a critical examination of theories, how-

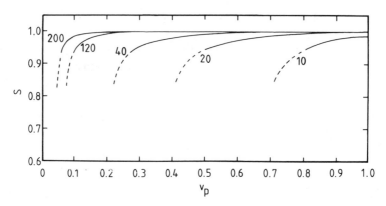

FIGURE 5
Variation of the order parameter S with polymer volume fraction v_p.
Values of the axial ratio x used in these calculations are given to
each curve. The broken curves indicate the results of calculations
extended over the concentration range where the biphasic
equilibrium should be expected. The junction between the solid and
broken curves corresponds to the nematic – isotropic phase
boundary: the value of S at this point defines the critical order
parameter (S_0). (Reproduced with permission from Ref. 40.)

ever, further accumulation of experimental data, including data on polymer
liquid crystals other than PBLG, is needed (cf. Chapter 6).

The effect of external flow fields on the isotropic–anisotropic equilibrium
also presents an interesting problem in relation to the fabrication process of
stiff-chain polymers. Marrucci and Ciferri[41] have estimated the excess free
energy arising from the frictional force acting upon individual rigid-rod
molecules, and introduced an additional term in the Flory "1956" expression.
They concluded from trial calculations that the effect of flow fields should
become distinct only in the range of dilute solutions.

3.1.2. POLYDISPERSE SYSTEMS

The Flory-Ronca theory is readily adapted to the treatment of polydisperse mixtures, such as are normally encountered in real systems.[42] For a
multicomponent rodlike solute system, Eq. (18) is valid provided that the
individual molecular quantities are properly replaced by the corresponding
averages. The usual self-consistency condition[43] should hold for each species
α, then

$$y_\alpha = (4/\pi) x_\alpha (f_2^\alpha / f_1^\alpha) \tag{43}$$

In the "1956" approximation, this relation is replaced by

$$\exp(-2/y_\alpha) = 1 - v_p(1 - \bar{y}_\alpha/\bar{x}_\alpha) \tag{44}$$

The lower of these solutions locates the minimum in Z. This expression indicates that the equilibrium value of y is independent of x; i.e., $y \equiv y_\alpha$ for all α with $x > y$. This result simplifies the treatment in this approximation.

At equilibrium between the isotropic and anisotropic phases, $\mu_i^i = \mu_i^a$ for the respective components in two phases: i.e., $\mu_s^i = \mu_s^a$ for the solvent, and $\mu_\alpha^i = \mu_\alpha^a$ for rods with $x > y$ as well as $x \leq y$. For a given distribution n_α/n_p, quantities characterizing the phases in equilibrium can be elucidated following the conventional procedure. However, it should be noted here that smaller rods with $x \leq y$ may remain in the anisotropic phase as an isotropic diluent. For such species, as briefly discussed above, y inevitably exceeds x over the range $1 \geq \sin \Theta > \pi/4$ according to the definition of y given in Eq. (23).

The partitioning of rodlike solute species between isotropic and anisotropic phases was first investigated for a binary mixture of rodlike components.[42] Flory and Frost[44] extended the treatment to systems having the most probable distributions and also to the Poisson distribution of rod lengths. Later, Moscicki and Williams[45] adapted the Flory theory to the case of a Gaussian distribution.

A theoretical phase diagram obtained[12] for the athermal ternary systems comprising a solvent $x_1 = 1$ and two rodlike solute components with $x_a, x_b = 100, 10$ is shown in Fig. 6. The boundaries of the biphasic region are heavy lined. The upper curve represents the isotropic phase, the lower the anisotropic phase. Representative tie lines for conjugate phases in the ternary systems are shown by light lines. Most remarkable is the presence of a region of three coexisting phases indicated by I, A_1, and A_2. Values of y less than unity may not be physically unacceptable according to strict interpretation of the model. In these cases, the partitioning of the components may be corrected by adopting the ideal mixing law ($y = 1$) for the anisotropic phase. The results thus obtained are shown by the dashed lines in Fig. 6. The only significant effect of restricting y to the range $y \geq 1$ is the displacement of the phase point A_1 to A_1^*. Teramoto and his co-workers[46] have determined ternary-phase diagrams for aqueous solutions of schizophyllan (a polysaccharide existing in triple helices in water). In the isotropic–anisotropic biphasic region, the immiscibility gap becomes sizeably widened by the polydispersity of the sample. When the ratio x_a/x_b is sufficiently large, a triphasic equilibrium is observed below the biphasic region. Although the agreement between theory and experiment is only qualitative, various characteristic features predicted by the theory are reproduced in the experimental phase diagram.

Numerous calculations for various polydisperse systems indicate that concomitantly with the broadening of the biphasic gap, partitioning of solute species should occur between the coexisting isotropic and nematic phases. The predicted fractionation of species has been universally confirmed but the selectivity is generally somewhat less than theory predicts[47] (cf. Chapter 6). Ternary systems containing two chemically heterogeneous rod components

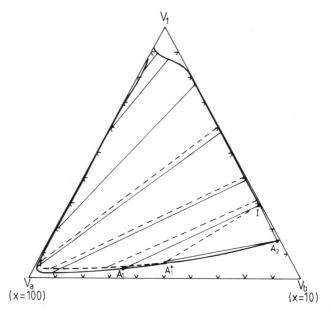

FIGURE 6

Ternary phase diagram calculated for the system (100, 10). Binodials and tie lines calculated without restriction on y are shown by solid lines; coexisting phases thus calculated at triphasic equilibrium are I, A_1, and A_2. The binodial for the anisotropic phase calculated with $y = 1$ and associated tie lines are dashed; coexisting phases at triphasic equilibrium are I, A_1^*, and A_2. (Reproduced with permission from Ref. 12. Copyright American Chemical Society.)

may also be treated by adding χ terms for the intermolecular interaction. Experimental observations indicate however that rods are quite incompatible except when they are chemically alike[48] (cf. Chapter 6).

3.1.3. MIXTURES OF RODS AND RANDOM COILS

Mixtures of rods and coils can be treated easily by the lattice model by first introducing the rods as outlined in Section 2.2. Thus the number of empty consecutive lattice sites is given by Eq. (5). The flexible coil may be introduced in the second step using the usual Flory-Huggins statistics, i.e., by a priori probabilities as given in Eq. (1). The remainder of the lattice sites then is filled with solvent molecules. The partition function derived from these considerations follows as[49]

$$Z_M = \frac{(n_0 - n_x(x_r - \bar{y}))!Z_{\text{orient}}}{(n_0 - n_x x_r - n_c x_c)!n_x!n_c!} n_0^{-n_x(\bar{y}-1)-n_c(x_c-1)} \tag{45}$$

with subscripts r for the rod and c for the coil. The resulting phase diagram for athermal mixtures was first calculated by Flory in the framework of the "1956" approximation.[49] Here we give the phase diagram (Fig. 7) for an athermal mixture of rods having an axial ratio of 100 with coils comprising

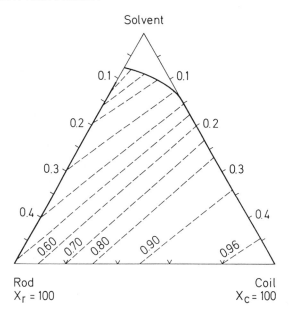

FIGURE 7
Composition of a phase diagram for an athermal system consisting of a rigid rod with axial ratio 100 and a random coil comprising 100 segments in a solvent.[49] Binodials are shown as heavy lines; coordinates are volume fractions. Tie lines are dashed. The phase diagram has been calculated using the Flory-Ronca treatment. (Reproduced with permission from Ref. 50. Copyright John Wiley & Sons, Inc.)

100 segments in a common solvent.[50] The isotropic phase tolerates an appreciable portion of the rodlike species if the concentration of the random coil is rather low. Most notable is the fact that the coils are virtually excluded from the ordered phase. The binodal for the nematic phase practically coincides with the axis connecting the rodlike solute with the solvent. These predictions of the lattice model have been fully verified by the experimental work of the Ciferri group[51] and by the Air Force group.[52] It must be noted that the strong demixing of rods and coils proceeds without assistance of enthalpic interactions; it is of purely entropic nature ("entropic demixing"). The gratifying agreement of theory and experiment underlines the basic validity of the lattice calculation and presents a further example for the broad applicability of the Flory theory. Recently, an extension of this model to polyelectrolyte chains has been given.[53]

3.1.4. SEMIRIGID MACROMOLECULES

As briefly pointed out in Section 3.1.1, real chain molecules invariably possess some degree of flexibility. Departures from rectilinearity may be characterized by finite values of the persistence length as observed in solution. According to Norisuye's group,[54] the persistence length of the schizophyllan triple helix is around 200 μm in aqueous media. Stable helical conformations, such as those of the polypeptide α-helix, also exhibit some departure from a perfect rigidity ($q = 150$ μm). In instances where the skeletal bonds are nominally colinear, bending of bond angles introduces an appreciable degree of flexibility. Motowoka et al.[55] reported a persistence length $q = 13$ μm for a polymer such as $+ \mathrm{PT(PBu_3)_2 - C \equiv C - C \equiv C} +_x$ in n-heptane. The latter polymer and its homologs are known to form lyotropic liquid crystals in trichloroethylene.[56] For sufficiently large macromolecules ($L/q \gg 1$, where L is the contour length) the effects of the partial flexibility are known to be dominant. For these molecules, as a first approximation, Flory has proposed the Kuhn chain model, a particularly simple scheme that provides intuitive insight into the tendency of a semirigid chain to induce formation of a nematic phase. Matheson and Flory[58-60] further extended the lattice theory to semirigid macromolecules consisting of rodlike sequences of units in combination with flexible (random coil) units. In this device, contributions arising from flexible segments have been properly considered in the free energy expression. Thus it has been demonstrated that the lattice theory is versatilely useful in treating thermodynamic properties of polymers over a wide range of flexibility from perfect rigidity to random coil. The semiflexibility of real polymer systems, which is most closely represented by a wormlike chain, has never been treated by Flory, however. Revisions along this line have been attempted by Ronca and Yoon.[29]

The Kuhn Chain Model. The model is also called random flight or freely jointed chain, which consists of bonds of appropriate length connected by flexible joints. The directions of neighboring bonds are completely uncorrelated, and the chain axis undergoes abrupt changes at occasional points along the chain. This obviously artificial model offers the distinct advantage of being susceptible to treatment within the framework of the lattice scheme presented above. The theory developed on this basis may be adapted to semirigid chains by the simple device of replacing the molecular axial ratio x by the axial ratio x_k of the Kuhn segment. The model comprises m rods, being of the same length, connected as described above. They are characterized by an axial ratio x_k, and the corresponding disorientation index y.[57]

The validity of the model has been critically studied for semiflexible polymers such as poly(n-hexylisocyanate) by Bianchi et al.[35,51] Cellulose and cellulose derivatives, which occasionally exhibit sharp bends in otherwise a rather stiff chain sequence, have also been extensively examined by this model. Justification for this simple model as a representation of any real chain rests on the supposition that the cumulative effect of many small departures from rectilinearity over a length of the real chain equal to a rodlike member of the model can be represented by the junction between two such members, that junction having the quality of permitting free orientation.

As first pointed out by Krigbaum,[61] however, the number of universal joints $m - 1$ recognized in this manner seems to create some problem in the

(a)

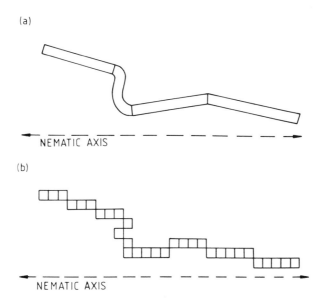

(b)

FIGURE 8
(a) Schematic representation of a semirigid chain containing three rodlike portions and one flexible section. (b) Representation of a semirigid chain on a lattice. (Reproduced with permission from Ref. 58. Copyright American Chemical Society.)

definition of the reference state. At the limit $v_p \to 1$ for the bulk nematic state, we obtain

$$-\ln Z/n_p = -\ln x_k m - 1 + m(2 + y - 2\ln y) \qquad (46)$$

The result suggests that the free energy of disorientation varies with the value of m, and becomes positive at $y = 1$ and $x_k = 7.3891$ for the range $m > 1$. This is unrealistic. Such an anomaly does not exist for $m = 1$; i.e., Eq. (46) reduces to zero by insertion of the above parameter set. The role of the universal joint in a densely packed medium, e.g., in the bulk state, can hardly be recognized in the lattice model. To circumvent these difficulties, Flory adopted a revised definition for the reference state in a later work.[60] The definition of the reference state does not affect consequences of the phase equilibrium, provided, of course, that the same reference state is employed for identical rods in different phases.

Chains with Rodlike Sequences at Fixed Location. Matheson and Flory[58] extended the lattice treatment to semirigid chains that contain inherently flexible (random coil) units at certain locations along the otherwise rigid chain. A molecule of the kind here considered is shown schematically in Fig. 8. The directions of the rodlike sequences are assumed to be mutually uncorrelated by the intramolecular connections through randomly coiled units of variable length: x_i^c and x_i^k are the numbers of random coil and rigid segments, respectively, the total number of segments in this molecule being

$$x_i = x_i^c + x_i^k \tag{47}$$

The internal configuration partition function for a coil segment is defined by z_c relative to $z_k = 1$ for a rodlike segment. The free energy expression therefore includes a contribution arising from such an internal chain flexibility

$$\sum_i x_i^c \ln z_c \tag{48}$$

in addition to those considered in the treatment of the universal joint model. The phase equilibrium for athermal solutions of a once-broken rod has been examined by this model.[58] In this treatment, the internal flexibility of the coil, z_c, was taken to be invariable between the two coexisting phases. The expressions reduce to those of the Kuhn model chain when flexible coil sections are replaced by a volumeless universal joint.

Chains with Interconvertible Rodlike and Random-Coil Sequences in Equilibrium.

Polymers exhibiting a helix–coil transition are a prototypical example of this category. A strong tendency to exclude coil sequences from the lyotropic nematic phase, as is found in an earlier investigation on separate rodlike and random-coil chains,[49,50] may produce an enhanced cooperativity in the helix–coil transition. A general formulation of theory has been presented by Flory and Matheson in the "1956" approximation.[59,60] Upon adoption of the lattice theory, the authors changed the state of reference from the conventionally accepted "perfect ordered parallel array" to one in which the rodlike molecules or sequences are randomly disoriented over the full range of solid angles, steric overlaps among these sequences being hypothetically ignored. Consequently, the term involving the internal configuration partition function of a coil segment, z_c, and the one responsible for the dispersion of chain ends, $-n_p \ln x$, are ignored in the above expression. As pointed out above, however, these revisions in the reference state should not affect the equilibrium properties of the system.

The conventional Zimm-Bragg terminologies are adopted to describe an intramolecular helix–coil transition, i.e., σ denoting the statistical weight for the helical state relative to the coil, and s being the weighting factor for initiation of a helical sequence. The free energy change due to introducing helical sequences into the polymer molecules requires inclusion of a term

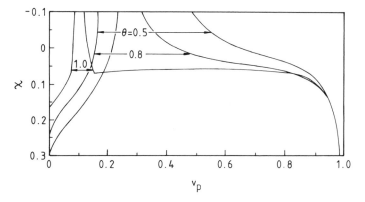

FIGURE 9
The effect on the binodal curves for isotropic – nematic equilibria
produced by changing s at constant σ. Three conjugate pairs
correspond to $s \geq 1.4$ ($\theta = 1$), $s = 1.0151$ ($\theta = 0.8$), and $s = 1.0$
($\theta = 0.5$). Invariant parameters are $\sigma = 10^{-4}$, $x = 100$, and $m = 10$.
(Reproduced with permission from Ref. 60. Copyright American
Chemical Society.)

such as

$$- \sum_i mx_i(\theta \ln s - \rho \ln \sigma) \qquad (49)$$

where m represents the number of repeat units involved in a helical sequence, θ is the fraction of polymer units in the helical conformation, and ρ
is the fraction of units that marks the beginning of a helical sequence. The
permutation term for helical and coil sequences of various lengths has also
been elucidated.

Minimization of the free energy with respect to the fractions of helical
sequences at a fixed helicity leads to the equilibrium distribution of helical
sequence lengths and the number of helical sequences. Expressions for the
chemical potentials of the components in the isotropic and fully helical,
nematic phases are derived, and binodal curves are constructed. The role of s
is especially interesting. The results calculated for $x = 100$, $m = 10$, $\sigma =$
10^{-4}, and three values of s are shown in Fig. 9. The first pair of binodals
($\theta = 1$) are identical with those for systems of rigid rods. Relaxation of
rigidity in the isotropic phase, as manifested in smaller rigid sequence lengths
$xm\theta/\rho$ and also lower volume fractions θ of rigid sequences, renders the
transition more gradual from the broad biphasic range for positive interactions $\chi \simeq 0$ and for $\chi \leq 0$. The transition range is shifted simultaneously to
higher concentrations. The principal result of this study is the pronounced
"conformational ordering" that is observed to accompany formation of an
anisotropic phase.

In this treatment, possible correlations between two consecutive helical sequences in the same chain are neglected. As the authors point out, this assumption may limit its application to more general chains.

3.1.5. RIGID RODS WITH FLEXIBLE SIDECHAINS

Another example for the versatility of the lattice approach is the treatment of rods substituted by flexible sidechains.[26, 27] There is now a bulk of experimental data available on these comblike polymers in which the stiffness of the mainchain is preserved but which exhibit sufficient solubility due to the appended sidechains.[62] The lattice calculation[27] proceeds as follows: The rodlike mainchains are first introduced according to the rules given in Section 2.2. The flexible sidechains follow by applying the methods of the Flory-

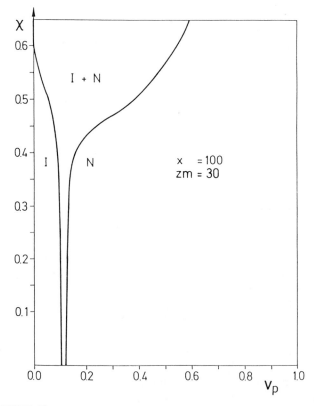

FIGURE 10
Influence of flexible sidechains on the phase behavior of rigid rods: phase diagram of rods with axial ratio 100 bearing sidechains. The parameter zm is the total number of segments of the sidechains per rod. (Reproduced with permission from Ref. 27. Copyright American Chemical Society.)

Huggins statistics. The only difference is given by the fact that the first segment may not be chosen freely. Hence, the expectation for finding a series of empty lattice sites for a rod bearing z sidechains each of which contains m segments is augmented by an additional factor as given in Eq. (1) to the power of $z \cdot m$. Starting from this, the partition function is evaluated as derived in Section 2.2.

The main result of this treatment is the finding that the sidechains are acting much in a way of a bound solvent, the volume fractions v_p^i and v_p^a being shifted to higher values accordingly. Another characteristic feature of the phase diagrams is the absence of nematic–nematic equilibria even in the case of a low volume fraction of sidechains. This is directly obvious when comparing Fig. 4 (rods without sidechains: $zm = 0$) to Fig. 10 (rods with sidechains: $zm = 30$). In addition to this, the wide biphasic gap at poor quality of the solvent has become considerably smaller. A detailed comparison with experiments[27] confirms these conclusions in a qualitative fashion, but a quantitative comparison is severely hampered by association in these systems.

It should be noted in the context of the section that an experimental determination of sidechain conformations has been attempted by using the deuterium NMR technique for PBLG in the lyotropic liquid crystalline state.[39] The spatial orientation of sidechains was found to remain unaffected by an increase in concentration from $v_p \simeq 0.15$ (B point) to 0.3.

3.2. Thermotropic Systems

3.2.1. NEAT LIQUIDS

In the subsequent section a detailed description of the treatment of thermotropic LCP's in the framework of the Flory approach will be presented. Special attention will be given to low molecular weight model systems consisting of nematic LMWLC. It will become obvious that the essential features of thermotropic LCP's can be discussed theoretically as well as experimentally using these model systems. Correspondence with LCP's is achieved through enlargement of the axial ratio x (cf. below).

As demonstrated in Section 2.4, a mean-field treatment of the anisotropic dispersion forces leads to the interaction energy given by Eq. (37). The combinatorial part of the partition function explicitly takes into account the presence of free volume in the system expressed in terms of the reduced volume $\tilde{V}$. If the nematic–isotropic transition temperature T_{NI} as well as $\tilde{V}$ at T_{NI} are known, T^* may be obtained by numerical solution of Eq. (42) as outlined in Section 2.4 for a given axial ratio x. The great importance of the free volume is seen when T_{NI} calculated for a given value of x and of T^* is plotted as a function of $\tilde{V}$ (Fig. 11).[17,21] Lowering $\tilde{V}$ is followed by an increase of the steric interactions among the rods followed by a strong rise of T_{NI}. It is thus obvious that the axial ratio of the LMWLC or the respective

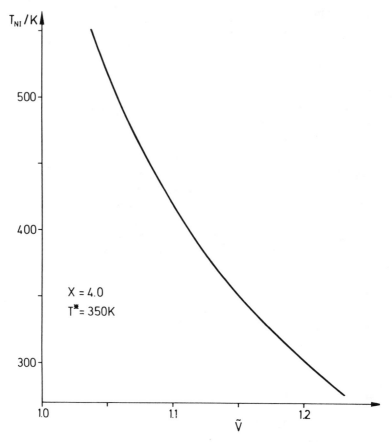

FIGURE 11

Nematic – isotropic transition temperature T_{NI} as a function of the reduced volume $\tilde{V}$. The characteristic temperature T^* is fixed to 350 K, and the axial ratio of the rod is 4.0. (Reproduced with permission from Ref. 17. Copyright Gordon and Breach Science Publishers.)

LCP is not sufficient to calculate the transition temperature T_{NI}; values of $\tilde{V}$ and T^* must be supplied too.

It has been shown that the characteristic temperature T^* can be related directly to thermodynamic and optical data through Eq. (38). In a comparison of T^* thus obtained with theory, one must bear in mind that only rodlike molecules without flexible parts are suitable for this purpose. Also, accurate data on the anisotropy of the polarizability $\Delta\alpha$ must be available for a meaningful test of Eq. (38). Table 1 gives a résumé of the data obtained on two homologous series of rodlike nematogens.[63, 64]

Table 1
Characteristic Data of LMWLC

n	T_{NI}	x	$\tilde{V}(T_{NI})$	$\dfrac{\Delta\alpha}{\alpha}$	σ	T^* (K)
4	523	3.9	1.38	0.96	0.07	573
5	691	4.8	1.50	1.02	0.066	630
6	838	5.5	1.56	1.13	0.054	650

n	T_{NI}	x	$\tilde{V}(T_{NI})$	$\dfrac{\Delta\alpha}{\alpha}$	σ	T^* (K)
3	373	3.8	1.216	0.54	0.13	343
4	527	5.1	1.284	0.58	0.10	316
5	737	6.4	1.364	0.60	0.092	306

Despite the experimental uncertainties, it is obvious that the geometrical constant σ is located within the range predicted by theory (cf. Section 2.4; see also Refs. 17 and 65). This finding demonstrates the validity of the lattice theory of thermotropic systems. The experimental data displayed in Table 1, furthermore, directly demonstrate the need to describe the nematic–isotropic transition in terms of the steric forces. The anisotropic dispersion forces per segment as expressed by the quantity T^* remain virtually constant throughout the oligomers of a given series. The strong rise of T_{NI} with ascending axial ratio then can be traced back to the increase of the steric interactions thus affected.

As has been outlined above, the Flory model seems to describe the nematic to isotropic transition in neat, thermotropic nematogens rather well. However, the order parameter S predicted by this approach is located between 0.6 and 0.7, which is significantly higher than typical values of low molecular weight liquid crystals ($S = 0.3$–0.4) at transition. This problem is not restricted to the Flory theory but seems to be common to all approaches starting from a system of rigid rods.[66] It has been pointed out by a number of authors (see Ref. 17 for an extended discussion) that this disagreement is due to the neglect of fluctuations in a mean-field approach rather than to insufficiencies in the physical description of the nematic phase. Although these fluctuations are predicted to be of minor importance for thermodynamics, they will have a profound influence on the observed order parameter. Estimates by Warner[67] indeed indicate that this effect should not be neglected. Another possible reason for the discrepancy between theory and experiment might be sought in molecular biaxiality. Also, there may be an influence of the imperfect shape of real nematogens on the order parameter. Again this problem may be treated in terms of the lattice theory,[68] leading to the conclusion that deviations from the ideal cylindrical shape will greatly reduce the magnitude of S. In addition, this distortion is followed by a much stronger dependence of S on temperature. Hence, a part of the discrepancy must arise from the idealization of nematogens or cylinders.

3.2.2. BINARY SYSTEMS

The considerations developed in the preceding section are again easily extended[21,43] to include mixtures of rodlike nematogens with equal T^*. The subject was first treated by Warner and Flory[43] at the limit of $\tilde{V} = 1.0$, i.e., without consideration for the free volume. Assuming $x = 1$ for one of the components, the expression reduces to that of a solvent–solute system with inclusion of the orientation-dependent attractive interactions. Calculations on long rods (e.g., $x = 50$) dispersed in a simple diluent lead to a phase diagram similar to those predicted previously to arise from isotropic attractive interactions between long-rod solute molecules (cf. Fig. 4). In the present scheme, the ordinate is expressed by the reciprocal reduced temperature $\tilde{T}^{-1}$ scaled by the axial ratio x in place of the familiar χ parameter. The complex behavior involving a critical point and a triple point persists down to an axial ratio just greater than $x = 20$. The width of the chimney representing biphasic equilibria tends to be broadened as x decreases. The treatment thus demonstrates that the characteristic features of the phase diagram for the polymer–diluent system can be reproduced by taking account of anisotropic dispersion interactions. For mixtures of short rods, consideration of the free volume, or unoccupied sites, become important. Flory and Irvine[21] have demonstrated the striking dependence of the nematic–isotropic transition on the free volume for a homologous series of poly(p-phenylenes), $H + C_6H_4 +_n H$, with $n = 4$–6. Biphasic equilibria in the three binary systems formed from these homologs were found to be in excellent agreement with predictions of theory, the same value of T^* being used for these comparisons. The theory has been further extended to treat mixtures of components for which T^* differs.[23] The validity of the treatment has been tested against experimental data obtained for three binary systems of oxybenzoate oligomers (Fig. 12).

The theory predicts a wide biphasic gap and concomitantly, a strong partitioning of the components between the nematic and isotropic phases. Experimental data, however, revealed that both features are much less

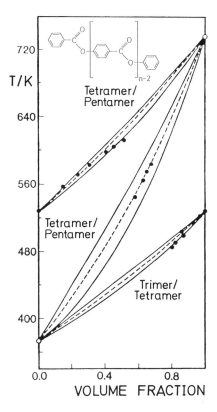

FIGURE 12
Phase diagrams of the three binary systems consisting of the
oxybenzoate trimer – tetramer, trimer – pentamer, and tetramer –
pentamer (trimer, $n = 3$; tetramer, $n = 4$; pentamer, $n = 5$). The
upper and lower curves for a given mixture present the volume
fractions of the coexisting isotropic and nematic phases, respectively.
The volume fraction plotted on the abscissa refers to the higher
oligomer. Filled circles are experimental temperatures of the
nematic – isotropic transition. Open circles are extrapolated
temperatures of the nematic – isotropic phase transition for the pure
trimer and pentamer (cf. Ref. 23 for details). The dashed lines
present the temperature of the nematic – isotropic transition
calculated assuming equal composition in the coexistent phases
(one-component treatment; see text for explanation). (Reproduced
with permission from Ref. 23.)

pronounced than anticipated by theory. For instance, the biphasic region in
binary mixtures of nematogens is rather small and is disregarded in most
experimental studies. Thus the mixture behaves like a one-component system. The resulting single transition temperature is displayed as a dashed line
in Fig. 11. Good agreement between theory and experiment is observed. The
absence of the wide biphasic gap seems to be due to nonequilibrium effects.

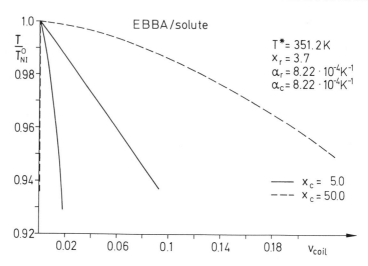

FIGURE 13

Theoretical phase diagrams of a mixture consisting of a thermotropic
nematogen and a coiled species. The parameters used in the
calculation correspond to the system[69] EBBA/PS. The quantity x_r
is the axial ratio of the nematogen; T^* its characteristic temperature
measuring the strength of anisotropic interaction and T_{NI} its
nematic – isotropic transition temperature; x_c denotes the number
of segments of the coiled species. The thermal expansion
coefficients of the rodlike and the polymeric species are denoted by
α_r and α_c, respectively. The segment fraction v_{coil} of the flexible
species has been chosen as the independent variable. (Reproduced
with permission from Ref. 69.)

3.2.3. MIXTURES OF NEMATIC LMWLC WITH FLEXIBLE COILS

The considerations given in Section 3.1.3 can be extended to include
mixtures of thermotropic nematogens and flexible coils by introducing free
volume and anisotropic interaction between the rods. The dilution of the
dispersion forces between the rods by the coils may be taken into account by
multiplying Eq. (37) by v_r, the volume fraction of rods in the systems[43, 69]:

$$\epsilon_{an}(\Theta) = -(kT^*/\tilde{V})v_r SP_2(\cos \Theta) \qquad (50)$$

The rodlike component is characterized by x_r and T^*, the coiled species by
its contour length x_c, which equals the number of segments occupied on the
lattice. The reduced volume $\tilde{V}$ of the mixture can be calculated in the first
approximation by assuming additivity of volumes. Figure 13 gives the right-

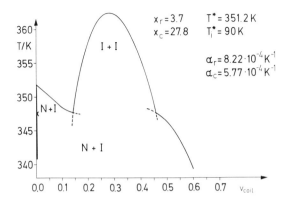

FIGURE 14

Theoretical phase diagram of a mixture of a nematogen and a polymer. The data given in the graph correspond to the system EBBA / PS 2100; the quantity T_i^* denotes the characteristic temperature of isotropic interaction, and v_{coil} is the segment fraction of the polymer. Dashed lines denote metastable continuations. (Reproduced with permission from Ref. 69.)

hand side of a theoretical phase diagram calculated using the data of a typical nematogen (EBBA) mixed with oligomeric polystyrene.

As in the case of lyotropic mixture (see Section 3.1.3), there is a strong exclusion of the coils from the ordered phase. The effect becomes more pronounced with increasing length of the coils, polymeric species are virtually excluded from the nematic phase. Experimental data (cf. Chapter 6) are in qualitative accord with these deductions. In the course of the foregoing considerations no net interactions between nematogen and the coils has been taken into account. Introducing this in terms of the usual interaction parameter χ leads to occurrence of liquid–liquid demixing in the isotropic phase (Fig. 14). Both liquid–liquid demixing together with nematic–isotropic phase separation leads at lower temperatures to a triphase line and a wide biphasic region. All features are in qualitative accord with the phase diagrams of a system such as PAA (*p*-azoxyanisole)|*n*-octadecane and PAA|*n*-tetracosane.[70]

The above discussion shows clearly that there are two reasons for incompatibility: (1) the incompatibility upon formation of an ordered phase ("entropic demixing," see Section 3.1.3), and (2) incompatibility due to isotropic interaction, which leads to the familiar demixing into two isotropic phases.[6] Both effects become even more pronounced when increasing the molecular weight. It is therefore found that mixtures of flexible polymers with LCP are usually totally incompatible.[5]

3.2.4. SEMIFLEXIBLE SYSTEMS

In his unfinished work[71] Flory attempted to extend his theory to semi-flexible polymers exhibiting a thermotropic nematic–isotropic transition. A typical example treated here is a polymer

consisting of two kinds of units, one rigid and the other flexible, capable of disrupting perpetuation of the axis of the rigid unit. The oxyethylene sequence ($-OCH_2CH_2-$) may assume sufficiently extended form (e.g., ttt) to be included with the rigid segments, with a statistical weight s^* compared with unity for the disordered form. The flexible sequences are short, so that the axial ratio (x_1) of one unit can be defined by the distance spanning from CH_2 to CH_2 in the nematic as well as in the isotropic state. In this respect this model differs from that depicted in Fig. 8, where substantial volumes are assigned to the flexible segments. The underlying concept has already been developed in the Flory-Matheson theory, which treats the helix–coil transition incident to the formation of a nematic phase. For simplicity, a system consisting of a single polymer component of identically large chain length is assumed. To account for the conformational flexibility characteristic of the above-mentioned LCP, Flory introduced a term such as

$$- \sum (\zeta - 1)\gamma_\zeta \ln s^* \tag{51}$$

in the reduced free energy expression. Here γ_ζ indicates the number of rigid sequences containing ζ rigid units, i.e., consisting of ζ rigid members joined by $\zeta - 1$ oxyethylene units in the extended conformation. The correspondence between Eqs. (49) and (51) is apparent: σ is unity and θ is not required in the latter treatment. In the isotropic phase, polymer chains are free from any external anisotropic constraint and the expression reduces to $-\bar{\zeta}\gamma \ln(1 + s^*)$.

The orientation-dependent attractive interactions were taken into account according to the formulation given in Eq. (9). The equilibrium distribution at fixed $\gamma = \Sigma \gamma_\zeta$ and fixed $\bar{\zeta}\gamma = \Sigma \gamma_\zeta$ was obtained for the thermotropic nematic state. Finally the expressions for the equilibrium between nematic and isotropic phases were elucidated by the conventional procedure. Flory left some handwritten notes that suggest his further effort to apply this relation to real liquid-crystalline polymer systems.

A solution to the theoretical scheme mentioned above was later furnished by Yoon.[72] Variations in such structural and thermodynamic quantities as the average rod length, the orientational order parameter, and the transition temperature have been elucidated as a function of s^*. An expression for the equilibrium between isotropic and perfectly ordered nematic phases was also derived. The results of calculations with $x_1 = 4$ and $\tilde{V} = 1.3$ clearly indicate the effect to "conformational ordering" that accompanies formation of an anisotropic phase. Yoon[72] compared these theoretical predictions with experimental data reported for mainchain polymer liquid crystals carrying spacers such as $-O(CH_2)_{10}O-$ and $-O(CH_2CH_2O)_3-$.

Vasilenko et al.[73] have treated thermotropic liquid crystals comprising polymers such as those depicted in Fig. 8. In these systems, the flexible component may serve as a diluent to some extent. The effect arising from a stiffening of the soft segment induced by the anisotropic environment was examined within the framework of the Matheson-Flory scheme. It has been concluded on this basis that an increase in the stiffness enhances the stability of the nematic mesophase. As is well-known, however, the conformational ordering of soft flexible spacers takes place highly cooperatively in the formation of an anisotropic phase. A satisfactory theory that takes account of this important effect has yet to be developed.[74]

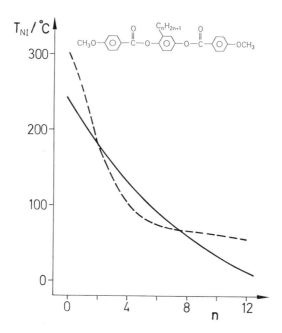

FIGURE 15

Temperature of the nematic–isotropic transitions versus n, the number of carbon atoms in the alkyl sidechains. The experimental data (crosses) have been taken from the work of Weissflog and Demus;[75] the solid line displays the result of the model calculation. (Reproduced with permission from Ref. 68.)

3.2.5. RODS WITH FLEXIBLE SIDECHAINS

The theory of rods with appended flexible sidechains as given in Section 3.1.5 can be augmented along the lines given in Section 2.4 to include thermotropic systems.[68] It has to be noted that in this approach the sidechains are treated explicitly in the frame of the lattice approach. They are not taken into account by enlarging the diameter of the mainchains. In the first approximation, the enthalpic interactions between main- and sidechains may be disregarded but the dilution of the anisotropic dispersion forces between the mainchains is taken into account with resort to Eq. (50). Figure 15 shows the nematic–isotropic transition temperature T_{NI} calculated as a function of the length of the sidechain for a given axial ratio x and characteristic temperature T^* of the mainchain.

The model calculation in Fig. 15 assumes a hydrocarbon sidechain with n carbon atoms contained therein. This enables a direct comparison with the data of Weissflog and Demus,[75] which surprisingly reveal a great stability of the nematic state even when the sidechain is longer than the mainchain. These experimental findings are in accord with theory, the result of which is displayed in Fig. 15. The reason for the unexpected stability of the nematic state even in the presence of flexible lateral substituents derives from the balance of the lowering of the steric and attractive forces by the sidechains and the increase of these interactions due to lowering the temperature (cf. Fig. 11 of Section 3.2.1).

Another interesting feature is the decrease of the order parameter S due to the presence of sidechains as well as its more pronounced dependence on temperature.[68] This suggests that a part of the discrepancy of theory and experiment with regard to S is due to the imperfection of molecular shapes, i.e., due to the idealization of real molecules as perfect cylinders.

4. CONCLUSION

The discussion in Section 3 has shown that the Flory lattice model is a highly versatile approach to various problems in liquid-crystalline systems. Despite the difficulties discussed in Section 2.3, the model works in a semiquantitative fashion over the entire range of concentrations. In particular, the Flory model has proved indispensable to treatments of mixtures of rods and coils and of more complicated systems, such as rods with flexible sidechains, or the helix–coil transition in ordered systems. The obvious disadvantage, of course, is the necessity of a discontinuous lattice to evaluate the partition function, which can be evaluated in a continuous frame when using the Onsager approach (cf. Chapter 3). Also, the treatment of semiflexibility encounters more difficulties in the Flory approach than in the Onsager treatment. On the other hand, the Onsager can only be extended to finite concentrations by introducing the decoupling approximation. A comparison of the prediction of both theories with experimental data in Chapter 6 will give a more detailed discussion of this problem.

ACKNOWLEDGMENT

One of the authors (A.A.) is very grateful to the Alexander von Humboldt-Stiftung who gave him the opportunity to participate in this work at the Max-Planck-Institut für Polymerforschung (Mainz). Financial support by the Bundesministerium für Forschung und Technologie, Projekt "Steife Makromoleküle," and by the Deutsche Forschungsgemeinschaft, Schwerpunkt "Thermotrope Flüssigkristalle," is gratefully acknowledged.

REFERENCES

1. P.J. Flory, *Proc. R. Soc. London*, A, **1956**, *234*, 73.
2. P.J. Flory, in *Polymer Liquid Crystals*, A. Ciferri, W.R. Krigbaum, R.B. Meyers, eds., Academic Press, New York, 1982, p. 103.
3. P.J. Flory, in *Recent Advances in Liquid Crystalline Polymers*, L.L. Chapoy, ed., Elsevier, London, 1985, p. 99.
4. H.C. Andersen, D. Chandler, and J.D. Weeks, *Adv. Chem. Phys.*, **1976**, *34*, 105; F. Kohler, *The Liquid State*, Verlag Chemie, Weinheim, 1972.
5. P.J. Flory, *Adv. Polym. Sci.*, **1984**, *59*, 1.
6. P.J. Flory, *Principles of Polymer Chemistry*, Cornell University Press, Ithaca, NY, 1953.
7. P.J. Flory, *Proc. R. Soc. London*, A, **1956**, *234*, 60.
8. P.J. Flory, *Proc. Natl. Acad. USA*, **1982**, *79*, 4510.
9. P.J. Flory and G. Ronca, *Mol. Cryst. Liq. Cryst.*, **1979**, *54*, 289.
10. J.P. Straley, *Mol. Cryst. Liq. Cryst.*, **1973**, *22*, 333.
11. M. Warner, *Mol. Cryst. Liq. Cryst.*, **1982**, *80*, 67.
12. A. Abe and P.J. Flory, *Macromolecules*, **1978**, *11*, 1122.
13. M. Warner, *Mol. Cryst. Liq. Cryst.*, **1982**, *80*, 79.
14. P.A. Irvine and P.J. Flory, *J. Chem. Soc.*, *Faraday Trans 1*, **1984**, *80*, 1821; M. Warner, *J. Chem. Phys.*, **1980**, *73*, 5874.
15. J.D. Parsons, *Phys. Rev. A*, **1979**, *19*, 1225.
16. A.R. Khokhlov and A.N. Semenov, *J. Stat. Phys.*, **1985**, *38*, 161.
17. M. Ballauff, *Mol. Cryst. Liq. Cryst.*, **1989**, *168*, 209.
18. W. Maier and A. Saupe, *Z. Naturforsch.*, A, **1959**, *14*, 882; **1960**, *15*, 287.
19. P.J. Flory and G. Ronca, *Mol. Cryst. Liq. Cryst.*, **1979**, *54*, 311.
20. E. Nies, L.A. Kleintjens, R. Koningsveld, R. Simha, and R.K. Jain, *Fluid Phase Eq.*, **1983**, *12*, 11.
21. P.J. Flory and P.A. Irvine, *J. Chem. Soc. Faraday Trans. 1*, **1984**, *80*, 1807.
22. P.J. Flory, R.A. Orwoll, and A. Vrij, *J. Am. Chem. Soc.*, **1964**, *86*, 3507.
23. M. Ballauff and P.J. Flory, *Ber. Bunsenges. Phys. Chem.*, **1984**, *88*, 530.
24. A. Nakajima, T. Hayashi, and M. Ohmori, *Biopolymers*, **1968**, *6*, 973.
25. E.L. Wee and W.G. Miller, *J. Phys. Chem.*, **1971**, *75*, 1446; W.G. Miller, C.C. Wu, E.L. Wee, G.L. Santee, J.H. Rai, and K.D. Goebel, *Pure Appl. Chem.*, **1974**, *38*, 37.
26. E.L. Wee and W.G. Miller, *Liq. Cryst. Ordered Fluids*, **1978**, *3*, 371.
27. M. Ballauff, *Macromolecules*, **1986**, *19*, 1366.
28. I. Uematsu, Y. Uematsu, *Adv. Polym. Sci.*, **1984**, *59*, 37.
29. G. Ronca and D.Y. Yoon, *J. Chem. Phys.*, **1982**, *76*, 3295; **1984**, *80*, 925; **1985**, *83*, 373.
30. H. Yamakawa , *Modern Theory of Polymer Solutions*, Harper & Row, New York, 1971.

31. A.R. Khokhlov and A.N. Semenov, *Physica*, *A*, **1981**, *108*, 546; **1982**, *112*, 605.
32. T. Odijk, *Macromolecules*, **1986**, *19*, 2313.
33. A. Teramoto, in *Frontiers of Macromolecular Science*, T. Saegusa, T. Higashimura, and A. Abe, eds., Blackwell, Oxford, 1989, p. 319.
34. T. Itou, A. Teramoto, *Macromolecules*, **1988**, *21*, 2225; T. Itou, T. Sato, A. Teramoto, and S.M. Aharoni, *Polym. J.*, **1988**, *20*, 1049; T. Sato, N. Ikeda, T. Itou, and A. Teramoto, *Polymer*, **1989**, *30*, 311; T. Sato and A. Teramoto, *Mol. Cryst. Liq. Cryst.*, **1990**, *178*, 143.
35. E. Bianchi, A. Ciferri, G. Conio, and W.R. Krigbaum, *Polymer*, **1987**, *28*, 813; G. Conio, E. Bianchi, A. Ciferri, and W. Krigbaum, *Macromolecules*, **1984**, *17*, 856.
36. S.-D. Lee and R.B. Meyer, *J. Chem. Phys.*, **1986**, *84*, 3443.
37. L. Onsager, *Ann. N.Y. Acad. Sci.*, **1949**, *51*, 627.
38. M.L. Sartirana, E. Marsano, E. Bianchi, and A. Ciferri, *Macromolecules*, **1986**, *19*, 1176; M.L. Sartirana, E. Marsano, E. Bianchi, and A. Ciferri, *Mol. Cryst. Liq. Cryst.*, **1987**, *144*, 263.
39. A. Abe and T. Yamazaki, *Macromolecules*, **1989**, *22*, 2138, 2145; in *The Materials, Science and Engineering of Rigid Rod Polymers*, W.W. Adams, R.K. Eby, and D.E. McLemore, eds., MRS Symposium Proceedings, Vol. 134, Materials Research Society, Pittsburgh, 1989, p. 53.
40. T. Yamazaki and A. Abe, *Polym. J.*, **1987**, *19*, 777.
41. G. Marrucci and A. Ciferri, *J. Polym. Sci., Polym. Lett.*, **1977**, *15*, 643.
42. P.J. Flory and A. Abe, *Macromolecules*, **1978**, *11*, 1119.
43. M. Warner and P.J. Flory, *J. Chem. Phys.*, **1980**, *73*, 6327.
44. P.J. Flory and R.S. Frost, *Macromolecules*, **1978**, *11*, 1126.
45. J.K. Moscicki and G. Williams, *Polymer*, **1981**, *22*, 1451; **1982**, *23*, 558.
46. T. Itou and A. Teramoto, *Polym. J.*, **1984**, *16*, 779; T. Itou and A. Teramoto, *Macromolecules*, **1984**, *17*, 1419; T. Kojima, T. Itou, and A. Teramoto, *Polym. J.*, **1987**, *19*, 1225.
47. S.M. Aharoni, E.K. Walsh, *Macromolecules*, **1979**, *12*, 271, *J. Polym. Sci., Polym. Lett. Ed.*, **1979**, *17*, 321; C. Balbi, E. Bianchi, A. Ciferri, and A. Tealdi, *J. Polym. Sci., Polym. Phys. Ed.*, **1980**, *18*, 2037; G. Conio, E. Bianchi, A. Ciferri, and A. Tealdi, *Macromolecules*, **1981**, *14*, 1084; S.M. Aharoni, *Polym. Bull.*, **1983**, *9*, 186; S. Sasaki, K. Tokuma, and I. Uematsu, *Polym. Bull.*, **1983**, *10*, 539.
48. E. Marsano, E. Bianchi, and A. Ciferri, *Macromolecules*, **1984**, *17*, 2886; S. Sasaki, M. Nagao, and M. Gotoh, *J. Polym. Sci., Polym. Phys. Ed.*, **1988**, *26*, 637; S.M. Aharoni, *Polymer*, **1980**, *21*, 21.
49. P.J. Flory, *Macromolecules*, **1978**, *11*, 1138.
50. M. Ballauff, *J. Polym. Sci., Polym. Phys. Ed.*, **1987**, *25*, 739.
51. E. Bianchi, A. Ciferri, G. Conio, E. Marsano, and A. Tealdi, *Macromolecules*, **1984**, *17*, 1526, and references cited therein.
52. W.F. Hwang, D.R. Wiff, C.L. Benner, and T.E. Helmeniak, *J. Macromol. Sci. Phys.*, *B*, **1983**, *22*, 231.
53. I.A. Nyskova and A.R. Khokhlov, *Vysokomol. Soedin.*, **1989**, *31*, 375.
54. T. Yanaki, T. Norisuye, and H. Fujita, *Macromolecules*, **1980**, *13*, 1462; Y. Kashiwagi, T. Norisuye, and H. Fujita, *Macromolecules*, **1981**, *14*, 1220.
55. M. Motowoka, T. Norisuye, A. Teramoto, and H. Fujita, *Polym. J.*, **1979**, *11*, 665.
56. S. Takahashi, M. Kariya, T. Yatake, K. Sonogashira, and N. Hagihara, *Macromolecules*, **1978**, *11*, 1063; S. Takahashi, E. Murata, M. Kariya, K. Sonogashira, and N. Hagihara, *Macromolecules*, **1979**, *12*, 1016; A. Abe, S. Tabata, and N. Kimura, *Polym. J.*, **1991**, *23*, 69.
57. P.J. Flory, *Macromolecules*, **1978**, *11*, 1141.
58. R.R. Matheson, Jr. and P.J. Flory, *Macromolecules*, **1981**, *14*, 954.
59. R.R. Matheson, Jr., *Biopolymers*, **1983**, *22*, 43.

60. P.J. Flory and R.R. Matheson, Jr., *J. Phys. Chem.*, **1984**, *88*, 6606.
61. W.R. Krigbaum, private communication, 1986.
62. M. Ballauff, *Angew. Chem., Int. Ed. Engl.*, **1989**, *28*, 253.
63. P.A. Irvine, P.J. Flory, and D.C. Wu, *J. Chem. Soc., Faraday Trans. 1*, **1984**, *80*, 1795.
64. M. Ballauff, D.C. Wu, P.J. Flory and E.M. Barrall, II, *Ber. Bunsenges. Phys. Chem.*, **1984**, *88*, 524.
65. P. Navard and P.J. Flory, *J. Chem. Soc., Faraday Trans. 1*, **1986**, *82*, 3367; P.J. Flory and P. Navard, *J. Chem. Soc., Faraday Trans. 1*, **1986**, *82*, 3381.
66. M.A. Cotter, *Mol. Cryst. Liq. Cryst.*, **1983**, *97*, 29.
67. M. Warner, *Mol. Phys.*, **1985**, *52*, 677.
68. M. Ballauff, *Liq. Cryst.*, **1987**, *2*, 519.
69. M. Ballauff, *Ber. Bunsenges. Phys. Chem.*, **1986**, *20*, 1053.
70. H. Orendi and M. Ballauff, *Liq. Cryst.*, **1989**, *6*, 479.
71. P.J. Flory, in *The Materials Science and Engineering of Rigid Rod Polymers*, W.W. Adams, R.K. Eby, and D.E. McLemore, eds., MRS Symposium Proceedings, Vol. 134, Materials Research Society, Pittsburgh, 1989, p. 3.
72. D.Y. Yoon and P.J. Flory, in *The Materials Science and Engineering of Rigid Rod Polymers*, W.W. Adams, R.K. Eby, and D.E. McLemore, eds., MRS Symposium Proceedings, Vol. 134, Materials Research Society, Pittsburgh, 1989, p. 11.
73. S.V. Vasilenko, A.R. Khokhlov, and V.P. Shibaev, *Macromolecules*, **1984**, *17*, 2270.
74. A. Abe, *Macromolecules*, **1984**, *17*, 2280; A. Abe, H. Furuya, and D.Y. Yoon, *Mol. Cryst. Liq. Cryst.*, **1988**, *159*, 151; A. Abe and H. Furuya, *Macromolecules*, **1989**, *22*, 2982; H. Furuya, T. Dries, K. Fuhrmann, A. Abe, M. Ballauff, and E.W. Fischer, *Macromolecules*, **1990**, *23*, 4122.
75. W. Weissflog and D. Demus, *Crystal Res. Technol.* **1984**, *19*, 55.

CHAPTER 5

Other Theories

G. RONCA*

*Dipartimento di Chimica, Politecnico di Milano,
20131 Milano, Italy*

and

A. TEN BOSCH

*Laboratoire de Physique de la Matière Condesée (CNRS,
UA 190), Université de Nice, 06034 Nice Cedex, France*

CONTENTS

1. INTRODUCTION

1.1. Other Theories: Why?

In this chapter we describe theories that are not based on the early approaches of Flory[1] and Onsager.[2] These theories differ from the work described in Chapters 3 and 4 in various ways, one being the use of a specific model to describe a single polymer molecule and to calculate its persistence length.

In Section 2 the liquid crystal (LC) behavior of a bend elastic chain is described. Here details of chemical structure discussed in Chapter 1 are neglected and the molecule is replaced by a uniform elastic line. The chemical interactions between the nearest-neighbor units are described solely by an elastic bending energy and the bend elastic coefficient of the chain

---

*It is tragic that Giorgio Ronca died shortly after completion of this chapter. He will be sadly missed by his many friends and associates all over the world.

defines the persistence length of a given chain. In addition an orientation-dependent Maier-Saupe-type potential[3] is included to induce alignment of the macromolecules. This potential has been already discussed in Chapters 3 and 4 and is well known in low molecular weight liquid crystals (LMWLC). The resulting model is an extension of the classic Maier-Saupe theory of rigid rods to include flexibility of chain molecules. In the present form the mean field is related to the space-average intersegmental interaction and is therefore adapted only to soft interactions. Even so, a variety of experimental trends can be given correctly (see Chapter 6), even though hard-core interactions, considered in Chapters 3 and 4, are neglected. From the single-chain model various physical properties can be calculated without further assumptions using the method of functional integration.

The above approach has recently been extended to more complex systems such as sidechain LC polymers (LCP) and elastomers. These are described in Section 3. In a sidechain LCP the rigid mesogens are linked to a bent elastic backbone chain. Experimental verification of the theory on sidechain LCP is given in Chapter 8.

Finally in Section 4 we survey theories based on the cubic lattice, pointing out the differences from the lattice approach used in Chapter 4. These theories are best suited for the description of segmented chains (cf. Chapter 7) with proper introduction of anisotropic interactions. Moreover, we present an elaboration of "persistent lattice chains" which predicts broad gaps and thermotropic transitions without anisotropic interaction. In fact, wormlike models can sometimes be used to predict the nematic phase transition of systems with negligible anisotropic interaction. Lattice models can provide not only needed support for the calculation of the combinatorial (steric) term of the partition function of an otherwise continuous system, but also suitable frames for the evaluation of the complete partition function, whose conformational part can be calculated on the lattice too. Lattice chains, like wormlike chains, are persistent molecules. The no-return condition on the simple cubic lattice gives rise to long persistence lengths if the bent conformation is made less favored energetically than the straight one. Nematic phase and smectic forms can be studied on the lattice model, which appears to show great flexibility for the analysis of complex molecular geometries.

Since the theory presented in Section 2 uses a functional integral representation of the wormlike chain that is different from the more chemical description outlined in Chapter 1, we present this alternative description in Section 1.2. A brief outline of the persistence length of lattice chains considered in Section 4 is then given in Section 1.3.

1.2. The Functional Integral Representation of Stiff Chains

The elastic chain[4,5] is described by a continuous space curve $\mathbf{r}(s)$ $(O \leq s \leq L)$ with respect to an arbitrary origin (O) of coordinates, where s measures the

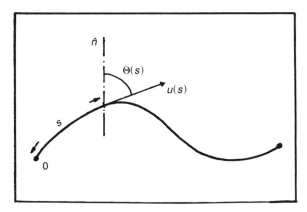

FIGURE 1
Model of an elastic wormlike chain

contour length along the chain and L is here the total contour length of the chain (Fig. 1). The vector $\mathbf{u}(s) = d\mathbf{r}/ds$ is tangent to the curve at point s. We consider first a single inextensible chain with

$$\mathbf{u}(s)^2 = 1$$

The potential bending energy of the chain follows a Hooke-type law written using E, the chain bending constant:

$$U_b = \frac{E}{2} \int \left(\frac{d\mathbf{u}}{ds} \right)^2 ds \tag{1}$$

For a single isolated chain, we can define the distribution function by a Boltzmann distribution

$$G(\mathbf{u}, \mathbf{u}', L) = \int_{\mathbf{u}(O)=\mathbf{u}'}^{\mathbf{u}(L)=\mathbf{u}} \delta \mathbf{u}(s) \exp\left[-\int ds \frac{E}{2kT} \left(\frac{d\mathbf{u}}{ds} \right)^2 \right] \tag{2}$$

giving the (unnormalized) probability for a configuration with, respectively, initial and final orientation $\mathbf{u}(O) = \mathbf{u}'$, $\mathbf{u}(L) = \mathbf{u}$ in the case of an inextensible chain. We introduce at this point the formalism of functional integration. The function G can be shown to satisfy the diffusion equation.[4,6]

$$\left(\frac{\partial}{\partial L} - \frac{kT}{2E} \Delta_{\mathbf{u}} \right) G(\mathbf{u}, \mathbf{u}', L) = \delta(\mathbf{u} - \mathbf{u}')\delta(L) \tag{3}$$

with the condition

$$\lim_{L \to O} G(\mathbf{u}, \mathbf{u}', L) \to \delta(\mathbf{u} - \mathbf{u}')$$

A solution of this equation is given by an expansion in eigenfunctions (the spherical harmonics) and singlechain properties such as the mean-square end-to-end distance $\langle R^2 \rangle$ can be calculated[6]:

$$\langle R^2 \rangle = 2qL\{1 - q/L[1 - \exp(-L/q)]\} \qquad (4)$$

It is found that elastic chains have a persistence length $q = E/kT$, which is necessarily temperature dependent. The chain becomes more flexible at high temperatures as the elastic energy becomes small relative to the thermal energy.

Dynamical properties of isolated chains such as intrinsic viscosity and light-scattering intensity have also been calculated in this formalism. For example, the more general distribution function $G(\mathbf{R}, O, \mathbf{u}, \mathbf{u}', L, O)$ for a chain conformation that starts at the origin in the direction $\mathbf{u}'$ and has a tangent $\mathbf{u}$ at $\mathbf{R}$ at the end of the chain at L has been studied in this model. It was possible to derive a series expansion in terms of the ratio of the total contour length to the persistence length.[7,8] In another approach, the condition of an inextensible chain is relaxed.[4] This model can be solved analytically but leads to a Gaussian end-to-end distribution.

If we consider other elastic potentials more general models are obtained.[4] The well-known extensible chains are described by an elastic energy for stretch

$$U_s = \frac{3}{2l} \int \left(\frac{d\mathbf{r}}{ds} \right)^2 ds \qquad (5)$$

where $\mathbf{r}(s)$ is the vector from a point s on the chain to an arbitrary origin and l is the bond length. This term has been neglected in most studies on stiff chains. Helicoidal structures with important torsional energies have been investigated by Yamakawa's group.[9,10] Various properties of this type of chain have been calculated, in particular the chain dimensions, the scattering functions, and related physical properties such as dipole moments.[11]

1.3. Persistence Length of Lattice Chains with No Return

On a simple cubic lattice we define the chain persistence length as

$$\frac{q}{d} = \left\langle \mathbf{l}_1 \cdot \sum_{i=1}^{\infty} \mathbf{l}_i \right\rangle$$

where $\mathbf{l}_i$ are the bond vectors each of unit length. Since correlation is lost at the first bend,[1] we obtain

$$\langle \mathbf{l}_1 \cdot \mathbf{l}_i \rangle = p^{i-1}$$

where p is the probability of the straight conformation:

$$p = \frac{1}{1 + 4\exp(-\varepsilon/kT)}$$

ε being the energy of the bent conformation. Application of the above result gives

$$q = \frac{1}{1 - p} = \frac{1 + 4\exp\left(-\dfrac{\varepsilon}{kT}\right)}{4\exp\left(-\dfrac{\varepsilon}{kT}\right)}$$

$$\frac{\langle R^2 \rangle_N}{d^2} = \left(\frac{1 + p}{1 - p}\right) N - \frac{2p}{(1 - p)^2}(1 - p^N)$$

where N is the number of lattice segments per chain, and $\langle R^2 \rangle$ is the mean square end-to-end distance.

2. ELASTIC WORMLIKE CHAINS WITH LONG-RANGE INTERACTIONS

2.1. Transition Properties of the Thermotropic Melt

In the melt (thermotropic systems) or in solution (lyotropic systems) the molecular chains are no longer isolated. In the philosophy of the wormlike chain, the short-range interactions between nearest-neighbor links in a single chain are taken into account by the bend elastic energy discussed in Section 1.2. The long-range interactions between links that are far removed from each other either on the same chain or on different chains must now be included, here with help of a mean-field theory.

In real systems, many different types of interaction occur between individual molecules: dipole, induced dipole, quadrupole, and in polyelectrolytes coulomb interactions. In spherical molecules, it is well known that the intermolecular potential consists of a strong repulsive interaction at small values of intermolecular separation r followed by an attractive potential well. A useful model potential is the Lennard-Jones model:

$$V(r) = \varepsilon\left[\left(\frac{\sigma}{r}\right)^{12} - \left(\frac{\sigma'}{r}\right)^{6}\right]$$

An extension to the orientation-dependent interactions in molecules with nonspherical symmetry is obtained by an expansion of the potential in

Legendre polynomials $P_j(\mathbf{u}_1, \mathbf{u}_2)$ in the angle between the molecular orientations of the molecules $\mathbf{u}_i = (\varphi_i, \theta_i)$ relative to an external direction[12]

$$V(r, \mathbf{u}_1, \mathbf{u}_2) = \sum_{j=0}^{\infty} V_j(r) P_j(\mathbf{u}_1 \cdot \mathbf{u}_2) \tag{6a}$$

The radial component $j = 2$ has also been described by a Lennard-Jones model with interaction parameters and distance parameters which can depend on j. In conventional isotropic polymers only the spherically symmetric interactions have been considered (the so-called excluded volume). In liquid crystals the existence of orientational ordering points to the importance of higher order harmonics and strong orientational interactions. Two approaches were taken historically. Onsager[2] concentrated on the repulsive part of the potential for the formation of ordered phases. Maier and Saupe[3] considered the attractive part to be dominant. Recent calculations on small molecular weight liquid crystals include both.[13] Care must be taken when using highly divergent potentials such as the rigid rod:

$$V(r, \mathbf{u}_1, \mathbf{u}_2) = \begin{cases} \infty & \text{if molecules intersect} \\ 0 & \text{otherwise} \end{cases}$$

In hard-sphere systems spurious divergencies in thermodynamical properties occur as the low-density solution is extended to the close-packed density of the spheres,[14] and a similar problem occurs for hard rods. This will be discussed further on.

The effect on macromolecules of quadrupole–quadrupole interactions derived from attractive van der Waals forces and repulsive excluded volume forces was first studied in relation to the helix–coil transition.[15] The intermolecular coupling was shown to lead to a first-order transition with a change from a nearly coiled to a nearly rigid conformation as a consequence of long-range nematic order. This idea was extended to the wormlike chain to investigate lipid membrane transitions[16] and later applied to liquid crystal polymers.[17–20]

We consider first the case of a pure monodisperse melt (thermotropic behavior).[21,22] In polymeric systems mean-field theory can be applied to include long-range interactions between segments. We derive a formula for the free energy of the system and replace long-range interactions by an appropriate mean field. The resistance to bend deformations is taken to be dominant and measured by an elastic coefficient E.

We introduce an order parameter to describe long-range organization of the orientation of the molecule. We calculate the dependence of the order parameter on temperature and thereby determine the transition temperature of the isotropic anisotropic transition. We show that in the limit of short rods the theory is equivalent to the mean-field theory of liquid crystals as proposed by Maier and Saupe. Only systems with uniform segment density N_p

(number of segments per unit volume) will be considered here. The segment volume is v and all lengths are measured in units of segment length a; L is then equivalent to the degree of polymerization.

In the case of a simple uniaxial potential between segments

$$V(r\mathbf{u}\mathbf{u}') = \omega_{pp}(r) + \varepsilon_{pp}(r)P_2(\mathbf{u})P_2(\mathbf{u}') \tag{6b}$$

where r denotes here the distance between interacting particles of orientation $\mathbf{u}$ and $\mathbf{u}'$. The polymer mean field (which minimizes the free energy) is

$$w_p(\mathbf{u}) = \omega_{pp} + \varepsilon_{pp}SP_2(\mathbf{u}) \tag{7}$$

where S is the usual nematic order parameter and the average interaction parameters are given by (1) the isotropic interaction

$$\omega_{pp} = \frac{1}{vkT} \int dr\, r^2 \omega_{pp}(r)$$

and (2) the anisotropic interaction

$$\varepsilon_{pp} = \frac{1}{vkT} \int dr\, r^2 \varepsilon_{pp}(r)$$

The average interaction parameters can include soft repulsive and attractive interactions, possibly using a cutoff hard-core diameter to insure convergence of the integral. The method could also be extended to obtain more complex definitions of the mean fields[23] containing the chain distribution functions.

The free energy per segment becomes

$$\frac{F}{kT} = -\frac{1}{L}\ln Q_p - \frac{\omega_{pp}}{2} - \frac{1}{2}\varepsilon_{pp}S^2 \tag{8}$$

where Q_p is a measure of the entropy of the chain given by a distribution function $G(\mathbf{r}\mathbf{u}, \mathbf{r}'\mathbf{u}', L)$ for a chain conformation of L segments with the origin given by position $\mathbf{r}$ tangent $\mathbf{u}$ and the point at L by $\mathbf{r}'\mathbf{u}'$.

$$Q_p = \int d\mathbf{r}\, d\mathbf{r}'\, d\mathbf{u}\, d\mathbf{u}'\, G(\mathbf{r}\mathbf{u}, \mathbf{r}'\mathbf{u}', L) \tag{9}$$

In the limiting case of rigid rods $q/L \to \infty$ then

$$-\ln Q_p = \int \ln f(\mathbf{u})f(\mathbf{u})\, d\mathbf{u} + L\varepsilon_{pp}S^2 \tag{10}$$

and the well-known Maier-Saupe model of liquid crystals is recovered (when

$L = 1$) with an orientation distribution $f(\mathbf{u}) = (1/Q_p)\exp[-\varepsilon_{pp}SP_2(\mathbf{u})]$ and no isotropic interactions $\omega_{pp} = 0$.

If the chain has finite elasticity the calculation of the polymer free energy contribution is more involved[16] and resolution requires numerical calculation of the probability for a chain with fixed tangents at the origin and at L similar to Eq. (2) of the isolated chain:

$$G(\mathbf{u},\mathbf{u}',L) = \int d\mathbf{r}\, d\mathbf{r}'\, G(\mathbf{r},\mathbf{u},\mathbf{r}',\mathbf{u},L)$$

with

$$G(\mathbf{u},\mathbf{u}',L) = \int_{\mathbf{u}(0)=\mathbf{u}}^{\mathbf{u}(L)=\mathbf{u}'} \delta\mathbf{u}(s)\exp\left[-\int_0^L ds\left(\frac{E}{kT}\left(\frac{d\mathbf{u}}{ds}\right)^2 + w_p(\mathbf{u})\right)\right] \quad (11)$$

which solves the equation [compare Eq. (3)]

$$\left[\frac{\partial}{\partial s} - \frac{1}{2q}\Delta_{\mathbf{u}} + \varepsilon_{pp}LSP_2(\mathbf{u})\right]G(\mathbf{u}\mathbf{u}'s) = \delta(s)\delta(\mathbf{u}' - \mathbf{u}) \quad (12)$$

An expansion of G in eigenfunctions and the use of spherical harmonics leads to a numerical solution for G $(\mathbf{u}\mathbf{u}'s)$. The system is completely determined at the transition by the value of L/q. The transition occurs at the temperature T_i for which the free energy will be equal for isotropic ($S = 0$) and anisotropic phases ($S \neq 0$). Defining the dimensionless mean-field parameter $\varepsilon_{pp} = -w/kT$ we find[21] (for a variation of L at constant q).

$$\frac{kT_i}{wq} \simeq f\left(\frac{L}{q}\right) = 0.15\left[1 - \frac{q}{3L}(1 - e^{3L/q})\right] \quad (13)$$

or (for a variation of q at constant L):

$$\frac{kT_i}{wL} = \frac{q}{L}f\left(\frac{L}{q}\right)$$

and for the critical order parameter S_0 at T_i

$$S_0 \simeq 0.36\left[1 - \frac{q}{3L}(1 - e^{-0.8L/q})\right] + 0.08\left(1 - \frac{q}{4.3L}(1 - e^{-4.3L/q})\right)\left(\frac{q}{L}\right)$$

We see the existence of two limiting cases $L/q \to 0$ and $L/q \to \infty$ which can be associated with two physical limits: (1) the LMWLC ($L/q \to 0$, $L = 1$) which corresponds to the well-known Maier-Saupe result:

$$\frac{kT_i}{w} \approx 0,22 : S_0 \sim 0,43$$

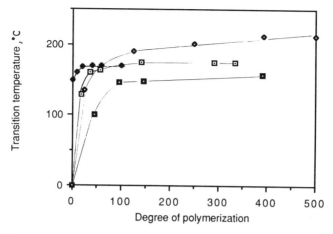

FIGURE 2

Transition temperature T_i^0 as a function of degree of polymerization taken from experiments on various LCP's: ◆ a segmented polyester DDA-9[54]; two cellulose derivatives; ◇ hydroxypropylcellulose[55] and ▣ acetoxypropylcellulose[56]; and ▪ polynonylisocyanate.[57]

and (2) the infinitely long chain ($L \rightarrow \infty$)

$$\frac{kT_i}{wq} \approx 0,15 : S_0 \sim 0,36$$

For a given LCP of persistence length q an increase of the transition temperature with chain length with a saturation at high molecular weight, i.e., for $L > q$, is predicted. This has been seen in experiments on thermotropic polymers and a few examples are given in Fig. 2. In comparing experiment and theory, the persistence length of the mesomorphic polymer can be taken from measurements (see Chapter 2) and w is fitted from the T_i for a given value of degree of polymerization DP. In applying the theory to segmented chains (such as DDA-9 in Fig. 2) an average persistence length of the order of the monomer length is assumed. In general we find the experimental values of T_i are lower than the theoretical values and increase more rapidly with DP.

We calculate[21] the existence of a minimum for the critical order parameter S_0 as a function of L/q and a value of S_0 bounded between two values: $0,34 < S_0 < 0,43$. Experimental measurements for polymers (see Chapter 6) generally yield order parameters that are higher. This may be due to neglect of steric hinderance, which generally raises the value of the order parameter. The use of the mean field to calculate the polymer contribution to the entropy Q_p also probably underestimates the real value, and the values from the Flory lattice model may be more correct especially for stiff polymers consisting of rodlike molecules. Furthermore strong distortions of the polymer have been automatically neglected by the finite expansion in spherical harmonics, valid only in the limit of slowly varying conformations of the polymer along the axis of preferred orientation.[24] In the Onsager approach (Chapter 3) a different expression for the elastic chain entropy is used. Equivalence to Eq. (9), which was derived from first principles, has not yet been investigated.

We have so far concentrated on the effect of soft orientation-dependent interactions. In the limit of rigid rods it is possible to include hard-core interactions for cylinders by redefinition of the mean field[25]

$$\bar{w} = w + \gamma_p N_p kT \tag{14}$$

The second term now takes the repulsive excluded volume into account for cylinders of diameter d. A shift of the transition temperature is found since as before $kT_i/\bar{w}L = 0.22$ so that

$$kT_i = \frac{wL}{4.3 - N_p\gamma_p} \tag{15}$$

where

$$\gamma_p = \frac{5\pi}{16}d(aL)^2$$

is the excluded volume parameter. It is obvious that the transition temperature will now diverge for a critical value L^c such that

$$L^c = \frac{4}{5}4.3\frac{d}{a}$$

We find then a critical DP of the order of 4 (depending on choice of diameter d) of the same order of magnitude as in other approaches (see Chapters 3 and 4). The question remains whether this absolute stabilization of the nematic phase is a real physical phenomenon, or simply due to the lack of high-density screening or chain flexibility, or because of real soft-core interactions for which no divergence occurs. A calculation of the transition at constant pressure instead of at constant volume used here could also have an effect (see also Chapter 3).

In a different method of solution of Eq. (8) the free energy expansion

$$F = AS^2 + BS^2 + CS^4 \tag{16}$$

was derived for the wormlike chain[26, 27] by expanding the exact expression for the partition function (Eq. 11) as a function of the order parameter. The coefficients A, B, C are then obtained as a function of T and of chain variables w, q, and L. This permits analytical calculation of transition properties such as critical temperature, order parameter, latent heat by use of expression (16) in place of Eq. (8). Agreement with the "exact" calculations using a numerical solution of the partition function is fair for the transition temperature and shows the same behavior in q/L with saturation at high L. Calculated critical order parameters are much larger, around 0.7–0.8 (see Fig. 6), and increase with L/q, passing from a rigid rod to a flexible limit, after passing through a small dip.

2.2. Screened Potential[21]

In a polymer system the effective mean-field potential on a chain will depend on the conformation of the segment units and on the total length or degree of polymerization.[5,11] This is because a polymer can adapt its conformation to the interaction of the surrounding medium similar to screening in electrolyte solutions. Many approaches to this question have been used in isotropic polymer systems.

In liquid crystal polymers, the bend elastic energy and the orientational part of the potential must be considered in addition to the isotropic interactions. In a simple Maier-Saupe potential [$j = 0, 2$ in the expansion Eq. (6b)] the renormalized mean fields parameters are[21,28]

$$\omega_{pp}^{s} = \frac{\omega_{pp}}{1 + L\omega_{pp}} \tag{17}$$

$$\varepsilon_{pp}^{s} = \frac{\varepsilon_{pp}}{1 + \dfrac{1}{5L} g_2 \varepsilon_{pp}} \tag{18}$$

with

$$g_2 = \frac{2qL}{3}\left[1 - \frac{q}{3L}(1 - e^{-3L/q})\right]$$

This screening calculation is valid only in the vicinity of the isotropic phase and includes local fluctuations of the order parameter but no long-range order. It cannot be expected to remain valid far below the phase transition, where fluctuations around the ordered state must dominate.

The self-consistent screened mean fields include the ability of the chain to adapt its conformation to intra- and interchain interactions and should replace ω_{pp} and ε_{pp} in the definition of the mean field (Eq. 7). For example the transition temperature is now given by (see Eq. 13)

$$\frac{k(T_i - T')}{wq} = f\left(\frac{q}{L}\right) \tag{19}$$

where $kT'/w = g_2/5L$. We find that screening stabilizes the nematic phase and shifts the transition to higher temperature.

Screening is of greatest importance for properties related to the polymer conformation. As will be discussed in Section 2.4 the relation between $\langle R^2 \rangle$ and L is modified and the effective persistence length becomes dependent on solvent interactions as well as on molecular weight. Elastic constants, being good measures of the effective potential of a chain, can also show screening effects (see Section 2.6).

2.3. Phase Diagrams[21,29,30]

We now consider the phase transition in mixtures of a liquid crystal polymer (p) with a nonmesomorphic solvent (s). The free energy of mixing can be obtained as discussed in the thermotropic case. The long-range potential includes isotropic solvent–solvent $\omega_{ss}(r)$ and polymer–solvent $\omega_{sp}(r)$ interactions. The polymer volume fraction is v_2. As before we calculate the mean fields that minimize the free energy

$$w_s = (1 - v_2)\omega_{ss} + v_2\omega_{sp}$$

for the solvent and

$$w_p(\mathbf{u}) = v_2\omega_{pp} + (1 - v_2)\omega_{sp} + v_2\varepsilon_{pp}SP_2(\mathbf{u}) \qquad (20)$$

for the polymer.

The isotropic mean-field parameters are given, as before, for the solvent:

$$\omega_{ss} = \frac{1}{kTv} \int dr\, r^2\omega_{ss}(r)$$

and similarily for ω_{sp}.

In a solution of a LCP of $DP\ L$ the free energy of mixing per segment becomes

$$\frac{F_M}{kT} = \frac{v_2}{L} \ln v_2 + (1 - v_2)\ln(1 - v_2)$$

$$- \frac{v_2}{L} \ln\left[Q_p \exp\left(v_2 L\omega_{pp} + (1 - v_2)L\omega_{sp}\right)\right] \qquad (21)$$

$$+ \frac{v_2^2}{2}\omega_{pp} + \frac{(1 - v_2)^2}{2}\omega_{ss} + v_2(1 - v_2)\omega_{sp} - \frac{v_2}{2}\varepsilon_{pp}S^2$$

From the model free energy, the phase diagrams can now be calculated as usual. The equilibrium order parameter is found by minimization of the free energy. Possible biphasic separation is given by equality of the chemical potential $\mu = \delta F_M/\delta v_2$ and the osmotic pressure $\Pi = F_M - v_2\mu$ in the two phases. The two phases can be both isotropic or isotropic in an anisotropic phase or anisotropic in an isotropic phase. Equation (21) applies to a solution of a LCP in a low molecular weight solvent or to a mixture with an extensible isotropic polymer as described by Eq. (5).

If both polymer components are in an isotropic phase, the Flory-Huggins model of polymer solutions[31] is recovered. As usual the Flory interaction parameter is given by $\chi = [\omega_{sp} - 1/2(\omega_{ss} + \omega_{pp})]$ and can be positive ("bad" solvents) or negative ("good" solvents). The decrease of mixing entropy for long chains leads to phase separation in the former solvents at high molecular weight. This occurs also in liquid-crystalline polymers and numerical calculations have been performed to investigate the role of chain flexibility and of the isotropic and anisotropic interactions.[30] Typical phase diagrams for a LCP and a nonmesogenic component may include a superposition of Flory-Huggins phase separation and at high polymer concentrations a linear dependence of the temperatures limiting the narrow biphasic zone near the liquid–crystal transition.

As illustrated in Fig. 3, the parameters for the LCP are T_i^0, L_p/q, χL_p. The ratio L_p/L_s of the lengths of the two components is also considered. Figure 3a shows that the biphasic gap widens with strong repulsion χL_p as shown in other theories (see Chapters 3 and 4). Figure 3b shows similar widening when L_p/q is increased all other parameters being constant. The biphasic gap is widened if the degree of polymerization of the polymeric solvent is increased (variation of L_p/L_s, not shown). This trend is consistent with the reported incompatibility of a mesogenic and a nonmesogenic polymer when the DP of the latter is increased (Chapters 4 and 6; Ref. 32).

The effect of molecular weight of the LCP was studied at high LCP concentrations.[29] It was shown that as the DP of the LCP increases, the transition temperature to the pure isotropic phase at constant v_2 increases, and the biphasic gap $v_2^a - v_2^i$ at constant temperature widens. This is supported by experimental evidence.[32]

In systems with a narrow biphasic gap in the range of temperature of interest, it is sometimes useful to use the "pseudo-transition".[33] At the pseudo-transition temperature T_p, the free energies of the isotropic and anisotropic phases are equal and as in the pure melt (Eq. 13) we find at sufficiently large L/q:

$$\frac{kT_p}{v_2 wq} = f\left(\frac{L}{q}\right) \approx 0.15 \tag{22}$$

which approximates the transition at zero biphasic separation. This would lead to a linear dependence of T_p on v_2, but experimentally a slower decrease was found.[34] We therefore include the temperature dependence of

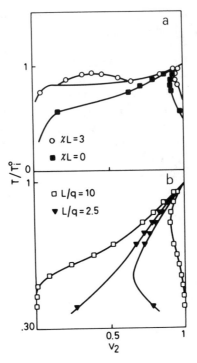

FIGURE 3

Theoretical phase diagram for a mesomorphic (p) – nonmesomorphic (s) mixture. (a) χL_p varies but $L_p/q = 2.5$ and $L_p/L_s =$
2.5, (b) L_p/q varies but $L_p/L_s = 10$ and $\chi Lp = 0$. (Reproduced
ith permission from Ref. 30.)

the persistence length $(q = E/kT)$. The critical concentrations in the mixture at constant temperature T can then be approximated by

$$v_2^i \approx v_2^a \approx \left(\frac{T}{T_i^0} \right)^2 \tag{23}$$

where T_i^0 is the transition temperature in the pure LCP. Using the results of
Eq. (13) or experimental values of T_i^0 we can then plot the dependence of
the critical concentration on DP. This is illustrated in Fig. 4. Good agreement with experiment has been found in cellulose derivatives.[34]

Mixtures between two mesomorphic components were also calculated[30]
and again biphasic zones were shown to widen as χ increased. The theory
has also been extended to ternary systems[35] but numerical calculations have
been performed so far only in the case of a LCP in a mixture of solvents.

If the liquid-crystalline components of the polymers are rigid and discon-
nected as in sidechain PLC's, then the orientation of the mesogen may follow

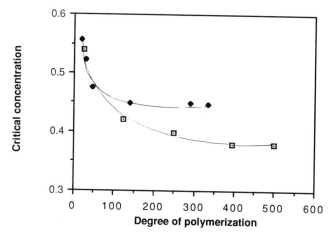

FIGURE 4

Critical polymer volume fraction v_2 calculated at the pseudotransition (see text) for a solution of a LCP in a simple solvent as a function of degree of polymerization using $v_2^i = [T/T_i^0]^2$, $T = 30°C$, T_i^0 from Fig. 2 for hydroxypropylcellulose ■, acetoxyproylcellulose ◆. (Data from Refs. 55 and 56.)

the rigid rod distribution as in Eq. (10). Examples of the possible phase diagrams have been calculated by Brochard et al.[33]

2.4. Chain conformations in LCP's

Long-range intra- or interchain interactions alter the conformation of the chain through screening effects and induce expansion or contraction of the chain relative to the isolated state. This effect can be measured through the mean square end-to-end distance $\langle R^2 \rangle$ (and mean square radius of gyration $\langle R_G^2 \rangle$). The literature on the calculation and measurement of end-to-end distance or radius of gyration in simple polymer systems is extensive.[11] For example, in the case of extensible chains, Flory proposed long ago that $\langle R^2 \rangle \approx L^{6/5}$ in dilute solutions with repulsive interactions.

In LCP systems two effects on the polymer conformation could occur due to the presence of orientation-dependent interactions. First a change in the *total* end-to-end vector would lead to spherical expansion or contraction of chain conformation. Second, a change in the *components* parallel and perpendicular to the direction of preferred orientation would lead to an anisotropic chain conformation. $\langle R^2 \rangle$ has been calculated for bend elastic chains using a perturbation expansion[36] and recently in the random Gaussian field approach.[28] Expansion effects occurring in isotropic solutions[37,38] are discussed in Chapter 2. Various authors[17, 22, 24, 39] have also suggested the possibility that the chain conformation is anisotropic in a nematic phase (see also Chapter 3). In the isotropic phase the polymer occupies a sphere. At the transition, the sphere should be distorted to an ellipsoid with a given orientation relative to the nematic director (chosen here as the coordinate z). Calculations of the anisotropy were performed for the model of inextensible wormlike chains using the mean-field model for the anisotropic interactions. From the distribution function $G(\mathbf{uu'}L)$ all the components of the tensor of the end-to-end vector $\mathbf{R}$ given by $\langle \mathbf{R}_i\mathbf{R}_i \rangle$ $(i, k = x, y, z)$ can be obtained and studied as a function of L/q, temperature, and concentration. All of the

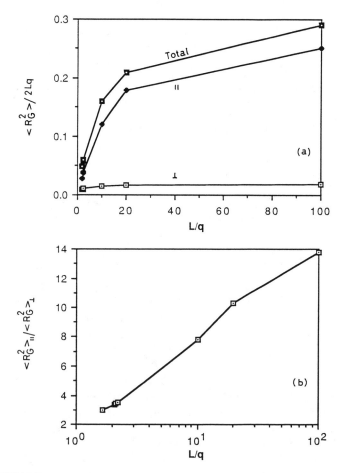

FIGURE 5

(a) Calculated anisotropy of the mean square radius of gyration at the transition temperature for the component parallel ($\blacklozenge$) or perpendicular ($\square$) to the director and for the total ($\blacksquare$) component. (b) Ratio of the parallel to the perpendicular components of the mean-square radius of gyration relative to the direction of preferred orientation. (Calculations courtesy of P. Maïssa.)

diagonal components $\langle R_\perp^2 \rangle = \langle R_x^2 \rangle = \langle R_y^2 \rangle$ and $\langle R_\parallel^2 \rangle = \langle R_z^2 \rangle$ vary with L/q in the same way as in the isolated chain between a rigid-rod limit proportional to L^2 and a flexible limit proportional to Lq. The ratio of $R_\parallel^2/R_\perp^2$ varies with L/q at T_i between ~ 3 for the rigid rods due to ordering, which effectively increases the projection on the director, and about 15 in the flexible limit. A discontinuous distortion at the transition is calculated with a weak temperature dependence in the nematic phase similar to that of the nematic order parameter. On the other hand, the calculated total value of $\langle R^2 \rangle = 2\langle R_\perp^2 \rangle + \langle R_\parallel^2 \rangle$ has a weaker variation at the transition temperature. The ratio of total anisotropic to isotropic mean square end-to-end distance varies from 1 for the LC limit ($L/q \to 0$, as expected) to ~ 2 in the long-chain limit. The same calculations can be done for the components of the mean square radius of gyration and are illustrated in Fig. 5.

Warner et al.[24] introduced the effect of hairpin defects, which would be the dominant mechanism in the disordering of polymer chains as the temperature is raised. As the isotropic phase is approached the polymer chains do not simply fluctuate more and more in the direction of preferred orientation but form 180° turns called hairpins. An exponential decrease of anisotropy of chain conformation with increasing temperature is predicted. It is also been suggested that macroscopic dielectric experiments will reveal an exponential variation of the susceptibility with temperature reflecting the activation of hairpin defects.[40]

2.5. Effect of External Fields on the Phase Transition

It is simple to extend the mean-field calculations in Section 2.1 to include external electric[41] and magnetic fields or elongational flow.[42] We include an interaction with the external field in the partition function of the polymer by an additional term in the mean field (Eq. 7) with v_f the strength of the external potential:

$$w_{pf}(\mathbf{u}) = -v_f P_2(\mathbf{u}) \tag{24}$$

Typically an external potential shifts the transition temperature and induces a small order in the isotropic phase. These effects appear to be small but will be strongest for elongational flow due to larger value of the coupling constant v_f (Fig. 6). The large values of the order parameter S are due to the use of a Landau-de Gennes expansion type calculation [see Eq. (16)], instead of a "direct" mean-field one [see Eq. (8)] in the results given in Fig. 6.

Magnetic birefringence in a liquid crystal polymer was also considered and measurements were used to determine the critical supercooling temperature T'' below which the isotropic state is unstable.[43] The difference $T_i - T''$ is small in LMWLC's but increases on addition of a polymeric component, thereby leading to a better agreement with predictions of mean-field theory. On the other hand, the slope of the Cotton Mouton coefficient as a function

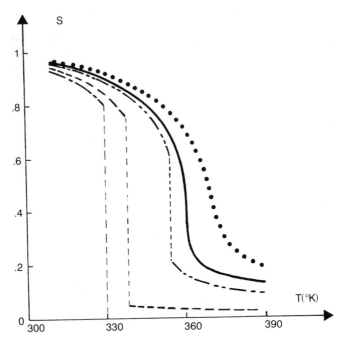

FIGURE 6
Calculated order parameter S in a LCP as a function of temperature on variation of an external applied field $v_f/w = 0$ (− −), 10^{-2} (——), 3×10^{-2} (—··), 3.72×10^{-2} (——) 5×10^{-2} (···).
(Reproduced with permission from Ref. 42.)

of T increases in contradiction to the theory. This was suggested to be evidence of a rigidification of the polymer chain at the transition.[44]

2.6. Elastic Constants

The direction of preferred orientation $\mathbf{n}$ can vary or can be forced to vary by the action of external forces and boundary conditions. The response of the liquid crystal can be described with a curvature elastic theory. The free energy density of the deformed liquid crystal is written:

$$F_d = K_s(\text{grad } \mathbf{n})^2 + K_t(\mathbf{n} \cdot \text{rot } \mathbf{n})^2 + K_b(\mathbf{n} \times \text{rot } \mathbf{n})^2 \qquad (25)$$

The three constants K_i represent the curvature elastic moduli for so called splay, twist, and bend deformations of the director $\mathbf{n}$. The moduli are connected to the effective interactions $V(\mathbf{r}, \mathbf{u}_1, \mathbf{u}_2)$ between two liquid crystal segments at distance $\mathbf{r}$ with orientations $\mathbf{u}_1$ and $\mathbf{u}_2$, and to the variation of the orientation distribution $f(\mathbf{u})$ as derived from the chain distribution $G(\mathbf{uu}'L)$.[21] For example:

$$K_s = \int V(\mathbf{ru_1u_2}) \frac{df(\mathbf{u_1})}{d\cos\Theta_1} \frac{df(\mathbf{u_2})}{d\cos\Theta_2} \mathbf{u}_{1x}\mathbf{u}_{2x}x^2 \, d\mathbf{u}_1 \, d\mathbf{u}_2 \, d\mathbf{r} \qquad (26)$$

where the direction $\mathbf{u}_i$ is described by the polar angles ϕ_i, Θ_i relative to the original uniform orientation. We can use an expansion in spherical harmonics $Y_j^m(\mathbf{u})$ of $V(\mathbf{r}, \mathbf{u}_1, \mathbf{u}_2)$ for the Maier-Saupe potential.

$$V(\mathbf{ru_1u_2}) = \sum_m V_2^m(\mathbf{r}) Y_2^m(\mathbf{u}_1) Y_2^m(\mathbf{u}_2) \qquad (27)$$

We find then from Eq. (26)

$$K_s = K_t = 2K_b = \frac{2}{3} N_p^2 S^2 F(022) \qquad (28)$$

with

$$F(022) = \int V_2^0(\mathbf{r}) r^4 \, dr \qquad (29)$$

In PLC's, we replace $V(\mathbf{ru_1u_2})$ by the effective screened interaction discussed in Section 2.2. For constant density, this leads to a variation of $K_i \approx L^2$ in the rigid-rod limit $L/q \to 0$ and $K_i \approx q^2$ for long chains ($q/L \to 0$).[45]

The elastic coefficients of orientation deformation at constant density do not depend on chain length in the simplest mean-field approximation as seen from Eq. (28). Three mechanisms can lead to chain length dependence of the effective mean field and therefore of the elastic constants. We discussed here the effect of screening which allows the molecule to adapt its configuration to minimize the internal interactions. Hard rod interactions consider the contact between rigid cylinders and will be discussed in Chapter 9. It has been suggested that due to steric hindrance the splay elastic constant should increase rapidly in liquid crystal polymers as the degree of polymerization is increased.[39] Finally a more subtle definition of the mean field including long-range segmental correlations as well as screening should be considered.

Recently other fluctuation properties of wormlike chains have been calculated: for example, the static structure factor in the nematic phase is obtained.[46] The correlation length is shown to be independent of the nematic interaction. The structure factor can be expanded for small wave vector $\mathbf{k}$ and the term in $\mathbf{k}^4$ can change in sign for strong nematic interaction. The same author also studied the elastic coefficients given by the static order parameter correlations.[47] In contrast to the usual Leslie Ericksen formulation using constant density the order parameter fluctuations as induced by density fluctuations were calculated. These were shown to increase with increasing degree of polymerization.

3. SIDECHAIN LIQUID CRYSTAL POLYMERS

3.1. Phase Transitions[48-52]

A new group of liquid crystal polymers was synthesized by attaching stiff nematic side chains to a flexible main chain. There are many similarities in the physical properties of sidechain and mainchain liquid crystal polymers: for example, the same dependence of transition temperature on degree of polymerization (see Chapter 8).

A molecular model was introduced using the wormlike chain (see Fig. 7).[51,52] In this model the backbone (B) is an elastic (elastic constant E) mesogenic (interaction parameter U_B) chain, the sidechain (A) is a stiff mesogenic (interaction parameter U_A) rod. The cross coupling between sidechain and mainchain consists of a nematic interaction U_c and an orientational interaction U_{AB} due to linkage of sidechain and mainchain and considered to reflect the flexibility of the spacer connecting A and B. The important length parameters (measured in units of the sectional length) are the length of the sidechain y, the number of segments in the mainchain per sidechain n, and the related volume fraction of isodiametric sidechains $Y = y/n + y$. Two order parameters now exist: on the sidechain S_A and along the mainchain S_B. The signs of S_A and S_B allow characterization of the different nematic phases: in N_I with $S_A > 0$, $S_B < 0$ the sidechains are oriented along the director and mainchains perpendicular to the director, in N_{II}, $S_A < 0$, $S_B > 0$ and we find the mainchains are oriented along the director and the sidechains are perpendicular, and in N_{III} where $S_A > 0$, $S_B > 0$, both are parallel to the director.

Intuitively one would expect U_B and U_C, as well as the ordering of the flexible mainchains, to be small. The hinge coupling U_{AB} considered here is assumed to be dominated by the orientation of the sidechain relative to the mainchain. The additional isotropic coupling due to linkage with the sidechains is not explicitly considered but could be included as in the calculation of phase diagrams discussed in Section 2.3.

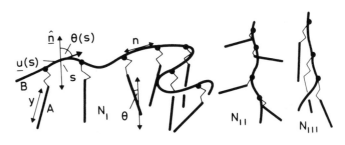

FIGURE 7
Nematic phases in a sidechain LCP. (Reproduced with permission from Ref. 49. Courtesy of Blackie Publ. Group)

The mean field on a sidechain is now simply:

$$w_A(\mathbf{u}) = -\{YU_A y S_A + [(1 - Y)U_C y + U_{AB}] S_B\} P_2(\mathbf{u}) \qquad (27)$$

and on a main chain at point s

$$w_B(\mathbf{u}(s)) = -\left\{(1 - Y)U_B S_B + \left(YU_C - \frac{U_{AB}}{n}\right) S_A\right\} P_2(\mathbf{u}(s)) \qquad (28)$$

The order parameters S_A and S_B can now be calculated by minimization of the free energy $F(S_A, S_B)$ for a given set of parameters.

The free energy of a repeat unit is given by

$$F = YF_A + (1 - Y)F_B \qquad (29)$$

where

$$yF_A = -kT \ln Z_A - \frac{1}{2}\langle w_A(\mathbf{u})\rangle \qquad (30)$$

$$L_B F_B = -kT \ln Z_B - \frac{1}{2}\left\langle \int_0^{L_B} w_B(\mathbf{u}(s))\, ds \right\rangle \qquad (31)$$

where $\langle\ \rangle$ denotes as usual the appropriate statistical average, and Z_A is the partition function of the rigid sidechain mesogens, given essentially by the mean field:

$$Z_A = \int d\cos\theta \exp[-w_A(\mathbf{u})] \qquad (32)$$

and for the mainchain of length L_B described by tangent vector $\mathbf{u}(s)$:

$$Z_B = \int \delta \mathbf{u}(s) \exp\left[-\int ds \left(\frac{E}{2kT}\left[\frac{d\mathbf{u}(s)}{ds}\right]^2 + w_B[\mathbf{u}(s)]\right)\right] \qquad (33)$$

The problem is now very similar to the (LCP + LMWLC) mixture.[17] Only the $L \to \infty$ solution was calculated and temperature versus Y diagrams were traced. In experiments, Y can be varied by changing the length of the sidechain or by variation of the distance between sidechains. Various first-order transitions between N phases are predicted (Fig. 8) with reorientation of sidechains ($N_{II} \to N_{III}$), mainchains ($N_I \to N_{III}$), or both ($N_I \to N_{II}$). Transitions to weakly ordered (primed) phases also occur.

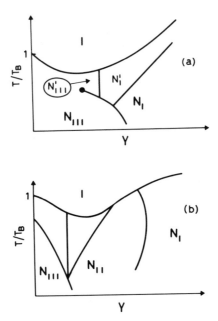

FIGURE 8
Phase transitions in a liquid crystal sidechain polymer; temperature
is reduced by the value of the transition temperature of the pure
backbone chain of length $y = 3$, volume fraction of sidechains Y,
coupling constants $U_A : U_B : U_C : U_{AB} = $ (a) $3 : 2 : 2 : 3$,
(b) $1 : 2 : 1 : 2 : 3$. (Reproduced with permission from Ref. 49.
Courtesy of Blackie Publ. Group)

Some results can be given as follows.

1. Effect of sidechain length: in short sidechains only N_{II} phases are
   found.
2. Effect of mainchain–sidechain coupling: large coupling removes the
   N_{II} phase in favor of the N_{III} phase.

Chain conformations can also be calculated as discussed previously. It
was found that the chain is prolate ($\langle R_\parallel^2 \rangle > \langle R_\perp^2 \rangle$) in N_{II} and N_{III} phases
and oblate in the N_I phase. In the N_I phase the coefficient of anisotropy
decreases as the coupling between mainchains increases.

Sidechain polymers often order in smectic phases with long-range order
of the positions of the mesogens. The smectic order of the mesogens is
incompatible with changes in the orientation of the mainchain. The mainchain conformation of sidechain polymer smectics has been considered.[52]
Effectively, the mainchains then see a repulsive periodic potential which
tends to spread the mainchain in the layers and reduce the hops between
layers.

The equation for the Green's function of the mainchains is then:

$$\left[\frac{\partial}{\partial s} - \frac{kT}{2E}\,\text{grad}_U^2 - \frac{c}{kT}P_2(\mathbf{u}_z) - \mathbf{u}_z\frac{\delta}{\delta z} - \frac{b}{kT}\cos k_0 z\right]G$$

$$= \delta(s)\delta(\mathbf{u}_z - \mathbf{u}_z^0)\delta(z - z_0) \tag{34}$$

b being the strength of the smectic potential, c that of the nematic coupling between mainchain segments, and k_0 the period of the smectic layers. $\mathbf{u}_z^0$ and z_0 describe the original configuration of the polymer. This equation is solved for $q \to \infty$ $L \to \infty$ and strong coupling c. It is found that $R_\parallel^2 \approx \exp(-kTE_L)$, a result similar to the hairpin result. The activation energy is found to be

$$E_L = \frac{8}{k_0}\left(3\sum bc\right)^{1/2} \tag{35}$$

where $\Sigma = \langle\cos k_0 r_z(s)\rangle$ is the smectic order parameter. For reviews on the chemistry of sidechain LCP's see Refs. 53–55.

3.2. Nematic Elastomers[49,56–58]

In such materials, the nematic polymers are cross linked to produce a network with remarkable coupling between mechanical and optical properties. A spontaneous distortion was predicted to occur in nematic elastomers below the transition temperature which causes a shift in the transition temperature. The distortion e in the direction of the director is calculated by minimization of the elastic free energy given by a Landau-de Gennes expansion[49]

$$F = a_0(T - T'')S^2 + BS^3 + CS^4 - USe + \frac{Ee^2}{2} \tag{36}$$

where S is the uniaxial order parameter of the mainchains and E and U are the modulus and coupling constants relative to the elastic strain. By minimization of F, the macroscopic strain $e_m = US/E$ of the elastomer is found to be proportional to the microscopic order parameter and leads to a contribution $\sim S^2$ in the Landau-de Gennes expansion. Therefore a shift occurs in $T'' \to T'' + U^2/2E$ and in the transition temperature of the nematic elastomer if the elastomer is formed in the nematic state.

If an external stress σ is applied, then an additional term $-\sigma e$ is present in the free energy. The results discussed in Section 2.5 on applying an external field to a nematic are now recovered as a function of σ, in particular the presence of a critical temperature for which the phase transition becomes of second order (Fig. 6). Above this critical value there is no longer a transition; the order parameter varies continuously with σ.

Warner et al.[56] related the macroscopic strain to the anisotropy of the polymer in the elastomer. As discussed in Section 2.4 in a nematic polymer the anisotropic interactions cause a change in the chain conformation or more specifically in the end-to-end vector. In a perturbation expansion, effective persistence lengths which are different in the directions parallel $q_{\parallel}$ and perpendicular $q_{\perp}$ to the director are calculated (for large L/q, the case of long chains with a Gaussian-like distribution):

$$\langle R_{\parallel}^2 \rangle = 2q_{\parallel}L \quad \text{and} \quad \frac{q}{q_{\parallel}} = 1 + \frac{2}{9}\Delta^2 + \cdots \tag{37}$$

$$\langle R_{\perp}^2 \rangle = 2q_{\perp}L \quad \text{and} \quad \frac{q}{q_{\perp}} = 1 - \frac{1}{9}\Delta^2 + \cdots \tag{38}$$

and the nematic coupling constant is $\Delta^2 = -3EU_BS/(kT)^2$, considering here only the contribution of the mainchains of length L for simplicity. Because of the crosslinking the polymer cannot achieve this conformation but is deformed by a strain λ with principal elements $\lambda_{\parallel}$ and $\lambda_{\perp}$. The strained vector is then $\mathbf{R}' = \lambda R$. Incompressibility of the network requires $\lambda_{\parallel}\lambda_{\perp}^2 = 1$. The free energy of distortion is calculated from the probability $P(\mathbf{R}')$ of finding two crosslinks connected by a vector $\mathbf{R}'$, assumed to be Gaussian and anisotropic in $\mathbf{R}_{\parallel}$ and $\mathbf{R}_{\perp}$:

$$F_{el} = -kT\langle \ln P(R') \rangle_0 \tag{39}$$

The average is taken in the uncrosslinked state. The free energy of distortion is a function of $q_{\parallel}, q_{\perp}$ and $\lambda_{\parallel}, \lambda_{\perp}$. For small distortion $\lambda_{\parallel} = 1 + e$. Then $q_{\parallel}$ and $q_{\perp}$ can be expressed in S leading to the free energy expansion in S and e. The coupling constants U, E can now be related to microscopic parameters, and the spontaneous distortion is found by minimization of this expression:

$$e_m = -\frac{\Delta^2}{9} \tag{40}$$

Therefore, if crosslinking occurs in the isotropic state an additive quartic term in S occurs and the transition temperature of the elastomer is lowered. If crosslinking occurs in the nematic state, the transition temperature will be changed by an amount proportional to the crosslink density and raised or lowered depending on the order present in the sample before crosslinking.

As discussed in Section 2.4, the presence of hairpins may cause exponential decay of parallel dimensions and therefore of the spontaneous strain as a function of increasing temperature. The elastic free energy for Gaussian wormlike chains was also extended to the two-component theory for combs taking the order of both the main- and sidechains into account. For experimental studies on LC elastomers see Refs. 59 and 60.

4. CUBIC LATTICE APPROACH

4.1. Concentrated Solutions of Persistent Chains

On a cubic lattice, we define the chain as a connected sequence of lattice segments. At each junction between adjacent segments straight bonds require no energy, whereas all bent conformations must be formed with an energy expense, ϵ. Each chain comprises X lattice sites. The lattice contains n_p polymer chains and n_s solvent molecules. This model was first considered by Flory.[61]

Interaction between chains was taken into account adapting molecules to the lattice in sequence, segment by segment, one chain after the other. The probability of accommodating each segment of the chain without overlap with molecules already present was taken equal to the volume fraction of free sites at each step. Comparison between isotropic melt and fully extended (crystalline) configuration shows that transition to the oriented state occurs at the temperature $kT = 1.183\epsilon$ for infinite chains. States of intermediate order are not considered in this treatment.

Introduction of intermediate order can be allowed in several steps. We can specify the configuration of all the n_p chains of the solution and fill the lattice using translational freedom. One chain has to be accommodated after the other, with an overlap probability increasing with concentration. This method, introduced by Di Marzio,[62] represents an improvement over the volume fraction argument of Flory.[61] It links the model to the geometry of the simple cubic lattice, which implies a loss of generality, but it also allows differentiation between states of different partial orientation. Once the conformation of the general chain is specified and the position of the first segment is given, the sequence of sites needed to accommodate the chain on the lattice is uniquely defined. If some of the sites of the sequence are already occupied by other chains, a new position must be tried for the first segment, until the sequence is all free. Along the lattice path reserved to the chain there are in general free sites and occupied submolecules. The mole fractions of free sites or occupied submolecules are not the same along the three lattice directions in the presence of macroscopic anisotropy. If the first site is free, the probability of having the lattice path of $X - 1$ segments accepted is:

$$P = \prod_{i=1}^{X-1} p_i \tag{41}$$

where p_i is the molar fraction of free sites along the lattice axis in the direction of the ith segment. Equation (41) raises no ambiguity. At each step of the filling process, i.e., when adapting each new chain to the lattice, the six mole fractions, two for each lattice direction, have to be calculated. Overall orientation of the segments may be kept fixed during the filling process; actually, what shows in the results is only the final average orientaion of the segments, because of several cancellation effects. For a system of n_s solvent molecules and n_p chains at concentration v_p with all conformations already specified, Di Marzio obtains[62] the combinatorial free energy ΔG_{comb}:

$$\frac{\Delta G_{comb}}{kT} = n_s \ln(1 - v_p) + n_p \ln(v_p/X)$$

$$- \frac{n_p X}{v_p} \sum_{i=1}^{3} \left[1 - \frac{(X-1)}{X} v_p \alpha_i \right] \ln \left[1 - \frac{(X-1)}{X} v_p \alpha_i \right] \quad (42)$$

where α_i is the overall fraction of chain segments oriented along the axis i of the simple cubic lattice. As particular cases of persistent chains we can consider rigid rods, containing X lattice sites. Equation (42) applies also to this particular system.[63] Different forms of Eq. (42) are generated considering systems of higher complexity.

ΔG_{comb}, given by Eq. (42), is *not* the complete free energy, at given values of α_i. A different set of conformations of all the molecules, yielding the same value of α_i (1, 2, 3), produces the same values of ΔG_{comb}. How many of these conformational states[64-67] exist, and to which expense of conformational energy they must be formed, one must specify, adding a suitable configurational energy ΔG_{conf}. This configurational free energy depends on the set α_i. Different sets of values α_i give rise to different values of the configurational free energy, which cannot be considered "constant" as is usually done in the theory of mixtures of ordinary polymers, if we want to explore the relative stability of states of different macroscopic orientation.

In the next section we consider a brief review of theories applying the Di Marzio method to the calculation of combinatorial entropies. The last section will be devoted to the analysis of solutions of homogeneous semiflexible chains. The concept of mole fraction of free sites, essential to the development of the Di Marzio theory, is of decisive importance in the Flory theory of rigid rods on lattices.[68] In this theory (cf. Chapter 4) rods are also accommodated to the lattice in successive steps. Each rod configuration is accepted if it does not overlap with previously adapted molecules. Allowance for continuous distribution of orientation is made by breaking the rod into a sequence of submolecular units connected stairwise and directed along the principal axis of orientation. Lattice statistics of free sites and occupied submolecules along this privileged direction are one dimensional. In the larger macroscopic orientation, occupied submolecules of the one-dimensional lattice are longer, and therefore fewer. The mole fraction of free sites is then larger, which makes accommodation of the general rod easier. Flory's and Di Marzio's formulas for the combinatorial entropy are formally similar, although thermodynamically nonequivalent, and give different results as shown comparing results of cubic lattice theories[64] and wormlike treatments of semiflexible chains based on the Flory model (see next sections).

4.2. Lattice Theories of Segmented Chains

As pointed by Agren and Martire,[69] many liquid crystals have a rigid central portion. The original Di Marzio paper on rigid rods yields an expression for the combinatorial free energy which needs implementation. For chain systems containing rigid units and flexible or semiflexible parts, more than one orientational order parameter may be needed. While a consistent theory of systems of polydisperse persistent chains is not yet available, introduction of multiple order parameters for sections of the same molecular unit appears to pose problems which make exact solutions rather cumbersome. Agren and Martire[69] were the first to study lattice models of particles with rigid, rodlike central cores and semiflexible pendant segments. The statistics for semiflexible pendant sections was developed using matrix methods.[70] In their treatment, conformational energy is enriched with additional constraints, assigning various degrees of preference to different orientations in space, in order to specify the coupling between conformation and external field of orientation. Agren and Martire show that molecules containing a number of rigid sites (5) slightly above the rigid-rod transition threshold have, at given pressure, transition temperatures affected by the degree of rigidity of the tail, which increases the temperature of transition to the ordered state only above a certain chain rigidity. The temperature raising effect is lost with longer rigid units, which tend to decrease the transition temperature uniformly. The entropy of transition per molecule invariably increases with the length of the semiflexible tail, the increase being more marked with flexible tails. More rigid tails and longer rigid units produce higher relative density changes at the transition. The lattice treatment by Agren and Martire shows features common to other lattice treatments of liquid-crystalline polymers: useful for comparison with experimental trends, hard to use for completely predictive purposes. Dowell and Martire[71, 72] reconsidered chains with rigid cores and semiflexible tails, observing that the entropy of transition appears to increase too rapidly with tail length in the Agren-Martire model. Tight connection to the conformational (trans–gauche) energetics of the tails was found to be responsible for these anomalies. A different model of the mean field that links the effective "trans" conformation of the tails to the orientation of the molecule is considered. In the case of complete flexibility,[71, 72] decrease of transition temperature with tail length was found excessive by comparison with experiment, at given pressure. The conclusion is therefore reached that experimental data suggest reduced flexibility of tails, although dominance of intrachain energetics (trans–gauche) appears to be misleading. In fact, Dowell and Martire find it more sensible to redefine the "trans bond" as one colinear with the rigid core. In order to obtain reasonably small values of the relative density change at the transition, the pressure has to be kept very high in their model. Small ratios between experimentally acceptable values and computationally usable pressure levels are common in these authors treatment. Introduction of energetic interaction between chains improves both the order parameter of the core and the density change at the transition.

The lattice model considered by Martire and Dowell lends itself to studies on the stability of isotropic–nematic, smectic A, and reentrant–nematic phases.[73, 74] Recourse to high values of the pressure must be kept in order to obtain sensible results. However, in lattice models, the meaning of this pressure is probably questionable if quantitative comparison with experimental values is attempted. In order to avoid these inconsistencies many authors prefer to work at constant volume. Using semiflexible tails with a proper definition of the trans state, Dowell reformulates the statistics of molecules containing rigid cores and semiflexible tails. The length of the cores is kept at values exceeding $X = 3.652$ reported by Alben[75] for spontaneous transition of the bulk of rods to the nematic state. Energetic interactions between different molecules are not necessary for the prediction of the occurrence of the smectic A state. Organization of rigid rods in layers of oriented cores coupled by semiflexible tails is considered allowing for various degrees of layered organization.[74] With decreasing temperature, the general trend is from the isotropic, to the nematic, to the smectic, to the reentrant–nematic phase. The existence of semiflexible tails is essential to the appearance of the smectic S_A phase. If the tails are too rigid, direct passage from the isotropic to the stable nematic phase is predicted, with no appearance of the smectic phase. As temperature is lowered, the level of layered organization of the smectic phase is also predicted to decrease, before passing to the reentrant–nematic phase. The width of the region of stability of the smectic phase is narrower for more rigid tails and ranges from a fraction of a degree to a few decades. The alternation of rigid cores and semiflexible tails provides a pattern of periodicity. All nematics have a critical point lying a few degrees below the isotropic–nematic transition temperature. Unstable fluctuations of the isotropic phase below the critical temperature are evidently enhanced by this sort of periodicity to the point of forming a stable smectic phase. The lattice treatment is certainly oversensitive to this sort of builtin periodicity. However, the temperature ranges calculated appear reasonable and the number of tail segments considered (5–20) is realistic. It would perhaps be illuminating to do these calculations also at constant volume, in order to avoid recourse to prohibitively high pressures. An increase of chain flexibility in the Dowell model stabilizes the smectic A phase but shifts orientational transitions to very low temperatures of questionable practical interest. Thermotropic effects of varying complexity have been studied for these treatments of chains with rigid cores. Two improvements seem necessary: (1) clear separation between conformational degrees of freedom and the macroscopic fields of orientation; and (2) exact thermodynamic coupling between the orientational order and a count of the molecule's effective degrees of freedom.

The analysis presented so far in this chapter applies to low molecular weight compounds. Boehm et al.[76] extended the lattice treatment based on the Di Marzio partition function to segmented chains containing many rigid units. Due to cancellation effects Eq. (42) maintains its validity even for chains containing sequences of rigid rods and flexible spacers. However, exact calculation of the configurational free energy discussed in the preceding section becomes more difficult. Boehm et al. solve the problem assuming that rodlike groups are randomly distributed along the polymer chain. In this way spacers effectively decouple orientations of consecutive rigid units, which are assumed to affect the conformations of the spacer chain introducing internal stress, larger in the nematic state. The method couples the conformations of the spacers and the orientation of the rigid rod to the macroscopic orientation of the system.

Conformational statistics of the segmented chain are not resolved completely. The average degree of orientation of rigid rods and semiflexible segments affects not only the combinatorial entropy but also the global energy of interaction of the chains which is calculated as the sum of an isotropic contribution plus an anisotropic part proportional to the square of the order parameter S of the rigid units. Calculations are done at constant pressure. Under certain conditions two different anisotropic nematic phases exist, both corresponding to energy minima. One is highly oriented and corresponds to nearly complete orientation of the spacers.

Dowell[77] has also extended her treatment to segmented polymers comprising many rigid units. Lack of resolution of the conformational structure of each molecule into exact counts of cooperative degrees of freedom is apparent from the results: modest values of the order parameter at the isotropic–nematic transition of infinite chain systems.

4.3. Homogeneous Semiflexible Chains on the Simple Cubic Lattice

For concentrated solutions of homogeneous semiflexible chains various definitions of order are possible. The configurational free energy must explore the degrees of freedom left free at fixed values of the α_i's, which characterize the combinatorial part. Therefore, the three α_i's suggest themselves as suitable order parameters. The three α_i are the fractions of segments oriented along the three axes of the cubic lattice. Denoting by Q the fraction of segments oriented along the preferred axis of orientation, we rewrite the

Di Marzio equation as:

$$\frac{\Delta G_{\text{comb}}}{kT} = n_s \ln(1 - v_p) + n_p \ln\left(\frac{v_p}{X}\right)$$

$$- \frac{n_p X}{v_p}\left[1 - \frac{(X - 1)}{X}v_p Q\right]\ln\left[1 - \frac{(X - 1)}{X}v_p Q\right]$$

$$- \frac{2n_p X}{v_p}\left[1 - \frac{(X - 1)}{2X}v_p(1 - Q)\right]\ln\left[1 - \frac{(X - 1)}{2X}v_p(1 - Q)\right]$$

$$(43)$$

A three-state spin vector[64, 65] $\boldsymbol{\sigma} = \boldsymbol{\Lambda}_i$

$$\boldsymbol{\Lambda}_1 = \begin{pmatrix} 1 \\ 0 \\ 0 \end{pmatrix} \qquad \boldsymbol{\Lambda}_2 = \begin{pmatrix} 0 \\ 1 \\ 0 \end{pmatrix} \qquad \boldsymbol{\Lambda}_3 = \begin{pmatrix} 0 \\ 0 \\ 1 \end{pmatrix} \qquad (44)$$

can be used to denote states of homonymous orientation of the $X - 1$ segments of each chain. The conformational energy of the general chain becomes

$$H = \varepsilon \sum_{m=1}^{X-2} \boldsymbol{\sigma}_m^T \mathbf{D} \boldsymbol{\sigma}_{m+1} \qquad (45)$$

where $\mathbf{D}$ is the conformational matrix

$$\mathbf{D} = \begin{pmatrix} 0 & 1 & 1 \\ 1 & 0 & 1 \\ 1 & 1 & 0 \end{pmatrix} \qquad (46)$$

The one-chain Boltzmann factor becomes

$$\mathbf{P} = \exp\left[-J \sum_{m=1}^{X-2} \boldsymbol{\sigma}_m^T \mathbf{D} \boldsymbol{\sigma}_{m+1}\right] \qquad (47)$$

where $J = (\varepsilon/kT) - \ln 2$. The constant $\ln 2$ is a degeneracy factor (there are two ways of turning in a given direction; there is only one way to go straight). The complete configurational partition function of the n_p chains is then written

$$Z(Q, J, X) = \sum_{\{\sigma_k(1)\}} \cdots \sum_{\{\sigma_k(n_p)\}} \exp\left[-J \sum_{j=1}^{n_p} \sum_{m=1}^{X-2} \boldsymbol{\sigma}_m^T(j) \mathbf{D} \boldsymbol{\sigma}_{m+1}(j)\right]$$

$$\times \delta\left[\sum_{j=1}^{n_p} \nu_3(j) - (X - 1)n_p Q\right] \qquad (48)$$

where $\nu_3(j)$ is the number of segments of the jth chain oriented in the preferred direction, and the weighting factor containing $\nu_3(j)$ is a delta function. We can express $\nu_3(j)$ in the form

$$\nu_3(j) = \boldsymbol{\sigma}_1^T(j)\mathbf{A}\boldsymbol{\sigma}_2(j) + \sum_{m=2}^{X-3} \boldsymbol{\sigma}_m^T(j)\mathbf{K}\boldsymbol{\sigma}_{m+1}(j) + \boldsymbol{\sigma}_{X-2}^T(j)\mathbf{A}^T\boldsymbol{\sigma}_{X-1}(j) \quad (49)$$

where

$$\mathbf{K} = \begin{pmatrix} 0 & 0 & 1/2 \\ 0 & 0 & 1/2 \\ 1/2 & 1/2 & 1 \end{pmatrix} \quad (50)$$

and:

$$\mathbf{A} = \begin{pmatrix} 0 & 0 & 1/2 \\ 0 & 0 & 1/2 \\ 1 & 1 & 3/2 \end{pmatrix} \quad (51)$$

accounts for the end effects of the linear molecule, which contains X lattice sites, $(X-1)$ segments, and $(X-2)$ junctions. We must substitute Eq. (49) in Eq. (48), introduce the Fourier representation of the delta function, and integrate over the Fourier variable using saddlepoint techniques. We obtain in this way

$$Z(Q, J, X) \propto \exp\left[-(X-1)n_p Q\alpha\right]\left[Z_c(\alpha, J, X)\right]^{n_p}, \quad (52)$$

where α is the saddlepoint value of $i\Omega$ and Ω is the Fourier variable of the delta expansion. Z_c is calculated as

$$Z_c(\alpha, J, X) = \sum_{\{\sigma_m\}} \exp\left[\boldsymbol{\sigma}_1^T(\alpha\mathbf{A} - J\mathbf{D})\boldsymbol{\sigma}_2\right.$$

$$\left. + \sum_{m=2}^{X-3} \boldsymbol{\sigma}_m^T(\alpha\mathbf{K} - J\mathbf{D})\boldsymbol{\sigma}_{m+1} + \boldsymbol{\sigma}_{X-2}^T(\alpha\mathbf{A}^T - J\mathbf{D})\boldsymbol{\sigma}_{X-1}\right] \quad (53)$$

and α is the solution of the nonlinear saddlepoint equation

$$Q = \frac{\partial}{\partial\alpha}\left[\frac{1}{(X-1)} \ln Z_c(\alpha, J, X)\right] \quad (54)$$

Equation (52) can be reduced to the form $(z)^{n_p}$ with the prefactor $\exp[-(X-1)Q\alpha]$. Correct normalization of the effective one-particle partition function is essential to the evaluation of the configurational partition function. From Eq. (53) we obtain

$$Z_c(\alpha, J, X) = \sum_{i,k} (\mathbf{G})_{ik} \tag{55}$$

G is the matrix

$$\mathbf{G} = \mathbf{ST}^{X-4}\mathbf{S}^T \tag{56}$$

where:

$$\mathbf{T} = \begin{pmatrix} 1 & e^{-J} & e^{\alpha/2-J} \\ e^{-J} & 1 & e^{\alpha/2-J} \\ e^{\alpha/2-J} & e^{\alpha/2-J} & e^{\alpha} \end{pmatrix} \tag{57}$$

$$\mathbf{S} = \begin{pmatrix} 1 & e^{-J} & e^{\alpha/2-J} \\ e^{-J} & 1 & e^{\alpha/2-J} \\ e^{\alpha-J} & e^{\alpha-J} & e^{3\alpha/2} \end{pmatrix} \tag{58}$$

Recourse to eigenvalues, eigenvectors, and their condition of completeness reduces the calculation of Eq. (56) to simple algebraic formulas. The configurational free energy can be written

$$\frac{\Delta G_{conf}}{kT} = n_p(X - 1)Q\alpha - n_p \ln[Z_c(\alpha, J, X)] \tag{59}$$

which must be added to Eq. (43). Calculation of phase equilibria in solution and transition temperatures in the bulk can be done searching anisotropic minima of the complete free energy, to be compared with the isotropic state using the free energy or the two chemical potentials (solvent and solute). Chain length influence persists at high X. This feature is not equally dominant in wormlike systems of persistent chains. Correct normalization of the configurational partition function corresponds to using fields of orientation whose global energetic effect must be subtracted from the partition function, to which they accede in order to enforce orientational constraint without favoring orientation energetically. This double task is effectively accomplished by suitable shift of the zero of the conformational energy of the segments which may point in different directions. The delta function method selects this zero automatically. Figures 9, 10, and 11 show the main result of this calculation for bulks and solutions of persistent lattice chains. The fraction g of bent configurations is chosen as a convenient order parameter in Figs. 9 and 10. Chains with fewer than four sites, consistently with Alben's[75] finding (we do not consider chains containing nonintegral values of X), show no nematic transition even in the bulk. As Fig. 9 shows, order tends to be higher for long molecules. Actually, Fig. 9 shows that the oriented phase tends to contain completely straight chains in this limit. The orienta-

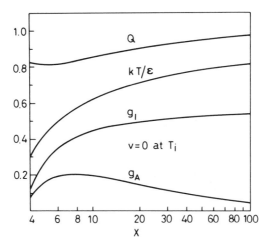

FIGURE 9
Fraction Q of oriented segments, reduced transition temperature
kT/ε, fraction of bent conformations of the isotropic phase g_1, and
fraction of bent conformations of the ordered phase g_A. All quantities
refer to bulk transitions of chains containing X lattice sites.
(Reproduced with permission from Ref. 65.)

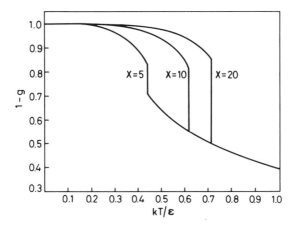

FIGURE 10
Fraction of straight bond conformations in the bulk for $X = 5$, 10,
and 20. (Reproduced with permission from Ref. 65.)

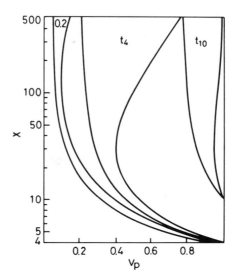

FIGURE 11

Phase coexistence at three different values of the reduced
temperature $t = kT/\varepsilon$. $t_4 = 0.3021$ and $t_{10} = 0.6209$ are the
predicted bulk transition temperatures for $X = 4$ and 10, respectively.
(Reproduced with permission from Ref. 65.)

tional order parameter (represented by Q) at the transition is always high
and approaches unity for long chains. For $X = 4$, Q is high (~ 0.8) but the
relative change of g is small at the transition. Therefore, the transition is
almost rodlike. Different results are obtained by Dowell and Martire,[72] who
find tail flexibility on one side and a high degree of extension on the other
side of the transition, because they work with partially rigid units. Figure 11
describes solution properties. Three temperatures have been chosen in
Fig. 11:

$$kT/\varepsilon = 0.2, \qquad t_4 = 0.3021, \quad \text{and} \quad t_{10} = 0.6209$$

The value $kT/\varepsilon = 0.2$ is low. At this temperature all chains with $x \geq 4$
are oriented in the bulk. The narrow strip at $kT/\varepsilon = 0.2$ gives the concentration gap as a function of chain length. Up to $X = 500$ this concentration gap
shows the typical features of rigid liquid-crystalline polymers, as calculated
using other models of persistent chains.[78] Wormlike chains having persistence length axial ratios[78] $q/d \simeq 50$ show incipient concentration isotherms
similar to that obtained from the lattice model at $kT/\varepsilon = 0.2$. The gap,
however, is generally smaller in the case of wormlike chains. At $kT/\varepsilon = 0.2$
the persistence length of the lattice chain is $q/d \sim 38$. For $kT/\varepsilon = 0.2$ at
$X > 500$ a general characteristic of the lattice model is observed: the enlargement of the gap without energetic contribution to the interaction between
the chains. This enlargement leaves the concentration asymptotes of the

incipient phase at values reminiscent of liquid-crystalline behavior but progressively shifts the nematic saturation curve to higher concentrations and orientations with increasing chain length. The effect starts at shorter chain length at higher temperatures, forcing the incipient isotherm to stay closer to the bulk state. For long enough chains at any temperature, the nematic saturation curve corresponds to highly oriented quasi-crystalline morphology of the nematic phase. This phase contains numbers of solvent molecules, bent conformations, and nonaligned segments proportional to $1/X$, where X is the number of lattice sites per chain. The reduced temperatures $t = 0.2$, t_4, and t_{10} are indicative of the conditions in studies on chains with rigid cores.[76] At these temperatures, for chains of modest length ($X \sim 30$), the nematic curve is still far from quasi-crystalline features. Calculation of phase equilibria for chains of actual infinite length does not yield solutions for the chemical potentials. At given concentration one can still study the relative stability of isotropic and nematic phases. For infinite chain systems the nematic phase of stable orientation becomes more stable than the isotropic at sufficiently low temperature,[64, 66] as also seen by Auriemma, Corradini, and Vacatello who use the Allegra[67] method to calculate the orientationally constrained partition function. Recourse to the condition of completeness of the eigenvectors[65] allows us to explore asymptotic regions of chain length not sufficiently characterized by the knowledge of the maximum eigenvalue. These regions are of interest for characterizing the terminal enlargement of the phase gap with very long chains. Direct comparison of free energies for infinite chain systems at fixed concentration gives only indications concerning the existence of oriented states more stable than the isotropic phase. Actual calculations must always be done with finite X,[65] without taking the limit $X \rightarrow 0$.

Future work in the field of lattice models of liquid-crystalline polymers must remedy several deficiencies of present treatments and elucidate some peculiarities of the model. As we have seen, the lattice model of long chains in solution predicts very broad gaps even without energetic interaction. The concentration asymptote of the incipient curve at high molecular weights is comparable to that predicted by wormlike treatments, but the saturation curve approaches the quasi-crystalline bulk. No such effect is predicted by wormlike treatments whose phase gap is always of the order of 10%.[78] Wormlike treatments of the Maier-Saupe type[17] or relying on calculations of steric effects[78, 79] predict enlargement of the gap only with introduction of interchain energetics. The idea[61] that the cubic lattice model is better suited for studying crystallization deserves consideration. On the other hand, narrow gaps up to 10^3 bonds are predicted by the lattice model at sufficiently low temperature. In general, suitable domains of the variables (temperature, concentration, chain length, and flexibility) always appear to exist, inside which the lattice model, whose adaptation to continuous geometries has been considered,[68] treats liquid-crystalline systems correctly. Explanation of the gap enlargement in terms of intrachain effects is suggested as a possibility by

Semenov and Khokhlov,[79, 80] who find transition to complete order in the case of chain systems governed by rotational isomeric conformational mechanisms. To this extent the lattice model appears to be applicable to systems with discrete structures to their conformations. The model presented in this section can be applied to calculations of nematic transitions for systems containing rigid cores. For example, simple modification of the terminal matrix A defined in Eq. (51) allows extension, *ceteris paribus*, to a polymer systems consisting of two rigid units connected by a flexible spacer. Similar topologies have been considered by Auriemma et al.[66] Other topologies can be treated in similar fashion. The complex pattern of interplay between the order parameter Q, the fraction of bent configurations g, the polymer volume fraction v_p, and the chain length X suggests limitation of the number of approximations. Possible anomalies must not be obscured but critically accepted as questionable features of the lattice model. The expression for the combinatorial free energy calculated by Di Marzio, as given by Eq. (42), must be changed for nonlinear chains or even for linear chains if focus shifts to smectic transitions.

ACKNOWLEDGMENTS

Critical review by Dr. P. Maïssa is gratefully acknowledged.

REFERENCES

1. P.J. Flory, *Proc. R. Soc. London*, **1956**, *234*, 60.
2. L. Onsager, *Ann. N.Y. Acad. Sci.*, **1949**, *51*, 627.
3. W. Maier and A. Saupe, *Z. Naturforsch.*, *A*, **1958**, *13*, 674.
4. K.F. Freed, *Adv. Chem. Phys.*, **1972**, *22*, 1.
5. S.F. Edwards, in *Molecular Fluids*, R. Balian, G. Weil, eds., Gordon and Breach, London, 1976, p. 151.
6. N. Saito, K. Takahaski and Y. Yunoki, *J. Phys. Soc. Jpn.*, **1967**, *22*, 219.
7. J. Shimada, M. Fujii, and H. Yamakawa, *J. Polym. Sci.*, **1974**, *12*, 2075.
8. W. Gobush, H. Yamakawa, W.H. Stockmayer, and W.S. Magee, *J. Chem. Phys.*, **1972**, *57*, 2839.
9. H. Yamakawa and M. Fujii, *J. Chem. Phys.*, **1977**, *66*, 2578, 2584.
10. M. Fujii, K. Nagasaka, J. Shimda, and H. Yamakawa, *J. Chem. Phys.*, **1982**, *77*, 986.
11. H. Yamakawa, *Modern Theory of Polymer Solutions*, Harper and Row, New York, 1971.
12. M. Nakagawa and T. Akehane, *Mol. Cryst. Liq. Cryst.*, **1982**, *90*, 53.
13. W. Gelbart, *J. Phys. Chem.*, **1982**, *86*, 4298.
14. J.K. Percus, in *Equilibrium Theory of Classical Fluids*, H.L. Frisch and J.L. Lebowitz, eds., W. Benjamin, New York, 1964, p. II-33.
15. P. Pincus, P.G. de Gennes, *J. Polym. Sci.*, **1978**, *65*, 85; Y. Kim and P. Pincus, *Am. Chem. Soc. Symp. Ser.*, **1978**, *74*, 127.
16. F. Jahnig, *J. Chem. Phys.*, **1979**, *70*, 3279.

17. A. Ten Bosch, P. Maïssa, and P. Sixou, *J. Chem. Phys.*, **1983**, *79*, 3462.
18. A. Ten Bosch, P. Maïssa, and P. Sixou, *Phys. Lett.*, **1983**, *94*, 298.
19. A. Ten Bosch, P. Maïssa, and P. Sixou, in *Polymeric Liquid Crystals*, A. Blumstein, ed., Plenum Press, New York, 1985, p. 109.
20. P. Sixou and A. Ten Bosch, in *Cellulose Structure Modification Hydrolysis*, R. Young and R. Rowell, eds., J. Wiley, New York, 1986, ch. 12, p. 205.
21. A. Ten Bosch and P. Maïssa, *Fluctuations and Stochastic Phenomena*, L. Garrido, ed., Lecture Notes in Physics, Vol. 268, Springer Verlag, Berlin, 1987, p. 333.
22. X.J. Wang and M. Warner, *J. Phys.*, *A*, **1986**, *19*, 2215.
23. A. Perera, G.N. Patey, and J.J. Weis, *J. Chem. Phys.*, **1988**, *89*, 6941.
24. M. Warner, J.M.F. Gunn, and A.B. Baumgartner, *J. Phys.*, *A*, **1985**, *18*, 3007.
25. H. Kimura, *J. Phys. Soc. Jpn.*, **1974**, *36*(5), 1280.
26. F. Jahnig, *Mol. Cryst. Liq. Cryst.*, **1981**, *63*, 157.
27. W. Rusakov and M.I. Shliomis, *J. Phys. Lett.* **1985**, *46*, L935.
28. A. Ten Bosch and P. Sixou, *J. Chem. Phys.* **1985**, *83*, 899.
29. A. Ten Bosch, J. Pinton, P. Maïssa, and P. Sixou, *J. Phys.*, *A*, **1987**, *20*, 4531.
30. P. Maïssa and P. Sixou, *Liq. Cryst.*, **1989**, *5*, 1861.
31. P.G. de Gennes, *Scaling Concepts in Polymer Physics*, Cornell University Press, Ithaca, New York, 1979.
32. M.J. Seurin, A. Ten Bosch, and P. Sixou, *Polym. Bull.*, **1983**, *9*, 450.
33. F. Brochard, J. Jouffroy, and P. Levinson, *J. Phys.*, **1984**, *45*, 1125.
34. M.J. Seurin, J.M. Gilli, A. Ten Bosch, and P. Sixou, *Polymer*, **1984**, *25*, 1073.
35. Baba Ainina, P. Maïssa, and P. Sixou, *Polymer*, to be published.
36. H. Yamakawa and W.H. Stockmayer, *J. Chem. Phys.*, **1972**, *57*, 2843.
37. T. Norisuye and H. Fujita, *Polym. J.*, **1982**, *14*, 143.
38. J.F. d'Allest, P. Maïssa, A. Ten Bosch, P. Sixou, A. Blumstein, R. Blumstein, J. Teixera, and L. Noirez, *Phys. Rev. Lett.*, **1988**, *61*(22), 2562.
39. P.G. de Gennes, in *Polymer Liquid Crystals*, A. Ciferri, W.R. Krigbaum, and R.B. Meyer, eds., Academic Press, New York, 1982, ch. 5, p. 115.
40. J.M. Gunn and M. Warner, *Phys. Rev. Lett.*, **1987**, *58*(4), 393.
41. X.J. Wang, M. Warner, *Phys. Lett.*, *A*, **1986**, *119*, 181.
42. P. Maïssa, A. Ten Bosch, and P. Sixou, *J. Polym. Sci. Polym. Lett.*, **1983**, *21*, 757; **1986**, *24*, 481.
43. J.M. Gilli, G. Maret, P. Maïssa, A. Ten Bosch, P. Sixou, and A. Blumstein, *J. Phys. Lett.*, **1985**, *46*, L329.
44. P.G. de Gennes, *Mol. Cryst. Liq. Cryst.*, **1984**, *102*, 95.
45. A. Ten Bosch and P. Sixou, *J. Chem. Phys.*, **1987**, *86*, 6556.
46. T. Shimada, M. Doi, and K. Okano, *J. Chem. Phys.*, **1988**, *88*, 2815.
47. T. Shimada, M. Doi, and K. Okano, *J. Phys. Soc. Jpn.*, **1988**, *57*(7), 2432.
48. S. Vasilenko, V. Shibaev, A. Khoklov, *Macromol. Chem.*, **1985**, *186*, 1951.
49. M. Warner, in *Sidechain Liquid Crystal Polymers*, C.B. McArdle, ed., Blackie, Glasgow and London, 1989, ch. 2, p. 7.
50. X.J. Wang and M. Warner, *J. Phys.*, *A*, **1986**, *19*, 2215.
51. W. Renz, *Mol. Cryst. Liq. Cryst.*, **1988**, *155*, 549.
52. W. Renz and M. Warner, *Phys. Rev. Lett.*, **1986**, *56*, 1268.
53. H. Finkelmann, in *Thermotropic Liquid Crystals*, G.W. Gray, ed., J. Wiley & Sons, New York, 1987.
54. G.W. Gray, in *Sidechain Liquid Crystal Polymers*, C.B. McArdle, ed., Blackie, Glasgow, and London, 1989, ch. 4, p. 106.
55. B. Reck and H. Ringsdorf, *Makromolec. Chem. Rapid. Commun.*, **1985**, *6*, 291.
56. M. Warner, K.P. Gelling, and T.A. Vilgis, *J. Chem. Phys.*, **1988**, *88*, 4008.
57. T. Gilling and M. Warner, *Mol. Cryst. Liq. Cryst.*, **1988**, *155*, 539.
58. W. Renz and W. Warner, *Proc. R. Soc. London, Ser. A*, **1986**, *417*, 213.
59. J. Schätzle and H. Finkelmann, *Mol. Cryst. Liq. Cryst.*, **1987**, *142*, 85.

60. J. Schätzle, W. Kaufhold, and H. Finkelmann, *Makromol. Chem.*, **1989**, *190*, 3269.
61. P.J. Flory, *Proc. R. Soc. London, Ser. A*, **1956**, *234*, 60.
62. E.A. Di Marzio, *J. Chem. Phys.*, **1962**, *36*, 1563.
63. E.A. Di Marzio, *J. Chem. Phys.*, **1961**, *35*, 658.
64. G. Ronca, *J. Chem. Phys.*, **1983**, *79*, 6326.
65. G. Ronca, *J. Polym. Sci., B*, **1989**, *27*, 1795.
66. F. Auriemma, P. Corradini, and M. Vacatello, *Gazz. Chim. Ital.*, **1989**, *116*, 569.
67. G. Allegra, *Macromol. Chem.*, **1968**, *117*, 12.
68. P.J. Flory, *Proc. R. Soc. London, Ser. A*, **1956**, *234*, 73.
69. G.I. Agren and D.E. Martire, *J. Chem. Phys.*, **1974**, *61*, 3059.
70. A. Wulf and A.G. de Rocco, *J. Chem. Phys.*, **1971**, *55*, 12.
71. F. Dowell and D.E. Martire, *J. Chem. Phys.*, **1978**, *68*, 1088.
72. F. Dowell and D.E. Martire, *J. Chem. Phys.*, **1978**, *68*, 1094.
73. F. Dowell, *Phys. Rev., A*, **1983**, *28*, 3520.
74. F. Dowell, *Phys. Rev., A*, **1983**, *28*, 3526.
75. R. Alben, *Mol. Cryst. Liq. Cryst.*, **1971**, *13*, 193.
76. R.E. Boehm, D.E. Martire, and N.V. Madhusudana, *Macromolecules*, **1986**, *19*, 2329.
77. F. Dowell, *Mol. Cryst. Liq. Cryst.*, **1988**, *155*, 457.
78. G. Ronca and D.Y. Yoon, *J. Chem. Phys.*, **1985**, *83*, 373.
79. A.N. Semenov and A.R. Khokhlov, *Polym. Sci. USSR*, **1986**, *28*, 150.
80. A.N. Semenov and A.R. Khokhlov, *Polym. Sci. USSR*, **1986**, *28*, 159.

EXPERIMENTAL BEHAVIOR AND PERFORMANCE OF THEORIES

CHAPTER 6

Phase Behavior of Rigid and Semirigid Mesogens

A. CIFERRI

Istituto di Chimica Industriale
Università di Genova
16132 Genova, Italy

CONTENTS

1. INTRODUCTION

There are a few issues raised by theory we hope may be resolved by experimental analysis: Can hard and soft anisotropic interactions be independently assessed? Is the concept of a critical axial ratio a realistic one? Which is the best model for chain rigidity? Does molecular dispersion occur within the mesophase, and is the role of isotropic interaction essential or not? In this chapter we consider experimental data for rigid or semirigid mesogens, which are mainchain, or backbone, LCP's suitably represented by the rod, wormlike, and freely jointed chain models. The segmented mesogens, which are also backbone LCP's but show an alternation of flexible and rigid sections, are considered in the following chapter. Discussion of these classes of LCP's in separate chapters has several justifications. First, there is the amount of data available, and the fact that rigid or semirigid mesogens are often studied as diluted systems, whereas the segmented LCP's are undiluted, thermotropic systems. Rigid and semirigid mesogens are also those which have been considered in applications involving ultrahigh mechanical properties, a feature not exhibited by mesogens having flexible spacers.[1]

Furthermore, theory tends to differentiate the two classes of LCP's since the repeating unit of rigid or semirigid mesogens is not, at variance with the case of segmented LCP's, a low molecular weight liquid crystal. In a sense, the former may more properly be regarded as an "intrinsic" polymeric liquid crystal, while the segmented mesogens may be regarded as a polymerized versions of LMWLC's. Interest in the latter, which began significantly after[2,3] the synthesis of the first rigid mesogens had been reported,[4] resulted from the exploration of structure–property relationships between the LMWLC units and the corresponding polymers (there was also an interest in reducing the high melting temperatures of rigid mesogens).

Analogies and differences between the two classes of mesogens start with the realization that both comprise a rigid segment, the length of which does not increase during polymerization of segmented LCP's (due to the decoupling effect of the spacer), while the reverse occurs for rigid or semirigid chains. Thus, the length of a rigid block of a segmented mesogen may be in the order of 10–30 Å, whereas it may be as large as a persistence length of several hundred angstroms for rigid or semirigid LCP's.[5] Consequently, earlier theories suggested that soft interactions are essential to the former systems, whereas hard repulsive interactions play the prevailing role in the latter systems. Yet this separation cannot be too rigid. Most theories now recognize that both hard and soft interactions occur in LMWLC's and LCP's, that thermotropicity can occur in lyotropic systems and vice versa, and that the decoupling effect of the flexible spacer may not be complete. Moreover, similar chemical groups may be involved in rigid, semirigid, or segmented LCP's, and while the repeating unit of the former is not a LMWLC, it is possible that mesogenic properties are achieved during the earlier stages of polymerization. In this respect, no studies are available on the behavior of very low oligomers of the rigid LCP's, or on polymers of LMWLC's without the flexible spacer.

Treatments for discotic LCP's displaying not only soft[6] but also hard interactions are not available. Onsager[7] could not apply his second virial approximation to discs. Quantitative data relating diameter/thickness ratios to mesophase properties are also lacking.

2. UNDILUTED MESOGENS

2.1. Oligomers

In Chapters 4 and 7 results for selected classes of LMWLC's are discussed. Here, the analysis is restricted to the issue of soft anisotropic vs. hard interactions. The classical Maier-Saupe theory[6] for LMWLC's postulated only orientation-dependent energies, whereas the classical treatments by Onsager[7] and Flory[8] postulated only repulsions due to molecular asymmetry of long, thin rods. These positions were surmounted by several authors[9–16] who considered the superimposition of hard and soft interactions for both low and high molecular weight mesogens. The verification of this superimposition is a fundamental issue that has important implications. In fact, it has been implied (cf. Chapter 5) that separation of the two contributions is elusive since the steric repulsion and the mean soft interaction per segment may both increase with the length of the molecule (the latter effect might result, for instance, from an increased electron delocalization in conjugated systems). Therefore, it is relevant to investigate whether experimental data for LMWLC's support the contention of independent roles of hard and soft interactions.

For a quantitative evaluation of hard interactions it is customary to use the length (L)/diameter (d) or axial ratio X

$$X = \frac{L}{d} \tag{1}$$

which can be determined from structural data. For soft interactions the characteristic temperature T^*, defined by

$$\epsilon(\Theta) = -kT^* v_p S\left(1 - \tfrac{3}{2}\sin^2\Theta\right) \tag{2}$$

is often used. Here $\epsilon(\Theta)$ is the orientation-dependent energy for a segment forming an angle Θ with the domain axis, k is the Boltzmann's constant, S is the order parameter

$$S = 1 - \tfrac{3}{2}\langle\sin^2\Theta\rangle \tag{3}$$

and v_p is the polymer volume fraction, which, for undiluted systems, may be replaced by the inverse of the reduced volume $\tilde{V}$, the ratio of the actual volume to the hard-core volume V^*.

Theory suggests[6, 10, 12, 17] that the ratio $\epsilon_{an}/\epsilon_{iso}$ of the orientation-dependent energy to the isotropic intermolecular energy for liquids is proportional to the square of the ratio $\Delta\alpha/\bar{\alpha}$ of the anisotropy of polarizability to the mean polarizability. The following relationship[18] may be used for an evaluation of T^*

$$kT^* \approx -0.05\bar{V}(\Delta\alpha/\bar{\alpha})^2\epsilon_{iso} \tag{4}$$

A few authors[10, 12, 18, 19] have used such an approach, obtaining $\Delta\alpha$ from depolarized Rayleigh scattering data, $\bar{\alpha}$ from the refractive index using the Lorentz-Lorenz relation, and ϵ_{iso} from the equation of state theory.[20] The limits of the rather approximative constant in eq. (4) have been discussed by Irvine and Flory.[18] $\tilde{V}$ may be obtained from the relationship[21]

$$\tilde{V} = \left[\frac{\gamma T}{3(1 + \gamma T)} + 1\right]^3 \tag{5}$$

where γ is the cubic expansion coefficient below the nematic–isotropic transition temperature T_{NI}. Alternatively, T^* may be derived from liquid crystal theory, once values of T_{NI}, X, and $\tilde{V}$ are known. For instance, according to the Maier-Saupe[6] (MS) theory, which considers only soft interactions[18]

$$T^* = 4.54T_{NI}\left(\tilde{V}_{NI}^2/X\right) \tag{6}$$

Suitable theoretical relationships for calculating T^* using the Flory-Ronca[13] (FR) theory, which includes both soft and hard interactions, and the Flory-Irvine theory,[21] which considers the effect of $\tilde{V}$, are illustrated in Fig. 1[22] (cf. also Chapter 4).

Table 1 includes experimental data for several LMWLC's (these data have also been used for a different analysis in Chapter 4). The variation of T_{NI} with X is displayed in Fig. 2. The following homologous series are included.

$(p\text{-P})$ $n = 4, 5, 6$

1

$(p\text{-HBA})$ $n = 3, 4, 5$

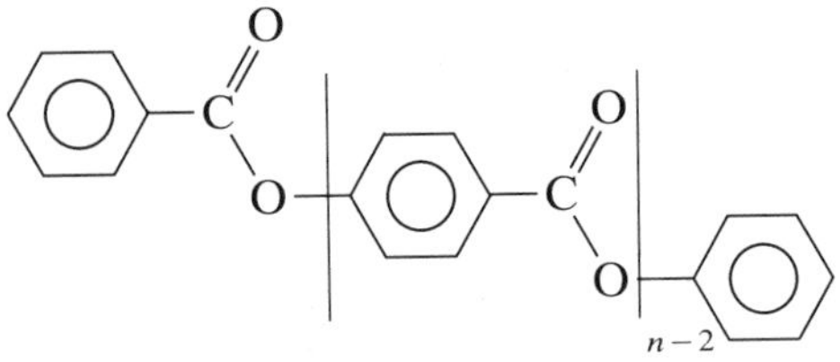

2

$(p\text{-HBAH})$

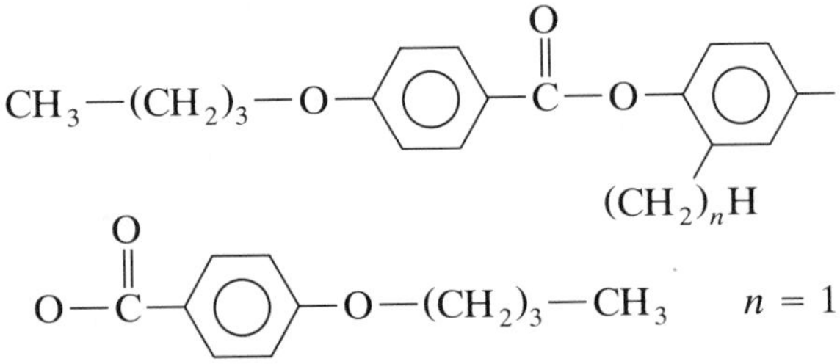

$n = 1, 2, 3, 4, 11$

3

For the p-phenylenes[18, 21] and the p-oxybenzoate[19] series, T^* parameters and reduced volumes were directly measured according to Eqs. (4) and (5), respectively. These T^* values are compared with those calculated from the FR and MS theories (Fig. 1 and Eq. 6). For the p-HBAH series no such comparison can be done and X was assumed to decrease with n due to an increase of the diameter. Although a more rigorous account of the role of sidechains is required (cf. Fig. 15 of Chapter 4), the approximation may not greatly affect the relative values of calculated T^* reported in Table 1. Data for B-4 and MBBA[24] are also included.

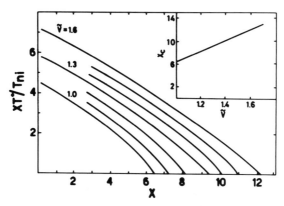

FIGURE 1

XT^*/T_{NI} vs. axial ratio at given value of reduced volume $\tilde{V}$. The inset shows the minimum axial ratio which stabilizes the mesophase at each $\tilde{V}$, when $T^*/T_{NI} = 0$. Calculations performed using Flory-Ronca and Flory-Irvine theories. (Reproduced with permission from Ref. 22.)

Table 1
Soft and Hard Interaction for LMWLC

Nematogen	T_{NI}, (K)	X	$\tilde{V}(T_{NI})$	T^* (K)[b] from $\Delta\alpha$	T^* (K)[c] from FR	T^* (K)[d] from MS
p-P[18, 21]						
4	523	3.9	1.38	440	573	1156
5	691	4.8	1.50	580	630	1470
6	838	5.5	1.56	—	650	1680
p-HBA[19]						
3	373	3.8	1.22	140	343	664
4	527	5.1	1.28	160	316	769
5	737	6.4	1.36	168	306	967
p-HBAH[23]						
1	476	3.6	$\langle 1.0 \rangle$	—	330	600
2	431	3.4	$\langle 1.0 \rangle$	—	329	575
3	399	3.2	$\langle 1.0 \rangle$	—	336	566
4	383	3.1	$\langle 1.0 \rangle$	—	346	561
11	344	3.0	$\langle 1.0 \rangle$	—	332	520
[a]B-4[24]	529	5.2	$\langle 1.0 \rangle$	—	125.	462
MBBA[24]	319	4.3	$\langle 1.0 \rangle$	—	140	337

[a]$C_6H_5CO(OC_6H_4CO)_2OC_6H_5$.

[b]From Eq. (4).

[c]From Fig. 1.

[d]From Eq. (6).

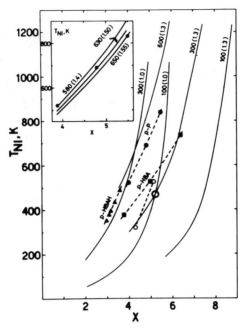

FIGURE 2

Experimental data of Table 1 showing T_{NI} vs. X for the series p-P, p-PBA, p-HBAH, B4, and MBA. Full lines are the theoretical expectations deduced from the relationships plotted in Fig. 1 at given T^* and $\tilde{V}$. The inset shows a particular selection of T^* and $\tilde{V}$ values enabling representation of the data for series p-P.

A peculiarity of the data collected in Table 1 is that T^* obtained from the anisotropy of polarizability is smaller and does not increase with X as rapidly as is the case with values calculated from the Maier-Saupe theory. It is not possible, therefore, to interpret the increase of T_{NI} with X solely on the basis of soft interaction. Instead, there are instances in which soft interactions stay constant (p-HBA series) and the increase in T_{NI} with X may be assumed to reflect the corresponding increase of hard interaction. The modest increase with X of the segment's mean interaction energy observed with the p-P series could be attributed to differences in the interactions of the two terminal phenyl groups and intermediate phenylene residues.[21] These effects should disappear when n is further increased.

On the other hand, the LMWLC's literature shows many examples of nematogens having similar axial ratios and quite different T_{NI} (cf. also Chapter 7). For instance, the H—$[C_6H_4]_5$—H (p-P5) compound in Table 1 can be compared with B-4, having similar X. There is a significant difference in T^* and this seems to be the basis for the difference in T_{NI} ($\tilde{V}$ was not measured for B-4; upward revision of the assumed value $\tilde{V} = 1$ to

1.3 would increase T^* to ~ 310 K, still far smaller than the value for p-P5). Thus, it appears that instances exist in which we can distinguish the independent roles of hard and soft interactions. Data on elastic constants (Chapter 9) also support the prevailing role of hard interactions. Unfortunately, however, direct measurements of T^* and $\tilde{V}$ are admittedly scarce, preventing a more convincing verification.

The accuracy of the Flory-Ronca theory in reproducing the observed trends is rather good. However, actual values of T^* derived from theory are smaller than those estimated from $\Delta\alpha$. The main problem in this type of comparison lies on the constant in Eq. (4), which has been assumed to be 0.05 on the basis of semiquantitative arguments[18, 19] but may vary between 0.02 and 0.16. The FR theory is also defective in the prediction of the order parameter (cf. Chapter 4). Alternative theories for the superimposition of soft and hard interactions may also be expected to be qualitatively in line with experiment, but a too strict quantitative analysis may again be deceiving.

The theoretical derivation has the merit of directing insight into isotropic interactions that adjust the density of the system. Its role, which may be appreciated using the Flory-Ronca theory, is of general validity (and may also be described in terms of external pressure[5]). For instance, the T^* value (630 K) reported for p-P5 at $\tilde{V} = 1.50$ would drop to ~ 230 K if the correction had been neglected (i.e., $\tilde{V} = 1$). On the other hand, inclusion of $\tilde{V}$ reduces T_{NI} at constant T^* as shown in Fig. 11 of Chapter 4. Further, note the inset in Fig. 2, which shows how the T_{NI} vs. X dependence is affected. To reproduce the latter dependence for the p-P series one must place the data for each homolog on a theoretical T_{NI} vs. X curve calculated, using the data in Fig. 1, for a particular value of $\tilde{V}$ and of T^*.

The curves in Fig. 2 suggest a "divergency," which, for each $\tilde{V}$, announces the so-called "critical axial ratio" (X^c), a noteworthy feature of all theories dealing with hard interaction[5, 24, 25] that is, of course, absent in the Maier-Saupe approach.[26] The value of X^c predicted by Flory and Ronca when $T^*/T_{NI} = 0$ increases with $\tilde{V}$ (inset in Fig. 1), being ~ 6.4 at $\tilde{V} = 1$ and ~ 12.2 at $\tilde{V} = 1.6$. Lower bounds are predicted by virial[5] and cubic lattice[16] theories (cf. Section 2.2). A corollary of the existence of a critical axial ratio is the existence of a range of "absolute stability" (i.e., $T_{NI} \to \infty$) for the nematic phase when $X > X^c$.

The evidence, discussed above, of independent contributions of soft and hard interactions, and the trend of data in Fig. 2 support the contention that X^c, and absolute stability, may be reached when n is further increased. However, a reliable determination of X^c may not be an easy task. Since T_{NI} is affected by $\tilde{V}$ and by X, constant volume measurements on sharp oligomer fractions are preferred. Also, the divergency could be more easily followed (cf. Fig. 2) with oligomers having low T^*. The data for series p-P and p-HBA fitted to the Flory-Ronca theory suggest values of X^c in line with the inset in Fig. 1 (e.g., $X^c \approx 10$ and ≈ 8 for p-P4 and p-HBA3, respectively). However, as stated above, the latter theory appears to overestimate T^*. Alternative approaches for determining X^c by back extrapolation of data corresponding to $X > X^c$ are discussed in Section 2.2.

As we proceed from oligomers to polymers, retention of a finite T_{NI} can be now be anticipated to be assisted by chemical modifications that limit an increase of the axial ratio (as is the case of segmented polymers), by free volume and dilution effects, as well as by conformational alterations causing large and negative dX/dT.

2.2. Polymer Melts

It is not the objective of this chapter to present a survey of the many chemical structures that have been reported to exhibit liquid crystallinity in both melts and solutions. These may be found in a few recent reviews[1, 27, 28] (a survey of the segmented polymers is included in Chapter 7). The field stability of undiluted mesophases is limited by the melting temperature T_m (T_{KS} or T_{KN}) and by the isotropization temperature T_i or T_{NI}. Sometimes, a glass rather than a melting temperature may be observed, and the isotropization temperature may not be reached. The concept of a "degree of liquid crystallinity" has not meet with success, molecular weight (MW) and compositional distributions being involved in those cases in which coexistence of isotropic and LC phases was reported.

As we increase the degree of polymerization (DP) of rigid mesogens (e.g., the p-HBA series, **2**) not only T_{NI} but also T_m increase, and it is more difficult to study the mesophase. For instance, all aromatic homopolyesters such as poly(p-oxybenzoate) (PHBA) (**2**), or poly(1, 4-phenylene terephthalate) (PPT) (**4**)

| 2 | 4 |

exhibit melting points of $\sim 600°C$ by fast ($80°C$ min^{-1}) differential scanning calorimetry (DSC).[28] Due to lack of solvents, chemical modification must then be used to lower T_m, without destroying the mesophase. Neglecting the use of flexible aliphatic spacers (segmented homopolyesters are considered in Chapter 7), the preferred approaches are substitution on the aromatic rings, copolymerization, and use of special units.

Asymmetric substitution with small halogens or alkyl groups up to four carbon atoms at the hydroquinone moiety leads to a T_m on the order of $400°C$.[29] However, for poly(2-n-alkyl-1,4-phenylene terephthalates) having hexyl to dedecyl substituents, T_m as low as $217°C$ were reported.[30] Also very effective is the substitution achieved in poly(phenyl-1,4-phenylene terephthalate) (5)[31, 32] (PPHT)

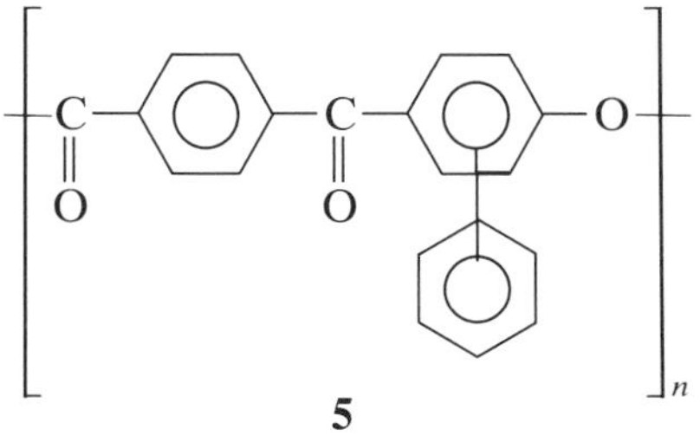

5

with T_m down to 340°C. Use of two acids (e.g., terephthalic and 4, 4'-biphen-yldicarboxylic) in addition to the substitution on hydroquinone leads to further reduction of T_m due to a conventional copolymerization effect.[29] Unsubstituted copolymers of type (7)[33]

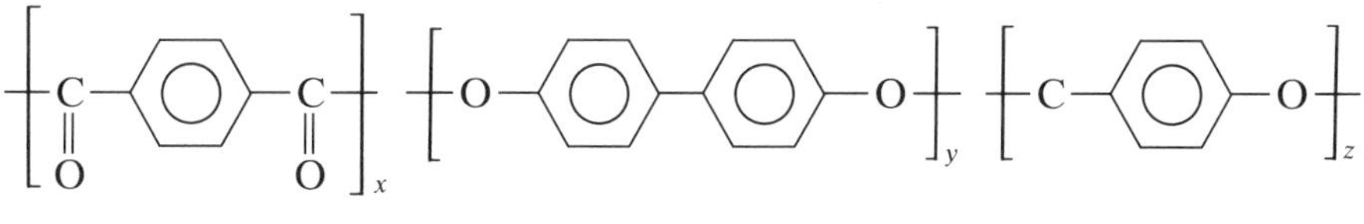

6

had T_m in the order of 380°C, and have been considered for applications.[33, 34]

Special monomers that reduce T_m include those capable of introducing a rigid kink such as m-hydroxybenzoic acid,[29] or kinked monomers such as 4,4'-oxydibenzoic acid[35] (7). Moreover, monomers such as 3,4'-dihydroxy benzophenone (8)[36] and, particularly, 2,6-oriented naphthalene derivatives (9)[37] have been recently used for processable LCP's.

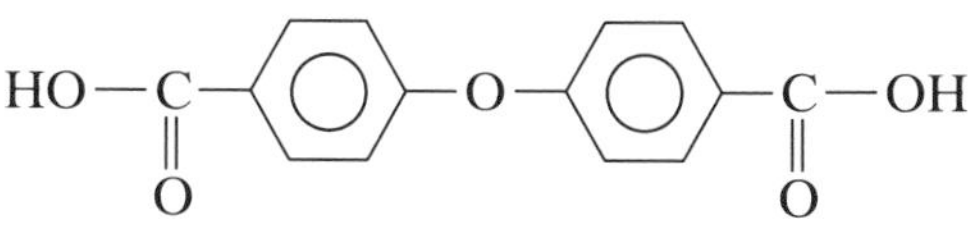

7 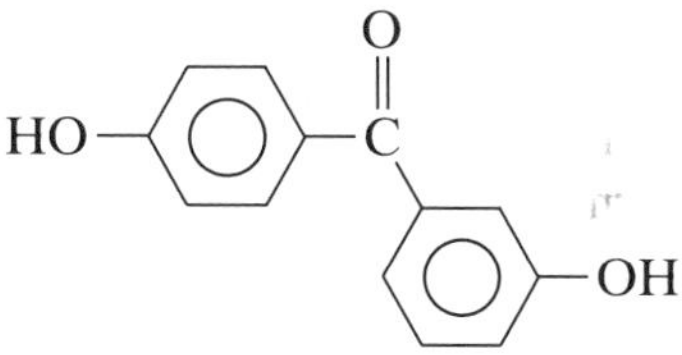   **8**

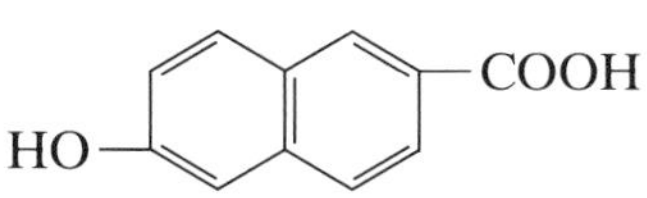

9

In the above examples the reduction of T_m may be attributed to conventional copolymerization and internal copolymerization effects and to specific alterations of chain conformation and diameter that prevent efficient packing in the crystalline state. The latter effects should also play a role in the stability of the mesophase. However, since T_{KN} is already very high, exploration of T_{NI} at still larger temperatures was not generally attempted (it is T_{NI}, not T_m, that is needed for verification of theoretical predictions). An exception is the case of PPHT (structure **5**) for which by fast DSC a T_{NI} temperature of $\sim 460°C$ was reported.[38, 39]

In addition to all aromatic polyesters, other polymeric mesogens form anisotropic melts. Cellulose derivatives and poly(n-hexyl isocyanate) (PHIC), which are usually studied as lyotropic systems (Section 3), also exhibit a measurable T_{NI} in the undiluted state. For instance, T_{NI} for cellulose derivatives is between 180° and 210°C, while for PHIC a value of $\sim 180°C$ was reported (cf. Table 2).[40-44] Moreover, T_{NI} was found to increase slightly with MW, asymptotic values being attained at MW $\sim 400,000$ (equivalent to ~ 70 persistence lengths, q), for cellulose derivatives,[45, 46] and at MW $\sim 200,000$ for PHIC[41] ($\sim 15q$).

We can now compare the above behavior with theories specifically developed for polymers. On the basis of the theory for rigid oligomers discussed in the preceding section, we should expect T_{NI} to stay above the measurable range if $X > X^c$. Polymer theories that use hard potentials for steric interaction do predict a critical axial ratio above which the mesophase is absolutely stable. On the other hand, the very concept of X^c is absent in theories based on a soft potentials for steric interaction.[25] Polymer theories will be more extensively discussed in connection with lyotropic systems in Section 3. Flory's theory[8] (cf. Eq. 7) yields the result that for undiluted rods $X^c = 6.4$ (the limit of the theory used in Section 2.1), and for undiluted freely jointed chains[40] $X^c = 6.7$. These values refer to dense packing and will be *increased* by free volume as discussed in Section 2.1.

Onsager's virial theory[7] cannot be extrapolated as such to concentrated solutions and melts. However, extrapolation is possible using an approach that essentially decouples orientational and translational degrees of freedom and that yields $X^c = 3.25$ for the freely jointed chain and $X^c = 50$ for the wormlike chain. Intermediate values are predicted for randomly broken worms (cf. Section 3). These values refer to minimal external pressure (with a small contribution of anisotropic interaction amounting to $\sim 10\%$ of the total interactions energy) and are *decreased* by increasing density. Comparison of the predictions of the two theories suggests that $X^c = 6.4$ of the lattice theory might be too large a number since even a smaller anisotropy should prevent formation of the isotropic phase for athermal rods at dense packing. Monte Carlo calculations appear to support the lower figure of the virial theory.[47]

While a considerable indetermination on the value of X^c exists, the above theories predict that for $X > X^c$, T_{NI} should diverge. For $X < X^c$, T_{NI} should be finite and, in principle, could be calculated a priori if the intensities of isotropic and anisotropic interactions were known.[5] Since finite T_{NI} were observed for such rigid polymers as PPHT (Table 2), one should

Table 2

Temperature Dependence of Persistence Length and Axial Ratio at T_{NI}[a]

System	Ref.	$d_{25°C}$, (Å)	T (°C) (range)	$\dfrac{d\ln q}{dT}$ (deg^{-1})	$T\left(\dfrac{d\ln q}{dT}\right)$	T_{NI} (°C)	$\left(\dfrac{2q}{d}\right)_{T_{NI}}$	T^* (K)
PPHT–DB + CP	38,39	5.5	25–140	−0.0038	−1.35	460	4.9	(217)
PHIC–1-CN	40	10.3	25–111	−0.011	−3.7	184	7.3[b]	0
PHIC–1-CN	40	10.3	25–111	−0.011	−3.7	184	7.6	0
PHIC–1-CN	40	16.4	25–111	−0.011	−3.7	184	4.1[b]	(235)
PHIC–1-CN	40	16.4	25–111	−0.011	−3.7	184	4.3	(210)
PHIC–toluene	41	10.3	25–99	−0.011	−3.6	180	12.9	0
PHIC–toluene	41	16.4	25–99	−0.011	−3.6	180	6.8	0
CA–DMAc	42	8.1	25–110	−0.007$_8$	−2.6	—	—	—
HPC–DMAc	43	10.4	25–104	−0.005	−1.7	210	4.8	(160)
APC–DMPh	44	12.0	25–150	−0.004$_5$	−1.6	182	4.5	(170)

[a]Reproduced from Ref. 22. Polymers: PPHT, poly(phenyl-1, 4-phenylene terephthalate); PHIC, poly(n-hexyl isocyanate); CA, cellulose acetate; HPC, hydroxypropylcellulose; APC, acetoxypropylcellulose. Solvents: DB + CP = 1 : 1 mixture of O-dichlorobenzene and p-chlorophenol; 1-CN, 1-chloronaphthalene; DMAc, N, N-dimethylacetamide; DCA, dichloroacetic acid; DMPh, dimethyl phthalate.

[b]The effect of the T dependence of d is included only in these entries. $d\ln(2q/d)/dT = -0.014$. In all other cases $d_T = d_{25°C}$.

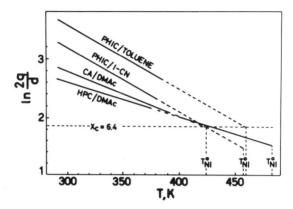

FIGURE 3
Temperature dependence of the axial ratio of the Kuhn segment
for HPC in DMAc,[43] CA in DMAc,[42] PHIC in 1-CN ($d = 10.3$ Å),[40]
PHIC in toluene ($d = 16.4$ Å).[41] (Reproduced with permission from
Ref. 22.)

conclude that thermal expansion effects and/or a temperature dependence
of the axial ratio are involved. Evaluation of data at constant volume would
be desirable. Yet, the analysis of role of $\tilde{V}$ in Section 2.1 (Fig. 1) suggests
that thermal expansion on X^c might not play a controlling role (within the
context of hard interactions). Thus, the temperature dependence of the
actual axial ratio has to be introduced.

Table 2 includes dilute solution data for the temperature coefficient of
the persistence length[48] q for PPHT, PHIC, and cellulose derivatives. Accounting also for the temperature dependence of the chain diameter, these
data are used for the plot in Fig. 3 of the axial ratio of the Kuhn segment
($2q/d$) vs. temperature. Extrapolation of $2q/d$ at the corresponding T_{NI} is
indicated in Fig. 3 and in Table 2. It appears that these independently
measured axial ratios at T_{NI} (4 ÷ 13) are compatible with the critical axial
ratios for the rod and the Kuhn model mentioned above. They appear to be
certainly smaller than those expected for the persistent chain. These results
allow an interesting interpretation of T_{NI}. The latter is simply the temperature at which the axial ratio that pertains to a semirigid chain has decreased
to a value at which hard interactions alone are not sufficient for supporting
the mesophase. The concept of a critical axial ratio gains support from this
interpretation. One could attempt an evaluation of T^* from the axial ratios
at T_{NI} using the approach in Section 1.1. This approach leads to the T^*
values included in Table 2. However, the approach is valid for oligomers and
is based on the debatable 6.4 value for X^c.

The observed small increase of T_{NI} with MW might not be easily
reconciled with theories that predict a divergence of T_{NI} when $X \gg X^c$.
However, it has been shown that for wormlike chains the self-consistent field

associated with the mesophase can generate a cooperative increase of the effective axial ratio (cf. Chapters 3 and 5) which increases with chain length L. Also the Ronca-Yoon theory (Section 3.1) predicts that T_{NI} will diverge or reach a plateau when L increases, depending whether the axial ratio of a limiting persistence length is, respectively, larger or smaller than 4.5. In fact, due to the large dq/dT we do expect small axial ratios or large L/q at T_{NI}.

It thus appears that a satisfactory interpretation of the observed trends may be made within the context of theories based on hard interactions provided a temperature coefficients is introduced for q. This is not an ad hoc assumption since the latter is independently measured. However, dq/dT is obtained in diluted solutions and its application to anisotropic melts may be questioned (the correlation is shown to be valid in the case of isotropic melts[49]).

A quite different interpretation of thermotropicity is given by Ten Bosch et al.,[25,50] who use a soft potential of the Maier-Saupe type and a wormlike chain model. This potential is essentially attractive but also includes a soft repulsive component (the latter was instead emphasized by Parson[51]). The T_{NI} is now basically controlled by soft interaction, and its a priori calculation is not simple. However, since no hard interaction is involved, T_{NI} should not diverge as MW is increased[26] but increase at first and than reach a finite limit. The effect is attributed to an increase of soft attraction due to efficient contacts over chain lengths only a few persistence lengths long.[52] The increase of T_{NI} with MW is also evident for segmented polymers[53-57] and is further discussed in Chapter 7. The Ten Bosch et al. theory yields the Maier-Saupe result (Eq. 6) in the limit $L/q \to 0$. Also included was a screening of quadrupolar interaction associated with a change from rigid to semirigid conformation which should occur at larger MW when q increases. These predictions appear to be in partial agreement with the observed trend of T_{NI} vs. MW (cf. Fig. 2 of Chapter 5).

Again is to be stressed that the relevance of hard vs. soft repulsions for the description of thermotropicity is mitigated in practical cases by the isotropic component. However, if large dq/dT are a general feature, a divergency of T_{NI} with MW might never be observed for polymers, even under constant volume conditions.

3. MESOGEN + SOLVENT SYSTEMS

The main features of an experimental phase diagram of a mesogenic polymer dissolved in a conventional solvent are schematized in Fig. 4.[58] In the vast majority of cases the transition from the isotropic to anisotropic phase is bridged by the narrow biphasic region, characterized by the conjugated polymer volume fractions v_2^i and v_2^a, and within which fractionation is occurring for polydisperse polymers. The narrow region may run almost parallel to the T axis or bend and possibly hit the axis ($v_2 = 1$) describing

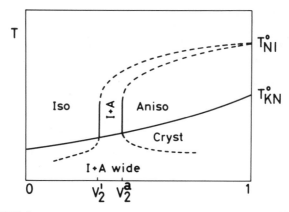

FIGURE 4

Schematic representation of the experimental features of phase diagrams for binary LCP – solvent systems.

undiluted systems at a finite T_{NI}°. In the latter case the system is both lyotropic and thermotropic. Some investigators report a wide region occurring at low temperature. However, the low-temperature boundary is often represented by the solubility line. We now discuss details of the diagrams for various systems, and their theoretical representation.

Theories used for lyotropic systems differ in their modeling of chain conformation and intersegmental interaction. In particular, continuous flexibility is considered by Khokhlov, Semenov, and Odijk[59-61] (KSO) and by Ten Bosch et al.,[50] while rodlike behavior is considered by Onsager[7] and by Flory.[24, 62] A hard + soft potential is generally used for the anisotropic intersegmental interaction, with the exception of Ten Bosch et al., who use only a soft potential. Isotropic interaction is added through a soft term of the van Laar form.[24]

3.1. Role of Chain Length and Flexibility

The combined role of chain length and flexibility may be appreciated in Fig. 5, illustrating the isothermal MW dependence of the critical concentration v_2^i for selected systems. Shown in parentheses are the corresponding persistence lengths. Fractionated and unfractionated samples are included. Within each system v_2^i decreases with MW. However, some scatter is exhibited by v_2^i vs. q. We can apply to these data the theoretical analyses based on the models of rod, freely jointed (Kuhn for simplicity), and various wormlike chains. Due to specific characteristics of the theory, the rod model should be restricted to systems with large q and low MW [e.g., poly(γ-benzyl-L-glutamate) (PBLG); poly(p-benzamide) (PBA); schizophyllan]. Similarly, the Kuhn model should only be applied to the limiting behavior exhibited at large MW, particularly

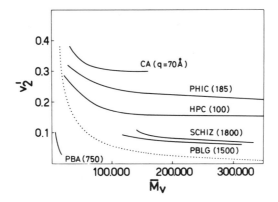

FIGURE 5
Variation in $\overline{M}_V$ of the critical polymer volume fraction at room temperature for cellulose acetate in DMAc,[42] PHIC in dichloromethane,[63] HPC in dichloroacetic acid,[43] PBLG in m-cresol[64] and dioxane,[65] PBA in DMAc[66] and in H_2SO_4,[67] schizophyllan in H_2O[68] (the corresponding persistence lengths are in parentheses). The dotted line is the prediction of Eq. (7) assuming an axial ratio corresponding to the length of the whole HPC molecule. (Adapted with permission from Ref. 22.)

for chains that may exhibit sudden but infrequent deviations from an extended conformation [e.g., cellulose acetate (CA); hydroxypropylcellulose (HPC); acetoxypropylcellulose (APC)].[69] Finally the classical worm model, representing a gradual accumulations of small conformational deviations, could be applied to the whole range of MW and q values investigated. Poly(n-hexyl isocyanate) (PHIC) is considered a wormlike chain although sites for occasional helix reversal have been postulated.[70]

3.1.1. ROD AND KUHN MODELS

Figure 6 shows the application of the rod model to rigid molecules restricting consideration to low v_2 and low MW for which the contour length L is smaller or comparable with $2q$, the size of the Kuhn segment. Experimental data similar to those in Fig. 5 are now plotted vs. the axial ratio X. The theoretical lines are those predicted by the simple expressions

$$v_2^i = \frac{8}{X}\left(1 - \frac{2}{X}\right) \approx \frac{6.4}{X} \quad \text{(lattice)} \qquad (7)$$

$$v_2^i \approx \frac{3.3}{X} \quad \text{(virial)} \qquad (8)$$

given by Flory[8] and Onsager[7] for athermal systems ($T^* = 0$, $\chi = 0$). Figure 6

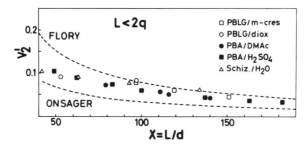

FIGURE 6

Critical polymer – volume fraction vs. axial ratio $X = L / d$ at room temperature for PBLG (d = 15.6 Å) in m-cresol[64] and in dioxane,[65] PBA (d = 5 Å) in DMAc + 3% LiCl[72] and in H_2SO_4,[67] and schizophyllan (d = 16.7 Å) in H_2O.[68] Broken lines are theoretical predictions from Eqs. (7) and (8).

clearly shows that experimental data tend to fall between the two theoretical curves, but the deviation from either is usually within a factor 2.

Before commenting on the performance of these theories let us consider in Figure 7 the applications of the Kuhn model[62,71] to data in the high-MW range and low q, when $L \ll 2q$. We select limiting v_2^i values (i.e., plateau in Fig. 5) and use Eqs. (7) and (8), but replace X with $X_K = 2q/d$, the axial ratio of the Kuhn segment (relevant q data are collected in Table 3). Moreover, for the freely jointed chain the constant in Eqs. (7) and (8) is, respectively, 6.7[41] and 3.25.[59] Both Fig. 6 and Table 3 show that most

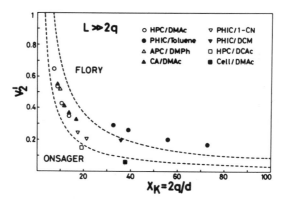

FIGURE 7

Limiting values of v_2^i (data at several temperatures) vs. axial ratio of the Kuhn segment for cellulosic derivatives and PHIC (d = 10.3 Å). Data from Table 2 and Refs. 63, 43, 41, 40, and 44. Broken lines are theoretical predictions from Eqs. (7) and (8) with $X_K = 2q / d$. (Reproduced with permission from Ref. 22.)

Table 3
Data for the Application of the Kuhn Model[a]

System	Ref.	d (Å)	q (Å)	$2q/d$	$v^i_{2,\,exp}$	$v^i_{2,\,theor}$[b]	$v^i_{2,\,theor}/v^i_{2,\,exp}$[b]
HPC–DMAc	73	10.4	70	13.5	0.35	0.52	1.5
HPC–DCA	43	10.4	100	19.2	0.15	0.38	2.5
CA–DMAc	42	8.1	70	17.3	0.33	0.42	1.3
APC–DMPh	44	12.0	60	10.0	0.52	0.68	1.3
PHIC–DCM	63	10.3	185	35.9	0.20	0.21	1.0
PHIC–toluene	63	10.3	375	72.8	0.17	0.11	0.7
PHIC–toluene	41	16.4	310	37.8	0.17	0.20	1.2
PHIC–1-CN[a]	40	10.3	110	21.4	0.21	0.34	1.6
PHIC–1-CN[a]	40	16.4	95	11.6	0.21	0.60	2.8
Cell–DMAc + LiCl	74,75	5.8	(252)	(86.9)	0.06	(0.09)	(1.5)

[a]Reproduced from Ref. 22. All data at 25°C, except for PHIC–1-CN (90°C).
[b]Calculated for the lattice model, Eq. (7).

experimental data again fall between the theoretical prediction of the lattice and virial theory. An exception is intentionally shown for the system PHIC–toluene to point out that considerable indetermination may arise from the value of the chain diameter d. For PHIC, upper and lower bounds for d are, respectively,[63] 16.4 and 10.3 Å. The former value would cause data points to fall between the two theoretical curves, as shown by the $v^i_{2,\,theor}/v^i_{2,\,exp}$ ratios in Table 3. The data for cellulose–DMAc + LiCl included in Table 3 will be considered in Section 3.5 because there is definite evidence of molecular association.

From the above analysis it appears that both lattice and virial theories for rods and freely jointed chains are rather good if an indetermination smaller than a factor of 2 can be accepted. In view of the indetermination on q and d,[22] this conclusion would not seem to be unacceptable. The treatment of partial rigidity is, of course, not a satisfactory one since the Kuhn model treats the chain as a collection of disassembled rods having the size of a statistical segment. The intermediate flexibility regime, and values of v^i_2 larger than the limiting value, cannot be represented. That a change of regime from rod to wormlike chain occurs on increasing L/q is suggested by the dotted line in Fig. 5 and by elastic constant and viscosity data (cf. Chapter 9).[76]

From Figs. 6 and 7 it appears that v^i_2 predicted by the virial theory is always the *lowest bound* ($v^i_{2,\,theor}/v^i_{2,\,exp} < 1$). It has long been recognized that virial theory cannot be expected to be valid at high concentration due to its limitation to the second virial coefficient and to the nonconvergence if the virial series. Recently, Itou et al.[77] determined the variation of the chemical potential of the solvent with the concentration of PHIC in toluene and concluded that even at the relatively low v^i_2 values observed for this system higher virial terms cannot be neglected. However, introduction of higher virial terms may be expected to decrease $v_{2,\,\text{theor}}^i$ further, thus worsening the agreement with experimental data. In fact, the maximum excluded volume (hence the virial coefficients) decreases with increasing concentration[78] (for two rods the decrease is from L^2d in dilute solution to Ld^2 at dense packing; for three rods the corresponding decrease is from $L^3d^3 \ln L/d$ to L^2d^4). That the introduction of higher virial terms decreases $v_{2,\,\text{theor}}^i$ is supported by calculations due to Odijk,[61] and by extension of virial theory to concentrated solutions using the decoupling approximation.[60, 51] From Table I of Ref. 60 we derive that the constant in Eq. (8) (~ 3.3 at very low v_2) decreases to ~ 2.4 at $v_2 \approx 0.5$.

Limitations of the lattice theory have also been pointed out. A central point remains the oversimplification of Flory's lattice model,[8] not surmounted by the exact treatment of the orientational distribution, the inclusion of free volume and soft anisotropic interaction[24] (cf. also Chapter 4). The observation that this theory provides an upper bound for experimental data ($v_{2,\,\text{theor}}^i/v_{2,\,\text{exp}}^i > 1$) is not easily justified. Free volume would increase $v_{2,\,\text{theor}}^i$, and T^* decrease it. However, in solution these effects are not so important (cf. Section 3.3). Recently it has been suggested[79] that taking polydispersity into account should reduce $v_{2,\,\text{theor}}^i$, thus improving the performance of the lattice over the virial theory.

Other lattice models[16, 80, 81] (cf. discussion in Chapter 5) should not offer a better performance. The insensitivity of the v_2^i vs. X plots in Figs. 6 and 7 upon the detailed chemical structure reveals that steric interactions play the predominant role. Thus, even the addition to the cubic lattice of the energies of internal rotation and of site–site interaction[81] is not warranted.

3.1.2. WORM MODELS

The Khokhlov-Semenov theory,[59, 60] and its elaboration by Odijk,[61] describes the wormlike behavior through a modification of the orientational term which prevents the tangential vector along a segment from escaping the restriction imposed on the director by the nematic field. In the original KSO theory[59, 61] (Chapter 3) the intersegmental interaction term of the free energy of the wormlike chain remained, instead, that given by Onsager for rods within the second virial approximation. Thus, the chain elongates (cf. Fig. 5 of Chapter 3) and loses entropy when it enters the mesophase. This results in a larger v_2^i, and lower order parameter, with respect to rods.

Figure 8 illustrates data of Conio et al.[63, 82] for unfractionated PHIC in toluene and in DCM plotted in a form suggested by the KSO theory

$$v_2^i = \frac{d}{2q} \left[\frac{3.34 + 11.94(L/2q) + 6.34(L/2q)^2}{(L/2q)(1 + 0.586L/2q)} \right] \qquad (9)$$

The plot includes data more recently reported by Itou and Teramoto[83] for fractionated PHIC samples in the same solvents. The two sets of data are in

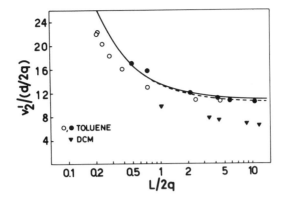

FIGURE 8

v_2^i vs. the ratio of contour length to Kuhn segment for the data of Conio et al.[63] for PHIC in toluene (●) and in DMC (▼) at room temperature. $d = 12.5$ Å, $q_{tol} = 375$ Å, $q_{DCM} = 185$ Å, $M_L = 63.5$ daltons Å. Data of Itou and Teramoto[83] (○) for PHIC in toluene at 25°C are included. The solid line is the prediction of Eq. (9). (Adapted with permission from Ref. 82, copyright Gordon & Breach Science Publishers, and Ref. 83, Copyright Am. Chem. Soc.)

excellent agreement and, in the case of toluene, fall close to the theoretical line with the assumption of a suitable (12.5 Å) diameter (similar values of q were used by the two groups of investigators). It is clear that Eq. (9) correctly represents the trend of the whole MW dependence of v_2^i, and, in this respect, the worm treatment appears superior to that based on rods (at low MW) and Kuhn models (at large MW). However, the quantitative agreement shown by the data in toluene is an apparent one since data in DCM are not well represented. Again, the indetermination on the diameter would render somewhat deceptive any claim of a strict quantitative agreement (plots with the assignment $d = 10.3$ Å were shown in Ref. 63).

Table 4 shows a more extensive comparison between the KSO theory and data for a variety of systems.[22] The $v_{2,\,theor}^i/v_{2,\,exp}^i$ ratio is often close to 1 and offers a better representation of data corresponding to the most rigid polymers (schizophyllan, PBA, PBLG) than is the case with Flory's theories. However, for more flexible polymers the $v_{2,\,theor}^i/v_{2,\,exp}^i$ ratio is considerably larger than one and the Kuhn model (Table 3) offers a better representation.

The poor performance of the KSO theory at large L/q ratios can only in part be rationalized in terms of the second virial approximation which should fail at the larger v_2^i prevailing with the more flexible systems.[77] In fact, as already pointed out, in a more recent version of the theory, Khokhlov and Semenov[60] have replaced the steric interaction term based on the second virial approximation with an approach related to that used by Parson[51] to extend the virial theory to arbitrary concentration and melts (decoupling approximation).

Table 4
Analysis of KSO Theory[a]

System	Ref.	L (Å)	L/q	$v^i_{2,\,exp}$	$v^i_{2,\,theor}$	$v^i_{2,\,theor}/v^i_{2,\,exp}$
HPC–DMAc	73	2542	36	0.35	0.81	2.3
HPC–DCA	43	2542	25	0.15	0.57	3.8
CA–DMAc	42	2289	33	0.33	0.33	1.9
PHIC–DCM	63	4377	24	0.20	0.31	1.5
PHIC–1-CN	40	4377	40	0.21	0.51	2.4
PHIC–toluene	62	4377	14	0.17	0.18	1.1
PBA–DMAc	72	704	0.94	0.042	0.057	1.4
		582	0.78	0.051	0.062	1.2
		394	0.52	0.072	0.076	1.1
Schizophyllan–H$_2$O	68	2221	1.23	0.062	0.072	1.2
		1559	0.86	0.077	0.083	1.1
		1052	0.58	0.091	0.083	1.0
		701	0.39	0.105	0.126	1.2
PBLG–m-cresol	64	2325	1.55	0.055	0.073	1.3
		1875	1.25	0.070	0.078	1.1
		1500	1.00	0.085	0.084	1.0

[a] Reproduced in part from Ref. 22.

The limiting value (at large MW) obtained for the worm model (given by $v^i_2 = 10.38/X_K$ within the second virial approximation[59] valid in very dilute solutions) decreases to $v^i_2 \approx 8.10/X_K$ using the new approximation valid up to $v_2 \approx 0.4$ (cf. Table III of Ref. 60). If one provisionally accepts the validity of the latter approximation, $v^i_{2,\,theor}$ is expected to decrease by ~ 20% in the concentration range represented in Table 4. However, a significantly larger disagreement is revealed by the $v^i_{2,\,theor}/v^i_{2,\,exp}$ data in the same table.

One possibility suggested by the above analysis is that the KSO theory overestimates the effect of flexibility. This possibility is in line with the observation that the same theory underestimates the order parameter (Section 3.4) and overestimates the critical axial ratio (Section 2.2). A plausible justification is the possibility that wormlike chains with large L/q exhibit, in certain solvents, sudden but infrequent bends, similarly to those mentioned above for cellulosic derivatives.[69, 70] Khokhlov and Semenov[84] have considered the behavior of special models, in particular a randomly broken wormlike chain including sharp bends occurring with some small probability at predetermined sites. A parameter ν characterizes the ratio of the Kuhn segments of a classical wormlike chain and of a chain with rotational isomerism based on segments comprised between predetermined bonds. With respect to the classical wormlike chain, the latter chain exhibits $v^i_{2,\,theor}$ smaller by about a factor 3 (cf. Table IV of Ref. 60), correspondingly larger order parameters, and a smaller critical axial ratio.[5] Thus, it is clear that by arbitrary selecting a proper ν value, virtual agreement between experimental data and theoretical predictions can be achieved (cf., however, Section 3.4).

In conclusion, as far as the representation of experimental data is concerned, the worm treatment and the combined rod + Kuhn treatments each have merits and demerits. In view of the indetermination on parameters much as d and q, the kind of agreement between theory and experiment may have already reached an acceptable level. A controversy remains on the artificiality of the lattice model. On the other hand, the good performance of the KSO theory heavily hinges on the validity of the decoupling approximation and perhaps on deviations from the worm conformation which need to be subjected to independent verification. Mansfield[85] has recently concluded that the hydrodynamic radius and the static structure factor may be very similar for a classical wormlike chain and for a chain incorporating abrupt kinks. Therefore, experimental assessment of special flexibility mechanisms might not be simple.

Ronca and Yoon[86] have also treated a wormlike chain using the lattice framework. They start by objecting to the validity of the classical Kratky-Parod chain, which exhibits a vanishing unperturbed mean-square end-to-end distance $\langle R^2 \rangle$ at infinite temperature. This implies[86] $T(d \ln \langle R^2 \rangle / dT) = -1$, or even smaller temperature coefficients if the bending force constant of the chain decreases with temperature [it is shown in Table 2 that experimental $T(d \ln \langle R^2 \rangle / dT)$ values are indeed smaller than -1]. Ronca and Yoon (RY) propose a chain for which

$$-1 < T\frac{d \ln\langle R^2 \rangle}{dT} < 0 \tag{10}$$

The new feature is that $T(d \ln\langle R^2 \rangle / dT) = 0$ at $T \to \infty$, implying a nonvanishing $\langle R^2 \rangle$ at high enough temperature.[86] This corresponds to a limiting cutoff length L_0, or axial $X_0 = L_0/d$, reflecting the geometrical constraints of bonded and nonbonded interaction at $T \to \infty$.

In the limits of Eq. (10), the RY theory predicts absolute stability $(T_{NI}^\circ \to \infty)$ for a chain having an axial ratio of the cutoff length $L_0/d > 4.5$ and an axial ratio of the contour length $L/d > \sim 100$. One problem with this theory is that a cutoff axial ratios as large as 4.5 may not be realistic. If one tries to enlarge the limits of Eq. (10) to include the large negative values of $T(d \ln\langle R^2 \rangle / dT)$ experimentally measured, one ends up with cutoff axial ratios smaller than 1.[22] This point may not invalidate other features of the theory, however. In fact, in the limit $L_0 \to 0$ the general conclusions of RY are similar to those obtained for the classical wormlike chain by Khokhlov and Semenov (KS).[5] Moreover, the MW dependence of v_2^i for PHIC in both toluene and DCM are rather well represented,[86] and the fitting using the classical limit $T(d \ln\langle r \rangle / dT) = -1$ is far superior to the fitting based on a cutoff length. If one considers that the order parameters predicted by RY are larger than those predicted by KS, it appears that with revision of the issue of the cutoff length, the RY theory may become a very useful tool.

An analysis of the theory by Ten Bosch et al.[50] based on wormlike chains and a soft potential for steric interaction is presented in the next section.

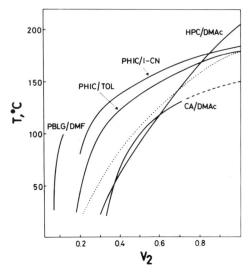

FIGURE 9

Variation of the nematic → isotropic transition temperature with the critical polymer volume fraction v_2^i for PBLG in DMF,[88] HPC in DMAc,[73] CA in DMAc,[42] PHIC in toluene,[41] and PHIC in 1-CN.[40] The dashed line is a theoretical prediction for the Kuhn model[40] fitted to T_{NI}^o and to $d \ln q / d \ln T$ of PHIC in 1-CN. (Reproduced with permission from Ref. 22.)

The experimental behavior of LC polyelectrolytes and relevant theoretical predictions (cf. Chapter 3) have not been assessed adequately. Recent emphasis has been placed on DNA at high ionic strength (0.3 M NaCl).[87] The relevance of the mesophase organization to in vivo assemblies was pointed out (cf. also Chapter 10). Phase diagrams can be considered only tentative, and the condensed counterion cloud complicates the assessment of volume fraction and axial ratios.[87]

3.2. Thermotropicity

The schematic diagram in Fig. 4 suggests a strong dependence upon temperature of the narrow region compositions. The actual behavior of several systems is illustrated in Fig. 9 (for clarity only v_2^i is plotted, but the behavior is that of the narrow region). The smallest thermotropic effect is shown by rigid PBLG,[88] and the largest by PHIC, whose critical v_2^i span the range from ~ 0.19 at 25°C to 1.0 at ~ 180° (T_{NI}^o).[22] Simple thermal expansion of the components could not account for the effect observed.[40]

How can we interpret a thermotropic effect occurring in solutions? Existing theories for the thermotropic effects in melts are discussed in Section 2.2. Since the results in Fig. 9 include melts, but mostly refer to solutions, it is appropriate to analyze in more detail the role of soft interaction on lyotropic systems. Soft interactions are usually attractive and can be either isotropic or anisotropic.[24, 60, 51] An assessment of the role of soft interaction can be made along the lines of theories based on a hard potential for steric interactions. For the characterization of the isotropic interaction we use the Θ temperature or the χ parameters of classical polymer theory (these are more fully discussed in Section 3), and for the anisotropic attractions we use the characteristic temperature T^* (cf. Eq. 2). The effect of χ, or Θ, may be appreciated in the detailed phase diagrams calculated by Flory[24] and Khokhlov and Semenov[5] (using the scheme in Fig. 4, one can merely replace the T axis with a $1/\chi$ axis). The invariable result is that only within the wide region (poor solvents $\chi \rightarrow 0.5$) a temperature dependence of v_2^i is predicted. However, the thermotropic effect observed experimentally (Fig. 9) corresponds to the narrow region and obviously has a trend different from that expected in the wide region (in the construction of the theoretical diagrams, χ parameters have been assumed identical in the two phases; removal of this assumption[58] produces only a very modest curvature of the narrow region toward high concentration).

The anisotropic component of the attractive interaction is generally much smaller than the isotropic one.[60] T^* is reduced to T^*v_2 in the presence of a diluent but still contributes to the stabilization of the mesophase. However, only a very small curvature of the narrow region is predicted,[60, 89] even for large T^*. Thus, it is clear that the curvature observed in Fig. 9 cannot be explained by introducing soft attractions in theories that include hard interactions.

Alternative interpretations are based on a temperature variation of the conformation or of the state of aggregation of the mesogen. The latter possibility has been considered (cf. Section 3.5), but no relationship has yet emerged. The former possibility is instead supported by the negative temperature coefficients of the persistence length measured in dilute solution. These may be related to a temperature dependence of the axial ratios if molecular dispersion prevails, and if essentially the same conformation occurs in nematic and isotropic phases. Table 2 includes $T(d \ln q/dT)$ values for several semirigid systems. The dashed line in Fig. 9 results from using a temperature-dependent Kuhn segment in connection with the lattice model (neglecting soft attractions). The agreement with the experimental trend of the PHIC–1-CN system is rather good, as also observed with PHIC in toluene,[41] CA in DMAc,[42] and HPC in DMAc.[43] Also, in the case of PBLG in DMF, thermotropicity was explained by a conformational effect.[88] The large temperature coefficients of the persistence length cannot be easily explained in terms of rigid or wormlike chains (cf. Eq. 10). They likely result from specific effect associated to alteration in the state of solvation of the chains by highly polar solvents.

An alternative interpretation for the strong dependence of v_2^i upon temperature derives from the theory of Ten Bosch et al.[50] (cf. Section 2.2 and

Chapter 5). They consider wormlike molecules with an elastic bending energy and can include the effect of dq/dT. However, since they use a soft potential for steric repulsion, a strong dependence of v_2^i upon T may be explained primarily by a dilution of soft interaction. The phase diagram illustrated in Fig. 3 of Chapter 5 shows that v_2^i changes with T over a wide composition range according to $v_2^i \approx (T/T_{NI}^\circ)^2$. Inclusion of dq/dT does not essentially modify this trend.[52] On a quantitative basis, this theory predicts values of v_2^i in the order of 0.4 when $T \approx 25°C$ and $T_{NI}^\circ \approx 200°C$ and the dependence of v_2^i upon DP for cellulose derivatives (Fig. 4 of Chapter 5) is well represented. However, the theory could predict an increase of v_2^i with q (cf. Fig. 3b, Chapter 5) which is opposite to the experimental findings (cf. Fig. 7). Also the width of the biphasic gap appears too large (this feature is also evident in theories using a hard potential when, in poor solvents, an effective isotropic attraction between polymer segments occurs). Predicted order parameters are between 0.34 and 0.43, although larger values may be obtained (cf. Eq. 16 of Chapter 5). Experimental values are on the order of 0.8 (Section 3.4). Also the predicted dependence of elastic constants upon DP is not in line with expectations (cf. Chapter 9).

In spite of the above discrepancies, it is interesting that the theory of Ten Bosch et al. can qualitatively reproduce several experimental features (cf. also Section 2.2). This justifies the use of the approximative Maier-Saupe potential for segmental interaction whenever a simple, unsophisticated analysis suffices. However, since the concept of a critical axial ratio is absent, the soft nature of steric repulsion does not seem adequate to describe the role of molecular asymmetry as successfully used by the other theories.

Still another mechanism was suggested by Viney et al.,[90] who reported a strongly bent narrow region for solutions of a polymer composed of alternating rigid units ($X \approx 3 \div 4$) and flexible spacers in the mainchain and in the sidechain. They attributed thermotropicity not to dq/dT for the isolated chain, but rather to the disruption of a cooperative alignment among neighboring rodlike units favored by the selection of extended conformations. Occurrence of anisotropic attraction was essential to their argument. A cooperative increase of the radius of gyration upon entering the mesophase is predicted by most theories of semirigid chains (cf. Chapters 3 and 5). For wormlike chains this elongation may be achieved without serious conformational energy variation. However, for chains endowed of trans–gauche isomerism, and particularly for chains undergoing coil to helix transitions,[91] a significant conformational rearrangement also occurs. The elongation of the flexible spacer in melts of segmented chains was documented by computational studies (cf. Fig. 11 of Chapter 1).[55]

3.3. Biphasic Region, Fractionation

The occurrence of a biphasic gap is a general thermodynamic requirement for phase transition involving two diluted phases.[92] The width of the gap is affected quite significantly by the quality of the solvent within the wide region, but it is almost unaffected by it in the narrow region to which the following considerations are restricted. Within the gap, the volume fraction of isotropic phase Φ changes from $\Phi = 1$ (pure isotropic) to $\Phi = 0$ (pure anisotropic) when the overall polymer volume fraction v_2 is increased. The conjugated compositions v_2^i and v_2^a do not change with Φ if the system is monodisperse. In this case v_2^a/v_2^i is ~ 1.5 and 1.35 according, respectively, to the lattice and virial theories for large X. However, if polydispersity occurs, v_2^i and v_2^a will change with Φ since, as suggested by Eq. (7), partitioning of components with larger (smaller) axial ratio in the anisotropic (isotropic) phase must occur. Moreover, the gap will widen with the disparity in size of the species involved. For a most probable distribution the lattice theory yields v_2^a/v_2^i larger than 2, depending upon the value of $\overline{M}_w$ and Φ.[93] Numerical calculations have also been performed for a Poisson distribution,[94] Gaussian distribution,[95] and bidisperse systems.[96, 97] Maximum width corresponds to the limits $(v_2^a)_{\Phi=0}$ and $(v_2^i)_{\Phi=1}$.

Numerous reports have confirmed the occurrence of fractionation,[66, 97–100] even if less efficient than predicted. For instance, Conio et al.[98] working with a PBA sample of $\overline{M}_w \sim 12,200$, report that, at $\Phi = 0.5$, $\overline{M}_w$ of polymer in the anisotropic phase was $\sim 13,100$ and that in the isotropic phase was $\sim 10,800$. The efficiency varied with the relative volumes of coexisting phases. In line with theoretical expectations,[70] the efficiency of fractionation also decreased[63] with increasing chain length for semirigid polymers such as PHIC, when v_2^i attains a limiting value and is only a function of q not affected by contour length. However, when fractionation was observed, the v_2^a/v_2^i ratio for polydisperse system was usually found[66, 88, 98–100] to be in a range (1.4 ÷ 1.9) close to that expected for monodisperse systems.

There was some doubt about the possibility of determining the maximum width $(v_2^a)_{\Phi=0}/(v_2^i)_{\Phi=1}$ using earlier viscosity and microscope observations.[66, 99, 101] Thus, Conio et al.[98] introduced an analytical technique based on the determination of Φ as a function of the overall v_2 (or the individual v_2^i and v_2^a), and extrapolation at $\Phi = 0$ and $\Phi = 1$. Latest results of these investigations,[79] including measurements at rather low Φ for polydisperse PBA, PBLG, and PHIC, are included in Fig. 10. For PBLG in dioxane data can be represented by a straight line down to $\Phi = 0.05$, and $(v_2^a)_{\Phi=0}/(v_2^i)_{\Phi=1}$ ~ 1.3. For PBA and PHIC an upward curvature is exhibited at low Φ, but still $(v_2^a)_{\Phi=0}/(v_2^i)_{\Phi=1}$ ratios are ~ 1.8 and ~ 1.9, respectively. Although larger than previously reported, these ratios are still much smaller than theoretical predictions for polydisperse rods [for a Gaussian distribution, broken lines 2 and 3 suggest $(v_2^a)_{\Phi=0}/(v_2^i)_{\Phi=1}$ to increase from ~ 2.3 to ~ 8 when $\overline{X}_w/\overline{X}_n$ increases from 1.08 to 1.30].

The behavior of bidisperse systems was investigated for the systems schizophyllan–H_2O[102] and PHIC–toluene.[97] A simple theoretical diagram for bidisperse rods calculated from the lattice theory is shown in Fig. 13 (Section 4.2). Figure 1 of Chapter 3 shows a similar diagram from the virial theory. The experimental diagram for PHIC in toluene has similar general features, but the diagram for schizophyllan in H_2O also included regions of triphasic

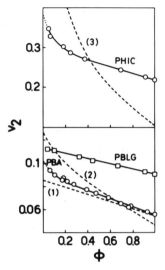

FIGURE 10

Variation of the volume fraction of isotropic phase with the overall polymer volume fraction within the narrow region. Data of Marsano et al.[79] for PBLG ($\bar{M}_w \approx$ 120,000) in dioxane (■), PBA ($\bar{M}_w \approx$ 10,000) in DMAc + 3% LiCl (○), and PHIC ($\bar{M}_w \approx$ 72,000) in benzene. Broken theoretical lines calculated[95] for (1) $X = 150$, $\bar{X}_w / \bar{X}_n = 1.00$; (2) $\bar{X}_n = 1.50$, $\bar{X}_w / \bar{X}_n = 1.08$; (3) $\bar{X}_n = 50$, $\bar{X}_w / \bar{X}_n = 1.30$. (Adapted with permission from Figs. 1 and 2 of Ref. 79, Copyright Gordon & Breach Science Publishers.)

(I–A–A) and biphasic (A–A) equilibria. The Japanese workers attempted to reproduce their data using the lattice theory for rods and the KSO theory for wormlike chains, assuming athermal behavior. In all cases, v_2^i and v_2^a were larger than the experimental ones, and the width gap v_2^a/v_2^i was smaller than predicted. These features are similar to those described above and in Section 3.1. While the lattice theory could predict the existence of regions I–A–A and A–A, the KSO theory could not. However, the latter theory offered a closer representation of the data, both in terms of a closer representation of the data, both in terms of a smaller $v_{2,\,\text{theor}}^i/v_{2,\,\text{exp}}^i$ and of a smaller gap width. In fact, partial flexibility (associated with a hard potential) may significantly contribute to narrowing the gap since for the wormlike chain a v_2^a/v_2^i value of ~ 1.09 was calculated as opposed to ~ 1.34 for rods and 1.50 for Kuhn chains (cf. Chapter 3).

Another possible justification for the smaller than predicted gap width is offered by Flory,[24] who suggests that orientational order may occur faster than partitioning, which is a slow diffusion-controlled process. An alternative possibility is suggested by the inclusion, first proposed by Itou and Teramoto,[102] of enthalpy parameters reflecting a favorable polymer–solvent interaction. For bidisperse but chemically similar polymers, the polymer–polymer interaction parameter χ_{23} (cf. Section 4) vanishes. However $\chi_{13} = \chi_{23}$ may be < 0 in the case of the strongly interacting solvents used to dissolve nematic polymers. Whereas the χ parameter has negligible influence on the width of the narrow region for monodisperse systems, it can reduce the gap width for dispersed systems. An example is given in Fig. 13 (Section 4.2).

3.4. Order Parameter

Studies of the order parameter for rigid molecules in solution have been reported for PBLG[103–107] and for PBA[108] using IR,[105, 106, 109] x-ray,[103] susceptibility,[104] and deuterium NMR[107] techniques. Results afford a more detailed test of the various theories than that based on phase diagrams.[109] These are not, however, simple measurements, and additional studies on fractionated samples[61] are desirable. Several of the techniques used for thermotropic polyesters (Chapter 7) lose sensitivity when a diluent is present. Macroscopic orientation of the director is often a problem.[103, 108] Rubbing and other surface treatments followed by the application of an H field have been used. Some polymers may be easily oriented homeotropically (PBLG), others homogeneously. Intrinsic polymer parameters such as flexibility and MW distribution do play a role and need detailed investigation. Some techniques present specific problems. For instance, IR spectroscopy is critically influenced by the choice of the direction of the transition moment.[106]

For comparison with theoretical predictions, the order parameter $S = 1 - 3/2\langle\sin^2\theta\rangle$ (Eq. 3) is usually measured in the concentration range between v_2^a and the solubility limit avoiding the biphasic region. Lee and Meyer[110] have tabulated values of S as a function of v_2 using the virial theory. In the case of the lattice theory, Flory and Ronca[111] gave relationships (solvable by iteration) between their disorientation parameter $\bar{y}$ and S

$$S = 1 - \left(\frac{3}{2}\right)\left(\frac{f_3}{f_1}\right)$$

$$f_n = \int_0^{\pi/2} \sin^n\theta \exp(-\beta\sin\theta)\, d\theta$$

$$\beta = \frac{4}{\pi}X\ln\left[1 - v_2 - \left(1 - \frac{\bar{y}}{x}\right)\right]$$

$$\bar{y} = \frac{4}{\pi}X\left(\frac{f_2}{f_1}\right)$$

(11)

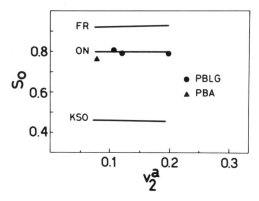

FIGURE 11

Variation of the order parameter S_0 determined by D-NMR at the v_2^a composition with v_2^a for PBLG in DMF at 30°C[107] and PBA in DMAc + 3% LiCl.[108] (Data from Refs. 107 and 108.) Data for PBG refer to three different molecular weights. Horizontal bars indicate levels predicted by the Flory-Ronca, Onsager, and Khokhlov-Semenov-Odijk theories.

where f_n is the $(n-1)$th moment of the distribution, and β governs the orientational distribution function. In the case of the KSO theory, Vroege and Odijk[109] give a value of $S \approx 0.46$ at v_2^a.

In Fig. 11, NMR data for PBLG and PBDG in DMF are compared with the above theoretical predictions.[107] Determined for samples deuterated at the amide hydrogen, S refers to the α-helical axis and is not affected by the sense of spiralization. The order parameter at v_2^a is plotted vs. v_2^a for three samples characterized by different axial ratios. The experimental value of S_0 (~ 0.8, nearly independent of v_2^a) is remarkably close to the prediction of the virial theory.

In the case of PBA, the order parameter was obtained in DMAc + 3% LiCl from the dicroic ratio measured by polarized IR spectroscopy.[108] S was found to increase from 0.76 at v_2^a ($= 0.076$, value shown in Fig. 11) to 0.83 at the solubility limit ($v_2 = 0.094$). These figures are also in line with Onsager's theory, which appears to be correct insofar as orientational distribution is concerned. The latter, however, predicts smaller v_2^a corresponding to the actual axial ratios. As already pointed out, this theory always gives a lower bound for v_2^i and v_2^a.

The lattice theory ($S_0 \approx 0.92$) overestimates the experimental values of S by $\sim 15\%$, whereas the KSO theory ($S_0 \approx 0.46$) underestimates it by $\sim 40\%$ (better is the performance of the Ronca-Yoon theory,[86] but still poorer is the performance of the theory of Ten Bosch et al.,[90] cf. Section 3.2). As expected, the FR and the KSO theories offer a better agreement for the critical concentration. Abe and Yamazaki attributed the overestimation of S_0 by FR to an overestimation of orientational distribution, and suggested a direct experimental elucidation of the latter.

When concentration is increased above v_2^q, the order parameter has been found to increase tending asymptotically to 1. The rate of increase is in line with theoretical predictions by the lattice and the virial theory.[106-108] Only in the case of the PBLG data by Murphy et al.,[103] the experimental value of S has been found to be smaller than 0.8 in a wide concentration range. Its value was estimated from the broadening of the x-ray diffraction streak in dioxane using planar alignment (homeotropic alignment was used by other investigators[105,106]). Kirov et al.[112] had observed that the orientation in homeotropic samples was better than for planar alignment.

The failure of the KSO theory is perplexing. As discussed in Section 3.1, a randomly broken wormlike chain may justify the large $v_{2,\text{theor}}^i / v_{2,\text{exp}}^i$ ratios observed with the most flexible polymers. The order parameter predicted for broken worms could be fitted to the experimental value with an ad hoc choice of the parameter ν.[84] However, for the rigid systems for which S was measured (PBLG and PBA) there seems no need of invoking a deviation from the classical worm conformation. Possibly the rigidity of PBLG is overestimated by the large q values adopted here (1500 Å[107] and 750 Å,[48] respectively; cf. Chapter 2). A problem remains, and its origin is unclear. It has also been considered by Khokhlov in Section 10 of Chapter 3.

3.5. Crystallization, Gelation

The experimental behavior in the low-temperature, wide region of binary systems (cf. Fig. 4) is not well understood. In general, as we proceed toward poorer solvents, the conventional liquid $\rightarrow$ liquid and crystallization equilibria may encroach on the formation of the mesophase. Papkov[113] pointed out that the rates of nucleation are in the order liquid > liquid crystal > crystal and therefore what is observed might not correspond to predictions of equilibrium theories. To complicate matters, a difficult to analyze gel "phase" is a common occurrence.[58,66,88] Theoretical guidelines should nevertheless be used.

The lattice[81] and the decoupling approximation[60] approaches predict that, upon lowering temperature, as the χ_{12} interaction parameter (Eq. 14) increases to slightly positive values revealing attractive isotropic interaction between polymer molecules, there will be a broad separation between the diluted isotropic and concentrated ordered solutions. Moreover, if $X > \sim 50$ there will also be a temperature gap between a critical T_c, at which two anisotropic phases form, and a triple point T_t ($< T_c$), at which the isotropic phase also coexists. These effects are expected at axial ratios large enough that the system is still far above the liquid–liquid θ temperature. Only if X becomes very small ($\sim X^c$) does the wide region occur at temperatures close to θ, and in this case a triple point appears, marking the occurrence of two isotropic and one anisotropic phases.[60]

From the above considerations it appears that if the wide region is gradually and slowly approached from the narrow one, liquid–liquid separation can be avoided. In fact, early report,[88, 114] claimed a verification of the behavior predicted in the wide region by the lattice theory. The formation of a PBLG gel was attributed to spinodal decomposition when the wide region is entered.[88, 115] There is no clear cut evidence for a wide region uncomplicated by gelation (for a possible exception cf. ref. 115[a]).

The superimposition of crystallization and mesophase equilibria was also considered in some detail.[116–118] Phase diagrams were calculated[118] including: (1) the isotropic → LC equilibrium for a freely joined chain exhibiting a temperature-dependent axial ratio, $\chi_{12} > 0$, and $T^* = 0$; (2) the depression of the melting temperature T_{KI}° in isotropic solution; and (3) the depression of the melting temperature T_{KN}° in anisotropic solution. It was shown that in general the wide region becomes metastable due to encroachment of the crystallization equilibria. However, any sluggishness in crystal nucleation would allow the LC precursor to appear first and direct the ensuing crystallization. This mechanism could provide the driving force for the self-assembly of biological fibers and membranes. The texture of the mesophase is often not altered by crystallization.[117]

Crystallization is sometimes involved in the formation of highly swollen gels.[119] Cellulose[120, 120a] and chitin[121] solutions have been shown to gel at concentrations well below those at which the mesophase is usually detected. It is noteworthy that an highly oriented (grandjean) cholesteric texture spontaneously developed within the chitin gel. The concurrent existence of a gel and liquid crystalline order suggested by these results is surprising. Recently[121a] a theory for liquid crystallinity developing within chemically crosslinked networks was formulated. The theory suggests that the critical concentration (within a swollen gel) is not largely affected by the crosslinkages. An extension of this approach to networks having labile junctions would be desirable.

Depending upon preparation, diluted solutions of cellulose in DMAc + LiCl exhibit either a molecular dispersion or stable aggregates consisting of about seven fully extended molecules with a side-by-side organization. In both cases, upon increasing concentration, association equilibria occur.[122] However, as the data in Table 3 indicate, the critical concentration shows a value that is normal for a rigid polymer. Also the correlation with the persistence length (measured in nonaggregated solutions) yields $v_{2,\,\text{theor}}^{i}/v_{2,\,\text{exp}}^{i} \approx 1.5$ in terms of the Kuhn model. The latter value is comparable to values obtained for other systems when aggregation or association was not evidenced. An axial ratio distribution corresponding to associated species might have to be considered.

The possibility that the mesophase is stabilized by aggregated, rather than by molecular, dispersions has been theoretically considered to explain the formation of nematic phases by cylindrical micelles. Above the cmc (critical micelle concentration) linear growth is coupled to alignment in the nematic field, and is controlled by micellar flexibility.[123] The process should be particularly relevant to supermolecular organization. A corresponding process could be envisioned for micellar bilayers on the basis of a theory for large discotic solutes.

4. COMPATIBILITY, BLENDS, AND COPOLYMERS

4.1. Thermodynamic Basis for Compatibility

In the foregoing sections main emphasis was placed on hard and soft *anisotropic* interaction. For the description of mixtures it is however essential to consider in great detail the role of the soft *isotropic* interactions that may be described by the χ parameter. In Section 3 the effect of solvent–polymer interaction on the phase equilibria of both monodisperse and polydisperse polymers was considered. The role of χ, however, is of far greater importance for systems involving chemically different polymers.

Let us consider again, in general terms, the thermodynamic components of mixing. Figure 12 illustrates how the entropic component in isotropic and anisotropic states is affected by the degree of polymerization for both polymer–solvent and polymer–polymer mixtures. ΔS_{mix}^{iso} acquires the ideal values for a mixture of two low molecular weight liquids ($X \approx 1$ in Fig. 12a), but decreases with increasing X, particularly when both components are polymers. Calculations of Fig. 12a were performed using the Flory-Huggins theory[124] for 50–50 athermal mixtures. In Fig. 12b, ΔS_{mix}^{aniso} was similarly calculated, using the approximate Abe-Flory theory,[96] for mixtures of rodlike molecules with a solvent, two rodlike molecules, and rods with coiled polymers. The following conclusions are apparent. (1) The tendency to mix

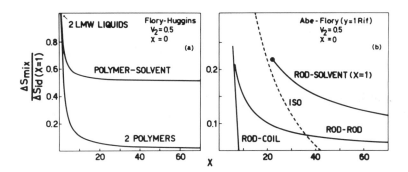

FIGURE 12
Variation of mixing entropy (referred to the ideal value) with the number of units in the polymer molecule for the indicated binary systems. (a) Isotropic phase, (b) anisotropic phase. Composition of systems is always 50 : 50. Athermal mixing.

strongly decreases with MW, but ΔS_{mix} remains positive (favorable to mixing), and is actually larger in the anisotropic than in the isotropic solution. (2) An important exception is the case of rod–coil mixtures, for which ΔS_{mix}^{aniso} becomes negative even at low X values. On an entropy basis, incompatibility is therefore expected only for mixtures of different conformers and it is due[24, 96] to the difficulty of accommodating the coils in the ordered mesophase of the rods.

Turning now to the enthalpic components it is important to differentiate the cases of systems with only symmetric interaction (described by χ), from that of systems with anisotropic interactions. The former are typical of isotropic phases and also of mesophases that are essentially stabilized by hard interactions (suitable chemical structures or diluted solutions). In these cases it is assumed[24] that

$$\chi^{iso} \approx \chi^{aniso} \tag{12}$$

According to polymer solution theory[124] for binary systems, χ_{12} is defined by the net change of energy accompanying formation of unlike $1, 2$ contacts out of the disappearance of like $1, 1$ and $2, 2$ contacts:

$$\chi_{12} = \frac{Z \Delta \omega}{RT} \tag{13}$$

$$\Delta \omega = \omega_{12} - \tfrac{1}{2}(\omega_{11} + \omega_{22}) \tag{14}$$

where Z is a coordination number. For ternary systems one needs parameters for all possible pairs: χ_{12}; χ_{13}; χ_{23}. Demixing is predicted to occur for polymer–solvent systems below the θ temperature when $\chi_{12} > \tfrac{1}{2}$, while in general demixing occurs when χ exceeds a critical value, e.g.,

$$\chi_{23} > \chi_{23}^c = \frac{1}{2}\left(\frac{1}{X_2^{1/2}} + \frac{1}{X_3^{1/2}} \right)^2 \tag{15}$$

which depends upon the degree of polymerization of the respective components. In solution, the composition at demixing is given by $v_p^{demix} = \chi_{23}^c / \chi_{23}$ (if $\chi_{12} = \chi_{13}$). Values of χ, experimentally determined or calculated[125–127] using Hildebrand solubility parameters, are generally positive. Thus, in spite of well-known limitations[124] affecting χ, it may be argued that ΔH_{mix}^{sym} will generally be unfavorable. It is the prevalence of ΔH_{mix}^{sym} over the small ΔS_{mix}^{iso}, which is causing the incompatibility generally observed with isotropic blends of conventional polymers. In view of Eq. (12), incompatibility may also be expected in the mesophase of two rodlike polymers since ΔS_{mix}^{aniso} is only slightly larger than ΔS_{mix}^{iso}.

A different situation might be anticipated for the enthalpic component in systems displaying anisotropic interactions. The orientation-dependent intermolecular energy defined by Eq. (2) is now operative, but the net exchange upon mixing two nematogens

$$\Delta \epsilon = \epsilon_{12} - \tfrac{1}{2}(\epsilon_{11} + \epsilon_{22}) \tag{16}$$

cannot be expected to be systematically positive since highly polar and similar structures are involved. In fact, even in the isotropic state (when anisotropic interaction vanishes) this class of compounds may yield near zero χ parameters (cf. Section 4.3.1). Moreover, the isotropic component of the soft interaction is active in both phases and, as a rule, the anisotropic component is much smaller than the isotropic one.[60, 128] Thus, ΔH_{mix}^{asym} for systems capable of asymmetric interaction will not be generally unfavorable, or offset the behavior controlled by ΔH_{mix}^{sym}.

From the above considerations it may also be anticipated that for systems such as sidechains LCP mixed with LMWLC, the enthalpy in *both* isotropic and anisotropic phases will contain an unfavorable component due to the mixing of the apolar mainchain with the LMWLC, and a favorable component due to the mixing of sidechains with the LMWLC. Mixing or demixing will be controlled by the balance of these components.

General thermodynamic arguments set forth by Brochard et al.[129] are consistent with the foregoing considerations. They used the Maier-Saupe formalism, whereas here (Fig. 12) the lattice model for the entropy of the mesophase was used. However, the trend of ΔS_{mix} of the various formalisms is similar, and the shortcomings of the basic theories have been discussed in Section 3. Here, we rather focus on the main conclusions concerning compatibility which appear to be controlled by isotropic interaction irrespective of the particular molecular theory. At variance with Brochard et al.,[129] we emphasize χ and fully exploit well established techniques for calculating isotropic interactions[125–127] (the problem in evaluating $\Delta\epsilon$ is the ϵ_{12} term, since ϵ_{11} and ϵ_{22} may be derived from the corresponding T_{NI}).

Before turning to a test of the above expectations for selected systems it is important to point out that several of these systems are important for technological applications ranging from electrooptics, support for LMWLC's in display devices, optical recording, membranes, plasticizers, and reinforced materials. These applications have been reviewed by Dutta et al.[130]

4.2. Ternary Mixtures of Lyotropic LCP's

Figure 13 illustrates the phase behavior for mixtures of rods as predicted by the lattice[96] theory assuming only entropy effects and athermal mixing (not only $T^* = 0$, but also all $\chi = 0$, a similar diagram from the virial theory[131] is shown in Fig. 1 of Chapter 3). One expects a fractionation, a widening of the biphasic region increasing with X_2/X_1, but at large rod concentration a single mesophase—i.e., compatibility—is expected. Figure 13 also includes the effect of a negative solvent–polymer interaction parameter χ_{13} or χ_{12}. Experimental results for mixtures of chemically identical homologs have been compared with the above predictions in Section 3.3. Here, we consider chemically different polymers dissolved in a solvent. Quite a number of polymer pairs were investigated (PHIC–PBLG, PBLG–PGA, HPC–CA, cellulose PBA, cellulose CA)[132] and HPC–ethyl cellulose,[133] but invariably incompatibility was observed. This is shown by the ternary diagram in Fig. 14

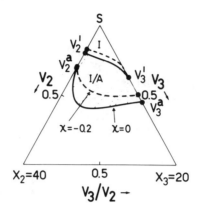

FIGURE 13
Theoretical diagrams for mixtures of polymers differing in axial ratio
X. Lattice theory. (Adapted with permission from Ref. 96. Copyright
Am. Chem. Soc.)

for the system cellulose acetate–hydroxypropyl cellulose–DMAc. The two
had similar persistence and contour lengths. The drastic difference between
the observed incompatibility and the predictions in Fig. 13 cannot easily be
attributed to semirigidity, or to differences between the lattice and virial
theory. The fact that demixing is observed already in the isotropic phase
clearly indicates that the classical incompatibility of conventional polymers is
prevailing. The theoretical predictions based on athermal solution are thus of
little use in real situations. Heterogeneous blends seem to be the rule.

The above conclusion can be put on a more quantitative basis by the
analysis of χ_{23} parameters for the system in Fig. 14. From molecular

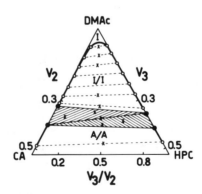

FIGURE 14
Experimental phase diagram for the cellulose acetate, hydroxypropyl
cellulose and N,N-dimethylacetamide system at 20°C. Dashed areas
represent three-phase equilibria. (Reproduced with permission from
Ref. 132. Copyright Am. Chem. Soc.)

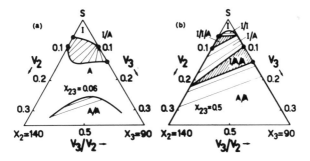

FIGURE 15
Theoretical diagram for mixtures of polymers differing in axial ratio calculated using the lattice theory assuming values of $\chi_{23} = 0.06$ (a) and $= 0.5$ (b). (Reproduced with permission from Ref. 134.)

attraction constants and Hildebrand solubility parameters χ_{23} was calculated[132] to be $= 0.24$. The critical χ_{23}^c (cf. Eq. 15) was instead $= 0.02$. Since $\chi_{23} > \chi_{23}^c$, incompatibility is expected at a $v_p^{demix} > 0.08$, in excellent agreement with the experimental finding. Mesophase formation occurs in the two demixed isotropic phases and the resulting anisotropic phases remain unmixed since for this system T^* may be assumed to be negligible, and Eq. (12) applies. Sasaki[134] fully substantiated this view by recalculating theoretical diagrams which include positive values of χ_{23}. Results, shown in Fig. 15a, reveal that for small values of χ_{23} formation of a single anisotropic phase is followed by demixing at larger polymer concentration. The latter behavior was verified in the case of mixtures of α-helical polyglutamates.[134] At still larger χ_{23}, (cf. Fig. 15b), incompatibility becomes apparent even in the isotropic state and mesophase formation occurs within triangular areas that are similar to those in Fig. 14 (in Fig. 15b the three-phase regions are bridged by a biphasic region, a situation that is not easily detectable in experimental cases).

The foregoing analysis is still of a semiquantitative nature and refinements could be introduced by considering more sophisticated evaluations of hard and soft interaction, of chain flexibility, or by using concentration-dependent χ parameters. However, in view of the limitations of the basic theories, a too good agreement with experimental data could also be attributed to a compensation of effects. In fact, ternary diagrams including χ parameters have been constructed using the virial theory.[97] Similarly, using the density functional expansion method of Ten Bosch et al.,[50] it has been shown that binary diagrams for mixtures of two nematogens (and even ternary diagrams, cf. Chapter 5) can reproduce experimental trends.

The extremely good agreement between "trends" resulting from the introduction of χ parameters in different molecular theories is a convincing proof that conventional incompatibility plays a determining role even for

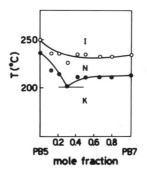

FIGURE 16
Experimental phase diagram for mixture of two polyesters in 10 with
$n = 5$ and $n = 7$. (Reproduced with permission from Ref. 135.
Copyright Am. Chem. Soc.)

lyotropic polymers. Thus, isotropic interaction should receive adequate consideration in any successful elaboration of the basic theories.

4.3. Binary Mixtures of Thermotropic Mesogens

4.3.1. BACKBONE LCP's

At variance with the situation in Section 4.2, thermotropic polyesters are often mutually compatible. Homogeneous blends may therefore be prepared and a depression of transition temperatures is achieved without the use of a solvent. This compatibility is not in contradiction with the general thermodynamic considerations set forth above and likely results from a not-so-unfavorable mixing enthalpy. As an example we may consider a blend of two segmented polyesters for which a complete phase diagram was reported by Watanabe and Krigbaum.[135] Compatibility was also exhibited by other systems involving two segmented homopolyesters,[136] and segmented polyesters with a LMWLC[137, 138] (random copolymers are discussed in Section 4.5.2).

Figure 16 represents binary mixtures of two nematic polymers ($\eta_{inh} = 0.5-0.8$)

$$\left[\!\!-O-\!\!\langle\bigcirc\rangle\!\!-\!\!\langle\bigcirc\rangle\!\!-O-\overset{\overset{O}{\|}}{C}-(CH_2)_n-\overset{\overset{O}{\|}}{C}-\!\!\right]_x$$

10

with $n = 5$ and $n = 7$. Compatibility is observed in the whole composition range, both in the nematic and in the isotropic phase. The depression of T_{NI} of PB7 is a rather small one, indicating minimal disruption of its nematic order by PB5, a reflection of the structural similarity of the two compounds. That the situation is close to ideality is confirmed by the calculation of the χ

parameter from the molecular attraction constants prevailing in the isotropic state: $\chi \approx 0$ was obtained.[139] Although these systems display strong intermolecular anisotropic forces, the exchange of energy upon mixing (Eq. 16) plays a negligible role so that entropy-driven compatibility results. This class of compounds also exhibits lower MW (hence larger mixing entropy) than is the case with the lyotropic systems.

The "compatibility rule"[140] used for identification of similar mesophases in the case of LMWLC's is also likely based on a large mixing entropy and the absence of an unfavorable mixing enthalpy. This situation is in significant contrast with the case of conventional polymers which are incompatible due to an unfavorable χ and a low ΔS_{mix} resulting from their large MW.

4.3.2. SIDECHAIN LCP's

The validity of the analysis based on the χ parameter can be explored also in the case of mixtures of sidechain LCP's and LMWLC's. Workers familiar with the compatibility rule and LMWLC's were surprised when the first example of incompatibility between a sidechain LCP and a LMWLC was observed.[141] A relevant system is a polydimethylsiloxane chain functionalized with a phenylbenzoate (A) and mixed with either B, C, or D:

11

Finkelmann et al.[142] studied system (A) ($n = 4$, $m = 1$) + (B) and reported compatibility over the whole composition range. However, Casagrande et al.[141] studied the same polymer mixed with (C) and reported miscibility gaps in both the isotropic and anisotropic phase. Their diagram is shown in Fig. 17. Sigaud et al.,[143] trying to explain this unexpected demixing, investigated a series of systems (A) + (D) over a range of values of n, m, n', m' and

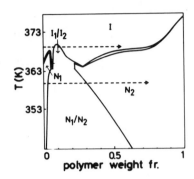

FIGURE 17
Experimental phase diagram for a sidechain LCP and a LMWLC
(formulas in 11, A $n = 4$, $n = 1 + C$). (Reproduced with permission
from Ref. 141.)

attempted a classification of situations leading to mixing or demixing.
Ringsdorf et al.[144] and Achard et al.[145] had also observed mixing and
demixing behavior related to the chemical nature of the backbone, of the
sidechain, and of the LMWLC.

A much simpler approach consists in considering first the relevant χ
parameters for the isotropic systems. For the system used by Casagrande
et al., Marsano and Ciferri[139] calculated

$$\chi_{iso} = \begin{cases} 0.98 & \text{at 298 K} \\ 0.80 & \text{at 368 K} \end{cases}$$

$$\chi^c = 0.62$$

Since $\chi > \chi^c$ (and $T < T_\theta$) this system is expected to demix at some composition (which could be evaluated[146]) already in the isotropic state, thus reflecting conventional incompatibility. This reluctance to mix due to isotropic
interaction is carried into the mesophase since the silicon chain is neither
oriented nor subjected to anisotropic interaction. Since the anisotropic contribution from Eq. (16) will not generally overcome this barrier, the system
stays demixed even in the mesophase.

Current theories for sidechain nematogens (Chapter 5) do not yet include soft isotropic repulsions (i.e., $\chi = 0$). One may speculate that inclusion
of $\chi > 0$ might eventually favor smectic mesophases, reflecting a microsegre-
gation of sidechains and mainchains. A similar effect was considered in
connection with mesogens composed of a rigid and a flexible block.[147] If a
LMWLC is added to a microsegregated systems, it may be expected to swell
the microphase containing the sidechains preferentially, in analogy with the
behavior of block copolymers.

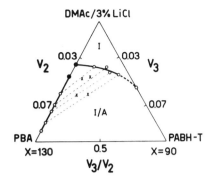

FIGURE 18
Experimental diagram for poly(p-benzamide) ($X = 130$),
polyterephthalamide of p-aminobenzhydrazide ($X = 90$) and
N,N-dimethylacetamide $+ 3\%$ LiCl at 20°C. (Reproduced with
permission from Ref. 149. Copyright Am. Chem. Soc.)

4.4. Mixtures of Mesogens and Coiled Polymers

4.4.1. TERNARY MIXTURES OF LYOTROPIC LCP's AND COILED POLYMERS

As indicated in Section 4.1, entropy should be drastically unfavorable to the mixing of rigid mesogens and coiled polymers in anisotropic phases. A theoretical ternary diagram[148] based only on the above considerations (i.e., $T^* = 0$, $\chi = 0$) is reproduced in Fig. 7 of Chapter 4. The conjugated composition of the anisotropic phase coincides with the axis representing the binary rod + solvent solution, and a single anisotropic phase cannot form. This expectation may be compared with the experimental diagram[149, 150] in Fig. 18 for the system PBA–polyterephthalamide of p-aminobenzyhdrazide (PABH-T) dissolved in DMAc $+ 3\%$ LiCl. This system is very close to an athermal one since a very small χ_{23} ($= 6 \times 10^{-4}$) was calculated. Moreover, χ_{23}^c was 0.014 and therefore the classical condition for miscibility in the isotropic phase applies. The observation that immiscibility appears when the first drop of mesophase is formed, and the total exclusion of the flexible polymer from the mesophase, are therefore most stringent proofs of the predicted demixing based solely on entropy considerations. Other diagrams showing features similar to those exhibited in Fig. 18 have been reported.[150-152]

There seems to be little hope of surmounting the incompatibility of rods and coils just described. In fact, soft interactions, either anisotropic or isotropic, will not act in the direction of favoring compatibility. The effect of anisotropic interaction will be considered in Section 4.4.2. Here we consider cases in which large positive values of χ_{23} reveal an effective soft repulsion between the components (cf. Eq. 14). Figure 19 illustrates a phase diagram[153]

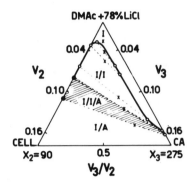

FIGURE 19
Experimental phase diagram for the system cellulose, cellulose
acetate, and *N,N*-dimethylacetamide + 7.8% LiCl at 20°C.
(Reproduced with permission from Ref. 153. Copyright Am. Chem.
Soc.)

for the system cellulose–cellulose acetate–DMAc + 7.8% LiCl. A rather
large χ_{23} (~ 3) was calculated, while χ_{23}^c was $= 4.2 \times 10^{-3}$. Since $\chi_{23}^c < \chi_{23}$
demixing is predicted to occur in the isotropic phase already at $v_p > 0.005$.
Two isotropic phases are in fact observed at $v_p > \sim 0.02$. When the combined polymer volume fraction is ~ 0.1, one isotropic phase transforms into
an anisotropic one, which is actually an intimate mixture of an isotropic and
an anisotropic phase. Cellulose acetate is excluded from the mesophase.
Coexistence of three phases was clearly evidenced for the system
PBLG–polystyrene–benzyl alcohol by Sasaki and Uzawa.[154] By including
values of $\chi_{23} > 0.2$ in the expressions used by Flory to calculate the athermal
diagram in Fig. 18, Sasaki and Uzawa were able to reproduce the appearance
of the *I–I* and the *I–I–A* regions. The quantitative fit of experiments with
theory was not a perfect one. However, as noted in Section 4.2, the results
provide ample evidence that soft isotropic interactions play a determining
role and should be included in any more elaborated version of the basic
theories presented in Section 3.

The occurrence of isotropic demixing is also suggested by ternary diagrams composed of poly(*γ*-benzyl-*α*, L-glutamate)–nylon 6–*m*-cresol[155] and of
copolyesters–polycarbonate–CHCl₃.[156]

A possibility for surmounting the incompatibility of rods and coils was
suggested by Nyrkova and Khokhlov,[157] but it has not yet been analyzed
experimentally. It is based on slightly charging the coil so that the mobility of
the counterions, and conformational extension, contribute favorably to ΔS_{mix}.

4.4.2. *BINARY MIXTURES OF LMWLC's*
AND COILED POLYMERS

The role of soft anisotropic interaction on the mixing of mesogens and
coiled polymers is best analyzed by considering binary mixtures involving a
LMWLC. Ballauff[158] has added the anisotropic attraction between molecules

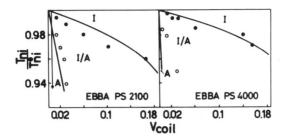

FIGURE 20
Comparison of theoretical phase diagrams (full lines) calculated by
Ballauff[158] with the experimental data of Kronberg et al.[159] for
systems composed of EBBA and two different fractions of
polystyrene. v_{coil} is the segment fraction of coils. Other relevant
parameters are given in the text. (Reproduced with permission from
Ref. 158. Copyright Gordon and Breach Science Publishers.)

of the mesogens to the steric part of the partition function used by Flory for
mixtures of rods and coils. Figure 20 shows his phase diagrams calculated
with parameters obtained for the system p-ethoxybenzylidine-p-n-butylani-
line (EBBA)–polystyrene (PS) investigated by Kronberg et al.[159] The theoretical lines represent the decrease of the transition temperature with increasing
the segment fraction of the coils. Parameters selected for EBBA were its T_{NI}°
($= 79.1°C$), its axial ratio ($X_r = 3.7$), its characteristic temperature T^*
($= 351.2$ K), and density and thermal expansion data for the assessment of
free volume (cf. Section 2). Parameters for the two sharp fractions of PS
investigated were the number of segments ($X_c = 27.8$ and 53, respectively,
for MW $= 2100$ and 4000) and thermal expansion data. The diagram clearly
shows that the biphasic gap is widened by an increase of the length of the
coiled polymer, and that already at MW $= 4000$ there is an almost complete
exclusion of the latter from the anisotropic phase of the LMWLC. Thus, the
basic incompatibility between rods and coils discussed in the preceding
section is retained when soft anisotropic interactions are operative.

Interesting speculations were made concerning a possible coupling between the anisotropic interaction of the mesogen and the isotropic interaction of the coil. In the range of low MW where some coil molecules enter the
mesophase, neutron-scattering studies by Dubault et al.[160] did not reveal any
anisotropization of the conformation of PS. de Gennes and Veyssie[161] suggested that PS chains form isotropic droplets locally destroying the nematic
order.[162] It has been also reported that the order parameter S decreases
along the nematicus line,[163] and attempts were made to introduce a χ
depending upon S,[161] or the concept of a pseudo clearing temperature.[162, 163]
However, Ballauff[158] pointed out that since the concentration of coils within
the mesophase is so low when $X_c > X_r$, it is the behavior of net liquids which
is indeed observed.

The theoretical analysis leading to the phase diagram in Fig. 20 is still
defective since although soft anisotropic interaction and mixing entropy

terms are considered, the corresponding χ term is not. Inclusion of even the latter component was performed by Ballauff[164] and this treatment represents the most complete account of all enthalpic and entropic components using the lattice framework. Experimentally observed[163] details such as demixing in the isotropic phase and a reentrant isotropic phase at low temperatures find a natural justification by recognizing that LMWLC's are enthalpically poor solvents for PS. A diagram calculated[164] assuming the same parameters valid for the EBBA–PS (2100) system considered in Fig. 20, but with the additional assumption of $\chi_{12} \approx 0.30$ (or $T_i^* \approx 90$ K since $\chi_{12} = T_i^*/T$ where T_i^* is a characteristic temperature of isotropic interaction), is given in Fig. 14 of Chapter 4. The features of this diagram are in semiquantitative agreement with observations made for the systems EBBA–polyethylene oxide[163] and p-azoxyanisole–n-octadecane (or n-tetracosane)[165] which exhibit isotropic demixing. It may be concluded that inclusion of the conventional χ term is mandatory even for systems displaying anisotropic interaction in order to explain the whole behavior.

Blends of LMWLC's and coiled polymers attract attention for technological applications.[130] Usually they are processed from the isotropic melt where compatibility is exhibited. Demixing is reported in the solid state of the polymer (either glassy or semicrystalline).

4.4.3. BINARY MIXTURES OF LCP's AND COILED POLYMERS

As expected, the behavior of these mixtures is similar to that described above (Sections 4.4.1 and 4.4.2). Seurin et al.[166] attempted to mix polyethylene glycol and cholesteric HPC at 110°C and reported immiscibility in the mesophase when the MW of PEG was larger than 1000. Chuah et al.[167] and Wiff et al.[168] reported immiscibility for PPBT and nylon 66 blends (clear films prepared by Chuah et al. phase separated above the melting point of nylon 66). Weiss et al.[169] reported segregation of segmented polyester fibers within a PS matrix in the solid state. Pracella et al.[170] and Paci et al.[171] studied solid state properties of blends of crystalline poly(butylene terephthalate) with a segmented polyester. In these cases partial miscibility in the isotropic phase was indicated, the mesophase was not investigated, and segregation occurred in the solid state. Note that the latter segregation is not necessarily evidence of immiscibility in the mesophase. Unless cocrystallization occurs, it is only the "extent" of segregation (and morphological and mechanical details) which may be controlled by miscibility in the precursor phases (cf. also Sections 4.5.1 and 4.5.2).

4.5. Copolymers

4.5.1. BLOCK COPOLYMERS

Exceptions to the prevailing incompatibility of two conventional coiled polymers may sometime be found.[125] For the rod–coil case, however, the unfavorable ΔS_{mix}^{aniso} leaves block copolymerization as the most viable route to

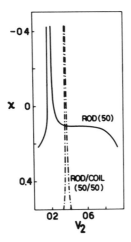

FIGURE 21

Binary polymer – solvent phase diagram calculated from the Matheson-Flory theory[71] for a rod of 50 units and for a block copolymer of 50 rigid and 50 flexible units. (Reproduced with permission from Ref. 172.)

efficient and thermodynamically stable mixing. Matheson and Flory[71] used the lattice theory $(T^* = 0)$ to predict the phase behavior of block copolymers composed of long rodlike and coiled section. Figure 21 shows, for instance, phase diagrams for a rod with $X = 50$ and for a copolymer composed of a rodlike block with $X = 50$ and a flexible block with 50 units. The polymers are in both cases dissolved in a conventional solvent. The figure reveals that the critical concentration of the block copolymer and the width of its biphasic gap are, respectively, larger and smaller than for the homopolymer. However, flexible blocks can enter a single anisotropic phase. The order parameter of the nematic phase is reduced by the presence of the block, but this theory[71] does not consider any orienting effect on the coil by the nematic field. For ternary systems involving rod–copolymer–solvent, compatibility is expected at v_p increasing with coil length.[172]

A main prediction of the above theory was verified by comparing the biphasic behavior of a blend of PBA and poly(m-phenylene isophthalamide) in DMAc + 3% LiCl with the behavior of a corresponding block copolymer having a 80/20 w/w monomer ratio[172] (Fig. 22). The volume fraction Φ, measured as a function of the overall polymer concentration, attains a limit of ~ 0.4 for the blend, but decreases to zero for the copolymer. Thus, the coiled component is admitted to the mesophase in the copolymer, but it is excluded in the blend.

Working with a copolymer having a block of PBA and a block of flexible PABH-T, Bianchi et al.[173] noticed that the value of the critical concentration of the purified copolymer was *smaller* than the value for the PBA prepolymer. They speculated the occurrence of somewhat extended conformations of

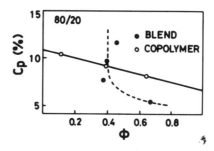

FIGURE 22
Variation of the volume fraction of isotropic phase Φ with overall
polymer concentration C_p for 80 : 20 blends of PBA and
poly(m-phenylene isophthalamide) (●), and for a corresponding
80 : 20 block copolymer (○). Solvent in DMAc + 3% LiCl. (Adapted
with permission from Figs. 1b and 1e of Ref. 172.)

the coiled block within the mesophase, leading to an increase of the axial
ratio attributable to the PBA block. Such a possibility was theoretically
considered by Vasilenko et al.[53] Moreover, homopolymer PABH-T polymerized in the presence of PBA appeared to form a metastable adduct.

The above results indicate that block copolymers may afford a most
interesting approach to the study of the detailed structure of liquid-crystalline systems. Additional interest in these systems derives from the potential
of materials involving rigid and flexible polymers. The complex technology
involved in high-performance composites could be significantly diversified by
the use of block copolymers. For instance, in the preparation of materials
based on a ductile matrix uniaxially reinforced with long rigid polymers, a
fine dispersion of the components (molecular composite) is essential in order
to achieve the maximum properties predicted by the rule of mixtures. Hwang
et al.[152] working with blends of 30% poly(p-phenylene benzobisthiazole)
(PPBT) and 70% flexible poly-2,5(6)benzimidazole (ABPBI) found that
large-scale segregation could be avoided only by rapidly spinning from a
diluted, isotropic solution. A triblock copolymer having 30% PPBT and 70%
ABPBI was later considered by Krause et al.[174] They did not investigate
compatibility in solution and probably the flexible block was too long to enter
the mesophase. Segregation in the solid state was still occurring. Nevertheless, a smaller scale segregation and improved adhesion between phases
resulted in mechanical properties significantly improved with respect to the
blend.

Mixtures of block copolymers with rods have received only limited
attention, but compatibility was exhibited.[172] No data are available for
mixtures of block copolymers and coils. On the theoretical side, Ballauff[175, 176]
has considered equilibria of comb- or starlike polymers composed of rigid
and coiled sections, as well as their mixtures with coiled homopolymers. The

stars formed a mesophase (see Fig. 10 of Chapter 4 and its similarity to Fig. 21), but the coiled homopolymer was excluded from it. Use of flexible sidechains to improve compatibility of rigid polymers was also suggested.[177]

4.5.2. RANDOM COPOLYMERS

Only scattered information is available on these systems. The evaluation of all thermodynamic components is a rather difficult task. Considering, for instance, only the isotropic interactions, the general case of a mixture of two copolymers AB + CD, where x is the volume fraction of component A in copolymer AB, and y is the volume fraction of component C in copolymer CD, may be described by an overall χ

$$\chi = xy\chi_{AC} + x(1 - y)\chi_{AD} + (1 - x)y\chi_{BC} + (1 - x)(1 - y)\chi_{BD}$$
$$- x(1 - x)\chi_{AB} - y(1 - y)\chi_{CD}$$

(17)

which is based on "segmental" interaction parameters.[126, 127] These considerations also apply for a single copolymer AB since a compositional distribution among molecules of a given sample may occur. In the latter case

$$\chi = (x - y)^2\chi_{AB}$$

The simultaneous occurrence of a MW distribution adds support to the possibility that segregation can occur even when a mixture is not prepared intentionally. An additional problem, relevant to the copolyesters which have been most extensively investigated, is the possibility of transesterification.[178] The latter may smooth out initial differences in compositional distribution, resulting in improved compatibility.

De Meuse and Jaffe[179] studied blends of two mesogenic random copolymers composed of p-hydroxybenzoic (HBA) and 6-hydroxy-2-naphthoic acid (HNA) residues. Samples used had different comonomer–mole ratios (e.g., 30:70, 58:42 and 75:25), but rather similar MW and MW distributions. Transesterification did not seem to be a significant factor. The T_{KN} temperatures were measured by DSC for mixtures of the two copolymer pairs 58:42 + 75:25 and 30:70 + 75:25. Both mixtures exhibited a tendency to cocrystallize (no eutectic) which was explained by occurrence of similar sequences of both HBA and HNA in adjoining chains. According to Hanna and Windle,[180] the larger the "matching length" the higher the melting temperature in copolymers. The effect causes an efficient molecular mixing, or "compatibility" in the solid state. The latter compatibility need not be related to the compatibility in the isotropic and in the nematic phase considered in preceding sections. In fact, mixing of the two PB-5 and PB-7 homopolyesters (cf. 10 and Fig. 16) revealed that each component crystallizes separately (eutectic) in spite of the compatibility exhibited in the nematic and the isotropic phases. On the other hand, Watanabe and Krigbaum[135] also found that for single random copolymers of PB-5, 7 (and similar copolymers) the two components cocrystallize to form a solid solution.

The occurrence of cocrystallization in the latter case was related[135] to the geometrical similarity of the units involved, and to the frequent occurrence of crystalline polymorphism for homopolymeric mesogens. No cocrystallization occurred for the copolymer PB-6, 12, where the repeating units were quite different in length. Also the nematic and smectic mesophases of the copolymers[135] were able to accommodate different units with minimal perturbation of the structure.

For the HBA–NHA copolymer[179] there was some evidence of compatibility in the mesophase for mixtures of the 58 : 42 + 75 : 25 copolymers, and of incompatibility for mixtures (30 : 70 + 75 : 25) showing a large compositional difference. In line with the discussion in Section 4.3, large segmental differences may offset the compatibility usually observed with mesogenic homopolymers.[181]

Most of the other blends investigated included a nematic copolyester and a coiled polymer. Extensively used was a copolyester formed by transesterification of poly(ethylene terephthalate) (PET) and p-acetoxybenzoic acid.[182] Kimura and Porter[183] and Huang et al.[184] reported that the more flexible PET-rich component of the PET–HBA copolymer (assumed to be revealed by the lower glass temperature $T_g \approx 326°C$) was compatible with poly(butylene terephthalate) or polycarbonate, whereas the HBA-rich phase (more rigid and with a $T_g \approx 460°C$) was not. This would be understandable in terms of the analysis in Section 4.1, but studies aiming at the solid-state properties of blends have often avoided a detailed analysis of the mesophase. Other studies involving PET–HBA copolymers and PET suggest that their basic incompatibility could only be surmounted by nonequilibrium situations,[185] or by extensive transesterification.[186, 187]

REFERENCES

1. W.J. Jackson, Jr., *Mol. Cryst. Liq. Cryst.*, **1989**, *169*, 23.
2. A. Roviello and A. Sirigu, *Gazz. Chim. Ital.*, **1977**, *107*, 333.
3. P.-G. de Gennes, *C.R. Hebd. Seances Acad. Sci.*, Ser. B, **1975**, *282*, 101.
4. S.L. Kwolek, U.S. Patent 3,671,542 (to du Pont Co.), 1972.
5. A.R. Khokhlov and A.N. Semenov, *Macromolecules*, **1986**, *19*, 373.
6. W. Maier and A. Saupe, *Z. Naturforsch.*, **1960**, *15*, 287.
7. L. Onsager, *Ann. N.Y. Acad. Sci.*, **1949**, *51*, 627.
8. P.J. Flory, *Proc. R. Soc. London*, Ser. A, **1956**, *234*, 73.
9. J.R. McColl and C.S. Shih, *Phys. Rev. Lett.*, **1972**, *29*, 85.
10. A. Wulf, *J. Chem. Phys.*, **1976**, *64*, 104.
11. W.M. Gelbart and A. Gelbart, *Mol. Phys.*, **1977**, *33*, 1387.
12. M. Warner, *J. Chem. Phys.*, **1980**, *73*, 5874.
13. P.J. Flory and G. Ronca, *Mol. Cryst. Liq. Cryst.*, **1979**, *54*, 311.
14. M.A. Cotter and D.C. Wacher, *Phys. Rev. A*, **1978**, *18*, 2669.
15. R.E. Boehm and D.E. Martire, *Mol. Phys.*, **1978**, *36*, 1.

16. P. Corradini and M. Vacatello, *Mol. Cryst. Liq. Cryst.*, **1983**, *97*, 119; *Gazz. Chim. Ital.*, **1986**, *116*, 569.
17. H. Imura and K. Okano, *J. Chem. Phys.*, **1973**, *58*, 2763.
18. P.A. Irvine and P.J. Flory, *J. Chem. Soc., Faraday Trans.*, **1984**, *80*, 1821.
19. M. Ballauff and P.J. Flory, *Ber. Bundsenges. Phys. Chem.*, **1984**, *88*, 530.
20. P.J. Flory, R.A. Orwoll, and A. Vrij, *J. Am. Chem. Soc.*, **1964**, *86*, 3507.
21. P.J. Flory and P.A. Irvine, *J. Chem. Soc., Faraday Trans.*, **1984**, *80*, 1807.
22. A. Ciferri and E. Marsano, *Gazz. Chim. Ital.*, **1987**, *117*, 567.
23. G. Costa, A. Minicucci, V. Trefiletti, and B. Valenti, *Liq. Cryst.*, **1990**, *7*, 629.
24. P.J. Flory, *Adv. Polym. Sci.*, **1984**, *59*, 1.
25. H. Kimura, *J. Phys. Soc. Jpn.*, **1974**, *36*, 1280.
26. A. Ten Bosch, Chapter 5, this volume.
27. H.R. Ringsdorf, B. Schlarb, and J. Venzmer, *Angew Chem.*, **1988**, *27*, 113.
28. W.J. Jackson, Jr., *Br. Polym. J.*, **1980**, *12*, 154.
29. J.R. Schaefgen, U.S. Patent 4,118,372 (to du Pont Co.), 1978.
30. J. Majnusz, J.M. Catala, and R.W. Lenz, *Eur. Polym. J.*, **1983**, *19*, 1043.
31. C.R. Payet, U.S. Patent 4,159,365 (to du Pont Co.), 1979.
32. W.J. Jackson, Jr., G.C. Gebeau, and H.F. Kuhfuss, U.S. Patent 4,153,779 (to Eastman Kodak Co.), 1979.
33. W. Volksen, J.R. Lyerla, Jr., J. Economy, and B. Dawson, *J. Polym.Sci., Polym. Chem. Ed.*, **1983**, *21*, 2249.
34. S.G. Cottis, R. Layton, and N.D. Field, U.S. Patent 4,563,508 (to Dart Industries), 1986.
35. J.J. Kleinschuster, U.S. Patent 3,991,014 (to du Pont Co.), 1976.
36. S.L. Wunder, S. Ramachandran, C.R. Gochanour, and M. Weinberg, *Macromolecules*, **1986**, *19*, 1696.
37. G.W. Calundann, in *High Performance Fibers: Their Origin and Development*, R.B. Seymour and G.S. Kirschenbaum, Eds., Elsevier Science Publishing Co., New York, 1986.
38. W.R. Krigbaum and T. Tanaka, *Macromolecules*, **1988**, *21*, 743.
39. W.R. Krigbaum, G. Brelsford, and A. Ciferri, *Macromolecules*, **1989**, *22*, 2487.
40. E. Bianchi, A. Ciferri, G. Conio, and W.R. Krigbaum, *Polymer*, **1987**, *28*, 813.
41. W.R. Krigbaum, H. Hakemi, A. Ciferri, and G. Conio, *Macromolecules*, **1985**, *18*, 973.
42. E. Bianchi, A. Ciferri, G. Conio, L. Lanzavecchia, and M. Terbojevich, *Macromolecules*, **1986**, *19*, 630.
43. M.A. Aden, E. Bianchi, A. Ciferri, and G. Conio, *Macromolecules*, **1984**, *17*, 2010.
44. G.V. Laivins and D.G. Gray, *Macromolecules*, **1986**, *18*, 1746.
45. A.J. Seurin, A. Ten Bosch, and P. Sixou, *Polym. Bull.*, **1983**, *9*, 450.
46. S.N. Bhadani, S.L. Tseng, and D.G. Gray, *Polym. Prepr.*, **1983**, *24*, 264.
47. D. Frenkel and B.M. Mulder, *Mol. Phys.*, **1985**, *55*, 1174, 1193.
48. G.L. Brelsford and W.R. Krigbaum, Chapter 2, this volume.
49. P.J. Flory, A. Ciferri, and R. Chiang, *J. Am. Chem. Soc.*, **1961**, *83*, 1015.
50. A. Ten Bosch, J.F. Pinton, P. Maissa, and P. Sixou, *J. Phys. A: Math. Gen.*, **1987**, *20*, 4531; P. Maissa and P. Sixou, *Liq. Cryst.*, **1989**, *5*, 1861.
51. J.D. Parson, *Phys. Rev. A*, **1979**, *19*, 1225.
52. A. Ten Bosch, personal communication.
53. S.V. Vasilenko, A.R. Khokhlov, and V.P. Shibaev, *Macromolecules*, **1984**, *17*, 2270.
54. A.R. Khokhlov, personal communication.
55. D.Y. Yoon and S. Bruckner, *Macromolecules*, **1985**, *18*, 651.

56. P.J. Flory, in *Materials Science and Engineering of Rigid Rod Polymers*, W.W. Adams, R.K. Eby, and D.E. McLemore, Eds., MRS Symposium Proceedings, Vol. 134, Materials Research Society, 1990.
57. R.E. Boehm, D.E. Martire, and N.V. Madhusudana, *Macromolecules*, **1986**, *19*, 2329.
58. A. Ciferri, W.R. Krigbaum and R.B. Meyer, Eds., *Polymer Liquid Crystals*, Academic Press, New York, 1982.
59. A.R. Khokhlov and A.N. Semenov, *Physica*, **1982**, *112A*, 605.
60. A.R. Khokhlov and A.N. Semenov, *J. Stat. Phys.*, **1985**, *38*, 161.
61. T. Odijk, *Macromolecules*, **1986**, *19*, 2313.
62. P.J. Flory, *Macromolecules*, **1978**, *11*, 1141.
63. G. Conio, E. Bianchi, A. Ciferri, and W.R. Krigbaum, *Macromolecules*, **1984**, *17*, 856.
64. J. Hermans, Jr., *J. Colloid Sci.*, **1962**, *17*, 638.
65. C. Robinson, J.C. Ward, and R.B. Bevers, *Disc. Faraday Soc.*, **1958**, *25*, 29.
66. C. Balbi, E. Bianchi, A. Ciferri, A. Tealdi, and W.R. Krigbaum, *J. Polym. Sci., Polym. Phys. Ed.*, **1980**, *18*, 2037.
67. S.L. Kwolek, P.W. Morgan, J.R. Schaefgen, and L.W. Gulrich, *Macromolecules*, **1977**, *10*, 1390.
68. T. Itou, K. Van, and A. Teramoto, *J. Appl. Polym. Sci., Appl. Polym. Symp.*, **1985**, *41*.
69. D.A. Brant, and K.D. Goebel, *Macromolecules*, **1972**, *5*, 536.
70. M.R. Ambler, D. McIntyre, and L.J. Fetters, *Macromolecules*, **1978**, *11*, 300.
71. R.R. Matheson and P.J. Flory, *Macromolecules*, **1981**, *14*, 954.
72. R. Bruzzone, Thesis, Institute of Industrial Chemistry, University of Genoa, 1986.
73. G. Conio, E. Bianchi, A. Ciferri, A. Tealdi, and M.A. Aden, *Macromolecules*, **1983**, *16*, 1264.
74. E. Bianchi, A. Ciferri, G. Conio, A. Cosani, and M. Terbojevich, *Macromolecules*, **1985**, *18*, 646.
75. C.L. McCormick, P.A. Callais, and B.H. Hutchinson, Jr., *Macromolecules*, **1985**, *18*, 2394.
76. S.-D. Lee and R.B. Meyer, *Phys. Rev. Lett.*, **1988**, *61*, 2217.
77. T. Itou, T. Sato, A. Teramoto, and S.M. Aharoni, *Polymer J.*, **1988**, *20*, 1049.
78. M. Ballauff, *Mol. Cryst. Liq. Cryst.*, **1989**, *168*, 209.
79. E. Marsano, G. Conio, and A. Ciferri, *Mol. Cryst. Liq. Cryst.*, **1988**, *154*, 69.
80. G. Ronca, *J. Polym. Sci., Polym. Phys. Ed.*, **1989**, *27*, 1795.
81. F. Dowell, *J. Chem. Phys.*, **1989**, *91*, 1316.
82. A. Ciferri, *Mol. Cryst. Liq. Cryst. Lett.*, **1990**, *7*, 139.
83. T. Itou and A. Teramoto, *Macromolecules*, **1988**, *21*, 2225.
84. A.R. Khokhlov and A.N. Semenov, *Macromolecules*, **1984**, *17*, 2678.
85. M.L. Mansfield, *Macromolecules*, **1986**, *19*, 854.
86. G. Ronca and D.Y. Yoon, *J. Chem. Phys.*, **1985**, *83*, 373.
87. T.E. Strzelecka, M.W. Davidson, and R.L. Rill, *Nature*, **1988**, *331*, 457.
88. W.G. Miller, Jr., J.H. Ray, and E.L. Wee, in *Liquid Crystals and Ordered Fluids*, Vol. 2, R. Porter and J. Johnson, Eds., Plenum, New York, 1974, p. 243.
89. M. Warner and P.J. Flory, *J. Chem. Phys.*, **1980**, *73*, 6327.
90. C. Viney, D.Y. Yoon, B. Rech, and H. Ringsdorf, *Macromolecules*, **1989**, *22*, 4088.
91. P.J. Flory and R.R. Matheson, *J. Phys. Chem.*, **1984**, *88*, 6606.
92. D.E. Martire, G.A. Oweimreen, G.J. Agreen, S.G. Rayan, and H.T. Peterson, *J. Phys. Chem.*, **1976**, *64*, 1456.
93. P.J. Flory and R.S. Frost, *Macromolecules*, **1978**, *11*, 1126.

94. R.S. Frost and P.J. Flory, *Macromolecules*, **1978**, *11*, 1134.
95. J.K. Moscicki and G. Williams, *Polymer*, **1982**, *23*, 558.
96. A. Abe and P.J. Flory, *Macromolecules*, **1978**, *11*, 1122.
97. T. Sato, N. Ikeda, T. Itou, and A. Teramoto, *Polymer*, **1989**, *30*, 311.
98. G. Conio, E. Bianchi, A. Ciferri, and A. Tealdi, *Macromolecules*, **1981**, *14*, 1084.
99. S.M. Aharoni and E.K. Walsh, *Macromolecules*, **1977**, *12*, 271.
100. T.I. Bair, P.W. Morgan, and F.L. Kilian, *Macromolecules*, **1977**, *10*, 1396.
101. R.R. Matheson, Jr., *Macromolecules*, **1980**, *13*, 643.
102. T. Itou and A. Teramoto, *Polym. J.*, **1984**, *16*, 779.
103. N.S. Murphy, J.R. Knox, and E.T. Samulski, *J. Chem. Phys.*, **1976**, *65*, 4835.
104. R.W. Duke, D.B. Dupré, and E.T. Samulski, *J. Chem. Phys.*, **1977**, *66*, 2748.
105. B.E. Volchek, A.V. Gribanov, A.T. Kol'Tsov, A.V. Purkina, G.P. Vlasov, and L.A. Ovsyannikova, *Vysokomol. Soyed.*, **1977**, *A19*(3), 519.
106. M.L. Sartirana, E. Marsano, E. Bianchi, and A. Ciferri, *Mol. Cryst. Liq. Cryst.*, **1987**, *144*, 263.
107. A. Abe and T. Yamazaki, *Macromolecules*, **1989**, *22*, 2145.
108. M.L. Sartirana, E. Marsano, E. Bianchi, and A. Ciferri, *Macromolecules*, **1986**, *19*, 1176.
109. G.J. Vroege and T. Odijk, *Macromolecules*, **1988**, *21*, 2848.
110. S.-D. Lee and R.B. Meyer, *J. Chem. Phys.*, **1986**, *84*, 3443.
111. P.J. Flory and G. Ronca, *Mol. Cryst. Liq. Cryst.*, **1979**, *54*, 289.
112. N. Kirov, P. Simova, and H. Ratajczak, *Mol. Cryst. Liq. Cryst.*, **1980**, *58*, 285.
113. S.P. Papkov, in *Contemporary Topics in Polymer Science*, Vol. 2, E.M. Pierce and J.R. Schaefgen, Eds., Plenum Press, New York, 1977.
114. A. Nakajiama, T. Hirai, and T. Hayashi, *Polym. Bull.*, **1978**, *1*, 143.
115. K. Tohyama and W.G. Miller, *Nature*, **1981**, *289*, 813.
115a. S. Fortin and G. Charlet, *Macromolecules*, **1989**, *22*, 2286.
116. S.P. Papkov, *Polym. Sci. USSR*, **1984**, *25*, 1210.
117. A. Ciferri and W.R. Krigbaum, *Mol. Cryst. Liq. Cryst.*, **1981**, *69*, 273.
118. A. Ciferri and W.R. Krigbaum, *Gazz. Chim. Ital.*, **1986**, *116*, 529.
119. A. Veiss, *The Macromolecular Chemistry of Gelatin*, Academic Press, New York, 1964.
120. A.N. Ritcey and D.C. Gray, *Biopolymers*, **1988**, *27*, 1363.
120a. C.R. La Marre, J.A. Cuculo, S.M. Hudson, and A. Ciferri, *Mol. Cryst. Liq. Cryst. Lett.*, in press.
121. E. Bianchi, A. Ciferri, G. Conio, and E. Marsano, *Mol. Cryst. Liq. Cryst. Lett.*, **1990**, *7*, 111.
121a. S.S. Abramchuk, I.A. Nyrkova, and A.R. Khokhlov, *Vysokomol. Soyed.*, **1989**, A32(5), 1759.
122. M. Terbojevich, A. Cosani, G. Conio, A. Ciferri, and E. Bianchi, *Macromolecules*, **1985**, *18*, 640.
123. T. Odijk, *J. Phys.*, **1987**, *48*, 125.
124. P.J. Flory, *Principles of Polymer Chemistry*, Cornell Univ. Press, Ithaca, NY, 1953.
125. D.R. Paul and S. Newman, Eds., *Polymer Blends*, Vol. I, Academic Press, New York, 1978.
126. G. Ten Brinke, F.E. Karasz, and W.J. Macknight, *Macromolecules*, **1983**, *16*, 1827.
127. D.R. Paul and J.W. Barlow, *Polymer*, **1984**, *25*, 487.
128. M.A. Cotter and D.C. Wacker, *Phys. Rev.*, **1978**, *18A*, 2669.
129. F. Brochard, J. Jouffroy, and P. Levison, *J. Phys.*, **1984**, *45*, 1125.

130. D. Dutta, H. Fruituala, A. Kohli, and R.A. Weiss, *Polym. Eng. Sci.*, **1990**, *30*, 1005.
131. H.N.W. Lekkerkerker, Ph. Coulon, R. Van Der Haegen, and R. Debliek, *J. Chem. Phys.*, **1984**, *80*, 3427.
132. E. Marsano, E. Bianchi, and A. Ciferri, *Macromolecules*, **1984**, *17*, 2886.
133. S. Ambrosino, T. Khallala, M.J. Seurin, A. Ten Bosch, F. Fried, P. Maïssa, and P. Sixou, *J. Polym. Sci., Polym. Lett.*, **1987**, *25*, 351.
134. S. Sasaki, M. Nagao, M. Gotoh, and I. Uematsu, *J. Polym. Sci., Polym. Phys. Ed.*, **1988**, *26*, 637.
135. J. Watanabe and W.R. Krigbaum, *Macromolecules*, **1984**, *17*, 2288.
136. J.-I. Jin, E.J. Choi, and K.Y. Lee, *Polym. J.*, **1986**, *18*, 99.
137. A.C. Griffin and S.J. Havens, *J. Polym. Sci., Polym. Lett.*, **1980**, *18*, 259.
138. E.R. George, R.S. Porter, and A.C. Griffin, *Mol. Cryst. Liq. Cryst.*, **1984**, *110*, 27.
139. E. Marsano and A. Ciferri, unpublished data.
140. H. Arnold and H. Sackmann, *Z. Phys. Chem.*, **1960**, *213*, 137, 145.
141. C. Casagrande, M. Veyssiè, and H. Finkelmann, *J. Phys. Lett.*, **1982**, *43*, L 671.
142. H. Finkelmann, H.J. Kock, and G. Rehage, *Mol. Cryst. Liq. Cryst.*, **1982**, *89*, 23.
143. G. Sigaud, M.F. Achard, F. Hardouin, M. Mauzac, H. Richard, and H. Gasparoux, *Macromolecules*, **1987**, *20*, 578.
144. H. Ringdorf, H.W. Schmidt, and A. Schneller, *Makromol. Chem. Rapid Commun.*, **1982**, *3*, 745.
145. M.F. Achard, S. Sigaud, P. Keller and F. Hardouin, International Conference on Liquid Crystal Polymers, Bordeaux, France, Paper 11P3, 1987.
146. H. Brody, *J. Appl. Polym. Sci.*, **1986**, *31*, 2753.
147. A.N. Semenov and S.V. Vasilenko, *Sov. Phys. JETP*, **1986**, *63*, 70.
148. P.J. Flory, *Macromolecules*, **1978**, *11*, 1138.
149. E. Bianchi, A. Ciferri, and A. Tealdi, *Macromolecules*, **1982**, *15*, 1268.
150. E. Bianchi, A. Ciferri, E. Marsano, and A. Tealdi, *Macromolecules*, **1984**, *17*, 1526.
151. S.H. Aharoni, *Polymer*, **1980**, *21*, 21.
152. W.F. Hwang, D.R. Wiff, C.L. Brenner, and T.E. Helminiak, *J. Macromol. Sci., Phys. B*, **1983**, *22*, 231.
153. E. Marsano, E. Bianchi, A. Ciferri, G. Ramis, and A. Tealdi, *Macromolecules*, **1986**, *19*, 626.
154. S. Sasaki and T. Uzawa, *Polym. Bull.*, **1986**, *15*, 517.
155. P.S. Russo and T. Chao, *Mol. Cryst. Liq. Cryst.*, **1988**, *157*, 501.
156. F. Schubert, K. Friendlich, M. Hess, and R. Kosfield, *Mol. Cryst. Liq. Cryst.*, **1988**, *155*, 477.
157. I.A. Nyrkova and A.R. Khokhlov, *Vysokomol. Soyed.*, **1989**, *29B*, 375.
158. M. Ballauff, *Mol. Cryst. Liq. Cryst.*, **1986**, *136*, 175.
159. B. Kronberg, J. Bassignana, and D. Patterson, *J. Phys. Chem.*, **1978**, *82*, 1714.
160. A. Dubault, R. Ober, M. Veyssie, and B. Cabane, *J. Phys.*, **1985**, *46*, 1227.
161. P.-G. de Gennes and M. Veyssie, in *Structural Order in Polymers*, IUPAC, F. Ciardelli and P. Giusti, Eds., Pergamon Press, Oxford, 1981.
162. F. Brochard, *C.R. Hebd. Seances Acad. Sci., Ser. B*, **1979**, *289*, 229, 299; **1980**, *290*, 485.
163. A. Dubault, C. Casagrande, and M. Veyssie, *Mol. Cryst. Liq. Cryst. Lett.*, **1982**, *72*, 189.
164. A. Ballauff, *Mol. Cryst. Liq. Cryst. Lett.*, **1986**, *41*, 15.
165. H. Orendi and M. Ballauff, *Liq. Cryst.*, **1989**, *6*, 479.
166. M.J. Seurin, J.M. Gill, A. Ten Bosch, and P. Sixou, *Polymer*, **1984**, *25*, 1073.
167. H.H. Chuah, T. Kyu, and T. Helminiak, *Polymer*, **1987**, *28*, 2130.

168. D.R. Wiff, W.F. Hwang, H.H. Chuah, and E.J. Soloski, *Polym. Eng. Sci.*, **1987**, *27*, 424.
169. R.A. Weiss, W. Huh and L. Nicolais, *Polym. Eng. Sci.*, **1987**, *27*, 684.
170. M. Pracella, E. Chiellini, G. Galli, and D. Dainelli, *Mol. Cryst. Liq. Cryst.*, **1987**, *153*, 525.
171. M. Paci, C. Barone, and P.L. Magagnini, *J. Polym. Sci.*, *Polym. Phys. Ed.*, **1987**, *25*, 1595.
172. W.R. Krigbaum, Zhang Shufan, J. Preston, G. Conio, and A. Ciferri, *J. Polym. Sci.*, *Polym. Phys. Ed.*, **1987**, *25*, 1043.
173. E. Bianchi, A. Ciferri, G. Conio, A. Tealdi, W.R. Krigbaum, and J. Preston, *Polym. J.*, **1988**, *20*, 83.
174. S.J. Krause, T.B. Haddock, G.E. Price, and W.W. Adams, *Macromolecules*, **1988**, *29*, 195.
175. M. Ballauff, *Macromolecules*, **1986**, *19*, 1366.
176. M. Ballauff, *J. Polym. Sci.*, *Polym. Phys. Ed.*, **1987**, *25*, 739.
177. M. Ballauff, *Polymers for Advanced Technology*, Vol. 1, VCH Publishers, New York, 1989.
178. G. Chen and R.W. Lenz, *Polymer*, **1985**, *26*, 1307.
179. M.T. De Meuse, and M.H. Jaffe, *Mol. Cryst. Liq. Cryst.*, **1988**, *157*, 535.
180. S. Hanna and A.H. Windle, *Polymer*, **1988**, *28*, 207.
181. R.R. Luise, *Polym. Liq. Cryst.*, *Farad. Disc.*, **1985**, *79*, 290.
182. W.J. Jackson, Jr. and H.F. Kuhfuss, *J. Polym. Sci.*, *Polym. Chem. Ed.*, **1976**, *14*, 2043.
183. M. Kimura and R.S. Porter, *J. Polym. Sci.*, *Polym. Phys. Ed.*, **1984**, *22*, 1697.
184. S. Huang, A.C. Griffin, and R.S. Porter, *Polym. Eng. Sci.*, **1989**, *29*, 55.
185. T. Kyu and P. Zhuang, *Polym. Commun.*, **1988**, *29*, 4, 99.
186. M. Hess, K. Friendlich, and R. Kosfield, Paper 7P8, Int. Conf. Liq. Cryst. Polym., Bordeaux, France, 1987.
187. Z. Zhou, X. Wu, and M. Yu, *18th Europhysics Conf. Macromol. Phys.*, **1987**, *11c*, 82.

Segmented-Chain Liquid Crystal Polymers

AUGUSTO SIRIGU

Dipartimento di Chimica, Università degli Studi di Napoli Federico II, 80134 Napoli, Italy

CONTENTS

1. INTRODUCTION

This chapter is devoted to presenting and discussing the mesomorphic properties of linear mainchain liquid-crystalline polymers (LCP's) constituted by an alternate sequence of "rigid" and "flexible" molecular sections. Most of the thermotropic mainchain LCP's synthesized so far belong to this class.

The rigid segments are formed by atomic groups of anisometric shape. In most cases they may be described as rods with small axial ratios that are connected in the polymer chain along their elongation axis. Very few cases have been reported of polymers containing rigid, rodlike segments that are included in the polymer chain with their elongation axes approximately orthogonal to the chain direction. Some discotic liquid-crystalline polymers may also be classified as of the segmented-chain type.

Rigidity, which is by no means absolute, may be restricted in most cases to the requirement that any conformational mobility does not drastically affect the overall shape, linearity, and elongation of the molecular segment. Actually, there seems to be no need, in principle, for any section of a linear macromolecule to be highly rigid for liquid-crystalline order to occur. Actually, that a linear polymer of finite length having uniform chain flexibility can produce a (nematic) liquid-crystalline order in the bulk has been theoretically predicted even if orientation-dependent van der Waals interactions are neglected.[1,2] Therefore, the inclusion of rigid segments in a polymeric chain may be considered a practical means of influencing, de facto, its overall flexibility and flexuosity.

Seemingly, the denomination of the rigid group as the "mesogen" implies that the liquid crystal properties of the polymer are univocally related to the presence of that molecular segments, irrespective of the chemical and structural nature of the flexible moiety. This is by no means the case. It may very easily happen that two polymers containing the same mesogenic group but different flexible sections exhibit different mesomorphic behavior, including one being mesogenic and the other nonmesogenic.

In conclusion, with this warning we shall use words such as "mesogen" or "rigid" without any literal implication, notwithstanding their largely conventional and allusive meaning.

2. POLYMER STRUCTURE AND MESOMORPHIC PROPERTIES

Virtually all segmented-chain LCP's are polycondensated, for a very practical reason. Polycondensation is a versatile way to connect two prebuilt molecular sections in alternating sequence just like flexible and rigid segments are. A simple idea is implicit in the basic procedure followed for the synthesis of most segmented-chain LCP's: the mesogenic potential of the rigid segment is known from previous work on low molecular weight analogues. However, this procedure is not the only one followed. Several polycondensation LCP's have been obtained by connecting molecular segments none of which contains the complete structure of the mesogen. This is just built up by the polymerization reaction.

By far the largest number of segmented-chain polymers are polyesters. Once again, this is related to chemical synthesis opportunities rather than to basic principles. In fact, other condensation polymers are known that are polyethers or polycarbonates, polyamides, or polyurethanes. Not infrequently "hybrid" structures such as polyether-esters or polyester-amides have been utilized. In most cases, as for low molecular weight liquid-crystalline compounds (LMWLC), the mesogen has an aromatic structure.

Table 1, which is not meant to be exhaustive, reports the chemical formulas, together with some key references, for a variety of segmented LCP's.

Table 1
Mesogenic Segmented-Chain Polymers

	Refs.[b]
I. R = —Ph—Ph—[c]	
—OOC(CH$_2$)$_n$COO—R—	5, 56, 79, 88, 120, 131
—COO(CH$_2$)$_n$OOC—R—	43, 47, 49
—O(CH$_2$)$_n$O—R—	68, 86, 114
—O(CH$_2$)$_n$OOCCH$_2$COO(CH$_2$)$_n$O—R—	63
—O(CH$_2$)$_n$OOCO(CH$_2$)$_n$OCOO(CH$_2$)$_n$O—R—	117, 143
—OC(CH$_2$)$_n$CO—R—	145
—O(CH$_2$)$_6$OOC—CH—COO(CH$_2$)$_6$O—R— CH$_2$CH=CH$_2$	8
—O(CH$_2$)$_6$OOC—CH—COO(CH$_2$)$_6$O—R— (CH$_2$)$_6$O—Ph—Ph—O(CH$_2$)$_3$CH=CH$_2$	8
—OOC—Ph—O(CH$_2$)$_n$O—Ph—COO—R—	118, 131
—O(CH$_2$)OOC(CH$_2$)$_2$COO(CH$_2$)$_2$O—R—	120
—O(CH$_2$)$_6$OOCNH—⬡—CH$_3$	65
—R—O(CH$_3$)$_6$OOC—NH	
II. R = —Ph—Ph—Ph—[c]	
—COO(CH$_2$CH$_2$O)$_n$OC—R—	48, 49
—COO(CH$_2$)$_n$OOC—R—	49
—COOCH$_2$C(CH$_2$CH$_3$)$_2$CH$_2$OOC—R—	49
—COOCH$_2$C(CH$_3$)$_2$CH$_2$OOC—R—	49
—OC(CH$_2$)$_n$CO—R—	154
III. R = —Ph—COO—Ph—[c]	
—OOC(CH$_2$)$_n$COO—R—	4, 41, 77, 113, 122, 131, 138
—O(CH$_2$)$_n$O—R—	40, 89, 131, 138
—O(CH$_2$CH$_2$O)$_n$—R—	138
—COO(CH$_2$)$_n$OOC—R—	76, 119
—COO(CH$_2$CH$_2$O)$_n$OC—R—	138
—OOCCH$_2$CH$_2$S(CH$_2$)$_n$SCH$_2$CH$_2$COO—R—	
—COO(CH$_2$)$_m$COO—R—	11, 134
IV. R = —Ph—COO—Ph—OOC—Ph—[c]	
—COO(CH$_2$)$_n$OOC—R—	MS-[116, 125]
—COO(CH$_2$CH$_2$O)$_n$OC—R—	70, 137
—OOC(CH$_2$CH$_2$O)$_n$CH$_2$CH$_2$COO—R—	70
—O(CH$_2$)$_n$O—R—	39, 55, 131 MS-[30, 71, 118, 124, 135]
—(OCH$_2$CH$_2$)$_n$O—R—	70, 132, 137
—O(CH$_2$)$_n$O—Ph—COO—R—	131
V. R = —Ph—OOC—Ph—COO—Ph—[c]	
—(CH$_2$)—R—	54
—COO(CH$_2$)$_n$OOC—R—	46, 61, 119, 127 MS-[125]
—COO(CH$_2$CH$_2$O)$_n$OC—R—	61, 70, 137

Table 1
Mesogenic Segmented-Chain Polymers (Continued)

	Refs.[b]
$-COOCH_2CH(CH_3)(OCH_2(CH_3)CH)_nOOC-R-$	61, 62
$-O(CH_2)_nO-R-$	71, 74, 82 MS-[3]
$-O(CH_2CH_2O)_n-R-$	70, 137
$-OCH_2Si(CH_3)_2OSi(CH_3)_2CH_2O-R-$	MS-[82]
$-CONH(CH_2)_nHNOC-R-$	139
VI. R $=-Ph-N=N-Ph-^c$	
$-OOC(CH_2)_nCOO-R-$	6, 31, 32 MS-[32]
$-O(CH_2)_nOOCCH_2COO(CH_2)_nO-R-$	63
$-O(CH_2)_6OOCCHCOO\ (CH_2)_6)O-R-$	
$\qquad CH_2CH=CH_2$	8
$-O(CH_2)_6OOC-CH-COO(CH_2)_6O-R-$	
$\qquad (CH_2)_6O-R-CN$	146
$-R'-OOC(CH_2)_8COO-R$	
$R'=-N=N-Ph-;$	
$-O-Ph-N=N-Ph-;$	
$-N=N-Ph-N=N-Ph-;$	129 MS-[129]
VII. R $=-Ph-N=ON-Ph-^c$	
$-OOC(CH_2)_nCOO-R-$	126, MS-(9, 10, 38, 126)
$-COO(CH_2)_nOOC-R-$	31
$-COO(CH_2CH_2O)_nOC-R-$	45
$-OOC(CH_2)_2-N(CH_3)-(CH_2)_6-N(CH_3)-$	
$(CH_2)_2COO-R-$	64
$-OOC(CH_2)_2-S-(CH_2)_2-S-(CH_2)_2COO-R-$	142
$-OOC(CH_2)_2-S-(CH_2)_2O(CH_2)_2-S-$	
$(CH_2)_2COO-R-$	142
$-OOC(CH_2)_2CH(CH_3)CH_2COO-R-$	MS-(9)
VIII. R $=-Ph-C(X)=N-N=(X)C-Ph-^c$	
X = H $\qquad -OOC(CH_2)_nCOO-R-$	MS-[136]
X = CH$_3$ $\qquad -OOC(CH_2)_nCOO-R-$	14, 80, 81, 87 MS-[136]
$-OOCO(CH_2)_nOCOO-R-$	14
X = CH$_2$CH$_3$ $\quad -OOC(CH_2)_nCOO-R-$	33, 87
IX. R $=-Ph-C(X)=(X')C-Ph-^c$	
X = X' = H $\qquad -COO(CH_2)_nOOC-R-$	49, 90, 115, 148
$\qquad -COO(CH_2CH_2O)_nOC-R-$	69, 85
X = CN, X' = H $\quad -OOC(CH_2)_nCOO-R-$	84
$\qquad -OOCCH_2CH_2CH(CH_3)CH_2COO-R-$	84
X = CH$_3$, X' = H $\quad -OOC(CH_2)_nCOO-R-$	14, 81, 140
$\qquad -O(CH_2)_nO-R-$	7, 130, 149
$\qquad -O(CH_2CH_2O)_n-R-$	128
X = X' = CH$_3$ $\qquad -OOC(CH_2)_nCOO-R-$	33
X = X' = CH$_2$CH$_3$ $\quad -OOC(CH_2)_nCOO-R-$	133
X. Mesogen containing group $-Ph-NHCO-^c$	
$-OOC-Ph-NHCO(CH_2)_x-OCNH-Ph-COO(CH_2)_y-$	26, 27
$-OOC(CH_2)_nCOO-Ph-NHCO-Ph-$	140
$-OOC(CH_2)_nCOO-Ph-CONH-Ph-NHOC-Ph-$	139
$-OOC(CH_2)_nCOO-Ph-NHOC-Ph-CONH-Ph-$	139
$-COO(CH_2)_nOOC-Ph-NHOC-Ph-CONH-Ph-$	139
$-O(CH_2)_n-O-Ph-CONH-Ph-OOC-Ph-$	39

Table 1
Mesogenic Segmented-Chain Polymers (Continued)

	Refs.[b]
XI. Mesogen containing group $-Ph-CH=N-Ph-$[c]	
$-OOC(CH_2)_8COO-Ph-CH=N-Ph-$	147
$-OOC(CH_2)_xCOO-Ph-COO-Ph-N=CH-$	
$Ph-O(CH_2)_yO-Ph-CH=N-Ph-OOC-Ph-$	42
$-O(CH_2)_nO-Ph-CH=N-Ph-$	
$OOC-Ph-COO-Ph-N=CH-Ph-$	42
$-OOC(CH_2)_nCOO-Ph-CH=N-Ph-$	MS-[121]
$-OOC(CH_2)_nCOO-Ph-CH=N-Ph-Ph-$	MS-[121]
$-OOC(CH_2)_nCOO-Ph-CH=N-Ph-O-Ph-$	MS-[121]
XII. Mesogen containing 2,6-(R1), 1,4-(R2), 2,3-(R3) substituted naphthalene[c]	
$-OOC(CH_2)_nCOO-R1-$	88
$-COO(CH_2)_nOOC-R1-$	90
$-COO(CH_2)_nOOC-Ph-OOC-R1-COO-Ph-$	61
$-COO(CH_2CH_2O)_nOC-Ph-OOC-R1-COO-Ph-$	61
$-COOCH_2CH(CH_3)-[OCH_2CH(CH_3)]_nOOC-$	
$Ph-OOC-R1-COO-Ph-$	61
$-O(CH_2)_nO-Ph-OOC-R1-COO-Ph-$	74
$-O(CH_2)_nO-Ph-COO-R1-OOC-Ph-$	75
$-O(CH_2)_n-Ph-COO-R2-OOC-Ph-$	75
$-O(CH_2)_nO-Ph-COO-R2-R2-OOC-Ph-$	118
$-O(CH_2)_nO-Ph-COO-R3-OOC-Ph-$	75
XIII. R = 1,4-cyclohexylene[c]	
$-OOC(CH_2)_nCOO-Ph-COO-R-OOC-Ph-$	123
$-COO(CH_2)_nOOC-Ph-OOC-R-COO-Ph-$	66, 127
$-O(CH_2)O-Ph-OOC-R-COO-Ph-$	75
XIV. Mesogen containing group $-C\equiv C-Ph-$[c]	
$-OOC(CH_2)_nCOO-Ph-C\equiv C-Ph-$	141
$-OOC(CH_2)_nCOO-Ph-C\equiv C-C\equiv C-Ph-$	144
$-OOC(CH_2)_2CH(CH_3)CH_2COO-Ph-C\equiv C-C\equiv C-Ph-$	144

[a]Not all of the polymers quoted in the text are reported in this table.
[b]MS-[ ] indicates that the mesogen contains lateral substituents.
[c] $-$ Ph $-$ = p-phenylene.

We shall now focus our attention on the vast problem of finding qualitative and quantitative relationships between polymer chain structure and liquid-crystalline behavior in the bulk. The experimental data concerning polymers having selected structural differences or analogies will be examined and the possible differences or analogies in the liquid-crystalline properties discussed. The stereochemical nature of the segments which constitute the polymer chain will be taken into account specifically. This will allow to detect whether and to what extent some specific chemical or geometrical feature has any intrinsic influence on the liquid crystal properties of the polymer in which it is contained. With the same spirit some reference will be made to the liquid crystal behavior of low molecular weight analogues.

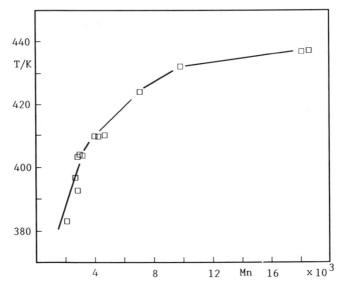

FIGURE 1
Isotropization temperature as a function of molecular weight for
nematogenic polyester **1**. (Adapted with permission from Ref. 10.
Copyright American Chemical Society.)

3. THE INFLUENCE OF MOLECULAR WEIGHT

The pattern of the experimental data pertinent to the point is rather
fragmentary and certainly insufficient to find a definite answer to all questions. By far the most largely available experimental data related to the
problem consist of isotropization temperatures (T_i) associated to solution
viscosity measurements or, less frequently, to average molecular weights
measured for polydisperse samples.[3-12] Although the data are not entirely
homogeneous there is a general agreement at least in one basic feature: for
relatively low molecular weights and within a limited range of values, T_i
depends on molecular weight. The entire set of data, which concerns both
homopolymers and random copolymers, contributes to defining the following
picture: T_i increases with increasing MW according to a nonlinear dependence with a decreasing gradient and a final leveling for MW in the order of
10^4 units. A specific example of this behavior is reported in Fig. 1. Most of
the experimental data concern nematogenic polymers; nevertheless, the essential feature, i.e., the existence of a limited range of MW within which T_i
increases with increasing MW, also applies to smectogenic polymers.[5,13] No
data are available about discotic polymers. The minimum value of MW at
which the high limit of T_i is attained is a valuable parameter for both
theoretical and practical purposes. Unfortunately, very few data are available

to try a more subtle analysis of the relationship, if any, between that value and the polymer chain structure. An interesting example of a possible such relationship is offered by a pair of homologous nematogenic polymers with formula[11]:

$$+F1-O-Ph-COO-Ph-CO-F2-OC-Ph-OOC-Ph-O+_{dp}$$

$$F1 = -OC-(CH_2)_2-S-(CH_2)_n-S-(CH_2)_2-CO- \quad n = 3, 4;$$

$$F2 = -O-(CH_2)_6-O-$$

A single methylene group differentiates the monomer unit of these polymers, yet the limiting T_i is attained for quite different molecular weights in the two cases: 4×10^3 for $n = 4$, corresponding to a degree of polymerization ~ 5, and $\sim 8 \times 10^3$ for $n = 3$, corresponding to an average degree of polymerization ~ 10. This appears to be a peculiar case of odd–even fluctuation of liquid-crystalline properties. In the region of low MW the average polymer chain is reduced to a few monomer units and the dependence of T_i appears to be more critical. In particular, the nature of chain terminations may take special relevance.

A systematic reduction of T_i was observed[10] for polymers **1**

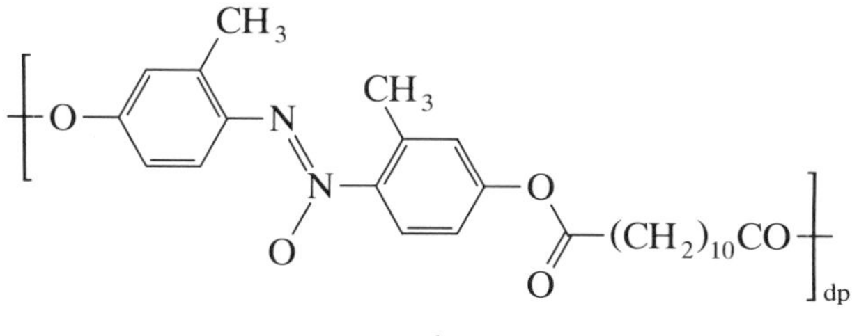

1

with a degree of polymerization ranging from ~ 6 to ~ 10 as the ratio between aromatic to aliphatic terminal groups increases at constant average molecular weight. As for any ordinary polymer, the melting temperature (T_m) of a mesogenic polymer depends on MW particularly at low values. There is no reason why this dependence should have a trend parallel to that followed by T_i. Therefore, not only the thermal stability but also the interval of stability of the mesophase depends on MW. This might occur to such an extent that the same polymer may exhibit enantiotropic $(T_i > T_m)$ or monotropic $(T_i < T_m)$ mesomorphism depending on molecular weight. A specific case concerns polymer **2**, a nematogenic polyether investigated by Percec and Nava,[12] which exhibits enantiotropic mesomorphism for number-average molecular-weight $M_n > 5000$

$$+Ph-C(CH_3)=CH-Ph-O-(CH_2)_{11}-O+_{dp}$$

2

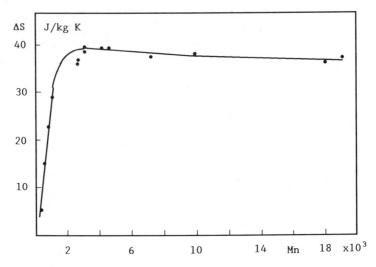

FIGURE 2
Isotropic – nematic transition entropy as a function of molecular
weight polymer **1**. (Adapted with permission from Ref. 10. Copyright
American Chemical Society.)

It is worth noting that to any practical purpose an enantiotropic to
monotropic switch might occur as a superimposed effect depending on the
thermal history. Not infrequently, a positive mesophase thermal stability
interval may be reduced to zero by annealing the polymer to increase its
melting temperature.

Experimental data on molar isotropization enthalpies (ΔH_i) and entropies (ΔS_i) as a function of MW are also available in the literature (Fig. 2
for ΔS_i as an example). There is a qualitative analogy between the dependence of enthalpy or entropy and temperature on MW. Once again, however
the correlation between polymer structure and molecular weight at which the
highest value for the ΔH_i or ΔS_i is attained is by no means obvious. As an
example, the molar isotropization enthalpy of the previously quoted poly(es-
ter β-sulfide) with $n = 3$ is essentially constant ($\Delta H_i = 4.5$ kJ mol^{-1}) within
the range of molecular weight included between $M_n = 1330$ and 7830.

Virtually all the polymers whose liquid-crystalline properties have been
examined are polydisperse. However, the influence of polydispersity on
mesophasic properties is still inadequately documented. Inadequacy concerns
particularly the quantitative relationship between polydispersity and T_i or
ΔH_i within the full range of molecular weight.

As far as low molecular weights are concerned, which define the most
critical aspect of the problem, remarkably useful information has been
gathered by investigating the liquid-crystalline properties of strictly monodisperse model compounds.

Table 2

Mesomorphic Behavior of Dimeric Molecules[a] as a Function of Spacer and End-Chain Length

	$R = -Ph-C(CH_3)=HC-Ph-$[b]										
$n \backslash p$	2	3	4	5	6	7	8	9	10	12	14
0				N	N	N	N				
2	N		N	N	N	N	N				
3				N	N						
4	S, N	S, N	S, N	N	N	N	N				
6	S		S	S*, N	S*, N	N	S, N		N*		
8				S*	S*	S*, N	S*	N*	S*, N	N	N

[a] Dimers: $CH_3-(CH_2)_nCOO-R-OOC-(CH_2)_p-COO-R-OOC(CH_2)_nCH_3$.

[b] N = nematic, S = smectic; asterisk indicates smectic polymorphism or monotropic smectic behavior for nematics. (Adapted with permission from Ref. 15.)

"Dimeric" molecules are the simplest model compounds that contain the basic structure characterizing a segmented-chain polymer, i.e., a flexible segment connecting two rigid ones. It seems reasonable to expect that the liquid-crystalline behavior of such model molecules, whose general formula is $T_1-M-F-M-T_2$ (M = mesogenic group, F = flexible spacer, T_1, T_2 = terminal groups, not necessarily different) might represent the parent polymer better than a monomeric model. This is what actually happens in most cases provided the terminal group is selected with care. This last point may turn out to be a crucial one since the very nature of the mesophasic behavior, together with the thermodynamic quantities related to it, may be influenced by the chain terminals. The following is a significant example.

Polyesters with formula **3** all exhibit nematic mesomorphism[14]

$$+Ph-C(CH_3)=CH-Ph-OOC-(CH_2)_p-COO \frac{}{dp} \qquad (p = 6-12)$$

3

Table 2 reports the mesophase types observed for a set of homologous dimeric compounds with formula **4**[15] as a function

$$H_3C(CH_2)_nCOO-M-OOC-(CH_2)_p-COO-M-OOC-(CH_2)_nCH_3$$

$$M = -Ph-C(CH_3)=CH-Ph-$$

4

of the length of spacer and terminal flexible group. The content of the table may thus be summarized: (1) for a given spacer length, smectic mesomorphism is favored by longer terminal chains; (2) the minimum terminal length at which smectic mesomorphism is observed decreases with decreasing spacer length.

It is apparent that the length of the terminal chain is a relevant parameter at least to the purpose of qualitatively reproducing the mesophasic behavior of a given polymer.

In this specific case, with an exception for $n, p = 4$, nematogenic model compounds have terminal chains shorter than the corresponding spacer. Included among these are molecules that are stoichiometrically identical to the reference polymer. These should be the best models. In contrast, a dimeric molecule whose terminal chains have the same length as the spacer (e.g., $p = n = 10$) would be a bad model for the polymer containing the same spacer: the polymer is nematogenic while the dimer is smectogenic.

In this connection, it is probably worth noting that a detailed analysis of the mesophasic behavior of a polydisperse polymer should take into account the possible presence of a significant fraction of low molecular weight oligomers whose mesogenic behavior may be not congruous with that of the high molecular weight fractions.

Dimeric model compounds have been utilized, also in relation to their polymeric homologues, particularly for investigating the role of chemical and structural parameters such as the length and the parity of the flexible chain segment.[15–21] Some of the most relevant results are discussed in Section 6.

As a further example for the need to utilize well-selected monodisperse model compounds we consider monomeric, dimeric, and tetrameric homologues of a nematogenic polymer containing 4-alkoxyphenyl 4'-alkoxybenzoate groups as monomer units[22]:

Monomer

$$C_5H_{11}O-Ph-COO-Ph-OC_5H_{11}$$

5

Dimer

$$C_5H_{11}O-Ph-COO-Ph-O(CH_2)_{10}O-Ph-OOC-Ph-OC_5H_{11}$$

6

Tetramer

$$C_5H_{11}O-Ph-COO-Ph-O(CH_2)_{10}-O-Ph-OOC-Ph-O\rceil$$

$$C_5H_{11}O-Ph-COO-Ph-O(CH_2)_{10}O-Ph-OOC-Ph-O(CH_2)\rfloor$$

7

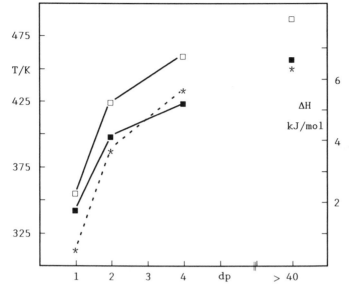

FIGURE 3

Melting (■) and isotropization (□) temperatures and isotropization enthalpy (∗) (normalized to 1 mol of rigid groups) as a function of degree of polymerization. Compounds **5 – 8**. (Adapted with permission from Ref. 22. (See also Ref. 110).

Polymer

$$\left[OC-Ph-O(CH_2)_{10}O-Ph-COO-Ph-O(CH_2)_{10}O-Ph-O \right]_{dp}$$

8

Monomer, dimer, and tetramer all exhibit a nematogenic behavior similar to the corresponding polymer. The isotropization temperature and the corresponding molar enthalpy (Fig. 3), normalized to a single monomer unit, show a drastic jump passing from monomer to dimer. This is a striking indication of the unique role played by the methylenic chain when it connects two rigid sections as it does within the polymer chain. This feature is by no means peculiar to the specific compound we are dealing with. On the contrary, it appears to be a general property at least for dimeric mesogens containing alkoxy or alkanoyloxy spacers of even parity.

As to polymers containing discotic mesogens in the main chain, the stabilizing effect resulting from polymerization is well documented. In the case of two discotic polymers containing either substituted triphenylene **(9)** or substituted benzene **(10)** rings as discotic mesogens,[23] the polymers exhibit higher discotic–isotropic transition temperature than the respective "monomeric" analogues **11**, **12**:

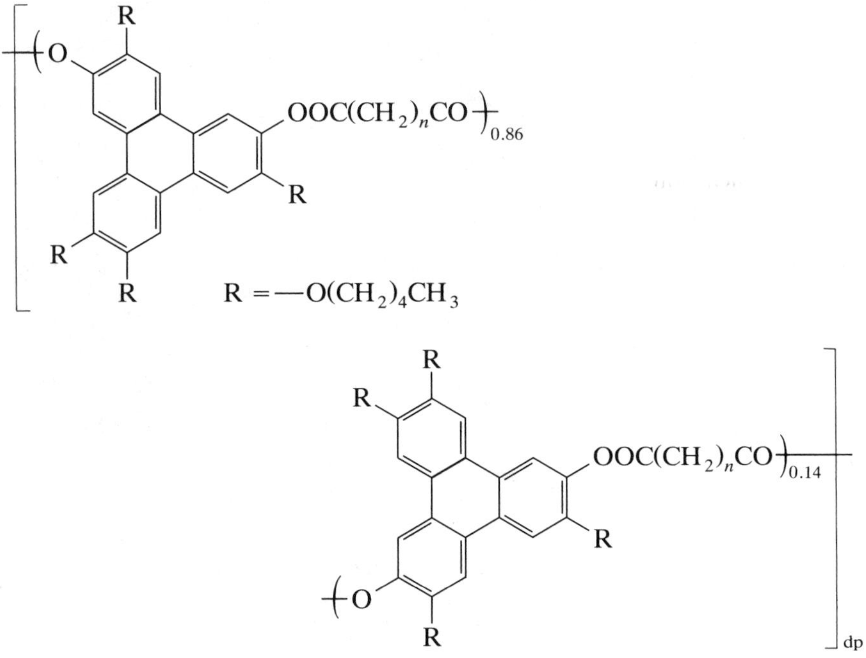

$$R = -O(CH_2)_4CH_3$$

9

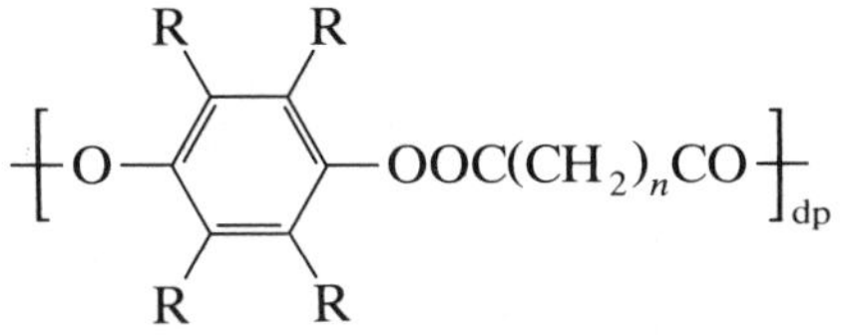

$$R = -OOC(CH_2)_6CH_3$$

10

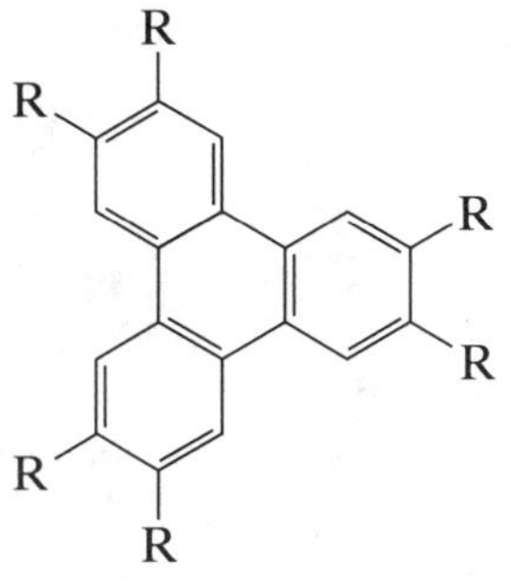

11

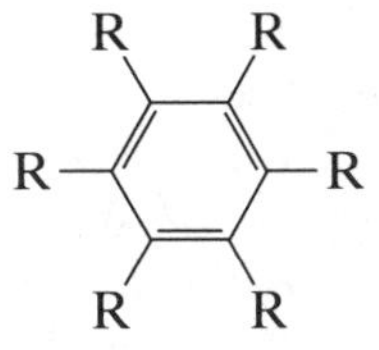

12

where $T_i(9, n = 10) = 493$ K,[23] $T_i(11) = 395$ K,[24] $T_i(10, n = 14) = 365$ K,[23] $T_i(12) = 356$ K.[25]

In addition to the thermal quantities related to isotropization another fundamental parameter appears to be dependent on MW in a somewhat similar manner. This is the order parameter. We shall discuss this point further in Section 10 and show again how dimeric model compounds may afford precious information.

In conclusion, it is quite evident that molecular weight is a relevant parameter that must be taken into full account. In the following presentation, when liquid-crystalline properties of different polymers are compared, it is implied that they have very close molecular weights or, more frequently, comparable solution viscosity, or that molecular weights are high enough to bring their relevance to a minimum.

4. THE INFLUENCE OF GEOMETRIC PARAMETERS

We shall now examine the influence that some geometric parameters of the monomer unit may exert over the liquid-crystalline properties of the polymer. The length and average cross sections of both the rigid and the flexible segments will be taken into account. It is obvious that geometrical differences arising, for instance, from different numbers of $-CH_2-$ groups or of p-phenylene units entail some other "nongeometric" differences in molecular properties, such as the electric polarizability or the multiplicity of the accessible chain conformations. Even a cursory inspection of the experimental data will show that polymers characterized by very similar geometric parameters may exhibit largely different mesophasic behavior as a consequence of a chemical diversity. Table 3 reports types of mesophase and T_i for a few selected examples. Notwithstanding the stereochemical affinities the differences of the liquid-crystalline properties are remarkable. The second polymer, whose melting temperature (T_m) is lower than the isotropization temperature of the quasi-homologous first polymer, exhibits no mesogenic behavior at all. It is apparent that chemical factors overcome and obfuscate the role of the geometric parameters, which, taken by themselves, offer no decisive indication either about the nature of the mesophase, if any, or about

Table 3
Different Liquid-Crystalline Properties Notwithstanding
Geometric Affinities in the Monomer Units

	Property	Refs.
$-Ph-N=N-Ph-OOC(CH_2)_8COO-$	$T_{NI} = 551$ K	38
$-Ph-N=N-Ph-COO(CH_2)_8OOC-$	Not mesogen	31
$-Ph-CH=N-Ph-OOC(CH_2)_8COO-$	$T_{SI} = 493$ K	147
$-Ph-NON-Ph-COO(CH_2CH_2O)_3OC-$	$T_{SI} = 453$ K	45
$-Ph-COO-Ph-OOC(CH_2)_8COO-$	$T_{NI} = 537$ K	41

Table 4
Influence of the Length of the Rigid Segment on the Isotropization Temperature

		Property	Refs.
1A	$-OOC-Ph-Ph-COO(CH_2)_n-$ ($n = 2, 4, 6$)	T_i (1A) $< T_i$ (1B)	
1B	$-OOC-Ph-Ph-Ph-COO(CH_2)_n-$		49
2A	$-O-Ph-COO-Ph-O(CH_2)_6-$	$T_i = 555$ K	40
2B	$-O-Ph-COO-Ph-OOC-Ph-O(CH_2)_6-$	$T_i = 653$ K	55
3A	$-O-Ph-COO-Ph-OOC-Ph-O(CH_2)_{10}-$	$T_i = 543$ K	55
3B	$-O-Ph-COO-Ph-Ph-OOC-Ph-O(CH_2)_{10}-$	$T_i = 647$ K	118

4A   Ti = 453 K   150

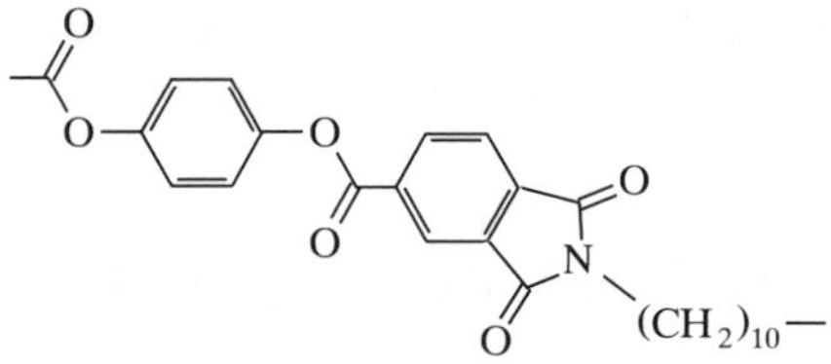

4B   Ti = 571 K   150

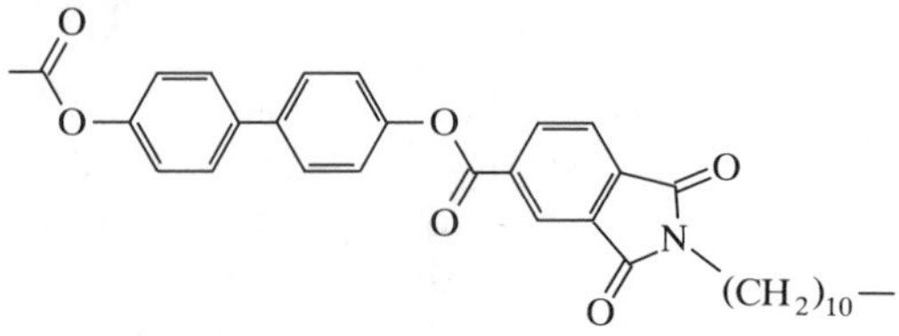

4C   Ti = 677 K   44

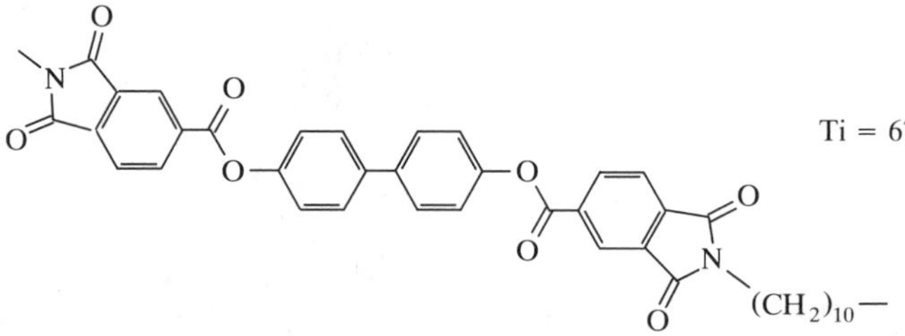

its thermal stability. Nonetheless, if our inspection is restricted as much as possible to classes of strictly similar compounds, the effect of possible interferences due to even small and localized differences of chemical structure can be minimized and the role played by the geometric parameters comes to light. The examples reported in Table 4 are representative of an entire array of cases showing that the thermal stability of the mesophase is an increasing function of the length of the rigid section of the monomer unit. This is true regardless of the nature of the mesophase.

Although in most cases comparison has been restricted to polymers exhibiting homologous mesomorphism, there is no real need for doing that. What we are really looking for is the temperature at which the amorphous liquid has the same free energy of the ordered one, whatever the structure of the latter may be. This is the case for polymers 1A, which are smectogenic, and 1B, which show also a nematic phase for $n = 2, 4$. In all cases $T_i(1A) <$ $T_i(1B)$. The length of the rigid sections characterizing the above-mentioned polymers lay within a very limited range. Polymers 1A and 4C, which correspond to the extreme values, have rigid sections whose lengths are in the ratio $\sim 1/2$. The same holds for the average axial ratios: ~ 2 for 1A, ~ 4 for 4C.

As will be discussed further on, T_i depends on the length of the flexible segment as well as on that of the rigid one. Specifically, shorter spacers favor higher temperatures. Therefore, thermotropic mesomorphism might show up with longer mesogens, unless chemical decomposition takes place, provided long spacers are used. However, the behavior of polymers 4A/C, which can be taken as a model, shows that, notwithstanding the considerable length of the methylenic spacer, the rapid increase of T_m and T_i with increasing length of the rigid segments is a serious obstacle in the way of obtaining thermotropic mesomorphism for a polymer whose rigid segment is much longer than it is for polymer 4C.

Most segmented LCP's, and LMWLC's as well, contain at least two phenyl groups in their rigid sections (e.g., polymers 1A and 2A) or some other group of roughly equivalent linear dimension (e.g., t-cyclohexyl groups connected as in **13**)

$$-Ph-COO-C_6H_{10}-OOC-Ph-$$

13

which built up a rigid segment with an average axial ratio $> \sim 2$. However, this is not a necessary requisite and liquid crystal properties may show up even when the rigid moiety has a smaller linear dimension. However, some peculiar features intervene that are illustrated by the following examples. Polymer **10**[23] is possibly the most simple example of a segmented-chain polymer to exhibit discotic mesomorphism. The simplest low molecular weight "monomeric" homologue, i.e., the benzenehexaalkanoate, has the same mesomorphic behavior.[25] The chemical structure of these compounds excludes the occurrence of intermolecular interactions of any peculiar kind. Therefore, the nature of the mesophase appears to be dominated entirely by the shape of the monomer unit. As to polymers **14**[26, 27]

$$+CONH-Ph-COO(CH_2)_nOOC-Ph-HNOC-(CH_2)_m+_{dp}$$

14

they are polyesteramides exhibiting smectic mesomorphism for specific values of n and m. It is very likely that intermolecular hydrogen bonding plays a decisive role. In this case, strong intermolecular interactions compensate a weak steric drive to mesomorphism.

A significant example of the consequences of similar interactions on the liquid crystal properties of low molecular weight compounds is offered by the phase behavior of methyl-substituted N,N'-dialkanoyl-1,3-benzendiamines.[28] Mesomorphism, particularly of the discotic type, is presented by molecules having a rigid core that, besides being rather small, is neither linear nor disclike and may even be unsymmetrically substituted.

5. RIGID GROUPS WITH LATERAL SUBSTITUENTS

Inserting substituents on the rigid segment modifies its electronic and steric features and, therefore, its mesogenic potential. Electronic and steric factors may have conflicting effects on the thermal stability of the meso-phase.[9, 29, 31–34, 118, 125] However, in general, the steric factor plays a predominant role.[29] A number of experimental data lead to the conclusion that the presence of one or more lateral substitutents reduces the thermal stability of the liquid-crystalline phase. This does not necessarily entail a reduction of the thermal stability interval. On the contrary, it may occur that because of a concomitant larger depression of T_m the stability interval is increased with respect to the unsubstituted homologue. Polymers bearing an intrinsically mesogenic segment as a lateral substituent have also been reported.[30]

The presence of substituents to the rigid segment may have a consequence not limited to the purely steric factor of increasing the average cross section of the segment. Most commonly, the mesogenic segments utilized to synthesize polymers have a symmetrical structure, usually characterized by an inversion center or a binary axis orthogonal to the elongation axis of the segment. The presence of a substituent may break that symmetry and, as a consequence of a polymerization reaction occurring with no steric control, constitutional disorder affects the polymer chain.

Constitutional disorder, as will be discussed further in Section 9, should have a comparatively larger effect on T_m, depressing it, than on T_i. Therefore, the presence of a single substitutent has a negative influence on T_i mainly because of the increased sterical hindrance of the rigid section of the monomer unit. The same factor as well as constitutional disorder contributes to depress T_m.

The following example may illustrate the point. Polymers 15 and their 3-methyl-substituted counterparts 16 are nematogenic.[31, 32]

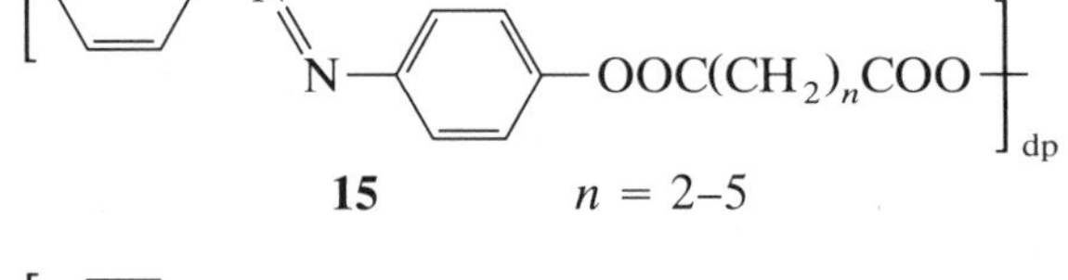

15          $n = 2-5$

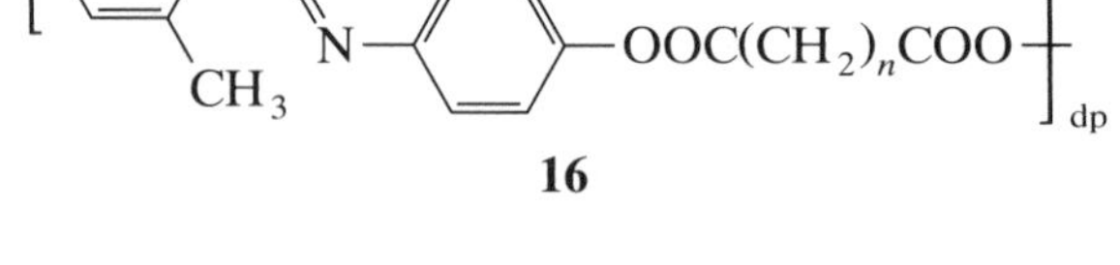

16

For any given spacer length, polymer **15** has higher T_m and T_i than the corresponding **16**. The average difference is 74 K for T_m and 58 K for T_i. Therefore, the average thermal stability interval of the nematic phase is higher by 16 K in favor of polymers **16**.

Progressing from unsymmetrically monosubstituted to symmetrically disubstituted mesogens, a quite analogous interplay between steric and entropic factors is detectable.

Let the following two couples of such polymers be used as example:

$$\text{+Ph}-\text{C(CH}_3)\!=\!\text{HC}-\text{Ph}-\text{OOC(CH}_2)_8\text{COO+}_{dp}$$

17

where $T_m \approx 483$ K, $T_i = 530$ K[33];

$$\text{+Ph}-\text{C(CH}_3)\!=\!(\text{CH}_3)\text{C}-\text{Ph}-\text{OOC(CH}_2)_8\text{COO+}_{dp}$$

18

with $T_m = 500$ K, $T_i = 454$ K[14] (virtual);

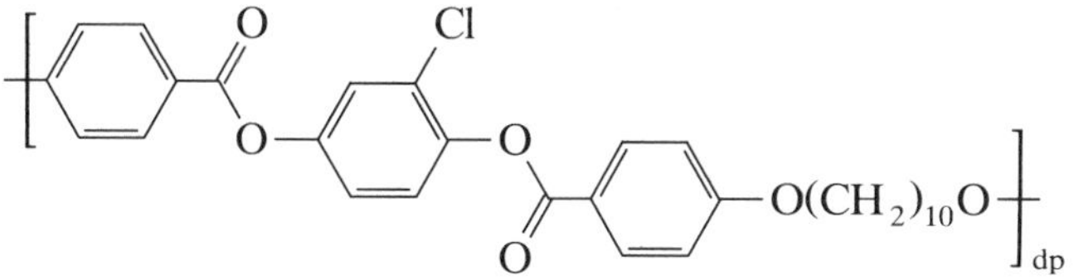

19[34] $T_m = 430$ K, $T_i = 552$ K;

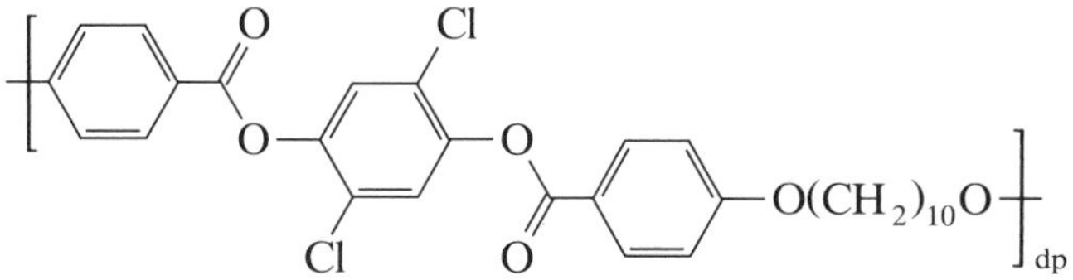

20[34] $T_m = 473$ K, $T_i = 528$ K.

Insertion of a second substituent has a drastic depressive effect on T_i in both cases. Polymer **18** is not even an enantiotropic mesogen. Its clearing temperature is a virtual value obtained by extrapolating the mesogenic behavior of structurally related random copolymers.

The effect on T_m is exactly the opposite. The diminution of melting entropy related to the symmetrical geometry of the monomer unit prevails. As a further argument let us consider the behavior of

$$\text{+Ph}-\text{C(CH}_3)\!=\!\text{N}-\text{N}\!=\!(\text{CH}_3)\text{C}-\text{Ph}-\text{OOC(CH}_2)_8\text{COO+}_{dp}$$

21

with T_m = 483 K, T_i = 545 K,[33] and:

$$+ Ph - C(CH_2CH_3) = N - N = (CH_3CH_2)C - Ph - OOC(CH_2)_8COO +_{dp}$$

22

with T_m = 440 K, T_i = 418 K (virtual).[14] Now both polymers have symmetric monomer units. The larger bulkiness of substituents of polymer **22** corresponds to a reduction of both melting and isotropization temperature (as for polymer **18**, this is a virtual value).

Let us now take into account a different case. Polymer **23**[35] is a very remarkable example of a class of liquid-crystalline polymers whose mesogenic section may take nonlinear geometries because of conformational mobility:

$$+ Ph - O - CH_2 - Ph - CH_2 - O - Ph - O - (CH_2)_n - O +_{dp} \quad n = 7-12$$

23

Taking into account the isolated mesogenic group only, rotation around the $PhO - CH_2Ph$ bond is not hindered enough to prevent the statistical weight of gauche conformations to be quite relevant at temperatures around 450–500 K.[36] However, this does not need to be entirely true for the liquid crystal polymer as well. It is likely that intramolecular constraints coming from the polymeric structure and the orientational field of the mesophase may have a cooperative straightening effect on the mesogen itself.

6. THE EFFECT OF THE SPACER LENGTH

The effect of the length of the flexible spacer on the liquid crystal properties of a polymer has been examined in a considerable number of cases. Two features are outstanding for the high frequency they are observed. First, within a homologous series of polymers, T_i decreases as the number of atoms forming the backbone chain (i.e., the length) of the flexible segment increases.

This statement is better qualified by the second: T_i fluctuates, with an amplitude depending on the chemical nature of the polymer, according to the even or odd parity of the number n of atoms forming the backbone chain of the flexible segment. In general, $T_i(n) > [T_i(n - 1) + T_i(n + 1)]/2$ for n even.

This behavior is not bound to any particular mesophase type. It has been observed both for nematogenic[11, 14, 37-42] and smectogenic polymers[43-45] (also[46-48] for the first feature only) or even in some case in which both mesomorphic forms are present.[5]

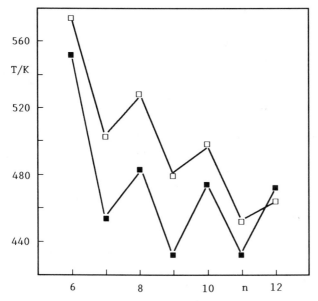

FIGURE 4

Melting (■) and isotropization (□) temperatures for nematogenic polyesters **24** as a function of number n of CH_2 groups in the spacer. (Adapted with permission from Ref. 14. Copyright Hüthig & Wepf Verlag.)

The thermal stability interval of the mesomorphic state (i.e., $T_i - T_m$) follows a less clearly defined trend. One trivial reason for this is related to the dependence of T_m on the thermal history of the polymer.

A typical example of "regular" behavior is that shown in Fig. 4 for a homologous series of nematogenic polyesters (**24**) containing α-methylstilbene as a mesogenic segment.[14]

$$+O-Ph-C(CH_3)=HC-Ph-OOC(CH_2)_n-CO\,]_{dp} \qquad n = 6\text{--}12$$

24

Melting temperature T_m and isotropization temperature T_i fluctuate with a parallel odd–even effect but they decrease for increasing n with a different gradient. For shorter spacers ($n < 10$ in this specific example), $dT_m/d_n < dT_i/d_n$, for both even and odd values of n. For longer spacers the trend is inverted. As a consequence, the thermal stability interval of the mesophase first increases with n, then decreases.

Not infrequently low and high n limits of enantiotropic mesomorphism are not or cannot be detected. For the specific case under discussion, $n = 12$ is quite clearly the high limit. This qualification comes from a simple and instructive observation. A polymer sample that has undergone no previous thermal treatment melts at a temperature lower than that appearing in Fig. 4 and even lower than T_i. Therefore, under such conditions, the polymer manifests a seemingly enantiotropic mesomorphism. However, the melting temperature can be made to rise closer to the limiting value by annealing the polymer in the solid state just below melting. The polymer melts to an isotropic liquid and mesomorphism is actually revealed as monotropic. As to the low n limit, provided any limit exists, no experimental data are available for $n < 6$. From a rough extrapolation of the trend shown in Fig. 4 it is not unlikely that even for $n = 4$ chemical instability prevents any reliable determination of T_m and T_i which should be quite high.

Liquid-crystalline behavior, usually as the property of only one phase of a liquid biphasic system, has been observed with polymers containing flexible segments of considerable length. This, for instance, is the case for polymer[49]:

$$+O-Ph-Ph-Ph-COO(CH_2CH_2O)_{10}-CO+_{dp}$$

whose liquid crystalline fraction isotropizes between ~ 343 K and ~ 390 K (as a comparison, the homologous polymer containing four oxyethylene groups in the monomer unit isotropizes at 526 K).

Analogous behavior has been observed also with low molecular weight compounds.[50-52]

The odd–even fluctuation of T_i is not restricted to polymeric mesogens. Table 5 reports some thermodynamic data concerning a set of homologous "monomeric," "dimeric," and polymeric alkanoates containing α-methylstil-

Table 5

Comparison of Thermodynamic Data Concerning Nematogenic Monomeric (M), Dimeric (D), and Polymeric (P) Homologues[a]

	M		D		P	
n	T_i (K)[b]	ΔH_i (kJ mol^{-1})[b]	T_i (K)[b]	ΔH_i (kJ mol^{-1})[b]	T_i (K)[b]	ΔH_i (kJ mol^{-1})[b]
6	382.8	0.77	460.4	6.77	575	9.59
7			425.7	2.64	503	2.72
8	361.5	0.62	442.8	6.86	528	8.66
9			420.0	2.90	479	3.18
10	367.7	1.01	430.4	6.71	498	7.37
11			414.9	3.53	452	3.39
12	361.0	1.24	421.4	6.87	464	6.57

[a] $M = CH_3(CH_2)_{n'}COO-R-OOC(CH_2)_{n'}CH_3$, $n' = (n + 2)/2$;
$D = CH_3(CH_2)_4COO-R-OOC(CH_2)_nCOO-R-OOC(CH_2)_4CH_3$;
$P = +R-OOC(CH_2)_nCOO+_{dp}$, $R = -Ph-C(CH_3)=HC-Ph-$.
[b] T_i (K) and ΔH_i (kJ mol^{-1}) are for nematic–isotropic transition. Adapted with permission from Ref. 53.

bene as a mesogenic core.[53] The amplitude of the odd–even effect increases from monomer to polymer but the largest increment occurs at the first step.

The dependence of ΔH_i on the length of the flexible spacer parallels that of T_i only as far as odd–even fluctuations are concerned (Table 5). If even or odd homologues are taken separately into account, no single trend emerges. Transition enthalpy may increase or decrease or be substantially constant with increasing spacer length and, within the same homologous series, even and odd subsets may show analogous or opposite trends. The only fairly frequent feature is that gradients are small.

Examination of the mesomorphic behavior of homologous polymers indicates as a general trend that increasing spacer length favors the stabilization of smectic mesomorphism over the nematic one. This feature may manifest itself with smectic mesomorphism completely replacing the nematic one for spacers longer than a certain value. This is the case for polymers $+OC-Ph-Ph-Ph-COO(CH_2)_n-O+_{dp}$ which are both nematogenic and smectogenic for $n = 2,4$ and only smectogenic for $n > 4$.[49] Otherwise, both mesomorphic forms may be exhibited enantiotropically[39,54,55] and the smectic–nematic (T_{SN}) and nematic–isotropic (T_{NI}) transition temperatures change with the spacer length with different average gradients.

The influence of the spacer parity may also show up with a peculiar odd–even effect on the nature of the mesophase. This is the case for some polyalkanoates of 4,4'-dihydroxybiphenyl,[5,56]

$$+O-Ph-Ph-OOC-(CH_2)_n-CO+_{dp} \qquad n = 5\text{--}12,$$

which are nematogenic for n odd and smectogenic for n even.

Let us now reinspect the data of Table 2 concerning a set of dimeric model molecules. Two features need to be underlined. (1) For any given flexible terminal chain, the relative stability of the smectic phase over the nematic one as a function of the spacer length follows a trend opposite to that mentioned for polymers. (2) Smectic mesomorphism is better favored by even spacers. Thus, it is evident that the application to polymeric mesogens of specific indications coming from the behavior of low molecular weight model compounds must be done with great care.

Rather more primitive is the pattern concerning columnar discotic mesomorphism of mainchain polymers. The onset of discotic behavior appears to be dominated by the structure of the mesogenic group much more than for any other mesophase. Nonetheless, even the few available experimental data indicate that the role played by the spacer is not irrelevant. Mesophase stability and molar isotropization enthalpy decrease with increasing spacer length[23,57] but, seemingly, too short a spacer may equally prevent discotic behavior from developing. Table 6 reports thermal data concerning polymers **9** and **10**.[23] On the other hand, x-ray diffraction studies of the discotic phase of **10** ($n = 14$)[58] and of its homopolymeric analogue containing 100% 2,6-linked triphenylene groups[59] agree on the value of 2.04 nm for the inter-

Table 6
Thermodynamic Data for Discogenic Polymers[a]

	9[c]			**10**[c]		
n[b]	T_g (K)	T_i (K)	ΔH_i (J g^{-1})	T_g (K)	T_i (K)	ΔH_i (J g^{-1})
7	327	d	d			
8	328	d	d			
10	328	368	18	323	493	19
12	327	370	19			
14		365	5	333	423	7
20	303	d	d	308	d	d

[a] Adapted with permission from Ref. 23. Copyright Hüthig & Wepf Verlag.
[b] n = CH$_2$ groups in the spacer.
[c] T_g = glass transition; T_i = discotic–isotropic transition;
ΔH_i = discotic–isotropic transition enthalpy.
[d] Nonmesogenic.
[e] Partially crystalline.

columnar distance and 0.35 nm for the intracolumnar disk separation. These are quite close to the values of 1.88 nm and 0.36 nm found by Levelut[60] for "monomeric" 2,3,6,7,10,11-hexakis(pentyloxy)triphenylene. Seemingly, a spacer of that length has little influence on the structure of the discotic phase.

7. SUBSTITUENTS AT THE FLEXIBLE SEGMENT

Inclusion of a substituent along the flexible segment or as a branch of it has some influence on liquid-crystalline properties. As a general trend, with a very peculiar exception, the thermal stability of the mesophase is depressed. The effect is progressive as the bulk size is augmented.

The following examples are taken to represent some of the ways the phenomenon may occur. To the different lateral bulk should be ascribed the different isotropization temperature found for polymers **25** and **26**: 621 K and 460 K, respectively.[49]

$$+OC-Ph-Ph-Ph-COO-CH_2-C(CH_3)_2-CH_2-O+_{dp}$$

25

$$+OC-Ph-Ph-Ph-COO-CH_2-C(CH_2CH_3)_2-CH_2-O+_{dp}$$

26

A similar effect is observed for adipate (**27**) and 3-methyladipate (**28**) polymers containing 2,2'-dimethylazoxybenzene groups as the mesogen. In this specific case, since the 3-methyladipate group is configurationally regular, the nematic mesomorphism of polymer **27** is maintained in polymer **28** as the cholesteric variant. As a consequence of the unsymmetrical substitution on the spacer and of the sterically uncontrolled polymerization, polymer **28** is constitutionally disordered. No data are available about any possible influence of this feature on mesophase stability.

The case for smectogenic polymers **29** and **30** is similar.

$$+Ph-OOC-Ph-COO-Ph-COO(CH_2CH_2O)-OC+_{dp}$$

29

$$+Ph-OOC-Ph-COO-Ph-COO(CH_2CH(CH_3)O)_2-OC+_{dp}$$

30

T_i is 608 K for **29**[61] and 563 K for **30**, which contains configurationally ordered flexible spacers.[62] A still lower temperature (538 K) is measured for the same polymer if configurational order is absent.[61] In some cases, lateral substituents may favor mesophase stability instead of depressing it. Polymer **31** is smectogenic with isotropization at 420 K.[63]

$$+O-Ph-Ph-O(CH_2)_6-OOC-CH_2-COO-(CH_2)_6+_{dp}$$

31

Substitution of one hydrogen atom of $-OOC-CH_2-COO-$ with an allyl group $-CH_2-CH=CH_2$ preserves the smectic nature of the mesophase but T_i decreases to 394 K.[8] The negative effect produced by the increased bulk is apparent. However, if the substituent group is **32**, the smectic phase isotropizes at 443 K.[8]

$$-CH_2-(CH_2)_5-O-Ph-Ph-O-(CH_2)_3-CH=CH_2$$

32

Several cases have been reported[64-67] in which the flexible spacer is modified by inclusion of a bulky group along its chain. That reported by Furuya et al.[67] concerning monodisperse oligomers [whose reference full polymer might be found in poly(4,4'-alkoxybiphenyl)[68]] is of interest for its implications in the odd–even effect.

The most common structure for a flexible spacer is a polymethylenic chain. The most common variant of this structure involves substitution of one or more CH_2 groups with oxygen atoms. Although experimental data are not entirely coherent, the most recurrent results indicate that such a substitution

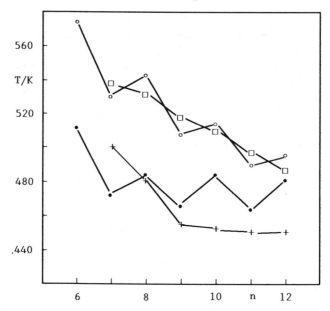

FIGURE 5

Melting temperatures (lower values) and isotropization temperatures (upper values) as a function of spacer length for nematogenic polymers **33** (●, ○) and **34** (+, □). The number of CH_2 groups in the spacer n for **33**, $n - 2$ for **34**. (Adapted with permission from Ref. 14. Copyright Hüthig & Wepf Verlag.)

is scarcely effective on mesophase stability if a single CH_2 is replaced. This is typically the case for polymers containing groups

$$-R-COO-(CH_2)_2-O-(CH_2)_2-OOC-,^{[45,61,69]}$$

or

$$-R-O-(CH_2)_2-O-(CH_2)_2-O-,^{[70]}$$

as compared to homologues

$$-R-COO-(CH_2)_5-OOC-^{[31,49,61]} \quad or \quad -R-O-(CH_2)_5-O-.^{[55,71]}$$

Some modification on mesophase stability and on the amplitude of the odd–even fluctuation is produced by a more extensive chemical change. Figure 5 reports T_m and T_i for two sets of polymers having the same rigid segment in the monomer unit but a different spacer:

$$+Ph-C(CH_3)=N-N=(CH_3)C-Ph-OOC-(CH_2)_n-COO+_{dp}$$

33

$$+Ph-C(CH_3)=N-N=(CH_3)C-Ph-OOCO-(CH_2)_{n-2}-OCOO+_{dp}$$

34

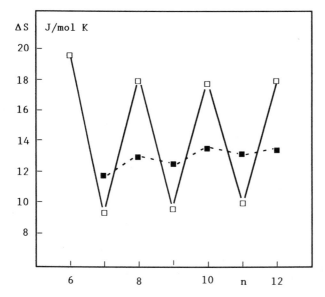

FIGURE 6
Molar isotropization entropy for polymers **33** (□) and **34** (■) as a function of spacer length. (Adapted with permission from Ref. 14. Copyright Hüthig & Wepf Verlag.)

A drastic depression of the odd–even fluctuation characterizes the change from ester to carbonate linking groups. Mesophase stability is slightly reduced for even spacers and slightly increased for the odd ones. The same trend (Fig. 6) is followed by ΔS_i.[14]

Totally analogous differences distinguish the mesophasic behavior of monodisperse model molecules of dimeric structure:

$$CH_3(CH_2)_4COO-R-OOC(CH_2)_nCOO-R-OOC(CH_2)_4CH_3$$

35

$$CH_3(CH_2)_4COO-R-OOCO(CH_2)_{n-2}OCOO-R-OOC(CH_2)_4CH_3$$

36

the rigid group R being the same as for polymers **33** and **34**.[16,17] Figures 7 and 8 report T_i and ΔS_i for two related sets of such dimers. It is apparent that for polymers and for dimeric model compounds the structural variation has its most relevant consequences on the conformational mobility of the spacer at the critical point of connection with the rigid segment.

Polymers containing group $-(CH_2CH_2O)_n-CH_2CH_2-$ in the spacer with $n > 1$ have lower melting temperatures than the corresponding methylenic homologues. As to mesophase stability, the pattern of the experimental

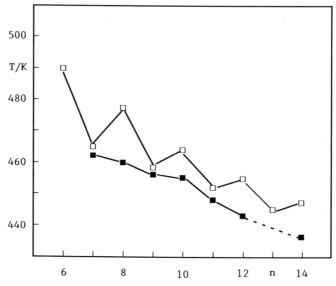

FIGURE 7
Isotropization temperature for nematogenic dimeric compounds **35**
(□) and **36** (■) as a function of spacer length. (Adapted with
permission from Ref. 16. Copyright Gordon & Breach Sci.
Publishers, and Ref. 17. Copyright John Wiley & Sons.)

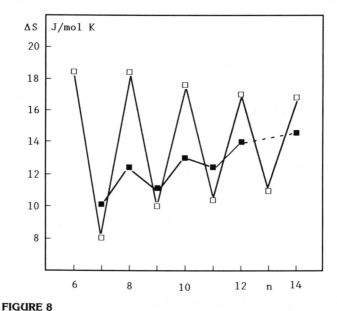

FIGURE 8
Molar isotropization entropy for nematogenic dimeric compounds
35 (□) and **36** (■) as a function of spacer length. (Adapted with
permission from Ref. 16. Copyright Gordon & Breach Sci.
Publishers, and Ref. 17. Copyright John Wiley & Sons.)

286

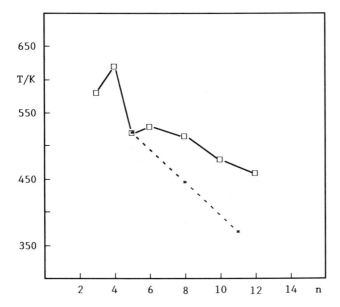

FIGURE 9
Isotropization temperature for smectogenic polymers **37** ($\square$) and **38**
($*$). (Data from Refs. 49, 85, 148.)

data does not allow any univocal conclusion. However, what seems to be a general trend is the steeper decrease of mesophase stability with increasing spacer length for polymers containing oxyethylenic spacers. Figure 9 contains a comparative set of data for smectogenic polyesters of stilbenedicarboxylic acid:

$$\left[OC-Ph-CH=HC-Ph-COO(CH_2)_n-O\right]_{dp}$$

37

$$\left[OC-Ph-CH=HC-Ph-COO(CH_2CH_2O)_mCH_2CH_2O\right]_{dp}$$

$$m = (n-2)/3$$

38

8. CONSTITUTIONAL ISOMERISM IN POLYESTERS

The structural peculiarity of mesogenic segmented-chain polymers, namely the alternate sequence of two drastically different molecular sections, makes polycondensation the most practical reaction process for their production. Actually, within the vast array of mesogenic polymers, all kinds of polycon-

Table 7
Comparison of Mesophase Stability for Couples
of Isomeric R—COO—F R—OOC—F Polyesters

	Polymer	Mesophase	T_i (K)	Refs.
1	—OC—Ph—Ph—COO(CH$_2$)$_6$—O—	S	502	49
2	—O—Ph—Ph—OOC(CH$_2$)$_6$—CO—	S	609	5
1	—OC—Ph—Ph—COO(CH$_2$)$_7$—O—	S	417[a]	43
2	—O—Ph—Ph—OOC(CH$_2$)$_7$—CO—	N	526	5
1	—OC—Ph—COO—Ph—COO(CH$_2$)$_6$—O—	N	463	119
2	—O—Ph—COO—Ph—OOC(CH$_2$)$_6$—CO—	N	588	43
1	—OC—Ph—N=N—Ph—COO(CH$_2$)$_8$—O—	b	—	31
2	—O—Ph—N=N—Ph—OOC(CH$_2$)$_8$—CO—	N	551	31
1	—OC—Ph—NO=N—Ph—COO(CH$_2$)$_7$—O—	S	474[c]	31
2	—O—Ph—NO=N—Ph—OOC(CH$_2$)$_7$—CO—	N	544	32

[a] Isotropic–smectic transition; some supercooling is possible.
[b] Not mesogenic: T_m = 505 K.
[c] Isotropic–smectic transition: T_m = 478 K, monotropic mesomorphism.

densates are present but polyesters are by far the most common. Ester linkages may be utilized for connecting rigid to flexible segments or for building the rigid segment itself or for both purposes together.

Two cases of constitutional isomerism concerning polyesters deserve some discussion because of their frequent occurrence. The first one concerns the two possible ways rigid and flexible segment may be connected: R—COO—F or R—OOC—F. The second differentiates the structure of rigid segments containing two phenylbenzoate groups:

—Ph—OOC—Ph—COO—Ph— —Ph—COO—Ph—OOC—Ph—

The experimental data on polymers distinguished by constitutional isomerism of the first type but homologues in any other respect are numerous (Table 7). With very few exceptions, they indicate that: (a) Isomer R—COO—F is most frequently smectogenic, while R—OOC—F is nematogenic; (b) mesophase stability is higher for isomer R—OOC—F than for R—COO—F.

As far as the second type of isomerism is concerned, a number of low molecular weight monomeric compounds containing either group

—Ph—OOC—Ph—COO—Ph—

or group

—Ph—COO—Ph—OOC—Ph—

as the mesogen have been investigated.[72,73] *p*-Phenylenedibenzoates constantly exhibit larger mesophase stability than p-substituted phenyltherphthalate homologues. Since these isomeric mesogens have virtually identical length and average cross section, no sterical reasons appear to be responsible for this feature. A possible explanation was given by Dewar and Goldberg[72] in terms of different modifications of the polarity of the carboxylic carbonyls produced by terminal substituents. Electron-donor terminal groups would enhance polarity of $-C{=}O$ groups of phenylenedibenzoates and have scarce influence on phenylterephthalates; electron-withdrawing groups would depress polarity of $-C{=}O$ groups of phenyltherephthalates and have little effect on phenylendibenzoates. As to polymeric compounds containing the same mesogens, a similar, although not equally clearcut, trend is detectable within the available data.[3, 55, 70, 71, 74, 75] Some inconsistency that may be traced in the data is related probably to exceedingly large differences in molecular weights of the homologous polymers that are compared.

9. COPOLYMERS

Most liquid-crystalline polymers of practical interest are copolymers. Actually, copolymerization offers a powerful and versatile means to vary composition and chain structure of a polymer with consequences on mesophase stability and, in some cases, on the nature of the mesophase itself. In the most simple instance, a segmented chain copolymer may be synthesized utilizing either two different rigid groups or two different flexible groups together. Such binary copolymers, having formula $+R_x(R')_{1-x}-F+_{dp}$ or $+R-F_x(F')_{1-x}+_{dp}$, where R and R' or F and F' vicariate each other at random are by far the most common. We shall focus our attention on copolymers of that type. To simplify classification, monomer units $-R-F-$ will be qualified as "mesogenic" (or "nonmesogenic") if the corresponding homopolymers exhibit (or do not exhibit) enantiotropic mesomorphism. A further distinction will be related to the nematic or smectic nature of the mesophase. Before doing that, however, let us examine more subtle forms of chemical disorder that either by purpose or de facto are produced in the polymerization process. If either the rigid or the flexible segment forming the polymer structure is not symmetric, chemical disorder may affect polymer chains if polymerization takes place in the absence of regiospecific control. This is what normally happens when, as an instance, a polyester is formed by interfacial condensation of a symmetric aliphatic dicarboxylic acid and an unsymmetric molecule, such as $HO-Ph-C(R){=}HC-Ph-OH$ or $HO-Ph-COO-Ph-OH$, whose two functional groups are regioselectively and chemoselectively distinguishable. As a consequence, several polymers among those mentioned so far as being homopolymers have an aregic structure and may be considered random copolymers. The almost complete absence of experimental data concerning regioregular homologues prevents any general evaluation of the consequences of this type of disorder on liquid-crystalline properties. However, two specific cases are worthy of note. Polyesters containing $-\text{OOC}-\text{Ph}-\text{OOC}-\text{Ph}-\text{COO}-$ as rigid segments were prepared[76] with either aregic (**39**) or syndioregic (**40**) structure.

$$\left[\text{OC}-\text{Ph}-\text{OOC}-\text{Ph}-\text{COO}(\text{CH}_2)_{10}-\text{O}\right]_{dp}$$

39

$$\left[\text{OC}-\text{Ph}-\text{OOC}-\text{Ph}-\text{COO}(\text{CH}_2)_{10}-\text{OOC}-\text{Ph}-\text{COO}-\text{Ph}-\right.$$
$$\left.\text{COO}(\text{CH}_2)_{10}-\text{O}\right]_{dp}$$

40

Both polymers melt at the same temperature (413 K) but, while the disordered form shows mesomorphic behavior within a limited monotropic range (T_i = 406 K) the syndioregic form shows none.

The second case is particularly interesting because it gives also the opportunity to point out a further mechanism by which chemical disorder can be produced along the polymer chain and to evaluate the consequences on the mesophasic behavior. The basic structure is that of an alkanoate of 4′-hydroxyphenyl-4-hydroxybenzoate:

$$\left[\text{O}-\text{Ph}-\text{COO}-\text{Ph}-\text{OOC}(\text{CH}_2)_5-\text{CO}\right]_{dp}$$

41

Carbon-13 NMR spectroscopy data[77] indicate that the polymer prepared by transesterification from $\text{CH}_3\text{COO}-\text{Ph}-\text{COO}-\text{Ph}-\text{OOCCH}_3$ and pimelic acid $\text{HOOC}(\text{CH}_2)_5\text{COOH}$ contains oxybenzoate diads

$$-\text{O}-\text{Ph}-\text{COO}-\text{Ph}-\text{COO}-$$

It is apparent that also the central ester linkage of the 4′-oxyphenyl-4-oxybenzoate is engaged by the reaction. As a consequence, the final polymer structure contains in random and aregic sequence groups

$$-\text{O}-\text{Ph}-\text{OOC}(\text{CH}_2)_5-\text{CO}-$$

having very low, if any, mesogenic potential, standard unaltered monomer units, and groups

$$-\text{O}-\text{Ph}-\text{COO}-\text{Ph}-\text{COO}-\text{Ph}-\text{OOC}(\text{CH}_2)_5-\text{CO}-$$

with higher mesogenic potential. "A posteriori" the significance of this result should be extended to analogous polymers synthesized previously by different authors[4,55] utilizing transesterification procedures. A regioregular polymer of the same basic composition could be prepared[77] by solution polycondensation of the acid chloride with

$$HO-Ph-OOC-Ph-OOC(CH_2)_5COO-Ph-COO-Ph-OH$$

Regular and disordered polymers have drastically different mesomorphic behavior. The clearing temperature for the disordered isomer (T_i = 661 K, upper limit of the optically observed transition) is much higher than for the regular one (T_i = 553 K) but the same holds for the thermal width of the biphasic region (119 K compared to 5 K), which is detectable for the disordered form by optical observation but not by DSC analysis.[78] Seemingly, chemical disorder is responsible for such a different behavior more than lack of regioregularity. In fact, the same polymer was synthesized (together with some homologues) by high-temperature solution polycondensation of 4'-hydroxyphenyl-4-hydroxybenzoate and the acid chloride.[41] This procedure does not involve the ester linkage of the phenylbenzoate group but is not regiospecific. Therefore, the polymer contains rigid segments of a single structure but their position along the backbone chain is aregic. Solution polycondensed polymers have lower clearing temperatures but also much narrower biphasic regions than homologues prepared by transester-ification.[4,41,55] The only significant difference in the liquid-crystalline properties between the aregic polymer containing pimeloate groups and its syndioregic homologue concerns isotropization temperature which is higher by 5 K for the disordered isomer.

9.1. Copolymers Whose Monomer Units Have the Same Rigid Group and Different Spacer

The most common and simple case is found for monomer units that both are nematogenic and differ from each other in having flexible spacers with homologous structure but different length.[79-82] Copolymers are nematogenic within the full range of composition. Isotropization temperatures are in most cases close to the composition weighted average. In respect to this, random copolymers behave as binary systems of low molecular weight mesogens which are reciprocally soluble in all proportions in the nematic phase.[83] Odd–even fluctuations of isotropization temperatures and molar enthalpy or entropy changes are also observed and their ubiquity can be appreciated looking at Figs. 10 and 11. Isotropization temperatures and entropy changes concern some nematogenic homo- and copolymers containing monomer units 42:

$$\left. + O-Ph-C(CH_3)=N-N=(CH_3)C-Ph-OOC-(CH_2)_n-CO \right. +$$

42

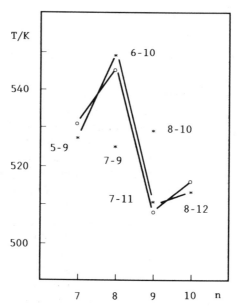

FIGURE 10
Isotropization temperature of binary copolymers (∗) and related homopolymers (○) **42**. Numbers beside asterisks indicate methylene units in the spacer present in equimolar proportion. (Adapted with permission from Ref. 81. Copyright Pergamon Press.)

Copolymers contain equimolar proportions of two spacers of different length. The liquid-crystalline properties of copolymers 5–9, 6–10, 7–11, and 8–12 closely correspond to those of the stoichiometrically equivalent homopolymers. Odd–even fluctuation occurs with the same sense and amplitude. Copolymers 7–9 and 8–10 have homopolymers $n = 8$ and $n = 9$, respectively, as stoichiometric counterparts. However, 7–9 is an "odd"-type polymer and 8–10 an "even" type; isotropization temperatures and molar entropies are consistent with that.

A fairly simple phase diagram may characterize nematogenic binary random copolymers also in case flexible units are not strictly homologous. Copolyesters[9, 84] containing azoxybenzene or 2,2′-dimethylazoxybenzene or α-cyanostilbene groups as the mesogen are characterized by having optically active 1,4-dicarboxy-2-methylbutane groups as one of the mutually vicariant spacers. All these copolymers are nematogenic in the full range of composition with a smooth variation of isotropization temperature. The presence of chiral groups of uniform configuration is responsible for the cholesteric structure which characterizes the liquid crystal phase for most part of the composition range.

Let us now examine the case of both monomer units being smectogenic. Because of the supposed random structure of the polymer chains we are

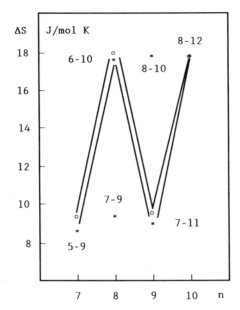

FIGURE 11
Isotropization entropy of binary copolymers (*) and related homopolymers (O) 42. Numbers beside asterisks indicate methylene units in the spacers present in equimolar proportions. (Adapted with permission from Ref. 81. Copyright Pergamon Press.)

faced by the question of whether a set of structurally aperiodic linear macromolecules may originate a phase structure that is monodimensionally periodic along a direction coincident with or related to that of the polymer chains. A repeated and not entirely obvious answer to this question comes from a fairly adequate set of copolymers irrespective of spacers being chemically homologous or not: smectic mesomorphism is stable within the full composition range.[45, 68, 69, 79, 85] The smectic structural period appears related to the length of the monomer units.

A second and complementary question is whether the smectic mesophase exhibited by random copolymers is a truly monophasic system in which monomer units of different nature are accommodated in the same smectic arrangement or it is rather a biphasic one, the two phases originating by the segregation of homopolymeric segments. Most available data are in favor of a monophasic structure. Isotropization temperature and molar enthalpy change, as well as the smectic structural spacing, show smooth variations with composition. A fair example is offered by a set of copolyalkanoates of 4,4'-dihydroxybiphenyl.[79] Their behavior is incompatible with the hypothesis that only a (homopolymeric) fraction of the system is involved in the smectic structure. However, if the two mutually vicariating spacers have drastically

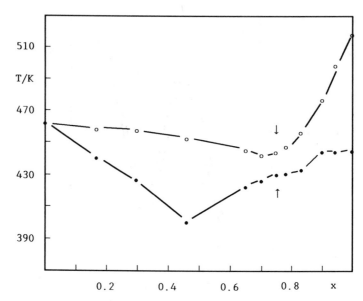

FIGURE 12
Melting temperature (●) and isotropization temperature (○) for
copolymers **43** as a function of composition. (Adapted with
permission from Ref. 85. Copyright Hüthig & Wepf Verlag.)

unlike stereochemical structures a quite different picture may show up. This
is the case for a set of copolymers having formula **43**[85]:

$$[(\!\!+\!OCH_2CH_2)_2\!-\!O\!-\!R\!+\!)_x\!+\!O(CH_2)_{12}\!-\!O\!-\!R\!+\!)_{1-x}]_{dp}$$

where

$$R = -OC-Ph-CH\!=\!HC-Ph-CO-$$

43

Spacers have quite unequal backbone chain length; besides, they are
chemically different.

The phase diagram (Fig. 12) shows a discontinuity around composition
$x = 0.75$. Coinciding with this a sharp discontinuity in the molar isotropization enthalpy and in the smectic periodicity also occurs. Two smectic phases
are formed, each stable within a definite range of composition. Only for
$x = 0.75$ both phases are found together. For compositions in the range
$x = 0–0.7$ isotropization enthalpy is proportional to the mole fraction of
dodecamethylenic spacer: $\Delta H(x) = \Delta H(0)\,(1 - x)$. This is what one should
expect if only a fraction of the system were arranged in a smectic structure.
However, the considerable variation of the smectic spacing with composition

and the absence, even at high x values, of any evidence for the existence of a smectic periodicity comparable to that characterizing homopolymer $x = 1$ do not support the view that the smectic phase might be formed by segregated homopolymeric ($x = 0$) sequences. A similar conclusion holds for copolymers in the composition range $0.78 < x < 1$.

In conclusion, notwithstanding the restriction imposed by a regular periodicity, the smectic structure is able to accommodate monomer units of different length with consequences on thermodynamic data becoming drastic only when largely different monomer units are involved.

9.2. Copolymers Whose Monomer Units Have the Same Spacer and Different Rigid Groups

Taking a few out of the numerous copolymers which belong to this class[33, 39, 86-90] let us examine first the case in which rigid segments have very similar linear dimensions but different mesogenic potentials. This diversity may stem from having unequal cross sections, as for groups R1 and R2, or from a more specific chemical difference as for groups R3 and R4:

$$R1 = -Ph-C(CH_3)=N-N=(CH_3)C-Ph-;$$

$$R2 = -Ph-C(CH_2CH_3)=N-N=(CH_3CH_2)C-Ph-$$

$$R3 = -Ph-COO-Ph-NHOC-Ph-;$$

$$R4 = -Ph-COO-Ph-OOC-Ph-$$

Homologous polyalkanoates $+O-R-OOC(CH_2)_nCO+_{dp}$ ($n = 6, 8,$ 10, 12) are nematogenic for $R = R1$ and nonmesogenic for $R = R2$.[87] The phase diagram of copolyalkanoates **44**:

$$[+O-R2-OOC(CH_2)_6CO+_x+O-R1-OOC(CH_2)_6CO+_{1-x}]_{dp}$$

44

is shown in Fig. 13 as an example. Within a large range of composition, copolymers exhibit enantiotropic mesomorphism of nematic nature; T_i changes almost linearly with composition. Copolymers containing longer spacers behave qualitatively in the same way. Extrapolation to $x = 1$ gives a virtual T_i of ~ 443 K for the "nonmesogenic" homopolymer. To explore the possible significance of this result it is worth noting that for the random copolymer

$$[+O-R2-OOC(CH_2)_4CO+_{0.5}+O-R2-OOC(CH_2)_8CO+_{0.5}]_{dp}$$

45

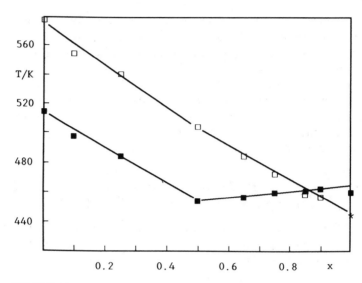

FIGURE 13
Melting (■) and isotropization (□) temperature for copolymers **44**
as a function of composition. (Adapted with permission from Ref.
87. Copyright Pergamon Press.)

which is the stoichiometric equivalent of homopolymer

$$+O-R2-OOC(CH_2)_6CO+_{dp},$$

the considerable melting point depression (consistent with the random chain
structure) allows detection of nematic mesomorphism with $T_i \sim 447$ K. By
the same procedure, two independent evaluations of the virtual isotropization temperature of "nonmesogenic" homopolymer

$$+O-R2-OOC(CH_2)_8CO+_{dp}$$

give the same value of ~ 420 K.

Let us now turn our attention to the phase behavior of copolymers[39]

$$[+O-R4-O(CH_2)_4+_x+O-R3-O(CH_2)_4+_{1-x}]_{dp}$$

46

Both homopolymers corresponding to the extreme compositions exhibit
enantiotropic mesomorphism; nematic for $x = 1$, both smectic and nematic
for $x = 0$. They have very close T_m and T_i; T_i is virtually independent of
composition. The rigid groups can vicariate each other with no consequences
at all on the overall stability of the mesophase. The thermal stability of the
smectic phase decreases with increasing x. This is caused presumably by the
progressive disruption of the intermolecular hydrogen-bonding pattern as
amide linkages are replaced by ester linkages. However, this circumstance

has little effect on the solid phase behavior. Isomorphous replacement of the two repeating units, which was proved by x-ray diffraction, explains the absence of a pseudo-eutectic minimum in the melting temperatures.[39]

Let us finally take into account copolymers containing two stereochemically different rigid groups. Attention will be restricted to two specific cases: (a) neither of the rigid groups is mesogenic; (b) only one rigid group is mesogenic.

Case a, a mesogenic copolymer containing "nonmesogenic" monomer units, is not a paradox but only an additional proof of the precarious meaning attached to the word mesogen.

Rigid groups

$$R1 = -Ph-C(CH_2CH_3)=N-N=(CH_3CH_2)C-Ph-$$

and

$$R2 = -Ph-C(CH_3)=(CH_3)C-Ph-$$

which are contained in copolymers:

$$[\text{(-O-R1-OOC(CH}_2)_8\text{CO-)}_x\text{(-R2-OOC(CH}_2)_8\text{CO-)}_{1-x}]_{dp}$$

47

have been qualified as "nonmesogenic" because homopolymers corresponding to $x = 0$ and $x = 1$ do not show any mesogenic behavior. On the contrary, copolymers are nematogenic within an appreciable ($.25 < x < .85$) range of composition.[33] Once again, melting point depression stemming from the randomness of the chain structure brings to light a virtual mesogenic power. Because of the nematic nature of the mesophase, the different length of the rigid segments does not play any relevant role and isotropization temperature shows a regular variation with composition.

To discuss case b, we shall take into account as the first example the mesomorphic behavior of some copolyalkanoates of 4,4'-dihydroxybiphenyl and 2,6-dihydroxynaphthalene:

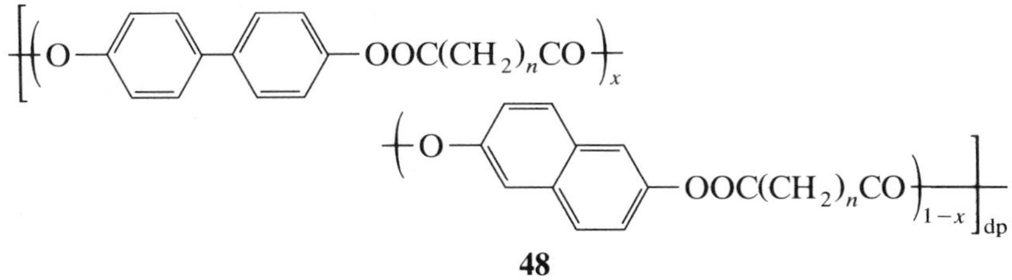

48

These copolymers are of particular interest since they arise from two rigid segments having different lengths and sharply different mesogenic potentials. In fact, while homopolyalkanoates of 4,4'-dihydroxybiphenyl exhibit a nematic phase for n odd and a highly ordered smectic S_H phase when n is even,[56] homopolyalkanoates of 2,6-dihydroxynaphthalene, at least for $n = 5$–8, do not show any mesomorphic behavior.[88] On the contrary, all copolymers are enantiotropically mesogenic within large composition ranges and the even series shows both nematic and S_H smectic mesomorphism. Taking copolymers with $n = 6$ as a reference, the stability of the smectic phase decreases with increasing content of nonmesogenic segments. It only matches the stability of the crystalline phase at $x \approx 0.3$. This is quite a remarkable feature if one takes into account that the lengths of the rigid segments are different by ~ 2.2 Å and the S_H phase has a rather regular "in layer" structure. Once again, the formation of smectic structures may occur with no need to include only sterically homologous units. However, chemical inhomogeneity and structural disorder have a negative influence not only on the stability of the phase but also on its order. Two features are noteworthy.

1. The smectic–isotropic transition entropy is remarkably decreased for copolymers: 15.8 J mol^{-1} K^{-1} for $x = 0.7$; 33.9 J mol^{-1} K^{-1} for homopolymer $x = 1$.

2. Nematic mesomorphism, whose thermal stability interval decreases with increasing x, is observed for copolymers containing as much as 70% of "smectogenic" units (very likely this holds for even higher values) and at temperatures that are almost 100 K above the melting temperature of the "nonmesogenic" homopolymer. The copolymeric structure favors the disruption of the smectic phase into the nematic one, which does not require any geometrical matching of the different monomer units. Both features are in contrast but not in contradiction with the previously discussed behavior of smectogenic copolymers, whose monomer units differ by the length of the flexible spacer. Those polymers, with a partial exception for one extreme case, are characterized by the persistence of smectic mesomorphism within the full composition range and by a smooth variation of the isotropization entropy.

10. ORIENTATIONAL ORDER IN THE NEMATIC PHASE

For an assembly of rigid rods with cylindrical symmetry, orientational order is unequivocally defined at any specific point and temperature by the statistical distribution function of the orientation of the rod axes. A single-order parameter, normally defined as the average quantity $S_{zz} = \langle 3\cos^2\theta - 1\rangle/2$, where θ is the angle between any specific rod axis and the average orientation of all rod axes at the same location, is sufficient for a quantitative definition of nematic order. Segmented-chain polymers have neither rodlike nor rigid backbone chains. They are flexuous and structurally heterogeneous and their constitutive segments have different conformational mobilities. Therefore, even with the assumption, which is not acceptable in some cases, that "rigid" segments are truly rigid, a complete definition of nematic order should include, besides the orientational order of the mesogen, the average conformational status of the spacers. Unfortunately, very few experimental data are available concerning specifically the last point. On the contrary, mesogen orientation has been measured by proton and/or deuterium NMR spectrometry for a significant number of polymers or related model compounds although not as extensively as would be necessary to explore thoroughly the influence of stereochemical parameters on orientational order. In addition, average chain orientation has been determined by the measure of "macroscopic" physical quantities such as magnetic susceptibility or electron density (by x-ray diffraction techniques).

Temperature dependence of orientational order is a most general behavior that polymers share with low molecular weight compounds. It is confirmed by all available measurements. A fine example is shown in Fig. 14, reporting order parameters measured as a function of the temperature ratio T/T_i (T is the actual temperature and T_i is the isotropization temperature) for a homologous set of polymeric and low molecular weight compounds. This remarkable set of data has been obtained by Kothe et al.[20] by application of multipulse dynamic NMR techniques to deuterated compounds whose formulas are given below:

$$P1 = + R - O(CH_2)_{10}O \, \}_{dp}$$

$$M1 = CH_3(CH_2)_4O - R - O(CH_2)_4CH_3$$

$$D1 = CH_3(CH_2)_4O - R - O(CH_2)_{10}O - R - O(CH_2)_4CH_3$$

$$D_5 = CH_3(CH_2)_4O - R - O(CH_2)_9O - R - O(CH_2)_4CH_3$$

$$R = - Ph - COO - Ph(Cl) - OOC - Ph -$$

For low molecular weight compounds, liquid-crystalline order is lost not only at $T > T_i$ but also at $T < T_m$ as crystallization takes place. At variance with this, Fig. 14 shows that on cooling the polymer below melting temperature a high degree of orientational order is permanently quenched. This adds to other evidence coming from DSC thermal analysis, particularly data concerning mesogenic random copolymers, pointing out the mesophasic nature of the noncrystalline fraction that is present in solid polymers in all cases, although in variable amounts.

Influences from molecular weight and odd–even effects are also contained in the data of Fig. 14. At any T/T_i a considerable increase of order parameter occurs in the progression from "monomer" M1 to "dimer" D1 to polymer P1; order parameters for D1 are regularly higher than for D5. Some data concerning nematogenic polymers and low molecular weight homologues are reported in Table 8 for a comparison. The overall picture appears coherent. The odd–even fluctuation in the order parameter measured or

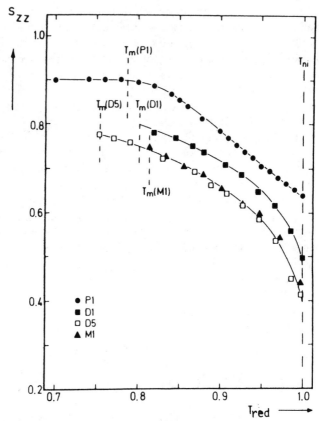

FIGURE 14
Orientational order parameter S_{zz} as a function of reduced
temperature $(T \, / \, T_i)$ for polymer P1 (●), dimer D1 (■), dimer D5
(□), and monomer M1 (▲). (Reproduced with permission from Ref.
20.)

extrapolated at $T/T_i = 1$ parallels a similar fluctuation of isotropization
temperature and enthalpy change.

The dependence of order parameter on molecular weight is qualitatively
similar to that characterizing isotropization temperature and enthalpy change
variation. The order parameter of polymer P1 was found to be independent
of molecular weight in the range $3000 < M_n < 10,000$.[19] On the other hand,
order parameters measured on unfractionated samples of a polyalkanoate of
4,4′-dihydroxy-2,2′-dimethylazoxybenzene with $3000 < M_n < 4000$, appear to
be influenced by the distribution of end groups rather than by the average
molecular weight itself.[10]

Information about conformational order of the flexible spacer may be
gathered by ^{2}H-NMR spectrometry. Assuming rotational isomeric approxi-

Table 8
Orientational Order Parameter (S_{zz}) for Nematogenic Polymers (P) and Dimeric
Model Compounds (D) as a Function of Reduced Temperature (T / T_i)

Polymer (P)/dimer (D)[a]			T_i (K)	S_{zz}			Refs.
				($T/T_i = 1$	0.95	0.90)	
P1		$n = 10$	552	0.64	0.71	0.78	20
		$n = 9$	543	0.54[b]	0.61	0.68	19
P2				0.79			107
			489	0.60[c]			110
				0.75	0.78		18
P3[d]			411	0.69	0.79	0.84	108
			438	0.6			10
D1	$CH_3(CH_2)_4O—$	$n = 10$	508	0.50	0.65	0.71	20
D5	$CH_3(CH_2)_4O—$	$n = 9$	508	0.42	0.58	0.65	20
D2	$CH_3(CH_2)_4O—$		421	0.49[c]			110
D3	$CH_3O—$		e	0.52	0.68	0.74	10

[a]See text for formulas P1, D1, D5; P2 = $+PhCOOPhO(CH_2)_{10}O+_{dp}$; P3 = 1; terminal
groups are given for dimers. All data (except [c]) from NMR measurements.
[b]Extrapolated value.
[c]From magnetic susceptibility measurements.
[d]Samples differ by molecular weight.
[e]Monotropic.

mation, any C—^{2}H bond vector pertaining to an aliphatic chain has four
allowed directions (with respect to the chain axis) which are correlated to the
conformational status of the chain. Any restriction imposed upon chain
conformations implies some ordering of the C—D bond vectors located at
one or more chain segments. This may be detected by ^{2}H-NMR techniques.
Ordering at a specific chain segment may be expressed conveniently[91, 92] by a
single "segmental" order parameter $S_{z'z'}$. Complete segmental disorder, i.e.,
equal probability for the four directions of the C—D bond vector located at
that specific chain segment, corresponds to $S_{z'z'} = 0$. On the other hand,
complete chain order, i.e., all-trans conformation, implies $S_{z'z'} = 1$ for all
segments. Figure 15 reports segmental order parameter $S_{z'z'}$ as a function of
T/T_i at the α and δ positions of monomer M1, dimer D1, and polymer P1.
The data have been obtained by Kothe et al.[20] by multipulsed dynamic NMR
techniques applied to α-deuterated or δ-deuterated homologues of M1, D1,
and P1. In all cases, as temperature increases conformational order decreases, approaching the minimum critical value corresponding to isotropization. As for orientational order, the polymer has the peculiar behavior of
preserving a high degree of conformational order frozen at temperatures
lying below T_m. With no relation to molar mass, at any specific value of T/T_i,
segmental order parameter at position α is larger than at position δ. There is
a peculiar sort of "flexibility gradient" along the chain with a progressive

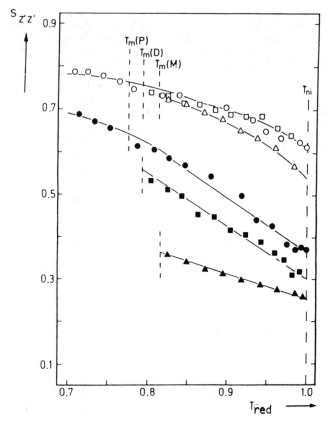

FIGURE 15
Segmental order parameter $S_{z'z'}$ as a function of reduced
temperature (T / T_i) for polymer P1: (○) α position, (●) δ position,
dimer D1: (□) α position, (■) δ position; monomer M1: (△) α
position, (▲) δ position. (Reproduced with permission from Ref.
20.)

weakening of the constraints imposed by the mesogen on conformational
mobility. Segments at α position, which are close to the mesogen, have order
parameters scarcely dependent on molecular weight. Actually, dimer and
polymer are virtually indistinguishable within a large range of T/T_i. In
contrast, monomer, dimer, and polymer have sharply different order parameters at position δ at whatever temperature. As temperature decreases, δ
segments of dimer and polymer reorder faster than the α ones. This leads
the corresponding order parameters of the polymer almost to convergence at
low temperature. In contrast with that, the δ segment of the pentyloxy
pendand chain of M1 undergoes only a moderate ordering before any
liquid-crystalline order is lost as crystallization takes place.

Table 9
Temperature Dependence of Nematic Order
for the Flexible Segment of a Nematogenic Polyester[a]

T/T_i	S_{zz}	$S_{CD}(\alpha)$	S_{CD} (int)
0.995	0.72	0.28	0.19
0.984	0.76	0.30	0.22
0.962	0.80	0.32	0.25
0.935	0.83	0.33	0.27
0.920	0.83	0.34	0.28
0.889	0.85[b]	0.35	0.31

[a]Adapted with permission from Ref. 94. Copyright American Chemical Society. See text for polymer and symbols.

[b]Extrapolated value.

The results concerning end-chain ordering of M1 are in full agreement with more detailed data, also obtained by deuterium magnetic resonance methods, on the dependence of segmental order on temperature and segment position for some 4,4'-dialkoxyazoxybenzene homologues.[93] The segmental order parameter undergoes a peculiar sort of odd–even fluctuation according to the parity of the segment position number, the first segment (i.e., the one close to the mesogen) having the highest order parameter.

Further experimental data are available on the different behaviors of α-methylenes and inner methylenes composing the spacers of a nematogenic polymer.[94] They concern a polyester obtained by condensation of perdeuterated dodecandioyl-d$_{20}$ dichloride with 2,2'-dimethyl-4,4'-dihydroxyazoxybenzene. The bond vector order parameter $S_{CD} = S_{zz} \langle P_2(\cos \alpha) \rangle$, where S_{zz} is the mesogen orientation order parameter and α is the angle that the C—D bond vector at any specific chain segment makes with the symmetry axis of the mesogen, is evaluated as a function of temperature utilizing deuterium NMR techniques. Data reported on Table 9 are specific for α-methylenes while no distinction is made among the internal ones. The pattern that emerges is in qualitative agreement with the picture outlined above.

Data reported on Table 8, specifically order parameters at $T/T_i = 1$, do not allow any unequivocal correlation to be made between order parameters and mesogen structure (the same holds if data reported in Ref. 109 for polymers and in Refs. 111 and 112 for dimers are also considered). If polymers are taken into account, the largest order parameter at isotropization is observed for polymer P2. This prominence does not correspond to anything similar if geometrical parameters of the rigid groups are compared. Polymer P2 has neither the longest mesogen nor the highest average axial ratio. On the other hand, mesogens have axial ratios that are rather close to each other. Therefore, it is not unlikely that intrinsic chemical diversity and unequal influences related to such factors as molecular weight distribution or uncertain definition of T_i, may obfuscate the contribution of purely geometric factors.

11. COMPARISON WITH THEORETICAL CALCULATIONS

A large part of this book is devoted to presenting and discussing theoretical models. Their abundance is in itself an indication of how hard the problem is of taking into full account, within a single approach, the variety of physical and chemical parameters that may be relevant to liquid crystallinity. Therefore, in the following short comparison between theory and experiment, reference will be made not to a single theoretical approach but to some of those dealing with flexible polymers. Theories of liquid-crystalline ordering in the melt that take specific account of the basic structural features of segmented-chain polymers have been developed by Corradini and Vacatello (the CV theory,[95] Vasilenko, Khokhlov, and Shibaev (VKS),[96] Bohem, Martire, and Madhusudana (BMM),[97] and Dowell (D).[98, 99] All of them utilize lattice combinatorial statistics to deal with molecular packing (cf. Chapter 5).

Other theories, such as those developed by Ronca and Yoon,[1, 100] Khokhlov and Semenov[2] or Ten Bosch et al.[101] for polymers with continuous flexibility, are discussed in Chapter 6 and will not be considered here. It should be pointed out (see below) that some of the experimental trends concerning segmented-chain polymers may find explanation also within theories for wormlike chains.

The CV theory makes use of a matrix multiplication scheme to evaluate the orientational and conformational partition function for various orientations of the polymer chains, or part of them, along a given lattice axis while the steric contribution is calculated according to Di Marzio's lattice statistics.[102] Only the rigid segments are taken into account for the calculation of orientation-dependent interactions utilizing an ad hoc modification of Ronca and Yoon's[100] treatment of wormlike chains with continuous flexibility. Therefore, at any given temperature, the free energy is set proportional to the square average order parameter of the rigid segments. The VKS theory is an extension, to the athermal melt, of Matheson and Flory's[103] treatment of segmented chain macromolecules in solution. At variance with Matheson and Flory, the possible ordering of the flexible segments induced by the self-consistent orientational field generated by the anisotropic melt is taken into account and brought to light. This is the most interesting contribution given by the VKS theory and it is in qualitative agreement with experiment. The BMM theory follows to some extent the VKS approach in modeling the polymer chain, assuming completely flexible junctions between monomer units. The BMM theory includes lattice occupation density and degree of polymerization as parameters, as well as short-range packing and long-range isotropic and anisotropic interactions. The latter contribution may be calculated taking into account pair interactions between rigid or flexible segments as well as cross interactions. However, rigid–rigid interactions were primarily considered since their contribution appears the most relevant one. The Di Marzio cubic lattice statistics is utilized to calculate packing contributions to the free energy taking as a reference state a hypothetical completely aligned configuration. As in the VKS approach, an extension of the flexible spacer along the preferred direction is assumed. It is described as the effect of an internal mechanical tension applied by the anisotropic environment generated by the nonrandom orientation of the rigid segments. As for the VKS theory, the onset, under certain conditions, of a highly ordered nematic phase in addition to the "ordinary" nematic one is expected. Since no such phenomenon has ever been observed for real polymers, any reference to the BMM theory made in the following discussion will concern the less ordered nematic phase only.

Dowell's theory follows a rather different approach insofar as realistic polymer structures seem to be taken into account instead of very simplified models. This entails the use of specific values for numerous parameters relevant to the calculation of dispersion interactions (which are dealt with in the framework of a localized mean-field approach) and chain conformations. Molecular packing is treated by means of cubic lattice statistics, continuous limits being taken with respect to number of molecules and number of lattice sites in the system. The theory includes one-dimensional positional ordering of rigid and flexible segments along the preferred orientation. This allows predictions about the onset of smectic order to be made (cf., however, Chapter 5).

The CV, BMM, and D theories (the VKS theory will not be taken into further account) have different predictive qualities. The latter has been utilized to calculate liquid-crystalline properties for specific "real" polymers. Therefore, while a close quantitative comparison with experiment is possible for those specific polymers, no general information may be inferred more safely than is allowed by the generalization of specific experimental results. In contrast, the very simplified molecular model assumed by the former two theories does not allow quantitative comparisons with the behavior of any specific polymer. However, general trends are calculated which we shall use for a comparison, although on a qualitative level. Before doing that, let us summarize as a reminder the most relevant experimental results about structure–property relationships for segmented polymers in bulk. They involve some of the physical and structural parameters taken into account by the theoretical calculations we are going to examine.

Molecular Weight

Molecular weight influences isotropization temperature, molar entropic and enthalpic changes, and order parameters. A sharp increase of these physical quantities occurring with molecular weight increasing within the first $\sim 10^4$ dalton is followed by a plateau region. In some cases entropies have been found also to decrease slightly for high molecular weights. However, no unequivocal evidence is available to exclude kinetic reasons.

Rigid Segment

Isotropization temperature increases with increasing length; cross section has an opposite influence. Most rigid segments of practical interest for the preparation of thermotropic polymers have small axial ratios. Therefore, the influence of the purely geometric parameter is easily obscured by electronic factors and/or by stereochemical features of the spacer.

Flexible Segment

Isotropization temperature is decreased by increasing the length of flexible segments. The trend is not linear and may undergo more or less drastic odd–even fluctuations depending on chemical structure. Analogous fluctuations characterize enthalpic and entropic changes. With spacers of the same parity (odd or even) these physical quantities are also influenced by spacer length, although to a lesser extent and in a way that may depend on the specific chemical structure.

Order Parameter

The orientational order parameter of the mesogenic core is influenced by molecular weight (at least in the range of low values of MW) and may undergo odd–even fluctuations according to the parity of the spacer. It depends on temperature, taking the minimum value at $T = T_i$ and increasing for $T < T_i$. The conformational order of the segments forming the spacer also depends upon their specific position along the chain.

We shall now examine to what extent experimental trends are accounted for by different theoretical approaches.

11.1. Influence of Molecular Weight

A smooth increase in nematic–isotropic transition temperature with increasing degree of polymerization in qualitatively good correspondence with the available experimental data is calculated by the CV[104] and D theories. Although the first of these calculations is performed for a symbolic polymer chain while the other concerns the specific "real" polymer

$$\text{-}\!\!\left[O-Ph-Ph-Ph-(CH_2)_4\right]\!\!\text{-}_{dp}$$

both theories calculate that an asymptotic limit of the isotropization temperature is closely approached for polymer chains containing ~ 100 monomer units. With the BMM approach, the trend followed by isotropization temperatures can be calculated from the ratios $T_{i(n)}/T_{i(m)}$ of the transition temperatures of different pairs of homologous polymers taking one of them as a reference. If dimer (m = 2) is taken as the reference, the aforementioned ratio decreases with increasing n down to a minimum (the degree of polymerization corresponding to the minimum depends on the polymer structure, i.e., on the number of units forming the rigid and flexible sections) then increases with n. Experimental data, particularly those concerning monodisperse oligomers,[22] do not conform to these calculations. The same theory, however, calculates a dependence of molar isotropization entropy on molecular weight in qualitative agreement with those experimental results[10] which show a small progressive decrease of the transition entropy for higher molecular weights. Unfortunately, it is not clear as yet whether this feature is a thermodynamic or a kinetic effect. In the latter event the decrease in transition entropy may be related to the metastable permanence of an "amorphous" fraction of the polymer at temperatures below T_i.

As far as the orientational order parameter is concerned, a dependence on molecular weight is calculated by D and BMM. According to Dowell's theory, the core order parameter at T_i of polymer

$$\left.\begin{array}{c}\text{+O—Ph—Ph—Ph—(CH}_2)_4\end{array}\right]_{\text{dp}}$$

is expected to increase with molecular weight following a trend analogous to that of T_i with ~ 0.71 as the limiting value. No specific experimental data are available for a check, but both the trend and the absolute values of the order parameter appear not unreasonable in comparison with data concerning different compounds.

The pattern offered by the BMM theory is different. It calculates a dependence of the orientational order parameter of the rigid segments on molecular weight which parallels the one previously outlined for the entropy change. Order parameters calculated for "oligomeric" species are much too high compared to measured values and, therefore, the resulting decreasing trend also has no experimental counterpart. Nevertheless, order parameters calculated for high degrees of polymerization are not unreasonable at all (e.g., rigid and flexible segments containing four units each, polymer volume fraction $v_p = 0.8$, degree of polymerization 100: order parameter at T_i = 0.64).

11.2. The Length of the Spacer

Theoretical predictions concerning the influence of the length of the flexible segments on the liquid crystal properties offer a fairly coherent picture. With a very peculiar exception, all theories calculate decreasing nematic–isotropic transition temperature with increasing spacer length if the other relevant parameters are kept constant. The knowledge based on experimental data would suggest that the parity (odd–even) of the spacer should be one of those parameters. However only Dowell's theory takes it into appropriate account and odd–even fluctuations of T_i are correctly calculated. The other theories may mimic odd–even effects only by including ad hoc parameters.

For instance, odd–even fluctuations of the anisotropic dispersion interactions involving the spacers produce parallel fluctuations of isotropization entropy or the order parameter as calculated according to the BMM theory. These inadequacies appear to be intrinsic to the polymer chain model assumed. Actually, the origin of the odd–even alternations for real polymers may be traced to their configurational properties if these properties are taken into full account even for a single molecule. Following two not completely equivalent approaches this has been done by Abe[105] and by Yoon and Bruckner[106] for polymers containing $-R-OOC-F-$, $-R-O-F-$, or $-R-COO-F-$ sequences. For any possible spacer conformation, statistically weighted at a specific temperature, orientational correlations of rigid groups are calculated. For polymers containing $-R-OOC-F-$ or $-R-O-F-$ sequences a higher fraction of spacer conformations favoring linearity and high chain extension[106] is calculated for even spacers than for the odd ones. Furthermore, entropy changes (at T_i) calculated including the conformational contribution stemming from the restricted number of spacer conformations allowed in the nematic state[106] are in better agreement with experiment than those including only combinatorial and mesogen orientation contributions[105] (cf. Chapter 1).

The hint at a peculiar exception made in the foregoing discussion concerns a specific single set of homologous polymers,

$$\{Ph-Ph-(CH_2)_n\}_{\overline{100}} \qquad (n = 22–27),$$

whose real behavior is unknown. The nematic–isotropic transition temperature is calculated by Dowell to increase with increasing n. For the same polymer, the occurrence of smectic polymorphism is also calculated with smectic–nematic transition temperature increasing with n. The difference $T_i - T_{SN}$ decreases as n increases. This is the only feature that conforms to experimental findings for other polymers.[39,54,55]

As to isotropization entropy, it is worth recalling that experimental data give multiple answers. Entropy may increase or decrease or remain virtually constant as spacer length varies. It is calculated by BMM as an increasing function (with decreasing gradient) of the length of the flexible segment.

Concerning the order parameter, there is a peculiar mismatch between theoretical predictions and experimental findings. All theoretical approaches calculate that the orientational order parameter at T_i decreases with increasing spacer length. Yet, no unambiguous experimental result is available for a comparison. In fact, while some significant experimental evidence is available concerning odd–even fluctuations affecting order parameters, such effects are not even treatable by the aforementioned theories, with the exception of Dowell's theory. The latter calculates orientational order parameters of mesogenic cores and flexible spacers for polymers

$$\{O-Ph-Ph-Ph-(CH_2)_n\}_{\overline{100}} \qquad n = 5–9$$

predicting odd–even fluctuations for both.

The orientational order parameter of the mesogenic group as calculated according to BMM decreases with increasing T/T_i. As an example, for a polymer with degree of polymerization 100, containing rigid groups and flexible spacers formed, respectively, by four and five units, order parameters are 0.607 at $T = T_i$ and 0.674 at $T/T_i = 0.5$. Any specific comparison with the behavior of real polymers would be pointless; nonetheless the calculated trend is in agreement with experiment.

A final remark concerns the qualitative analogies between the predictions of theories for segmented and for wormlike chains. The increase and leveling off of T_i with MW observed here was also observed for polymers such as poly(n-hexylisocyanate) and hydroxypropylcellulose (Chapter 6). Theories that emphasize the role of steric repulsions for wormlike chains[1,2] predict this effect for low values of the persistence length q ($2q/d$ below a critical value). Again, the effect is attributed to the self-consistent field of the mesophase causing an elongation ("stiffening"; Chapter 3) increasing with chain length L. Moreover, q values at T_i are generally rather small (due to large dq/dT; Chapter 6) and probably comparable to the length of the rigid segments considered here. Thus, closeness of at least a few features of the two models is suggested. Further, the above theories[1,2] directly relate a decrease of q (or chain rigidity) to a decrease of T_i, and this effect may also be regarded as qualitatively consistent with the reduction of T_i with increasing spacer length.

Theories for wormlike chains emphasizing only anisotropic attractions[101] also predict an increase of T_i with chain length due to increasing contacts up to moderate values of the L/q ratio (Chapter 5). Superimposition of experimental data for segmented polymers to the theoretical T_i vs. L/q dependence of Ten Bosch et al. is shown in Fig. 2 of Chapter 5.

REFERENCES

1. G. Ronca and D.Y. Yoon, *J. Chem. Phys.*, **1984**, *80*, 925.
2. A.R. Khokhlov and A.N. Semenov, *Macromolecules*, **1986**, *19*, 373.
3. G. Chen and R.W. Lenz, *J. Polym. Sci., Polym. Chem. Ed.*, **1984**, *22*, 3189.
4. W.R. Krigbaum, R. Kotek, T. Ishikawa, H. Hakemi, and J. Preston, *Eur. Polym. J.*, **1984**, *20*, 225.
5. J. Asrar, H. Toriumi, J. Watanabe, W.R. Krigbaum, and A. Ciferri, *J. Polym. Sci., Polym. Phys. Ed.*, **1983**, *21*, 1119.
6. N. Hiruma, K. Funaki, N. Koide, and K. Iimura, *Rep. Prog. Polym. Phys. Jpn.*, **1984**, *27*, 245.
7. V. Percec, H. Nava, and H. Jonsson, *J. Polym. Sci., Polym. Chem. Ed.*, **1987**, *25*, 1943.
8. R. Zentel and G. Reckert, *Makromol. Chem.*, **1986**, *187*, 1915.
9. A. Blumstein, S. Vilasagar, S. Ponrathnam, S.B. Clough, R.B. Blumstein, and G. Maret, *J. Polym. Sci., Polym. Phys. Ed.*, **1982**, *20*, 877.
10. R.B. Blumstein, E.M. Stickles, M.M. Gauthier, and A. Blumstein, *Macromolecules*, **1984**, *17*, 177.

11. G. Galli, E. Chiellini, A.S. Angeloni, and M. Laus, *Macromolecules*, **1989**, *22*, 1120.
12. V. Percec and H. Nava, *J. Polym. Sci.*, *Polym. Chem. Ed.*, **1987**, *25*, 405.
13. R.W. Lenz, A.K. Rao, S. Bhattacharya, M.B. Polk, and N. Venkatasubramanian, *Liq. Cryst.*, **1989**, *4*, 317.
14. A. Roviello and A. Sirigu, *Makromol. Chem.*, **1982**, *183*, 895.
15. R. Centore, A. Roviello, and A. Sirigu, *Liq. Cryst.*, **1988**, *3*, 1525.
16. J.A. Buglione, A. Roviello, and A. Sirigu, *Mol. Cryst. Liq. Cryst.*, **1984**, *106*, 169.
17. C. Carfagna, P. Iannelli, A. Roviello, and A. Sirigu, *J. Therm. Anal.*, **1985**, *30*, 1317.
18. S. Bruckner, J. Campbell Scott, Do Y. Yoon, and A.C. Griffin, *Macromolecules*, **1985**, *18*, 2709.
19. K. Mueller, B. Hisgen, H. Ringsdorf, R.W. Lenz, and G. Kothe, *Mol. Cryst. Liq. Cryst.*, **1984**, *113*, 167.
20. K. Kohlhammer, K. Muller, and G. Kothe, *Liq. Cryst.*, **1989**, *5*, 1525.
21. G.R. Luckhurst, in *Recent Advances in Liquid Crystalline Polymers*, L.L. Chapoy, Ed., Elsevier, Amsterdam, 1985.
22. A.C. Griffin, S.L. Sullivan, and W.E. Hughes, *Liq. Cryst.* **1989**, *4*, 677.
23. W. Kreuder, H. Ringsdorf, and P. Tschirner, *Makromol. Chem. Rapid Commun.*, **1985**, *6*, 367.
24. C. Destrade, M.C. Mondon, and J. Malthete, *J. Phys. (Paris)*, *C-3*, **1979**, *40*, 17.
25. S. Chandrasekhar, B.K. Sadashiva, K.A. Suresh, N.V. Madhusudana, S. Kumar, R. Shashidhar, and G. Venkatesh, *J. Phys. (Paris)*, *C-3*, **1979**, *40*, 120.
26. S.M. Aharoni, *Macromolecules*, **1988**, *21*, 1941.
27. S.M. Aharoni, *Macromolecules*, **1989**, *22*, 686.
28. H. Kawada, Y. Matsunaga, T. Takamura, and M. Terada, *Can. J. Chem.*, **1988**, *66*, 1867.
29. R.W. Lenz, *Pure Appl. Chem.*, **1985**, *57*, 1537.
30. B. Reck and H. Ringsdorf, *Makromol. Chem. Rapid Commun.*, **1986**, *7*, 389.
31. K. Iimura, N. Koide, and R. Ohta, *Rep. Prog. Polym. Phys. Jpn.*, **1981**, *24*, 231.
32. J. Asrar, O. Thomas, Q. Zhou, and A. Blumstein, *Proc. Macro-IUPAC*, Amherst, 1982.
33. A. Roviello, S. Santagata, and A. Sirigu, *Makromol. Chem. Rapid Commun.*, **1983**, *4*, 281.
34. R.W. Lenz, *Faraday Disc. Chem. Soc.*, **1985**, *79*, 21.
35. H. Jonsson, P. Werner, U.W. Gedde, and A. Hult, *Macromolecules*, **1989**, *22*, 1683.
36. V. Petraccone and B. Pirozzi, private communication.
37. A.C. Griffin and S.J. Havens, *J. Polym. Sci.*, *Polym. Phys. Ed.*, **1981**, *19*, 951.
38. A. Blumstein and O. Thomas, *Macromolecules*, **1982**, *15*, 1264.
39. A.H. Khant, J.E. McIntyre, and A.H. Milburn, *Polymer*, **1983**, *24*, 1610.
40. A.C. Griffin and S.J. Havens, *Mol. Cryst. Liq. Cryst. Lett.*, **1979**, *49*, 239.
41. R. Kotek and W.R. Krigbaum, *J. Polym. Sci.*, *Polym. Phys. Ed.*, **1988**, *26*, 1173.
42. J.I. Jin and J.H. Park, *Eur. Polym. J.*, **1987**, *23*, 973.
43. J. Watanabe and M. Hayashi, *Macromolecules*, **1988**, *21*, 278.
44. H.R. Kricheldorf and R. Pakull, *Makromolecules*, **1988**, *21*, 551.
45. N. Koide, R. Ohta, and K. Iimura, *Polym. J.*, **1984**, *16*, 505.
46. C.K. Ober, J.I. Jin, and R.W. Lenz, *Makromol. Chem. Rapid Commun.*, **1983**, *4*, 49.
47. W.R. Krigbaum and J. Watanabe, *Polymer*, **1983**, *24*, 1299.
48. C. Noel, C. Friedrich, L. Bosio, and C. Strazielle, *Polymer*, **1984**, *25*, 1281.
49. P. Meurisse, C. Noel, L. Monnerie, and B. Fayolle, *Br. Polym. J.*, **1981**, *13*, 55.
50. H. Hoshino, J.I. Jin, and R.W. Lenz, *J. Appl. Polym. Sci.*, **1984**, *29*, 547.
51. J.C.W. Chien, R. Zhou, and C.P. Lillya, *Macromolecules*, **1987**, *20*, 2340.

52. Y.G. Lin, R. Zhou, J.C.W. Chien, and H.H. Winter, *Macromolecules*, **1988**, *21*, 2014.
53. J.A. Buglione, P. Iannelli, A. Roviello, and A. Sirigu, *Gazz. Chim. Ital.*, **1983**, *113*, 393.
54. A. Fradet and W. Heitz, *Makromol. Chem.*, **1987**, *188*, 1233.
55. L. Strzelecki and D. van Luyen, *Eur. Polym. J.*, **1980**, *16*, 299.
56. W.R. Krigbaum, J. Watanabe, and T. Ishikawa, *Macromolecules*, **1983**, *16*, 1271.
57. G. Wenz, *Makromol. Chem.*, *Rapid Commun.*, **1985**, *6*, 577.
58. O. Herrmann-Schoenherr, J. Wendorff, W. Kreuder, and H. Ringsdorf, *Makromol. Chem.*, *Rapid Commun.*, **1986**, *7*, 97.
59. B. Hueser, T. Pakula, and H.W. Spiess, *Macromolecules*, **1989**, *22*, 1960.
60. A.M. Levelut, *J. Phys. Lett.*, **1979**, *40*, 81.
61. A.Yu. Bilibin, A.V. Tenkovtsev, O.N. Piraner, E.E. Pashkovsky and S. Skorokhodov, *Makromol. Chem.* **1985**, *186*, 1575.
62. B. Gallot, G. Galli, and E. Chiellini, *Makromol. Chem. Rapid Commun.*, **1987**, *8*, 417.
63. B. Reck and H. Ringsdorf, *Makromol. Chem. Rapid Commun.*, **1985**, *6*, 291.
64. G. Galli, M. Laus, A.S. Angeloni, P. Ferruti, and E. Chiellini, *Makromol. Chem.*, *Rapid Commun.*, **1983**, *4*, 681.
65. P.J. Stenhouse, E.M. Valles, S.W. Kantor, and W.J. MacKnight, *Macromolecules*, **1989**, *22*, 1467.
66. K. Clausen, J. Kops, K. Rasmussen, K.H. Rasmussen, and J. Sonne, *Macromolecules*, **1987**, *20*, 2660.
67. H. Furuya, K. Asahi, and A. Abe, *Polym. J.*, **1986**, *18*, 779.
68. T. Shaffer and V. Percec, *J. Polym. Sci., Polym. Lett. Ed.*, **1985**, *23*, 185.
69. A. Roviello, S. Santagata, and A. Sirigu, *Makromol. Chem., Rapid Commun.*, **1984**, *5*, 141.
70. Z. Jedlinski, J. Franek, and P. Kuziw, *Makromol. Chem.*, **1986**, *187*, 2317.
71. S. Antoun, R.W. Lenz, and J.I. Jin, *J. Polym. Sci., Polym. Chem. Ed.*, **1981**, *19*, 1901.
72. M.J.S. Dewar and R.S. Goldberg, *J. Org. Chem.*, **1970**, *35*, 2711.
73. J.P. Schroeder and D.W. Bristol, *J. Org. Chem.*, **1973**, *38*, 3160.
74. T. Kato, G.M.A. Kabir, and T. Uryu, *J. Polym. Sci., Polym. Chem. Ed.*, **1989**, *27*, 1447.
75. J.I. Jin, E. Choi, and S. Ryu, *J. Polym. Sci., Polym. Chem. Ed.*, **1987**, *25*, 241.
76. C. Ober, R.W. Lenz, G. Galli, and E. Chiellini, *Macromolecules*, **1983**, *16*, 1034.
77. J.S. Moore and S.I. Stupp, *Macromolecules*, **1988**, *21*, 1217.
78. P.G. Martin and S.I. Stupp, *Macromolecules*, **1988**, *21*, 1222.
79. J. Watanabe and W.R. Krigbaum, *Macromolecules*, **1984**, *17*, 2288.
80. A. Roviello and A. Sirigu, *Eur. Polym. J.*, **1979**, *15*, 61.
81. P. Iannelli, A. Roviello, and A. Sirigu, *Eur. Polym. J.*, **1982**, *18*, 745.
82. B.W. Jo, J.I. Jin, and R.W. Lenz, *Eur. Polym. J.*, **1982**, *18*, 233.
83. R.L. Humphries, P.G. James, and G.R. Luckhurst, *Symp. Faraday Soc.*, **1971**, *5*, 107.
84. N. Hiruma, T. Michihata, N. Koide, and K. Iimura, *Rep. Prog. Polym. Phys. Jpn.*, **1984**, *27*, 247.
85. C. Carfagna, A. Roviello, S. Santagata, and A. Sirigu, *Makromol. Chem.*, **1986**, *187*, 2123.
86. T.D. Shaffer, M. Jamaludin, and V. Percec, *J. Polym. Sci., Polym. Chem. Ed.*, **1985**, *23*, 2913.
87. P. Iannelli, A. Roviello, and A. Sirigu, *Eur. Polym. J.*, **1982**, *18*, 753.
88. J. Watanabe, K. Ikeda, and W.R. Krigbaum, *J. Polym. Sci., Polym. Phys. Ed.*, **1987**, *25*, 19.
89. W. Zhang, J.I. Jin, and R.W. Lenz, *Makromol. Chem.*, **1988**, *189*, 2219.

90. W.J. Jackson, Jr., and J.C. Morris, *J. Polym. Sci., Polym. Chem. Ed.*, **1988**, *26*, 835.
91. P. Meier, E. Ohmes, and G. Kothe, *J. Chem. Phys.*, **1986**, *85*, 3598.
92. A. Saupe, Z. *Naturforsch.*, *A*, **1964**, *19*, 161.
93. N. Boden, R.J. Bushby, and L.D. Clark, *Chem. Phys. Lett.*, **1979**, *64*, 519.
94. E.T. Samulski, M.M. Gauthier, R.B. Blumstein, and A. Blumstein, *Macromolecules*, **1984**, *17*, 479.
95. P. Corradini and M. Vacatello, *Mol. Cryst., Liq. Cryst.*, **1983**, *97*, 119.
96. S.V. Vasilenko, A.R. Khokhlov, and V.P. Shibaev, *Macromolecules*, **1984**, *17*, 2270.
97. R.E. Boehm, D.E. Martire, and N.V. Madhusudana, *Macromolecules*, **1986**, *19*, 2329.
98. F. Dowell, *Mol. Cryst. Liq. Cryst.*, **1988**, *155*, 457.
99. F. Dowell, *J. Chem. Phys.*, **1989**, *91*, 1316.
100. G. Ronca and D.Y. Yoon, *J. Chem. Phys.*, **1982**, *76*, 3295.
101. A. Ten Bosch, P. Maïssa, and P. Sixou, *Phys. Lett.*, **1983**, *94*, 298.
102. E.A. Di Marzio, *J. Chem. Phys.*, **1961**, *35*, 658.
103. R.R. Matheson, Jr. and P.J. Flory, *Macromolecules*, **1981**, *14*, 954.
104. F. Auriemma, Doctoral Thesis, University of Napoli, **1990**
105. A. Abe, *Macromolecules*, **1984**, *17*, 2280.
106. D.Y. Yoon and S. Bruckner, *Macromolecules*, **1985**, *18*, 651.
107. S. Bruckner, *Macromolecules*, **1988**, *21*, 633.
108. A.F. Martins, J.B. Ferreira, F. Volino, A. Blumstein, and R.B. Blumstein, *Macromolecules*, **1983**, *16*, 279.
109. R. Capasso, P. Iannelli, A. Roviello, and A. Sirigu, *J. Polym. Sci., Polym. Phys. Ed.*, **1987**, *25*, 2431.
110. G. Sigaud, D.Y. Yoon, and A.C. Griffin, *Macromolecules*, **1983**, *16*, 875.
111. R. Capasso, P. Iannelli, A. Roviello, and A. Sirigu, *Macromolecules*, **1985**, *18*, 2773.
112. H. Toriumi, H. Furuya, and A. Abe, *Polym. J.*, **1985**, *17*, 895.
113. L. Strzelecki and L. Liebert, *Eur. Polym. J.*, **1981**, *17*, 1271.
114. T.D. Shaffer and V. Percec, *Makromol. Chem.*, **1986**, *187*, 111.
115. E. Amendola, C. Carfagna, A. Roviello, S. Santagata, and A. Sirigu, *Makromol. Chem. Rapid Commun.*, **1987**, *8*, 109.
116. R.S. Ghadage, S. Ponrathnam, and V.M. Nadkarni, *Polym. Commun.*, **1988**, *29*, 116.
117. M. Sato, K. Kurosawa, K. Nakatsuchi, and Y. Ohkatsu, *J. Polym. Sci., Polym. Chem. Ed.*, **1988**, *26*, 3077.
118. B.W. Jo, R.W. Lenz, and J.I. Jin, *Makromol. Chem. Rapid Commun.*, **1982**, *3*, 23.
119. C. Ober, J.I. Jin, and R.W. Lenz, *Polym. J.*, **1982**, *14*, 9.
120. A. Blumstein, K.N. Sivaramakrishnan, R.B. Blumstein, and S.B. Clough, *Polymer*, **1982**, *23*, 47.
121. D. Sek, *Eur. Polym. J.*, **1984**, *20*, 805.
122. D. Van Luyen, L. Liebert, and L. Strzelecki, *Eur. Polym. J.*, **1980**, *16*, 307.
123. D. Braun and U. Schuelke, *Makromol. Chem.*, **1986**, *187*, 1145.
124. A. Furukawa and R.W. Lenz, *Makromol. Chem., Makromol. Symp.*, **1986**, *2*, 3.
125. Qi-Feng Zhou and R.W. Lenz, *J. Polym. Sci., Polym. Chem. Ed.*, **1983**, *21*, 3313.
126. A. Blumstein, M.M. Gauthier, O. Thomas, and R.B. Blumstein, *Faraday Disc. Chem. Soc.*, **1985**, *79*, 33.
127. K. Tani, N. Koide, and K. Iimura, *Rep. Prog. Polym. Phys. Jpn.*, **1984**, *27*, 243.
128. T.D. Shaffer and V. Percec, *J. Polym. Sci., Polym. Chem. Ed.*, **1987**, *25*, 2755.
129. H.K. Hall, Jr., T. Kuo, R.W. Lenz, and T.M. Leslie, *Macromolecules*, **1987**, *20*, 2041.

130. V. Percec, T.D. Shaffer, and N. Nava, *J. Polym. Sci., Polym. Lett. Ed.*, **1984**, *22*, 637.
131. D. Van Luyen and L. Strzelecki, *Eur. Polym. J.*, **1980**, *16*, 303.
132. W. Xueqiu, W. Hojung, and L. Shijin, *Liq. Cryst.*, **1988**, *3*, 1267.
133. M. Sato, *J. Polym. Sci., Polym. Chem. Ed.*, **1988**, *26*, 2613.
134. A.S. Angeloni, E. Chiellini, G. Galli, M.Laus, and G. Torquati, *Makromol. Chem., Makromol. Symp.*, **1989**, *24*, 311.
135. J.E. McIntyre, P.E.P. Maj, and J.G. Tomka, *Polymer*, **1989**, *30*, 732.
136. M. Marcos, F. Navarro, L. Oriol, and J.L. Serrano, *Makromol. Chem.*, **1989**, *190*, 305.
137. Z. Jedlinski, J. Franek, A. Kulczycki, A. Sirigu, and C. Carfagna, *Macromolecules*, **1989**, *22*, 1600.
138. A.S. Angeloni, D. Caretti, M. Laus, E. Chiellini, and G. Galli, *Polym. J.*, **1988**, *20*, 1157.
139. D. Sek and A. Volinska, *Eur. Polym. J.*, **1989**, *25*, 9.
140. A. Roviello and A. Sirigu, *Makromol. Chem.*, **1979**, *180*, 2543.
141. A.H. Al-Dujaili, A.D. Jenkins, and D.R. Walton, *J. Polym. Sci., Polym. Chem. Ed.*, **1984**, *22*, 3129.
142. M. Laus, P. Ferruti, G. Galli, and E. Chiellini, *J. Polym. Sci., Polym. Lett. Ed.*, **1984**, *22*, 587.
143. M. Sato, K. Nakatsuchi, and Y. Ohkatsu, *Makromol. Chem. Rapid Commun.*, **1986**, *7*, 231.
144. Y. Ozcayir and A. Blumstein, *J. Polym. Sci., Polym. Chem. Ed.*, **1986**, *24*, 1217.
145. T.D. Shaffer and V. Percec, *Polym. Bull.*, **1985**, *14*, 367.
146. I.G. Voigt-Martin, H. Durst, B. Reck, and H. Ringsdorf, *Macromolecules*, **1988**, *21*, 1620.
147. K.N. Sivaramakrishnan, A. Blumstein, S.B. Clough, and R.B. Blumstein, *Polym. Prepr. (ACS)*, **1978**, *19*, 190.
148. W.J. Jackson, Jr. and J.C. Morris, *J. Polym. Sci., Polym. Chem. Ed.*, **1987**, *25*, 575.
149. T.D. Shaffer and V. Percec, *Makromol. Chem. Rapid Commun.*, **1987**, *6*, 97.
150. H.R. Kricheldorf, R. Pakull, and S. Buchner, *J. Polym. Sci., Polym. Chem. Ed.*, **1989**, *27*, 431.

CHAPTER 8

Liquid-Crystalline Sidechain Polymers

H. FINKELMANN

Institut für Makromolekulare Chemie,
Universität Freiburg, Stefan-Meier-Str. 31,
D-7800 Freiburg, Germany

CONTENTS

1. INTRODUCTION

The term "liquid crystal sidechain polymers" (LCSP's) classifies polymers that have mesogenic moieties linked as side groups to the polymer backbone. According to the established classification of low molecular weight liquid crystals (LMWLC), the mesogenic moieties can have either a rigid rodlike or a disklike structure, both of which may cause the thermotropic liquid crystalline state. If the mesogenic moiety exhibits an amphiphilic structure, the lyotropic liquid-crystalline state may be observed in solution due to micellar aggregation.[1,2]

In this chapter we will consider only LCSP's with rigid rodlike mesogenic moieties and will discuss some selected fundamental properties. The discussion of the LCSP's and their properties mainly comes from the following two basic aspects:

1. In contrast to liquid crystal mainchain polymers (LCMP's), the axial ratio of the rigid rodlike mesogenic moiety of LCSP's remains unchanged when comparing monomer and polymer. Consequently, the same holds for the anisotropic dispersion interactions which may serve as a basis for the theoretical description of the LC state. Actually, the experiments reflect

many similarities between monomers and polymers. For example, nearly all the polymorphic variants that are known for LMWLC are also identified for polymers. However, the linkage of the rods to the backbone causes some basic differences. Translational as well as rotational motions of the mesogenic moieties become restricted, which will directly influence the state of order and structural modifications of the LC state. These aspects will be considered in Sections 2 and 3.

2. In most cases the chemistry of the LCSP backbone does not differ from that of conventional flexible polymers. Experiments with isotropic melts or isotropic solutions of LCSP's do not indicate any noticeable deviations from flexible chain properties. However, in the liquid-crystalline state, the backbone must adopt—at least locally—the anisotropic phase structure and must depart from the isotropic, statistical chain conformation. Consequently, chain entropy will act against LC phase structure and uniform director alignment. This aspect of the LCSP is most clearly exemplified with elastomers and is discussed in Section 4.

2. CHEMICAL CONSTITUTION AND PHASE TRANSITIONS

2.1. Chemical Constitution

The simple structural concept of LCSP's is to introduce any functional group into any LMWLC. The functional group has to be capable of either a polymerization reaction or a side reaction with a suitably functionalized polymer (Fig. 1).

The LMWLC may exhibit a stable or metastable (monotropic) LC phase and may be chosen from any one of the known LC molecules.[3] The functional group may be substituted at the end of the mesogenic moiety (end on) or laterally to the rigid rod (side-on LCSP). Additional modifications can be realized with "twins" or other structures. The polymers may have linked the LMWLC at every single monomer unit yielding homopolymers. Copolymers with mesogenic or nonmesogenic comonomers having a statistically irregular arrangement of the monomer units (statistical copolymers) or a regular arrangement of segments (block copolymers) may be synthesized. This brief summary illustrates the broad variety of feasible macromolecular architectures with respect to the chemistry of the backbone, the mesogenic molecules, and the means of linking them together. For all these structures the LC state is observed to exhibit basically the same systematic classifications as LMWLC's. The variety of chemical structures used for the synthesis of LCSP's have been reviewed.[4-6]

For LMWLC's the phase structure and the temperature regime of the LC state is determined solely by the chemical constitution of the mesogenic moiety and their substituents. However, for LCSP's the degree of polymerization (DP) of the polymer backbone as well as the linkage between the

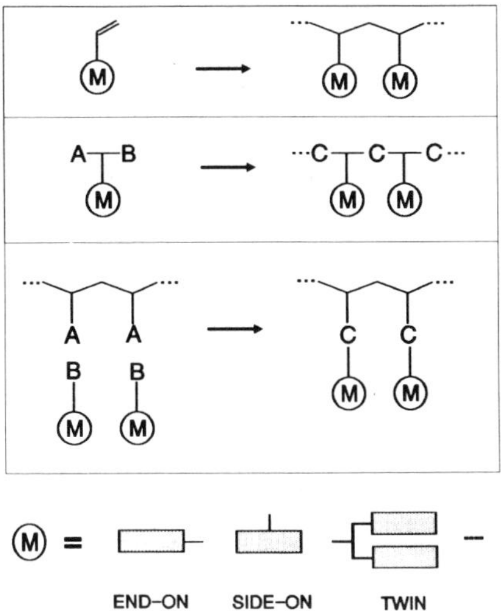

FIGURE 1
Synthesis of LCSP: polyaddition, polycondensation, and side reactions of polymers of mesogenic molecules M. (A, B: functional groups.)

mainchain and mesogenic moieties additionally influence the anisotropic state. The effect of the linkage will be discussed in detail in Section 3. A qualitative explanation of the DP dependence of the LC to isotropic phase transformation will be given in the next section.

2.2. Liquid-Crystalline to Isotropic Phase Transformation

Numerous experiments have been performed to analyze the dependence of the LC–isotropic phase transformation temperature T_i on the DP of the polymer. However, the number of quantitative results is too limited to obtain a detailed insight into this relationship for all different types of LCSP. A general conclusion is that T_i is strongly affected in the regime of oligomers with DP $\gtrsim 10$, while for $10 < DP < 100$, the transformation temperature approaches a value that remains constant for DP > 100.

The same holds for LC–LC transformations, e,g., smectic to nematic. A typical example is shown in Fig. 2[7] for fractionated oligomers of:

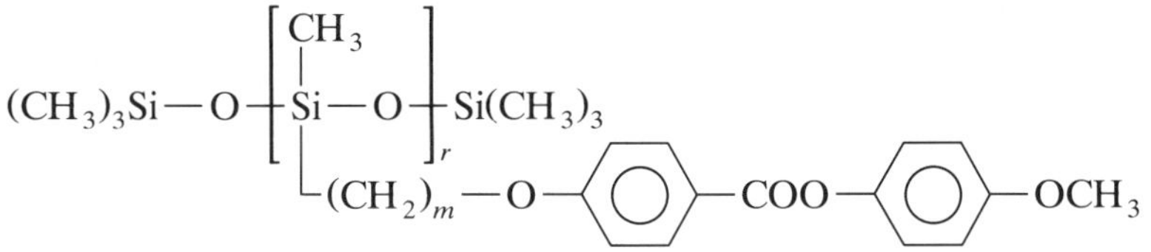

1

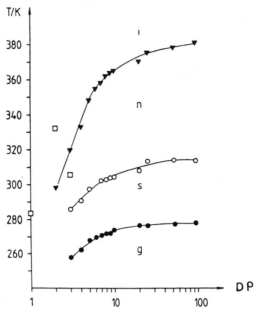

FIGURE 2
Phase transformation temperatures of fractionated polysiloxanes **1**
with $m = 6$ as function of DP (g = glassy, s = smectic, n = nematic,
i = isotropic). (Reproduced with permission from Ref. 7. Copyright
American Chemical Society.)

For all of these experiments it must be realized that the terminal group of
the macromolecule or oligomer may additionally influence the phase transformation temperature. In the example illustrated in Fig. 2, the bulky
trimethylsiloxane end group will definitely contribute to the phase behavior.
The experimental results, furthermore, indicate that the highly ordered
smectic phases of polymers are less sensitive to changes in DP than the
nematic phase, giving the sequence

$$\frac{\Delta T_{\text{NI}}}{\Delta \text{DP}} > \frac{\Delta T_{\text{SI}}}{\Delta \text{DP}} > \frac{\Delta T_{\text{SN}}}{\Delta \text{DP}} \tag{1}$$

These results clearly resemble the phase transformation (PT) behavior of
LMWLC's, where the first-order phase transformation can be described by
the Clausius-Clapeyron equation[7]

$$\left(\frac{dP}{dT_{\text{tr}}}\right) = \frac{\Delta H}{T_{\text{tr}}\, \Delta \mathscr{V}} \tag{2}$$

where ΔH is the specific phase transformation enthalpy and $\Delta \mathscr{V} = \mathscr{V}' - \mathscr{V}''$ is the difference between the specific volumes of the coexisting phases at the phase transformation temperature. For LMWLC's it has been generally established that

$$\left(\frac{dP}{dT}\right)_{NI} < \left(\frac{dP}{dT}\right)_{SN} \approx \left(\frac{dP}{dT}\right)_{SI} \tag{3}$$

which resembles the sequence of Eq. (1). The link between Eqs. (1) and (3) is the specific volume of the liquid-crystalline phase at the phase transformation. For $\mathscr{V}'(T, P)$ along the coexisting curve, we have to differentiate $\mathscr{V}'$ with respect to T. With the specific isobaric expansion coefficient γ and the isothermal specific compressibility β at the phase transformation we obtain

$$\left(\frac{d\mathscr{V}'}{dT}\right)_{tr} = \mathscr{V}'_{tr}\left[\gamma_{tr} - \beta\left(\frac{dP}{dT}\right)_{tr}\right] \tag{4}$$

which directly relates the change of the phase transformation temperature to the specific volume.

For the LCSP, $\mathscr{V}$ decreases with an increasing degree of polymerization as indicated in Fig. 3 for the system described in Fig. 2.[7] In other words, the

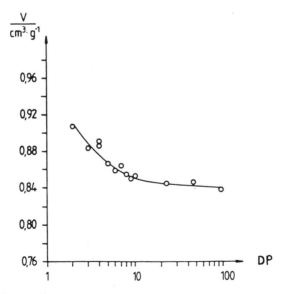

FIGURE 3
Specific volume V as function of DP at $T = 298$ K for polysiloxanes
1 ($m = 6$). (Reproduced with permission from Ref. 7. Copyright
American Chemical Society.)

systematic variation of specific volume with pressure observed in LMWLC's obviously also holds for LCSP's, where the specific volume changes with DP.

For the nematic to isotropic transformation the Maier-Saupe model[8, 9] also directly links the specific volume of the coexisting nematic phase with the phase transformation temperature. The thermodynamic relationship which results from the calculation of the dipole–dipole dispersion interactions yields the numerical equations for the phase transformation at constant volume (free energy $\Delta F = 0$):

$$\frac{\varepsilon(\Theta)}{kT_{NI}, \mathscr{V}_{NI}^2} = 4.54 \quad \text{and} \quad S_0 = 0.43 \tag{5}$$

where $\varepsilon(\Theta)$ is the orientation-dependent part of the dispersion interaction for the molecule, k is the Boltzmann constant, and S_0 is the nematic order parameter at T_{NI}. Due to the small volume changes at the nematic to isotropic phase transformation, Eq. (5) is a good approximation at the phase transformation under constant pressure ($\Delta G = 0$). The values of $\varepsilon(\Theta)$ $(T_{NI}, \mathscr{V}_{NI})$ change only slightly with the relative jump in the volume $\Delta\mathscr{V}_{NI}/\mathscr{V}_{NI}$. If we assume that the quantity $\varepsilon(\Theta)$ in Eq. (5) remains unchanged in going from the monomer to the corresponding polymer (the mesogenic group is not involved in any structural changes during polymerization), the relation

$$\frac{T_{NI, mon}}{T_{NI, pol}} \approx \frac{\mathscr{V}_{NI, pol}^2}{\mathscr{V}_{NI, mon}^2} \tag{6}$$

should be valid. The experimental results can actually be described sufficiently with this simple relation,[10] although it is only a rough estimation, i.e., assuming the same order parameter at T_{NI} for monomer and polymer (Eq. 5). It should be pointed out, however, that additional careful PVT measurements of suitable monomers, oligomers, and polymers are necessary to clarify the T_{NI}(DP) relation. It is interesting to compare the above conclusions with the assessment of free-volume effects for oligomers and LCMP's (see Chapter 6).

For all nematic systems the Maier-Saupe relation (Eq. 5) predicts an order parameter of $S_0 = 0.43$ at T_{NI}. Numerous experiments on LMWLC's have proved that S_0 deviates from this model depending on the chemistry of the mesogenic moiety. If we compare the temperature variation of the order parameter for the monomeric LMWLC and for the corresponding LCSP, a systematic shift is observed. All experiments indicate that the absolute values of S, related to a reduced temperature T/T_{NI}, are always lower for the polymer. An example is shown in Fig. 4,[11] where the dashed line additionally indicates the theoretical curve of $S(T)$ according to the Maier-Saupe theory

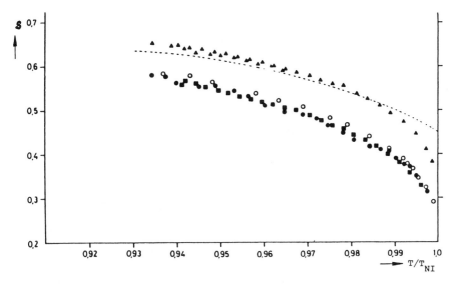

FIGURE 4
Temperature dependence of the nematic order parameter S for polysiloxanes 1 ($\bullet$, $m = 3$; $\bigcirc$, $m = 4$; $\blacksquare$, $m = 6$) as indicated in Fig. 2 and the LMWLC

$$C_6H_{13}O-\bigcirc-COO-\bigcirc-OC_6H_3$$

($\blacktriangle$). (Reproduced with permission from Ref. 11.)

for systems with $\Delta\mathscr{V}_{NI}/\mathscr{V}_{NI} \approx 0.004$. Obviously the linkage of the LC moieties to the backbone causes the same systematic deviation. This systematic decrease of S obviously cannot be related to the chemical constitution of the mesogenic moiety because no change occurs during polymerization. This means that in the frame of the Maier-Saupe model $\varepsilon(\Theta)$ is not affected by polymerization.

An explanation may be given by the expansion of the Maier-Saupe theory with respect to the orientation distribution function of the mesogenic moieties. Humphries et al.[12] have extended the Maier-Saupe pair potential $V(\Theta)$ for cylindrical molecules with

$$V(\Theta) = \sum V_L \bar{P}_L P(\cos \Theta); \qquad L = 2, 4 \ldots \qquad (7)$$

where Θ is the angle between the rod and the main ordering direction. Neglecting higher terms than $L = 4$ one obtains

$$V(\Theta) = V_2\{\bar{P}_2(\cos \Theta) + \lambda\bar{P}_4 P_4(\cos \Theta)\} \qquad (8)$$

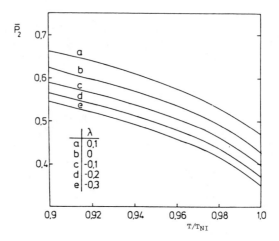

FIGURE 5
Theoretical curves of $S(T)$ for different values of λ [for $\lambda = 0$, $S(T)$ coincides with the Maier-Saupe theory]. (Reproduced with permission from Ref. 12.)

Table 1
Nematic–Isotropic Phase Transformation Entropies ΔS_{NI}
for Some LMWLC and Polysiloxanes

	ΔS_{NI} (J mol^{-1} K^{-1})
$\diagup\!\!\!\diagup\!\!\!\diagdown$—O—⟨◯⟩—COO—⟨◯⟩—OC$_6H_{13}$	4.6
$H_{13}C_6$—O—⟨◯⟩—COO—⟨◯⟩—OC$_6$H$_{13}$	4.4
$H_{13}C_6$—O—⟨◯⟩—COO—⟨◯⟩—OC$_5$H$_{11}$	3.5
$H_{13}C_6$—O—⟨◯⟩—COO—⟨◯⟩—OC$_2$H$_5$	3.6

$$\cdots -\underset{\underset{(CH_2)_m-O-\langle\bigcirc\rangle-COO-\langle\bigcirc\rangle-OCH_3}{|}}{\overset{\overset{CH_3}{|}}{Si}}-O-\cdots$$

$m = 3$	2.4
$m = 4$	1.8
$m = 5$	2.9
$m = 6$	2.9

322

where $\lambda = V_4/V_2$ is a measure of the relative influence of the fourth Legendre polynomial. The addition of the P_4 term compared to the Maier-Saupe potential, causes, with increasing positive (negative) λ, an increase (decrease) of the order parameter $\bar{P}_2 = S$ at a given reduced temperature. The theoretical curves[12] are given in Fig. 5.

The trend parallels the experimental findings, suggesting that the systematic shift of S for the monomer–polymer systems may be due to a broadening in the orientation distribution function.

A change of λ in Eq. (8) also influences such thermodynamic properties as the phase transformation entropy ΔS_{NI} and temperature T_{NI}. With a negative λ, not only S, but also ΔS_{NI} and T_{NI} decrease. For the systems shown in Fig. 4, the phase transformation entropies are compared in Table 1 with some LMWLC's having the same mesogenic moiety. Actually the hexyloxy-substituted benzoic acid phenylester (order parameter $S_{NI} = 0.38$) exhibits a larger ΔS_{NI} than the polymers with $S_{NI} = 0.29$.

Although the examples mentioned in this section qualitatively verify the considerations, additional systematic experiments on the order parameter and thermodynamic properties of monomer–polymer systems must be carried out to get a better understanding of the LC to isotropic phase transformation.

2.3. Glass Transition

In most cases, the bulky side groups of LCSP's prevent crystallization of the polymer at low temperatures. Under normal experimental conditions the liquid-crystalline melt can be supercooled with respect to the melting temperature. Partially crystalline polymers can only be obtained from annealing experiments. At lower temperatures the LC melt will undergo a glass transition.

The glass transition temperature (T_g) strongly depends on the chemical structure of the polymers. Besides mainchain flexibility the length and flexibility of the flexible spacer essentially determine the glass transition temperature. Short, flexible spacers strongly elevate T_g nearly independently of the chemistry of the mainchain, while for long flexible spacers the nature of the backbone becomes important. Copolymerization with nonmesogenic comonomers, as well as low molar mass additives, decrease T_g.

Detailed investigations of the glass transition by NMR,[13] dielectric relaxation spectroscopy,[14] and optical methods[11] indicate that translational motions of the mesogenic moieties and the polymer backbone cease simultaneously, assuming a homogeneous liquid-crystalline phase below T_g. In the glassy state only local reorientation processes and rotational motions of molecular fragments remain. The glass exhibits the anisotropic state of order and structure that existed during the vitrification process of the LC phase. Polymers aligned macroscopically, e.g., by electric or magnetic fields keep their orientation during the vitrification process.

Table 2

Phase Transition Temperatures, Enthalpies ΔH_i, and Change
of the Isobaric Specific Heat at T_g for Some Polymers

$$\text{Polymer: } CH_3 - \overset{\overset{\displaystyle CH_2}{|}}{\underset{|}{C}} - \overset{\overset{\displaystyle O}{\|}}{C} - O - (CH_2)_m - O - \bigcirc\!\!-\!\!\bigcirc - R$$

m	R	Phase Transitions (K)	Δc_p (kJ mol^{-1} K^{-1})	ΔH_i (kJ mol^{-1})
6	H	$T_g\,313\,T_i$	0.14	—
2	OCH_3	$T_g\,390\,T_n\,420\,T_i$	0.10	1.1
6	OC_5H_{11}	$T_g\,373\,T_s\,399\,T_i$	0.06	8.5
6	OC_6H_{13}	$T_g\,—\,T_s\,427\,T_i$	—	11.3

Thermodynamic investigations of the change of the isobaric specific heat ΔC_p at the glass transition give some information about the structure of the LC phase which exists above T_g. In the nematic phase, where the mesogenic sidechains have only long-range orientational order, the polymer backbone only slightly deviates from the chain conformation of the corresponding isotropic phase (see also Section 4). Accordingly, the experimental values of ΔC_p at T_g are similar for an isotropic and nematic polymer (Table 2).

For the smectic polymers, which have long-range positional order in one dimension (S_A, S_C), restricted mobility of the backbone and the mesogenic moiety is indicated by a reduced change in the specific heat at T_g compared to nematic and isotropic polymers. Finally, for highly ordered smectic phases, which also exhibit a large ΔH_i, molecular mobility is obviously strongly depressed and under normal DSC experimental conditions no change in ΔC_p is found.

3. STRUCTURE OF LC PHASES

Disregarding any structural anomalies that may arise from an anisotropic backbone arrangement in the liquid-crystalline state and looking only at the arrangement of the mesogenic side groups, nearly all LC phases known for LMWLC's have been identified for LCSP's. If the mesogenic groups are hinged via a flexible spacer to the mainchain, the polymers normally exhibit the same polymorphism observed for the corresponding LMWLC having the chemical structure of the monomer unit. Exceptions are often observed for nematic systems. In most cases the nematic phase region of the monomer is reduced in favor of smectic phases for the polymer. Nevertheless, similar to the strategy for the synthesis of LMWLC's, systematic variations in the length of the flexible spacer, the mesogenic moiety, and their substituents enable the realization of the polymorphism known for LMWLC's.

In this section we shall not refer to well-known structures which have been extensively reviewed recently.[4] We shall concentrate instead on structures that are not analogous to LMWLC's due to strong interactions or linkages between backbone and side groups. Three aspects will be considered: (1) the contribution of backbone anisotropy, (2) translational restrictions of the side groups, and (3) rotational restrictions of the side groups.

3.1. Backbone Anisotropy and LC Phase Structure

As already mentioned, the statistical chain conformation in the isotropic state is not consistent with the anisotropic LC phase structure. This can be observed directly if a conventional nonmesogenic polymer is dissolved in a nematic solvent. Even if in the isotropic state the components are completely miscible, phase separation occurs in the nematic state[15] (see Chapters 4 and 6). For LCSP's no phase separation can occur and the backbone conformation must adopt an anisotropic conformation according to the phase structure. X-ray,[16] neutron scattering experiments,[17] and director reorientation in the magnetic field[18] prove the departure from spherical coil conformation. Prolate as well as oblate backbone coils have been observed in the nematic state depending on the chemistry of the flexible spacer and the mesogenic group. Basically the same conclusion can be obtained from x-ray experiments of fibers that are prepared from the LC melt. During the spinning process of the fiber, the backbone becomes oriented in the shear gradient, causing a parallel (perpendicular) orientation of the nematic director for a polymer having a prolate (oblate) coil in the melt under equilibrium conditions.

The molecular origin for the different chain conformations is delicate and will be discussed in Section 4.2.1 in more detail for elastomers. A theoretical explanation has been given recently by Warner,[19] which is outlined in Chapter 5. In this theory the cross-coupling between the rodlike sidechain and the mainchain causes different structures of the nematic phase. These structures are classified by the order parameters of the sidechain S_A and of the mainchain S_B. For $S_A > 0$, $S_B < 0$ the backbone is an oblate spheroid and the phase is called the N_I phase (see Fig. 7, Chapter 5). The prolate phases are N_{II} and N_{III} with $S_A < 0, S_B > 0$ and $S_A, S_B > 0$, respectively. In the theory it is assumed that the backbone has a nematic interaction with the sidechains. Consider the conventional LCSP with polyacrylate, polymethacrylate, or polysiloxane mainchains, where in the sense of the Maier-Saupe theory the anisotropy of polarizability of the backbone units can be neglected compared to that of the mesogenic moieties. For the LCSP's these assumptions of strong nematic-like interaction between main- and sidechains are unlikely. Consequently all these polymers should have the same N phase which is in contrast to the experiments. As outlined in Section 4.2.1 small variations of the spacer length and the mesogenic group cause changes from N_I to N_{III}, which cannot be explained with this theory.

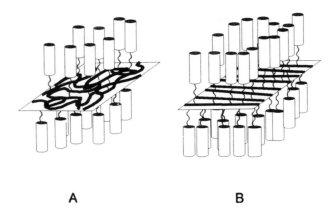

A   **B**

FIGURE 6
Schematic representation of smectic polymers having a flexible (A)
and an orientationally ordered (B) backbone.

Warner's theory will, however, be of interest for the "combined LC polymers" synthesized for the first time by Reck and Ringsdorf,[20] where mesogenic moieties are both along the mainchain and linked as side groups. If a N_I phase actually exists for these polymers (up to now only N_{III} phases are identified), an additional aspect may become important: strong interaction between the backbones may also cause a nematic ordering of the main chain. This additional orientation should be even more pronounced for smectic phases, where the polymer backbone must be arranged in layers as shown schematically in Fig. 6.

Figure 6a shows a smectic phase as assumed for conventional LCSP's, where the backbone adopts a more or less two-dimensional, statistical arrangement. If the chains become orientationally ordered in addition, and if this orientation is transferred from one layer to the neighboring layers (Fig. 6b), a new phase will be observed that can be identified simply by its biaxial optical behavior.

3.2. Translational Restriction

The linkage of the mesogenic molecule drastically restricts their translational motions and their translational diffusion processes are strongly correlated with the neighboring molecules of the backbone. Nevertheless, these restrictions do not prevent the formation of known liquid-crystalline structures with a systematic variation very similar to LMWLC's. However, one requirement has to be fulfilled to obtain the liquid-crystalline state for the polymers as described in Section 2.1: the rigid mesogenic molecules must be linked to the monomer units of the polymer backbone via a flexible spacer. The spacer may consist, e.g., of an alkyl, alkyloxy, or siloxane chain. If no flexible spacer

FIGURE 7
Schematic representation of a boardlike and bottle brush structure of LC sidechain polymers.

exists, the position of the rods will be fixed with respect to the monomer unit and fluctuations of the center of mass of the rods are limited to a fixed radius. As indicated by space-filling models, additional steric hindrance of the rods prevents their arrangement along the backbone independently of neighboring side groups. Two extreme arrangements may be conceived which are schematically shown in Fig. 7.

(1) The polymer backbone becomes strongly stiffened and the mesogenic groups are perpendicular and cylindrically arranged around the backbone. This structure for a LCSP without a spacer resembles a bottle brush and was suggested for the first time by Cser and Hardy (a periodical helical structure).[21] In it the N_{II} phase occurs where $S_A < 0$, $S_B > 0$. (2) The mesogenic molecules are also constrained in a perpendicular position to the backbone, but they are arranged parallel to each other. This arrangement causes a "boardlike" structure of the macromolecule.

For both structures the tight linkage of the bulky side groups causes a stiffness of the mainchain. Owing to the immobility of the side groups, the anisomeric element is no longer the monomer unit but whole segments of the backbone. In principle nematic phases may exist by an orientational long-range order of the bottle brushes or boards. A smectic arrangement of the boards is reasonably similar to conventional smectics, while the bottle brushes may become packed in a hexagonal structure that corresponds to the hexagonal H_1 phase of cylindrical micelles. Recent calculations by Renz[22] arrive at the conclusion that the N_{II} phase is thermodynamically unstable. Careful x-ray measurements on polymers rule out the proposed periodical helical structure.[23] The boardlike or ribbon-like structure is corroborated by experiment. First, these polymers exhibit extremely high glass transition temperatures (up to ~ 200°C),[24] which are strongly elevated compared to polymers having the same mesogenic side groups but flexible spacers. Furthermore, all these polymers exhibit smectic structures almost exclusively, independently of the chemical constitution of the mesogenic group. In this regard no systematic relationship can be found between phase structure and structure of the mesogenic moiety obtained for the same polymers having flexible spacers. Compared to the monomers, the LC to isotropic phase transformation temperature is elevated to very high values which cannot be explained by the arguments given in Section 2.2. Finally, x-ray experiments confirm the board-like macromolecular structure.[25]

3.3. Rotational Restrictions

In the nematic, chiral nematic (cholesteric), and smectic A and C phases of LMWLC's, translational and rotational motions of the molecules are restricted only by the anisotropic dispersion and/or repulsion interactions with neighboring molecules. For these phases it can be assumed that due to the low potential barrier, there exists a nearly unhindered rotation of the molecules around their long molecular axes. Although the molecular structure of the mesogenic molecules rather resembles a board (biaxial structure), their symmetry can be regarded as being cylindrical. Theoretically it has been predicted by Freizer[26] that at low temperatures the potential barrier for rotation of the long axis becomes sufficiently large that the biaxial nature of the molecule can no longer be neglected. A second-order uniaxial nematic to biaxial nematic phase transformation takes place. Similarly, a smectic A phase should become biaxial. However, these transformations are expected to occur at temperatures where the LC phases are no longer stable with respect to the crystalline or glassy state. An elevation of the biaxial to uniaxial nematic transformation temperature is observed, if the conventional structure of the LMWLC is optimized with respect to molecular biaxiality. Actually the biaxial nematic phase has been observed recently.[27, 28]

For LCSP's rotational restrictions of the mesogenic groups can be directly affected by chemistry in the following ways:

1. The linkage of the mesogenic groups via a short flexible spacer. The long-axis rotation is no longer determined only by intermolecular interactions but also by the spacer.
2. The mesogenic group is attached via lateral substituents to the polymer backbone (see Fig. 1).

The effect of the spacer length on the restriction of the long-axis rotation of the mesogenic group has been studied in detail on chiral nematic polymers.[10] According to theory[29, 30] the helicoidal (twisted nematic) structure of a cholesteric phase sensitively depends on order parameters that are directly related to the rotation of the molecules around their long molecular axis. In the case of nonhindered rotation, no cholesteric twist should exist. Increasing hindered rotation causes at least local phase biaxiality and increasing twist of the cholesteric structure. The twist of the cholesteric phase, characterized by the pitch p, can be easily measured spectroscopically according to

$$\lambda_R = \bar{n}p$$

where λ_R is the wavelength of circularly polarized light that is reflected by a helicoidal phase, and $\bar{n}$ is the mean refractive index. In the case of a local biaxial cholesteric phase (the overall symmetry being still uniaxial) the pitch is given by[30]

$$\frac{1}{p} \approx -\frac{\pi(\chi)\bar{P}_2 - \frac{2}{3}\delta(\chi)\bar{D}}{\delta(\sigma)\bar{P}_2 - \frac{1}{2}\pi(\sigma)\bar{D}} \tag{9}$$

where the molecular quantity χ is related to the chirality of the molecules (dipole–quadrupole interactions). This term is nonzero only when the molecules are chiral. σ describes the dipole–dipole interactions similar to the Maier-Saupe theory.[9] The term $\delta(\chi, \sigma)$ can be regarded as anisotropy and $\pi(\chi, \sigma)$ as flatness of χ or δ; $\bar{P}_2$ is the normal Maier-Saupe order parameter S, while the order parameter $\bar{D}$ is related to the rotation of the molecules along their long molecular axis. Any changes of $\bar{D}$ directly influence the helicoidal structure.

Equation (9) contains too many unknown quantities for clear experimental evaluation on low molar mass cholesteric phases. For polymers, however, it is a helpful theoretical basis for the interpretation of experiments. If we analyze the cholesteric pitch of polymers that differ only in the length of the flexible spacer (e.g., by the number of methylene groups), the molecular quantities χ and σ should remain essentially constant. As indicated in Fig. 4, the same holds true for the order parameter S. Consequently, if the pitch of these polymers is altered by varying the spacer length, this alteration should be directly related to a change in $\bar{D}$, and we can analyze restrictions of rotational motions of the mesogenic group.

Experiments have been carried out with so-called "induced cholesteric phases," where a nematic host phase is converted into a cholesteric phase by chiral guest molecules. Copolymers with the nematogenic groups of different spacer lengths were synthesized with increasing mole fraction, x_{ch}, of chiral comonomers. For these systems, the helical twisting power[10]

$$\text{HTP} = \left(\frac{dp}{dx_{ch}}\right)_{x_{ch} \to 0} \tag{10}$$

that characterizes the ability of a chiral molecule to induce the cholesteric twist into the nematic host phase can be directly related to Eq. (9). Expanding the orientation-dependent energy of a molecule in a one-component

Table 3

HTP of Polysiloxanes **1** Copolymerized with the Chiral Comonomer Units

$$CH_3-\underset{\underset{O}{|}}{\overset{|}{Si}}-(CH_2)_3-COO-cholesterol$$

and the Corresponding Monomer Mixture

	HTP, $10^2\left(\dfrac{dp^{-1}}{dx_{ch}}\right)_T$ (nm^{-1})
Copolymer $m = 3$	2.67
$m = 4$	2.23
$m = 6$	2.00
Monomer mixtures	1.22

phase as calculated by Vertogen for mixtures, one obtains[7]

$$HTP \propto \frac{\pi_{21}(\chi)\,\bar{P}_2^{(2)}\bar{P}_2^{(1)} - \frac{2}{3}\delta_{21}(\chi)\,\bar{D}^{(2)}\bar{D}^{(1)}}{\delta_{22}(\sigma)\left(\bar{P}_2^{(2)}\right)^2 + \frac{1}{2}\pi_{22}(\sigma)\left(\bar{D}^{(2)}\right)^2} \qquad (11)$$

where the indices (1) and (2) refer to the chiral (1) and nematogenic (2) molecules. Equation (11) has the same form as Eq. (9). Results for the polymers previously discussed are listed in Table 3.

While the monomer mixture of LMWLC's having the same chemistry exhibits the lowest HTP, in copolymers HTP increases with decreasing length of the flexible spacer. It should be pointed out that the HTP for the polymer with the shortest spacer is extremely high, and that these high values can only be observed for LMWLC's having completely different chemistry.[31] Here the strong effect is observed only by varying the length of the alkyl chain of the spacer, which causes restriction of rotational motions of the mesogenic moiety. However, these restriction are not sufficient to convert the uniaxial cholesteric one into a biaxial cholesteric phase.

A consequent continued restriction of rotational motions is based on a new class of LMWLC synthesized recently by Weissflog et al.[32] Contrary to conventional modifications of LMWLC's, the mesogenic moieties are substituted laterally with long alkyl chains without destroying the LC phase structure. The introduction of a functional group at the end of the lateral chain allows synthesis of polymers having the mesogenic group linked to the backbone through a lateral arrangement as indicated in Fig. 1.[33,34] Rotation of the mesogenic groups around their long molecular axes is prevented by this chemical modification and evaluation of the optical properties of nematic phases clearly indicates phase biaxiality. The biaxial structure is stable up to the nematic to isotropic phase transformation without changing from biaxial to uniaxial. These preliminary experiments must be continued and accompanied by quantitative measurements. The experimental problem preventing quantitative determinations is the macroscopic alignment of the two directors of the biaxial phase.

Interesting aspects are expected in mixtures of these polymers with uniaxial nematic LMWLC's for studies of the uniaxial to biaxial phase transformation. Additionally, the concept of restricting long axis rotation by chemical constitution can be transferred to smectic phases, where a biaxial analogue should exist to the smectic A phase.

4. LC ELASTOMERS

Above the glass transition temperature in the melt of a conventional flexible polymer the backbone adopts the statistical chain conformation. A crosslinking reaction does not affect the backbone conformation, but translational diffusion of the chains is restricted. Segmental motions remain except at, and in the vicinity of, the crosslinks. The same should hold for LCSP's that are crosslinked in the isotropic state or in isotropic solution, provided that the crosslink density still allows segmental mobility. The interesting aspect of these elastomers is whether a mechanical deformation that influences the chain conformation is reflected in the properties of the elastomers in the liquid-crystalline state. These properties will be discussed following a brief introduction to the chemistry of LC elastomers.

4.1. Chemical Constitution and Phase Behavior

The synthesis of LC elastomers can follow the well-known method for the synthesis of conventional networks. The basic problem is to avoid network defects, such as dangling chains or elastically inactive loops, which cannot be prevented with the simple synthetic routes normally applied. A convenient way to obtain suitable elastomers is the copolymerization of a LMWLC with another functional comonomer, yielding a functionalized linear LCSP in the first reaction step (Fig. 8). These linear polymers can be analyzed with respect to their DP and phase transition behavior before crosslinking with a suitable crosslinker.

The phase behavior of the elastomers mimics the phase behavior of the corresponding linear LCSP provided that the contour length between adjacent netpoints is sufficiently high compared to the persistence length of the chain and that the crosslinking agent does not disturb the LC order.

An interesting aspect has been described theoretically by Warner[35] with respect to the nematic to isotropic phase transformation temperature (see also Chapter 5). If the crosslinking reaction is performed in the nematic

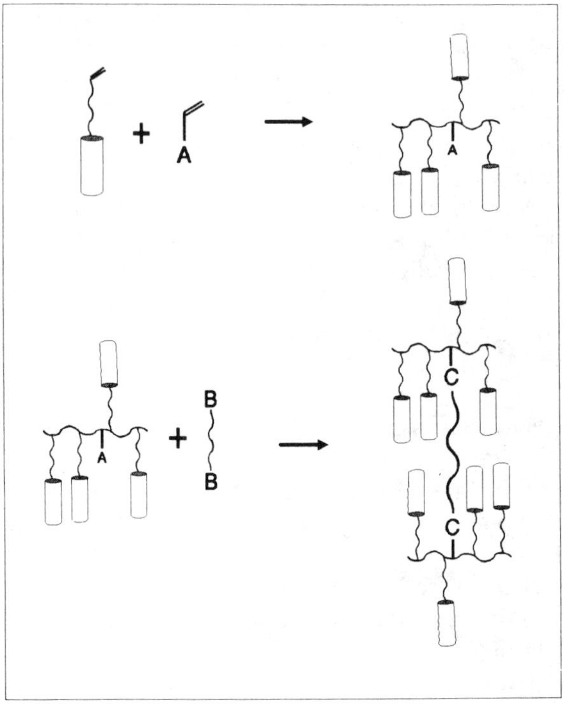

FIGURE 8
Schematic synthesis route for an elastomer via a linear copolymer
having the functional monomer units A.

state, an anisotropic network structure becomes chemically locked in. The transformation temperature of this network is expected to occur at temperatures higher than T_{NI} for a network prepared in the isotropic state or in an isotropic solution. We will come back to this problem in Section 4.2.2.

4.2. Mechanical Field Effect

For linear LCSP's the spherical shape of the chain in the isotropic phase becomes oblate or prolate at the isotropic to nematic phase transformation as discussed in Section 3.1. While in the melt, linear polymers can easily undergo any change of backbone conformation. However, in a network, the above change requires a complete rearrangement. On the other hand, by applying a mechanical field to an elastomer, the network chains will rearrange according to the symmetry of the external field. The LC organization of the sidechains will be forced to adjust to this symmetry. In other words, the mechanical deformation of the elastomer will influence the director orientation and the state of order of the system which is correlated with the phase transformation temperature.

4.2.1. DIRECTOR ORIENTATION

Consider a LCSP network synthesized in the isotropic state or in an isotropic solution. Then the backbone conformation equals the conformation of a conventional isotropic system. If this elastomer is brought into the nematic state by lowering the temperature or removing the solvent, the mesogenic groups become oriented along their long molecular axes. The backbone must adopt this structure where the deviation from the statistical coil conformation to the prolate or oblate shape costs entropy. The equilibrium condition will emerge from the minimization between the difference in chain entropy and the elastic free energy of the nematic structure. The experiments reveal that this equilibrium condition is an entirely disordered nematic structure.[36] The elastomer is completely turbid, indicating larger domain sizes, and the x-ray pattern resembles that for powder samples. Presuming that no network inhomogeneities are actually introduced during the preparation process of the elastomer, the isobaric expansion coefficient of the macroscopic sample of the elastomer should be isotropic. Consequently, the network chains become only locally anisotropic and deviate from the statistical chain conformation of the isotropic state, while the overall structure is still isotropic.

Applying a uniaxial mechanical field (elongation or compression), a distinct interaction between stress and network structure is obtained as shown in Fig. 9[37] for a nematic polymer at different temperatures. Three parts of the stress–strain curve can be identified. In part A at low strain λ, the polydomain structure remains stable while in the region labeled B the nonordered sample becomes a macroscopically ordered monodomain sample as evidenced by IR dichroism measurements. Interestingly, a threshold mechanical field is necessary to induce the orientation process, which is very similar to the effect of an electric or magnetic field on LMWLC's. At this threshold stress a remarkable change in the dimensions of the elastomer occurs, depending on the orientation of the director of the nematic order with respect to the deformation axis. For the sample shown in Fig. 9, the director becomes aligned parallel to the stress axis and the sample's length changes at constant stress by approximately 20%. Because the volume remains approximately constant, the other dimensions perpendicular to the stress axis have to decrease. Another important feature can be derived from Fig. 9. In region C, uniformly aligned sample exists above the threshold field. Extrapolating the linear $\sigma(\lambda)$ relation to $\sigma = 0$ yields the length of the uniformly aligned elastomer without mechanical field (dashed line) at the given temperature. This monodomain state is thermodynamically unstable with respect to the polydomain sample (below the threshold field) but reflects the macroscopic dimensions of the elastomer as a function of the nematic state of order. This fictitious length of the monodomain sample is shown in

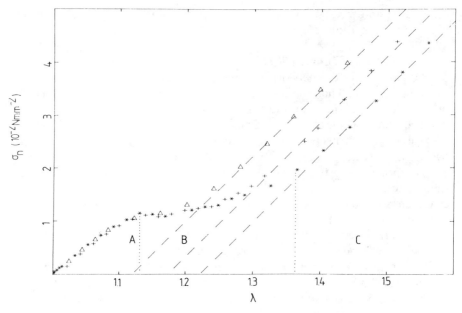

FIGURE 9

Nominal stress σ_n vs. strain λ in the nematic phase of LC polymethacrylates with the mesogenic monomer units:

$\triangle$, $T = 324$ K; $+$, $T = 326$ K; $*$, $T = 333$ K. (Reproduced with permission from Ref. 37.)

Fig. 10 as a function of the reduced temperature and suggests a potential spontaneous elongation of over 20% across the transition.

With this result we have a direct link to the results mentioned in Section 3.1: Different methods have proved that the spherical coil of a LCSP in the isotropic state becomes prolate or oblate as theoretically explained by Warner. Applied to the elastomers, an elongation of the sample along the director reflects the prolate departure from spherical coil (N_{III} phase). Consequently, a shrinkage should reflect the oblate departure (N_I phase). Systematic investigations[36] on nematic polysiloxane elastomers (crosslinked linear poly-

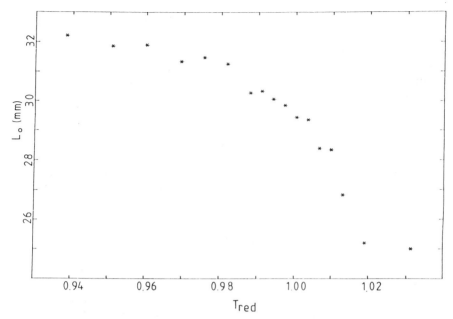

FIGURE 10
Length L_0 extrapolated at $\sigma = 0$ from data in region C of Fig. 9 (monodomain structure) vs. the reduced temperature $T_{red} = T / T_{NI}$. (Reproduced with permission from Ref. 37.)

mers from **1**), deviating only in the length of the flexible spacer, revealed that an even number of atoms in the spacer (4 or 6) produce the N_I phase, while spacers with odd numbers of atoms (5 or 7) produce the N_{III} phase. These results cannot be explained in the framework of the Warner theory, because the cross-coupling between the mainchain and the side group is not affected by this variation. Obviously delicate changes in the conformation of the spacer with respect to the mainchain cause the prolate or oblate backbone shape. The mesogenic groups and their interactions are also involved in this orientation process. Adding small amounts of a mesogenic comonomer or LMWLC substituted with the polar CN group to the nonpolar elastomer changes the orientation from N_{III} to N_I above a critical concentration of about 5%.[36] These changes additionally indicate that only sensitive variations of the chemical constitution of the elastomers influence the conformational interactions between mainchain and side groups.

4.2.2. PHASE TRANSFORMATION

In 1975 when the synthesis of LC polymers was in its infancy, de Gennes pointed out that crosslinking of backbone nematogens should yield materials with exceptional properties.[38, 39] The basic idea is to describe the free energy as function of the nematic order parameter S, of the mechanical deformation $e = \lambda - 1$, and the applied stress σ. Stress-induced isotropic–nematic phase transformation or a shift of T_{NI} with stress is predicted. These ideas are also valid for LCSP and are also discussed by Warner[19] (see Chapter 5). According to de Gennes, for elastomers the free energy expansion takes the form

$$F(S) = F(S)_{e=0} - USe + \tfrac{1}{2}Ee^2 - \sigma e \qquad (12)$$

where U is the coupling coefficient between mesogenic groups and the network and E the elastic modulus. Even without a mechanical field ($\sigma = 0$) a spontaneous deformation of the network should occur in the nematic state, since minimizing F with respect to e gives $e_m = US/E$.[35] With the equilibrium value of e_m, Eq. (12) becomes

$$F(S) = F_0 + \tfrac{1}{2}a_0(T - T'')S^2 + \tfrac{1}{3}BS^3 + \tfrac{1}{4}CS^4 - (U^2/2E)S^2 \qquad (13)$$

where a_0, B, and C are constant and T'' is a hypothetical second-order phase transformation temperature slightly below T_{NI}.

If a mechanical field is applied ($\sigma \neq 0$), an additional deformation occurs besides the spontaneous deformation. Minimizing F with respect to e gives the equilibrium value of $e_m = (\sigma + US)$. Neglecting terms in σ^2 for moderate values of σ we get

$$F(S, \sigma) = F_0 + \tfrac{1}{2}a_0(T - T'')S^2 + \tfrac{1}{3}BS^3 + \tfrac{1}{4}CS^4 - \frac{U^2}{2E}S^2 - \frac{\sigma U}{E}S \qquad (14)$$

where the additional term in S^2 also causes a shift in T_{NI}. With Eq. (14) the order parameter can be calculated as a function of temperature and applied mechanical field as shown in Fig. 11.[37] Furthermore, it can be calculated that a mechanical critical point (cp) exists with

$$S_{cp} = -\frac{B}{3C}$$

$$T_{cp} - T_{NI} = \frac{B^2}{9a_0C} \qquad (15)$$

$$\sigma_{cp} = -\frac{B^3U}{27C^2U}$$

The formalism of the mechanical field on S is similar to the formalism of the influence of an electric or magnetic field on the order parameter.[40] However, for the electric or magnetic field the experimental verification of the theory is limited due to the weak coupling between the external field and the order

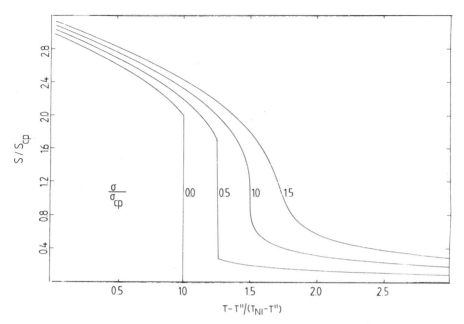

FIGURE 11
Reduced order parameter S / S_{cp} vs. normalized temperature
$(T - T'') / (T_{NI} - T'')$ for different values of external mechanical field
σ/σ_{cp}. (Reproduced with permission from Ref. 37.)

parameter. For example, for a magnetic field it can be estimated that T_{NI} is only shifted by some millikelvins.

Experimental results on elastomers are shown in Fig. 12, where the order parameter S (determined by FTIR–dichroism measurements) is plotted as a function of temperature for different nominal stresses.[37] Actually the mechanical field strongly influences the state of order and the nematic–isotropic phase transformation temperature as predicted by theory. Future measurements need to clarify the magnitude of the coupling constant U and their relation to the chemical constitution of the elastomers, especially with respect to the spacer.

In Fig. 12 the values of $S(T)$ for $\sigma = 0$ are obtained by extrapolation of measurements for monodomain samples above the threshold field. If one compares this curve with Fig. 10, it can be seen that both S and L_0 exhibit the same temperature dependence. Obviously the macroscopic sample dimensions are correlated with the order parameter. This is shown in Fig. 13 where S vs. L_0/L_{i0} for the monodomain sample yields a straight line. This has been theoretically predicted by Renz and Warner.[41] The local correlation of the LC polymer, expressed by the order parameter S, should linearly depend on the anisotropy of the radius of gyration in the elastomer experiments as detected by the macroscopic variation of the sample dimensions.

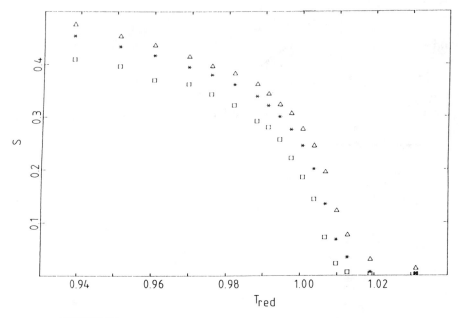

FIGURE 12

Nematic order parameter S vs. reduced temperature $T_{red} = T / T_{NI}$ different levels of nominal stress, σ_n: $\square$, 0, $*$, 2.5 $\times$ 10^{-2}; $\triangle$, 4.5 $\times$ 10^{-2} (in N mm^2). (Reproduced with permission from Ref. 37.)

It has been mentioned above that T_{NI} should differ for elastomers crosslinked in the isotropic or nematic state. From experiments on the elastomers discussed previously one can roughly estimate this effect. The preceding experiments indicate that a nematic monodomain elongates the network by approximately 20% compared to the isotropic state. If this anisotropy of the networks becomes chemically introduced by crosslinking in the nematic state, T_{NI} should be elevated accordingly. The amount of the shift in T_{NI} should equal the change brought about by a corresponding elongation of the elastomer prepared in the isotropic state. This value is approximately 1.5 K.

Besides the above properties, the interaction of the mechanical field and the state of order brings about many interesting new aspects. Recently Brand[42] pointed out that helielectricity is expected to be available from the mechanical deformation of cholesteric elastomers. Furthermore, interesting properties will result from ferroelectric chiral smectic C phases, such as ferroelectric films or films for nonlinear optics exhibiting noncentrosymmetric phase structures. In addition to the mechanical field effects of uniaxial symmetry, new features can be observed from experiments with other field symmetries, e.g., shear experiments.[43] This brief summary indicates that the

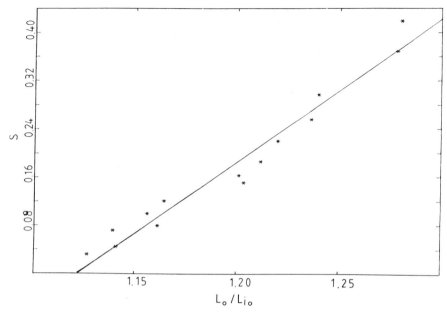

FIGURE 13

Local correlation vs. global correlation. The nematic order parameter S is plotted vs. the relative length L_0 / L_{i0} of the monodomain sample. (L_{i0} refers to the sample length in the isotropic state.) (Reproduced with permission from Ref. 37.)

theory as well as the experiments on LC elastomers are still developing, and interesting new results can be expected in the future.

REFERENCES

1. E. Jahns and H. Finkelmann, *Colloid Polym. Sci.*, **1987**, *265*, 304.
2. H. Finkelmann and E. Jahns, in *Polymer Association Structures*, ACS Symposium Series 384, M.A. El Nokaly, Ed., American Chemical Society, Washington, DC, 1989, Ch. 1.
3. D. Demus, H. Demus, and Z. Zaschke, *Flüssige Kristalle in Tabellen*, VEB Deutscher Verlag für Grundstoffindustrie, Leipzig, 1976.
4. V. Percec and C. Pugh, in *Side Chain Liquid Crystal Polymers*, C.B. McArdle, Ed., Blackie, Glasgow, London, 1989.
5. H. Finkelmann, in *Thermotropic Liquid Crystal*, G.W. Gray, Ed., John Wiley & Sons, New York, 1987.
6. G.W. Gray, in *Side Chain Liquid Crystal Polymers*, C.B. McArdle, Ed., Blackie, Glasgow, London, 1989.
7. H. Stevens, G. Rehage and H. Finkelmann, *Macromolecules*, **1984**, *17*, 851.
8. A. Saupe, Dissertation, Freiburg, 1958.
9. W. Maier and A. Saupe, *Z. Naturforsch.*, **1958**, *13A*, 564.

10. H. Finkelmann, Habilitationsschrift, Clausthal, 1984.
11. H. Finkelmann and G. Rehage, *Adv. Polym. Sci.*, **1984**, *60/61*, 99.
12. R.L. Humphries, P.G. James, and G.R. Luckhurst, *J. Chem. Soc. Faraday Trans.* *2*, **1972**, *68*, 1031.
13. C. Boeffel and H.W. Spiess, in *Side Chain Liquid Crystal Polymers*, C.B. McArdle, Ed., Blackie, Glasgow, London, 1989.
14. C.M. Haws, M.G. Clark, and G.S. Attard, in *Side Chain Liquid Crystal Polymers*, C.B. McArdle, Ed., Blackie, Glasgow, London, 1989.
15. F. Brochard, *C. R. Hebd. Séances Acad. Sci.*, *Ser. B*, **1979**, *289*, 229.
16. H. Mattoussi, R. Ober, M. Veyssie, and H. Finkelmann, *Europhys. Lett.*, **1986**, *2*, 233.
17. F. Moussa, J.P. Cotton, F. Hardouin, P. Keller, M. Lambert, G. Pépy, M. Mauzac, and H. Richards, *J. Phys.*, **1987**, *48*, 1079; R.G. Kirste and H.G. Ohm, *Macromol. Chem. Rapid Commun.*, **1985**, *6*, 179.
18. P. Fabre, C. Casagrande, M. Veyssié, and H. Finkelmann, *Phys. Rev. Lett.*, **1984**, *53*, 993.
19. M. Warner, in *Side Chain Liquid Crystal Polymers*, C.B. McArdle, Ed., Blackie, Glasgow, London, 1989.
20. B. Reck and H. Ringsdorf, *Makromol. Chem. Rapid Commun.*, **1985**, *6*, 291.
21. F. Cser, K. Nyitrai and G. Hardy, in *Advances in Liquid Crystal Research and Applications*, L. Bata, Ed., Pergamon Press, Oxford, 1980, p. 845.
22. W. Renz, private communication.
23. H. Finkelmann and H.J. Wendorff, *Polym. Sci. Technol.*, **1985**, *28*, 295.
24. V.P. Shibaev and N.A. Platé, *Adv. Polym. Sci.*, **1984**, *60/61*, 173.
25. P. Zugenmaier and J. Mügge, in *Recent Advances in Liquid Crystalline Polymers*, L.L. Chapoy, Ed., Elsevier, London, 1985.
26. M.J. Freizer, *Phys. Rev. Lett.*, **1970**, *24*, 1041.
27. S. Chandrasekhar, B.K. Sodashiva, B.R. Ratna, and V.N. Raja, *Pramana J. Phys.*, **1988**, *30*, L491.
28. K. Praefke, B. Kohne, B. Gündogan, D. Demus, S. Diele, and G. Pelzl, *Mol. Cryst. Liq. Cryst. Lett.*, **1990**, *7*, 27.
29. W.J.A. Goossens, *J. Phys.*, **1979**, *C3*(40), 158.
30. B.W. van der Meer and G. Vertogen, *Phys. Lett.*, **1976**, *59A*, 279.
31. G. Heppke, D. Lötzsch, and F. Oestereicher, *Z. Naturforsch.*, **1986**, *41*, 1214.
32. W. Weissflog and D. Demus, *Cryst. Res. Technol.*, **1984**, *19*, 55.
33. F. Hessel, R.P. Herr, and H. Finkelmann, *Makromol. Chem.*, **1987**, *188*, 1597.
34. Q.F. Zhon, H.M. Li, and X.D. Feng, *Macromolecules*, **1987**, *20*, 233.
35. M. Warner, K.P. Gelling, and T.A. Vilgis, *J. Chem. Phys.*, **1988**, *88*, 4008.
36. J. Schätzle and H. Finkelmann, *Mol. Cryst. Liq. Cryst.*, **1987**, *142*, 85.
37. J. Schätzle, W. Kaufhold, and H. Finkelmann, *Makromol. Chem.*, **1989**, *190*, 3269.
38. P.G. de Gennes, *C. R. Hebd. Seances Acad. Sci.*, *Ser. B*, **1975**, *28*, 101.
39. P.G. de Gennes, in *Polymer Liquid Crystals*, A. Ciferri, W.R. Krigbaum, and R.B. Meyer, Eds., Academic Press, New York, 1982.
40. E. Gramsbergen, L. Longa, and W. de Jeu, *Phys. Rep.*, **1986**, *135*, 195.
41. W. Renz and M. Warner, *Proc. R. Soc. London*, *Ser. A*, **1986**, *417*, 213.
42. H. Brand, *Makromol. Chem. Rapid Commun.*, **1989**, *10*, 441.
43. H. Brand, private communication.

PART IV

PHYSICS

CHAPTER 9

Elastic and Viscous Properties of Lyotropic Polymer Nematics

SIN-DOO LEE

Bellcore, 331 Newman Springs Road,
Red Bank, NJ 07701 USA

and

ROBERT B. MEYER

The Martin Fisher School of Physics, Brandeis University,
Waltham, MA 02254 USA

CONTENTS

1. INTRODUCTION

Concentrated solutions of long, rigid or semirigid rodlike polymers may exhibit one or more liquid-crystalline phases between a conventional liquid and a crystalline solid. Study of these polymer liquid crystals (LCP's) provides us with fundamental knowledge about the intrinsic properties of polymers and low molecular weight liquid crystals (LMWLC's). Also, the high degree of anisotropy in their elasticity and viscosity is of great significance for both the discovery of new macroscopic structural phenomena and the industrial application of these materials.

Measurements of the basic mechanical properties of these systems should be useful both as a basis for understanding their phenomenology and as a

343

guide to the development of theory relating their molecular and macroscopic properties. In this chapter, some of consequences of constructing a nematic phase from solutions of long rodlike polymers are explored at the molecular level. We will concentrate on understanding the role of molecular properties in determining macroscopic parameters that clearly distinguish LCP's from LMWLC materials. Essentially the only molecular information used is the great length of the molecules and the degree of flexibility. Therefore, fairly simple theoretical models in a moderate concentration limit, neglecting detailed intermolecular interactions, may be nearly right. In these models, simple geometrical parameters, such as the degree of chain rigidity, the length-to-diameter ratio L/d, and the volume fraction v_2 of the polymer in solution determine all the novel anisotropic properties reflecting structural features of their liquid-crystalline phases. For the most part, systems with a high degree of orientational order and fully extended chains will be considered.

In the following two sections, theoretical descriptions of mechanical parameters such as elastic moduli and viscosities are presented, starting from the basic concepts, and carrying on with efforts to describe real systems, at liquid-like densities, with short as well as long molecules, semiflexible as well as rigid ones. The fourth section will discuss the experimental methods such as the Fredericks transition and quasi-elastic Rayleigh scattering for determining the viscous and elastic coefficients. The results for elastic moduli and viscosities that clearly demonstrate the distinction between rigid and semiflexible behavior of a mainchain nematic LCP's will be also presented. The conclusion section looks ahead to unanswered questions.

2. ELASTIC MODULI AND CHAIN RIGIDITY

We will consider nematic solutions of neutral, rigid, or semiflexible polymers and describe their elastic properties in terms of the excluded volume effect. Details of the phase behavior such as the effect of charge and an external field on the isotropic–nematic transition were discussed in Chapter 3.

2.1. Hard-Rod Model

The starting point for theories of lyotropic nematic LC's is the hard-rod model, first presented by Onsager,[1] based on the virial expansion of the free energy. This views the interaction between molecules as arising entirely from the excluded-volume effect. The appearance of the nematic phase is the result of maximizing the entropy of the system; in the nematic phase, rotational entropy is sacrificed to increase the configurational entropy of molecular positions. In this approach, all that matters are two-body interactions, which are treated in a mean-field fashion. For relatively short rods, this Onsager treatment makes physically unrealistic predictions because the critical packing density for the isotropic–nematic transition becomes greater than the maximum close-packing density. For such a system, the isotropic–nematic transition will obviously be preempted by the liquid–solid transition. A reasonable way of generalizing the Onsager description might be a proper scaling[2-5] of the equation of state for hard spheres, which relates the geometrical shape anisotropy to the effective excluded-volume effect and thus the stability of the nematic phase. The results are in good agreement with recent computer simulations.[6-8]

To describe the elastic properties of the nematic phase, a simple theory of the curvature elasticity, at the level of the Onsager approximation (the second virial approximation), was first developed by Priest[9] and Straley.[10] In a deformed nematic LC, the increase in the free energy due to long-wavelength distortions will be proportional to the square of the associated wavevector because the symmetry of the system ensures that distortions corresponding to positive and negative wavevectors are equivalent. To that order of the wavevector, the increase in the free energy caused by distortions may be calculated by keeping the orientational distribution function constant (stationary) apart from rotations of the local preferred direction, $\mathbf{n}$, called the director. In such a calculation, the rotational entropy may be neglected, and all that is taken into account is the change in the two-body excluded volume produced by spatial distortions of the director field. Then, the elastic moduli can be evaluated from knowledge of the accurate orientational distribution function obtained self-consistently in a molecular field.[11] The numerical results are summarized in Table 1 as a function of the degree of orientational order $S = \langle P_2(\mathbf{a} \cdot \mathbf{n}) \rangle$. Here P_2 and $\mathbf{a}$ represent the second-order Legendre polynomial and the orientation of molecules, respectively. The average $\langle \ \rangle$ was taken over the orientational distribution function. All three elastic moduli K_i ($i = 1, 2, 3$) are scaled with respect to kT/d where k is Boltzmann's constant and T is absolute temperature.

In this mean-field approach K_1 and K_2 are only slightly dependent on the degree of orientational ordering, while K_3 diverges to infinity at perfect order. This is intuitively reasonable. For perfectly parallel molecules, at a low enough, fixed volume fraction, twist and splay distortions produce no interparticle interferences, so that those elastic moduli vanish. For any finite degree of order they remain small. Bend, on the other hand, creates strong interference effects for any degree of order. Moreover, at perfectly parallel order, the singular behavior of the coupling between two molecules leads to a change in the free energy that is proportional to the absolute value of the bend distortion rather than quadratic in the bending, which implies an infinite bend elastic modulus. At a degree of order less than perfect, the bend modulus is finite, but it diverges rapidly at large order parameter. This behavior is physically reasonable and does not appear to be a consequence of the mean-field approximation.

Table 1
Elastic Moduli K_i as a Function of the Dimensionless Concentration $Q = v_2(L / d)$
(or the Order Parameter S) in a Hard-Rod Theory[a]

Concentration, Q	Order parameter, S	Splay, K_1	Twist, K_2	Bend, K_3
3.60	0.598	0.465	0.155	1.558
3.70	0.656	0.552	0.184	2.115
3.80	0.697	0.623	0.208	2.740
3.90	0.729	0.684	0.228	3.334
4.00	0.755	0.739	0.246	3.948
4.20	0.794	0.838	0.279	5.251
4.50	0.835	0.967	0.322	7.429
4.75	0.859	1.065	0.355	9.477
5.00	0.878	1.156	0.385	11.76
5.25	0.892	1.244	0.415	14.29
5.50	0.904	1.328	0.443	17.09
6.00	0.923	1.490	0.497	23.55
6.50	0.936	1.646	0.549	31.24
7.00	0.946	1.798	0.599	40.29
7.50	0.953	1.948	0.649	50.80

[a]Data from Ref. 4. K_i are scaled with respect to kT/d.

In a highly ordered state, it is possible to derive analytic expressions for K_i in terms of v_2 and L/d. To see the leading order behavior of K_i in v_2 and L/d, choosing a simplified Gaussian form for the orientational distribution function, the two-body excluded-volume effects lead asymptotically to[12]

$$K_1 \approx \frac{kT}{d} \frac{7}{8\pi} v_2 \left(\frac{L}{d} \right) \approx 3K_2 \tag{1a}$$

$$K_3 \approx \frac{kT}{d} \approx \frac{kT}{d} \frac{4}{3\pi^2} v_2^3 \left(\frac{L}{d} \right)^3 \tag{1b}$$

In the above expressions, all terms of higher order in d/L and end effects of the molecules have been ignored. This criterion is consistent with the second virial approximation. It is clear that the relative difference between the analytical calculations and the numerical results for K_i decreases with increasing v_2 or L/d. As already mentioned before, K_3 exhibits the strongest dependence on v_2 and L/d.

For a nematic short-rod LC's at liquid-like densities, Onsager's low-density limit is obviously not appropriate, and terms beyond the leading order in the virial series should be taken into account. The density-functional formalism has been recognized as a powerful tool for this purpose.[13-16] Following the functional scaling in a density-functional approximation,[15] the effective elastic moduli contain a scaling factor $\alpha(\eta)$, responsible for higher order packing entropies, where $\eta = cV$ with c the concentration and V the volume of a hard rod. The scaling factor $\alpha(\eta)$ can be derived from a compressibility factor and the direct pair correlation function of an equivalent system of hard spheres. For example, $\alpha(\eta) = (4 - \eta)/4(1 - \eta)^4$ for the Carnahan-Starling[17] equation of state for hard spheres. Note that $\alpha(\eta)$ is more singular than $(1 - \eta)^{-1}$ to provide accurate data for pressure. In the low-density limit ($\eta \ll 1$), $\alpha(\eta) \approx 1$, and thus the results exactly reproduce those in the second virial approximation. Recent density-functional calculations, performed by Somoza and Tarazona,[16] suggest that higher orders in d/L of the excluded-volume coupling between two rods are also important for adequately describing the elastic properties of a nematic LC of short rods. Moreover, the relation $K_1 \approx 3K_2$ can be broken by the higher order terms of d/L, which agrees with the computer simulation results.[18]

Beyond the Onsager picture of the elastic moduli, for longer, more flexible chains such as many currently studied polymers, or for more concentrated solutions and melts, other theoretical ideas are needed. Here we consider only the possibility of semiflexible chains, which are nonrigid but are still fully extended in the nematic phase. There are two ideas in this case. First, the splay elastic modulus has an additional component,[19] ΔK_1, arising from a single particle contribution to the entropy. Splay at constant density requires relative compression and dilation in spatial distribution of the chain ends, which reduces their entropy. As the molecules become long, there are fewer chain ends available, so splay becomes difficult. Therefore, ΔK_1 increases linearly with both L/d and v_2. Also, K_1 is roughly independent of both the degree of nematic order and chain rigidity in the highly ordered state. This contribution exists for hard rods as well as for more flexible chains.

It should be noted that de Gennes[20] proposed a model for the splay modulus for semiflexible molecules, based on intermolecular strain free energy rather than chain end entropy, which predicts

$$\Delta K_1 \approx \Omega L^2 \approx \frac{kT}{d}\left(\frac{\Omega}{ckT}\right)v_2\left(\frac{L}{d}\right) \qquad (2)$$

where Ω^{-1} is the osmotic compressibility and c is the concentration of chain ends. For fully extended chains, the leading behavior of Ω is linear in c, so there is no disagreement between the qualitative description of Meyer's and de Gennes's models in the case of solutions. de Gennes's model, however, contains an idealization in that the analysis assumes no other chain ends are next to each polymer along its entire length L. His expression is precisely correct only for a perfectly layered structure (supersmectic) in which all the chains are aligned into layers of spacing L, but the concept that forming a continuous curvature from discrete molecules leads to some elastic strains must be also true for the nematic structure. As discussed before, Meyer has relaxed this condition, allowing interdigitation of the polymer chains with one another, and predicted that K_1 should increase essentially with L, not L^2, for a fixed volume fraction v_2.

2.2.   Effect of Chain Rigidity

Let us discuss how the chain rigidity affects the elastic properties. In contrast to the hard rods, for polymers that are semiflexible but still fully extended parallel to the nematic director, the individual polymers bend to follow the director distortions. This implies that bending elastic energy is stored in the polymer chains. If each polymer chain is characterized by an elastic modulus E to bend with the director, then $K_3 \approx 2v_2 E/d^2$. In terms of the persistence length $q = 2E/kT$ (see Ref. 21), $K_3 \approx v_2(q/d)(kT/d)$; K_3 becomes independent of chain length and linear in v_2. For deriving formal expressions for K_i, however, we need to analyze the configurational statistics of a semiflexible polymer in a space-dependent nematic field. Such an analysis is complicated even for constant nematic fields (see Chapter 3). Thus, in practice, the scaling nature[12, 22] of a semiflexible chain can be utilized to obtain the elastic moduli for semiflexible chains from those for hard rods, which results in

$$K_2 \approx \frac{kT}{d} v_2^{1/3} \left(\frac{q}{d} \right)^{1/3} \tag{3a}$$

$$K_3 \approx \frac{kT}{d} v_2 \left(\frac{q}{d} \right) \tag{3b}$$

For the splay modulus, the direct application of the scaling argument leads to $K_1 \approx 3K_2$, whereas the splay modulus is certainly dependent on L.

Also, recent mean-field calculations by Grosberg and Zhestkov[23] for long persistent chains predict that $K_1 \approx K_3 \approx v_2(q/d)(kT/d)S^2$ and $K_2 \approx K_1/10$ in the limit of low orientational order ($S \ll 1$). While for high degree of the order ($S \to 1$), $K_3 \approx v_2(q/d)(kT/d)S$, finite, but K_1 increases exponentially with v_2 and q/d. They argued that this rapid increase in K_1 with v_2 is due to the presence of hairpin defects produced by splay distortions in nematic LCP's. A definite test of this prediction would require a systematic measurement of the elastic moduli on a well-controlled nematic LCP as a function of the concentration.

We now briefly discuss the consequences of the theoretical predictions described above. As the polymers become semiflexible, the ΔK_1 contribution to splay also becomes dominant, since the two-body excluded-volume contributions to splay are limited, while ΔK_1, whose origin lies in a single-body entropic effect, remains unaffected and is still proportional to L/d as long as the chains remain fully extended. Thus in this limit, the ratio of splay to bend elastic moduli should be relatively large and linearly proportional to chain length, rather different from the hard-rod limit, in which this ratio would be small and decreasing with increasing chain length. For imperfect orientational ordering, the crossover from rigid to semiflexible behavior then occurs at

$$\frac{L}{d} \approx \left(\frac{3\pi^2}{4v_2^2}\frac{q}{d}\right)^\delta \quad \left(\delta > \frac{1}{3}\right) \tag{4}$$

Notice that the crossover occurs for $L < q$, which implies the effective length scale is not simply the persistence length. Within the semiflexible regime, the ratio of splay to bend elastic moduli should be

$$\frac{K_1}{K_3} \approx \frac{L}{q} \tag{5}$$

In this regime, the twist K_2 should still remain small and independent of L. The theories for semiflexible chains thus predict qualitatively different behavior of mechanical properties of a nematic LCP with L/d and v_2 than those for rigid rods.

3. ANISOTROPIC VISCOSITIES

In this section we describe the fundamental ideas and theories for the dynamics of nematic LCP's. For nematic LMWLC's, it has been known that the constitutive equation of nematic LC's is entirely different from that of isotropic liquids (see Ref. 24). The first phenomenological theory for the hydrodynamics of nematic LC's was constructed by Ericksen[25] and Leslie.[26] In what follows, we briefly review a theoretical description of the viscous properties of LCP's and discuss the characteristic features that distinguish them from LMWLC's.

3.1. Molecular Kinetic Approach

Recently, a molecular kinetic description of the dynamic behavior of long rodlike polymers in concentrated solutions was made by Doi[27] at the level of the Onsager approximation. For describing the viscous properties of nematic LC solutions, the model calculations of Marrucci[28] (see also Chapter 11), based on Doi's pioneer work, give predictions reminiscent in spirit to those of Straley[10] for elastic moduli. Here we describe nematodynamic viscosities in an extended version[29] of the Doi model, consistent with the phase space kinetic theory,[30,31] in terms of molecular parameters such as the concentration, the length, and the degree of orientational ordering.

The constitutive equation of nematic LCP's can be derived on the basis of two equations; one is a generalized diffusion equation, which governs the time evolution of the orientational distribution function in the presence of a flow field under consideration, and the other is the stress tensor, which involves some kind of statistical average over the distribution function. The stress tensor is generally composed of the elastic, the hydrodynamic viscous, and the solvent contributions. The elastic stress can be calculated by the change in the Onsager-type free energy under a virtual deformation, and it may be considered as a dominant term. However, the viscous stress, derived from the hydrodynamic energy dissipation, may not be negligible in some nematic LCP's. The role of this term in the nematodynamic viscosities will be discussed in the next section. By comparing the resultant constitutive equation with the Ericksen-Leslie equation, the scaled Leslie coefficients with respect to $ckT/2\overline{D}$, with $\overline{D}$ the effective rotational diffusion coefficient, are given by

$$\alpha_1 = -(2 - \mu)R$$

$$\alpha_2 = -(1 + 1/\Gamma)S$$

$$\alpha_3 = -(1 - 1/\Gamma)S$$

$$\alpha_4 = (2/105)[7(3 + \mu) - 5(3 + 2\mu)S - 3(2 - \mu)R] \tag{6}$$

$$\alpha_5 = (2/7)[(5 + \mu)S + (2 - \mu)R]$$

$$\alpha_6 = -(2/7)(2 - \mu)(S - R)$$

where μ is a dimensionless parameter measuring the strength of the effective hydrodynamic interaction.[29] Here the parameter Γ (less than 1) is related to the stability of the simple shear flow, and R represents the equilibrium second-order parameter $\langle P_4(\mathbf{a} \cdot \mathbf{n}) \rangle$ where P_4 denotes the fourth-order Legendre polynomial. Since Γ is smaller than 1, the steady-state Couette flow is unstable. More precisely, it loses the stability even at very low shear velocities. Instead, an instability such as the indefinite tumbling process of

Table 2
The Leslie Coefficients α_i for a Nematic LC of Rigid Rods

Parameter[a]	Refs. 28 and 61	Refs. 62 and 63	Ref. 29 ($\mu = 1$)
α_1	$-2S^2$	$-2R$	$-R$
α_2	$-2S(1 + 2S)/(2 + S)$	$-(1 + 1/\Gamma)$	$-(1 + 1/\Gamma)$
α_3	$-2S(1 - S)/(2 + S)$	$-(1 - 1/\Gamma)$	$-(1 - 1/\Gamma)$
α_4	$2(1 - S)/3$	$2/35(7 - 5S - 2R)$	$2/105(28 - 25S - 3R)$
α_5	$2S$	$2/7(5S + 2R)$	$2/7(6S + R)$
α_6	0	$-4/7(S - R)$	$-2/7(S - R)$

[a]α_i are scaled with respect to $ckT/2\overline{D}$.

the director[32,33] can be realized. All the interesting phenomena associated with the rheology problem will be covered in Chapter 11. It is noted that the Parodi relation,[34] $\alpha_3 + \alpha_2 = \alpha_6 - \alpha_5$, is satisfied. Several other theoretical predictions for α_i, corresponding to $\mu = 0$, are compared with the case of $\mu = 1$ in Table 2.

3.2. Asymptotic Expressions

As in the case of the elastic moduli, it is also possible to obtain simple asymptotic expressions for the Leslie coefficients in a Gaussian approximation. In a highly ordered nematic state, these expressions give exact leading behavior of the nematodynamic viscosities. Their qualitative behaviors in the long-chain limit will be discussed and compared with other theoretical descriptions in this section.

Experimentally it is not easy to measure all of the Leslie coefficients. What are often measured are the combinations of them (see Ref. 24). For example, they are the Miesowicz viscosities for simple shear (η_a, η_b, and η_c), the viscosity of the elongational flow (ν_1), and the effective viscosities (η_{splay}, γ_1, and η_{bend}) associated with the three types of director distortions. With the choice of a Gaussian distribution function, several viscosities for shear and elongational flow can be obtained in terms of only the dimensionless concentration $Q = \upsilon_2(L/d)$, leaving out a common viscosity $\eta^*(\eta_s, \upsilon_2, L/d)$ with η_s the solvent viscosity as follows:

$$\eta_a \approx \pi Q^{-1}$$

$$\eta_b \approx \mu \pi Q^{-1}$$

$$\eta_c \approx 8Q + [(3 + 2\mu)/2]\pi Q^{-1} \qquad (7)$$

$$\nu_1 \approx 2\mu Q + [(32 - 9\mu)/8]\pi Q^{-1}$$

The effective viscosities associated with the three normal modes are

$$\eta_{\text{splay}} \approx 8Q + [(11\mu - 8)/2\mu]\pi Q^{-1}$$

$$\gamma_1 \approx 8Q + (11/2)\pi Q^{-1} \qquad (8)$$

$$\eta_{\text{bend}} \approx \mu \pi Q^{-1}$$

In Table 3, ratios of the effective nematodynamic viscosities for finite μ are collected and compared with those of existing theories ($\mu = 0$). The Leslie coefficients in the infinite chain limit ($L \to \infty$), proposed by Meyer,[19] require that $\alpha_1 \to -\infty$, $\alpha_2 \to -\infty$, and $\alpha_5 \to \infty$, while α_3, α_4, and α_6 remain finite. In terms of the Miesowicz viscosities, η_a and η_b are finite, while η_c is infinite

LEE AND MEYER

Table 3
Ratios of Effective Viscosities for a Nematic LC of Rigid Rods
in a Gaussian Approximation

Ratio	Refs. 62 and 63 $(Q \to \infty)$[a]	Infinite chain limit $(L \to \infty)$	Ref. 29 $(Q \to \infty)$[a]
η_a/η_b	Const. Q^2	Finite	$1/\mu$
η_a/η_c	$\pi/8Q^{-2}$	0	$\pi/8Q^{-2}$
η_b/η_c	Const. Q^{-4}	0	$\mu\pi/8Q^{-2}$
$\eta_{\text{splay}}/\gamma_1$	Const. $-$ Const. Q^{-2}	Finite	$1 - \pi/2\mu Q^{-2}$
γ_1/η_c	$1 + \pi/2Q^{-2}$	Finite	$1 + (4 - \mu)\pi/8Q^{-2}$
$\eta_{\text{bend}}/\gamma_1$	Const. Q^{-4}	0	$\mu\pi/8Q^{-2}$
ν_1/η_c	$\pi/2Q^{-2}$	Finite	$\mu/4 + (16 - 6\mu - \mu^2)\pi/32Q^{-2}$

[a]Q denotes the dimensionless concentration $v_2(L/d)$ and $0 < \mu < 1$ is a dimensionless parameter.

because a velocity perpendicular to the director with a gradient along the director produces a shear that tends to cut the molecules. Also, in terms of the effective viscosities, $\eta_{\text{splay}} \to \gamma_1 \to \infty$, and $\eta_{\text{bend}} \to \eta_b$ is finite. Furthermore, the elongational flow viscosity ν_1 is required to diverge and ν_1/η_c should be finite, but these requirements fail in the existing theories, as shown in Table 3. The ratio ν_1/η_c may serve as a basis for critically testing several theories in the long-chain limit. The actual value of the parameter μ can be determined by the strength of the effective hydrodynamic interaction.

The viscous properties of nematic LC solutions of semiflexible polymers have been much less studied than those of rigid rods. Some of the results were first obtained by Semenov[35] for a solution of long persistent chains. In his theory, just as in the case of rigid rods, a reptational kinetic equation was used for the time evolution of the orientational distribution function of the unit tangential vector along the polymer chain in the continuum limit. Again, the large-scale motion of a given polymer chain was assumed to be reptation along its intrinsic contour surrounded by the neighbors. One of the remarkable predictions is that the ratio of α_3/α_2 for semiflexible persistent chains is always positive and decreases with increasing the order parameter S. This result is qualitatively different from that for rigid rods. Also, there exists a transition region for the flow stability as a function of the order parameter, which gradually expands with increasing chain flexibility. An experimental test of this prediction should be important to improve or extend existing theories for describing the dynamic properties of flexible polymers or polymer melts.

As far as qualitative features are concerned, in fully extended semiflexible polymers η_c and γ_1 are essentially unchanged from the hard-rod limit. However, if the molecules are allowed to wrap gently around one another, η_a and η_c will be increased relative to η_b. There is no quantitative description of those effects yet.

4. POLY(BENZYL GLUTAMATE) NEMATIC LIQUID CRYSTALS

In this section we summarize systematic measurements[36, 37] of the elastic moduli and viscosities that clearly demonstrate a crossover from rigid to semiflexible behavior of a mainchain nematic LCP, a solution of poly(benzyl glutamate) (PBG) in mixed organic solvents, as the role of chain flexibility increases with molecular length. We also discuss an earlier experimental work[38, 39] on tobacco mosaic virus (TMV), which can be considered an ideal system of rigid rods, and compare them with PBG. The experimental methods include quasi-elastic Rayleigh depolarized scattering and the Fredericks transition.

The most extensively studied class of LCP's is that of the synthetic polypeptides, which exhibit liquid-crystalline phases in their rodlike helical conformations. Due to its ready availability and good solubility characteristics, PBG has been extensively studied,[36, 37, 40–49] and it is currently a well-characterized LCP. Here a rather complete picture of the viscous and elastic behavior of PBG nematic LC's is given in a systematic way.

Above a certain volume fraction of the polymer, PBG forms a lyotropic LC in a number of organic solvents and mixed-solvent systems, including benzene, nitrobenzene, chloroform, pyridine, N,N-dimethylformamide (DMF), dichloroacetic acid, m-cresol, dioxane, and dichloromethane. It has been shown that in all circumstances in which PBG forms the liquid-crystalline phase it is in the extended α-helical molecular conformation. The persistence length of PBG in several solvents has been found[50–53] to be in the range 750–1800 Å (see also Chapter 2), indicating that the polymer may possess limited rigidity. The internal degrees of freedom in the sidechain yield a variety of sidechain secondary structures and lead to considerable variation in the diameter of PBG in solution. The diameter of α-helical PBG is about 15–25 Å, determined by x-ray measurements.[50] The average length-to-diameter ratio, L/d, is approximately a tenth of the degree of polymerization (DP).

We studied nematic LC solutions of PBLG of several molecular weights in the range 6.6–21.0×10^4, giving $L/d = 32$–100. Freeze-dried racemic PBG with 50–50 weight ratios of PBLG and PBDG ($MW = 15.0 \times 10^4$) was also prepared. We used a solvent mixture composed of 18% dioxane and 82% dichloromethane to suppress the cholesteric helicity, and added to this a few percent of DMF to prevent the polymer from aggregating.[54] No evidence of aggregation was seen. The solvent compensation of the helicity may not be expected to yield the perfect nematic phase since other factors, such as temperature and concentration, also play a role in determining the sense and pitch of the cholesteric helix. The pitch of the helix decreases as the concentration increases. In practice, what can be achieved is to make the sample thickness be on the order of the pitch of the resulting cholesteric helix, and thus suppress static twisting in samples with rigid boundary

Table 4

The Average Molecular Weights, the Degree of Polymerization, and Ratios
of the Elastic Moduli of the PBG Nematic LC's $(v_2 \approx 0.16)^a$

Sample	Molecular weight $(\overline{M}_W \times 10^{-4})$	DP	Volume fraction v_2	Ratio of elastic moduli		
				K_3/K_1	K_3/K_2	K_1/K_2
1-1	7.0	320	0.159	0.84	10.7	12.5
1-2	8.5	390	0.158	1.14	16.5	14.5
1-3	9.2	420	0.157	1.32	19.9	14.8
1-4	11.0	500	0.155	1.44	23.1	16.1
1-5	12.7	580	0.156	1.43	24.0	17.2
1-6	15.8	720	0.154	1.21	25.3	22.4
1-7	16.5	750	0.152	1.14	25.4	23.2
1-8	19.0	870	0.158	0.97	26.7	26.6
1-9	21.0	1,000	0.154	0.83	27.3	31.2

$^a K_3/K_1$ and K_3/K_2 were determined from intensity measurements, and K_1/K_2 were deduced from the intensity correlation function composed of the splay and twist modes. Data from Refs. 36 and 37.

conditions. The average molecular weights and the degree of polymerization of PBG we studied are collected in Table 4 and Table 5.

For a nematic LCP of very long molecules, it has been argued[19] that the namatic director must lie parallel to a surface, because condensation of many chain ends at the surface costs a great deal of entropy. Therefore, the homeotropic alignment will not be favored unless there is a strong binding energy for chain ends at the surface. The development of homeotropy at the surface will therefore depend both on molecular chain length and on the detailed chemistry of the surface.

For PBG LC's, however, the previous experiments suggest that all of the standard procedures for producing parallel surface alignment that have proved successful in LMWLC's have yielded only the homeotropic

Table 5

The Average Molecular Weights, the Degree of Polymerization, and Ratios
of the Elastic Moduli of the PBG Nematic LC's $(v_2 \approx 0.20)^a$

Sample	Molecular weight $(\overline{M}_W \times 10^{-4})$	DP	Volume fraction v_2	Ratio of elastic moduli		
				K_3/K_1	K_3/K_2	K_1/K_2
2-1	7.0	320	0.203	1.05	17.8	12.5
2-2	8.5	390	0.196	1.38	24.7	18.4
2-3	12.7	580	0.202	1.41	29.3	22.2

$^a K_3/K_1$ and K_3/K_2 were determined from intensity measurements, and K_1/K_2 were deduced from the intensity correlation function composed of the splay and twist modes. Data from Refs. 36 and 37.

alignment.[55, 56] This is probably due to some binding of the polymer ends to glass. Following the technique developed by Taratuta et al.,[57] we achieved the planar alignment of PBG LC's, parallel to the glass surface coated with an inert plasma-polymerized ethylene film, by placing the sample, just after filling, in about a 20 kG magnetic field. Although initial uniformity of the alignment produced by the magnetic field was somewhat diminished after the sample was taken out of the field, a strong memory effect remained in the direction of the aligning field. The strength of the uniform anchoring was enhanced by applying a thin layer of silicon oxide, evaporated obliquely onto the glass surface prior to coating with polyethylene. We used PBG sample cells, typically 50 μm thick, with planar as well as homeotropic boundary conditions to carry out both the external field effect and light-scattering experiments on the same sample cell.

4.1. Quasi-elastic Light Scattering

There are several ways[24] of measuring the viscous and elastic coefficients of LC's. Among them, quasi-elastic depolarized Rayleigh scattering has been a very effective method, particularly for LCP's formed from solutions of long, rigid, or semirigid polymers such as PBG, because the high anisotropy in their viscoelasticity produces unusual static and dynamic responses to the external electric and magnetic fields.[44]

Long ago, the Osray Liquid Crystal Group[58, 59] predicted theoretically and confirmed experimentally that long-wavelength fluctuations of the nematic director give rise to two overdamped periodic distortion modes, associated with splay–bend and twist–bend elastic distortions of nematic LC's. These orientational fluctuations cause strong depolarized scattering of the light. Since the two uncoupled fluctuation modes are both overdamped, their time dependence obeys a diffusion-type differential equation derived from hydrodynamic equations. Experimentally, these time-dependent fluctuations lead to a frequency modulation of the scattered light and can be detected with current optical techniques. The time scale $(1-10^{-6}$ s) makes it ideal to use the photon correlation technique. Measurements of both the mean scattering intensities and their time dependences in appropriate geometries enable us to determine ratios of elastic moduli to one another, and ratios of elastic moduli to effective viscosities associated with the elastic distortion modes.

We studied two scattering geometries[45] in samples with parallel boundary conditions. In the first the nematic director is perpendicular to the scattering plane, with the incident polarization parallel to the director, and the scattered polarization parallel to the scattering plane. The plane of the sample is oriented so that the scattering wavevector is parallel to the glass windows. In the second geometry, everything is the same as in the first, except that the sample is rotated with respect to an axis normal to its surface so that the director is parallel to the scattering wavevector.

The first geometry allows us to see scattering from a superposition of pure splay and pure twist distortions. The ratio of the amplitudes of these distortions depends on the ratio of twist and splay elastic moduli, and their relaxation times depend on their effective diffusivities. The relative amplitudes are proportional to $\cos^2(\theta_s/2)K_1\mathbf{k}^2$ for splay and $\sin^2(\theta_s/2)/K_2\mathbf{k}^2$ for twist, where $\mathbf{k}$ and θ_s are the scattering wavevector and angle, respectively. In the second geometry we see scattering from a pure bend distortion. The amplitude for pure bend is proportional to $\cos^2(\theta_s/2)/K_3\mathbf{k}^2$. Also, the relaxation time of the bend distortion determines another effective diffusivity. Keeping the entire scattering geometry fixed and switching from the first sample orientation to the second, we can compare the amplitudes of the pure bend distortion to the splay and twist distortions as follows:

$$\frac{a_1 + a_2}{a_3} = \frac{K_3}{K_1} + \frac{K_3}{K_2} \tan^2\left(\frac{\theta_s}{2}\right) \tag{9}$$

where a_1, a_2, and a_3 are the amplitudes of splay, twist, and bend signals, respectively. The measurements were performed at a number of scattering angles to confirm the correct angular dependence of the scattering intensities and relaxation times and were repeated at least 10 times at each scattering angle.

Then, K_3/K_1 and K_3/K_2 can be determined from Eq. (9). At small scattering angles the second term in Eq. (9) is suppressed by the angular factor and K_3/K_1 is measured directly. In addition, the value for K_1/K_2 is also determined from the nonlinear least-squares fitting of the splay–twist

Table 6

Ratios of Effective Viscosities Determined from the Relaxation Rates of the Intensity Correlation Functions in Combination with the Ratios of the Elastic Moduli of the PBG Nematic LC's ($v_2 \approx 0.16$)[a]

Sample	DP[b]	$\eta_{\text{splay}}/\gamma_1$	$\gamma_1/\eta_{\text{bend}}$	γ_1 (poises)	η_{bend} (poises)	η_c/η_b
1-1	320	0.85	108	27	0.25	92
1-2	390	0.88	136	39	0.28	120
1-3	420	0.92	140	49	0.35	129
1-4	500	0.94	170	70	0.41	160
1-5	580	0.97	148	86	0.58	144
1-6	720	0.99	187	141	0.77	185
1-7	750	1.00	203	173	0.85	203
1-8	870	1.00	254	223	0.88	254
1-9	1,000	1.00	311	274	0.88	311

[a]Assuming that $K_2 = 0.6 \times 10^{-7}$ dyn, the absolute values for γ_1 and η_{bend} are deduced from the relaxation rates. Data from Refs. 36 and 37.

[b]$L/d \approx$ DP/10.

Table 7
Ratios of Effective Viscosities Determined from the Relaxation Rates of the Intensity
Correlation Functions in Combination with the Ratios of the Elastic Moduli
of the PBG Nematic LC's ($v_2 \approx 0.20$)

Sample	DP[b]	$\eta_{\text{splay}}/\gamma_1$	$\gamma_1/\eta_{\text{bend}}$ (poises)	γ_1 (poises)	η_{bend}	η_c/η_b^b
2-1	320	0.92	166	45	0.27	153
2-2	390	0.93	207	71	0.34	193
2-3	580	1.00	254	139	0.55	254

[a]Assuming that $K_2 = 0.6 \times 10^{-7}$ dyn, the absolute values for γ_1 and η_{bend} are deduced from the relaxation rates. Data from Refs. 36 and 37.
[b]$L/d \approx DP/10$.

intensity correlation function to a combination of two exponentials. These two measurements are in good agreement with each other. Our experimental results for ratios of the elastic moduli are collected in Table 4 and Table 5. Ratios of effective viscosities, determined from the time dependences of the intensity correlation functions in combination with the ratios of the elastic moduli, are presented in Table 6 and Table 7 as a function of L/d. We checked that the relaxation rates were proportional to $\mathbf{k}^2$, confirming the diffusive character of the elastic distortion modes. It is also noted the large anisotropy in the relaxation rates made the separation of the twist and splay modes relatively easy.

4.2. The Fredericks Transition

In the previous section, all the ratios of the elastic moduli to one another and the orientational diffusivities of PBG nematic LC's were determined. Knowing an absolute value for one of the elastic moduli or viscosities, obtained by other independent experimental methods, we can now determine the absolute magnitudes of all the remaining elastic and viscous parameters of PBG nematic LC's. The Fredericks transition provides a simple means for determining materials parameters for nematic LC's, provided that one can prepare well-aligned samples with the nematic director strongly anchored at the parallel substrates.

Application of an external electric or magnetic field of sufficient strength on well-aligned nematic samples induces distortions of pure splay, twist, or bend. If the experimental geometry is appropriately selected so that the alignment imposed by the surface differs from the preferred alignment in the presence of the external field,[24] the onset of realignment in the bulk of the sample occurs at a critical strength of the field. This critical field strength can determine the corresponding elastic modulus (splay, twist, or bend) from a knowledge of the dielectric or diamagnetic anisotropy. For example, with homeotropic boundary conditions and a magnetic field in the plane of the sample, the critical field strength is given by

$$H_c = \frac{\pi}{h}\left(\frac{K_3}{\Delta\chi}\right)^{1/2} \tag{10}$$

where h is the sample thickness and $\Delta\chi$ is the anisotropy of the diamagnetic susceptibility. Hence, an accurate measurement of the critical field strength H_c can be used to determine the bend modulus K_3 if h and $\Delta\chi$ are separately known.

The magnetic field experiments were performed in the homeotropic region of the sample in the geometry corresponding to a bend elastic distortion.[47,60] It is important to note that all the field and light-scattering experiments can be performed on a single assembled sample of PBG nematic LC's, so that the data can be combined unambiguously. Six samples with different concentrations were studied,[43] and the samples were made of racemic PBG ($L/d \approx 30$) solutions, containing no DMF solvent, in which some end-to-end aggregations of polymers might exist. The critical field strength was measured for each sample. The quantity $H_c h^2/\pi^2 = K_3/\Delta\chi$ was found to stay essentially constant (≈ 100 G^2 cm^2), changing only very slightly, in the range of $v_2 = 0.15$–0.32. Assuming that $\Delta\chi$ scales linearly with concentration, K_3 is expected to be a linear function of v_2. However, strictly speaking, $\Delta\chi$ depends on the order parameter S as well as the concentration.

A published value[42] of the diamagnetic anisotropy $\Delta\chi$ was used to determine the absolute magnitude of K_3 as a function of v_2. Knowing K_3, the estimated magnitude of K_2 is very weakly dependent on v_2 ($\approx 0.6 \times 10^{-7}$ dyn); it increases only a few percent with the concentration changing by a factor of two. A similar result of very slight concentration dependence was obtained with a different method;[41] a magnetic field-induced unwinding of a cholesteric structure was used to determine K_2 in PBG nematic LC's over a similar concentration range. Therefore, instead of K_3, the value for K_2 will be used for extracting the absolute magnitudes of all other viscous and elastic coefficients of PBG nematic LC's from the light-scattering data.

4.3. Crossover Behavior

First we discuss the elastic moduli. The measured K_1 and K_3 are of the same order of magnitude, about ten times larger than K_2. However, the most striking result is the behavior of K_3/K_1, as shown in Table 4, which initially increases with L/d, reaches a maximum, and then decreases. To interpret this behavior, we look at K_1 and K_3 separately. Recent experimental works on PBG LC's have shown that K_2 remains essentially constant in the molecular weight range[43] of 9.6–24.6×10^4 and exhibits no dependence on the concentration,[47] as discussed in the previous section. Thus K_2 might be expected to remain rather constant in the range of values we studied.

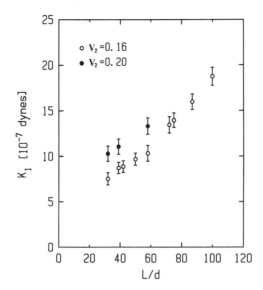

FIGURE 1
Estimated values for K_1 as a function of L/d, assuming that $K_2 = 0.6 \times 10^{-7}$ dyn, in PBG systems. (Reproduced with permission from Ref. 36.)

Assuming K_2 constant, with a literature value[42,47] of $K_2 = 0.6 \times 10^{-7}$ dyn, we determined the absolute magnitudes of K_1 and K_3 from Tables 4 and 5, which were plotted in Figs. 1 and 2 as a function of L/d. K_1 exhibits nearly linear dependence on L/d over the entire range studied. For K_3, a crossover from a rapidly increasing dependence to a saturation with increasing L/d is observed. The crossover begins at $L/d \approx 50$.

Combining the above arguments on the behavior of the elastic moduli K_1 and K_3, we expect that around the crossover region, $K_1 \approx K_3$, which agrees with the data. The persistence length of PBG gives $q/d \approx 50$–120, in good agreement with our data, since the crossover should begin for L/d somewhat less than q/d. The previous studies[47] of the concentration dependence of the elastic moduli were performed for samples near the crossover length and are consistent with the interpretation given here. For the PBG nematic LC with $L/d \approx 30$, K_1 and K_3 are within experimental accuracy both linear in v_2 such that $K_3/K_1 \approx 0.64$. K_2 remains small compared to either K_1 or K_3 and is almost independent of v_2. Assuming a model of semiflexible but fully extended chains in solution, the measured ratio of K_3/K_1 implies that $L/q \approx 0.6$, which leads to $q/d \approx 50$. This is consistent with the literature values for q, giving $q/d \approx 50$–120, in various solvents. Moreover, if there are considerable end–end aggregations of PBG polymers in the mixed solvents containing no DMF, the average molecular length L_{av} will be significantly increased; i.e., $L_{av}/d > 30$, probably close to 50.

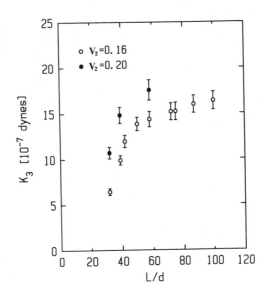

FIGURE 2
Estimated values for K_3 as a function of L/d, assuming that
$K_2 = 0.6 \times 10^{-7}$ dyn, in PBG systems. (Reproduced with
permission from Ref. 36.)

We compare the behavior of the measured elastic moduli of PBG
nematic LC's with existing theoretical predictions. The measured elastic
moduli of PBG nematic LC's are collected in Table 8 in comparison to the
theoretical predictions. As shown in Table 8, the obvious interpretation of
our results is that the short PBG molecules act as rigid rods, while above a
certain length, as the molecules become more strongly coupled to the mean
nematic ordering, their intrinsic flexibility makes them bend, so that the bend
modulus saturates, while the splay modulus keeps increasing linearly with
L/d.

Table 8

Comparison of the Elastic Moduli of the PBG Nematic LC's with Existing Theoretical
Predictions for Rigid Rods as Well as for Semiflexible Chains as a Function
of L/d ($v_2 \approx 0.16$)[a]

Ratio	PBG $L/d = 30{-}50$	Rigid rods (Refs. 10 and 11)	PBG $L/d = 50{-}100$	Semiflexible chains (Ref. 12)
K_3/K_1	$(L/d)^\alpha$	$[v_2(L/d)]^\beta$	$1/(L/d)$	q/L
K_1/K_2	(L/d)	3	(L/d)	$v_2^{2/3}(L/d)(q/d)^{-1/3}$
K_3/K_2	$(L/d)^{1+\alpha}$	$[v_2(L/d)]^\beta$	Constant	$v_2^{2/3}(q/d)^{2/3}$

[a]The exponents α and β lie in the range between one and two (Data from Ref. 37).

We now examine the behavior of effective viscosity coefficients as a function of L/d. For LMWLC's, understanding the relative values of viscosities is difficult, but for very long chains, some simplifications are expected,[19] which we see in our data. The viscosity associated with splay, η_{splay}, is found to approach that for twist, γ_1, with increasing L/d. The splay distortion involves cooperative director rotations coupled to limited sliding of the polymers parallel to one another, the two processes facilitating each other. In the limit of very long chain length, the viscosity for pure rotation of the director, γ_1, becomes extremely large compared to η_b, the shear viscosity for sliding of the polymers along one another, so that it dominates the behavior of the splay viscosity, as we observe. Moreover, one of the other simple shear viscosities, η_c, should approach γ_1 in the long-chain limit. The ratio η_c/η_b, identical to the ratio $\eta_{\text{splay}}/\eta_{\text{bend}}$ which we measured, is found to be on the order of 10^2, which supports our conclusions about the splay viscosity. The bend distortion is the only one that has a low viscosity, which approaches η_b, as L increases, another characteristic of the very long chain limit.

Still, assuming K_2 constant, we extract absolute values for viscosities from our data. The chain length dependences of the viscosities γ_1 and η_{bend} are illustrated in Table 6 and Table 7. An interesting feature is that the anisotropy between γ_1 and η_{bend} is huge, and η_b (similar to K_3) exhibits a saturation at $L/d \approx 70$. An approximately quadratic dependence for γ_1, and two different dependencies for η_{bend} on L/d are observed. For the PBG nematic LC with $L/d \approx 30$, previous concentration studies[47] found that the anisotropic viscosities show three distinctly different patterns of v_2 dependence; a roughly quadratic dependence for γ_1 and η_c, a linear one for η_a, and no strong v_2 dependence for η_b at all.

The main features are generally in accord with the following qualitative ideas. For highly parallel molecules, in the rigid rod regime, η_c and γ_1 are large, and both should grow as $v_2^2(L/d)^2$, by a simple geometrical argument. Also in this regime, η_b is small but increases with L/d due to interparticle interference effects. As the polymer becomes longer and therefore semiflexible but fully extended, η_c and γ_1 grow with $(L/d)^2$ in a way that is essentially unchanged from the rigid rod limit as long as chain entanglements are not very strong. However, for η_b, once the polymers bend with the director field, interparticle interference effects no longer grow with chain length, and η_{bend} becomes identical to η_b. In the absence of entanglement effects, η_b eventually saturates, becoming independent of L/d. This should occur for $L \approx q$, which is what we observe. If the polymers are allowed to gently wrap up around one another, η_a will increase, relative to η_b, with v_2. In addition, the observed independence of η_b on v_2 can be qualitatively interpreted by realizing that there are two competing factors in determining η_b. Mean interparticle distance decreases with increasing v_2, which leads to an increase in the interparticle interference affects, thus increasing the shear viscosity η_b. On the other hand, the degree of orientational order increases with v_2, which leads to a reduction in the interparticle interference. For

Table 9
Comparison of Ratios of Several Viscosities of PBG Nematic LC's and a TMV System
with Molecular Kinetic Descriptions[a]

Ratio	PBG	TMV	Infinite chain limit (Ref. 19)	Molecular kinetic (Refs. 62 and 63)	Theory (Ref. 28)
$\eta_{\text{splay}}/\gamma_1$	0.85–1.00	—	1	Finite	1
$\eta_{\text{bend}}/\gamma_1$	< 0.01	0.007	0	0	0
η_b/η_c	≤ 0.01	0.002	0	0	0
γ_1/η_c	≈ 1	0.95	1	1	1
ν_1/η_c	—	0.21	Finite	0	$\mu/4$

[a]Data from Ref. 37. $Q = v_2(L/d)$ and $0 < \mu < 1$ is a dimensionless parameter. The nematic order parameter S of TMV system is 0.92 (see Ref. 38).

polymers that are slowly twisting along their axes, the flow described by η_a is inhibited while that described by η_b is still easy. The results for ratios of several viscosities for PBG and TMV are also compared with molecular kinetic descriptions,[28, 29, 61–63] together with the infinite chain limit,[19] in Table 9. It is noted that for $L/d = 50$ the PBG LC already approaches a behavior characteristic of the infinite chain limit.

5. CONCLUSION

As the molecules become long, the crossover from rigid to semiflexible behavior of the anisotropic viscoelastic coefficients for nematic LCP's is expected, and confirmed in a PBG nematic LC. For a PBG nematic LC, the crossover begins, for $L/d \approx 50$, and this system is also exhibiting behavior characteristic of the infinite chain limit. As shown in Table 8 and Table 9, the experimental results are in reasonably good agreement with current theoretical predictions, even though quantitative comparison is still hard to achieve. Particularly, a precise theoretical picture, capable of explaining the observed behavior of the anisotropic viscosities, is currently absent.

We see that for both elasticity and viscosity, the bend distortions of an individual polymer, coupled to the director distortions, play a significant role in determining the mechanical properties of this system. The crossover behavior will be not only a characteristic of PBG nematic LC's but a universal behavior of other nematic LCP's formed from solutions of long semirigid molecules. Our interpretation of the data may not carry over to the cases of nematic melts or of more flexible polymer nematic LC's, but our conclusions represent a useful initial confirmation of the simple geometric ideas that are being widely used to develop models for the mechanical properties of all nematic LCP systems.

All the experiments described here were done at room temperature. No attempts to control the temperature of the sample accurately were made.

However, the temperature may be an interesting parameter for the complete description of the macroscopic properties of LCP's. Most liquid-crystalline polymer systems are not perfectly athermal but exhibit some degree of thermal behavior, discussed in Chapter 7. For example, the persistence length is directly affected by variation in temperature (see, for example, Chapters 2 and 6), so the study of bending fluctuations of a polymer chain may provide valuable information on its flexibility mechanism in the nematic state. Another interesting study might be the solvent dependence of the persistence length, associated with the change in polymer conformation.[48]

Finally, although the macroscopic properties of mainchain polymer, lyotropic or thermotropic, nematic LC's have been extensively investigated, studies of other classes of LCP's made up of sidechain polymers or block copolymers are still at an early stage. The compatibility problem in these systems was covered in Chapter 6, but further studies will contribute significantly to a basic understanding of the structural orders and the associated new phenomena in complex macromolecular fluids.

ACKNOWLEDGMENTS

We are grateful to all our colleagues at Brandeis University studying liquid crystals. The ability to carry out quantitative experiments on the PBG system resulted from the collective experience of various experiments at Brandeis University over many years. We are also grateful to Professor E.T. Samulski for helpful suggestions for preventing PBG aggregation. This research was supported in part by the National Science Foundation through Grant No. DMR-8803582, and by the Martin Fisher School of Physics, Brandeis University.

REFERENCES

1. L. Onsager, *Ann. N.Y. Acad. Sci.*, **1949**, *51*, 627.
2. J.D. Parsons, *Phys. Rev. A*, **1979**, *19*, 1225.
3. M. Baus, J. Colot, X. Wu, and H. Xu, *Phys. Rev. Lett.*, **1984**, *59*, 2184.
4. S.-D. Lee, *J. Chem. Phys.*, **1987**, *87*, 4972.
5. S.-D. Lee, *J. Chem. Phys.*, **1988**, *89*, 7036.
6. D. Frenkel, B.M. Mulder, and J.P. McTague, *Phys. Rev. Lett.*, **1982**, *52*, 287.
7. D. Frenkel and B.M. Mulder, *Mol. Phys.*, **1985**, *55*, 1171.
8. D. Frenkel, H.N.W. Lekkerkerker, and A. Stroobants, *Nature*, **1988**, *332*, 822.
9. R.G. Priest, *Phys. Rev. A*, **1973**, 7, 720.
10. J.P. Straley, *Phys. Rev. A*, **1973**, 8, 2181.
11. S.-D. Lee and R.B. Meyer, *J. Chem. Phys.*, **1986**, *84*, 3443.
12. T. Odijk, *Liq. Cryst.*, **1986**, *1*, 553.
13. A. Poniewierski and J. Stecki, *Mol. Phys.*, **1979**, *39*, 1931.
14. U.P. Singh and Y. Singh, *Phys. Rev. A*, **1986**, *33*, 3481.
15. S.-D. Lee, *Phys. Rev. A*, **1989**, *39*, 3631.

16. A.M. Somoza and P. Tarazona, *Phys. Rev. A*, **1989**, *40*, 4161.
17. N.F. Carnahan and K.E. Starling, *J. Chem. Phys.*, **1969**, *51*, 635.
18. M.P. Allen and D. Frenkel, *Phys. Rev. A*, **1988**, *37*, 1813.
19. R.B. Meyer, in *Polymer Liquid Crystals*, A. Ciferri, W.R. Krigbaum, and R.B. Meyer, eds., Academic Press, New York, 1982.
20. P.G. de Gennes, *Mol. Cryst. Liq. Cryst. Lett.*, **1977**, *34*, 177.
21. P.J. Flory, *Statistical Mechanics of Chain Molecules*, Wiley, New York, 1969.
22. T. Odijk, *Polym. Commun.*, **1985**, *26*, 197.
23. A.Y. Grosberg and A.V. Zhestkov, *Polym. Sci. USSR*, **1986**, *28*, 97.
24. P.G. de Gennes, *The Physics of Liquid Crystals*, Clarendon Press, Oxford, 1974.
25. J.L. Ericksen, *Arch. Ration. Mech. Anal.*, **1960**, *4*, 231.
26. F.M. Leslie, *Arch. Ration. Mech. Anal.*, **1968**, *28*, 265.
27. M. Doi, *Polym. Sci., Polym. Phys. Ed.*, **1981**, *19*, 229.
28. G. Marrucci, *Mol. Cryst. Liq. Cryst.*, **1982**, *72*, 153.
29. S.-D. Lee, *J. Chem. Phys.*, **1988**, *88*, 5196.
30. C.F. Curtiss, R.B. Bird, and O. Hassager, *Adv. Chem. Phys.*, **1976**, *35*, 31.
31. C.F. Curtiss and R.B. Bird, *J. Chem. Phys.*, **1981**, *74*, 2016.
32. G. Marrucci, *Pure. Appl. Chem.*, **1985**, *57*, 1545.
33. G. Marrucci and P.L. Maffettone, *Macromolecules*, **1989**, *22*, 4076.
34. O. Parodi, *J. Phys. (Paris)*, **1970**, *31*, 581.
35. A.N. Semenov, *Sov. Phys. JETP*, **1988**, *66*, 712.
36. S.-D. Lee and R.B. Meyer, *Phys. Rev. Lett.*, **1988**, *61*, 2217.
37. S.-D. Lee and R.B. Meyer, *Liq. Cryst.*, **1990**, *7*, 15.
38. S. Fraden, A.J. Hurd, R.B. Meyer, M. Cahoon, and D.L.D. Caspar, *J. Phys. Colloq. (Paris)*, **1985**, *46*, C3-85.
39. A.J. Hurd, S. Fraden, F. Lonberg, and R.B. Meyer, *J. Phys. (Paris)*, **1985**, *46*, 905.
40. C.G. Sridar, W.A. Hines, and E.T. Samulski, *J. Chem. Phys.*, **1974**, *61*, 947.
41. D.B. Dupre and R.W. Duke, *J. Chem. Phys.*, **1975**, *63*, 143.
42. N.S. Murthy, J.R. Knox, and E.T. Samulski, *J. Chem. Phys.*, **1976**, *65*, 4835.
43. H. Toriumi, K. Matsuzawa, and I. Uematsu, *J. Chem. Phys.*, **1984**, *81*, 6085.
44. R.B. Meyer, F. Lonberg, V. Taratuta, S. Fraden, S.-D. Lee, and A.J. Hurd, *Disc. Faraday Chem. Soc.*, **1985**, *79*, 125.
45. V. Taratuta, A.J. Hurd, and R.B. Meyer, *Phys. Rev. Lett.*, **1985**, *55*, 246.
46. F. Lonberg and R.B. Meyer, *Phys. Rev. Lett.*, **1985**, *55*, 718.
47. V. Taratuta, F. Lonberg, and R.B. Meyer, *Phys. Rev. A*, **1988**, *37*, 1831.
48. R. Parthasarathy, D.J. Houpt, and D.B. Dupre, *Liq. Cryst.*, **1988**, *8*, 1073.
49. H. Hakemi and A. Roggero, *Polymer*, **1990**, *31*, 84.
50. H. Block, *Poly(γ-benzyl-L-glutamate) and Other Glutamic Acid Containing Polymers*, Gordon and Breach, London, 1983.
51. H. Nakamura, Y. Husimi, G.P. Jones, and A. Wada, *J. Chem. Soc., Faraday Trans. II*, **1977**, *73*, 1178.
52. M.G. Vitovskaya and V.N. Tsvetkov, *Eur. Polym. J.*, **1976**, *12*, 251.
53. T. Sato and A. Teramoto, *Kobunshi*, **1988**, *37*, 278.
54. E.T. Samulski, private communication, 1987.
55. Y. Uematsu, J. Tomizawa, F. Kidokora, and T. Sasaki, *Polym. J.*, **1979**, *2*, 53.
56. D.B. Dupre, in *Polymer Liquid Crystals*, A. Ciferri, W.R. Krigbaum, and R.B. Meyer, eds., Academic Press, New York, 1982.
57. V. Taratuta, G. Srajer, and R.B. Meyer, *Mol. Cryst. Liq. Cryst.*, **1985**, *116*, 245.
58. Orsay Group on Liquid Crystals, *Phys. Rev. Lett.*, **1969**, *51*, 816.
59. Orsay Group on Liquid Crystals, *J. Chem. Phys.*, **1969**, *51*, 816.
60. F. Lonberg, Ph.D. Thesis, Brandeis Univ., Waltham, Massachusetts, 1986.
61. M. Doi, *Faraday Symp. Chem. Soc.*, **1983**, *18*, 49.
62. N. Kuzuu and M. Doi, *J. Phys. Soc. Jpn.*, **1983**, *52*, 3486.
63. N. Kuzuu and M. Doi, *J. Phys. Soc. Jpn.*, **1984**, *53*, 1031.

CHAPTER 10

Defects and Textures in Liquid Crystalline Polymers

MAURICE KLÉMAN

Laboratoire de Physique des Solides, Bâtiment 510,
Université de Paris-Sud, 91405 Orsay Cédex, France

CONTENTS

1. INTRODUCTION

The study of *defects* (generic name given to the local imperfections that break the order of the molecular arrangement) has played an important role since the beginning of our understanding of the structural and physical properties of low molecular weight liquid crystals (LMWLC; typical molecular length 30 Å); it was, in fact, the observation of defects in the polarizing microscope that enabled G. Friedel[1] and his contemporaries to elucidate and classify the structures of what G. Friedel baptized the *nematic*, the *cholesteric*, and the *smectic* phases, long before his findings were confirmed by x-ray diffraction studies. Since then, our understanding of the relationship between defects and structure has deepened and a complete theory has been elaborated for all ordered media, which relates defects of any dimensionality (point, line, or wall-like defects, configurations or solitons, etc.) to the generic singularities of the order parameter, via the topology of an adequate order parameter space.[2,3] Liquid crystal polymers (LCP) have therefore the same topologically stable defects as LMWLC's, since they have the same structural properties. However all observations point to the fact that the textures and defects of LCP's are vastly different from those of LMWLC's and also differ very much from one LCP to another. While the same structure in a nematic LMWLC and a nematic LCP, say, imply equal topological stability for line defects (disclinations) of the same strength $\mathscr{S}$, or for point defects of the same topological charge, things are indeed different with regard to *energetical stability*; these differences show up in (a) the relative occurrence of defects of a given type, since each defect, being a metastable configuration of the order parameter, carries an energy that depends, in large scales, on the stiffness constants of the material; (b) the nature of the *core* of the defect, where the order of the liquid crystal is usually replaced by the (dis)order of the higher temperature phase on a scale of the order of a coherence length ξ,[4] but which can also suffer various types of other arrangements; (c) the *mobility* of the defect, which always involves molecular processes, etc. Also, the mutual organizations of defects (which are called *textures*) depends on energetical considerations and physicochemical conditions (as anchoring at boundaries, etc.); the same ingredients enter the observational study of instabilities, flow properties, etc. We conclude therefore that the specific properties of defects met in LCP's should be directly related to their specific molecular configurations, which vary much from one chemical species to another. The origin of the stability of the liquid-crystalline order in polymers is much discussed today (see the relevant chapters in this volume), and a thorough study of defects should therefore shed some light on this question. A purpose of this review is also to help to raise relevant questions.

It is fair, however, to mention at once that the amount of results of a heuristic nature originating in the study of defects in LCP's is very small, and that very few generic conclusions have even been reached, except that the observed defects pertain to the expected topological classes. The experiments are difficult because of the high-temperature range in which many of the compounds exist and because of their high viscosity, so equilibrium textures are obtained long after the sample has been brought to the temperature of observation, if they are ever obtained. Also, most of the compounds are polydisperse in a way that is not usually known, so that the transition temperatures between the various phases are badly defined and two-phase regions often occur.

Most of the following will bear on mainchain polymers (either thermotropic or lyotropic), whose defects display more differences from the defects of LMWLC's than sidechain polymers, at least with regard to static properties. In sidechain polymers the mesomorphic properties are carried by the small sidechains; and, indeed, static observations show that, at first sight, most of the properties of defects are akin to those met in LMWLC's, while the viscoelastic properties[5] are ruled by the conformational properties of the polymeric backbone, which are still quite obscure, as well as the coupling between the backbone and the sidechains (but see Ref. 6). Concerning mainchain polymers, our review will include observations on (a) various thermotropic melts, such as homo- or copolyesters; (b) semiflexible polymers in solution, e.g., poly(p-phenylene terephthalamide) in sulfuric acid; (c) colloidal suspensions of rodlike polymers, e.g., tobacco mosaic virus (TMV); (d) semiflexible polymers in solutions of chiral molecules, most of them being of biological interest, e.g., poly(γ-benzyl L- or D-)glutamate (PBLG, PBDG), hydroxypropylcellulose (HPC), collagen, DNA. Some of the polymers belonging to the last category give nematics N or cholesterics N*, depending on the solvent, the concentration, the pH, etc.

The specific properties of defects in LCP's are due to a number of factors, such as the scarcity of chain ends and their anisotropic viscoelastic properties, which are all related, of course, to the great length of the molecules and to the character of rigidity or flexibility of the chain. Statistical models of the order parameter and of the liquid-crystalline transitions have been developed recently (see, for example, de Gennes,[7] Wang and Warner,[8] Renz,[9] and relevant chapters in this book). The variation of the Frank constants and of the viscosities in function of the chain length L, chain radius d, volume fraction of the polymer v_2, and persistence length q have been established by a number of authors: Straley,[10] in the line of the model of Onsager and Flory for rigid rods in solution; Odijk,[11] for semiflexible chains in solution (see also Chapter 9); Meyer,[12] and de Gennes[13] for thermotropic semiflexible polymers. Measurements of these viscoelastic constants have been made, mostly using the Fredericks transition under a magnetic field (Meyer et al.[14]; Sun and Kléman[15]) or under an electric field (Patel and Dupré[16]) or using Rayleigh light scattering (Lee and Meyer[17]).

For rodlike polymers in solution, the theory predicts that the ordering of the chains affects primarily the bend deformation constant K_3, which should be the largest, while $K_1 = 3K_2$. Hurd et al.[18] find $K_3/K_2 \approx 42$ and $K_1/K_2 \approx 2.5$ for TMV. They also obtain large anisotropies for the viscosity which correspond with the theory.

For semiflexible polymers in solution with large enough volume fractions v_2, and for thermotropic polymers, the theory predicts, in contrast to rodlike polymers, a large K_1 to which the major contribution comes from a single-particle entropy effect: splay at constant density requires segregation of "bottom" from "top" ends of molecules in the region of splay.[12] K_3 is limited by the persistence length and does not diverge. K_2 retains a low value, as in small molecule nematics (cf. Chapter 9). The orders of magnitude expected from this theory have been obtained in polyesters[15] and tested with success versus v_2 in PBG.[17]

2. GENERALITIES CONCERNING DEFECTS IN PARTIALLY ORDERED MEDIA

As already mentioned, the question of defects and textures can usually be treated under two headings[2,3,19-21]: (a) their classification with regard to the criterion of topological stability, which is related to the symmetry properties of the order parameter (see Refs. 20 and 21 for a description of the symmetries of the various liquid crystalline phases); and (b) their material-dependent properties, which include their energetical stability and the nature

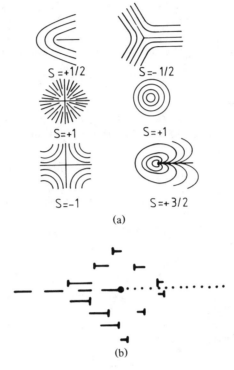

FIGURE 1
Typical configurations of the director in the vicinity of the core of a disclination line of strength $\mathscr{S}$. (a) wedge disclinations, (b) a model of a twist disclination.

of the order in the core. We discuss these topics in this section, taking into account as far as possible the differences between LCP's and LMWLC's originating in the anisotropy of the elastic constants of the former.

2.1. Topological Stability of Defects in Nematics

In uniaxial nematics, the line defects are of two types: the lines of half integral strength $\mathscr{S} = \pm \frac{1}{2}, \pm \frac{3}{2}, \ldots$, about which the director rotates by an angle of $2\pi\mathscr{S}$ and which are topologically stable, and the lines of integral strength $\mathscr{S} = \pm 1, \pm 2, \ldots$, about which the director rotates by an angle $2\pi\mathscr{S}$ and which are not topologically stable; specifically, this means that, for an integer line, the director can "escape" into the third dimension (Figs. 1 and 2) leaving the core nonsingular. If this process occurs (it is material dependent) the integral lines show up a blurred contrast under the polarizing microscope; they are then referred to as *thicks*, while the half integral lines

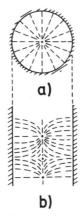

FIGURE 2
Model of a nonsingular core for a line of integral strength in an uniaxial nematic; (a) transversal cut, (b) meridian cut with escapes along two opposite directions, and singular points at the transition between the two modes of escape. Radial geometry for the director.

are called *thins* because the core region scatters light strongly (Fig. 3a). All the half-integral lines are topologically equivalent (it is possible to transform smoothly a half-integral line of any strength into a line of opposite strength[22]). The same is a fortiori true for integral lines. The $\mathscr{S}$ lines combine and merge according to the rules of addition of the numbers $\mathscr{S}$ mod 1, i.e., according to the rules of multiplication of the abelian group with two elements Z_2.[2] For more details, see the approach to topological stability via the homotopy theory of defects.[2, 3, 20, 21]

It is usual to make a distinction between wedge lines (Fig. 1a), which are parallel to the rotation vector, and twist lines (Fig. 1b), which are orthogonal to it. Wedge lines are visible in Schlieren textures (in which the lines are all perpendicular to the sample boundaries; Fig. 3b), and twist lines in thread textures (in which the lines are parallel to the sample boundaries; Fig. 3a). Transforming smoothly a wedge $\mathscr{S}$ line to a wedge $-\mathscr{S}$ line requires passing through a twist $|\mathscr{S}|$ line.[22]

Point defects can be visualized easily as originating on integral lines at the encounter of two opposite "escapes" (Fig. 2b).

While the classification and algebra of lines and points in uniaxial nematics is quite easy to grasp physically, this is not so for defects in biaxial nematics and cholesterics, which are both locally defined by three directors, forming a tripod. In brief, line defects (in both cases) are classified by the quaternion group Q and combine and merge according to the rules of multiplication of this group.[23] However lines of half-integral strength can still be defined[20, 24] (there are three sets of such lines, each one corresponding to

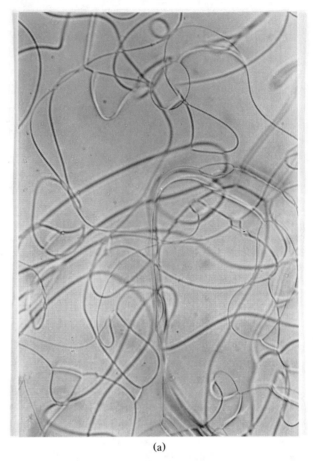

(a)

FIGURE 3
Polarizing microscopy. (a) Thicks and thins in a typical LMWLC.
Thread texture. (b) Schlieren texture. (Courtesy P. Oswald.)

one of the directors), but lines of integral strength divide into two classes: those of strength $\mathscr{S} = (2n + 1)2\pi$ are now topologically stable, those of strength $\mathscr{S} = 4n\pi$ are not. Therefore only those latter can appear as nonsingular in biaxial nematics. Additional important differences of topological origin between biaxial and uniaxial nematics are: first, the absence of singular points in biaxial nematics (they are not topologically stable) and, second, the obstruction to the crossing of two mobile $\mathscr{S} = \pm \frac{1}{2}$ lines that do not belong to the same director. None of those properties has so far been used to characterize a biaxial nematic, but it is important to have them in mind since there are experimental indications[25] that LCP's are favorite candidates for biaxiality.

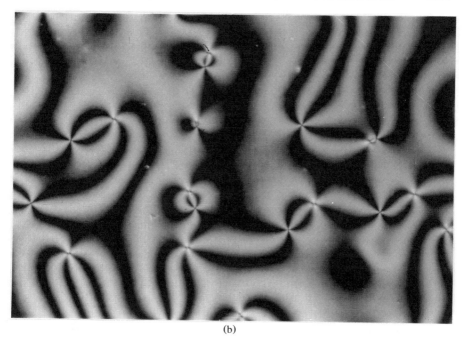

(b)

FIGURE 3 continued

2.2. Material-Dependent Properties in Uniaxial Nematics

The energy of a singular line of strength $\mathscr{S}$ is of the form:

$$W = \alpha \pi K_\alpha \mathscr{S}^2 \ln \frac{R}{r_c} + w_c \qquad (1)$$

where α is some geometrical coefficient, K_α some combination of the Frank constants K_i ($i = 1, 2, 3$), R a typical macroscopic length (a distance between defects), r_c the size of the region where the order parameter is broken (the core), and w_c the core energy.

The energy carried by the deformation around a nonsingular line (necessarily of integral strength) is of the form:

$$W = \beta 2 \pi K_\beta \mathscr{S} \qquad (2)$$

and does not depend on any length (the deformation spreads over all the available space); of course, the core energy vanishes, and K_β is a combination of Frank constants and β a geometrical coefficient.

It is clear at first sight that any line of integral strength will favor a singular core, if $K_\beta \gg K_\alpha$. In LMWLC's, where all the Frank constants are of the same order of magnitude, this inequality is not satisfied and one always observes nonsingular integral lines; most often they form Friedel's nuclei and carry singular points. According to Dzyaloskinskii,[26] the only wedge $\mathscr{S} = +1$ lines that are stable versus three-dimensional perturbations have a circular or a radial geometry. In the circular geometry, the energy of the nonsingular line is precisely:[27]

$$W = \pi\left(K_2 + K_3\frac{k}{\sin k}\right); \qquad \sin^2 k = \frac{K_3 - K_2}{K_3} \tag{3}$$

when assuming $K_3 > K_2$. In the radial geometry, we have:

$$K_1 > K_3 \qquad W = \pi\left(K_1 + K_3\frac{k}{\tanh k}\right); \qquad \tanh^2 k = \frac{K_1 - K_3}{K_1} \tag{4}$$

$$K_1 < K_3 \qquad W = \pi\left(K_1 + K_3\frac{k}{\tan k}\right); \qquad \tan^2 k = \frac{K_1 - K_3}{K_1} \tag{5}$$

These expressions and the former ones do not at once tell us the geometry that will be stable. Take as an example a situation in which K_1 is slightly larger than K_3. In principle, the radial geometry described by Eq. (4) should be favored. However a circular geometry with a singular core is still possible, as well as a nonsingular circular geometry. In order to decide which possibility will be realized, we have to compare $\pi K_3 \ln(R/r_c) + w_c$ (Eq. 1) and W given by Eq. (3) to the value above in Eq. (4). Similar comparisons can be made for other situations depicted above and for $\mathscr{S} = -1$ lines. We see that the result depends on the nature and size of the core and on the *anisotropy* of the Frank coefficients. However, note immediately that if singular integral lines are favored, they will have a strong tendency to split into half-integral lines, since the energy varies now with $\mathscr{S}^2$ (Eq. 1). Therefore we expect that in all cases when the Frank constants indicate a large anisotropy, and if there exist core arrangements of not too prohibitive an energy, half-integral lines (thins) will be much more numerous than integral ones, and that those integral lines will be singular. This is obviously not the case in LMWLC nematics, where the anisotropy is small and nonsingular integral lines (and singular points) are indeed predominant over other defects. However these remarks are relevant to LCP's.

We shall not discuss the question of the core of disclinations in LMWLC's[19, 20] but we will return to it for LCP's. However, let us quickly mention *point defects*; their energy scales as $K_\gamma R$, where K_γ is a suitable Frank constant coefficient and R a typical macroscopic length, as above. The integral of the Frank free energy does not diverge on the core: in other words there is no mathematical core. However, there is a stable physical core of molecular dimensions; a simple calculation, in which it is assumed that the core energy density is some constant ϵ, indeed yields $r_c^2 \approx K_\gamma/4\pi\epsilon$ and an energy $K_\gamma(R - 2r_c/3)$, smaller than $K_\gamma R$.

2.3. Defects in Cholesterics

There is, structurally speaking, very little difference between a twisted conventional nematic and a cholesteric at a scale smaller than the pitch p; optical observations made on samples small compared to p show up thicks and thins of the same nature as in a nematic. At larger scales, however, there are other features, more inherent in a cholesteric because of its three essential characteristics: the layered structure, the tendency toward continuous cores, and the local tendency to double twist. Topologically, the line defects, as already stated, are classified by the quaternion group, like the disclination lines in a biaxial nematic, and it is usual to refer to the types of elementary defects carried by the three directions of the local trihedron which defines the orientation of a cholesteric as λ, χ, and τ lines (Fig. 4).

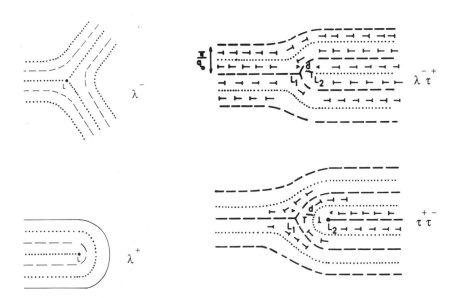

FIGURE 4
Some models of disclination lines in a cholesteric. The bars represent the λ director; the length of the bars is proportional to the projection of the unit λ vector on the plane; the head carried by the bar indicates that the director λ is at some angle to the plane, the head itself is supposed to be on the side of the observer. Therefore the cholesterics which are pictured for the $\tau^+\tau^-$ and $\lambda^-\tau^+$ are right handed. The χ axis is always in the plane of the drawing.

λ is a vector along the local molecular axis (crudely, along the molecular length), χ is along the axis of twist, and $\tau = \lambda \wedge \chi$. χ and τ are of course immaterial directors in an uniaxial cholesteric, but biaxial cholesterics have been discovered.[28]

2.3.1. THE INCIDENCE OF THE LAYERED STRUCTURE

Being periodic along the χ axis, a cholesteric frequently shows domains that are akin to the focal domains of smectics, with a larger flexibility, since the thickness of the "layers" can suffer larger distortions than in a smectic.[29] The corresponding textures (polygonal textures) have been described in detail.[30] Let us note immediately that they seem less frequent in biopolymers in solution than in conventional cholesterics.[31] The crucial ingredient seems here to be the flexibility of the layers, which have to suffer large (and even singular) curvature deformations along the so-called focal lines. The layers' bending involves the coefficient K_3, which is large in most biopolymers, e.g., polypeptides (PBLG; the persistence length q is of the order of 1500 Å; cf. Chapter 2) or polynucleotides (DNA; $q \approx 600$ Å). In xanthan, however, polygonal textures are frequent. However all the biopolymers just cited show *spherulites*, which appear during growth from the isotropic solution.[32] The classical model of spherulites is due to Frank and Pryce (see Robinson et al.[33]); the layers are along concentric spheres, and the molecular orientation on these spheres necessarily involves a defect of total strength $\mathscr{S} = 2$ (it is topologically impossible to draw a continuous field of directors on a sphere). Therefore one has either a diametral disclination of strength $\mathscr{S} = 1$, piercing the spherulite in two points, or a radial disclination of strength $\mathscr{S} = 2$, piercing the spherulite in one point. In this latter case, one can make the configuration continuous by neglecting the three directors, λ, τ, and χ (see Section 2.3.2). This is the most frequent situation met with biopolymers. Note that in a spherulite the Gaussian curvature of the layers is positive, while it is negative along focal lines.

2.3.2. CONTINUOUS CORE

Concerning disclinations, we have mentioned that in typical cholesterics a *continuous core* is favored.[34] This is always topologically possible for an $\mathscr{S} = 2n$ (with n an integer) line, and the spherulites offer an illustration of this property. For $\mathscr{S} = \frac{1}{2}$, λ^+ and λ^- lines (Fig. 4) are favored over τ^+ and τ^- lines: the material director is indeed nonsingular in a λ line. This is also true in biopolymers; however, these lines cannot avoid splay, as a simple calculation easily shows. Since the splay coefficient is necessarily large, these lines frequently occur in pairs in biopolymers ($\lambda^+\tau^-$ or $\lambda^-\tau^+$), forming dislocations of small Burgers' vector.[31]

2.3.3. DOUBLE TWIST

The double twist is represented in Fig. 5: any direction perpendicular to the axis of the cylinder is an axis of helicity, and the director configuration

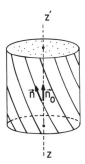

FIGURE 5
The cylindrical-double twist geometry.

reads, in cylindrical coordinates,

$$n_r = 0; \qquad n_\theta = -\sin \psi(r); \qquad n_z = \cos \psi(r) \qquad (6)$$

with $\psi(0) = 0$. This is the configuration of a $\lambda(\mathscr{S} = 1)$. The integral lines of **n** are along helices of chirality opposite to the chirality of the director about the radii. This structure presents a certain amount of stability in typical cholesterics, which can be phenomenologically attributed to a surface term in the free energy

$$\rho f = \frac{1}{2}K_1(\text{div }\mathbf{n})^2 + \frac{1}{2}K_2\left(\mathbf{n} \cdot \text{curl }\mathbf{n} + \frac{2\pi}{p}\right)^2 + \frac{1}{2}K_3(\mathbf{n} \wedge \text{curl }\mathbf{n})^2$$

$$- \frac{1}{2}K_{24}\,\text{div}(\mathbf{n}\,\text{div }\mathbf{n} + \mathbf{n} \wedge \text{curl }\mathbf{n}) \qquad (7)$$

where p is the pitch. In cylindrical coordinates, the K_{24} term reads $+(K_{24}/2r)[d(\cos^2 \psi)/dr]$; this quantity integrates, between $r = 0$ and $r = r_0$, to

$$-\pi K_{24}\left(1 - \cos^2 \psi_0\right) \qquad (8)$$

and is negative for any value of $\psi_0 \neq 2\pi n$, when K_{24} is positive.

If $K_{24} > 0$, double-twist cylindrical geometries are the favored geometries for nucleation of the cholesteric phase in the isotropic phase. This is especially true if K_1 is large compared to K_3, as in the biopolymers we have considered, since the double-twist geometry of Fig. 5 is splayless. However, this configuration necessarily has a limited extent ξ, since the gain in energy due to K_{24} is counterbalanced by the bend term K_3. This argument may well be another element of an explanation for the nucleation of the cholesteric phase in the form of spherulites with either a diametral disclination (which has the topology of the double-twist cylinder) or a radial disclination (two double-twist cylinders side by side).

When K_{24} is positive and large enough, new phases with thermodynamically stable double-twist textures may appear. These phases of defects are the *blue phases* first described by Saupe[35]; they exist in a very small range of temperature between the isotropic and the cholesteric phases. Three blue phases (BP) are known: BPI and BPII, which are cubic, and BPIII, which is probably disordered but is claimed to be thermodynamically stable. The cubic structures are fairly well understood: the building blocks are finite cylinders of double twist, which can arrange locally, for example, three of them along the quaternary axes of the cube.[36] If their lateral size is limited to $\psi_0 = \pi/4$, they fit nicely along their contacts, but the intermediary region along the three-fold axis cannot be filled along the continuous molecular directions: a disclination of strength $\mathcal{S} = -\frac{1}{2}$ appears in this region. This structure is called "frustrated," since the best local order is satisfied only along the axes of the cylinders of double twist, and the whole structure contains defects. Frustration phenomena are known in other situations[37] (polytetrahedral complex alloys phases, metallic glasses, etc.).

The stability of the blue phases has been discussed[38] within the framework of a Landau theory of phase transitions, as a function of the ratio $\kappa \propto \xi/p$, where ξ is a coherence length and p the pitch. ξ is a "racemic" correlation length that measures the tendency to parallel alignment, as opposed to helical alignment. The larger κ is, the greater the tendency for the appearance of a blue phase. Our discussion of the polymeric chiral liquid crystals will allow us to fill in this picture; double-twist geometries have indeed been observed in LCP's, some of them closely related to the cylindrical double-twist geometry, but others of a completely different nature (for example DNA in the chromosome of dinoflagellates) as we shall see later.

2.4. Defects in A Smectics (SmA's)

We give a very short description of defects in SmA's, since there are yet very few results concerning defects in SmA LCP's.

2.4.1. FOCAL LINE DEFECTS

In A smectics, topologically stable line defects can be classified under the two usual headings of disclinations and dislocations. Because of the strong constraint on the thickness of the layers, however, which are more difficult to deform elastically than to curve, the most common (and first recognized[1]) type of defect is the *focal line*, which is a special type of disclination around which the layers keep a constant thickness and are therefore parallel, although they suffer large curvature deformations. Focal lines in SmA's go by pairs, an ellipse E and a branch of hyperbola H, which are cofocal and located in two perpendicular planes. The line segments joining any point A on E to any point B on H are perpendicular to the layers, which curve along

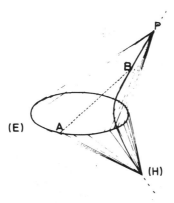

FIGURE 6
The geometry of a focal domain. (Reproduced from Ref. 1.)

so-called Dupin cyclides. The whole geometry constitutes a *focal domain* (Fig. 6), which is a type of object described a long time ago by G. Friedel.[1]
The free energy of a SmA reads

$$\rho f = \frac{1}{2} K_1 (\sigma_1 + \sigma_2)^2 + \frac{1}{2} B \left(\frac{\partial u}{\partial n} \right)^2 - K_{24} \sigma_1 \sigma_2 \qquad (9)$$

where σ_1 and σ_2 are the principal curvatures at a point of a layer; $\sigma_1 \sigma_2$ is the Gaussian curvature. The splay term vanishes if the layer is a minimal surface, with $\sigma_1 + \sigma_2 = 0$; it can be made small if σ_1 and σ_2 are of opposite signs. This is indeed what happens in focal domains, where the layers are locally saddle shaped. Furthermore, the elastic term $(1/2)B(\partial u/\partial n)^2$ is strictly zero, except of course in the cores of the focal lines, which have to be treated apart. The "saddle–splay" K_{24} term is generally neglected since it can be reduced to a surface term; however, it favors the nucleation of focal domains if K_{24} is negative.

2.4.2. EDGE DISLOCATION

Dislocations in SmA phases have many features that make them differ from dislocations in ordinary solids. The energy of an *edge dislocation*[20, 39] (Fig. 7a) of Burgers' vector $b = nd_0$ (d_0 the thickness of an elementary layer) reads

$$W = \frac{K_1 b^2}{2 \lambda_1 r_c} + W_c \qquad (10)$$

where $\lambda_1 = (K_1/B)^{1/2}$ is a penetration length and W_c the contribution of the core to the total energy.

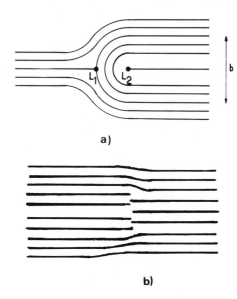

a)

b)

FIGURE 7
The geometry of an edge dislocation in a SmA: (a) core split into
two disclinations, (b) core split along the glide plane.

The usual model of the core assumes that it is split into two disclinations, L_1 and L_2, of opposite signs, as in Fig. 7. In this model, r_c is on the order of the distance between L_1 and L_2 and scales as b; the elastic energy is then proportional to b, and the core energy reads:

$$W_c = \frac{\pi K_1}{2} \ln \frac{b}{2d_0} + w_c \qquad (11)$$

where w_c is a new core energy for the disclinations which does not depend on b. This behavior of W favors large Burgers' vectors, as it has indeed often been observed.[39] The first term on the right hand side of Eq. (11) is pure curvature energy (of L_2, where the layers are parallel). The strain energy of L_1 can also be minimized (at the expense of curvature energy) by some instability along the line, which can be described in turn as some (longitudinal) splitting of the line into focal domains.

Polymeric smectics with side mesomorphic groups may have a large effective K_1 due to the presence of the backbone sitting in the layer[40] or perpendicular to the layer.[41] If this is the case, a different splitting of the core might be favored, more akin to a Peierls-Nabarro splitting along the glide plane (i.e., perpendicularly to the layers), as in dislocations in ordinary crystals[42] (Fig. 7b). The energy of the core W_{CPN} depends then on the surface energy along the faulted glide plane.[43] According to Lejcek,[44] W_{CPN} scales as

$K_1[b^2/(\lambda_1^3 r_c)^{1/2}]$, i.e., with $K_1(b/\lambda_1)^{3/2}$ if $r_c \approx b$. There is still a tendency to form dislocations with a large Burgers' vector in this model, as long as $\lambda_1 \gg b$, i.e., if λ_1 is much larger than the repeat distance. Dislocations with multiple Burgers' vectors of a few layers have been observed by high-resolution electron microscopy techniques in films of a few hundred angstroms thickness of a mainchain–side group smectic LCP.[41, 45]

Values of K_1 and B are dramatically lacking for smectic LCP's.

2.4.3. SCREW DISLOCATION

An obvious displacement field for a screw dislocation is, as in usual dislocation theory:

$$u = \frac{b\theta}{2\pi} \qquad (12)$$

The line energy, calculated to second order in a SmA, is zero. Thus, to this order, it is restricted to a core energy; screw dislocations of small Burgers' vector should therefore be frequent in SmA LCP's, as they are typical smectics.[46]

Taking higher order elasticity into account, screw dislocations are well understood within two limits:

1. When the Burgers' vector is small compared to λ_1, the layers take the shape of minimal surfaces for which div $\mathbf{n} = 0$; the only contribution to the energy comes from $\mathbf{B}$. A helicoid:

$$\varphi = -\frac{b\theta}{2\pi} + z \qquad (13)$$

[where $\varphi = \varphi(r)$ is a phase-variable constant on each layer, z is the coordinate along the dislocation, and θ a polar angle] is such a minimal surface and represents rightly a screw dislocation. The energy reads:

$$W = \frac{Bb^4}{128}\left(\frac{1}{r_c^2} - \frac{1}{R^2}\right) + w_c \qquad (14)$$

where R is the external radius of the sample. The b^4 behavior insures that, with this model, only dislocations of very small Burgers' vector are stable. The order of magnitude of Eq. (16) is 1000 times smaller than for the edge dislocation of the same Burgers' vector. Since K_1 is probably so large in polymers with mesogenic sidechains, this type of model of screw dislocation should be favored.

2. When b is large compared to λ_1, the layers prefer to stack parallel to one another, with a constant thickness. This condition is reminiscent of the constraint which leads to focal domains, but here we further impose the presence of a screw dislocation. Screw dislocations with giant Burgers'

vectors have been observed in A smectics.[47] They are constructed as follows (for details, see Ref. [21], Chapter 5). One starts from a *parent layer* σ_0, having the shape of a ruled helicoid (a minimal surface), with pitch b, and one stacks a set of layers on this parent layer at constant distance d_0 one from each other. The normals to the set of parallel layers σ_i are straight lines. There is an analogy between the set of layers and a set of wavefronts, between normals and light rays; there is therefore a focal surface enveloped by the normals; in fact, the normals meet two helices H_1 and H_2 of pitch b, which are singular lines of the geometry and cusp lines of the focal surface (which has many sheets). H_1 and H_2 are, in an actual geometry which avoids the focal surface, the only visible singularities: the layers fold around these lines as they do around a disclination (see Fig. 8). Let us emphasize the difference from the former model, where div $\mathbf{n} = 0$: all the layers are helicoids and therefore, if $b = nd_0$ there are n such nested helicoids, which are not parallel surfaces; in the continuous limit we have Eq. (13). Clearly the axis $r = 0$, on which all these helicoids meet, is a singular axis, and a core model has to be devised. In contrast, when $\partial u / \partial n = 0$ (parallelism of layers), there is only one layer in the shape of an helicoid, passing through the axis $r = 0$, and no singularity on the axis.

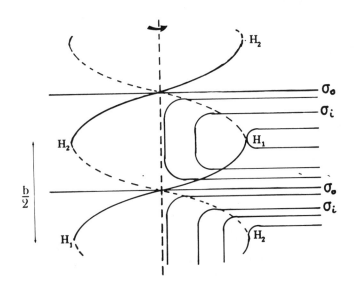

FIGURE 8
Meridian cut of a parallel stacking of layers σ_i on a parent layer σ_0 which has the shape of a ruled helicoid of pitch b. The layers fold around the two helices H_1 and H_2 which are the cusp lines of the focal surface of the stacking. σ_0 is the surface generated by the horizontal lines (also labeled σ_0) twisting about the vertical with a pitch b.

If λ_1 is large compared to d_0 (as it probably is in LCP's), there is little chance that this model will be favored. However, we have described this geometry in some detail, since it will prove relevant in another context (double-twist frustration in cholesteric biopolymers; see Section 3.2.1).

3. OBSERVATIONS AND MODELS FOR DEFECTS AND TEXTURES IN LCP's

3.1. Nematic Polymers

3.1.1. THICKS AND THINS IN MAINCHAIN POLYMERS; ABSENCE OF SINGULAR POINTS

Most of the observations point to the predominance of thin line defects, which are $\mathscr{S} = \pm \frac{1}{2}$ line defects, or singular $\mathscr{S} = \pm 1$ lines; this is in agreement with the discussion above for anisotropic media. Thick lines are seldom observed.

The $\mathscr{S} = \pm \frac{1}{2}$ defects are clearly documented in TMV nematic solutions (freeze etching observations[48]) where K_3 is much larger than the other Frank constants, and in the thread texture of the segmented C_x polyester,[49,50] for $x = 5$

$$CH_3CO {+\!\!\!-} O{-}O{-}COO{-}O{-}CO{-}(CH_2)_x{-}CO {-\!\!\!+}_n OH; \qquad n \sim 24$$

(where, in contrast, it is K_1 that is by far the largest Frank constant[15]) as well as in certain copolyesters,[51,52] for example, of the type designated "*B*-ET" (supplied by Eastman Kodak as X-7G) and containing 60 mol% *p*-oxybenzoate and 40 mol% ethylene terephthalate. They have also been observed in the Schlieren texture of the same copolyesters.

In the polyester mentioned above and for large x ($x = 14$, say) the viscosity is extremely high and the sample does not anneal at all during the optical microscopy observations; the local orientation does not vary even after long annealing in the isotropic phase. However, x-ray diffraction gives evidence for the existence of a nematic phase; the molecules are probably tightly correlated by coiling around one another, and these entanglements subsist in the isotropic phase while the extent of the correlations decrease. For $x = 5$ the texture varies with the degree of polymerization: for shorter chains ($M_w \approx 1000$) one observes a typical LMWLC thread texture, with thins and thicks. In the course of time the threads have a tendency to disappear and give place to a well-resolved texture of Friedel's nuclei (*plage à noyaux*), with only integral lines and singular points. However, for longer chains ($M_w \approx 10,000$ and more) integral lines or nuclei are extremely infrequent (the occasional presence of thicks has helped to identify thins as being

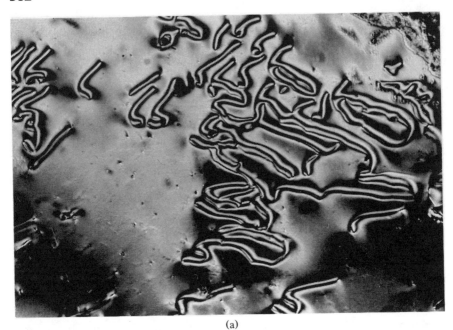

(a)

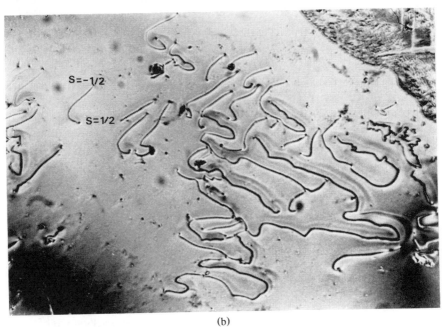

(b)

FIGURE 9
$\mathscr{S} = -\frac{1}{2}$ and $\mathscr{S} = +\frac{1}{2}$ cores at the free extremities of half-integral
lines in a free droplet (a) between crossed nicols, (b) unpolarized
light. Polyester (1) with $x = 5$. (Courtesy G. Mazelet-Parizé.)

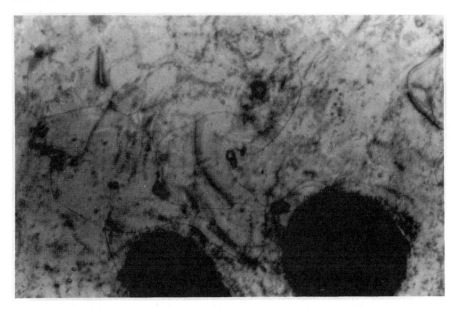

FIGURE 10
Half-integral and integral lines in the X-7G copolyester. (Courtesy
F. Lequeux. Reproduced from Ref. 80, with permission.)

of the half-integral type[49]) and most of the defects are half-integral lines,
either loops floating in the bulk and tending to collapse in a few minutes
after their appearance (these loops have a twist character), or lines attached
to either the glass covers or (in free droplets) the free boundary[50] (Fig. 9).

In such copolymers as X-7G, integer lines have been observed in their
threadlike form[53]; when they are in association with half-integral lines, they
obey the algebraic laws required by their merging (Fig. 10). Integer lines have
also been observed in Schlieren textures (*plages à noyaux*), more conspicuously when the sample is frozen to the nematic state from the isotropic
phase.[51,52,54] The core of the nuclei (*noyaux*) appears to be rather large and
the whole contrast is much fuzzier than in a usual Schlieren texture in a
LMWLC. However, this behavior seems to be proper to the copolyesters
cited above. It is difficult to assess without doubt that the integral lines
observed in these copolyesters are nonsingular. In the case of threads, at
least, their contrast under the polarizing microscope is quite fuzzy but does
not disappear completely when the polars are removed; this may point
toward their singular character.

Thin threads have been observed[55] in lyotropic solutions (in sulfuric acid)
of semiflexible polymers, (polyazomethines, polyterephtalamides, etc.) and in
a nematic aromatic copolyester[56] of a remarkably high molecular weight and
low viscosity ($M_w \approx 220,000$), based on methylhydroquinone, pyrocathecol,

and terephthalic acid. These lines may be singular *integer* lines, as claimed by the authors, on the basis that small micron-size loops are seen disappearing by a progressive attenuation of their optical contrast. However, direct measurements of the strengths are lacking. Skoulios et al.[55] have argued that K_3 is very large in their sulfuric solutions of semiflexible polymers, and have subsequently proposed a model of pure radial integer lines.

Singular points have never been reported in nematic polymers. According to our discussion above concerning the relationship between singular points and integral lines in an uniaxial nematic, this might indicate that most of the thins observed are not integral lines.

It is interesting to notice that singular points have not been reported either in those copolyesters in which singular integral and half-integral lines are both visible (see Fig. 10). It has been claimed by Windle et al.[25] that these copolyesters are biaxial nematics. This interpretation is perfectly consistent with the present observations of defects: singular points are topologically unstable in biaxial nematics, and nonsingular integral lines should be of strength multiple of 2 ($\mathscr{S} = \pm 2, \pm 4, \dots$). It is quite possible, by an extension of the arguments we have developed for anisotropic uniaxial nematics, that those lines are not energetically stable, in either their singular or their nonsingular avatars, in biaxial nematics.

3.1.2. CORES OF DISCLINATIONS IN MAINCHAIN POLYMERS

It is evident that, since the order parameter is broken there, the cores of defects should be preferred regions for the presence of chain ends and, even, of their segregation. In LMWLC's, the core of disclinations is at least of molecular size and its radius increases with temperature, but systematic experimental studies are lacking. We want to comment on two observations on the cores in LCP's.

The freeze–fracture experiments of Zasadzinski et al.[48] have shown that the $\mathscr{S} = |\frac{1}{2}|$ twist lines cores are of molecular size in TMV nematic solutions: the viruses reorient abruptly by 90° at the core, remaining in the plane of the disclination line. The wedge disclination core is several virus lengths in diameter and much more disordered, the viruses twisting out of the plane perpendicular to the line and into the direction along the disclination line. The twist disclination lines seem more frequent than the wedge ones, which can be related to the smaller value of K_2 (compared to K_1 and to K_3, which is the largest Frank coefficient).

The polarizing microscope observations (Fig. 9) by Mazelet and Kléman[50] of the C_5 polyester (1) reveal that in free droplets the cores of the wedge parts of the half-integral lines are very large; the $\mathscr{S} = +\frac{1}{2}$ and the $\mathscr{S} = -\frac{1}{2}$ differ widely; the size of the core of $\mathscr{S} = +\frac{1}{2}$ wedge segments is much larger than the size of the cores of $\mathscr{S} = -\frac{1}{2}$ wedge segments. In the first ones, the molecules seem to stay in the plane perpendicular to the line and the chain ends segregate in the core, while the off-core geometry implies essentially a bend and twist deformation (K_2 is small; K_3 is larger than K_2 but much

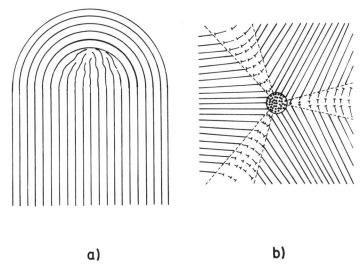

a)   b)

FIGURE 11
Models for the cores of half-integrals lines (a) $\mathscr{S} = +\frac{1}{2}$, (b) $\mathscr{S} = -\frac{1}{2}$.
(Reproduced from Ref. 50, with permission of the publishers,
Butterworth-Heinemann Ltd. ©.)

smaller than K_1). A schematic model is given Fig. 11a. The $\mathscr{S} = -\frac{1}{2}$ cores show up a typical three-fold symmetry with three spikes emerging from the core; these spikes have been interpreted as three wall-like regions where the chain ends segregate and twist out of the plane perpendicular to the line and into the direction parallel to the line; in the central part of the core itself the molecules are probably aligned along the core (Fig. 11b). These models are inferred from the contrast observed at large scales; furthermore (a) the calculations they suggest[50] seem to corroborate the models to some extent; (b) the large mobility of the $\mathscr{S} = -\frac{1}{2}$ and, in contrast, the vanishing mobility of the $\mathscr{S} = +\frac{1}{2}$ are in accordance with this model. To move an $\mathscr{S} = -\frac{1}{2}$ core we only have to change the molecular direction locally, while a mobile $\mathscr{S} = +\frac{1}{2}$ has to drag with it all the chain ends gathered inside the core.

3.1.3. TEXTURES IN NEMATIC MAINCHAIN POLYMERS
We return with more details to the question of ensembles of defects (textures) in a LCP. Individual defects in LCP's show up large differences with individual defects in LMWLC's of the same symmetry. This statement is also true for their textures.

Starting from the isotropic high-temperature phase, the nematic phase that first appears is usually very disordered at the micrometer size, in a sample of a few tens of microns thick. There is no clear consensus on the nature of this texture, which appears to be made of small regions having a

size typical of the long-range correlations, probably separated by disclinations. This disordered phase coarsens in the course of time when the
temperature is kept constant. It yields a Schlieren texture of a very fuzzy
nature in mainchain copolyesters, where integer lines and half-integer lines
can be recognized.[51,54,57] The very detailed observations of Shiwaku et al.[58]
in X-7G point in fact to a large predominance of $\mathscr{S} = |\frac{1}{2}|$ lines, some
$\mathscr{S} = +1$ lines, very few $\mathscr{S} = -1$ lines. In some homopolyesters, thin lines
appear after some time, but they are more readily obtained when the sample
is prepared directly in the nematic phase, by introducing the material by
capillarity between the glass plates.[49]

Apart from the highly disordered textures characteristic of the
nematic–isotropic (N $\rightleftarrows$ Iso) transition, two types of well-characterized textures are currently distinguished in LCP's: (1) a threaded (or line) texture
made of individually recognizable disclinations and (2) an ill-defined texture
made probably of an entanglement of disclinations, and which, when relax-
ing, gives rise to the line texture. Such textures, when they do not exist
originally, are obtained as a result of some strong action on the specimen
(shear or brutal compression) and have been observed and described in detail
in lyotropic nematics of the polyazomethine or polyaramide type in sulfuric
acid[55] and in some (thermotropic) copolyesters,[59] where the ill-defined texture is designated a worm texture. The relaxation time τ of the ill-defined
texture (which can be obtained by shearing or compressing the specimen)
shows a remarkable behavior: it does not depend, seemingly, on any other
parameter than the density of free chain ends ρ and, in thermotropics, on the
temperature. For example, it does not depend directly on the viscosity. τ
increases when the density of free ends $\rho \approx (Ld^2)^{-1} \sim (v_2/M_w)$ decreases.
This behavior has been critically tested in lyotropics,[60] in which a threshold
ratio $(v_2/M_w)_c \approx 10^{-5}$ has been discovered, below which τ becomes so long
that the ill-defined texture does not disappear in the time of an experiment.
This is tentatively explained by Millaud et al.[55] as due to a longer time of
diffusion of the free ends toward the cores of the defects when ρ is smaller.

In thermotropics,[59] the behavior of τ has been tested with respect to the
molecular weight M_w, the viscosity, and the value of the applied shear. Worm
textures that do not decay in the course of time have been observed for large
M_w. Furthermore, τ increases when T decreases, a fact which seems to
indicate that the ill-defined texture has to be "activated" from the line
texture. Shear goes in the same direction as temperature, in this respect,
since it provides the energy necessary to overcome some barriers.

Alderman and Mackley[59] have also reported on the changes in optical
textures under variable shear together with the subsequent relaxation behavior at the cessation of flow. Some observations, such as the nucleation and
multiplication of defects, are reminiscent of those observed in LMWLC
nematics,[61] at least at low shearing rates. However, others appear unique to
LCP's, in particular the fact that the shear has a significant and specific effect
on the small-scale texture, and presumably on the microstructure.[59] More

precisely, with increasing shear, one observes: (a) the appearance of the above-mentioned "worm texture," a disordered polydomain texture at the scale of a few microns, i.e., below the size of the specimens and independent of it. The worm density increases with increasing shear rate. (b) A sharp transition occurs between the worm texture to a birefringent texture (with optical axes along the direction of shear), called *"ordered texture,"* made presumably of a very high density of suboptical oriented defects of the type seen in the worm texture. The shear rates at which these transitions occur decrease with decreasing temperature and decreasing thickness of the sample. Finally the relaxation behavior is very peculiar and consists, in high enough molecular weight nematics ($M_w \sim 20,000$), of a *"banded texture"* perpendicular to the shear direction, after cessation of shear in the ordered texture; the banded texture relaxes to the worm texture and back finally to the quiescent original state with few disclinations. The banded texture itself seems to be a specific uniform texture that, like all other textures observed, always occurs with the same specific characteristics under a given set of shear and thermal conditions.

Banded structures (of another sort?) were observed in thin films of random copolyesters by diffraction contrast in electron microscopy.[62] Annealed specimens show up walls that tend to be either parallel or perpendicular to the original shear direction, with a characteristic rotation of the molecules out of the plane, interpreted by the authors as a splay–splay compensation of a type described in Ref. 18. Comparison of electron and optical microscopy pictures and x-ray diffraction patterns have led the authors to infer that copolyesters they have observed are biaxial,[25] with orientation correlations about all three axes (multiaxiality). It is quite possible that the copolyesters used by Alderman and Mackley[59] in their large-scale shearing experiments are also biaxial. In this respect, new observations of disclination lines are clearly needed, and it may well be that the differences observed between the textures in copolyesters and those in homopolyesters are related to the different natures of the molecular correlations.

3.2. Cholesteric Polymers

We have noted in Section 2.3 some of the characteristic defects that are observed in biopolymers. In this section we want to stress the existence of frustrated geometries in the same type of materials: they seem to be of two sorts.

Livolant[63] has recently described in great detail the elongated "precholesteric" textures that appear, during the process of concentrating a solution of DNA in water, between the isotropic and the true cholesteric phase. These precholesteric textures exhibit characteristics similar in many respects to the double-twisted cylindrical geometries alluded to above.

In the next section we will discuss in some detail another frustrated geometry, which has as yet no analogue in LMW cholesterics and is met within the chromosome of the dinoflagellate *Prorocentrum micans*, one of those in vivo arrangements that are conspicuously cholesteric.[64] The origin of the frustration is also double twist, but it is here achieved with a geometry "orthogonal" in some sense to the cylindrical one.

Let us just mention, for the sake of completeness, another domain of intense study in biopolymers: the appearance of band instabilities in sheared cholesteric solutions of polymers (PBLG in *m*-cresol, HPC in water) perpendicular to the shearing flow.[65-68] These bands show many similarities with the bands that show up in LCP nematics (see Section 3.1.3; Refs. 57, 59, and 60; and Chapter 11, this volume): they appear after the cessation of the shear flow, above some critical value $\dot{\gamma}_c$, and originate also most probably in a change in the texture of the defects, described long ago by Onogi and Asada[69] as an arrangement of polydomains and more recently as a clustering of disclinations[70] (probably more numerous in the $\dot{\gamma} > \dot{\gamma}_c$ regime than below). There are, however, few detailed direction observations of the defect texture itself and of its relationship with the bands; the origin of the instability is not completely elucidated either.

3.2.1. A FRUSTRATED CHOLESTERIC MODEL FOR THE CHROMOSOMES OF DINOFLAGELLATES

In Fig. 12, the helical axis is globally along the axis of the chromosome. However, one also observes at the periphery a double helical furrow with the same chirality as the cholesteric DNA, which indicates discrepancies with respect to a perfect cholesteric stacking. These discrepancies have been analyzed[71] using as a starting point the assumption that locally the molecules of DNA like to be equidistant. As indicated above and discussed again below, this property is the same as double twist, but it generates in the present case a molecular configuration that is quite different from the blue phase and analogous to the stacking of layers met in Section 2.4.3 (in fine) in our discussion of the screw dislocation of large Burgers' vector in a SmA phase. (See also Ref. 72 for an independent description of the chromosome.)

The geometry of the chromosome can indeed be described as including (1) a central parent sheet σ_0 (see Fig. 12) built from rectilinear DNA strands that rotate helically along the long axis of the chromosome. This object is a twisted sheet of constant thickness, and its midsurface is a ruled helicoid. (2) A stacking occurs on the parent surface of other twisted sheets σ_i of the same thickness, made of DNA molecules that have rotated by some amount about the normal to the parent surface, this rotation increasing with the distance to the parent surface. By this process one clearly obtains a double-twist geometry (one twist along the axis of the helicoid, another twist normal to the sheets) whose geometrical size is limited by the focal surface of the normals to the sheets; the sheets play the same role as the layers in the SmA

FIGURE 12

Schematic molecular assembly of the molecules in the parent surface σ_0 of the double-twisted arrangement in the chromosome of a dinoflagellate. The long axis of the chromosome is along the vertical and is an axis of twist for the whole geometry. The layers σ_i parallel to σ_0 are not drawn; the molecular directions rotate from one layer σ_i to the next σ_{i+1} along the normals to the layers. Therefore these normals are also axes of twist.

screw dislocation (Fig. 8), except that there is a richer structure in the sheets than in the layers. The two cuspidal edges of the focal surface are the sites of the two helical furrows we have described above, which can also be considered two helical $\mathscr{S} = +\frac{1}{2}$ disclination lines about which the sheets are folded.

The double-twist geometry we have just described is very different from the double-twist cylindrical geometry observed with short chiral molecules in the blue phase and in the precholesteric stages of Livolant.[63] While the latter are favored if $K_1 > K_3$ (since div $\mathbf{n} = 0$ in the cylindrical geometry), the chromosome double-twisted geometry is favored when $K_1 < K_3$. The reason that the chromosome exhibits an effective K_1 that is small is not straightforward: K_1 should be infinite in principle in a polymeric liquid crystal with infinitely long molecules. However, we must remember that the chromosome is far from being made of pure DNA, but that there are a number of (nonhistone) DNA-binding proteins around which the DNA double helix can fold to form "hairpins."

A very similar geometry shows up in the twisted β sheets of some fibrous or globular proteins: similar stackings of sheets have indeed been noticed in silk fibroin.[73] It is therefore intriguing to speculate that the *finite size* of these proteins, as well as the finite size of the chromosome of dinoflagellates, is due to the intrinsic frustration of the corresponding structures.

3.2.2. EQUIDISTANCE OF MOLECULES IN POLYMERIC CHOLESTERIC PHASES: SUPERSTRUCTURES AND SELF-ASSEMBLY

The double-twist structures described in Section 3.2.1 are ways of achieving a dense packing of chiral objects on a local scale. In fact, the molecules are quasi-parallel. This tendency toward a dense parallel packing is reflected in x-ray diffraction patterns: a local hexagonal order has been demonstrated in cholesteric phase solutions of PBLG and other biological polymers, e.g., DNA.[74]

Hexagonal order and cholesteric order are incompatible, but this frustration can be relieved on same local scale: a very small modification of Fig. 12 would make it a helical stacking of small hexagonal fiber domains; in fact, it would be enough that what we describe as DNA molecules in this figure be already hexagonal packings of such molecules, on a microscopic scale. This would be a double-twist chiral superstructure of hexagonal structures. The same phenomenon has been observed at much larger scales: very concentrated solutions of biological polymers are hexagonal, not cholesteric, according to x-ray diffraction patterns;[75] also in the optical microscope one observes typical hexagonal textures, in the form of hexagonal domains, but, at larger scales, these domains often appear to pack helically.[76]

More generally, we expect that a structure which minimizes energy at some local scale ξ can show up some kind of hierarchy of structures at higher and higher scales. Such hierarchies were advocated long ago for collagen.[77]

3.2.3. IDENTITY OF DOUBLE-TWIST LOCAL ORDER AND EQUIDISTANCE OF POLYMERS

In fact, double twist and compact stacking are of the same nature. This is straightforwardly demonstrated when considering the geometry of α-helices at a scale of a few strands. These strands assemble to form a string as in Fig. 13, where we have represented the case of five strands. It is clear that such a geometry is a geometry of close contact for molecules that are not straight. They are not parallel, but they are equidistant. Clearly also, the number of neighbors of the central molecule depends on the degree of torsion; this number tends to $n = 6$ when the molecules become parallel (hexagonal stacking) and there is a continuous series of conformations between double twists and with a large degree of torsion and hexagonal order (parallelism).

These considerations shed a new light on the possible existence of various types of frustrated organizations in LCP's, according to the number of neighbors n, the persistence length q, and the chirality p.[71] The blue phase is only one of those, where the coherence length ξ, which scales with the persistence length for a polymer, is much larger than p. It is also

FIGURE 13
A string is made of equidistant strands.

intriguing to speculate that the grainy textures or the dense disclinated structure can be the result of such frustrations.

3.2.4. THE CURVED SPACE REPRESENTATION OF FRUSTRATION IN DOUBLE-TWISTED CHOLESTERICS

Frustrated media exhibit domains separated by defects; however, frustration can be relieved in a curved crystal (i.e., a crystalline arrangement in a curved space) where the order is satisfied not only locally but extends to the whole space.[37] Kléman and Sadoc[78] have shown that the frustration of amorphous metallic glasses is relieved in a three-dimensional spherical crystal tiled with regular tetrahedra; Sethna et al.[79] have similarly proposed to relieve the cholesteric frustration of blue phases in a three-dimensional spherical crystal decorated with a field of unit vectors. More precisely, if S^3, the three-dimensional sphere, is represented by the analytical expression

$$x_0^2 + x_1^2 + x_2^2 + x_3^2 = R^2 \tag{15}$$

the field of unit vectors

$$\mathbf{n}(\mathbf{r}) = \frac{1}{R}(-x_1, x_0, x_3, -x_2) \tag{16}$$

satisfies double-twist and is homogeneous in all S^3; any field obtained by applying a constant rotation to $\mathbf{n}(\mathbf{r})$ is another double-twisted homogeneous field which relieves frustration, with pitch $p^* = 2\pi R$. Adding a central inversion yields another field

$$\mathbf{n}(\mathbf{r}) = \frac{1}{R}(-x_1, x_0, -x_3, x_2) \tag{17}$$

which is equally double-twisted but has an opposite pitch.

The double twist is apparent when one considers the integral lines of $\mathbf{n}(\mathbf{r})$; they form a family of great circles of S^3 (also called Clifford parallels) which are in mutual skew positions, right or left according to the sign of p^*. Since all the great circles are equivalent in S^3, now any great circle is an axial line for the local double-twist geometry. One can also show that it is possible to select subsets of great circles that cover surfaces in a number of ways; among them we have embedded tori,[71] which are locally like the sheets of the unfrustrated geometry of the chromosomes.

4. CONCLUSION

In spite of its difficulties, the physics of polymer liquid crystals is certainly a domain of study from which new ideas and facts on the nature of partial order should emerge. Isolated disclinations and dislocations in LCP's already have created a wealth of new problems. Semiflexible mesogenic polymers (which have been the main objects considered above) raise also problems of correlated orientation of a completely new nature, which are certainly at the origin not only of a complex viscoelastic behavior, but even of unexpected static organizations, where disclinations play a prominent role, probably at different scales, and where the concept of frustration seems to be often relevant. We have described some of these organizations above.

REFERENCES

1. G. Friedel, *Ann. Phys. (Paris)*, **1922**, *18*, 273.
2. G. Toulouse and M. Kléman, *J. Phys. Lett.*, **1976**, *37*, L149; M. Kléman and L. Michel, *Phys. Rev. Lett.*, **1978**, *40*, 1387.
3. L. Michel, *Rev. Mod. Phys.*, **1980**, *52*, 617.
4. M. Kléman, in *Dislocations 1984*, P. Veyssière, L. Kubin, and J. Castaing, Ed., Editions du CNRS, Paris, 1984, p. 1.
5. P. Fabre, C. Casagrande, M. Veyssié, and H. Finkelmann, *Phys. Rev. Lett.*, **1984**, *53*, 993.
6. L. Noirez and P. Davidson, in *Workshop on LCP's*, Laboratoire Léon Brillouin, Saclay, France, 1989.
7. P.G. de Gennes, *Mol. Cryst. Liq. Cryst. Lett.*, **1984**, *102*, 95.
8. X.F. Wang and M. Warner, *J. Phys., A, Math. Gen.*, **1986**, *19*, 2215.
9. W. Renz, in *Workshop on LCP's*, Laboratoire Léon Brillouin, Saclay, France, 1989.
10. J.P. Straley, *Phys. Rev., A*, **1973**, *8*, 2181.

11. T. Odijk, *Liq. Cryst.*, **1986**, *1*, 553.
12. R.B. Meyer, in *Polymer Liquid Crystals*, A. Ciferri, W.R. Krigbaum, and R.B. Meyer, Eds., Academic Press, New York, 1982, Ch. 6.
13. P.G. de Gennes, in *Polymer Liquid Crystals*, A. Ciferri, W.R. Krigbaum, and R.B. Meyer, Eds., Academic Press, New York, 1982, Ch. 5.
14. R.B. Meyer, F. Lonberg, V. Taratuta, S. Fraden, S.D. Lee, and A.J. Hurd, *Faraday Disc. Chem. Soc.*, **1985**, *79*, 125.
15. Z.M. Sun and M. Kléman, *Mol. Cryst., Liq. Cryst.*, **1984**, *111*, 321.
16. D.L. Patel and D.B. Dupré, *J. Polym. Sci., Polym. Lett. Ed.*, **1979**, *17*, 299.
17. S.-D. Lee and R.B. Meyer, *Phys. Rev. Lett.*, **1988**, *61*, 2217.
18. A.J. Hurd, S. Fraden, F. Lonberg, and R.B. Meyer, *J. Phys.*, **1985**, *46*, 905.
19. S. Chandrasekhar and G. Ranganath, *Adv. Phys.*, **1986**, *35*, 507.
20. M. Kléman, *Rep. Prog. Phys.*, **1989**, *52*, 555.
21. M. Kléman, *Points, Lines and Walls*, Wiley, New York, 1983.
22. For an illustration of this topological phenomenon, see Y. Bouligand, in *Physics of Defects*, R. Balian, M. Kléman, and J.P. Poirier, Eds., North Holland, Amsterdam, 1981, p. 695.
23. G. Toulouse, *J. Phys. Lett.*, **1977**, *38*, L37.
24. Y. Galerne, *Mol. Cryst. Liq. Cryst.*, **1988**, *165*, 131.
25. A.H. Windle, C. Viney, R. Golombok, A.M. Donald, and G.R. Mitchell, *Faraday Disc. Chem. Soc.*, **1985**, *79*, 55.
26. I.E. Dzyaloshinskii, *Sov. Phys. JETP*, **1970**, *31*, 773.
27. P.E. Cladis and M. Kléman, *J. Phys.*, **1972**, *33*, 591.
28. A.M. Figueiredo Neto, Y. Galerne, A.M. Levelut, and L. Liebert, *J. Phys. Lett.*, **1985**, *46*, L499.
29. T. Lubensky and P.G. de Gennes, quoted in *The Physics of Liquid Crystals*, P.G. de Gennes, Oxford Univ. Press, Oxford, 1974, p. 245.
30. Y. Bouligand, *J. Phys.*, **1974**, *35*, 959.
31. F. Livolant, *J. Phys.*, **1986**, *47*, 1605.
32. Y. Bouligand and F. Livolant, *J. Phys.*, **1984**, *45*, 1899.
33. C. Robinson, J.C. Ward, and R.B. Beevers, *Disc. Faraday Soc.*, **1958**, *25*, 29.
34. J. Rault, *Phil. Mag.*, **1973**, *28*, 11.
35. A. Saupe, *Mol. Cryst. Liq. Cryst.*, **1969**, *7*, 59.
36. See for example: S. Meiboom, M. Sammon, and W.F. Brinkman, *Phys. Rev.*, **1983**, *A27*, 438.
37. M. Kléman, *Adv. Phys.*, **1989**, *38*, 605.
38. H. Grebel, R.M. Hornreich, and S. Shtrikman, *Phys. Rev.*, **1983** *A28*, 1114.
39. M. Kléman and C.E. Williams, *J. Phys. Lett.*, **1974**, *35*, L49.
40. P. Davidson, P. Keller, and A.M. Levelut, *J. Phys.*, **1985**, *46*, 939.
41. I.G. Voigt-Martin, H. Durst, B. Reck, and H. Ringsdorf, *Macromolecules*, **1988**, *21*, 1620.
42. J. Friedel, *Dislocations*, Pergamon Press, Oxford, 1964.
43. M. Kléman, *J. Phys.*, **1974**, *35*, 595.
44. L. Lejcek, *Czech. J. Phys.*, *B*, **1982**, *32*, 767.
45. I.G. Voigt-Martin and H. Durst, *Macromolecules*, **1989**, *22*, 168.
46. M. Allain, *J. Phys.*, **1985**, *46*, 225.
47. C.E. Williams, *Phil. Mag.*, **1975**, *32*, 313.
48. J.A.N. Zasadzinski, M.J. Sammon, R.B. Meyer, M. Cahoon, and D.L.D. Caspar, *Mol. Cryst. Liq. Cryst.*, **1986**, *138*, 211.
49. M. Kléman, L. Liébert, and L. Strzelecki, *Polymer*, **1983**, *24*, 295.
50. G. Mazelet and M. Kléman, *Polymer*, **1986**, *27*, 714.
51. C. Viney and A.H. Windle, *J. Mater. Sci.*, **1982**, *17*, 2661.
52. C. Noël, F. Lauprêtre, C. Friedrich, B. Fayolle, and L. Bosio, *Polymer*, **1984**, *25*, 808.

53. F. Lequeux and M. Kléman, unpublished.
54. M.R. Mackley, F. Pinaud, and G. Siekmann, *Polymer*, **1981**, *22*, 437.
55. B. Millaud, A. Thierry, and A. Skoulios, *J. Phys.*, **1978**, *39*, 1109.
56. C. Noël, C. Friedrich, F. Lauprêtre, J. Billard, L. Bosio, and C. Strazielle, *Polymer*, **1984**, *25*, 263.
57. C. Noël, F. Lauprêtre, C. Friedrich, B. Fayolle, and L. Bosio, *Polymer*, **1984**, *25*, 808.
58. T. Shiwaku, A. Nakai, H. Hasegawa, and T. Hashimoto, *Macromolecules*, **1990**, *23*, 1590.
59. N.J. Alderman and M.R. Mackley, *Faraday Dis. Chem. Soc.*, **1985**, *79*, 149.
60. B. Millaud, A. Thierry, and A. Skoulios, *J. Phys. Lett.*, **1978**, *40*, L607.
61. D.J. Graziano and M.R. Mackley, *Mol. Cryst. Liq. Cryst.*, **1984**, *106*, 103.
62. A.M. Donald and A.H. Windle, *Polymer*, **1984**, *25*, 1235; *J. Mater. Sci.*, **1984**, *19*, 2085.
63. F. Livolant, *J. Phys.*, **1987**, *48*, 1051.
64. F. Livolant and Y. Bouligand, *Chromosoma*, **1980**, *80*, 97.
65. G. Kiss and R.S. Porter, *J. Polym. Sci.*, *Polym. Symp.*, **1978**, *65*, 193.
66. B. Ernst and P. Navard, *Macromolecules*, **1989**, *22*, 1419.
67. G. Marrucci, A. Grizutti, and A. Buonaurio, *Mol. Cryst. Liq. Cryst.*, **1987**, *153*, 263.
68. E. Marsano, L. Carpaneto, A. Ciferri, and Y. Wu, *Liq. Cryst.*, **1988**, *3*, 1561.
69. S. Onogi and T. Asada, in *Rheology*, Vol. 3, G. Astarita, G. Marrucci, and L. Nicolais, Eds., Plenum Press, New York, 1980, p. 647.
70. B. Ernst, P. Navard, T. Hashimoto, and T. Takebe, *Macromolecules*, **1990**, *23*, 1370.
71. M. Kléman, *J. Phys.*, **1985**, *46*, 1193; *J. Phys. Lett.*, **1985**, *46*, L723.
72. J. Friedel, *Proc. 6th Gen. Conf. Eur. Phys. Soc.*, J. Santà and J. Pantoflicek, Eds., Union of Czech. Math. and Phys., Prague, 1984.
73. B. Lotz, A. Gonthier-Vassal, A. Brack, and J. Magoshi, *J. Mol. Biol.*, **1982**, *156*, 345.
74. E.T. Samulski and A.V. Tobolsky, in *Liquid Crystals and Plastic Crystals*, Vol. 1, G.W. Gray and P.A. Windsor, Eds., Ellis Horwood Ltd., Chichester, 1975, p. 174.
75. P. Saludjian and V. Luzzati, in *Polyaminoacids*, G.D. Fasman, Ed., Marcel Dekker, New York, 1967, p. 157.
76. F. Livolant and Y. Bouligand, *J. Phys.*, **1986**, *47*, 1813.
77. A. Keller and L.J. Gathercole, in *The Periodontal Ligament in Health and Disease*, B.K. Berkovitz, Ed., Pergamon Press, New York, 1982, p. 103.
78. M. Kléman and J.-F. Sadoc, *J. Phys. Lett.*, **1979**, *40*, L569.
79. J.P. Sethna, D.C. Wright and N.D. Mermin, *Phys. Rev. Lett.*, **1983**, *51*, 67.
80. M. Kléman, *Liq. Cryst.*, **1989**, *5*, 399.

CHAPTER 11

Rheology of Nematic Polymers

G. MARRUCCI

Dipartimento di Ingegneria Chimica,
Università di Napoli Federico II,
Piazzale Tecchio, 80125 Napoli, Italy

CONTENTS

1. INTRODUCTION: MOLECULAR AND MACROSCOPIC ORDER

A well-known rheological property of liquid crystals is that their viscosity abruptly drops at the transition from the isotropic to the nematic phase. Figure 1 shows the typical diagram of the viscosity as a function of temperature.[1] When the temperature of the isotropic phase is decreased, the viscosity steadily increases up to the isotropic–nematic transition, where it suddenly drops to a lower value, to begin increasing again when temperature is lowered in the nematic phase.

A similar behavior is shown in the lyotropic case.[2] In Fig. 2, the solution viscosity at a constant temperature is plotted vs. the polymer concentration. When the concentration in the isotropic phase is increased, the viscosity rises steeply up to the transition. Somewhere in the concentration interval where two phases coexist, it begins to drop to a smaller value. It then keeps decreasing well within the nematic phase, to finally increase again at even larger concentrations.

The lower viscosity exhibited by liquid-crystalline polymers (LCP's) in the nematic phase is one of their attractive features. Although LCP's generally

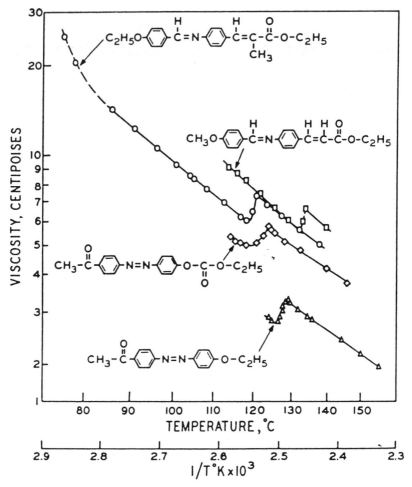

FIGURE 1
Viscosity jump at the isotropic – nematic transition. (Reprinted with
permission from Ref. 1.)

have a fairly rigid chain structure, which forms the basis of their exceptional
properties in the solid state, they can be processed in the nematic phase with
relative ease. The same chains in the isotropic phase would often be unpro-
cessable.

Nevertheless, the rheological behavior of LCP's in the nematic phase is
much more complex than the mere concept of a lower viscosity can describe.
To begin with, their viscosity is, as for most polymeric liquids, a function of
the shear rate. Differently from ordinary polymers, however, the curve of
viscosity vs. shear rate has the typical shape reported in Fig. 3.[3] At low values
of the shear rate, $\dot{\gamma}$, the nematic LCP is shear thinning; i.e., the viscosity

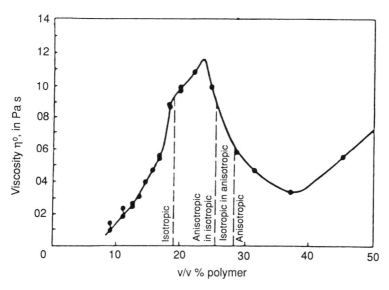

FIGURE 2

Viscosity vs. concentration of 50:50 copolymer of *n*-hexyl and *n*-propylisocyanate in toluene. (Reprinted from Ref. 2 by permission of the publishers, Butterworth & Co. Ltd. © 1980.)

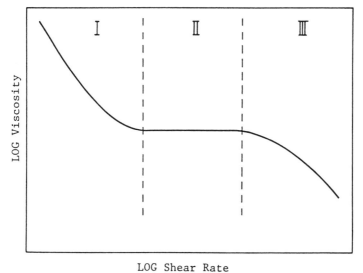

LOG Shear Rate

FIGURE 3

The typical viscosity curve of a nematic LCP. (Reprinted with permission from Ref. 3.)

decreases with increasing shear rate (region I). There then follows a region where the viscosity is almost constant with $\dot{\gamma}$ (region II). Finally, at even larger shear rates, the material becomes shear thinning again (region III). Ordinary polymers do not show a region I behavior; i.e., their viscosity always approaches a constant value as the shear rate approaches zero.

Through optical observations, this behavior of the viscosity has been linked to a very important characteristic feature of LCP's, which distinguishes them from low molecular weight liquid crystals (LMWLC).[3] Before reporting the main conclusions of these experiments, however, it is useful to spend a few words on the general structure of LCP's in the nematic phase.

As is well known, nematics are optically anisotropic substances. At any point of a uniaxial nematic, the optical tensor is axially symmetric around a special direction, indicated by a unit vector **n**, called the director. For elongated, rodlike molecules, the director usually coincides with the average orientation of the molecular axis at the point considered. (The spread of molecular orientations about the director is measured by the order parameter, see Chapters 6 and 7.)

If the director is uniform throughout the sample, then the material forms a defect-free, undistorted, "single crystal." This is seldom the case, however. Frequently, **n** varies in space, i.e., the liquid crystal is distorted, either because of nonuniform boundary conditions on **n**, which alone impose the distortion; or because of a conflict between a condition at the boundary and some imposed external field, each attempting to drive **n** in a different direction; or, finally, because there are defects (point or line disclinations) where the director field is discontinuous (see Chapter 10).

When there are many defects, or a complex distortion pattern, in a liquid-crystalline sample, we speak of a polydomain structure: the rough equivalent of the polycrystalline situation in solid crystals. A prominent difference between the nematic phase of a LMWLC and that of a LCP is the apparent stability of the polydomain structure in the latter case. In a LMWLC, bounding surfaces permitting, it is a relatively simple task to get rid of all distortions. The driving force for the elimination of distortions in the crystal is the Frank elasticity; i.e., the energy of the crystal attains an absolute minimum when all defects and distortions are absent. In contrast, defects are an essentially permanent feature of LCP's. Their elimination in a few situations[4,5] has required an extremely long and artful procedure.

It is not even clear whether defects are stabilized only by the large viscosity of LCP's as compared to the relative weakness of the Frank elasticity forces, or whether new factors linked to the macromolecular nature of these substances enter the picture. Be this as it may, it is an established fact that all LCP samples are polydomains, with a domain size (the average distance over which the director is virtually uniform) typically on the order of a few microns or less. As a consequence of the polydomain structure, a LCP sample in the rest state is macroscopically isotropic, i.e., it is globally unoriented, although, of course, it remains nematically oriented locally.

Returning to the behavior of the viscosity with shear rate, and to the associated results of optical experiments,[3] it has been found that, throughout region I and part of region II, the polydomain structure is preserved in spite of the flow: no significant net orientation of the director is induced by the flow process. At higher shear rates, conversely, the flow orients the director in the shear direction throughout the sample, as if the various domains had coalesced into a single one.

An "if" was used in the previous sentence because the apparently monodomain situation only exists during flow and for some time after the flow has been stopped. Given sufficient rest time, the globally random polydomain structure is recovered. Often, however, another well-known peculiarity of LCP's shows up during relaxation after a shear or an elongational flow process. A fairly regular banded texture is formed, where the bands are orthogonal to the shear (or elongation) direction, and are spaced a few microns apart.[6-11] Microscopic analysis has shown that, in the banded texture, the director continuously oscillates spatially, about the direction imposed by the previous flow.[7,8] The banded texture eventually vanishes, yielding to the disordered polydomain situation.

This brief excursus through a complex phenomenology highlights some important concepts that are peculiar to LCP's. First of all, we must bear a clear distinction between molecular and macroscopic order (above the micron level, say). The order parameter measures the former, i.e., the spread of orientations of nematogenic units in the polymer molecules about their average local orientation (the local director). In a relaxed sample, the order parameter is expected to be the same everywhere (with the exception of so-called defect cores). In other words, the material has the same degree of molecular order, characteristic of its nematic state at the given temperature and concentration, uniformly throughout the sample.

The behavior of the director in space characterizes the macroscopic order of the material. In this respect, relaxed LCP's are completely disordered and show no net orientation at the level of any sizable volume of material (1 mm^3, say). If brought to the solid state under these conditions, most properties, mechanical ones for instance, are correspondingly isotropic.

A flow process can modify this situation, however. For example, the director can be aligned to a virtually single direction. Thereby, if the solid state is achieved before a significant relaxation has occurred, a highly anisotropic solid can be obtained. The well-known Kevlar fiber is a typical example.

The effect of flow upon the director is common to LCP's and LMWLC's, although important differences exist that will be considered in a following section. In LCP's, however, we expect flow to also be able to alter the order parameter, which is never the case in LMWLC's. The reason for this expectation is that, as is true for polymers in general, the molecular relaxation times can be quite large, so that a sufficiently fast flow will have a direct influence upon molecules. It is well known that ordinary polymers, which only admit an isotropic liquid phase, can nevertheless be oriented in a fast flow. The order parameter, which is zero at equilibrium, becomes nonzero during flow (and decays back to zero during relaxation). Similarly, we should expect the order parameter of a LCP, although already nonzero at equilibrium, to be altered in one way or another in a fast flow.

The rest of this chapter is organized as follows. We first present further evidence of the complex rheology of LCP's (see also the review paper by Wissbrun[12]), emphasizing the prominent differences with respect to the rheology of ordinary polymers on the one hand, and to that of LMWLC's on the other. Next, we summarize the theoretical results available today, which begin to shed some light on this complexity. The chapter ends with an indication of the areas where further work appears necessary. The subject material here reviewed obviously reflects preferences of the author. The objective is not one of completeness but rather to introduce the reader to the main aspects of a fascinating, still largely unexplored subject.

2. LIQUID-CRYSTALLINE VS. ORDINARY POLYMERS

We have already shown differences between LCP's and ordinary polymers in the viscosity curve of Fig. 3. Even more striking is the behavior of normal stresses in a shear flow. It is known that, in shearing polymeric liquids, normal stresses develop in the material, as well as tangential ones. For ordinary polymers, the so-called primary normal stress difference is invariably a positive quantity, the positive sign implying a traction in the direction of shear or, equivalently, a compression in the gradient direction. In ordinary polymers, the primary normal stress difference is a steadily increasing function of the shear rate.

Figure 4 shows a typical curve of this normal stress difference, called N, for a LCP.[13-16] At low shear rates, N is a positive, increasing function of $\dot{\gamma}$. Then, at some value of the shear rate, it starts decreasing and soon changes its sign. When $\dot{\gamma}$ is increased further, N switches again from negative to positive values, resuming its steady growth. With respect to the regions defined in Fig. 3, the shear rate interval where N is negative falls approximately at the beginning of region III.

Next we show the shear stress, $\sigma(t)$, and the normal stress difference, $N(t)$, during the startup of a shear flow. In ordinary polymers, these transient responses are relatively uneventful. At low shear rates, both $\sigma(t)$ and $N(t)$ grow monotonically in time toward their respective steady-state values. At higher shear rates, $\sigma(t)$ first grows to a maximum, then decreases toward a steady value, whereas $N(t)$ keeps a simple monotonic shape. At still higher shear rates, finally, also $N(t)$ shows a tiny overshoot. In any event, the transient response only lasts a few units of shear at most. (Shear units are given by the nondimensional product $\dot{\gamma}t$.)

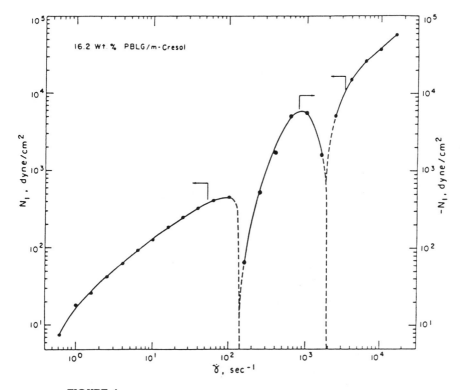

FIGURE 4
The primary normal stress difference vs. the shear rate. (Reprinted with permission from Ref. 13. Copyright J. Wiley & Sons, Inc.)

Figure 5 shows a typical example of shear startup in LCP's. At all shear rates, both $\sigma(t)$ and, more prominently, $N(t)$ undergo several oscillations before the steady state is reached.[16-18] The duration of the transient, particularly for the normal stress response, may be as large as 100 shear units, or even more.

The oscillation period of either $\sigma(t)$ or $N(t)$ shows an important regularity: it is (virtually) inversely proportional to $\dot{\gamma}$. In other words, if several curves of $\sigma(t)$, or $N(t)$, obtained at different shear rates, are plotted vs. shear units $\dot{\gamma}t$, rather than vs. time t, they go hand in hand, i.e., maxima and minima of all curves occur "simultaneously," though their values remain $\dot{\gamma}$ dependent.[18]

As regards the levels of these maxima and minima, particularly that of the initial peak, an apparent irreproducibility is found. Indeed, the initial response of the material significantly depends on its previous history over a time scale that is apparently indefinite. The only way to obtain reproducible results is that of "wiping off" the effects of the uncontrolled past history by using a preshear.[16, 19]

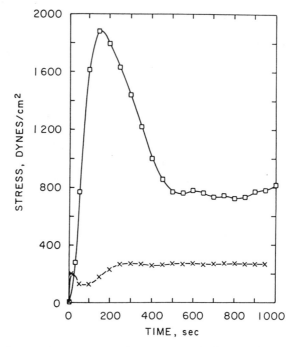

FIGURE 5

HPC (40 wt%) in acetic acid. Startup of a shear flow with $\dot{\gamma} =$ 0.27 s^{-1}. Upper curve: primary normal stress difference. Lower curve: shearing stress. (Reprinted with permission from Ref. 17.)

Similar problems are encountered in dynamical–mechanical experiments. These are made by imposing an oscillating shear of small magnitude (to obtain linearity) on to the material, and by measuring the in-phase and out-of-phase stress responses as a function of frequency ω. The results are expressed either in terms of elastic and loss moduli or, equivalently, as a complex viscosity η^*. For ordinary polymers, the functions $\eta^*(\omega)$ and $\eta(\dot{\gamma})$ happen to be linked to one another. The Cox-Merz rule states that, for equal values of ω and $\dot{\gamma}$, the modulus of $\eta^*(\omega)$ equals $\eta(\dot{\gamma})$. Although not fully explained theoretically, this empirical rule applies well to ordinary polymers.

Figure 6 shows that this is not the case for LCP's.[16, 20, 21] The curve of the modulus of η^* is far apart from that of η. η^* can be either above η, as in the case shown in Fig. 6, or the other way around in other systems. However, the Cox-Merz rule seems not to be obeyed by LCP's. Furthermore, the function $\eta^*(\omega)$, unlike $\eta(\dot{\gamma})$, is not unique to the material and suffers reproducibility problems analogous to those described above for the initial startup response.[16]

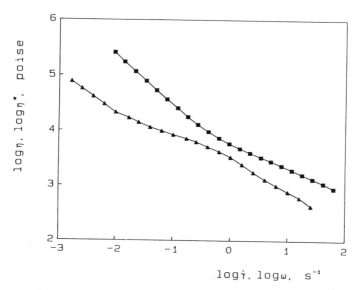

FIGURE 6

HPC (50 wt%) in water. Upper curve: complex viscosity. Lower curve: steady shear viscosity. (Reprinted with permission from Ref. 16.)

It is apparent at this point that LCP rheology is very different from that of ordinary polymeric liquids. It should finally be noted that these differences are not due to chemical peculiarities of the LCP chain structure per se; instead, they are intrinsic to the nematic phase of these polymers. Suffice it to mention that LCP's in the isotropic phase behave in the same way as ordinary polymers.

3. POLYMERIC VS. LOW MOLECULAR WEIGHT NEMATICS

Since the peculiar behavior of LCP's shows up only when they form a nematic phase, the last paragraph of the previous section might lead one to expect strong similarities with the behavior of LMWLC's to be found. On the contrary, the properties they have in common are very few. A significant similarity certainly exists; i.e., in both cases the flow field can align the director. As shown in a following section, however, even this common aspect of their possible behavior reveals important differences.

Before we compare the two classes of materials, we briefly recall what is known about the flow properties of LMWLC's in the nematic phase. Here the situation is more fortunate because a constitutive equation of general applicability is in fact available. The Leslie-Ericksen (LE) equation[22-25] (see references for details) put the following concepts into mathematical form:

1. The viscous interaction between the local velocity gradient $\nabla \mathbf{v}$, the local director $\mathbf{n}$ and its rate of change $\dot{\mathbf{n}}$ is linear in both $\nabla \mathbf{v}$ and $\dot{\mathbf{n}}$. The most general expression describing this linearity contains six constitutive parameters, known as Leslie coefficients, which play a role in nematics analogous to the single viscosity coefficient in isotropic liquids.
2. The local director also interacts elastically with the surrounding material if distortions are present. This interaction, the same that exists under static conditions, involves $\nabla \mathbf{n}$ and $\mathbf{n}$. It is expressed through three constitutive parameters: the splay, twist, and bend constants of Frank elasticity.

The set of equations of LE theory, involving, as it does, $\mathbf{n}$, $\dot{\mathbf{n}}$, $\nabla \mathbf{n}$, and $\nabla \mathbf{v}$, a pressure term, plus several material constants, is mathematically rather intricate and can only be solved under specially simplified conditions. Nevertheless, several significant predictions can be made, which appear to be well confirmed by experiments on LMWLC's.

One such prediction can be obtained on the basis of dimensional analysis only.[26] When performing a dimensional analysis of a problem where the material is not changed, all constitutive parameters with equal dimensions can be lumped into a single one, because the ratio of all others to that chosen form nondimensional quantities which stay constant in the problem. Thus, in the case at hand, we will only take one Leslie coefficient α, and one elastic constant K. Now consider the flow of a nematic in capillaries. From measured values of the pressure drop per unit length of the capillary tube, the shear stress at the wall of the capillary can be obtained through a simple force balance. We want to relate this wall stress σ to the volumetric flow rate F.

Since there are no inertia effects, the problem only involves the dimensional quantities σ, F, α, K, and D, where D is the capillary diameter. With these five quantities, only two independent nondimensional groups can be formed. We choose $\sigma D^2 / K$ and $\alpha F / KD$. Therefore, the required relationship must be of the form

$$\sigma D^2 / K = f(\alpha F / KD) \qquad (1)$$

Although dimensional analysis cannot predict the form of the function f (thus leaving unspecified the dependence of σ on F), Eq. (1) contains an important prediction. It states that, if $\sigma(F)$ data are obtained in capillaries of different diameters, and they are plotted as σD^2 vs. F/D, all such data must fall on a single curve.

This scaling law is well obeyed by LMWLC's. The same data show that, in general, the relationship $\sigma(F)$ is nonlinear, i.e., that nematics behave as non-Newtonian fluids. On the other hand, it is well known that ordinary non-Newtonian fluids in steady shear flows display a one-to-one correspondence between shear stress and shear rate. This implies that, for flows in capillaries, the relationship among σ, F, and D, is of the form

$$\sigma = f(F/D^3) \tag{2}$$

Comparison of Eqs. (1) and (2) shows the profound difference between the scaling law obeyed by LMWLC's, on the one hand, and ordinary non-Newtonian fluids on the other.

To say the same thing in different words, let us consider the apparent viscosity, which, apart from a constant numerical factor, is the ratio between σ and F/D^3. Equation (2) shows that, for any given value of the shear stress σ, the apparent viscosity of ordinary non-Newtonian fluids does not depend on the capillary diameter. Conversely, Eq. (1) reveals that the same is not true for LMWLC's. For them, the apparent viscosity also depends on the size of the apparatus: the capillary diameter in this example.

In order to understand the physics of this result, we must first return to the Leslie-Ericksen theory to recall a few of its elementary features. The first of them is as follows. Consider the shear flow of a LMWLC, the director of which is held fixed, uniformly throughout the sample, by means, e.g., of a strong magnetic field. As a consequence of the linearity alluded to in point 1 above, the viscosity that is measured under these conditions is independent of the shear rate (and of the size of the apparatus). It changes, however, if the orientation of the director is varied with respect to the shear (see point 1). For whatever orientation of the director, the measured viscosity is a suitable linear combination of the Leslie coefficients. Particularly well known are the three Miesowicz viscosities, which are obtained by orienting **n** either along the shear direction or along the gradient, or perpendicularly to both of them.

A second important result of LE theory has to do with director alignment due to shear. Consider the shear flow of a LMWLC the director of which is acted upon only by the shear itself. Then, if the ratio of the Leslie coefficients α_2 and α_3 is positive

$$\alpha_2/\alpha_3 > 0 \tag{3}$$

(which is the case most frequently encountered), the director spontaneously aligns as in Fig. 7, the angle Θ being determined by the equation

$$\tan \Theta = (\alpha_3/\alpha_2)^{1/2} \tag{4}$$

Notice (for future reference) that Θ does not change by changing the shear

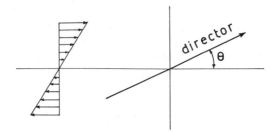

FIGURE 7
Alignment of the director in a shear flow.

rate, i.e., Θ is a material property. With typical values of α_2 and α_3 in LMWLC's, Θ is a small angle, of the order of a few degrees.[25]

We can now return to the question of why the apparent viscosity may depend on the size of the apparatus. Consider for example the parallel plate geometry of Fig. 8a, in which the nematic at rest is in the homotropic configuration, i.e., with the director orthogonal to the walls. Further assume that the anchoring of the director at the walls is a strong one, i.e., the orthogonal orientation at the wall will persist under flow conditions as well.

Figure 8b shows a line tangent to the director, all across the thickness of the nematic layer, when a shear flow is applied. At any point in the nematic, the orientation of the director results from a compromise between the aligning tendency of the shear flow, which would put **n** at the angle Θ, and the reaction of Frank elasticity to the distortion (compare point 2 above), arising because of the boundary condition of a strong anchoring.

If the thickness of the layer is large enough, the orientation far from the wall is Θ. The distortion is localized in a boundary layer, the thickness of

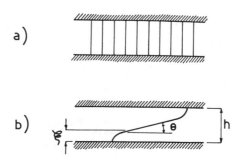

FIGURE 8
Shear flow of an aligning nematic: (a) static homotropic conditions; (b) director profile along the thickness of the sheared layer.

which, ξ, is of order

$$\xi = (K/\sigma)^{1/2} \qquad (5)$$

where σ is the applied shear stress and K is one of the elasticity constants. (The bend and splay constants appear in the exact solution of the problem, but the order of magnitude is the same for both of them.)

Remembering now that the local viscosity depends on the orientation of the director with respect to the shear, and that the overall apparent viscosity is a suitable average over local values, it becomes clear why the apparent viscosity for fixed σ may vary with sample thickness, h. Indeed, if h is much larger than ξ, the contribution of the boundary layer is negligible and the apparent viscosity essentially coincides with that characteristic of the orientation Θ. At the opposite extreme, if h is much smaller than ξ, the homotropic orientation remains virtually unaltered throughout the sample thickness in spite of flow, and the apparent viscosity becomes that pertaining to a director held constant along the shear gradient direction (one of the Miesowicz viscosities).

The same argument can be used to understand why LMWLC's are non-Newtonian in spite of their intrinsic linearity. Indeed, consider now the case where h is fixed and σ is varied. Since ξ varies with σ according to Eq. (5), ξ will become much larger than h as σ approaches zero, thus generating the homotropic orientation and the associated Miesowicz viscosity. Conversely, as σ becomes large, ξ decreases, and the viscosity corresponding to the angle Θ is approached.

If ξ and h are of comparable magnitude, i.e., in the case where the distortion is important throughout the thickness of the layer, the apparent viscosity can be kept constant with varying σ only if h is also varied in such a way that the ratio ξ/h stays constant. Indeed, if this ratio is preserved, the distortion profiles are self-similar. This is the meaning of the scaling law with capillary diameter shown by Eq. (1).

It is now time to return to our polymeric nematics to ask the following questions. Do LCP's ever obey LE theory? In particular, since LE theory is linear, is it at least approached in the limit of slow flows? Do LCP's ever show the scaling law with apparatus size just discussed?

The answer to these questions seems generally negative. The viscosity curve, such as that of Fig. 3, is independent of apparatus geometry and size. It appears to be an intrinsic property of the material, just as in ordinary polymers, not a compromise between the orientation due to flow and that imposed by the walls, as in LMWLC's. Size effects occasionally observed[27] in some capillary measurements on thermotropic LCP's were not reproduced.[28]

In principle, however, it is disturbing that LE theory does not seem to be approached, not even in the limit of very slow flows. The general condition for a linear theory to hold true is that molecular distributions remain close to equilibrium in spite of flow. This is certainly the case of LMWLC's, the molecules of which relax very quickly. Polymers, in contrast, behave nonlinearly, since their relaxation times can be very large, especially in concentrated systems. Ordinary polymers, however, always approach linearity in slow flows, i.e., under conditions such that even their sluggish macromolecules succeed in remaining close to the equilibrium state. Why, then, do slow flows of LCP's not exhibit the behavior predicted by LE theory?

A possible solution of the mystery might be the polydomain structure of LCP's, and the fact that they appear to be tumbling nematics at low shear rates; i.e., the following inequality applies to them

$$\alpha_2/\alpha_3 < 0 \tag{6}$$

instead of that of Eq. (3).

The tumbling situation, seldom encountered in LMWLC's, implies that shear alone (i.e., without considering Frank elasticity) would make the director rotate indefinitely in time. Thus, tumbling nematics are profoundly different from the shear orienting ones so far considered. They are inherently unstable and give rise, generally at least, to time-dependent flow and orientation fields.

Under special conditions, and by accounting for Frank elasticity, time-independent conditions are predicted by LE theory also for a tumbling nematic.[29, 30] Figure 9 shows the orientation of the director along the thickness of a layer in one such prediction.[29] The tumbling tendency of the director due to shear is counteracted by the elastic torque of the distortion. Instead of tumbling in time, the director winds up along the gradient direction. Figure 9 shows the case where the director makes a few turns between the confining walls. By increasing either the shear stress or the sample thickness, more turns become necessary. We will discuss possible implications of the tumbling nature of LCP's at low shear rates in the last section of the chapter.

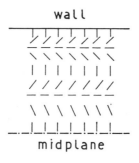

FIGURE 9
Schematic of the director field during the shear flow of a tumbling nematic.

4. MOLECULAR MODELING. RODLIKE POLYMERS

The rheology of LCP's can be approached from the theoretical side with the tools of molecular modeling. The basic model, in fact the only one so far developed to any significant extent, is that of the rigid rod. It is apparent from the start that such a model is too crude a representation of LCP's, the molecules of which are often semirigid (wormlike chains) or else contain flexible spacers between the rigid mesogenic groups (segmented chains). On the other hand, rheological theory for LCP's is still in an initial stage, somehow comparable to the early days of equilibrium theories, where the rodlike polymer model also played an important role in providing the basic understanding.

The first molecular property to be considered in the dynamics of rodlike polymers is their angular, or rotational, diffusivity. In extremely dilute systems, with the rods well separated, the rotational diffusivity D_0 only results from rod–solvent frictional interactions. It depends on rod length L, i.e., on polymer molecular weight, through the equation

$$D_0 = kT/\zeta L^3 \ln(L/d) \qquad (7)$$

where ζ is the friction coefficient per unit length of the rod, d is rod diameter, and kT is Boltzmann constant times absolute temperature. (Here and in the following, numerical coefficients are omitted in most equations, the aim being to show dependencies rather than to calculate values.) The logarithmic term varies weakly with L. Thus, the rod length dependence of D_0 is essentially with the inverse cube.

A reason for being interested in the angular diffusivity D is that for both dilute and concentrated solutions, the rod contribution to viscosity is given by the simple relationship

$$\eta = ckT/D \qquad (8)$$

where c is the number of rods per unit volume. From Eqs. (8) and (7), there follows the well-known result that the intrinsic viscosity of rodlike polymers is essentially proportional to the square of their molecular weight.

When rod concentration is increased, but much before the isotropic–nematic transition is reached, a new dynamic effect becomes important. Rods bump one into another in their rotational Brownian motion. These "topological" interactions decrease the rotational diffusivity. The effect becomes progressively more important with increasing concentration, the more so the longer are the rods. Detailed calculations[31] result in the equation ($c > 1/L^3$)

$$D = D_0/L^6 c^2 \qquad (9)$$

Combining this result with Eqs. (8) and (7) gives for the viscosity

$$\eta = kTc^3L^6/D_0 \propto w^3M^6 \tag{10}$$

where w is polymer concentration by weight, and M the molecular mass. Equation (10) shows how fast is the growth of η with increasing w in the isotropic phase of rodlike polymers.

Another important concept concerning the rotational diffusivity in concentrated systems is its sensitivity to the orientational distribution of the rods. If the rods are not randomly oriented, not only does the diffusivity increase on the average, but it even becomes a function of the particular orientation of a rod. Ignoring the latter aspect, one may write[32]

$$D_{aniso} = D_{iso}/\langle \sin \varphi \rangle^2 \tag{11}$$

where D_{aniso} represents an average diffusivity of the rods under anisotropic conditions, D_{iso} that for the isotropic case (given by Eq. 9), and φ is the angle between any two rods in the system; $\langle \ \rangle$ indicate the ensemble average.

Equation (11) indicates that, for rods roughly parallel to one another, the probability of any of them bumping into another in its rotational motion is much reduced with respect to the isotropic situation. The rotational diffusivity correspondingly increases. The upper limit of D_{aniso} with decreasing $\langle \sin \varphi \rangle$ is not infinity, however, as the approximate relationship of Eq. (11) might suggest. The maximum value is in fact D_0, attained when the topological interactions among neighboring rods have effectively vanished.

Although these concepts were first applied to the anisotropy induced by either a magnetic field (Kerr effect), or by flow, in otherwise isotropic rod systems, they go over to the nematic phase as well. Thus, since also Eq. (8) continues to hold true in nematics, it becomes clear why a sudden drop in the viscosity is observed at the isotropic–nematic transition. The factor responsible for the drop is the rotational diffusivity, which suddenly increases at the transition as a consequence of the orientation.

The viscosity may even continue to decrease after the transition (see Fig. 2). In fact, with increasing polymer concentration after the transition, an additional increase of the order parameter takes place, and thus $\langle \sin \varphi \rangle$ is further reduced. This effect can more than offset the reduction of D_{iso} due to a larger concentration, the net result being an enhancement of D_{aniso}.

So far, we have left vague which viscosity we were talking about. A better specification is not irrelevant since we are dealing with systems that, depending on conditions, exhibit different values of the viscosity. For what concerns the isotropic phase, Eq. (8) gives in fact (to within a numerical factor of order unity) the zero-shear viscosity. With increasing the shear rate, the viscosity decreases, and Eq. (8) no longer applies.

Also for the nematic phase, Eq. (8) (with $D = D_{aniso}$, of course) only applies to the linear limit, corresponding to LE theory. As we have mentioned in the previous section, however, even in that limit there exists a whole range of viscosity values, depending on the orientation of the director with respect to the shear. In other words, the numerical coefficient in Eq. (8) varies with director orientation. It can be shown that the maximum value is of order unity, whereas the minimum is much smaller and decreases with larger order parameters (see Chapter 9). Now, since the viscosity value usually measured is closer to the minimum than to the maximum, it can be concluded that the drop in viscosity at the transition actually results from two concurrent effects.

The simple considerations presented in this section, mainly based on results obtained by Doi, only refer to viscosity in the linear range. They only explain the behavior shown in fig. 2 (and, by analogy, that in Fig. 1), particularly the drop in viscosity which takes place at the transition. A more difficult task is that of explaining the complex rheological behavior exhibited by LCP's in the nonlinear range. The first step in this direction was again taken by Doi. A summary of his theory is presented in the next section.

5. DYNAMICS OF RODLIKE POLYMERS: THE DOI THEORY

When dealing with rodlike polymers in general, the fundamental quantity to be considered is the orientational distribution function of the rods, $f(\mathbf{u})$. If $\mathbf{u}$ is the unit vector specifying rod orientation, $f(\mathbf{u})\,d\Omega$ gives the fraction of rods within the solid angle $d\Omega$ in the neighborhood of $\mathbf{u}$. Of course, the integral of $f(\mathbf{u})$ over the full solid angle 4π must be unity. Also, since $\mathbf{u}$ and $-\mathbf{u}$ correspond to the same orientation, we must have $f(\mathbf{u}) = f(-\mathbf{u})$ in all cases.

The dynamics of rodlike polymers in an arbitrary flow was considered long ago by Kirkwood and Auer[33] for the case of dilute solutions. In the equilibrium state, the solution is isotropic, i.e., $f(\mathbf{u}) = \text{constant} = 1/4\pi$. Under nonequilibrium conditions, $f(\mathbf{u})$ obeys the "diffusion" equation:

$$\partial f/\partial t = D_0 \nabla^2 f - \nabla \cdot (f\dot{\mathbf{u}}) \qquad (12)$$

where ∇^2 and $\nabla \cdot$ indicate the Laplacian and divergence operators, respectively, in $\mathbf{u}$ space. The vector $\dot{\mathbf{u}}$ is the rate of change of vector $\mathbf{u}$ due to flow. Neglecting minor terms linked to rod thickness, it is given by

$$\dot{\mathbf{u}} = \mathbf{G} \cdot \mathbf{u} - (\mathbf{u} \cdot \mathbf{G} \cdot \mathbf{u})\mathbf{u} \qquad (13)$$

where $\mathbf{G}$ is the velocity gradient (in physical space) due to flow.

The interpretation of Eq. (12) is simple if one considers that f is but a rod "concentration" in $\mathbf{u}$ space. Equation 12 states that the change in time of f results from a convective term due to flow, counteracted by diffusion, which continuously attempts to reestablish the uniform equilibrium distribution. In Eq. (13), linking $\dot{\mathbf{u}}$ to $\mathbf{u}$ through the velocity gradient, the second term may be viewed as a "correction" to the first, arising from the fact that, $\mathbf{u}$ being a unit vector, $\dot{\mathbf{u}}$ is forced to be orthogonal to $\mathbf{u}$.

If $\mathbf{G}$ is independent of time (in a Lagrangean sense), then Eq. (12) always admits a time-independent solution, representing the nonuniform orientational distribution of the rods in a steady flow. This distribution strikes a balance between the convective and diffusion terms. Significant distortions from the equilibrium distribution will be found if the magnitude of $\mathbf{G}$ is on the order of D_0 or larger.

Once the distribution has been found, it can be used to calculate average values of any $\mathbf{u}$-dependent quantity. The average of the quantity $Q(\mathbf{u})$ is indicated as $\langle Q \rangle$ and is obtained from the integral over the full solid angle (or the unit sphere)

$$\langle Q \rangle = \iint Q(\mathbf{u}) f(\mathbf{u}) \, d\Omega \qquad (14)$$

Of particular interest are the averages corresponding to macroscopically observable properties. In the dilute case, the contribution of rodlike polymers to the stress tensor σ is given by

$$\sigma/ckT = 3\langle \mathbf{uu} \rangle + (1/D_0)\mathbf{G} : \langle \mathbf{uuuu} \rangle \qquad (15)$$

The first term of this expression is called the "elastic" stress, because it derives from the entropic free energy change due to anisotropy. The second term is the "viscous" stress, arising from the rod–solvent relative motion due to rod inextensibility. The frictional nature of the viscous term is better appreciated when considering that the prefactor ckT/D_0 is equivalent (compare Eq. 7) to $c\zeta L^3 \ln(L/d)$, where ζ is a friction coefficient. Also, the viscous stress vanishes instantaneously upon stopping the flow ($\mathbf{G} = \mathbf{0}$), whereas the elastic stress relaxes to zero in the course of time, following the parallel relaxation of the distribution function.

The set of Eqs. (12), (13), and (15) can be viewed as a constitutive equation for the stress in the continuum sense, since it links σ to $\mathbf{G}$, albeit via the intermediate "molecular" quantity $f(\mathbf{u})$. Actual solution of this set of equations shows that, even in the dilute case so far considered, the behavior is non-Newtonian in fast flows, i.e., when the magnitude of $\mathbf{G}$ is larger than D_0.

Increasing the concentration, we find the so-called semidilute regime, where topological interactions among neighboring rods are important (see previous section), whereas excluded volume interactions (and energetic ones even more) can still be neglected. This range of concentration is determined by the approximate inequalities $1/L^3 < c < 1/L^2d$; i.e., it is a significant range only for very long rods ($L/d \gg 1$).

The dynamics in the semidilute regime were considered by Doi and Edwards.[32] The essential change to be made in the equation determining the distribution function $f(\mathbf{u})$, Eq. (12), consists in replacing D_0 with D_{aniso} of the previous section. The change is not irrelevant, because D_{aniso} itself contains an average over $f(\mathbf{u})$, thus making Eq. (12) nonlinear.

Physically, however, the main changes arise from the lower value of the diffusivity in the isotropic state as given by Eq. (9), the implication being that the semidilute solution behaves non-Newtonianly much sooner, i.e., as soon as the magnitude of $\mathbf{G}$ is larger than D. Notice further that Eq. (15) remains unaltered. In particular, since the friction coefficient ζ has not changed, the viscous stress term still keeps the $1/D_0$ prefactor (not to be replaced by $1/D$, or $1/D_{aniso}$). It follows that the viscous stress may often be neglected: roughly, as long as the magnitude of $\mathbf{G}$, although larger than D, remains smaller than D_0.

We finally consider the concentration range that includes the isotropic–nematic transition. As is known from equilibrium theories, $L^2 d$ gives the order of magnitude of the excluded volume of a rod in the isotropic phase. Thus, as c approaches values on the order of $1/L^2 d$ or larger, excluded volume interactions become important, and eventually induce the transition.

These interactions, and energetic ones as well, can be represented in the form of a mean-field scalar potential, $V(\mathbf{u})$, acting on a rod oriented along $\mathbf{u}$, and driving it toward some average orientation of all other rods. In his theory,[34] Doi chose the simplest possible form for this potential, namely

$$V(\mathbf{u}) = -UkT\langle \mathbf{uu}\rangle : \mathbf{uu} \tag{16}$$

where U is the nondimensional intensity of the potential. If $V(\mathbf{u})$ is viewed as representing the excluded volume interaction only, then U is proportional to cL^2/d, but Eq. (16) is an approximate form in such a case. On the other hand, since Eq. (16) is a quadratic form of the Maier-Saupe type, it enjoys a more general status. It may be interpreted as incorporating also nematogenic interactions of energetic origin. U would also depend on temperature in such a case. Notice further that $V(\mathbf{u})$ has an absolute minimum if all rods are perfectly aligned, and that $V(\mathbf{u}) = V(-\mathbf{u})$, as it should.

The central part of Doi's theory is the pair of equations replacing Eq. (12) and Eq. (15). The diffusion equation is replaced by the following Smoluchowski equation:

$$\partial f/\partial t = D_{aniso}\nabla\cdot[\nabla f + f(\nabla V/kT)] - \nabla\cdot(f\dot{\mathbf{u}}) \tag{17}$$

In Eq. (17), the new term accounts for the torque ∇V exerted upon the rods by the nematogenic potential. Similarly, the stress equation becomes

$$\sigma/ckT = 3\langle\mathbf{uu}\rangle + \langle\mathbf{u}\nabla V/kT\rangle + (1/D_0)\mathbf{G}:\langle\mathbf{uuuu}\rangle \tag{18}$$

(The last term, i.e., the viscous stress, neglected in the original paper,[34] is accounted for in the book by Doi and Edwards.[35])

The set of these two equations [together with Eq. (11) for D_{aniso}, Eq. (13) linking $\dot{u}$ to G, and Eq. (16) for the potential] can again be viewed as a constitutive equation relating σ to G via the molecular distribution function $f(u)$. The power, and beauty, of the Doi theory is that the same set of equations applies to both the isotropic and the nematic phase. Across the transition, the change in rheological properties is quite dramatic, yet such major differences in behavior emerge "spontaneously" from a single theory.

The above equations are also very complex, however. Thus, in order to proceed with the calculations, Doi's theory included a mathematical simplification (a decoupling of the average $\langle \mathbf{uuuu} \rangle$ into $\langle \mathbf{uu} \rangle \langle \mathbf{uu} \rangle$), which has eventually proved unacceptable. Some uneasiness about this approximation was soon apparent. Indeed, in the linear limit in which exact calculations are possible, it was found a positive sign for the α_3 Leslie coefficient,[36, 37] implying that rodlike polymer nematics are of the tumbling type at low shear rates. Conversely, with the decoupling approximation, α_3 was found to be negative,[38] i.e., the polymeric nematic would belong to the flow-aligning category. In fact, flow alignment was predicted to occur at all values of the shear rate, in both the linear range and the nonlinear one.[34]

For this reason, and others that will be apparent in the following section, we do not report results obtained with the decoupling approximation. Instead, we proceed by showing a different simplifying procedure, which has proved to be qualitatively satisfactory.

6. RODLIKE POLYMERS IN SHEAR: TWO-DIMENSIONAL DESCRIPTION

A fundamental feature of a shear flow (as opposed to elongational, or stretching, flows) is that of inducing a permanent tumbling of suspended particles of whatever shape. Roughly, this motion consists in a rotation of the particle about the vorticity axis (the axis perpendicular to both the shear direction and that of the gradient), though other, more complex, aspects of this motion are also present in the general case.

It is believed that the essence of the behavior of rodlike polymers in shear is preserved if the situation is artificially restricted to two dimensions, i.e., if the convenient assumption is made that all rods are parallel to the shear plane (the plane of Fig. 10, containing both the shear and the gradient directions). Due to the shear, the rods will rotate in the shear plane with an angular velocity which, again neglecting minor terms linked to rod thickness, is given by

$$\dot{\theta} = -\dot{\gamma} \sin^2 \theta \tag{19}$$

where θ is the angle in Fig. 10, and $\dot{\gamma}$ is the shear rate.

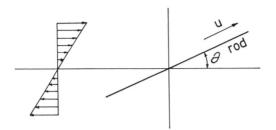

FIGURE 10
A rodlike molecule in the shear plane. θ is the angle with the shear direction.

Equation (19) replaces Eq. (13) in our case. The two-dimensional version of Eq. (17) then becomes

$$\partial f/\partial t = D\,\partial(\partial f/\partial\theta + f/kT\,\partial V/\partial\theta)/\partial\theta + \dot{\gamma}\,\partial(f\sin^2\theta)/\partial\theta \qquad (20)$$

where $D = D_{\text{aniso}}$ is understood. In Eq. (20), $f(\theta)$ takes the place of $f(\mathbf{u})$, and the Maier-Saupe potential may be written

$$V(\theta) = -UkT(\langle\cos 2\theta\rangle\cos 2\theta + \langle\sin 2\theta\rangle\sin 2\theta) \qquad (21)$$

Equation (20) is much easier to handle than Eq. (17). It even admits an analytical, time-independent solution given by

$$F(\theta) = C\{I(\theta) + A\}\exp\{-g(\theta)\} \qquad (22)$$

where C is a normalization constant, and

$$g(\theta) = G\left(\theta - \tfrac{1}{2}\sin 2\theta\right) - U(\langle\cos 2\theta\rangle\cos 2\theta + \langle\sin 2\theta\rangle\sin 2\theta) \qquad (23)$$

$$I(\theta) = \int_0^{\theta} \exp\{g(x)\}\,dx \qquad (24)$$

$$A = I(\pi)/(\exp\{\pi G\} - 1) \qquad (25)$$

G being a nondimensional shear rate ($G = \dot{\gamma}/2D$).

The form of Eq. (22) is not explicit, however, since $f(\theta)$ also appears in the averages $\langle\cos 2\theta\rangle$ and $\langle\sin 2\theta\rangle$. A procedure to complete the calculations is available in.[39] The most important result of these calculations is as follows: *A time-independent solution does not always exist*. It does exist, for all values of G, in the isotropic phase ($U < 2$), and in a small segment of the nematic range ($2 < U < 2.41$). Conversely, for $U > 2.41$, the time-independent solution *exists only at high shear rates*. At low shear rates, the steady-state solution is replaced by a periodic one, corresponding to *tumbling* of the director.

To avoid possible confusion, it is perhaps worth emphasizing the difference between tumbling of the individual rods and tumbling of the whole rod distribution (or of the director). As previously mentioned, individual rods always tumble in a shear flow. Their orientational distribution can be stationary, however, as long as the rods that leave an orientation are replaced by an equal number of other rods, reaching that same orientation.

In the isotropic phase, a steady shear flow always generates a stationary distribution. In the nematic phase, conversely, two outcomes (actually three, see below) are possible. Instead of remaining fixed in time, the distribution itself tumbles. High shear rates favor the stationary solution, low shear rates favor tumbling. (In a small transition range between these two main regimes, a third situation is found, where the director oscillates up and down.[40, 41])

Needless to say, the stationary solution prevailing at high shear rates corresponds to a flow-orienting situation. Several differences with respect to LMWLC's should be noted, however. In the first place, a LMWLC is either of the flow-aligning type or of the tumbling one, independently of the magnitude of the shear rate. Rodlike polymers, conversely, switch from one situation to the other, depending on G. Moreover, in the flow-aligning range, the small angle that the director forms with the shear direction also depends on G, and it can even become negative, whereas this angle is fixed at a positive value in LMWLC's (see Eq. 4).

Another important result of the two-dimensional analysis is the following: The flow alters the spread of the distribution with respect to equilibrium (order parameter). In the nematic phase, depending on G, the spread can either decrease or increase. In the latter case, *the first normal stress difference becomes negative.*

It is perhaps worth emphasizing this rheological peculiarity that distinguishes the nematic phase from the isotropic one. Indeed, in the isotropic phase, where molecular orientations are completely random at equilibrium, a flow process can only induce some degree of order. In a shear flow, such an ordering process results in a positive-valued normal stress difference. Conversely, a nematic phase already enjoys a degree of molecular order (orientational) under equilibrium conditions. Therefore, a flow process can either improve on the preexisting order or, on the contrary, reduce it. These two opposite possibilities give rise to normal stress differences, opposite in sign, in a shear flow.[39]

Figure 11 shows the normal stress difference N vs. the shear rate G as calculated from the model. In the tumbling region, where N is periodic in time, the time average over the tumbling period has been reported in Fig. 11. As discussed in the following section, this averaging is somehow justified by the polydomain situation. The general shape of the curve in Fig. 11, showing two signs changes with increasing G, is remarkably similar to that observed in

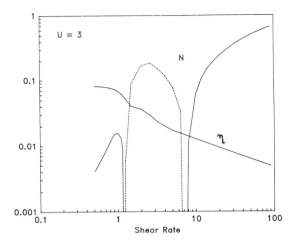

FIGURE 11
Model predictions of normal stresses and viscosity. The dotted curve corresponds to negative values of the normal stress difference, i.e., $-N$ is plotted instead of N. (Adapted with permission from Ref. 39. Copyright Am. Chem. Soc., and from Ref. 40.)

LCP's (see Fig. 4). According to these calculations, the transition from the tumbling regime to the flow-aligning situation takes place (roughly halfway) in the negative-N range of shear rates.

Figure 11 also shows the corresponding prediction for the viscosity curve. Here, the comparison with experiment is less favorable. The viscosity shows a low-shear plateau, followed by a shear thinning region at high shear rates, in much the same way as for ordinary polymers. There is no trace of the region I behavior which characterizes LCP's (see Fig. 3). We will come back to this discrepancy in the next section. Two points of agreement with experiment should be noted, however. One of them is the relative position of the viscosity and N curves. The negative N range roughly falls at the beginning of the shear-thinning zone (region III), as experimentally observed. The other point of agreement is the peculiar kink in the viscosity curve, occurring at the onset of the stationary solution. A similar kink can be noted in some experimental results.[13, 15, 16, 42]

It should finally be mentioned that the possible, obviously legitimate, reservations about the validity of these two-dimensional calculations have recently been removed by the work of Larson,[41] who carried out the numerical solution of Eq. (17) in steady shear flows using an expansion in spherical harmonics of the three-dimensional distribution function. Larson's results fully confirm the two-dimensional calculations in all the essential points. Moreover, since Larson has used a different nematogenic potential (that of

Onsager instead of Maier-Saupe), his results also show that the main predictions of the theory are indeed robust. They turn out to be independent of relatively secondary assumptions. Working in three dimensions, Larson could also calculate the second normal stress difference, N_2. He found that N_2 is opposite in sign to N, at virtually all shear rates. Thus, when N becomes negative, N_2 is positive. Some recent experiments, although highly preliminary, can perhaps be interpreted as confirming this prediction.[43]

7. POLYDOMAIN THEORY

The theory of Doi, and all results so far presented (with the exception of the time-averaging procedure alluded to in the previous section), explicitly refer to a monodomain situation. Spatial gradients of the director, and the associated effects of Frank elasticity, are ignored.

Simple (and simplistic) ways of accounting for the polydomain situation are as follows. In the tumbling regime, the director of each domain performs a cyclic motion, spending different times at the various orientations in the cycle. The calculations of the monodomain theory give us all details, including the stress response at each orientation along the cycle. It is then surmised that a "snapshot" of the polydomain sample would show a spatial distribution of the directors which essentially matches the distribution in time along the tumbling cycle. Thus, the time averaging of the stress response of a single domain also gives the average instantaneous response (independent of time) of the polydomain sample. This ergodic assumption was used in the previous section.

In the nontumbling regime, i.e., at the high shear rates where a stationary monodomain solution is found, the transient response of a polydomain during startup of the flow has been calculated in the following way.[40] First, the transient startup response of a single domain is calculated using Eq. (20). As one might have expected, this response is found to depend upon the initial orientation assigned to the director. By assuming that, in the polydomain sample, the initial orientations are randomly distributed, the startup response of the polydomain is then calculated by averaging the single domain results over the initial distribution of domain orientations.

Figure 12 shows some results of these calculations. The curves in Fig. 12 exhibit damped oscillations, so typical of LCP's in startup flows (see Fig. 5). Moreover, just as shown by Doppert and Picken,[18] among others, the maxima and minima of the curves obtained for different values of G occur (approximately) at the same values of Gt.

These encouraging results from simple approaches to the polydomain situation should not conceal the fact that Frank elasticity is not explicitly accounted for. In LCP's, stresses due to Frank elasticity are expected to be

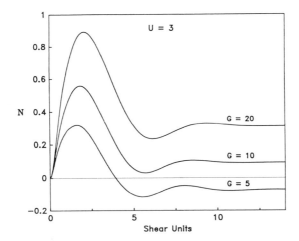

FIGURE 12

Model predictions of transient normal stresses in startup of shear flows. (Reprinted with permission from Ref. 40.)

rather weak with respect to viscous ones, so that they can perhaps be neglected at high shear rates. Even so, do they remain negligible at low shear rates as well? We believe that the answer is negative, for at least two reasons.

The first reason has to do with transient behavior in the tumbling regime. Let us attempt calculating the transient response for a startup in that range of shear rates. One might think of applying the same procedure as used at high shear rates. Starting from an initial random distribution of directors, each of them evolving in time in a known manner (from the monodomain calculations), the average over them should give the evolution in time of the polydomain sample. If this is done, the response never reaches a steady state; instead, it approaches a permanent oscillatory behavior where the director distribution cyclically reproduces itself. This situation is analogous to that of a viscous suspension of elongated non-Brownian particles.[44] In both cases, a way out of the difficulty is that of invoking interparticle interactions. In our case, interdomain interactions are naturally provided by Frank elasticity. It has been shown[40] that accounting for these interactions in a simple (albeit arbitrary) way is sufficient to transform the permanent oscillation into a damped one, approaching a steady state.

The second reason is the tumbling regime per se. As mentioned in a previous section, there exist analyses, based on LE theory, of steady solutions in shear and converging flows of tumbling nematics.[29,30] A recent work[45] shows that, although these results do not apply as such to LCP's, they may form the basis for interpreting the tumbling behavior of LCP's at low shear rates. In particular, the drop in viscosity in region I of Fig. 3 would result from a progressive loss of importance, as the shear rate increases, of Ericksen stresses due to Frank elasticity with respect to viscous stresses linked to the Leslie coefficients.

8. CONCLUDING REMARKS

In spite of some successes, reviewed in the previous sections, our theoretical understanding of the rheology of LCP's remains very primitive, certainly insufficient for a good control of the technological processes that might fully exploit the potential of these new materials. It may be worth concluding with a list of areas where work is needed in order to provide significant advancement.

To begin with, we lack some form of extension of these rheological theories to the semirigid case. The change from rodlike to wormlike chains is certainly not irrelevant. Infinitely long wormlike chains are predicted by Semenov[46] to be shear aligning at low shear rates, i.e., they would show the opposite behavior of rodlike polymers which, as we have long discussed, are predicted to be tumbling nematics in that range of shear rates.

For most if not all mainchain LCP's, either rigid, or semirigid, or segmented, it seems highly probable that the peculiar qualitative features of their rheological behavior is to be attributed to the rigidity of the nematogenic moieties. In favor of this conjecture, one can invoke the "universality" of the observed behavior (in its qualitative aspects) as well as the fact that such behavior is indeed predicted by a rigid-rod theory. Quantitatively, however, the predictions of the rodlike polymer theory cannot be expected to apply to actual LCP's, the molecules of which are not really rodlike. In particular, the dependence of most parameters on chain length, or molecular weight, is expected to be strongly influenced by flexibility. There are difficulties in obtaining this information, on a quantitative basis, even experimentally.

A satisfactory interpretation of relaxation phenomena is also lacking. In particular, the ubiquitous banded texture is of unknown origin. Why do flow-oriented LCP's abandon a state that should be one of minimum energy? Domain size is too large for Brownian motion to be responsible for randomization of the director field. Do defects survive the flow orientation process, thus providing a driving force for randomization (via the banded texture) due to Frank elasticity? Such an interpretation has been suggested,[11] but there is no direct proof of its validity. An excellent review of what is known today about defects and textures in LCP's is provided by Kléman.[47]

It should finally be mentioned that molecular theories, successful as they may eventually be in providing a basic understanding, cannot be used as such in modeling the complex flows encountered in the applications. Thus, from them, some simpler, yet effective, constitutive relation must be extracted for engineering purposes.

ACKNOWLEDGMENTS

Work presented herein has been supported by the Ministry of University and Research, Rome.

REFERENCES

1. R.S. Porter and J.F. Johnson, in *Rheology*, Vol. 4, F.R. Eirich, Ed., Academic Press, New York, 1967.
2. S.M. Aharoni, *Polymer*, **1980**, *21*, 1413.
3. S. Onogi and T. Asada, in *Rheology*, Vol. I, G. Astarita, G. Marrucci, and L. Nicolais, Eds., Plenum Press, New York, 1980, pp. 127–147.
4. K. Se and G.C. Berry, *Mol. Cryst. Liq. Cryst.*, **1987**, *153*, 133.
5. S.D. Lee and R.B. Meyer, Chapter 9, this volume.
6. G. Kiss and R.S. Porter, *Mol. Cryst. Liq. Cryst.*, **1980**, *60*, 267.
7. C. Viney and A.H. Windle, *Polymer*, **1986**, *27*, 1325.
8. P. Navard and A.E. Zachariades, *J. Polym. Sci., Polym. Phys.*, **1987**, *25*, 1089.
9. C.R. Fincher, *Mol. Cryst. Liq. Cryst.*, **1988**, *155*, 559.
10. E. Marsano, L. Carpaneto, and A. Ciferri, *Mol. Cryst. Liq. Cryst.*, **1988**, *158*, 267.
11. P.L. Maffettone, N. Grizzuti, and G. Marrucci, *Liq. Cryst.*, **1989**, *4*, 385.
12. K.F. Wissbrun, *J. Rheol.*, **1981**, *25*, 619.
13. G. Kiss and R.S. Porter, *J. Polym. Sci., Polym. Phys.*, **1980**, *18*, 361.
14. A.D. Gotsis and D.G. Baird, *Rheol. Acta*, **1986**, *25*, 275.
15. P. Moldenaers, Ph.D. Thesis, Leuven, Belgium, 1987.
16. N. Grizzuti, S. Cavella, and P. Cicarelli, *J. Rheol.*, **1990**, *34*, 1293.
17. A.B. Metzner and G.M. Prilutski, *J. Rheol.*, **1986**, *30*, 661.
18. H.L. Doppert and S.J. Picken, *Mol. Cryst. Liq. Cryst.*, **1987**, *153*, 109.
19. J. Mewis and P. Moldenaers, *Mol. Cryst. Liq. Cryst.*, **1987**, *153*, 291.
20. H. Aoki, J.L. White, and J.F. Fellers, *J. Appl. Polym. Sci.*, **1979**, *23*, 2293.
21. P. Moldenaers and J. Mewis, *J. Rheol.*, **1986**, *30*, 567.
22. J.L. Ericksen, *Arch. Rat. Mech. Anal.*, **1960**, *4*, 231.
23. F.M. Leslie, *Quart. J. Mech. Appl. Math.*, **1966**, *19*, 357; *Arch. Rat. Mech. Anal.*, **1968**, *28*, 265.
24. O. Parodi, *J. Phys.*, **1970**, *31*, 581.
25. P.G. de Gennes, *Physics of Liquid Crystals*, Clarendon Press, Oxford, 1975.
26. J.L. Ericksen, *Trans. Soc. Rheol.*, **1969**, *13*, 9.
27. K.F. Wissbrun, G. Kiss, and F.N. Cogswell, *Chem. Eng. Commun.*, **1987**, *53*, 149.
28. D.S. Kalika, L. Nuel, and M.M. Denn, *J. Rheol.*, **1989**, *33*, 1059.
29. T. Carlsson, *Mol. Cryst. Liq. Cryst.*, **1984**, *104*, 307; Ph.D. Dissertation, Chalmers Univ., Goteburg, 1984.
30. A.D. Rey and M.M. Denn, *Liq. Cryst.*, **1989**, *4*, 253.
31. M. Doi, *J. Phys.*, **1975**, *36*, 607.
32. M. Doi and S.F. Edwards, *J. Chem. Soc., Faraday Trans. 2*, **1978**, *74*, 560; **1978**, *74*, 918.
33. J.G. Kirkwood and P.L. Auer, *J. Chem. Phys.*, **1951**, *19*, 281.
34. M. Doi, *J. Polym. Sci., Polym. Phys.*, **1981**, *19*, 229.
35. M. Doi and S.F. Edwards, *The Theory of Polymer Dynamics*, Clarendon Press, Oxford, 1986.
36. A.N. Semenov, *Sov. Phys. JETP*, **1983**, *58*, 321.
37. N. Kuzuu and M. Doi, *J. Phys. Sov. Jpn.*, **1983**, *52*, 3486; **1984**, *53*, 1031.
38. G. Marrucci, *Mol. Cryst. Liq. Cryst.*, **1982**, *72L*, 153.

39. G. Marrucci and P.L. Maffettone, *Macromolecules*, **1989**, *22*, 4076.
40. G. Marrucci and P.L. Maffettone, *J. Rheol.*, **1990**, *34*, 1217; **1990**, *34*, 1231.
41. R.G. Larson, *Macromolecules*, **1990**, *23*, 3983.
42. G.C. Berry, *Mol. Cryst. Liq. Cryst.*, **1988**, *165*, 333.
43. J.J. Magda, S.G. Baek, and R.G. Larson, paper presented at the 61st Annual Meeting of the Society of Rheologists, Montreal, October, 1989.
44. J. Happel and H. Brenner, *Low Reynolds Number Hydrodynamics*, Noordhoff Int. Publ., Leyden, 1973.
45. G. Marrucci, *Macromolecules*, submitted.
46. A.N. Semenov, *Sov. Phys. JETP* **1987**, *66*, 712.
47. M. Kléman, Chapter 10, this volume.

MAIN SYMBOLS

USED IN ALL CHAPTERS

c	concentration
d	diameter of a polymer chain
DP	degree of polymerization
e	mechanical deformation
E	elastic modulus of elastomer
E	chain bending elastic constant
k	Boltzmann constant
K_i	Frank elastic constants
L	length of a polymer chain
LC	liquid crystal
LCP	liquid crystalline polymer
LMWLC	low molecular weight liquid crystal
MW	molecular weight
$M_w, \overline{M}_w$	weight-average molecular weight
n	nematic director
N_A	Avogadro's number
P_2	second order Legendre polynomial
q	persistence length
$\langle R^2 \rangle$	mean-square end-to-end distance
$\langle R_G^2 \rangle$	mean-square radius of gyration
S	orientational order parameter in nematic phase
S_0	order parameter at transition point
T	absolute temperature
T_m	melting temperature
T_i	isotropization temperature
$T_{KN}(T_{KN}^\circ)$	crystal $\rightarrow$ nematic transition temperature (in bulk)
$T_{NI}(T_{NI}^\circ)$	nematic $\rightarrow$ isotropic transition temperature (in bulk)
Tg	glass temperature
$v_2\ (v_p)$	volume fraction of polymer
$v_2^i\ (v_p^i)$	v_2 value in conjugated isotropic phase
$v_2^a\ (v_p^a)$	v_2 value in conjugated anisotropic phase
$V(\Theta)$	Maier–Saupe potential
X, x	axial ratio of rodlike particle
$\dot{\gamma}$	shear rate
λ	Kuhn segment length (chapters 2, 3)
Θ	angle between director and segment axes

CHAPTER 1

E_{tot}	total energy of the molecule
r_j	distance between non-bonded atoms
$2U_0$	barrier of rotation
V	interactions of the non-bonded atoms
W	remaining energy contributions
ΔW_{rot}	change in energy due to the torsion about a near single bond
ψ_s	molecular orbital
φ_i	atomic orbital
φ, ϕ	rotation angles (also $\psi, \theta, \alpha, \beta, \gamma, \delta$)

CHAPTER 2

A_2	second virial coefficient
B, B'	unreduced and reduced binary cluster parameter
D_0	diffusion coefficient
dn/dc	refractive index increment
f_0	friction coefficient
$I(k)$	excess scattered intensity
K, ν	constant and exponent relating intrinsic viscosity and molecular weight
k_1	magnitude of scattering vector
l	segment length
M_L	molar mass per unit length
N	number of persistence lengths
N'	number of Kuhn lengths
n	number of chain segments
n_s	solvent refractive index
$P(k)$	particle scattering function
$\langle R_{G,0}^2 \rangle$	unperturbed mean-square radius of gyration
R_H	hydrodynamic radius
$\langle R_z \rangle$	z-component average of end-to-end vector
s_0	sedimentation coefficient
$\bar{v}$	partial specific volume
z	excluded volume parameter
α_H, α_D	proton and deuterium coherent scattering lengths
α_R^2	expansion factor for $\langle R^2 \rangle$
$\alpha_{R_G}^2$	expansion factor for $\langle R_G^2 \rangle$
α_η^3	viscosity expansion factor
β	binary cluster integral
∂^2	molecular optical anisotropy
∂_0^2	segment optical anisotropy

Δn	birefringence
Γ^{-1}	average relaxation time
$[\eta]$	intrinsic viscosity
η_0	solvent viscosity
θ	scattering angle
λ_0	wavelength of light
ρ_2	polymer density
ρ_0	solvent density
ρ_v	depolarization ratio
ϕ	bond angle

CHAPTER 3

$B(\gamma)$	second virial coefficient of two segments forming an angle γ with each other.
$f(\mathbf{n})$	orientational distribution function for the chain segments.
F	free energy of a system.
N_2	number of chains.
r_D	Debye screening radius of polyelectrolyte solution.
V	volume of the system.
$w = (v_2^a/v_2^i - 1)$	relative width of the phase separation region.
ε	dielectric constant of the solvent.
μ	chemical potential.
Π	pressure (osmotic pressure).
$\varkappa$	ratio of anisotropic and isotropic components of the attractive forces between the links of the chain
σ	linear charge density of polyelectrolyte chain.

CHAPTER 4

a	quantity defined by Eq. (16)
f_p	integrals over orientational distribution
n_p	number of polymer molecules
n_s	number of solvent molecules
n_x	number of molecules with axial ratio x
n_{xy}	number of molecules with axial ratio x having an orientation y
p^*	characteristic pressure
s	weighting factor for initiation of a helical sequence
s^*	statistical weight for the disordered conformation
$\tilde{T}$	reduced temperature; $\tilde{T} = T/T^*$
T^*	characteristic temperature for anisotropic interactions

V_s^*	hard core volume of particle per segment
$\tilde{V}$	reduced volume: $\tilde{V} = V/V^*$, with V^* hard core volume of particle
v_r	volume fraction of rods in mixture with coils ($v_c = 1 - v_r$)
v_s	volume fraction of solvent molecules
v_x	volume fraction of molecules with axial ratio x
v_x^i, v_x^a	volume fraction as above in isotropic and anisotropic phase, respectively
x_c	number of segments per monomer of coiled species
y	disorder index
$\bar{y}$	average value of disorder parameter
Z	partition function
Z_{comb}	combinational part of partition function
Z_{orient}	orientational part of partition function
α	mean polarizability
$\Delta\alpha$	anisotropy of polarizability

CHAPTER 5

a	segment length
A, A^T	matrices of constraint; saddle point variable; fraction of lattice segments oriented along direction i
b	strength of smectic potential
c	strength of nematic coupling of main chain segments
d	lattice constant; square root of cross-sectional area of chain
$\mathbf{D}$	conformational matrix; symbol of delta-function
$f(\mathbf{u})$	orientation distribution function
$G(\mathbf{u}, \mathbf{u}', L)$	orientation distribution function of bending elastic chains
G	matrix; configurational free energy; combinatorial free energy
H	conformational energy of the lattice chain
J	Boltzmann coupling coefficient
K	matrix of constraint
$\mathbf{l}_i$	"ith" bond vector on the lattice
L_p	LCP DP
L_s	solvent DP
L^c	critical DP for nematic phase transition
N_p	segment density (number of segments per unit volume)
n	number of segments in mainchain per sidechain
n_s	number of solvent molecules
n_p	number of polymer molecules; number of lattice segments along the preferred axis that belong to jth chain; Fourier variable
p	probability of the straight conformation on the lattice

p_i	molar fraction of free sites
$\mathbf{P}$	probability and Boltzmann factor
$\mathbf{P(R)}$	probability of finding two cross links connected by $\mathbf{R}$
$P_j(\mathbf{u})$	Legendre polynomial
Q	fraction of lattice segments oriented along the preferred axis
Q_p	chain partition function
S_A	order parameter of sidechain
S_B	order parameter of mainchain
S_A	smectic A phase; spin vector; transposed spin vector
T_p	pseudo transition temperature
U	coupling constant between distortion and order
U_A	nematic interaction parameter of sidechains
U_B	nematic interaction parameter of backbone
U_C	nematic interaction parameter of sidechains and mainchains
U_{AB}	orientational interaction parameter of sidechains and mainchains
$V_j(r)$	radial component interaction of order j
v_f	external field coupling constant in mean field
w	mean field interaction parameter
$w_p(\mathbf{u})$	polymer mean field
w_s	solvent mean field
$w_A(\mathbf{u})$	mean field on sidechain
$w_B(\mathbf{u}(s))$	mean field on mainchain at s
Y	volume fraction of sidechains
y	length of sidechain
$Y_j^m(\mathbf{u})$	spherical harmonics
$Z(Q, J, X)$	configurational partition function
ε	energy of the bent (gauche) conformation
ε_{pp}	space average anisotropic interaction
Δ	nematic coupling constant
γ_p	excluded volume parameter
$\Delta_1, \Delta_2, \Delta_3$	spin vectors
σ	external stress; spin vector of the mth segment; summation; summation over the spin configurations of the first chain
ω_{pp}	space average isotropic interaction between LCP segments

CHAPTER 6

L_0	cut off length
T^*	characteristic temperature for soft interaction
$\tilde{V}$	reduced volume

V^*	hard core volume
X^c	critical axial ratio
X_K	axial ratio of Kuhn segment
X_r	axial ratio of rod
X_c	axial ratio of coil
x	volume fraction of A in AB copolymer
y	volume fraction of C in CD copolymer
$\bar{y}$	Flory's disorientation parameter
Z	coordination number
$\bar{\alpha}$	mean polarizability
β	parameter of orientational distribution function
γ	cubic expansion coefficient
$\epsilon(\Theta)$	orientation dependent energy
$\epsilon_{11}, \epsilon_{22}$	anisotropic interaction parameters for pure component
Θ	Flory's Θ temperature
ν	ratio of Kuhn segment for worm and broken wormlike chains
ω_{11}, ω_{22}	isotropic interaction parameters for pure components
$\chi, \chi_{12}, \chi_{23}, \chi_{32}$	isotropic interaction parameters for mixing
χ_{23}^c	critical interaction parameter for two polymers
Φ	volume fraction of isotropic phase

CHAPTER 7

$S_{zz}, S_{z'z'}$	order parameters
ΔS_i	isotropization entropy
ΔH_i	isotropization enthalpy
M_n	number-average molecular weight

CHAPTER 8

a_0, B, C	Landau expansion coefficient
D	order parameter (Eq. 9)
F	free energy
G	free enthalpy
$H, \Delta H$	enthalpy, phase transformation enthalpy
htp	helical twisting power
l, L_{i0}, L_0	sample length (deformed, undeformed, extrapolated at $\sigma = 0$)
$\bar{n}$	mean refraction index
p	pitch of cholesteric helix

P	pressure
T''	2nd order transition temperature (Eq. 13)
T_{cp}	critical temperature
U	coupling coefficient
$\mathscr{V}, \Delta\mathscr{V}$	specific volume, volume change at phase transformation
x_{ch}	mole fraction of chiral comonomers
β	specific isothermal compressibility
γ	specific isobaric expansion coefficient
δ	anisotropy term (Eq. 9)
ΔC_p	specific isobaric heat change
$\varepsilon(\Theta)$	orientation-dependent part of the dispersion interaction
λ	elongation; ratio V_4/V_2 in Eq. (10)
λ_R	wavelength of reflection of cholesteric phase
π	flatness term (Eq. 9)
σ	stress; interaction term in Eq. (9)
χ	chirality term (Eq. 9)

CHAPTER 9

$\mathbf{a}$	molecular axis
$a_i \ (i = 1 \text{ to } 3)$	scattering amplitudes
$\overline{D}$	effective rotational diffusion coefficient
h	cell thickness
H_c	the bend Fredericks threshold
k	scattering wavevector
L_{av}	average length of the molecules
P_4	fourth order Legendre polynomial
Q	dimensionless concentration
R	second orientational order parameter
V	volume of a molecule
$\alpha_i \ (i = 1 \text{ to } 6)$	Leslie coefficients
Γ	parameter for the stability of a shear flow
ΔK_1	an additional splay modulus
$\Delta\chi$	diamagnetic anisotropy
η	packing fraction
η^*	a common viscosity factor
η_s	solvent viscosity
(η_a, η_b, η_c)	Miesowicz viscosities
$(\eta_{\text{splay}}, \gamma_1, \eta_{\text{bend}})$	effective viscosities
μ	parameter for the hydrodynamic interaction
ν_1	elongational viscosity
θ_s	scattering angle
Ω	inverse of the osmotic compressibility

CHAPTER 10

b	modulus of the Burgers' vector
N	nematic
N*	cholesteric
N_B	biaxial nematic
Q	quaternion group
r_c	core radius
$\mathscr{S}$	strength of a disclination
Z_2	abelian group with two elements
λ, χ, τ	unit vectors along the 3 specific directors in a cholesteric
λ^-	disclination line along λ with strength $\mathscr{S} = -\frac{1}{2}$
λ^+	disclination line along λ with strength $\mathscr{S} = +\frac{1}{2}$
τ^-	disclination line along τ with strength $\mathscr{S} = -\frac{1}{2}$
τ^+	disclination line along τ with strength $\mathscr{S} = +\frac{1}{2}$
$\kappa = \xi/p$	ratio of the racemic correlation length to the pitch in a cholesteric
$\lambda_1 = (K_1/B)^{1/2}$	smectic penetration length
ξ	coherence length
σ_1, σ_2	principal curvatures at a point of a layer

CHAPTER 11

A	see Eq. (25)
C	normalization constant
D	rotational diffusivity; capillary diameter
F	volumetric flow rate
f	function, orientational distribution
G	nondimensional shear rate
G	velocity gradient
h	layer thickness
I	see Eq. (24)
N	first normal stress difference
N_2	second normal stress difference
$\dot{\mathbf{n}}$	rate of change of the director
Q	$\mathbf{u}$ = dependent quantity, see Eq. (14)
t	time
U	intensity of Maier–Saupe potential
u	rod orientation vector
$\dot{\mathbf{u}}$	rate of change of $\mathbf{u}$ due to flow
v	velocity
w	concentration by weight

ζ	friction coefficient per unit rod length
η	shear viscosity
η^*	complex viscosity
Θ	director orientation in shear plane
θ	rod orientation in shear plane
$\dot{\theta}$	rate of change of θ due to shear
ξ	boundary layer thickness
σ	shear stress; stress tensor
φ	angle between two rods
Ω	solid angle
ω	frequency

ACKNOWLEDGMENTS

The preparation of a multiauthors book aiming at an integrated outlook is an extremely difficult task. Even an attempt to reach a consensus on a few controversial issues would not have been possible without the commitment of the authors. Most of them participated in minimeetings and spent considerable more time on the book than is usually required in the preparation of scattered chapters.

Giorgio Ronca joined this project when several chapters were almost ready and we didn't have a description of cubic lattice treatments. He left us shortly after completing his contribution. The interaction lasted too short a time, yet enough to reveal the depth of his soul and of his culture, and his concern for issues of human and moral value.

The editorial task was greatly facilitated by the assistance of several people at the Istituto di Chimica Industriale in Genoa, and at the College of Textiles in Raleigh. Beth Vincelette at VCH displayed indispensable patience, insight and enthusiasm for the project.

INDEX